THE INTERNATIONAL POPULATION CENSUS BIBLIOGRAPHY: REVISION AND UPDATE, 1945–1977

TEXAS BIBLIOGRAPHY II

STUDIES IN POPULATION

Under the Editorship of: H. H. WINSBOROUGH

Department of Sociology
University of Wisconsin
Madison, Wisconsin

THE INTERNATIONAL POPULATION CENSUS BIBLIOGRAPHY: REVISION AND UPDATE, 1945–1977

TEXAS BIBLIOGRAPHY II

compiled by

DOREEN S. GOYER
Social Science Research Associate III,
Librarian of the Population Research Center
University of Texas at Austin
Austin, Texas

ACADEMIC PRESS
A Subsidiary of Harcourt Brace Jovanovich, Publishers
New York   London   Sydney   Toronto   San Francisco   1980

ACADEMIC PRESS, INC.
111 Fifth Avenue, New York, New York 10003

United Kingdom Edition published by
ACADEMIC PRESS, INC. (LONDON) LTD.
24/28 Oval Road, London NW1 7DX

Library of Congress Cataloging in Publication Data

Goyer, Doreen S.   Date.
    International population census bibliography, revision and
update, 1945-1977.

    (Studies in population)
    Edition for 1965-1967 by the Population Research Center,
University of Texas.
    1. Census—Bibliography.   2. Population—Statistics
—Bibliography.   I. Title.   II. Series.
Z7164.D3G69   1979   016.312   79-25890
ISBN 0-12-294380-5

PRINTED IN THE UNITED STATES OF AMERICA

80 81 82 83   9 8 7 6 5 4 3 2 1

Dedicated to two
fine friends,
Eliane and Saminho.

CONTENTS

PREFACE

Until the 1950s, few population demographic researchers had access to the data contained in censuses from countries other than their own. As a result, population censuses as a body of literature suffered from neglect both in bibliographic and content description. Growing scientific interest and concern about the world's population and resource limits have generated an unprecedented demand for the solid foundation of fact that is the essence of national population censuses and related statistical activities. Census materials, however, are not widely available; the need for comprehensive reference tools that are easily accessible to libraries and individuals is obvious. A researcher looking for a specific census publication in the past has had to go to a variety of sources to find it. None of these sources were complete, nor were they often available in other libraries or research centers. These sources, compiled by different organizations, were an attempt to meet specific research needs of their own users. Now the demand for general census information and the production of census materials has increased more rapidly than have any individual organization's attempts to maintain either a generalized set of census materials or a comprehensive listing of where such census information might be located. These two goals are what we here at Texas have tried to do. First, we have collected as many censuses as possible. Second, with the publication of this bibliography, we are producing a guide to where the information is located.

Eighteen years ago, when the Population Research Center was organized under the auspices of the Department of Sociology at the University of Texas, the directors felt that, in addition to demographic and ecological research, the center should try to collect all bona fide censuses from all nations. With funding from the university's General Libraries, they began microfilming all early censuses available and purchased as many of the circa 1960 printed volumes as finances permitted. The difficulties encountered in determining what had been printed, and when, led them to prepare the *International Population Census Bibliography* (six volumes and one supplement). Lack of funding curtailed census acquisition after a National Science Foundation grant expired in 1967. Nonetheless, whenever possible, the center continued to purchase current censuses.

The center received an NICHD five-year grant in 1971, which included funds for a full-time librarian and renewed census acquisition. During this grant period, a user-oriented library was established and card files were made of all new census publications acquired or cited in a variety of sources. In 1971 the International Census Collection had 49% of all known bona fide national population censuses ever taken. By 1975 our holdings increased to 75%. Since then, through acquisition of new census reports, microfilm of earlier census items, and a large gift of older censuses, we are now holding 80% or more. When we received a five-year renewal of the original NICHD grant, I began to prepare a revision and update of the original bibliography that covers the period 1945 to 1977, or approximately three decades. This is that volume.

In addition to the financial support from the NICHD center grant and the facilities provided by the Population Research Center, I would like to acknowledge the help contributed by my friends and colleagues from APLIC–International and the over fifty libraries who responded to my questionnaire. Working closely with Mary Beth Reilly of Research Publications, Inc., has proven beneficial to both of us, a cooperation that I hope continues over the years. Richard Hankinson and the superb publication *Population Index* were invaluable aids. Finally, I must not forget my library assistants over the last two years, Elaine Domschke, Helen Fredlein, and Bob Kelley, who ably handled the desk and freed me to tackle the bibliography.

The typing of the camera-ready copy is mine; any typographical errors must rest on my shoulders.

Doreen S. Goyer

INTRODUCTION

CHOICE OF ENTRIES

The objective of citing "all known, bona fide, national, population censuses" was adhered to as firmly as possible. At times, however, it was difficult to determine what to call a census and whether to include it.

The United Nations lists four major criteria for a census: (1) individual enumeration, (2) universality within a defined territory, (3) simultaneity, and (4) defined periodicity (*Principles and Recommendations for the 1970 Population Censuses,* 1967). There are valid reasons why many countries cannot strictly hold to them. Therefore, one of the difficulties confronted is exemplified by the following. One year there is a census of the European, or nonindigenous, population; a year or two later there is a census of African, or indigenous, population. While neither can be called a true census, could the term be loosely applied when such a pairing has occurred, even though the simultaneity is violated? In the *Revision and Update* we decided to include the reasonable pairing, or else past population statistics for many countries, especially the new African nations, would not be listed. We also decided to include sample censuses of the size of the British 1966 Sample Census, the Hong Kong 1966 By-Census, and the Taiwan 1970 and 1975 Sample Censuses because of their comprehensive nature and because they fill the statistical gap between decade censuses. Secondary sources have been cited only when no official statistical publications exist.

The choice of countries and territories included in this volume was obvious in all cases of sovereign nations. A few have no citations, but we felt that a bit of information might be helpful. A determination, however, had to be made about territories. It was decided that the geographic entity should be included if it fulfilled at least one of the following:

a. It attained independent/sovereign status during the 1945–1977 period (e.g., most of the African countries).

b. It took and published its own census (e.g., Scotland).

c. It changed from one administrative jurisdiction to another during this period (e.g., Ryukyu Islands, from the U.S. to Japan).

d. It published a separate set (or volume) of census results even though the census was conducted by the main administrative body (e.g., Bermuda, 1970).

e. It took a census independent of the mother country (e.g., Trust Territory of the Pacific Islands, 1973, or American Samoa, 1974).

Presentation

The presentation of the country entries does not follow the continental division used in the original IPCB. (Appendix A is a continental division listing.) Rather, it is strictly alphabetical, generally by the most common geographical name used in English; that is, Rhodesia is used instead of Southern Rhodesia or Zimbabwe–Rhodesia because the term Nothern Rhodesia has not been used for a number of years in the first case and there has not been enough time for familiarity to have developed in the second case. (The variant name cross-reference, Appendix B, will lead one to the entry name.)

Individual entries that were censused with a larger group, for example, the Commonwealth Caribbean countries and the French Overseas Territories, have partial citations under the individual country or territory name and a referral to the master set by the number assigned. When only a few entities are involved, the citation is complete but the number assigned is that of the master set. For example, American Samoa, 1970, is numbered (U.S.) 1970.1-1-54/58 because that is the number of the specific U.S. census volume that contains the results for the territory. Because Guam, the Virgin Islands, the Canal Zone, and the Trust Territory of the Pacific Islands are also included, this one volume cannot stand in five places at once.

Time Coverage

The time coverage of this work includes the censuses taken during the years 1945 through 1977. There are one or two exceptions. Jamaica, 1943, was included to complete the West Indies (Commonwealth Caribbean) set of 1945. Any publications giving results (preliminary or otherwise) of censuses taken after 1977 that appeared before publication of this work will have been included also.

Features of the Bibliography

The long form official name of the country, the name and address of the most current known official statistical agency, and of the publications distributor are listed for each entry.

Once the decision was made to include a census, the reports were viewed to exclude preliminary result publications unless (1) no final reports had been published because it was too early for them to have appeared; (2) final reports were never issued; or (3) the preliminary report was of sufficient length (30 pages or more) to contain significant data that were not repeated in the final reports or it contained data in a convenient summary form on a single page that were spread over several tables in the final reports.

Within the country entry, the publications were first divided by the year of the census whose results they contained. If the census/sample spanned more than one year, the latest date was assigned. The reports, then, were grouped into (1) preliminary and/or publications concerning the administration of the census, such as works containing definitions or directories; (2) the main set (a) in order of the numbering sequence printed on the volume or (b) when no integral numbering system was present, in a logical order, such as sample tabulation results separate from complete tabulation results, arranged by publication data; and (3) special reports or monographs issued by the official statistical agency that were not numbered as part of the main set.

As a general rule, citations are headed by the corporate entry. The vast majority of census publications are "authored" by official governmental agencies and are cited under the country (given in English) and the agency (in the appropriate language), for example, Czechoslovakia, Federální Statistický Úřad. In some cases, to save space (and my patience) the initials of some statistical agencies were used only after the full form had been introduced. Such initialisms also were indicated in the "Statistical Agency" listing, for example, Institut National de la Statistique et des Études Économiques (INSEE). I also chose to use the name of the agency that was printed on the volume itself, rather than the latest version of the corporate entry that many libraries prefer. (The latest version is that of the "Statistical Agency" in all but a few cases.)

Titles published in English are printed across the full page. Those that are in a foreign language are printed in the original language in the left column so that the English translation occupying the right can be consulted with greater ease than in the original IPCB. All languages that do not use the romanized alphabet are transliterated, if possible. In some cases (e.g., Japan) the reports are bilingual with English. In such cases the titles are treated as those written in English and printed across the full page.

The place of publication is cited if known. The publisher, because it is usually the same agency that authored the publication, is left out. One of my inconsistencies, however, was to cite the printer if it was readily available, but I did not feel it necessary to seek it out if it was not at hand. The date of publication was one of the more annoying items to determine. It is surprising how many published works contain no date of publication anywhere in the physical volume, much less on the title page. My order of preference for the date was (1) the one on the title page, or front cover; (2) the date included in the printer's identification elsewhere in the publication; (3) the date of the preface or foreword; and (4) that cited by another publication. When none of those were available, the standard practice of the use of "n.d." (no date) was used. The pagination of census reports occasionally can be the only item distinguishing one report from another of the same date and title. Generally the numbers (both Roman and Arabic) cited are those printed in the volume. Unnumbered pages were often counted and inserted in brackets if of a significant number. Volumes which were variously paged and too long to sum up were noted as "var. pag."; those that could be reasonably totaled were enclosed in brackets ([87]p.).

In order to conserve space, subnational volumes (of states, provinces, etc.) have reduced citations: date and page numbers only. In some cases they are only listed in order, designated by the country's usage or alphabetically according to the language of the text, for example, Chiapas follows Colima (Mexico, 1970). The purpose for including the subnational names instead of stating only that such volumes exist is to be consistent in the numbering system I designed not only for the bibliography, but to serve as a shelflist as well. The original IPCB numbering system precluded the possibility of inserting late publications into their proper position based on their relationship to the other volumes of the set. The pattern I developed contains the qualities of the decimal system—ever ready to expand, and, if at all possible, mnemonic. Each item cited has a unique number within the country's entry. For example, India, 1961 is the set with the greatest number of publications for any one census as yet to appear. Its publications have been listed in the following fashion. The Census Papers start the entry; the first item is number 1961.1-62-1. The "1961" is obvious, the ".1" refers to the first group, Census Papers, the "-62" refers to the date of appearance used by the Indian agency, the "-1" continues the pattern established. Hence, India 1961.1-62-1 means "Census of India, 1961. Census Paper No. 1 of 1962." If one day a Census Paper No. 2 of 1962 were to be found, it could be labeled 1961.1-62-2 with no interference with the surrounding numbered volumes and put in its proper place on the shelf. The final results constitute the next group and follow the same pattern based on the internal numbering system set forth by the agency. 1961.2-1-1-A(1) is "Census of India, 1961, [final report], Volume I–India, Part 1-A general report, section 1." By comparison, 1961.2-25-1 is "Census of India, 1961, [final report], Volume 25–Pondicherry, Part 1 General report," and so forth.

Finally, in this, I hope, not-too-complicated explanation of the features of this volume, I wish to elaborate a bit on the location citations. The code symbols used are of my own design. The Key to Locations follows this introduction. I wish to emphasize here that this book is not a union catalog of census publications. This would imply that every library that has a copy of any one item cited is listed with the citation. To do this would consume immense amounts of time and labor. My only intention was to indicate at least one library for each item; if more were known, these, too, were cited. Even my modest intention was not totally fulfilled since there are gaps—perhaps not too many, but more than I would have liked. As a further aid to finding a library with a copy of the item you wish, please consult my publication, *National Population Censuses, 1945-1976: Some Holding Libraries,* (Clarion, Pa: APLIC, 1979). A spinoff of my work on this bibliography, it lists 54 libraries in the U.S. that have part or all of the publications for the country and census year listed. Please check first with the library listed that is located nearest you to see if what you want is there.

Limitations

In some cases, the publications cited were not available for personal consultation, so if there were any doubts about including it or not, I chose to be safe and leave it in. Correspondingly, any specific bibliographic data were treated in the same way. I tried to make this bibliography as complete and as accurate as possible. I console myself with the fact that no nation in the world has ever had a perfect census either.

KEY TO LOCATIONS

BC U.S. Bureau of the Census Library
Federal Office Building, No. 3 Rm. 2471
Washington, D.C. 20233 (301) 763-5040

Berkeley University of California
General Library
Government Documents Department (401) 863-2167
Berkeley, California 94720 -2168

CPC Carolina Population Center Library
University of North Carolina
University Square–East
Chapel Hill, North Carolina 27514 (919) 933-3081

CU Columbia University Libraries
Reference Department
535 West 114th Street
New York, New York 10027 (212) 280-2241

EB Encyclopedia Britannica Statistical Library
425 North Michigan Avenue
Chicago, Illinois 60611 (312) 321-7279

EGCC Economic Growth Center Collection
Yale University Library
Box 1958, Yale Station
New Haven, Connecticut 06520 (203) 436-2457

E–W East–West Population Institute
1777 East–West Road
Honolulu, Hawaii 96848 (808) 947-8144

Harvard Harvard College Library
Documents Division, Widener Library
Cambridge, Massachusetts 02138 (617) 495-2089

IASI Inter-American Statistical Institute—OAS
Focal Point for Statistical Information
1725 Eye Street, N.W. (202) 393-8450
Washington, D.C. 20006 Ext.8333

InU Indiana University Libraries
Tenth Street and Jordan Avenue
Bloomington, Indiana 47401 (812) 337-3403

JB–F	International Monetary Fund/International Bank for Reconstruction and Development Joint Library. (Joint Bank-Fund Lib.) 1818 H Street, N.W. Washington, D.C. 20433	
LC	Library of Congress Washington, D.C. 20540	(202) 426-5000
Mass.	University of Massachusetts Library Amherst, Massachusetts 01003	(413) 545-0058
NWU	Northwestern University Melville J. Herskovits Library of African Studies Evanston, Illinois 60201	(312) 492-7684
NYPL	New York Public Library Economic and Public Affairs Division Fifth Avenue and 42nd Street New York, New York 10018	(212) 790-6343
OPR	Office of Population Research—Library 21 Prospect Avenue Princeton, New Jersey 08540	(609) 452-5517
PC	Population Council Library 1 Dag Hammarskjold Plaza New York, New York 10017	(212) 644-1620
PRC	Population Research Center University of Texas Austin, Texas 78712	(512) 471-5514
PSC	Population Studies Center Demography Library University of Pennsylvania 3718 Locust Walk (CR) Philadelphia, Pennsylvania 19174	(215) 243-5375
PUL	Princeton University Library Princeton, New Jersey 08540	(609) 452-3180
SIC	Southern Illinois University—Carbondale Delyte W. Morris Library Carbondale, Illinois 62901	(618) 453-2522
SU	Stanford University Libraries Government Documents Department Stanford, California 94305	(717) 532-1474 -1462

TXU	University of Texas General Libraries
	Austin, Texas 78712
	  Benson Latin American Collection
	  Asian Collection
		(512) 471-3813
		-3818
		-3135

UFL	University of Florida Libraries Documents Department/Latin American Documents Library West Gainesville, Florida 32611	(904) 392-0366 -0367

UH–A   University of Hawaii Library
            Asia Collection
            2550 The Mall
            Honolulu, Hawaii 96822   (808) 948-7205
UN   Dag Hammarskjold Library, United Nations
            P.O. Box 20, Grand Central Station
            New York, New York 10017   (212) 754-5321
Yale   Yale University Library
            Box 1603 A, Yale Station
            New Haven, Connecticut 06520   (203) 436-8335

Commercial Microform Publishers of Censuses
RIR   Redgrave Information Resources
                Corporation
            53 Wilton Road
            Westport, Connecticut 06880   (203) 226-6963
RPI   Research Publications, Inc.
            12 Lunar Drive
            Woodbridge, Connecticut 06525   (203) 397-2600

AFGHANISTAN

Republic of Afghanistan   Capital: Kabul.
Statistical Agency: Central Statistics Office
                     Prime Ministry/P.O. Box No. 2002
                     Kabul,
Publications distributor: same

The first census, planned for 1978, was postponed until July 1979. There was
a census of Kabul City (1965) and the Afghan Demographic Survey, 1971-1974.

     Afghanistan. Ministry of Planning. Department of Statistics.
1965.1   Kabul household sample survey [1344 (i.e., 1965)].   Kabul, [1968].
   ___p. [UN

     Note: There also has been a reference to "Kabul population pilot pro-
ject results, 1344 (1965)." It is not known if these titles are of
the same or of different publications.

     Afghanistan. Ministry of Planning. Department of Statistics.
  .2   Lashkar Gah household sample survey. Kabul, 1969.   ___p. [UN

     Afghanistan. Ministry of Planning.
1966.1   Population and manpower resources in Afghanistan, 1345-1350 (1966/
  67-1971/72).   Kabul, 1345 (1967). 18p. [JB-F

     [Afghanistan. Central Statistics Office].
     National demographic and family guidance survey of the settled popu-
lation of Afghanistan, 1972-1973. n.p., 1975. 3v.
1973.1-1   Demography, [by] Solomon Chu, Robert N. Hill, and Saxon Graham.
  180p. [LC, OPR
  .1-2   Methodology. Solomon Chu, Robert N. Hill and Paul A. Martino,
  editors.   ___p. [LC
  .1-3   Tables. Paul A. Martino and Susan F. Schultz, editors. 118p.
  [LC, OPR
  .1-4   [Not applicable].

     Afghanistan Council. The Asia Society.
1974.1   Demographic research in Afghanistan: a national survey of the settled population, by Graham B. Kerr.   New York, 1977. [6], 100p.
  [OPR

     The next census is scheduled for May-June 1979.

ALBANIA

People's Socialist Republic of Albania   Capital: Tirana
Statistical Agency: Bureau of Statistics
                      [Drejtoria e Statistikës]
                      Commission of State Planning
                      Tirana,
Publications Distributor: Kriban and Sogner
                          Box 68
                          D8 München 34, German Federal Republic.

There are no separate official publications for the Albanian censuses. Data
can be found in the statistical yearbooks and secondary sources listed below.

    Albania.   Drejtoria e Statisti-
       kës.
1958.1   Anuari statistikor i R. P.   Statistical annual of the Peo-
    Sh., 1958.   Tirana, 1958.   ple's Republic of Albania, 1958.
    312p.   [LC

    U.S.   Joint Publications Research Service.
 .1a   Translation and glossary of Albanian statistical yearbook, 1958.
New York, 1959. Pp. a-b, 1-90. (JPRS: 940-D) [

    Albania.   Drejtoria e Statisti-
       kës.
    Anuari statistikor i R. P.   Statistical annual of the Peo-
    Sh., [year].   Tirana, 1959-   ple's Republic of Albania, [year].
    1962.
1959.1   ..., 1959. 1959. xv, 267, 23p. [TXU, LC
 .1a Translation. 1959. xxxix, 124p. [TXU
1960.1   ..., 1960. 1960. xviii, 369p. [TXU, LC
 .1a Translation.   [
1961.1   ..., 1961. 1962. xvii, 351p. [TXU, LC
 .1a Translation. 1962. xliv, 142p. [TXU

    [The volume for 1962 was not issued. The title of the series was
changed in 1963. The first issue included 1962 figures.]

    Albania.   Drejtoria e Statisti-
       kës.
    Vjetari statistikor i R. P.   Statistical yearbook of the Peo-
    Sh., [year].   Tirana, 1964-1967 ple's Republic of Albania, [year]
1963.1   ..., 1963. 1964. xviii, 42p. [TXU, UN, PRC, OPR, RPI
 .1a Translation. li, 168p. [TXU, UN, PRC, OPR, RPI
1964.1   ..., 1964. 1964. xix, 486p. [TXU, UN, PRC, OPR, RPI
 .1a Translation. 1965. xv, 83p. [TXU, OPR
1965.1   ..., 1965. 1965. xix, 487p. [TXU, OPR
 .1a Translation. xv, 80p. [TXU, OPR
1966.1   ..., 1966. 1967. xv, 160p. [TXU, OPR
 .1a Translation. ix, 36p. [TXU, OPR

[The next volumes were issued in a double-year series.]

1968.1   ..., 1967-68. 1968. xv, 151p. [TXU, OPR
   .1a   Translation. 22p. [TXU
1970.1   ..., 1969-70. 1970. xiii, 152p. [TXU, OPR
1972.1   ..., 1971-72. 1973. xv, 214p. [TXU, OPR

[The following was a special jubilee volume.]

Albania. Drejtoria e Përgi-
      jithshine e Statistikës.
1973.1   30 vjet Shqipëri Socialiste,   Thirty years of Socialist Albania,
      1973. Tirana, 1974. 239p.   1973.
                                              [TXU, OPR

Secondary sources.

1953 Silaev, E.D.
      [Albania: economic and geographical characteristics]. Edited by
      B.P. Tihomirov. Moscow, Government Geographical and Literary Print-
      ing House, 1953. 1974p. map. [

1957 Bardi, H.
      Recensamintele populaţiei in   Population censuses in the Peo-
      Republica Popularā Albania. IN: ple's Republic of Albania.
      Revista de Statistica (Bucharest)   [PRC, BC, RPI
      (1957)7:3-20.

      Milo, P.
      Popullsia e Republikës Popull-   The population of the People's
      lore të Shqipërisë sipas regjis-   Republic of Albania according
      trimit të Tetorit 1955. IN: to the census of October 1955.
      Ekonomia Popullore (Tirana) 4   [NYPL, BC, PRC, RPI
      (5):53-69.

1962 Sheri, F. and Sh. Imami.
      Një përshkrim i shkurtër i   Short description of the history
      historikut të statistikës në   of statistics in our country.
      vendru tonë. IN: Ekonomia   [NYPL
      Popullore (Tirana) 9(4):54-68.

1963 Dibra, Jaho and Pasko Vako.
      Përbërja demografike e popull-   Demographic characteristics of
      sisë sipas regjistrimit të per-   the population according to the
      gjithshëm të vitit 1960. IN: general census of 1960.
      Ekonomia popullore (Tirana) 10   [NYPL
      (6):81-91.

1964 S[auvy], A[lfred]
      La population de l'Albania.   The population of Albania.
      IN: Population (Paris) 19(3):   [PRC
      583-584.

1965   Dibra, Jaho and Pasko Vako.
           La population de l'Albanie   The population of Albania accord-
        d'après les recensements de   ing to the censuses of 1955 and
        1955 à 1960. IN: Population   1960.
        (Paris) 20(2):253–264.   [PRC

1974   Sheri, F.
           Popullsia e Shqipërisë. Ti-   The population of Albania.
        rana, 1974.   p.   [

        Koziński, Leszek A.
           Urbanization in East-Central Europe after World War II.   IN: East
        European quarterly 8(2):129–153.   [TXU

1975   ?
             ?
        IN: Demografie (Prague) 17(4):
        368–369.   [NYPL, LC

        Sivignon, Michel
           Quelques données démographi-   Some demographic data on the
        ques sur la République Populaire   People's Republic of Albania.
        d'Albanie. IN: Revue de geo-   [NYPL, PRC
        graphie de Lyon 45(1):61–74.

        Hofsten, Erland
           Demographic transition and economic development in Albania.   IN:
        European demographic information bulletin 6(3):147–158.   [TXU

1976   S[auvy], A[lfred].
           La population de l'Albanie   The population of Albania in
        en transition. IN: Population   transition.
        (Paris) 31(1):193–195.   [PRC

ALGERIA

Democratic and Popular Republic of Algeria   Capital: Algiers.
Statistical Agency: National Bureau of Statistics and Accounting.
                      [Direction Nationale des Statistiques et de la
                          Comptabilité Nationale.]
                      Chemin Ibn Badis--El Biar
                      B.P. 478
                      Alger,
Publications Distributor: same

        Algeria. Service de Statistique
            Générale.
1948.1   Résultats définitifs du de-   Final results of the population
    nombrement de la population du   enumeration of October 31, 1948.
    31 octobre 1948.   Alger, Impr.   [UN, PRC, RPI
    Officielle, 1949. 15p.

        Algeria. Service de Statistique
            Générale.
        Résultats statistiques du   Statistical results of the enu-
    dénombrement de la population,   meration of the population taken
    effectué le 31 octobre 1948.   on October 31, 1948.
    Alger, V. Heintz, Ancienne Impr.,
    1950-1954. Vols. I-IV.
    .2-1   Population légale ou de   De jure or permanent resident
    résidence habituelle. Réper-   population. Statistical index
    toire statistique des communes   of the communes of Algeria.
    d'Algérie. 1950. xxxiv, 148p.   [UN, NYPL, LC, PRC, RPI
    .2-2   Population non musulmane.   Non-Muslim population. Marital
    État civil et activité profes-   status and occupational activity.
    sionnelle. 1952. 93, 120p.   [UN, NYPL, LC, PRC, RPI
    .2-3   Population musulmane.   Muslim population. Marital sta-
    État civil et activité profes-   tus and occupational activity.
    sionnelle. 1954. 94, 122p.   [BC, NYPL, LC, PRC, RPI
    .2-4   Familles. 1954. 204p.   Families.
                                          [UN, NYPL, LC, PRC, RPI

        Algeria. Service de Statistique
            Générale.
        Résultats statistiques du   Statistical results of the cen-
    recensement de la population   sus of the population of Octo-
    du 31 octobre 1954.   Alger, l'   ber 31, 1954.
    Impr. Baconnier Frères, [1957-
    1960]. Vols. I-III.
1954.1-1   Population légale ou de   De jure or permanent resident
    résidence habituelle. Réper-   population. Statistical index
    toire statistique des communes   of the communes of Algeria.
    d'Algérie. n.d. xlviii, 277p.   [TXU, LC, Berkeley, JB-F, RPI
    .1-2   Sexe, âge, état matrimo-   Sex, age, marital status, place
    nial, lieu de naissance, instruc-   of birth, education.
    tion. n.d. 143p.   [LC, PRC, UN, JB-F, RPI

1954.1-3   Population active. n.d.   Economically active population.
             259p.   [LC, BC, PRC, RPI

             Algeria. Service de Statistique
                  Générale.
1960.1   Premiers résultats du recense-   First results of the census of
           ment de la population de 1960.   population of 1960. (Final re-
           (Résultats définitifs). Alger,   sults).
           n.d. 32p.   [

             Algeria. Service de Statistique
                  Générale.
  .2   Dénombrement de la population.   Population enumeration. Final
           Résultats définitifs. Arrêté du   results. Decree of September 1,
           ler septembre 1961 authentifiant   1961, authenticating the results
           les résultats du dénombrement de   of the population enumeration
           la population effectué du 15 sep-   taken September 15 to October 1,
           tembre au ler octobre 1960. (Tab-   1960. (Corresponding tables
           leaux correspondants joint).   attached).
           Alger, 1961. 32p. (Extraits du   [UN, PRC, RPI
           R.A.A., no. 74, du 15 septembre
           1961.)

             France. Centre d'Études et d'In-
                  formation des Problèmes Hu-
                  mains dans les Zones Arides.
1961.1   La population des départe-   The population of the Saharan
           ments sahariens. Paris, 1962.   departments.
           3 vols. in 1.
           (1. La population légale. [4],   (1. The de jure population. 2.
           18p. 2. Les structures: sexes,   The structures: sex, age groups,
           groupes d'âge, catégories socio-   socio-occupational categories.
           professionnelles. [1], 67p. 3.   3. Statistic study.)
           Étude statistique. 30p.)   [UN, JB-F, RPI

             Algeria. Direction des Statis-
                  tiques. CNRP.
1966.1   Recensement général de la   General population census, 1966.
           population, 1966. Situation de   Situation of residence by commune.
           residence par commune. Alger,   [LB-F
           1967. 54p.

             Algeria. Direction des Statis-
                  tiques. CNRP.
  .2   Recensement général de la   General population census, 1966.
           population, 1966. Pyramides des   Age pyramids by five-year groups.
           âges par groupes quinquennaux,   Complete tabulation. Urban zones
           exploitation exhaustive, zones   of Greater Algiers.
           urbaines du Grand Alger. (113   [
           pyramides). Alger, 1968.

Algeria. Direction des Statis-
      tiques. CNRP.
   Recensement général de la
population et de l'habitat, 1966.
Résultats de l'exploitation par
sondage. Alger, 1968. 2v. in 1.

General population and housing
census, 1966. Results of the
sample tabulation.

1966.3-1   Données statistiques sur
la population. 118p.

Statistical data on the population.
[UN, PRC, OPR, RPI

.3-2   Données statistiques sur
l'habitat. Pp. 122-161.

Statistical data on housing.
[UN, PRC, OPR, RPI

Algeria. Direction des Statis-
      tiques. CNRP
   Recensement général de la
population et de l'habitat (1966).
Résultats du sondage (1/10e).
[Alger, 1967-1968]. Vols. 1-4.

General population and housing
census (1966). Results of the
one-in-ten sample.

.4-1   Démographie générale, instruction. 1967. ix, 291p.

General demography, education.
[UN

.4-2   Caractéristiques socio-
économiques et de la population.
1968. vi, 89p.

Socio-economic and population
characteristics.
[UN, JB-F, RPI

.4-3&4   Caractéristiques démographiques et culturelles des femmes et enfants de moins d'un an.
/Habitat. 1968. iv, 161p.

Demographic and cultural characteristics of women and infants
of less than one year of age./
Housing.
[UN, JB-F, RPI

Algeria. Direction des Statis-
      tiques. CNRP.
   Recensement général de la
population et de l'habitat (1966).
Résultats exhaustifs. Serie I.
[Alger, 1969-1970]. Vol. 1-17
in 18v.

General population and housing
census (1966). Complete tabulation results.

1966.5-1 through 1966.5-16. 1. Wilaya d'Alger. 183p./2. Ville d'Alger.
234p./3. Wilaya d'Annaba. 225p./4. Aurès. 223p./5. Constantine.
267p./6. El-Asnam. 251p./7. Médéa. 276p./8. Mostaganem. 265p./9.
Oasis. 299p./10. Oran. 218p./11. Saida. 201p./12. La Saoura. 226p./
13. Sétif. 287p./14. Tiaret. 202p./15. Tizi-Ouzou. 287p./16. Tlem-
cen. 218p. [NWU, PSC

   Résultats de l'Algérie
entière. 1970. 2 parts.

Results for Al Algeria.

.5-17-1   Population. 665, [7]p.

Population.
[UN, NWU, PRC, RPI

.5-17-2   Habitat. [5], pp. 666-
789.

Housing.
[UN, NWU, PRC, RPI

Algeria. Direction des Statis-
      tiques. CNRP.
   Recensement général de la
population et de l'habitat (1966).

General population and housing
census (1966). Series A-D.

Série A-D in 17v.
    Série A. Résultats divers.   Series A. Miscellaneous results.
Vol. 1-8.

1966.6-A-1   Population totale par com-   Total population by commune ac-
mune selon sexe et âge. 1969.   cording to sex and age.
96p.   [NWU

.6-A-2   Population totale par   Total population by Wilaya, urban
wilaya, secteur urbain et rural,   and rural sector, according to
selon sexe et âge. 1969. 35p.   sex and age.
                                   [NWU

.6-A-3   Résultats généraux pour   General results for the whole of
l'ensemble de l'Algérie présen-   Algeria presented by Wilaya.
tés par wilaya. 1970. 535p.   [UN, NWU, RPI

.6-A-4   Rapport général et metho-   General report and methodology.
dologie. 1971. 130, [102]p.   [UN, NWU, PRC, RPI

.6-A-5   Population totale par com-   Total population by commune, ac-
mune, selon sexe et âge (de 0 à   cording to sex and age (from 0
19 ans détaillé). 1970. 207p.   to 19 years of age detailed).
                                 [UN, NWU

.6-A-6   Caractéristiques socio-   Socio-economic characteristics.
économiques. Tableaux supplé-   Supplementary tables.
mentaires. 1971. 535p.   [UN, NWU, RPI

.6-A-7   Données supplémentaires   Supplementary data on housing.
sur l'habitat. 1971. 364,[2]p.   [UN, NWU, RPI

.6-A-8   Population non Algérienne.   Non-Algerian population.
1971. 545p.   [UN, NWU, RPI

.6-A-9   Aperçu général. 1971.   General overview.
    p.   [

    Série B. Population et habi-   Series B. Population and housing
tat des villes et chefs-lieux.   of cities and administrative cen-
Vol. 1-5 in 7v.   ters.

.6-B-1   Population des villes et   Population of cities and adminis-
chefs-lieux. Données générales.   trative centers. General data.
1970. 195p.   [UN, NWU, RPI

    État and structure de la   Status and structure of the popu-
population des chefs-lieux ur-   lation of urban and semi-urban
bains et semi-urbains. 1971.   administrative centers.
Tomes 1-2.

.6-B-2-1   635p.   [UN, NWU, RPI
.6-B-2-2   626p.   [UN, NWU, RPI
.6-B-3   L'habitat dans les chefs-   Housing in urban and semi-urban
lieux urbains et semi-urbains.   administrative centers.
1971. 623p.   [UN, NWU, RPI

.6-B-4   État et structure des   Status and structure of house-
ménages et familles des villes.   holds and families in cities.
1972. 289p.   [UN, NWU, RPI

.6-B-5

.6-B-6

Série C. Ménages et familles.
Vol. 1-2 in 3v.
État et structure des familles en Algérie. Tomes 1-2.
1966.6-C-1-1   510p.
.6-C-1-2   323p.
.6-C-2   État et structure des ménages en Algérie. 1972. 490p.

Série D. Carte district.
Vol. 1-2.
.6-D-1   Population.

.6-D-2   Habitat.

Algeria. Direction des Statistiques. CNRP.
.7   La population active au recensement de 1966. Alger, 1970. 154p. (Série occasionnelle).

Algeria. Commissariat National aux Recensements et Enquêtes Statistiques.
.8-1   Code géographique national de l'Algérie au recensement de 1966.   Alger, 1969.   49p.

Algeria. Direction des Statistiques et de la Comptabilité Nationale. Commissariat National aux Recensements et Enquêtes Statistiques.
1977.0-1 Deuxième recensement général de la population et de l'habitat. Résultats préliminaires par commune.   Alger, 1977. 39p.

Series C. Household and families.
Status and structure of families in Algeria.
[NYPL, LC, OPR, NWU
[NYPL, LC, NWU, RPI
Status and structure of households in Algeria.
[NYPL, NWU, RPI
Series D. Regional maps.

Population.
[
Housing.
[

The economically active population in the census of 1966.
[NWU

National geographic code of Algeria at the 1966 census.   Commune code.
[NWU

Second general population and housing census.   Preliminary results by commune.
[

AMERICAN SAMOA

Capital: Pago Pago

Statistical Agency: Development Planning Office
                     Pago Pago (Tutuila Island),
                              &
                     U.S. Bureau of the Census
                     Washington, D.C. 20233
Publications Distributor: same

U.S. Bureau of the Census.
1950.1-2-51/54. Census of population: 1950. A report of the seventeenth
     decennial census of the United States. Volume II. Characteristics
     of the population. Part 51-54. Territories and possessions (Alaska,
     Hawaii, Puerto Rico, American Samoa, Canal Zone, Guam, and Virgin
     Islands). 1953. var. pag. [PRC, TXU, BC, RPI

American Samoa. Governor.
1956.1   Census of American Samoa, September 25, 1956. n.p., n.d. 22p.
     [PRC, RPI

U.S. Bureau of the Census.
1960.1-1-54/57. Census of population: 1960. The eighteenth decennial
     census of the United States. Volume I. Characteristics of the popu-
     lation. Part 54-57. Outlying areas (Virgin Islands, Guam, American
     Samoa, and Canal Zone). 1963. [218]p. [PRC, BC, LC, RPI

U.S. Bureau of the Census.
1970.1-1-54/58. Census of population: 1970. Volume I. Characteristics
     of the population. Part 54-58. Guam, Virgin Islands, American Samoa,
     Canal Zone, Trust Territory of the Pacific Islands. 1973. var. pag.
     [PRC, BC, LC

American Samoa. Development Planning Office.
1974.0-1   The 1974 census of American Samoa: enumerator's instruction
     book. Prepared by Michael Levin. Pago Pago, 1974. ii, 36p. 2 maps.
     [E-W, PRC

American Samoa. Development Planning Office.
1974.1   Report on the 1974 census of American Samoa. Part 1: Basic
     information. [Pago Pago], 1974. iii, 162p. [PRC, E-W

ANDORRA

                                          Capital: Andorra la Vella
Statistical Agency: Tourists' Information Bureau
                      [Sindicat d'Iniciativa]
                      Andorra la Vella,

   Censuses are reputed to have been taken in 1948, 1954, and 1971 but
no official publications have been located.

ANGOLA

People's Republic of Angola   Capital: Luanda
Statistical Agency: Bureau of Statistical Services
                     [Direcção dos Serviços de Estatıstica]
                     Caixa Postale 1215
                     Luanda,
Publications Distributor: same

    Angola. Repartição Técnica de
        Estatística Geral
      II recenseamento geral da   Second general census of popula-
population, 1950. Luanda, Im-   tion, 1950
prensa Nacional, 1953-1956.
Vols. I-V.
1950.1-1   População segundo o tipo   Population according to racial/
somático e o sexo; familias e   ethnic types and sex; families
convivências, prédios e fogos.   and households, buildings and
1953. 129, 5p. 2 maps.   houses.
                                           [PRC, LC, Harvard, Yale, NWU,
                                           JB-F, RPI

  .1-2   População civilizada, pre-   Non-indigenous population, de
sente, segundo as idades e a re-   facto, by age and religion.
ligião. 1955. 155p.   [PRC, LC, Yale, Harvard, NWU
                                           JB-F, RPI

  .1-3   População civilizada, pre-   Non-indigenous population, de
sente, segundo o grau de instru-   facto, by education and marital
ção e o estado civil. 1955.   status.
401p.   [PRC, LC, Harvard, Yale, NWU
                                           JB-F, RPI

  .1-4   População não civilizada,   Indigenous population, according
segundo as idades, a religião,   to age, religion, groups of
os grupos as mulheres que gera-   women with children and education
ram filhos e a instrução, por   by commune or parish.
concelhos ou circunscrições.   [PRC, LC, Harvard, Yale, NWU,
1955. 174p.   JB-F, RPI
  .1-5   Familias e convivências,   Families and households, de jure
população de residência habitual   and de facto populations, accord-
e população presente, segundo a   ing to nationality. De facto
nacionalidade. População portu-   Portuguese population according
guesa, presente, segundo a natu-   to origin. Foreign population,
ralidade. População estrangeiro,   according to origin, age, mari-
segundo a naturalidade, idades,   tal status, religion, education,
estado civil, religião, instru-   and livelihood.
ção e meios de vida. 1956.   [PRC, LC, Harvard, Yale, NWU,
531p.   JB-F, RPI

    Angola. Repartição de Estatís-
        tica Geral.
      3° recenseamento geral da   Third general population census,
população, 1960. Luanda, Im-   1960.
prensa Nacional, 1964-1969.

Vols. 1-4, anexo.

1960.1-1   População segundo os grupos étnicos, estado civil e idades. 1964. 202p.

Population according to ethnic groups, marital status and age.
[PRC, LC, Harvard, NWU, JB-F, RPI

.1-2   População segundo as nacionalidades e naturalidades. 1967. 54p.

Population according to nationality and origin.
[PRC, LC, Harvard, NWU, JB-F, RPI

.1-3   População residente segundo a religião, os grupos linguísticos e a fecundidade. 1968. 118, [3]p.

Resident population according to religion, linguistic groups and fertility.
[PRC, LC, Harvard, NWU, JB-F, RPI

.1-4   População residente segundo as condições perante o trabalho. 1969. 138, [3]p.

Resident population according to economic activity.
[PRC, LC, Harvard, NWU, JB-F, RPI

.1-5   Anexo. Inventário de prédios e fogos. 1967. 85, [3]p.

Annex. Inventory of buildings and housing.
[PRC, LC, Harvard, NWU, JB-F, RPI

Angola. Direcção dos Serviços de Estatística.

1970.0-1 População de Angola. Recenseada em 1970, segundo os distritos e os concelhos ou circunscrições. Apuramento provisório. [Luanda, 1971?] 7p.

Population of Angola. Censused in 1970, according to districts and the communes or parishes. Provisional verification.
[OPR

[See also: Portugal 1970.3.]

ANTIGUA

State of Antigua (West Indies)   Capital: St. John's
Statistical Agency: Statistics Division
                     Ministry of Planning, Development and External
                        Affairs
                     St. John's,
Publications Distributor: same

       Jamaica. Central Bureau of Statistics.
1946   West Indian census, 1946.   Kingston, Government Printer, 1948–
       1950.
           [See Commonwealth Caribbean Nos. 1946.1-A and 1946.1-F].

       Jamaica. Department of Statistics.
1960   West Indies population census.   Kingston, Government Printer,
       n.d.
           [See Commonwealth Caribbean Nos. 1960.2-A-1 and 1960.2-A-2].

       Note: Antigua did not participate in the 1970 Commonwealth Caribbean
       census program.

       Antigua. Ministry of Planning, Development and External Affairs.
             Statistics Division.
           Census of population, 1970.   St. John's, 1974–1975. Vols. I–III.
1970.1-1   I.   Housing characteristics. 1974. 21p. [UN, PRC, JB-F
    .1-2   II. Social and demographic characteristics. 1974. 21p. [PRC,
       UN, OPR
    .1-3   III. Economic characteristics. 1975. 21p. [UN, PRC

—

ARGENTINA

Argentine Republic   Capital: Buenos Aires
Statistical Agency: National Institute of Statistics and Censuses
                     [Instituto Nacional de Estadística y Censos (INEC)]
                     Secretaria de Estado de Programación y Coordinación
                          Económica
                     Hipólito Yrigayen 250--Piso 12
                     Buenos Aires,
Publications Distributor: same

    Argentina. Dirección Nacional
       de Estadística y Censos.

IV censo general de la nación, 1947. Buenos Aires, 1951. Nos. 1-2.	Fourth general census of the nation, 1947.
1947.1-1 Resultados generales del censo de población. 1951. 40p.	General results of the population census. [TXU, NYPL, PRC, JB-F, RPI
.1-2 Comparación de los resultados del censo de población. 1951. 30p.	Comparison of the results of the population census. [TXU, NYPL, SU, PRC, JB-F, RPI

    Argentina. DNEC.

IV censo general de la nación. Buenos Aires, Talleres Gráficos de Guillermo Kraft, 1948-1952. Tomos I-III.	Fourth general census of the nation.
.2-1 I. Censo de población. n.d. 727p.	Population census. [PRC, TXU, NYPL, RPI
.2-2 II. Censo agropecuario. n.d. xxxiv, 491p.	Agricultural census. [JB-F, TXU, PRC, RPI
.2-3 III. Censos: industrial, de comercio... 1952. 452p.	Industrial and commercial censuses... [JB-F, TXU, PRC, RPI

    Argentina. DNEC.

1960.0-1 Censo nacional de población, 1960: antecedentes, normas y procedimientos. Buenos Aires, 1965. 80p.	National census of population, 1960: antecedents, norms and procedures. [PRC, TXU, NYPL, RPI

    Argentina. DNEC.

.1 Censo nacional 1960: características principales de la población obtenidas por muestreo. Buenos Aires, 1963. xii, 200p.	National census 1960: main characteristics of the population obtained by sample. [PRC, JB-F, RPI

    Argentina. DNEC.

Censo nacional de población, 1960. Buenos Aires, 1965. Tomos I-IX in 11v.	National census of population, 1960.

.2-1   I. Total del país. xliv,   Whole country.
   117p.   [PRC, TXU, RPI
1960.2-2 through 1960.2-9. [Number of volumes for each zone as noted.]
     2. Gran Buenos Aires-Capital Federal. 317p./3. Zona Pampeana--
     Buenos Aires, La Pampa. 360p./4. Zona Central--Córdoba, Santa Fé.
     liii, 286p./5. Zona Mesopotámica--Corrientes, Entre Ríos, Misiones.
     lx, 380p./6. Zona Chaquena--Chaco, Formosa, Santiago del Estero.
     lxi, 382p./7-1. Zona Noroeste, parte 1^a--Catamarca, Jujuy. lxxi,
     240p./7-2. Zona Noroeste, parte 2^a--La Rioja, Salta, Tucumán. [iv],
     pp. 241-626./8. Zona Cuyana--Mendoza, San Juan, San Luis. lxii,
     368p./9-1. Zona Patagónica, parte 1^a--Chubat, Neuquén, 1965. lxxii,
     237p./9-2. Zona Patagónica, parte 2^a--Río Negro, Santa Cruz, Tierra
     del Fuego. 1965. pp.[238]-592. [PRC, TXU, NYPL, RPI

Argentina. Instituto Nacional de
     Estadística y Censos (INEC)
1970.0-1 Manual de censista: censo na-   Enumerator's manual: national
     cional de población, familias, y   census of population, families,
     viviendas, 30 de setiembre de 1970.   and housing, September 30, 1970.
     Buenos Aires, 197?. xi, 211p.   [BC

Argentina. INEC.
     Censo nacional de población,   National census of population,
     familias y viviendas, 1970. Re-   families, and housing, 1970.
     sultados obtenidos por muestra.   Results obtained from sampling.
     Buenos Aires, 1974. 25v.
   .1-1   Total del país. 56p.   Whole country.
                                               [PRC, JB-F
1970.1-2 through 1970.1-26. 2. Capital Federal. 26p./3. Buenos Aires.
     51p./4. Gran Buenos Aires. Area Metropolitana. 26p./5. Catamarca.
     26 p./6. Córdoba. 26p./7. Corrientes. 26p./8. Chaco. 26p./9.
     Chubut. 26p./10. Entre Ríos. 26p./11. Formosa. 26p./12. Jujuy.
     26p./13. La Pampa. 26p./14. La Rioja. 26p./15. Mendoza. 26p./16.
     Misiones. 26p./17. Neuquén. 26p./18. Río Negro. 26p./19. Salta.
     26p./20. San Juan. 26p./21. San Luis. 26p./22. Santa Cruz. 26p./
     23. Santa Fé. 26p./24. Santiago del Estero. 26p./25. Tucumán. 26p./
     26. Tierra del Fuego. 21p. [IASI, BC, PRC, OPR

AUSTRALIA

Commonwealth of Australia.   Capital: Canberra ACT
Statistical Agency: Australian Bureau of Statistics
                      P.O. Box 10
                      Belconnen, ACT, 2616,
Publications Distributor: Government Printing Office
                      Box 17
                      Canberra, ACT, 2600,

     Australia. Commonwealth Bureau of Census and Statistics.
       Census of the Commonwealth of Australia, 30th June 1947.   Can-
    berra, L.F. Johnson, Government Printer, n.d. Vols. I-III.
1947.1-1   I. Comprising parts I-XVI of the detailed tables.   928p.
    [TXU, RPI
  .1-2   II. Comprising parts XVII-XIX of the detailed tables. pp.
    929-1602. [TXU, RPI
  .1-3   III. Comprising parts XX-XXVIII of the detailed tables, sta-
    tistician's report, Australian life tables. pp. 1603-2174, 386, 19p.
    [TXU, PRC, RPI

     Australia. Commonwealth Bureau of Census and Statistics.
       Census of the Commonwealth of Australia, 30th June 1954.   Can-
    berra, A.J. Arthur, Government Printer, 1955-1958. Vols. I-VIII
    and Australian life tables in 40v.
      I. New South Wales. 5 parts.
1954.1-1-1   Analysis of population in local government areas, etc. 1955.
    2, 191p. [PRC, RPI
  .1-1-2   Cross-classifications of the characteristics of the population.
    1957. 2, 168p. [PRC, RPI
  .1-1-3   Analysis of dwellings in local government areas, etc. 1956.
    2, 196p. [PRC, RPI
  .1-1-4   Cross-classifications of the characteristics of the dwellings
    and of householders. 1957. 2, 63p. [PRC, RPI
  .1-1-5   Population and occupied dwellings in localities with a popula-
    tion of 50 persons or more. 1955. 51, 3p. [PRC, RPI

    The above pattern is repeated for each of the States. II. Victoria.
    (1954.1-2-1 through 1954.1-2-5)/III. Queensland. (1954.1-3-1 through
    1954.1-3-5)/IV. South Australia. (1954.1-4-1 through 1954.1-4-5)/
    V. Western Australia. (1954.1-5-1 through 1954.1-5-5)/VI. Tasmania.
    (1954.1-6-1 through 1954.1-6-5). [PRC, RPI
      VII. Territories.
  .1-7-1   Northern Territory: population. 1957. 2, 114p. maps. [PRC
  .1-7-2   Northern Territory: dwellings and householders. 1957. 2,
    36p. [PRC, RPI
  .1-7-3   Australian Capital Territory: population. 1957. 2, 109p.
    [PRC, RPI
  .1-7-4   Australian Capital Territory: dwellings and householders.
    1957. 37, 1p. [PRC, RPI
  .1-7-5   External territories (Papua, New Guinea, Norfolk Island and
    Nauru): population and dwellings. 1958. 30p. [PRC, RPI

VIII. Australia.
1961.1-8-1   Cross-classifications of the characteristics of the popula-
        tion. 1957. 192, 2p. [PRC, RPI
   .1-8-1s Supplement to part 1. Cross-classifications of the character-
        istics of the population: race. 1958. 33, 1p. [PRC, RPI
   .1-8-2   Cross-classifications of the characteristics of dwellings and
        of householders. 1957. 76, 2p. [PRC, RPI
   .1-8-4   Australian life tables, 1953-1955. n.d. 20p, [PRC, RPI

    Australia. Commonwealth Bureau of Census and Statistics.
        Census of the Commonwealth of Australia, 30th June 1961.   Can-
    berra, A.J. Arthur, Government Printer, 1962-1965. Vols. I-VIII in
    38v.
        I. New South Wales.
1961.1-1-1   Analysis of population in local government areas and in non-
        municipal towns of 1,000 persons or more. 1963. 7, 124p. map.
        [PRC, RPI
   .1-1-2   Cross-classifications of the characteristics of the popula-
        tion. 1965. 266p. [PRC, RPI
   .1-1-3   Analysis of dwellings in local government areas and in non-
        municipal towns of 1,000 persons or more. 1964. 8, 138p. [PRC, RPI
   .1-1-4   Cross-classifications of the characteristics of dwellings and
        householders. 1965. 75p. [PRC, RPI
   .1-1-5   Population and dwellings in localities. 1963. 66p. [PRC, RPI

    The above pattern is repeated for each of the States. II. Victoria.
    (1961.1-2-1 through 1961.1-2-5)/III. Queensland. (1961.1-3-1 through
    1961.1-3-5)/IV. South Australia. (1961.1-4-1 through 1961.1-4-5)/
    V. Western Australia. (1961.1-5-1 through 1961.1-5-5)/VI. Tasmania.
    (1961.1-6-1 through 1961.1-6-5) [PRC, RPI
        VII. Territories.
   .1-7-1   Northern Territory: population. 1965. 188p. [PRC, RPI
   .1-7-2   Northern Territory: dwellings and householders. 1964. 70p.
        [PRC, RPI
   .1-7-3   Australian Capital Territory: population. 1965. 182p.
        [PRC, RPI
   .1-7-4   Australian Capital Territory: dwellings and householders.
        1964. 58p. [PRC, RPI
   .1-7-5   External Territories [Papua, New Guinea, Nauru, Norfolk Island,
        Christmas Island, and Cocos (Keeling) Islands]: population and
        dwellings. 1965. 59p. [PRC, RPI
        VIII. Australia.
   .1-8-1   Cross-classifications of the characteristics of the popula-
        tion. 1965. 302p. [PRC, RPI
   .1-8-2   Cross-classifications of the characteristics of dwellings and
        of householders. 1965. 79p. [PRC, RPI
   .1-8-3   Population and dwellings in localities. 1964. 204p. [PRC,RPI

    Australia. Commonwealth Bureau of Census and Statistics.
        Census of population and housing, 30th June 1966. Canberra,
    Government Printer, 1970-1973. Vols. 1-6 in 38v.

      1. Population: single characteristics. Parts 1-11.
1966.1-1-1   Age. 1970. 41p. [PRC, BC, RPI
.1-1-2   Marital status. 1970. 21p. [PRC, BC, RPI
.1-1-3   Birthplace. 1970. 73p. [PRC, BC, RPI
.1-1-4   Nationality. 1970. 63p. [PRC, BC, RPI
.1-1-5   Period of residence. 1970. 25p. [PRC, BC, RPI
.1-1-6   Educational attainment. 1970. 19p. [PRC, BC, RPI
.1-1-7   Religion. 1970. 39p. [PRC, BC, RPI
.1-1-8   Occupational status. 1970. 23p. [PRC, BC, RPI
.1-1-9   Industry. 1970. 107p. [PRC, BC, RPI
.1-1-10 Occupation. 1970. 121p. [PRC, BC, RPI
.1-1-11 Race. 1971. 30p. [PRC, BC, RPI
      2. Population: related characteristics. Parts 1-5.
.1-2-1   Growth and distribution of the population. 1973. 23p. [PRC, BC, RPI
.1-2-2   Demographic data. 1972. 40p. [PRC, BC, RPI
.1-2-3   The overseas-born population. 1970. 89p. [PRC, BC, RPI
.1-2-4   The work force. 1971. 60p. [PRC, BC, RPI
.1-2-5   Families and households. 1972. 39p. [PRC, BC, RPI
.1-3 3. Housing. 1972. 172p. [PRC, BC, RPI
      4. Population and dwellings in local government areas. Parts 1-7.
1966.1-4-1 through 1966.1-4-7. 1. New South Wales./2. Victoria./3. Queensland./4. South Australia./5. Western Australia./6. Tasmania./7. Northern Territory and Australian Capital Territory. [PRC, BC, RPI
      5. Population and dwellings in localitites. Parts 1-8.
1966.1-5-1 through 1966.1-5-7. [One volume for each of the areas listed in 1966.1-4 above.] [PRC, RPI
.1-5-8   Australia. 1970. 39p. 6 folding maps. [PRC, BC, RPI
.1-6 6. Statistician's report. [Never published.]

Australia. Commonwealth Bureau of Census and Statistics.
    Census of population and housing, 30 June 1966. Bulletins. Canberra, 1967-1968. [The results contained in the following were not duplicated in the final report volumes.]
1966.2-10-1 Census of the Territory of Norfolk Island, 30 June 1966. Summary of population. 1968. 12p. [PRC, RPI
.2-11-1 Census of the Territory of Christmas Island, 30 June 1966. Summary of population. 1968. 12p. [PRC , RPI
.2-12-1 Census of the Territory of Cocos (Keeling) Islands, 30 June 1966. Summary of population. 1968. 12p. [PRC, RPI
.2-13-1 Census of Nauru, 30 June 1966. Summary of population. 1968. 12p. [PRC , RPI
.2-14   The Aboriginal population of Australia. Summary of characteristics. 1969. 32p. [BC , RPI

Australia. Commonwealth Bureau of Census and Statistics.
1966.3 Catalogue of census tabulations. n.d. 292p. [PRC

Australia. Commonwealth Bureau of Census and Statistics.
1971.1 Census of population and housing, 30 June 1971. Final population totals for states and territories of Australia. Canberra, 1972. 1p. [PRC

Australia. Commonwealth Bureau of Census and Statistics.
    Census of population and housing, 30 June 1971. Bulletin.
(Final reports).   Canberra, 1972-1975. Vols. 1-14 in 67v.
    1. Summary of population. 1972. Parts 1-9.
1971.2-1-1 through 1971.2-1-9. 1. New South Wales./2. Victoria./3. Queens-
    land./4. South Australia./5. Western Australia./6. Tasmania./7. Nor-
    thern Territory./8. Australian Capital Territory./9. Australia.
    [PRC, BC
    2. Summary of dwellings. 1972. Parts 1-9.
1971.2-2-1 through 1971.2-2-9. [One volume for each area listed in 1971.
    2-1 above] [PRC, BC
    3. Demographic characteristics. 1973. Parts 1-9.
1971.2-3-1 through 1971.2-3-9. [One volume for each area listed in 1971.
    2-1 above] [PRC, BC
    4. Birthplace. 1973. Parts 1-9.
1971.2-4-1 through 1971.2-4-9. [One volume for each area listed in 1971.
    2-1 above] [PRC, BC
    5. Labour force. 1973. Parts 1-9.
1971.2-5-1 through 1971.2-5-9. [One volume for each area listed in 1971.
    2-1 above] [PRC, BC
    6. Population and dwellings in local government areas and urban
    centres. 1974-1975. Parts 1-9 in 8v.   [Parts nos. 7 and 8 are in
    one volume.]
1971.2-6-1 through 1971.2-6-9. [One volume for each area listed in 1971.
    2-1 above except where noted.] [PRC, BC
    7. Characteristics of the population and dwellings. Local
    government areas. 1973. Parts 1-8.
1971.2-7-1 through 1971.2-7-8. [One volume for each area listed in 1971.
    2-1 above except Australia as a whole.] [PRC, BC
    .2-8 8. Characteristics of the population and dwellings. Common-
    wealth electoral divisions. Australia. 1973. xxi, 377p. [PRC,
    BC
    .2-8s   Supplement. Western Australia and Australian Capital Terri-
    tory, 1974 boundaries. 1975. xiii, 63p. [PRC, BC
    .2-9 9. The Aboriginal population. Characteristics of the aboriginal
    and Torres Strait Islander population. 1973. xix, 20p. [PRC, BC
    10. Families and households. [Not published]
    11. Fertility. [Not published]
    12. Geographic distribution. [Not published]
    .2-13 13. Maps. 1972. 21 maps. [PRC
    14. Catalogue of 1971 census tabulations. 1974. 2 parts.
    .2-14-1   (Preliminary). ix, A173, B179p. [PRC
    .2-14-2   Supplement. [105]p. [PRC

Australian Bureau of Statistics.
    1976 census of population and housing. Population and dwellings
in local government areas and urban centres. (Preliminary). 1977-
1978. Parts 1-8.
1976.0-1-1 through 1976.0-1-8. 1. New South Wales./2. Victoria./3. Queens-
    land./4. South Australia./5. Western Australia./6. Tasmania./7. Nor-
    thern Territory./8. Australian Capital Territory. [PRC

Australian Bureau of Statistics.
   1976 census of population and housing. Characteristics of the
population: local government areas. (Preliminary). 1978. Parts
1-9.
1976.0-2-1 through 1976.0-2-9. [One volume for each area listed in 1976.0-1
above plus one for all Australia.] [PRC

Australian Bureau of Statistics.
   1976 population census. Information paper.   Canberra, 1977-197 .
Nos. 1-20.
1976.0-3-1   Availability of census results. n.d. 4p. [PRC
   .0-3-2   Release of data on microfiche.
   .0-3-3   Release of data on microfiche. Supplement. 1977. 6, [2]p.
   [PRC
   .0-3-4   Release of data in printed publications.
   .0-3-5   Availability of maps.
   .0-3-6   Release of data on magnetic tape.
   .0-3-7   Preliminary details of special summaries on magnetic tape.

   .0-3-8   Second release of data on magnetic tape.
   .0-3-9-1 Classification of characteristics.
   .0-3-9-2 Industry classification extract. 1977. 30p. [PRC
   .0-3-9-3 Occupation classification extract. 1977. 24p. [PRC
   .0-3-9-4 Classification of educational qualifications. 1978. 22p. [PRC
   .0-3-10 1976 census glossary of terms.
   .0-3-11 Service charges.
   .0-3-12 Child minding.
   .0-3-13 Dwelling structure.
   .0-3-14 Family. 1978. 4p. [PRC
   .0-3-15 Income. 1978. 5p. [PRC
   .0-3-16 Internal migration.
   .0-3-17 Journey to work.
   .0-3-18 Languages.
   .0-3-19 Racial origin. 1979. 4p. [PRC
   .0-3-20 LGA code list. 1978. [4], 118p. [OPR

AUSTRIA

Federal Republic of Austria.   Capital: Vienna
Statistical Agency: Central Statistical Office of Austria
                    [Österreichische Statistische Zentralamt]
                    Neue Hofburg, Heldenplatz
                    A-1014 Wien 1,
Publications Distributor: Carl Ueberreuter Druck und Verlag
                    Post fach 60
                    A-1095 Wien,

Austria. Statistisches Zentral-
    amt.
    Volkszählungsergebnisse 1951.   Results of the population census
Wien, Ueberreuter (Heft 1-11),   of 1951.
Österreichische Staatsdruckeri
(Heft 12-14), 1951-1953. Heft
1-14.
1951.1-1   Vorläufige Hauptergebnis-   Preliminary main results of the
se der Volkszählung vom 1. juni   population census of June 1,
1951 nach Gemeinden. 1951.   1951 by communities.
164p.   [PRC, UN, RPI
    Ergebnisse der Volkszäh-   Results of the population census
lung vom 1. juni 1951 nach Ge-   of June 1, 1951, by communities.
meinden. 1952. 9v.
1951.1-2 through 1951.1-10. 2. Vorarlberg. 7p./3. Burgenland. 16p./4.
Kärnten. 14p./5. Salzburg. 9p./6. Tirol. 13p./7. Niederösterreich.
53p./8. Oberösterreich. 21p./9. Steiermark. 35p./10. Wien. 7p.
[PRC, UN, RPI
    .1-11   Österreich. Sammelband   Austria. Summary volume for
    der Heft 2-10. var. pag.   parts 2-10.
                                         [PRC, LC, BC, UN, RPI
    .1-12   Tabellenband I. Demogra-   Tables I. Demographic section
    phischer Teil. 1953. 154p.   [PRC, UN, RPI
    .1-13   Tabellenband II. Berufs-   Tables II. Occupational statis-
    statistischer Teil. 1953. 244p.   tics section.
                                         [PRC, UN, RPI
    .1-14   Ergebnisse der Volkszäh-   Results of the population census
    lung vom 1. juni 1951. Text-   of June 1, 1951. Text volume.
    band. 1953. 123p.   [PRC, UN, RPI

Austria. Statistisches Zentral-
    amt.
    .2   Organisation, Technik und   Organization, technique and meth-
    Methodik der Volkszählung vom   odology of the population census
    1. juni 1951. Wien, 1957. 149p.   of June 1, 1951.
                                         [PRC, BC, UN, RPI

Austria. Statistisches Zentral-
    amt.
    .3   Ortsverzeichnis von Österreich.   Register of places in Austria,
    Bearbeitet auf grund der Ergeb-   prepared from the results of the

nisse der Volkszählung vom 1.
juni 1951.   Wien, 1953.   335p.

population census of June 1, 1951.
[PRC, UN, RPI

Austria.   Statistisches Zentral-
        amt.
        Volkszählungsergebnisse 1961.
Wien, Ueberreuter (Heft 1), Ös-
terreichische Staatsdruckerei
(Heft 2-17), 1961-1966.

Results of the population census,
1961.

1961.1-1   Vorläufige Hauptergebnisse der Volkszählung vom 21.
märz 1961 nach Gemeinden.   1961.
150p.
        Ergebnisse der Volkszäh-
lung vom 21. märz 1961.

Preliminary main results of the
population census of March 21,
1961, by communities.
[TXU, PRC, UN, RPI, RIR
Results of the population census
of March 21, 1961.

1961.1-2 through 1961.1-10.   2. Burgenland.   1963. 69p./3. Vorarlberg.   1963.
60p./4. Tirol. 1963.   69p./5. Salzburg.   1963.   62p./6. Kärnten.
1963.   67p./7. Niederösterreich. 1963.   116p./8. Oberösterreich.
1964.   76p./9. Steiermark.   1964.   86p./10. Wien.   1964.   65p. [PRC,
TXU, RPI, RIR
.1-11   Österreich.   1964.   60p.

Austria.
[PRC, TXU, BC, RPI, RIR

.1-12   Die Haushalte in Österreich.   1964.   24p.
.1-13   Die Zusammensetzung der
Wohnbevölkerung Österreichs
nach allgemeinen demographischen und kulturellen Merkmalen.
1964.   94p.

Households in Austria.
[PRC, TXU, BC, RPI, RIR
Composition of Austrian resident
population by general demographic
and cultural characteristics.
[PRC, TXU, RPI, RIR

.1-14   Die Berufstätigen nach
der beruflichen Zugehörigkeit.
1964.   930p.
.1-15   Die Berufstätigen nach
ihrer wirtschaftlichen Zugehörigkeit.   1964.   176p.
.1-16   Wohngemeinde--Arbeits-
gemeinde der Beschäfligten in
Österreich.   1965.   505p.
.1-17   Die Wohnbevölkerung Österreichs nach Einkommensquel-
len und wirtschaftlicher Zugehörigkeit.   1966.   208p.

The economically active by occu-
pation.
[PRC, TXU, BC, RPI, RIR
The economically active by indus-
try.
[PRC, TXU, BC, RPI, RIR
Place of residence--place of work
of the employed in Austria.
[PRC, TXU, BC, RPI, RIR
The Austrian resident population
by source of income and economic
activity.
[PRC, TXU, BC, RPI, RIR

Austria.   Statistisches Zentral-
        amt.
.2   Ortsverzeichnis von Österreich.   Bearbeitet auf grund
der Ergebnisse der Volkszählung vom 21. märz 1961.   Wien,
Österreichische Staatsdruckerie,
1965.   xx, 536p.

Register of places in Austria
prepared from the results of the
census of March 21, 1961.
[PRC, LC, UN, RPI

Austria. Statistisches Zentral-
    amt.
      Ergebnisse der Volkszählung   Results of the population cen-
vom 12. mai 1971. Wien, 1971-   sus of May 12, 1971.
1974. Heft 1-21.

1971.1-1   Endgültige Ergebnisse über   Final results of the resident
die Wohnbevölkerung nach Gemein-   population by communes (with
den (mit der Bevölkerungsentwich-   population growth since 1869).
lung seit 1869). Wien, Öster-   [PRC
reichischen Staatsdruckerei, 1971.
45p.

      Hauptergebnisse für...   Main results for...
Wien, Ueberreuter, 1972-1974.

1971.1-2 through 1971.1-10. [One volume for each of the following areas.]
2. Burgenland. 1972. 71p./3. Vorarlberg. 1973. 67p./4. Tirol.
1973. 82p./5. Salzburg. 1973. 67p./6. Kärnten. 1973. 75p./7.
Oberösterreich. 1973. 111p./8. Wien. 1974. 99p./9. Steiermark.
1974. 115p./10. Niederösterreich. 1974. 143p. [PRC

.1-11   Hauptergebnisse für Öster-   Main results for Austria.
reich. 1974. 69p.   [PRC

.1-12   Wohngemeinde--Arbeitsge-   Place of residence--place of
meinde der Beschäftigten in   work of the employed in Austria.
Österreich. 1974. 451p.   [PRC

.1-13   Berufspendelverkehr. 1974.   Commuting workers.
125p.   [PRC

.1-14   Die Berufstätigen nach   The economically active by occu-
beruflichen und wirtschaftlichen   pational and industrial charac-
Merkmalen. 1974. 209p.   teristics.
                                             [PRC

.1-15   Ausländer. 1974. 63p.   Foreigners.
                                           [PRC

.1-16   Familien. 1974. 69p.   Families.
                                           [PRC

.1-17   Haushalte. 1974. 38p.   Households.
                                           [PRC

.1-18   Der Bildungsstand der Be-   The structure of the population.
völkerung. 1974. 237p.   [PRC

.1-19   Wohnbevölkerung nach eini-   Resident population according to
gen demographischen und wirtschaft-   some demographic and economic
lichen Merkmalen. 1974. 33p.   characteristics.
                                           [PRC

.1-20   Binnenwanderung 1966-1971.   Internal migration, 1966-1971.
1974. 70p.   [PRC

.1-21   Schüler und Studenten.   Pupils and students.
1974. 159p.   [PRC

Austria. Statistisches Zentral-
    amt.
.2   Systematisches verzeichnis der   Systematic catalog of occupa-
Berufe. Überarbeitete Neuauflage   tions. Revised new editions of
des systematischen Verzeichnisses   the systematic list of occupa-
der Berufe 1961 (mit einem alpha-   tions 1961 (with an alphabetical

betischen Anhang). Ausgabe
1971. Wien, Ueberreuter,
1972. xxxii, 216p.

appendix). 1971 edition.
[PRC, UFL

Austria. Statistisches Zentral-
amt.
1971.3 Volkszählung 1971--Tabellen-
programm: Tabellenköpfe der
Publikations- und Arbeits-tabel-
len. Nach der Stand vom August
1972. Wien, 1972. 198p.

Population census of 1971--pro-
gram of tables: titles of published and work tables. As of
August 1972.
[

Austria. Statistisches Zentral-
amt.
.4 Volkszählung 1971--Tabellen-
verzeichnis nach dem Stand vom
September 1977. Wien, 1977.
224p.

Population census of 1971--list
of tables as of September 1977.
[PRC

BAHAMAS

Commonwealth of the Bahamas.   Capital: Nassau, New Providence
Statistical Agency: Department of Statistics   Island
                      Cabinet Office
                      P.O. Box N3904
                      Nassau
Publications Distributor: same

        Bahamas.   Supervisor of the Census.
1953.1   Report on the census of the Bahama Islands, taken on the 6th Dec-
        ember, 1953.   Nassau, New Providence, the Nassau Guardian, 1954.
        10, [20]p.   [BC, PRC, RPI

        Bahamas.   Department of the Registrar General
1963.1   Report on the census of the Bahama Islands taken 15th November,
        1963.   Nassau, 1965.   [321]p.   [PRC, RPI

        Bahamas.   Department of Statistics.   Census Office.
1970.1   Commonwealth of the Bahama Islands.   Report of the 1970 census of
        population.   Nassau, 1972.   xxxi, 481, 5p.   [PRC, BC, JB-F

        Bahamas.   Department of Statistics.
        Census monograph[s from the 1970 census of population].   Nassau,
        [1973-   ].   Nos. 1-
1970.2-1   Manpower and income.   1973.   p.   [BC
   .2-2   Demographic aspects of the Bahamian population 1901-1974.
        1976.   iii, 53p.   [PRC

BAHRAIN

State of Bahrain   Capital: Manama
Statistical Agency: Statistical Bureau
                     Ministry of Finance and National Economy
                     P.O. Box 235
                     Manama,
Publications Distributor: Information Department
                           Government of Bahrain
                           P.O. Box 253
                           Manama,

        Bahrain. Government.
1950.1   Census 1950. [Taken on March 3, 1950].   Manama, Government
        Offices, 1950. 15p. [UN, PRC, RPI

        Bahrain. Government.
1959.0-1 Population census, 1959. n.d. 22p. [OPR

        R.S. Porter, O.B.E. [Information supplied by the Government of
            Bahrain].
    .1   The third population census of Bahrain, May 1959.   Beirut, Middle
        East Development Division, 1961. 67p. [BC, OPR, PRC, RPI

        Bahrain. Government. Finance Department.
1965.1   4th census of population, 1965.   [Manama], 1965. 62p. [UN, PRC
        RPI

        Bahrain. Government. Finance Department. Statistical Bureau.
    .2   The fourth population census of Bahrain. A brief analytical and
        comparative study.   [Manama], 1969. 5, 44p. [UN, BC, PRC, JB-F, RPI

        Bahrain. Ministry of Finance and National Economy. Statistical
            Bureau.
1971.1   Results of the fifth population census.   Manama, 1971. 61p.
        [

        Bahrain. Ministry of Finance and National Economy. Statistical
            Bureau.
    .2   Statistics of the population census, 1971.   [Manama], 1972. xii,
        166p. [PRC, LC, JB-F

BANGLADESH

People's Republic of Bangladesh   Capital: Dacca
Statistical Agency: Bangladesh Bureau of Statistics
                     Secretary (Ex-Officio) Ministry of Planning
                     (Statistics Division)
                     Secretary Building
                     Dacca-2,
Publications Distributor: Controller of Printing
                           Bangladesh Government Press
                           Tajgaon, Dacca,

     Pakistan. Office of the Census Commission.
        Census of Pakistan, 1951.   Karachi, Manager of Publications,
     1951-1956. Volumes I-IX.
1951.1-1   General report and tables for Pakistan, showing provincial
     tables. n.d. viii, 115p. tables. [PRC, RPI
   .1-3   East Bengal. Report and tables. n.d. var. pag. [TXU, RPI
   .1-8   East Pakistan. Tables [of economic characteristics]. n.d.
     var. pag. [TXU, RPI
   .1-9   Administrative report. Part 1. The Census Commissioner's
     report. Part 2. The report of the provincial superintendents of
     Census Operations. n.d. x, 237p. [PRC, BC, RPI

     Pakistan. Office of the Census Commissioner.
        Census of Pakistan, 1951. Village lists for East Bengal [Pro-
     vince]. Karachi, n.d. Nos. 1-17.
1951.3-2-1 through 1951.3-2-17. [One volume for each of the following
     districts.] 1. Bakerganj. [2], 124p./2. Bogra. [3], 110p./3. Chit-
     tagong. [4], 54p./4. Chittagong Hill Tracts. [4], 17p./5. Dacca.
     [2], 222p./6. Dinajpur. [2], 92p./7. Faridpur. [2], iii, 142p./8.
     Jessore. [4], ii, 116p./9. Khulna. [4], iii, 87p./10. Kushtia. [4],
     56p./11. Mymensingh. [2], 308p./12. Noakhali. [2], 85p./13. Pabna.
     [2], 118p./14. Rajshahi. [2], 186p./15. Rangpur. [2], 177p./16.
     Sylhet. [2], 300p./17. Tippera. [2], 190p. [PRC, BC, RPI

     Pakistan. Office of the Census Commissioner.
        Census of Pakistan, 1961. Karachi, Manager of Publications,
     1963-1964. Vols. 1-9.
1961.1-1   Population. Pakistan. Tables and report. 1963. xii, [422]p.
     [TXU, PRC, RPI
   .1-2   Population. East Pakistan. Tables and report. 1964. v,
     [1054]p. [PRC, TXU, RPI
   .1-4   Non-agricultural labour force. Pakistan. 1964. (iv, 287p.
     [TXU, PRC, RPI
   .1-5   Non-agricultural labour force. East Pakistan. 1964. 1231,
     15, [xvii]p. [TXU, PRC, RPI
   .1-8   Housing 1960. Pakistan. 1963. (iii), [161], (xi)p. [TXU,
     PRC, RPI
   .1-9   Housing 1960. East Pakistan. 1963. v, [605]p. [TXU, PRC,
     RPI

Pakistan. Office of the Census Commissioner.
    Population census of Pakistan 1961. District census reports.
[Each report contains 5 parts].   Karachi, Manager of Publications,
n.d. 17 parts.
1961.3-E-1 through 1961.3-E-17. [One volume for each of the following dis-
    tricts.] 1. Bakerganj. [11], xli, 554p./2. Bogra. [11], xliii,
    323p./3. Chittagong. [11], xxxv, 403p./4. Chittagong Hill Tracts.
    [12], xlv, 236p./5. Comilla. [6], xli, 659p./6. Dacca. [10], xlviii,
    677p./7. Dinajpur. [11], xlvi, 483p./8. Faridpur. [20], xxxviii,
    489p./9. Jessore. [11], xlv, 478p./10. Khulna. [17], xlv, 433p./
    11. Kushtia. [15], xlvii, 334p./12. Mymensingh. [9], xlv, 971p./
    13. Noakhali. [10], xlviii, 329p./14. Pabna. [11], xliii, 381p./
    15. Rajshahi. [13], xxxviii, 652p./16. Rangpur. [8], il, 505p./
    17. Sylhet. [12], xlvi, 800p. [TXU, RPI

Bangladesh. Census Commission.
    Bangladesh census of population--1974. Bulletins.   Dacca, 1974-
    1976. Nos. 1-3.
1974.1-1   Provisional results. 1974. ii, 59p. maps, charts. [PRC, BC
    .1-2   (Age, sex, literates, labour force, households.) [1975].
    [vi], 218p. [PRC, BC, UN, E-W
    .1-3   Union population statistics. [1976]. 455p. [UN, OPR

Bangladesh. Census Commission.
    .2   1974 Bangladesh population census report: national volume.
    Dacca, 1977. xi, 673p. [E-W, OPR

[The 1974 census publications will also include District census reports, and a Report on field operation, enumeration and administration.
Reports on Housing, Labour force and Establishments will not be published according to Mr. Rahman of the Census Commission.

BARBADOS

                                                    Capital: Bridgetown
Statistical Agency: Barbados Statistical Service
                     3d floor, National Insurance Building
                     Fairchild Street
                     Bridgetown,
Publications Distributor: same

        Jamaica. Central Bureau of Statistics.
1946   West Indian Census 1946.
                [See Commonwealth Caribbean Nos. 1946.1-A and 1946.1-C.]

        Trinidad and Tobago. Central Statistical Office.
1960   Eastern Caribbean population census, 1960.
                [See Commonwealth Caribbean Nos. 1960.1-1-A and C.
                                        1960.1-2-Ba
                                        1960.1-3-Ba-1, 2, and 3.]

        West Indies. University. Census Research Programme.
1970   1970 population of the Commonwealth Caribbean.
                [See Commonwealth Caribbean Nos. 1970.1-1
                                        1970.1-2-?
                                        1970.1-3
                                        1970.1-4-4 and 16
                                        1970.1-5
                                        1970.1-6-2
                                        1970.1-7
                                        1970.1-8-a, b, and c
                                        1970.1-9-2
                                        1970.1-10-1 and 4.]

        Barbados. Statistical Service.
            Commonwealth Caribbean population census, 1970. Barbados. Preli-
        minary bulletins. Garrison, St. Michael, 1972-1974.
1970.2-1   Housing. 1972. iii, 17p. [PRC,
    .2-2   Working population, part I. 1972. iii, 13p. [PRC, OPR
    .2-3   Working population, part II. 1972. iii, 15p. [PRC, OPR
    .2-4   Population. 1973. iii, 12p. [PRC
    .2-5   Education. 1974. ii, 21p. [PRC

BELGIUM

Kingdom of Belgium.   Capital: Brussels
Statistical Agency: National Statistical Institute
                     [Institut National de Statistique]
                     Rue de Louvain, 44
                     1000 Bruxelles,
Publications Distributor: same

Belgium. Institut National de
    Statistique.
    Recensement général de la   General census of population,
population, de l'industrie et   industry and business of Decem-
du commerce au 31 décembre 1947.   ber 31, 1947.
Bruxelles, [publisher varies],
1949-1954. Vols. I-XIV in 16v.

1947.1-1   Exposé des méthodes. Popu-   Explanation of methods. Popula-
lation densité, étendue terri-   tion density, extent of territory
toriale et contenance imposable   and taxable real estate, by com-
du sol et des bâtiments, par   mune. Census of ecclesiastics.
commune. Recensement des reli-   [PRC, TXU, UN, RPI
gieux. Impr. A. Puvrez, 1949.
415p.

.1-2   Recensement des maisons   Census of houses and other
et autres bâtiments par commune   buildings...
...   [UN

.1-3   Recensement des logements.   Census of housing. Distribution
Répartition des logements d'   of dwellings by number of occu-
après le nombre d'occupants et   pants and number of rooms.
le nombre de pièces. Impr. Van   [PRC, TXU, UN, RPI
Muysewinkel, 1951. 229p.

.1-4   Répartition de la popula-   Distribution of the population
tion suivant l'état civil, la   by marital status, nationality,
nationalité, le degré d'instruc-   educational attainment and birth-
tion et le lieu de naissance.   place.
Impr. Van Muysewinkel, 1951.   [PRC, TXU, UN, RPI
247p.

.1-5   Répartition de la popula-   Distribution of the population
tion par âge. Impr. Van Muyse-   by age.
winkel, 1951. 449p.   [PRC, TXU, UN, RPI

.1-6   Recensement des ménages.   Census of households.
Impr. A. Puvrez, 1951. 205p.   [PRC, TXU, UN, RPI

.1-7   Recensement des familles.   Census of families.
Impr. A. Puvrez, n.d. 131p.   [PRC, TXU, UN, RPI

.1-8   Répartition de la popula-   Distribution of the population
tion d'après l'activité et la   by economic activity and occupa-
profession. Impr. Van Muyse-   tion.
winkel, 1953. 359p.   [PRC, TXU, UN, RPI

.1-9   Recensement du Commerce.   Census of business.
2 tomes.   [UN

.1-10   Recensement de l'indus-   Census of industry.
trie. 2 tomes   [UN

        Salaires dans l'industrie.   Wages in industry.
   Impr. A. Puvrez, 1952.   2 tomes.

1947.1-11-1   167p.   [PRC, TXU, UN, RPI
  .1-11-2   407p.   [PRC, TXU, UN, RPI
  .1-12   Salaires dans le commerce.   Wages in business.
   Impr. A. Puvrez, 1951.   229p.   [PRC, TXU, UN, RPI
  .1-13   Recensement des diplômés   Census of high school graduates.
  des l'enseignement supérieur.   [PRC, TXU, RPI
  Impr. Van Muysewinkel, 1952.   79p.
  .1-14   Recensement général de la   General census of population of
  population au 31 décembre 1947.   December 31, 1947.   Distribution
  Répartition au point de vue des   by national languages spoken.
  langues nationales parlées.   Impr.   [PRC, TXU, RPI
  du Moniteur Belge, 1954.   155p.

  Belgium.   Institut National de
         Statistique.
        Recensement général de la popu-   General population census of
  lation au 31.12.1961.   Bruxelles,   December 31, 1961.   [Also pub-
  Impr. V. Tengrootenhuysen, Wil-   lished in Flemish.]
  rijk, 1963-1966.   Vols. 1-10 in
  19v.

1961.1-1   1. Chiffre de la population.   Population figures.
  1963.   283p.   [PRC, TXU, BC, RPI, RIR
  .1-1s   Tiré-à-part: Evolution   Supplement: evolution of popu-
  du chiffre de la population des   lation figures for Belgian com-
  communes belges au cours de la   munes from 1831 to 1961.
  période 1831-1961.   1963.   69p.   [PRC, TXU, BC, RPI, RIR
  .1-2   2. Bâtiments.   2 tomes.   Buildings.
                            [PRC, TXU, BC, RPI, RIR
       3. Recensement des logements: Census of housing.
  .1-3-1   Royaume, province, ar-   ...Kingdom, province, district.
  rondissement.   1965.   213p.   [PRC, TXU, BC, RPI, RIR
  .1-3-2   Principaux résultats par   ...Main results by commune.
  commune.   1965.   115p.   [PRC, TXU, BC, RPI, RIR
       4. Répartition de la popula-   Population distribution by mari-
  tion selon l'état civil et la   tal status and nationality:
  nationalité:
  .1-4-1   Royaume, province, ar-   ...Kingdom, province, district.
  rondissement.   1966.   146p.   [PRC, TXU, BC, RPI, RIR
  .1-4-2   Principaux résultats   ...Main results by commune.
  par commune.   1965.   127p.   [PRC, TXU, BC, RPI, RIR
       5. Répartition de la popula-   Population distribution by age:
  tion par âge:
  .1-5-1   Royaume, province, ar-   ...Kingdom, province, district.
  rondissement.   1965.   301p.   [PRC, TXU, BC, RPI, RIR
  .1-5-2   Principaux résultats   ...Main results by commune.
  par commune.   1964.   111p.   [PRC, TXU, BC, RPI, RIR
       6. Recensement des ménages   Census of households and family
  et des noyaux familiaux: nuclei:
  .1-6-1   Royaume, province, ar-   ...Kingdom, province, district.
  arrondissement.   1966.   33p.   [PRC, TXU, BC, RPI, RIR

1961.1-6-2   Principaux résultats
   par commune. 1965. 116p.
.1-7 7. Recensement des familles.
   1966. 176p.
      8. Repartition de la popula-
   tion d'après l'activité, la
   profession et l'état civil:
.1-8-1   Royaume, province, arrondissement. 1966. 330p.
.1-8-2   Principaux résultats
   par commune. 1965. 368p.
.1-9 9. Migrations alternantes:
   mobilité géographique de la
   main-d'oeuvre. 1965. 159p.
      10. Enseignment:
.1-10-1   Royaume, province, arrondissement. 1966. 268p.
.1-10-2   Principaux résultats
   par commune. 1965. 168p.

   Belgium. Institut National de
      Statistique.
      Recensement de la popula-
   tion, 31 décembre 1970. Bruxelles, Impr. Van Muysewinkel,
   1973-1975. Vols. 1-15 in 3lv.
1971.1-1 1. Chiffres de la population.
   1973. 232p.
      2. Recensement des logements:
.1-2-a   Royaume, provinces, arrondissements et régions lin-
   guistiques. 1975. 182p.
.1-2-b   Principaux résultats
   par commune. 1975. 145p.
      3. Lieu de naissance et de
   residence:
.1-3-a   Royaume, provinces,
   arrondissements et régions lin-
   guistiques. 1975. 103p.
.1-3-2   Principaux résultats
   par commune. 1974. 53p.
      4. Population selon la natio-
   nalité:
.1-4-a   Royaume, provinces,
   arrondissements et régions lin-
   guistiques. 1974. 271p.
.1-4-b   Principaux résultats
   par commune. 1974. 54p.
      5. Population selon l'état
   civil et par âge:
.1-5-a   Royaume, provinces,
   arrondissements et régions lin-
   guistiques. 1974. 254p.

...Main results by commune.
[PRC, TXU, BC, RPI, RIR
Census of families.
[PRC, TXU, BC, RPI, RIR
Population distribution by in-
dustry, occupation and marital
status:
...Kingdom, province, district.
[PRC, TXU, BC, RPI, RIR
...Main results by commune.
[PRC, TXU, BC, RPI, RIR
Commuting: geographic mobility
of the labor force.
[PRC, TXU, BC, RPI, RIR
Educational attainment:
...Kingdom, province, district.
[PRC, TXU, BC, RPI, RIR
...Main results by commune.
[PRC, TXU, BC, RPI, RIR

Census of population, December
31, 1970. [Also published in
Flemish]

Population figures.
[PRC, OPR
Census of housing:
...Kingdom, provinces, districts
and linguistic regions.
[PRC, OPR
...Main results by commune.
[PRC, OPR
Birthplace and residence:

...Kingdom, provinces, districts
and linguistic regions.
[PRC, OPR
...Main results by commune.
[PRC, OPR
Population according to nation-
ality:
...Kingdom, provinces, districts
and linguistic regions.
[PRC, OPR
...Main results by commune.
[PRC, OPR
Population according to marital
status and by age:
...Kingdom, provinces, districts
and linguistic regions.
[PRC, OPR

1971.1-5-b   Principaux résultats   ...Main results by commune.
        par commune. 1974. 193p.   [PRC, OPR
        6. Ménages et noyaux fami-   Households and family nuclei:
        liaux:
.1-6-a   Royaume, provinces,   ...Kingdom, provinces, districts
        arrondissements et régions lin-   and linguistic regions.
        guistiques. 1975. 131p.   [PRC, OPR
.1-6-b   Principaux résultats   ...Main results by commune.
        par commune. 1975. 100p.   [PRC, OPR
.1-7 7. Fécondité des mariages.   Fertility of marriages.
        1975. 66p.   [PRC
        8. Population active: Economically active population:
.1-8-a   Royaume, provinces,   ...Kingdom, provinces, districts
        arrondissements et régions lin-   and linguistic regions.
        guistiques. 1975. 348p.   [PRC, OPR
.1-8-b   Principaux résultats   ...Main results by commune.
        par commune. 1974. 381p.   [PRC, OPR
.1-9 9. Mobilité géographique de   Geographic mobility of the labor
        la main-d'oeuvre. 1974. 260p.   force.
                                                 [PRC, OPR
        10. Niveau d'instruction de   Educational level of the popula-
        la population: tion:
.1-10-a   Royaume, provinces,   ...Kingdom, provinces, districts
        arrondissements et régions lin-   and linguistic regions.
        guistiques. 1975. 234p.   [PRC, OPR
.1-10-b   Principaux résultats   ...Main results by commune.
        par commune. 1975. 288p.   [PRC, OPR
.1-11 11. Personnes à charge.   Dependent persons.
        1975. 68p.   [PRC, OPR
.1-12 12. Handicapes physiques.   The physically handicapped.
        1975. 107p.   [PRC
.1-13 13. Données par secteurs sta-   Data by statistical sections of
        tistiques des communes. 1975.   communes.
        537p.   [PRC, OPR
        14. [Not published]
        15. Secteurs statistiques par   Statistical sections by communes,
        commune, superficie et population.   area and population.
        1973. Parts 1-9 in 11v.
1971.1-15-1 through 1971.1-15-9. [One volume for each province except Bra-
        bant which is divided into three parts.] 1. Antwerpen. 52p./2a. Arr.
        Hal-Vilvorde, Louvain. 56p./2b. Bruxelles-capitale. 28p./2c. Arr.
        de Nivelles. 32p./3. Prov. de Hainaut. 104p./4. Liège. 89p./5.
        Limburg. 50p./6. Luxembourg. 61p./7. Namur. 77p./8. Oost-Vlaanderen.
        69p./9. West-Vlaanderen. 61p. [PRC

        Belgium. Institut National de
            Statistique.
.2   Recensement de la population   Census of population and hous-
        et des logements, 31 décembre,   ing, December 31, 1970; synop-
        1970; cartes synoptiques des   tic maps.
        secteurs statistiques par com-   [PRC
        mune. Bruxelles, 1973. 71p.

BELIZE

Colony of Belize.   Capital: Belmopan.
Statistical Agency: Central Planning Unit
                      Colony of Belize
                      Belmopan,
Publications Distributor: same

Jamaica.   Central Bureau of Statistics.
1946   West Indian census, 1946.   Kingston, Government Printer, 1948-
          1950.
          [See Commonwealth Caribbean Nos. 1946.1-A and 1946.1-E.]

Jamaica. Department of Statistics.   Jamaica Tabulation Centre.
1960   West Indies population census, 1960.   Census of British Honduras,
          7th April, 1960.   Kingston, n.d.
          [See Commonwealth Caribbean Nos. 1960.2-BH-1 and 1960.2-BH-2.]

West Indies.   University.   Census Research Programme.
1970   1970 population census of the Commonwealth Caribbean.   Kingston,
          Herald Ltd., 1973-   .
          [See Commonwealth Caribbean Nos. 1970.1-1
                                          1970.1-2-?
                                          1970.1-3
                                          1970.1-4-5 and 16
                                          1970.1-5
                                          1970.1-6-2
                                          1970.1-7
                                          1970.1-8-a, b, and c.
                                          1970.1-9-2
                                          1970.1-10-1 and 4.]

BENIN

People's Republic of Benin.   Capital: Porto Novo, Cotonou
Statistical Agency: Central Bureau of Statistics
                      [Direction Centrale de la Statistique]
                      B.P. 377
                      Cotonou,
Publications Distributor: same

            France.   INSEE [and] Service Colonial des Statistiques.
1946   Résultats du recensement de 1946...
            [See French Overseas Territories, Nos. 1946.1-1, 2 and 3.
                                                  1946.2].

            France.   INSEE.
1951   Le recensement de la population...
            [See French Overseas Territories, No. 1951.1].

            French West Africa.   Service de la Statistique Générale.
            Recensement de la population...
            [See French Overseas Territories, No. 1951.2].

            French West Africa.   Haut-Commissariat Général.
1956   Premiers résultats définitifs...
            [See French Overseas Territories, No. 1956.1].

            France.   INSEE.   Service de
                 Coopération.
1961.1   Enquête démographique au   Demographic survey of Dahomey,
            Dahomey, 1961.   Résultats défi- 1961.   Final results.
            nitifs.   Par J. Nemo.   Paris,   [PRC, JB-F, NWU, RPI
            1964.   vi, 309, [8]p.

            France.   INSEE.
    .2   Données de base sur la situa-   Basic data on the demographic
            tion démographique au Dahomey en situation of Dahomey in 1961.
            1961.   Paris, 1962.   87p.   [NWU, RPI

            Dahomey.   Service de Statistique.
1964.1   Résultats provisoires du re-   Provisional results of the cen-
            censement de Cotonou (juin 1964) sus of Cotonou (June 1964) and
            et estimation de la population   the estimate of the population
            Dahomey au 1er janvier 1964.   of Dahomey on January 1, 1964.
            Cotonou, 1964.   10p.   [

            [A national census was proposed for 1978, but no citations have been
            seen.]

BERMUDA

Colony of Bermuda.   Capital: Hamilton
Statistical Agency: Statistical Office
                     Finance Department
                     Hamilton,
Publications Distributor: same

     Bermuda. Census Committee.
1950.1   Census of Bermuda, 23rd October, 1960. Report of census and sta-
     tistical tables compiled in accordance with the Census Act 1950.
     n.p., n.d. 118p. [UN, PRC, RPI

     Bermuda. Census Committee.
1960.1   Census of Bermuda, 23rd October, 1960. Report of census and sta-
     tistical tables compiled in accordance with the Census Act, 1950.
     Hamilton, Bermuda Government, 1961. 136p. [PRC, BC, RPI

     West Indies. University. Census Research Programme.
1970   1970 population census of the Commonwealth Caribbean.   Kingston,
     Herald Ltd., 1973-
        [See Commonwealth Caribbean Nos. 1970.1-1
                                         1970.1-2-?
                                         1970.1-3
                                         1970.1-4-10 and 16
                                         1970.1-6-3
                                         1970.1-7
                                         1970.1-8-a, b, and c.
                                         1970.1-9-3
                                         1970.1-10-2 and 4.]

     Bermuda. Census Office.
1970.2   Report of the population census, 1970.   Hamilton, Bermuda Govern-
     ment, 1973. 265p. [BC, PRC

BHUTAN

Kingdom of Bhutan   Capital: Thimphu
Statistical Agency: Ministry of Development
                     Royal Government of Bhutan
                     Thimphu,
Publications Distributor: same

     Bhutan. Government.
1969.1   Census report, 1969, Bhutan.   Thimphu, 1969. 8p. [Berkeley

BOLIVIA

Republic of Bolivia   Capital: La Paz
Statistical Agency: National Statistical Institute
                    [Instituto Nacional de Estadística]
                    Ministerio de Planificación y Coordinación.
                    Calle Bolívar, no. 688
                    La Paz,
Publications Distributor: same

     Bolivia. Dirección General de
        Estadística y Censo.
1950.1   Resultados generales del   General results of the popula-
    censo de población de la Repú-   tion census of the Republic of
    blica de Bolivia levantado el   Bolivia taken September 5, 1950.
    día 5 de septiembre de 1950.   [PRC, TXU, JB-F, RPI
    La Paz, Editorial Fénix, 1951.
    139p.

     Bolivia. Dirección General de
        Estadística y Censo.
 .2   Censo demográfico 1950.   Demographic census 1950.
    La Paz, Editorial "Argote,"   [PRC, BC, RPI
    1955. xxxii, 252, [6]p.

     Bolivia. Instituto Nacional de
        Estadística.
1976.1   Censo nacional de población   National census of population
    y vivienda 1976. Resultados   and housing, 1976. Anticipated
    anticipados por muestreo. La   results based on sample tabula-
    Paz, 1977. 77p.   tion.
                            [PRC, OPR

     Bolivia. Instituto Nacional de
        Estadística.
     Resultados del censo nacio-   Results of the national census
    nal de población y vivienda 1976. of population and housing, 1976.
    La Paz, 1978-   . Vol. I-XII.
1976.2-1 through 1976.2-9. [Departamento de...] 1. Chuquisaca./2. La Paz./
    3. Cochabamba./4. Oruro./5. Potosí./6. Tarija./7. Santa Cruz./8. Beni./
    9. Pando. [
 .2-10   Resumen nacional. Pobla-   National summary. Population
    ción y vivienda.   and housing.
                            [
 .2-11   Resumen nacional. Habi-   National summary. Inhabitants
    tantes por sexo, hogares y vi-   by sex, households and housing
    viendas según provincias, can-   by province, canton, city, popu-
    tones, ciudades, centros pobla- lated centers and dispersed popu-
    dos y población dispersa.   lation.
                            [
 .2-12   Resumen nacional. Evalu-   National summary. Census evalu-
    ación censal.   ation.
                            [

BONIN ISLANDS

The islands were returned to Japan in 1968 by the U.S.   They are now listed
under the prefecture of Tokyo-to.

        U.S.   Department of the Navy.
1952-65.1   Population statistics for Bonin Islands (for the years 1952-
        1965).   [Enclosure to Chief of Naval Operations letter Ser. 332POB2
        of (no date)].   2 typewritten pages.   [PRC

        Japan.   Bureau of Statistics.
1970.1-3-13   1970 population census of Japan.   Volume 3.   Part 13.
        Tokyo-to.   Tokyo, 1972.   xviii, 714p.   maps.   [PRC

        Japan.   Bureau of Statistics.
1975.1-3-13   1975 population census of Japan.   Volume 3.   Part 13.
        Tokyo-to.   Tokyo, 1977.   [10], xiv, 580p.   maps.   [PRC

BOPHUTHATSWANA

Capital: Mmabotho

No country but South Africa has recognized this black homeland as a separate nation as yet.

The 1970 South Africa census has figures for economic regions and districts (Bantu Homelands) that correspond more or less to this area. See economic area No. 65-70, Bophuthatswana, also South Africa 1970.2-19-4 (Tswana).

BOTSWANA

Republic of Botswana   Capital: Gaborone
Statistical Agency: Government Statistician
                     Central Statistics Office
                     Private Bag 24
                     Gaborone,
Publications Distributor: same

Bechuanaland Protectorate Government.
1946.1   Report on the census of the Bechuanaland Protectorate, 1946. By
C.W. Cousins.   Mafeking, 1952. xxii, 68p. [UN, LC, PRC, RPI

1956.1   [No report published.]

[Bechuanaland Protectorate Government. Population Census Office]
1964.1   Report on the census of the Bechuanaland Protectorate, 1964.
Bulawayo, Rhodesia, Mardon Printers (PVT), Ltd., 1965. vii, 130p.
Folding map. [UN, NWU, PRC, RPI

Botswana. Central Statistics Office.
1971.1   Report on the population census, 1971.   Gaborone, Government
Printer, 1972. vii, 194, [164]p. Appendix A1-A114, and 3 separate
cartograms. [PRC, NWU, BC, OPR, JB-F

Botswana. Central Statistics Office.
1975.1   Report of the census of Selebi Pikwe (1975).   Gaberone, 1975.
[6], 46, [68], A44p. [PRC

[Note: This census was undertaken to fill an important information
gap left by the 1971 population census.]

The next census is projected for 1981.

BRAZIL

Federative Republic of Brazil   Capital: Brasilia
Statistical Agency: Brazilian Statistical Institute
        [Instituto Brasileiro de Estatística]
        Fundação IBGE
        Avda. Franklyn Roosevelt 166
        20.000 Rio de Janeiro, RJ,
Publications Distributor: IBGE - Diretoria de Divulgação
        Dep. de Distribuição
        Avda. Brasil, 15.671
        Lucas ZC-91
        20.000 Rio de Janeiro, RJ,

Brazil. IBGE. Serviço Nacional
  de Recenseamento.
  VI recenseamento geral do   Sixth general census of Brazil.
Brasil. Censo demográfico: Demographic census: selection
seleção dos principais dados. of principal data.
Rio de Janeiro, Serviço Grá-
fico, 1951-1953. 23v.
1950.1-1 Estados Unidos do Brasil. United States of Brazil.
  1953. x, 85p.   [JB-F, RPI
1950.1-2 through 1950.1-23. [One volume for each of the following areas.]
  2. Territórios Federais (Acre, Amapá, Fernando Noronha, Guaporé, Rio
  Branco). 1952. xvi, 116p./3. Amazonas. 1952. vii, 28p./4. Pará.
  1952. vii, 34p./5. Maranhão. 1952. vii, 34p./6. Piauí. 1952.
  vii, 28p./7. Ceará. 1951. vii, 42p./8. Rio Grande do Norte. 1951.
  vii, 30p./9. Paraíba. 1951. vii, 32p./10. Pernambuco. 1952. viii,
  40p./11. Alagoas. 1952. viii, 30p./12. Sergipe. 1951. vii, 28p./
  13. Bahia. 1952. viii, 56p./14. Minas Gerais. 1953. viii, 88p./
  15. Espírito Santo. 1951. viii, 30p./16. Rio de Janeiro. 1951.
  viii, 36p./17. Distrito Federal. 1951. vii, 13p./18. São Paulo.
  1953. viii, 76p./19. Paraná. 1953. viii, 36p./20. Santa Catarina.
  1952. viii, 46p./21. Rio Grande do Sul. 1952. viii, 46p./22. Mato
  Grosso. 1952. vii, 30p./23. Goiás. 1952. vii, 34p. [JB-F, TXU
  PRC, RPI

Brazil. IBGE. Serviço Nacional
  de Recenseamento.
  VI recenseamento do Brasil, Sixth census of Brazil, 1950.
  1950. Rio de Janeiro, Serviço
  Gráfico, 1954-1958. Vols. I-XXX
  in 51v.
  .2-1 Brasil: censo demográfico. Brazil: demographic census.
    1956. xxxii, 334p.   [PRC, TXU, RPI
  .2-2 Brasil: censo agrícola.   Brazil: agricultural census.
    1956. xxxvi, 135p.   [PRC, TXU, RPI
  .2-3-1 Brasil: censo industrial. Brazil: industrial census
    1957. xxxvi, 284p.   [PRC, TXU, RPI
  .2-3-2 Brasil: censos comercial Brazil: censuses of commerce
  e dos serviços. 1957. lxiv, and services
  330p.   [PRC, TXU, RPI

.2-4   Brasil: transportes e   Brazil: transportation and com-
comunicações. 1958. xxx, 111p.   munication.
                                       [PRC, TXU, RPI
.2-5   Anexos (não editado).   Annexes (never published).
1950.2-6 through 1950.2-30-2. [One or more volumes for each state.]
6. Território do Guaporé: censos demográfico e econômicos. 1957.
lxx, 259p./7. Território do Acre. 1957. lxxi, 286p./8. Estado do
Amazonas. 1956. lxxii, 366p./9. Território do Rio Branco. 1957.
lxvii, 243p./10-1. Estado do Pará. 1956. xxv, 117p./10-2. Estado
do Pará: censos econômicos. 1956. lxi, 324p./11. Território do
Amapá: censos demográficos e econômicos. 1957. lxviii, 253p./
12-1. Estado do Maranhão: censo demográfico. 1955. xxv, 118p./
12-2. Estado do Maranhão: censos econômicos. 1956. lx, 318p./13.
Estado do Piauí: censos demográfico e econômicos. 1956. lxxiii,
364p./14-1. Estado do Ceará: censo demográfico. 1955. xxv, 131p./
14-2. Estado do Ceará: censos econômicos. 1956. lxi, 332p./15-1.
Rio Grande do Norte: censo demográfico. 1956. xxv, 97p./15-2. Rio
Grande do Norte: censos econômicos. 1956. lxi, 274p./16-1. Paraíba: censo demográfico. 1955. xxv, 101p./16-2. Estado da Paraíba:
censos econômicos. 1956. lxi, 278p./17-1. Estado de Pernambuco:
censo demográfico. 1955. xxv, 125p./17-2. Estado de Pernambuco:
censos econômicos. 1956. lx, 342p./18-1. Estado de Alagoas: censo
demográfico. 1955. xxv, 97p./18-2. Estado de Alagoas: censos econômicos. 1956. lx, 278p./
19. Estado de Sergipe: censos demográfico e econômicos. 1956.
lxxiii, 374p./20-1. Estado da Bahia: censo demográfico. 1955. xxv,
162p./20-2. Estado da Bahia: censos industrial, comercial e dos
serviços. 1956. xlvii, 210p./21-1. Estado de Minas Gerais: censo
demográfico. 1954. xxix, 283p./21-2. Estado de Minas Gerais: censo agrícola. 1955. xxvii, 469p./21-3. Estado de Minas Gerais:
censos industrial, comercial e dos serviços. 1955. xlvii, 256p./
22-1. Estado do Espírito Santo: censo demográfico. 1955. xxv, 98p./
22-2. Estado do Espírito Santo: censos econômicos. 1956. lx, 276p./
23-1. Estado do Rio de Janeiro: censo demográfico. 1955. xxv,
121p./23-2. Estado do Rio de Janeiro: censos econômicos. 1956. lxi,
356p./24-1. Distrito Federal: censo demográfico. 1955. xxiii, 88p./
24-2. Distrito Federal: censos econômicos. 1956. lxi, 287p./25-1.
Estado de São Paulo: censo demográfico. 1954. xxxi, 266p./25-2.
Estado de São Paulo: censo agrícola. 1955. xxv, 485p./25-3. Estado
de São Paulo: censos industrial, comercial e dos serviços. 1955.
xlvii, 257p./26. Estado do Paraná: censos demográfico e econômicos.
1955. lxxiii, 496., [10]p./27-1. Estado de Santa Catarina: censo
demográfico. 1955. xxv, 106p./27-2. Estado de Santa Catarina: censos econômicos. 1956. lxi, 284p./28-1. Estado do Rio Grande do Sul:
censo demográfico. 1955. xxv, 134p./28-2. Estado do Rio Grande do
Sul: censos econômicos. 1956. lx, 370p./29. Estado de Mato Grosso:
censos demográfico e econômicos. 1956. lxxii, 376p./30-1. Estado
de Goiás: censo demográfico. 1956. xxv, 118p./30-2. Estado de
Goiás: censos econômicos. 1956. lx, 326p. [PRC, TXU, RPI

Note: The 1960 demographic census was delayed in publication, hence
there are three corporate main entries: Serviço Nacional de Recensea-

mento (imprints 1967 and early 1968, part 1), Departamento de Censos (imprints 1968, part 2), and Departamento de Estatística de População (1976? imprints).

Brazil. IBGE. Departamento de Estatística de População.
VII recenseamento geral de 1960. Série nacional. Rio de Janeiro, Serviço Gráfico, 1967-1977?. Vols. I-IV in 5v.

Seventh general census of 1960. National series.

1960.1-1   Censo demográfico de 1960. Brasil. 1976? xlii, [6], 138p. specimen forms.

Demographic census of 1960. Brazil.
[PRC, UN, RPI

.1-2-1   Censo agrícola de 1960. Brasil. 1967. xix, [5], 37p.

Agricultural census of 1960. Brazil.
[PRC, UN, RPI

.1-2-2   Censo agrícola de 1960. Brasil. 1967. xx, [2], 125p.

Agricultural census of 1960. Brazil.
[UN, RPI

.1-3   Censo industrial de 1960. Brasil. 1967. xvi, 127p. specimen form.

Industrial census of 1960. Brazil.
[PRC, UN, RPI

.1-4   Censos comercial e dos serviços de 1960. Brasil. 1967. xxviii, 234p. specimen forms.

Censuses of business and of services of 1960. Brazil.
[PRC, UN, RPI

Brazil. IBGE. Departamento de Estatística de População.
VII recenseamento geral do Brasil. Série regional. Volumen I. Censo demográfico. Rio de Janeiro, 1967-1977? Tomos I-XIX in 25v.

Seventh general census of Brazil. Regional series. Volume I. Demographic census.

1960.2-1-1-1 through 1960.2-1-19. [One or more volumes for each state.] 1-1. Rondônia-Roraima-Amapá. 1967. xxii, 223p./1-2. ... 1968. xxxvii, 199p./2-1. Acre-Amazonas-Pará. 1967. xxvii, 291p./2-2. ... 1968. xxxvii, 257p./3-1. Maranhão-Piauí. 1968. xxi, 253p./ 3-2. ... 1968. xxxvii, 221p./4. Ceará. 197?. xlii, [4], 125p./ 5. Rio Grande do Norte-Paraíba. 197?. xlii, [4], 251p./6. Pernambuco. 197?. xlii, [4], 125p./7. Alagoas-Sergipe. 197?. xlii, [4], 227p./8. Bahia. 197?. xlii, [4], 137p./9. Minas Gerais. 197?. xlii, [4], 177p./10-1. Espírito Santo. 1967. xxvii, 103p./10-2. ... 1968. xxxvii, 87p./11. Rio de Janeiro. 197?. xlii, [4], 113p./12-1. Guanabara. 1968. xx, 121p./12-2. ... 1968. xxxvii, 117p./13. São Paulo. 197?. xlii, [4], 185p./14. Paraná. 197?. xlii, [4], 137p./15-1. Santa Catarina. 1968. xx, 157p./15-2. ... 1968. xxxvii, 129p./16. Rio Grande do Sul. 197?. xlii, [4], 137p./ 17. Mato Grosso. 197?. xlii, [4], 113p./18. Goiás. 197?. xlii, [4], 137p./19. Distrito Federal. 197?. xlii, [4], 95p. [PRC, UN

[Volumes II, III and IV of the regional series are of the Agricultural, Industrial and Business and Services censuses, respectively.]

Brazil. IBGE. Departamento
    de Censos.
    VIII recenseamento geral -   Eighth general census - 1970.
1970. Brasil. Série nacional.   Brazil. National series.
Rio de Janeiro, Serviço Gráfico,
1973-1975. Nos. 1-4, 6, 7.
1970.1-1   Censo demográfico. Brasil.   Demographic census. Brazil.
    1973. lxxiii, 267p. specimen   [PRC
    forms. map.
  .1-2   Censo predial. Brasil.   Building census. Brazil.
    1974. xvii, 74p.   [PRC
  .1-3   Censo agropecuário. Bra-   Agricultural and livestock cen-
    sil.   sus. Brazil.
      [PRC
  .1-4   Censo industrial. Brasil.   Industrial census. Brazil.
    1974. xxvi, 287p.   [PRC
  .1-5

  .1-6   Censo comercial. Brasil.   Business census. Brazil.
    1975. xvii, 157p.   [PRC
  .1-7   Censo dos serviços. Bra-   Services census. Brazil.
    sil. 1975. xvii, 71p.   [PRC

Brazil. IBGE. Departamento
    de Censos.
    VIII recenseamento geral -   Eighth general census - 1970.
1970. Série regional. Rio de   Regional series.
Janeiro, Serviço Gráfico, 1972-
1973. Tomos I-XXIV in 28v.
1970.2-1-1 through 1970.2-1-24. [One or more volumes for each state.]
    1. Rondônia-Roraima-Amapá. 1973. lxxi, 678p./2. Acre. 1973.
    lxxiii, 226p./3. Amazonas. 1973. lxxiv, 293p./4. Pará. 1973.
    lxxiv, 421p./5. Maranhão. 1973. lxxv, 461p./6. Piauí. 1972. lxxv,
    381p./7. Ceará. 1973. lxxvi, 621p./8. Rio Grande do Norte. 1972.
    lxxvi, 471p./9. Paraíba. 1973. lxxvi, 503p./10. Pernambuco. 1972.
    lxxvii, 551p./11. Alagoas. 1972. lxxv, 383p./12. Sergipe. 1972.
    lxxiv, 363p./13. Bahia. 1973. lxxx, 845p./14-1. Minas Gerais.
    1973. lxxxviii, 191p./14-2. ... 1973. xxvi, 593p./14-3. ...
    1973. xxiv, 676p./15. Espírito Santo. 1973. lxix, 387p./16. Rio
    de Janeiro. 1973. lxix, 441p./17. Guanabara. 1973. xci, 194p./
    18-1. São Paulo. 1973. lxxxvi, 191p./18-2. ... 1973. xxiv,
    501p./18-3. ... 1973. xxii, 478p./19. Paraná. 1973. lxxix,
    807p./20. Santa Catarina. 1973. lxxvii, 575p./21. Rio Grande do
    Sul. 1973. lxxviii, 783p./22. Mato Grosso. 1973. lxix, 427p./23.
    Goiás. 1973. lxxvi, 605p./24. Distrito Federal. 1973. lxxv,
    218p. [PRC

Brazil. IBGE. Departamento
    de Censos.
  .3   Metodologia para o recensea-   Methodology for the 1970 census.
    mento de 1970. Rio de Janeiro,   [
    Serviço Gráfico, 1970.   p.

Brazil. IBGE. Departamento
de Censos.

1970.4   VIII recenseamento geral,
1970. Código de municípios.
Rio de Janeiro, Serviço Gráfico, 1971. 242p.

Eighth general census, 1970.
Register of municipalities.
[

BRITISH INDIAN OCEAN TERRITORY

Capital: Administered from
Victoria, Seychelles.

Originally created in 1965 of the Chagos Archipelago (purchased from
Mauritius) and Aldabra, Farquhar and Des Roches Islands (acquired
from the Seychelles) the group was returned to the Seychelles when
it became independent in 1976.

Since the population is transient, there have been no censuses.

BRITISH VIRGIN ISLANDS

Colony of the Virgin Islands   Capital: Road Town, Tortola.
Statistical Agency: Government of the British Virgin Islands
                      Office of the Financial Secretary
                      Road Town, Tortola,
Publications Distributor: same

1946
      Jamaica.   Central Bureau of Statistics.
      West Indian census, 1946.   Kingston, Government Printer, 1948-
      1950.
         [See Commonwealth Caribbean Nos. 1946.1-A and 1946.1-F.]

1960
      Jamaica.   Department of Statistics.   Jamaica Tabulation Centre.
      West Indian population census, 1960.   [Leeward Islands] ...
         [See Commonwealth Caribbean Nos. 1960.2-BV-1 and 2.]

1970
      West Indies.   University.   Census Research Programme.
      1970 population census of the Commonwealth Caribbean...
         [See Commonwealth Caribbean Nos. 1970.1-1
                        1970.1-2-?
                        1970.1-3
                        1970.1-4-14 and 16
                        1970.1-6-3
                        1970.1-7
                        1970.1-8-a, b, and c
                        1970.1-9-4
                        1970.1-10-3 and 4]

BRUNEI

State of Brunei (Sultanate)   Capital: Bandar Seri Begawan
Statistical Agency: Economic and Statistics Section
                      State Secretariat
                      Bandar Seri Begawan,
Publications Distributor: Department of Information
                            State Secretariat
                            Bandar Seri Begawan,

            Sarawak & Brunei. Census Superintendent.
1947.1   A report on the 1947 population census. By J.L. Noakes. Kuch-
            ing, Sarawak, Government Printer, 1950. xi, 282p. [TXU, UN, PRC,
            RP]

            [Borneo. Joint Census Department]. Brunei Census Advisor.
1960.1   Report on the census of population taken on 10th August, 1960.
            By L.W. Jones, Census Advisor. Kuching, Sarawak, Government Print-
            ing Office, 1961. 180p. folding map, tables. [TXU, UN, PRC, JB-F,
            RP]

            Brunei. Economic and Statistics Section. State Secretariat.
1971.1   Report on the census of population, 1971. Bandar Seri Begawan,
            Star Press, 1973. xiii, 260p. [BC, PRC, E-W, OPR
      .2   [Households and housing]

BULGARIA

People's Republic of Bulgaria.   Capital: Sofia.
Statistical Agency: Central Statistical Office
                      [Tsentralno Statistischesko Upravlenie]
                      10, 6th September Street
                      Sofia,
Publications Distributor: Committee for Integrated Social Information System
                            Council of Ministers
                            2, P. Volov Street
                            Sofia,

Bulgaria. Tsentralno Statisti-
     chesko Upravlenie.

1946.0-1 Predvaritalni rezultati ot   Preliminary results of popula-
prebroiavane na naselenieto na   tion census, December 31, 1946.
31.XII.1946. Broi na naselenie-   Population size by localities.
to po naseleni mesta.   Sofia,   [PRC, UN, RPI
1947. 107p.

Bulgaria. Tsentralno Statisti-
     chesko Upravlenie.

.1   Prebroiavane na naselenieto   Population census taken on Dec-
na 31.XII.1946. Obshti rezul-   ember 31, 1946. General results.
tati. Naselenie po vuzrast,   Population by age, marital status
semeino polozhenie i viara.   and religion.
Sofia, 1949. 212p.   [UN, RPI

Bulgaria. Tsentralno Statisti-
     chesko Upravlenie.

.2   Rezultati ot prebroiavane na   Results of the population census
naselenieto na 31.XII.1946.   of December 31, 1946.
Kniga II.   Sofia, DUI, 1970.   [
50p.

Bulgaria. Tsentralno Statisti-
     chesko Upravlenie.

1956.0-1 Predvaritelni rezultati ot   Preliminary results of the popu-
prebroiavane na naselenieto na   lation census taken on December
1.XII.1956. Broi na naselenie-   1, 1956. Population size by
to po naseleni mesta.   Sofia,   localities.
1957. 104p.   [UN, PRC, RPI

Bulgaria. Tsentralno Statisti-
     chesko Upravlenie.

     Prebroiavane na naselenieto   Population census taken on Decem-
na 1.XII.1956. Obshti rezultati.   ber 1, 1956. General results.
Sofia, State Printing House
"Naouka i Izkoustvo," 1959-1961.
4v.

1956.1-1   Naselenie po vuzrast i
semeino polozhenie. 1959.
770p.
.1-2   Semeistva, kategorii naselenie, natsionalnost i ravnishte
na obrazovanie. 1960. 591p.
.1-3   Zanaiatie, obshtestveni i
vuzrastovi grupi i ravnishte na
obrazovanie. 1960. 1067p.
.1-4   Otrasli, obshtestveni i
vuzrastovi grupi, ravnishte na
obrazovanie i natsionalnost.
1961. 346p.

Bulgaria. Tsentralno Statisti-
chesko Upravlenie.
Predvaritelni rezultati ot
prebroiavaneto na naselenieto i
zhilishtnia fond na 1.XII.1965.
Sofia, 1966. 3v.
1965.0-1   Broi na naselenieto po
naseleni mesta. 254p.
.0-2   Broi na naselenieto po
naseleni mesta, pol i osnovni
vuzrastovi grupi. 362p.
.0-3   Broi na sgradite i zhi-
lishtnata plosht v tiah po
naseleni mesta. 351p.

Bulgaria. Tsentralno Statisti-
chesko Upravlenie.
.1   Rezultati ot prebroiavaneto
na naselenieto na 1.XII.1965.
Tri protsentova reprezentativna
razrabotka.   Sofia, 1966. 114p.

Population by age and marital
status.
[SU, PRC, UN, LC, RPI
Households, population categories,
nationality and educational level.
[SU, PRC, UN, LC, RPI
Economic, social and age groups
and educational level.
[SU, PRC, UN, LC, RPI
Economic branches, social and
age groups, educational level
and nationality.
[SU, PRC, UN, LC, RPI

Preliminary results of the census of population and housing
taken on December 1, 1965.

Population size by localities.
[Berkeley, PRC, RPI
Population size by localities,
sex and basic age groups.
[Berkeley, PRC, RPI
Number of buildings and their
floor space area by localities.
[Berkeley, PRC, RPI

Results of the census of popula-
tion taken on December 1, 1965.
Three percent sample tabulations.
[Berkeley, PRC, RPI

Bulgaria. Central Statistical Office.
.1a   Returns of the 1 December 1965 population census in the People's
Republic of Bulgaria. Three percent advanced sample tabulations.
Sofia, 1966. 111p. [UN, LC, PRC, RPI

Bulgaria. Tsentralno Statisti-
chesko Upravlenie.
Rezultati ot prebroiavane na
naselenieto na 1.XII.1965g.
Okrug... Sofia, 1967-1968.
28v.

Results of the population census
of December 1, 1965. District...

1965.2-1 through 1965.2-28. 1. Blagoevgrad./2. Burgas./3. Varna (and city)./
4. Veliko Turnovo./5. Vidin./6. Vratsa./7. Grabovo./8. Kurdzhali./9.
Kyustendil./10. Lovech./11. Mikhailovgrad./12. Pazardzhik./13. Pernik./
14. Pleven./15. Plovdiv (and city)./16. Razgrad./17. Ruse./18. Silis-

tra./19. Sliven. 1967./20. Smolyan./21. Sofia City./22. Sofia. 1968./
23. Stara Zagora./24. Tolbukhin./25. Turgovishte./26. Khaskovo./27. Shu-
men. 1967./28. Yambol. 1967. [

Note: Citations were seen only for Nos. 19, 22, 27 and 28. It is
not known if remainder were ever published.

Bulgaria. Tsentralno Statisti- 　　chesko Upravlenie. 　　Rezultati ot prebroiavane na naselenieto na 1.XII.1965. Sofia, 1968-1969. Vol. I- 1965.3-1-1	Results of the population census, December 1, 1965.
	[
.3-1-2　　　Plodovitost na omuzhe- nie zheni, razvedenite i vdovite na vuzrast ot 15 do 54g. 1968. viii, 567p.	Fertility of women--married, di- vorced and widowed, age 15-54. [
.3-1-3　　　Migratsiia na nasele- nieto prez perioda 1.XII.1956g. --1.XII.1965g. Obsho na N.R. Bulgariia i po okruzi. 1969. viii, 428p. .3-2	Migration of the population dur- ing the period from December 1, 1956 to December 1, 1965. Whole country and regions. [LC
	[
Balevski, Dano. 1975.0-1　　　Prebroiavane: 1975: re- zultati, prespektivi. -1.Izd.- Sofia, Partizdat, 1976. 119p. (Vŭprosi na denia).	Census, 1975. Results, perspec- tive. [LC
Bulgaria. Tsentralno Statisti- 　　chesko Upravlenie. .0-2　　　Osnovnite rezultati ot pre- broiavaneto na naselenieto i zhi- lishtniia fond v kraia na 1975 g. Sofia, 1975. In: Statistika, 23(3), pp. 3-16.	Basic results from the population and housing census taken on Dec- ember 2, 1975. [
Bulgaria. Tsentralno Statisti- 　　chesko Upravlenie. 　　Demografska i ikonomicheska kharakteristika na naselenieto v N.R. Bulgaria. Prebroiavane na naselenieto i zhilishchna fond kum 2 dek. 1975g. Sofia, 1977-1978. Vol. I-II.	Demographic and economic charac- teristics of population in the People's Republic of Bulgaria. Census of population and housing, December 2, 1975.
.1-1　　　I. 1977. 498p.	[PRC
.1-2　　　II. 1978. 547p.	[PRC

BURMA

Socialist Republic of the Union of Burma.   Capital: Rangoon
Statistical Agency: Central Statistical Organisation
                       New Secretariat
                       Strand Road
                       Rangoon,
Publications Distributor: Government Book Depot
                             212 Theinbyu Street
                             Rangoon,

The 1953-55 multi-stage census of the Union of Burma was interrupted
by political unrest.   The first stage covered 248 towns, i.e., the
urban areas, in Burma and 4 towns in Kachin State.   A series of 20
reseases was published.   The material was synthesized into the following publications:

Burma.   Census Department.
1953.1   Towns classified by population with decennial variations from 1881
          to 1953.   Tangoon, Government Printing and Stationery, 1954.   19p.
          [UN, RPI

Burma.   Census Department.
   .2   Union of Burma.   1953 stage census.   Population.   Series A.   Union
          urban, 252 towns.   General data on age, sex, race, marital status,
          number of industries and farmers.   Rangoon, Union Government Print-
          ing and Stationery, 1955.   [viii], x, 351p.   3 maps.   [BC, JB-F, UN,
          PRC, RPI

Burma.   Central Statistical and Economics Department.   Census Division.
          Union of Burma.   First stage census, 1953.   Rangoon, Government
          Printing and Stationery, 1957-1958.   Vols. I-IV.
   .3-1   I.   Population and housing.   1957.   xlviii, 295p.   folding map.
          [BC, JB-F, UN, PRC, RPI
   .3-2   II.   Industry, cottage industry and home consumed production
          industry.   1958.   v, 138p.   [BC, JB-F, UN, PRC, RPI
   .3-3   III.   Chin special division, population, housing and home eco-
          nomy.   n.d.   75p.   [TXU, JB-F, UN, RPI
   .3-4   IV.   Agriculture.   n.d.   lxxv, [5], 172p.   [BC, UN, PRC, RPI

Burma.   Central Statistical and Economics Department.   Census Division.
          Summary anaysis of the 1953 census.   Rangoon, nd.d   Parts 1-
   .4-1

   .4-2

   .4-3&4   Agriculture/Housing.   [JB-F

The second stage covered 2143 village-tracts in Burma and 1016 in
Kachin State (15 percent of the total rural area).   Some advance re-
leases were published (see below) but there has been no citation to
indicate the issuance of the proposed synthesized version comparable

to the 1953 set. The remaining stages were discontinued in 1955.

Burma. Central Statistical and Economics Department. Census Division.
     Advance publications, 1954 census stage. Series A.   Rangoon,
     1956-   . (Advance release No. 1-8).
1954.1-1   Population [totals by divisions, districts, and townships].
     [1956]. [200]p. [
  .1-2

  .1-3   Kachin State population and households. 1956. 2, 2p. plu
     14 tables. [UN, RPI
  .1-3s   Supplement. 1956. 1p. plus 2 tables. [
  .1-4   [Not applicable]
  .1-5   Housing.
  .1-6   [Not applicable]
  .1-7   [Not applicable]
  .1-8   Nuptiality, fertility, literacy, labor-force status. 1957. 6,
     3, 112p. [

Note: No publications have been issued as yet from the 1973 census
according to a letter early in 1978 to the East-West Center.

BURUNDI

Republic of Burundi   Capital: Bujumbura
Statistical Agency: Department of Statistical Studies
                     [Département des Études Statistiques]
                     Ministère des Affaires Étrangères de la Cooperation
                       et du Plan
                     B.P. 1156
                     Bujumbura,
Publications Distributor: same

The censuses of 1952 and 1958 are of the non-indigenous population
only. There were demographic inquiries in 1965 and 1970-71.

Belgian Congo. Gouvernement Géné-
      ral. Section Statistique.
1952.1   Résultats du recensement général   Results of the general census
de la population non-indigène du   of the non-indigenous population
Congo Belge et du Ruanda-Urundi   of the Belgian Congo and of
du 3 janvier 1952./Resultaten van   Ruanda-Urundi of January 3, 1952.
de algemene telling van de niet-   [UN, PRC, RPI
inlandse bevolking van Belgisch-
Kongo en Ruanda-Urundi op 3 jan-
uari 1952. [Leopoldville], 1952.
87p. (Bulletin mensuel des statistiques du Congo Belge et du
Ruanda-Urundi, 3ème année, No. 21)

Belgian Congo. Direction de la
      Statistique.
Résultats du recensement de la   Results of the census of the
population non-indigène au 3-1-   non-indigenous population of
1958./Uitslagen van de telling van   January 3, 1958.
de niet-inlandse bevolking op 3-1-
1958. [Leopoldville], 1959-1960.
Fasc. a-f. (BMSG du Congo Belge
et du Ruanda-Urundi, série speciale, no. 1)
A. Race blanche/Blanke Ras.   A. White race.
1958.1-A-1   a. Population par natio-   Population by nationality and
nalité et groupe professionnel.   occupational group.
1959. [2], 136p.   [BC, PRC, RPI
.1-A-2   b. Population par natio-   Population by nationality and
nalité et groupe professionnel.   occupational group. Mission-
Missionnaires. 1959. 9, pp.   aries.
137-255.   [BC, PRC, RPI
.1-A-3   c. Population par âge...   Population by age... Population
Population suivant durée du sé-   according to duration of resi-
sour... 1959. 12, pp. 259-351.   dence.
                                          [BC, PRC, RPI
.1-A-4   d. Population active...   Economically active population...
Agents d'entreprise... 1959.   Business agents...
14, pp. 349-488.   [BC, PRC, RPI

.1-A-5   e. Chefs de ménage...   Household heads...
    1960. 14, pp. 490-646.   [BC, PRC, RPI
.1-B Population totale des autres   Total population of other races.
    races. 1960. 14, pp. 650-700.   [BC, PRC, RPI

    Burundi. Government.
1965.1   Enquête démographique du   Demographic survey of Burundi
    Burundi (par sondage), 1965.   (by sample), 1965.
    Paris, 1966. 82p.   [
    [Also published in Bujumbura, 1968.   82p.] [Yale

    Burundi. Ministère du Plan.
         Dept. des Statistiques.
1970.0-1 Enquête démographique Burun-   Demographic survey, Burundi 1970-
    di 1970-71: méthodologie--ré-   71: methodology--provisional
    sultats provisoires. Redacté   results.
    par M.Y. Lambert. Paris, SEAE,   [NWU, OPR
    INSEE, 1972. 67p.

    Burundi. Ministère du Plan.
         Dept. des Statistiques.
    Enquête démographique Burun-   Demographic survey, Burundi 1970-
    di 1970-1971.   Paris, INSEE,   1971.
    1974. 2v.
.1-1   Habitat-Population. 416p.   Housing-Population.
                                          [NWU
.1-2   Méthodologie de l'enquête: Methodology of the survey: appen-
    annexes. 225p.   dices.
                                          [NWU

The next census was proposed for 1978 but no publications have been
seen as yet.

CAMBODIA

Democratic Kampuchea   Capital: Phnom Penh
Statistical Agency: National Institute of Statistics and Economic Research
                     [Institut National de la Statistique et des Recherches
                        Économiques (INSERE)]
                     B.P. No. 105
                     Phnom-Penh
Publications Distributor: same

       France.   INSEE [and] Service des Statistiques.
1946   Les français d'origine métropolitaine...
            [See French Overseas Territories, No. 1946.2]

       Cambodia.   Direction de la Sta-
            tistiques et des Études
            Économiques.
              Enquête démographique au Cam-   Demographic survey of Cambodia.
       bodge. [Phnom Penh], n.d. 2ov.
1960.1-1   Plan d'enquête [et résul-   Plan of the survey [and results].
       tats] (avril 1959). 6p. mimeo.   [PRC, RPI
       .1-2   Mouvement de la population   Population change in Cambodia.
       du Cambodge. Estimations pour   Estimates for a 12 month period
       une période de 12 mois (15 avril   (April 15, 1958 to April 15, 1959).
       1958 à 15 avril 1959). 1p. (D-   [PRC, RPI
       32).
       .1-3   Population du Cambodge en   Population of Cambodia in April
       avril 1959. Population du pays   1959. Population of the whole
       entièr par âge et par sexe. 1p.   country by age and sex.
       mimeo. (D-33)   [PRC, RPI
       .1-4   Mortalité au Cambodge.   Mortality in Cambodia. Estimates
       Estimations pour une période de   for a 12 month period (April 15,
       12 mois (15 avril 1958 à 15 avril   1958 to April 15, 1959).
       1959). 1p. mimeo. (D-34)   [PRC, RPI
       .1-5   Natalité au Cambodge. Esti-   Natality in Cambodia. Estimates
       mations pour une période de 12   ...
       mois (15 avril 1958 à 15 avril   [PRC, RPI
       1959). 1p. mimeo. (D-35)
       .1-6   Ménages ruraux au Cambodge.   Rural households in Cambodia.
       1p. mimeo.   [PRC, RPI
       .1-7   Population rurale du Cam-   Rural population of Cambodia by
       bodge par profession du chef de   occupation of head of household.
       ménage. 17p. _mimeo.   [PRC, RPI
       .1-8   Population rurale du Cam-   Rural population of Cambodia by
       bodge par type de logement (avril   type of dwelling (April 1958).
       1958). 6p. mimeo.   [PRC, RPI
       .1-9   Population de la ville de   Population of Phnom-Penh City.
       Phnom-Penh... 19p. mimeo.   [PRC, RPI
              Population de la ville de...
1960.1-10 through 1960.1-20. 10. Battambang (Sept. 1959). 5p./11. Kampot
       (Dec. 1958). 3p./12. Kampong-Chhnang (Feb. 1960). 4p./13. Kompong-
       Speu (Aug. 1958). 3p./14. Kratie (Mar. 1959). 3p./15. Prey-Veng

(Nov 1959). 5p./16. Pursat (Sept. 1959). 5p./17. Siem-Reap (Oct. 1958). 3p./17a. Siem-Reap (May 1960). 5p./18. Stung-Treng (Mar. 1959). 3p./19. Takeo (Feb. 1959). 3p./20. Svay-Rieng (Nov. 1959). 5p. [PRC, RP]

Cambodia. Direction du Recen-
      sement de la Population.
1962.0-1 Résultats préliminaires du   Preliminary results of the gen-
recensement général de la popu-   eral census of the population,
lation, 1962. [Phnom-Penh,   1962.
1963]. [4], 91p.   [BC, RP]

Cambodia. Institut National de
      la Statistique et des Re-
      cherches Économiques.
    Résultats finales: recense-   Final results: census of 1962.
ment de 1962. [Phnom-Penh],
1965. 13v. mimeo.
1962.1-1 through 1962.1-13. 1. Municipalités de Bokor, Kep, Sihanoukville. 38p./2. Prov. de Battambang. 55p./3. Prov. de Koh-Kong. 28p./4. Prov. de Kompong-Speu. 59p./5. Prov. de Kratie. 35p./6. Prov. de Mondolkiri. 22p./7. Prov. de Phnom-Penh. 100p./8. Prov. de Prey-Veng. 52p./9. Prov. de Pursat. 37p./10. Prov. de Rattanakiri. 26p./ 11. Prov. de Siemreap. 50p./12. Prov. de Stung-Treng. 28p./13. Prov. de Takeo. 51p. [

Cambodia. INSERE.
.2   Résultats finales du recense-   Final results of the general
ment général de la population,   census of the population, 1962.
1962. [Phnom-Penh], 1966.   [BC, OPR, RP]
885p.

George S. Siampos.
.3   Report: the population of Cambodia, 1945-1980.   Phnom Penh, 1968. 7, 85p. [UN, RP]

Khmere. Republic. INSERE.
.4   Additif aux résultats du re-   Addition to the results of the
censement général de la popula-   general census of population,
tion, 1962. Phnom-Penh, [1970].   1962.
[4], 47, [3]p.   [BC, RP]

CAMEROON

United Republic of Cameroon   Capital: Yaoundé
Statistical Agency: Bureau of Statistics and National Accounts.
                     [Direction de la Statistique et de la Comptabilité
                              Nationale]
                     B.P. 660
                     Yaoundé,
Publications Distributor: same

         France. INSEE [and] Service Colonial des Statistiques.
1946   Résultats du recensement...
            [See French Overseas Territories, Nos. 1946.1-1, 2, and 3.
                                    1946.2]

         France. INSEE.
1951   Le recensement de la population...
            [See French Overseas Territories, No. 1951.1]

         France. INSEE.
  .2   Premier résultats du re-   First results of the 1951 census
         censement de 1951 dans les   in the overseas territories (non-
         territoires d'outre-mer (popu-   indigenous population): part 2.
         lation non originaire): 2ème   Togo-Cameroon.
         partie, Togo-Cameroun.   Paris,   [UN, RPI
         n.d. [12], 87, [2]p. (Bulle-
         tin mensuel de statistique d'
         outre-mer, supplément série
         "statistique," No. 15)

         Cameroon. Service de la Statis-
              tique Générale.
  .3   Note sur le résultat du re-   Note on the result of the census
         censement des européens; popu-   of Europeans: European popula-
         lation européenne par sexe et   tion by sex and age.
         par âge. IN: Bulletin de la   [UN, RPI
         statistique général du Cameroun,
         2ème année, No. 9. Pp. 537-545.

         Cameroon. Service de la Statis-
              tique Générale.
  .4   Population européenne des   The European population of the
         principales villes de l'AOF et   main cities of the French West
         du Cameroun. IN: BSG du Came-   Africa and the Cameroon.
         roun, 2ème année, No. 10. P.573.   [UN, RPI

         Cameroon. Service de la Statis-
              tique Générale.
  .5   Résultats du recensement géné-   Results of the general census of
         ral des européens et assimilés   Europeans and the assimilated of
         du 12 novembre 1951. IN: BSG   November 12, 1951.
         du Cameroun, 2ème année, No. 12.   [UN, RPI
         Pp. [623]-[650].

Cameroon. Service de la Statis-
     tique Générale.
    Résultats du recensement de
la ville de Douala (1955-1956).
Population autochtone. Yaoundé,
n.d. Fasc. 1-2.

Results of the census of the city
of Douala (1955-1956). Native
population.

1956.1-1   Résultats par secteurs et
quartiers. 96p. folding map.

Results by sectors and neighbor-
hoods.
[UN, OPR, RPI

  .1-2   Résultats d'ensemble. 42p.

Results for the total population.
[UN, OPR, RPI

Cameroon. Service de la Statis-
     tique Générale.
  .2   Résultats du recensement de
la sub-division de M'Balmayo
(1956). (Population autochtone).
Yaoundé, 1958. 129p.

Results of the census of the sub-
division of M'Balmayo (1956).
(Native population).
[UN, OPR, RPI

Cameroon. Service de la Statis-
     tique Générale.
1957.1   Résultats du recensement de
la ville de Yaound;e (1957).
Population autochtone. [Yaoun-
dé, 1958]. 151p. folding map.

Results of the census of the
city of Yaoundé (1957). Native
population.
[TXU, BC, OPR, RPI

Cameroon. Service de la Statis-
     tique Générale.
  .2   Résultats du recensement de
la population non originaire du
15 janvier 1957. Yaoundé, 1960.
[3], xi, [3], 109p. folding map.

Results of the census of the non-
indigenous population of January
15, 1957.
[TXU, RPI

Cameroon. Service de la Statis-
     tique Générale.
1958.1   Résultats du recensement de
la ville d'Ebolowa, 1958. Population autochtone. Yaoundé,
1958. 124p.

Results of the census of the
city of Ebolowa, 1958. Native
population.
[UN, TXU, OPR, RPI

Cameroon. Service de la Statis-
     tique Générale.
1962.1   La population de Yaoundé.
Résultats définitifs du recensement de 1962. Paris, INSEE,
1970. xxiii, 376p.

The population of Yaoundé. Final
results of the census of 1962.
[OPR, RPI

Cameroon. Service de la Statis-
     tique.
  .2   Enquête démographique: Adamaoua, sud Bénoué (résultats
principaux). Yaoundé, 1962.
32p.

Demographic survey: Adamaoua,
South Bénoué (Main results).
[LC, BC, PRC, RPI

Cameroon.   Direction de la
          Statistique.
1964.1   La population du Cameroun oc-   The population of Western Camer-
cidental; principaux résultats   oon; main results of the demo-
de l'enquête démographique du   graphic inquiry of Western Cam-
Cameroun occidental de 1964.   eroon of 1964.
Yaoundé, 1965. 183, A94p.   [LC, NWU, OPR, PRC, RPI

.1a   [English translation of the above.] 1965. 203, 94p. [LC, OPR,
PRC, RPI

Cameroon.   Direction de la
          Statistique.
.2   La population du pays Bami-   The population of the Bamiléké
léké et des départements limi-   country and of the surrounding
trophes. Principaux résultats   departments. Main results of
de l'enquête démographique de   the demographic survey of 1965.
1965.   Paris, INSEE, 1966.   [NWU, RPI
[6], 173p.

Cameroon.   Service de la Statis-
          tique.
.3   Enquête démographique au Cam-   Demographic survey in Cameroon;
eroun; résultats définitifs pour   final results for the North
la région nord, 1962-1964.   region, 1962-1964.
Paris, INSEE, 1968. 135p.   [LC, NWU, PRC, JB-F, OPR, RPI

Cameroon.   Service de la Statis-
          tique.
.4   Enquête démographique au Cam-   Demographic survey in Cameroon;
eroun; résultats définitifs pour   final results for the South-East
la région sud-est, 1962-1964.   region, 1962-1964.
Paris, INSEE, 1968. 143p.   [LC, NWU, OPR, PRC

Cameroon.   Service de la Statis-
          tique.
      La population du Cameroun oc-   The population of Western Camer-
cidental. Résultats de l'en-   oon. Results of the demographic
quête démographique de 1964.   survey of 1964.
Paris, INSEE, 1969. 3v.
.5-1   I. 1969. xviii, 295p.   [EGCC, OPR, RPI
.5-2   II. 1969. ii, 352p.   [EGCC, OPR, RPI
.5-3   Notes de synthèse. 1969.   Notes of synthesis.
[4], 352p.   [EGCC, OPR, RPI

Cameroon.   Bureau Central du
          Recensement.
1976.0-1 Recensement général de la   General census of population and
population et de l'habitat: housing: manual of instructions
manual d'instructions aux agents   for enumerators.
recenseurs. [Yaoundé, 1976].   [
25p. 2 foldout sheets.

Cameroon. Bureau Central du
        Recensement.
1976.1   Principaux résultats du   Main results of the general cen-
recensement général de la popu-   sus of population and housing.
lation et de l'habitat d'avril   [UN, OPR
1976.   Yaoundé, 1978.   33p.

CANADA

Dominion of Canada.   Capital: Ottawa.
Statistical Agency: Statistics Canada
                     Tunney's Pasture
                     Ottawa, Ontario, K1A OT6,
Publications Distributor: Publications Distribution
                     (of the above)

    Newfoundland. Government.
       Eleventh census of Newfoundland and Labrador, 1945.   Ottawa,
    Dominion Bureau of Statistics, 1949. Vol. I-II.
1945.1-1   I. Population. xvi, 252p. [PRC
   .1-2   II. Agriculture and fisheries. 211p. [PRC

    Canada. Dominion Bureau of
        Statistics.
       Neuvième recensement du Cana-   Ninth census of Canada, 1951.
    da, 1951. Ottawa, Edmond Clou-
    tier, 1953-1956. Vol. I-XI in
    14v.
1951.1-1   I. Population: caracté-   Population: general character-
    ristiques générales. 1953.   istics.
    xvii, 916p. maps. charts.   [PRC
   .1-2   II. Population: classe-   Population: cross-classifications
    ments recoupés des caractéris-   of characteristics.
    tiques. 1953. xiii, 1018p.   [PRC
   .1-3   III. Logements et fami-   Housing and families.
    lles. 1953. xxiii, 1077p.   [PRC
   .1-4   IV. Main-d'oeuvre: Oc-   Labour force: occupations and
    cupations et industries. 1953.   industries.
    xv, 1058p.   [PRC
   .1-5   V. Main-d'oeuvre: gain   Labour force: earnings and em-
    et emploi des salariés. 1953.   ployment of wage-earners.
    xv, 824p.   [PRC

    [Volumes VI through IX are results of the census of agriculture.]

   .1-10   X. Revue générale. 1956.   General review.
    xiii, 588, [402], [103]p.   [PRC
   .1-11   XI. Rapport administratif.   Administrative report.
    1955. 291p. map.   [PRC

    Note: In 1956, Canada began to issue each volume as a series of sep-
    arate bulletins. The covers could be removed and the volume bound in
    consecutive tables. The following entries are for the volumes as a
    whole rather than as individual bulletins.

    Canada. Dominion Bureau of
        Statistics.
       Recensement du Canada de   Census of Canada, 1956.
    1956.   Ottawa, Edmond Cloutier,

1957-1960.   Vol. I-IV in 58v.

1956.1-1   I. Population. Caractéristiques générales, ménages et
familles. 1957-1958. (Bulletins 1-1 through 1-22).

Population. General characteristics, households and families.
[PRC

.1-2   II. Recensement de l'agriculture. 1957-1958. (Bulletins
2-1 through 2-11).

Census of agriculture.
[Harvard

.1-3   III. Rapport analytique.
1958-1960. (Bulletins 3-1
through 3-10).

Analytical reports.
[TXU

.1-4   IV. Caractéristiques de
la population et des logements
par secteur de recensement.
1957-1958. (Bulletins 4-1
through 4-15).

Population and housing characteristics by census tracts.
[TXU

Canada. Department of Citizenship and Immigration. Indian Affairs
         Branch.
1959.1   Census of Indians in Canada, 1959.   Ottawa, Queen's Printer, 1961.
45p. [

Canada. Dominion Bureau of
         Statistics.
Recensement du Canada de 1961.
Ottawa, Roger Duhamel, 1962-1971.
Vol. I-VII in 16 parts (179v).
     I. Population. 1962-
1963. Parts 1-3.

1961 census of Canada.

Population.

1961.1-1-1   Répartition géographique. (Bulletins 1.1-1 through
1.1-11).

Geographic distribution.
[PRC

.1-1-2   Caractéristiques générales. (Bulletins 1.2-1 through
1.2-11).

General characteristics.
[PRC

.1-1-3   Classement recoupé des
caractéristiques. (Bulletins
1.3-1 through 1.3-13)

Cross-classifications of characteristics.
[PRC

     II. Ménages et familles
et caractéristiques de l'habitation. 1962-1965. Parts 1-2.

Households and families and housing characteristics.

.1-2-1   Ménages et familles.
(Bulletins 2.1-1 through 2.1-
13).

Households and families.
[PRC

.1-2-2   Caractéristiques de
l'habitation. (Bulletins 2.2-1
through 2.2-13).

Housing characteristics.
[PRC

     III. Main-d'oeuvre et
salariés. 1963-1966. Parts 1-
3.

Labour force and wage earners.

1961.1-3-1   Main-d'oeuvre: professions. (Bulletins 3.1-1 through 3.1-17).   Labour force: occupations. [PRC

.1-3-2   Main-d'oeuvre: industries. (Bulletins 3.2-1 through 3.2-15).   Labour force: indistries. [PRC

.1-3-3   Salariés: salaire et emploi. (Bulletins 3.3-1 through 3.3-15).   Wage earners: earnings and employment. [PRC

.1-4   IV. Population échantillon: migration, taille de familles, revenu. (Bulletins 4.1-1 through 4.1-11).   Population sample: migration, family size, income. [PRC

[Volumes V and VI are results of the censuses of agriculture and commerce, respectively.]

VII. Revue générale. 1963-1971. Parts 1-2.   General review.

.1-7-1   Revue générale: population et main-d'oeuvre. (Bulletins 7.1-1 through 7.1-15).   General review: population and labour force. [PRC

.1-7-2   Revue générale: habitation, familles, agriculture, commerce. Administration. (Bulletins 7.2-1 through 7.2-13).   General review: housing, families, agriculture, commerce. Administration. [PRC

Canada. Dominion Bureau of Statistics.
Recensement du Canada de 1961. Série des secteurs de recensement. Ottawa, 1963. Parts 1-23.   1961 census of Canada. Census tract series.

1961.2-1 through 1961.2-23. 1. St. John's. 11p./2. Halifax. 12p./3. Saint John. 12p./4. Montreal. 84p./5. Quebec. 24p./6. Sherbrooke. 11p./ 7. Trois-Rivières. 11p./8. Hamilton. 23p./9. Kingston. 11p./10. Kitchener. 11p./11. London. 18p./12. Oshawa. 11p./13. Ottawa. 24p./ 14. Sudbury. 11p./15. Toronto. 72p./16. Windsor. 17p./17. Winnipeg. 29p./18. Regina. 12p./19. Saskatoon. 12p./20. Calgary. 12p./21. Edmonton. 18p./22. Vancouver. 30p./23. Victoria. 12p. [PRC

Canada. Dominion Bureau of Statistics.
1961 census of Canada. Census monographs. Ottawa, 1967-1970. 14v.

.3-1   Trends in Canadian marketing.
.3-2   Urban development in Canada. By L.O. Stone. 1967. xxi, 293p. [PRC
.3-3   Historical estimates of the Canadian labour force. By F.T. Denton and S. Ostry. 1967. viii, 49p. [PRC
.3-4   The occupational composition of the Canadian labour force. By S. Ostry. 1967. 90p. [

1961.3-5   Tendance et facteurs de   Trends and factors of Canadian
        la fécondité au Canada. By J.   fertility.
        Henripin. 1968. xxxi, 425p.   [PRC
    .3-6   Provincial differences in labour force participation. By S.
        Ostry. 1968. viii, 37p. [PRC
    .3-7   Unemployment in Canada. By S. Ostry. 1968. 83p. [
    .3-8   The female worker in Canada. By S. Ostry. 1968. x, 63p.
        [PRC
    .3-9   Incomes of Canadians. By J.R. Podoluk. 1968. xxiv, 356p.
        [PRC
    .3-10   Geographic composition of the Canadian labour force. By S.
        Ostry. 1968. xi, 41p. [PRC
    .3-11   Working life tables for Canadian males. By F. T. Denton and S.
        Ostry. 1969. viii, 56p. [PRC
    .3-12   Migration in Canada, Part I, Some regional aspects. By L.O.
        Stone. 1969. xxiv, 407p. [PRC
    .3-13   Internal migration in Canada, Part II, Demographic analyses.
        By M.V. George. 1970. xv, 251p. [PRC
    .3-14   The impact of immigration on Canada's population. By W. Kal-
        bach. 1970. xxxiv, 465p. [PRC

    Canada. Dominion Bureau of
        Statistics.
        Recensement du Canada de 1966.   1966 census of Canada.
    Ottawa, The Queen's Printer,
    1967-1971. Vol. I-V.
1966.1-1   I. Population - Caracté-   Population - General characteris-
        ristiques générales. 1967-1969.   tics.
        (Bulletins 1-1 through 1-16)   [PRC
    .1-2   II. Population - Ménages   Population - Households and fami-
        et familles. 1968-1971. (Bull-   lies.
        etins 2-1 through 2-14).   [PRC

    [Volumes III through V are results of the census of agriculture.]

    Canada. Statistics Canada.
        Recensement du Canada de 1971.   1971 census of Canada.
    Ottawa, 1972-1978. Vol. I-VI in
    21 parts (226v).
        I. Population. 1972-1976.   Population.
    Parts 1-5.
1971.1-1-1   Répartition géographi-   Geographic distribution.
        que. 1972-1974. (Bulletins   [PRC
        1.1-1 through 1.1-12).
    .1-1-2   Caractéristiques géné-   General characteristics.
        rales. 1973-1976. (Bulletins   [PRC
        1.2-1 through 1.2-9).
    .1-1-3   Caractéristiques géné-   General characteristics.
        rales. 1973-1976. (Bulletins   [PRC
        1.3-1 through 1.3-7).

1971.1-1-4   Classement recoupé des caractéristiques. 1973-1976. (Bulletins 1.4-1 through 1.4-12).

Cross classifications of characteristics.
[PRC

.1-1-5   Classement recoupé des caractéristiques. 1974-1976. (Bulletins 1.5-1 through 1.5-11).

Cross classifications of characteristics.
[PRC

II. Ménages, familles et habitation. 1973-1977. Parts 1-4.

Households, families and housing.

.1-2-1   Ménages. (Bulletins 2.1-1 through 2.1-12).

Households.
[PRC

.1-2-2   Familles. (Bulletins 2.2-1 through 2.2-13).

Families.
[PRC

.1-2-3   Caractéristiques du logement. (Bulletins 2.3-1 through 2.3-8).

Housing characteristics.
[PRC

.1-2-4   Caractéristiques du logement. (Bulletins 2.4-1 through 2.4-9).

Housing characteristics.
[PRC

III. Caractéristiques économiques. 1974-1977. Parts 1-7.

Economic characteristics.

.1-3-1   Population active et revenu des particuliers. Répartition de base. (Bulletins 3.1-1 through 3.1-14)

Labour force and individual income. Basic distributions.
[PRC

.1-3-2   Population active: professions. (Bulletins 3.2-1 through 3.2-13).

Labour force: occupations.
[PRC

.1-3-3   Population active: professions. (Bulletins 3.3-1 through 3.3-10).

Labour force: occupations.
[PRC

.1-3-4   Population active: activités économiques. (Bulletins 3.4-1 through 3.4-10).

Labour force: industries.
[PRC

.1-3-5   Population active: activités économiques. (Bulletins 3.5-1 through 3.5-11).

Labour force: industries.
[PRC

.1-3-6   Revenu des particuliers. (Bulletins 3.6-1 through 3.6-12).

Income of individuals.
[PRC

.1-3-7   Population active-- Antécédents de travail. (Bulletins 3.7-1 through 3.7-14).

Labour force activity--work experience.
[PRC

.1-4   IV. Recensement de l'agriculture. 1973-1976. Parts 1-5.

Census of agriculture.

V. Études schématiques: 1976-   . Parts 1-3.

Profile studies.

.1-5-1   Caractéristiques démographiques. (Bulletins 5.1-1 through 5.1-11).

Demographic characteristics.
[PRC

.1-5-2   Caractéristiques économiques. (Bulletins 5.2-1
through 5.2-11).

Economic characteristics.
[PRC

.1-5-3   Familles, logement,
agriculture. (Bulletins 5.3-1
through 5.3-9).

Families, housing, agriculture.
[PRC

.1-6   VI. Rapport administratif. 1976. 434p.

Administrative report. 1976.
[PRC

Canada. Statistics Canada.
    Recensement du Canada de 1971.
Série des secteurs de recensement. Ottawa, 1973-1974.
Series A-B. [A - 100 percent
data; B - sample data.]

1971 census of Canada. Census
tract series.

1971.2-1a through 1971.2-29b. [Two volumes for each of the following areas].
1. St. John's./2. Halifax./3. Saint John./4. Montreal./5. Quebec./6.
Sherbrooke./7. Trois-Rivières./8. Brantford./9. Hamilton./10. Kingston./
11. Kitchener and Guelph./12. London./13. St. Catharines-Niagara./14.
Oshawa./15. Ottawa-Hull./16. Peterborough./17. Sarnia./18. Sault Ste.
Marie./19. Sudbury./20. Thunder Bay./21. Toronto./22. Windsor./23. Winnipeg./24. Regina./25. Saskatoon./26. Calgary./27. Edmonton./28. Vancouver./29. Victoria. [PRC

Canada. Statistics Canada.
    Recensement du Canada de 1971.
Série spéciale. Ottawa, 1972-
1978. Parts SG, SF, SE, SP.

1971 census of Canada. Special
series.

.3-1   Géographie. (Bulletins
SG-1 and SG-2).

Geography.
[PRC

.3-2   Familles. (Bulletins SF-
1 through SF-3).

Families.
[PRC

.3-3   Caractéristiques économiques. (Bulletins SE-1 through
SE-3).

Economic characteristics.
[PRC

.3-4   Population. (Bulletins
SP-1 through SP-7).

Population.
⌐PRC

Canada. Statistics Canada.
    Recensement du Canada de 1971
Manuels de travail. Ottawa,
1970-1972. 3v in 4.

1971 census of Canada. Working
manuals.

.4-1   Classification des activités économiques, révisée 1970.
1970. 278p.

Standard industrial classification manual, revised 1970. [Eng-
lish version has 309p.]
[PRC

    La classification des pro-
fessions, recensement du Canada,
1971. 1971. 2v.

Occupational classification manual, census of Canada 1971.

.4-2-1   [Occupation groups]. 1971. 111p. [PRC
.4-2-2   [Classified and alphabetical index]. 1971. 455p. [PRC

.4-3   Dictionnaire des termes   Dictionary of the 1971 census
du recensement. 1972. 82, 88p.   terms.
                                        [PRC

Canada. Statistics Canada.
    Recensement du Canada de 1976.   1976 census of Canada. Enumera-
Listes de référence des secteurs   tion area reference lists.
de dénombrement. Ottawa, 1976-
1977. 5 parts in 11v.
1976.0-1   Subdivisions de recense-   Census subdivisions.
     ment. (Atlantic provinces, Que-   [PRC
     bec, Ontario, Western provinces
     and the Territories). 4v.
.0-2   Secteurs de recensement.   Census tracts.
     1976. 96p.   [PRC
.0-3   Secteurs de recensement   Provincial census tracts.
     provinciaux. (Atlantic provin-   [PRC
     ces, Quebec, Ontario, Western
     provinces and the Terr.). 4v.
.0-4   Composantes (Regions metro-   Components (Census Metropolitan
     politaines et agglomérations de   Areas and Census Agglomerations).
     recensement). 1976. 32p.   [PRC
.0-5   Régions urbaines par divi-   Urban areas by Census Division.
     sion de recensement. 1977.   [PRC
     103p.

Canada. Statistics Canada.
    Recensement du Canada de 1976.   1976 census of Canada.
Ottawa, 1977-1979. Vol. 1-10 in
107v.
.1-1   I. Population: réparti-   Population: geographic distri-
     tion géographique. (Bulletins   bution.
     1.1 through 1.12).   [PRC
.1-2   II. Population: carac-   Population: demographic charac-
     téristiques démographiques.   teristics.
     (Bulletins 2.1 through 2.9).   [PRC
.1-3   III. Logements et ména-   Housing and households.
     ges. (Bulletins 3.1 through   [PRC
     3.11).
.1-4   IV. Familles. (Bulletins   Families.
     4.1 through 4.6).   [PRC
.1-5   V. Activités économiques.   Labour force activity.
     (Bulletins 5.1 through 5.9).   [PRC
     VI. Secteurs de recense-   Census tracts.
ment. 1978. 32v. (Bulletins
6.1 through 6.32).
1976.1-6-1 through 1976.1-6-32. 1. Brantford./2. Calgary./3. Chicoutimi-Jon-
     Quiere./4. Edmonton./5. Guelph./6. Halifax./7. Hamilton./8. Kitchener./
     9. Kingston./10. London./11. Moncton./12. Montréal./13. Oshawa./14.
     Ottawa-Hull./15. Peterborough./16. Québec./17. Regina./18. St. Cathar-
     ines-Niagara./19. St. John's./20. Saint John./21. Sarnia./22. Saskatoon./

23. Sault Ste. Marie./24. Sherbrooke./25. Sudbury./26. Thunder Bay./
27. Toronto./28. Trois-Rivières./29. Vancouver./30. Victoria./31. Windsor./32. Winnipeg. [PRC

1976.1-7   Secteurs de recensement provinciaux, cartes de référence. (Bulletins 7.1 through 7.8)

Provincial census tracts. [PRC

.1-8   Bulletins supplémentaires: géographiques et démographiques. (Bulletins 8SG. 1 and 8SG.2) (8SD.1 through 8SD.4).

Supplementary bulletins: geographic and demographic. [PRC

.1-9   Bulletins supplémentaires: logements et familles. (Bulletins 9SH.1 and 9SF.1 through 9SF.5).

Supplementary bulletins: housing and families. [PRC

.1-10   Bulletins supplémentaires: caractéristiques économiques. (Bulletins 10SE.1 through 10SE. 8).

Supplementary bulletins: economic characteristics. [PRC

[Volumes XI, XII and XIII are results of the census of agriculture.]

CANTON AND ENDERBURY

The islands are jointly administered by the United Kingdom and the United States. The U.S. censuses for 1950 and 1960 carry only total munber of inhabitants in Table 1 of the U.S. Summary volume for those years. Canton was enumerated by the British in 1947 and 1963 in the Gilbert and Ellice Islands censuses.

Gilbert and Ellice Islands Colony.
1947.1   A report on the results of the census of the population, 1947. By F.N.M. Pusinelli.   Suva, Fiji, Government Press, 1951. ii, 103p. [PRC

Gilbert and Ellice Islands Colony.
1963.1   A report on the results of the census of population, 1963.   Suva, Fiji, Government Press, 1964. 267p. [PRC

In 1967 Canton joined Enderbury as uninhabited islands; there are no permanent residents.

CAPE VERDE

Republic of Cape Verde   Capital: Praia.
Statistical Agency: Department of Statistical Services
                     [Repartição dos Serviços de Estatística]
                     Praia,
Publications distributor: same

        Portugal. Instituto Nacional
            de Estatística
1950.1   Censos da população do im-   Population censuses of the Por-
        perio colonial portugues de 1950.   tuguese colonial empire of 1950.
        2: População da Colónia de Cabo   2: Population of Cape Verde.
        Verde. In: Buletim mensal do   [Summary results]
        I.N.E. Ano 23, no. 3. Março de   [TXU
        1951. Pp. 9-13.

        Cape Verde. Serviços de Adminis-
            tração Civil. Secção de
            Estatística.
        VIII recenseamento geral da   Eighth general census of popula-
        população da Provincia de Cabo   tion of the Province of Cape
        Verde em 1950.   Praia, Imprensa   Verde in 1950.
        Nacional, 1953-   . Vols. I- .
        .2-1   I. [Resumo descritivo e   Descriptive summary and first
        primeiros resultados definitivos].   final results.
        1953. 134p.   [PRC, Boston U., NWU
        .2-2   II.

        Cape Verde. Serviços de Adminis-
            tração Civil. Secção de
            Estatística.
1960.1   IX recenseamento geral do popu-   Ninth general census of popula-
        lação, 1960.   Lisboa, Comissão   tion, 1960.
        para os Inquéritos Agrícolas no   [UN, NWU
        Ultramar, 1975. 209p.

        Portugal. Instituto Nacional de Estatística.
1970   [1970 recenseamento da população...
            [See Portugal 1970.3.]

CAYMAN ISLANDS

Capital: Georgetown
Statistical Agency: Department of Finance and Development
                Georgetown, Grand Cayman,
Publications Distributor: same
                [See also Jamaica]

Jamaica. Central Bureau of Statistics.
1943.1   Eighth census of Jamaica and its dependencies, 1943. Population, housing and agriculture. Kingston, Government Printer, 1945. twenty-eight, cii, 571p. 4 folding maps. [TXU, NYPL, RPI

Jamaica. Department of Statistics. Jamaica Tabulation Centre.
1960.   West Indies population census, 1960. Census of the Cayman Islands, [See Commonwealth Caribbean, Nos. 1960.2-C-1 and 2.]

West Indies. University. Census Research Programme.
1970   1970 population census of the Commonwealth Caribbean...
          [See Commonwealth Caribbean, Nos. 1970.1-1
                                        1970.1-2-?
                                        1970.1-3
                                        1970.1-4-13 and 16
                                        1970.1-6-3
                                        1970.1-7
                                        1970.1-8-a, b, and c.
                                        1970.1-9-4
                                        1970.1-10-3 and 4.]

CENTRAL AFRICA

Central African Empire   Capital: Bangui
Statistical Agency: Bureau of General Statistics and of Economic Studies
                      [Direction de la Statistique Générale et des Études
                          Économiques]
                      B.P. 954
                      Bangui,
Publications Distributor: same

    There was a demographic survey (1959-60) but it excluded the eastern
portion of the country, the nomadic areas, and Bangui town. Bangui
was censused in 1955-56.

France. INSEE.
1946   Résultats du recensement...
    [See French Overseas Territories, Nos. 1946.1-1, 2, and 3.
                       1946.2]

France. INSEE.
1951   Le recensement de la population...
    [See French Overseas Territories, No. 1951.1]

France. INSEE.
1956.1   Recensement et démographie   Census and demography of the prin-
des principales agglomérations   cipal African agglomerations. IV.
africaines d'AEF. IV. Bangui.   Bangui.
Paris, n.d. [58]p.   [OPR

Central Africa. Ministère de
    l'Intérieur.
1960.1   Enquête démographique en Ré-   Demographic survey in the Central
publique Centrafricaine, 1959-   African Republic, 1959-1960.
1960. Résultats définitifs.   Final results.
By Marcel Lafarge. Paris,   [NWU, OPR, RPI
Ministère de la Coopération,
1964. 262p.

Central Africa. Ministère de
    l'Intérieur.
    Recensement général de la   General census of the population
population de la République   of the Central African Republic.
Centrafricaine. Paris, 1964-
1969. Parts 1-3.
1963.1-1   Résultats pour la région   Results for the Lobaye, Upper
de Lobaye, Haute Sangha, 1961-   Sangha region, 1961-1963.
1963.   Paris, INSEE, 1964.   [PRC, JB-F, NWU, RPI
    [2], 392p.
  .1-2   Résultats pour la région   Results for the Ouham, Ouham-
de Ouham, Ouham-Pende, Nana-   Pende, Nana-Membere (Baboua)
Membere (Baboua).   Paris, INSEE,   region.
1968. 35, 104p.   [PRC, JB-F, RPI

1963.1-3   Résultats pour la région   Results for the Upper-Kotto, Birao,
          de Haute-Kotto, Birao, Obo-Zemio,   Obo-Zemio, Sub-prefecture Rafai
          sous-prefecture de Rafai.   Paris,   region.
          INSEE, 1969. 91p.   [PRC, JB-F, NWU, RPI

Note: "The difficulties of approach caused that area which was
covered by the Demographic Survey taken in 1959-60 to be excluded."

          Central Africa.   Direction de la
               Statistique Générale et
               des Études Économiques.
             Répertoire des villages de   List of the villages of the Cen-
          l'Empire Centrafricain (recense-   tral African Empire (census of
          ment de 1975).   Bangui, n.d.   1975).
             3v.
1975.1-1   1.   [
    .1-2   2.   [
    .1-3   3.   [

CEUTA AND MELILLA

Spanish Plazas in North Africa.
Statistical Agency: See Spain.

        Spain.   Instituto Nacional de Estadística.
1950   Censo de la población...
            [See Spain, No. 1950.1-1]

        Spain.   Instituto Nacional de Estadística.
1960   Censo de la población...
            [See Spain, No. 1960.4-1]

        Spain.   Instituto Nacional de Estadística.
1970   Censo de la población...
            [See Spain, Nos. 1970.1
                           1970.2
                           1970.3-1
                           1970.3-2-51/52.
                           1970.3-3
                           1970.3-4-51/52]

CHAD

Republic of Chad   Capital: N'Djamena (Fort Lamy)
Statistical Agency: General Statistics Service
                     [Service de la Statistique Générale]
                     B.P. 453
                     N'Djamena,
Publications Distributor: same

The demographic survey of 1964 covered most of the country and coupled
with the Fort Lamy (now N'Djamena) census of 1962 can be considered
sufficient in absence of a full census for that decade.

France. INSEE.
1946   Résultats du recensement...
           [See French Overseas Territories, Nos. 1946.1-1, 2, and 3.
                                               1946.2]

France. INSEE.
1951   Le recensement de la population...
           [See French Overseas Territories, No. 1951.1]

France. INSEE.
1962.0-1   Recensement démographique   Demographic census of Fort Lamy,
de Fort Lamy, mars-juillet 1962:   March-July 1962: provisional
résultats provisoires.   Paris,   results.
1964. 78, [12]p.   [JB-F, NWU, RPI

France. Bureau pour le Develop-
            pement de la Production
            Agricole.
1963.1   Enquête démographique par   Demographic survey by sampling
sondage 1963. Zone des cuvettes   1963. Area of lacustrine depres-
lacustres et quadis du Lac Tchad.   sions and wadis of Lake Chad.
Rapport définitif.   Paris,   Final report.
        p.   [

Chad. Service de Statistique.
     Enquête démographique au   Demographic survey of Chad, 1964.
Tchad 1964. Résultats défini-   Final results.
tifs.   Paris, INSEE, 1966.
2v in 1.
1964.1-1   Analyse des résultats.   Analysis of results.
    ii, 307p.   [JB-F, LC, NWU, OPR
    .1-2   Tableaux statistiques   Detailed statistical tables.
détaillés. iii, 196p.   [JB-F, LC, NWU, OPR

The circa 1970 census has been postponed due to factors beyond the
control of the statistical authorities.

CHANNEL ISLANDS (JERSEY, GUERNSEY, ALDERNEY AND SARK)

Bailiwick of Jersey; Bailiwick of Guernsey.   Capital: St. Helier, St. Peter Port

Statistical Agency: Census Office
                     States of Guernsey Board of Administration
                     Grange House
                     St. Peter Port,
Publications Distributor: same (for home printed results)
                           See England and Wales (for other printed reports).

     Great Britain. General Register Office
1951.1   Census 1951. Report on Jersey, Guernsey, and adjacent islands.
     London, HMSO, 1956. li, 55p. specimen forms. [PRC, RPI

     Great Britain. General Register Office.
1961.1   Census 1961. Report on Jersey, Guernsey, and adjacent islands.
     London, HMSO, 1966. xiv, 83p. [PRC, BC, RPI

     Guernsey. Census Office.
1971.1   Census 1971. Report on the Bailiwick of Guernsey.   St. Peter
     Port, 1971. 172p. [PRC, OPR

     Guernsey. States Office.
1976.1   Guernsey census, 1976.   St. Peter Port, 1977. 58p. [OPR

     Jersey. Etat Civil Committee.
  .2   Report of the census for 1976. [St. Helier], 1977. 62p. (R.C.
     Series II). [LC

CHILE

Republic of Chile   Capital: Santiago
Statistical Agency: National Statistical Institute
                     [Instituto Nacional de Estadística]
                     Casilla 7597-Correo 3
                     Santiago,
Publications Distributor: Subdirección Técnica
                           Instituto Nacional de Estadística
                           Casilla 6177-Correo 22
                           Santiago,

Chile. Servicio Nacional de
        Estadística y Censos.
    XII censo general de pobla-   Twelfth general census of popula-
ción y I de vivienda. Santiago,   tion and first of housing.
n.d.   Tomos I-VI.
1952.1-1   I. Resumen de país. 1956   General summary for the country.
    269, [3]p. specimen forms.   [TXU, PRC, JB-F, RPI
    .1-2   II. Nucleo Central I.   Central nucleus I. Far North
    Norte Grande y Norte Chico. Pro-   and Near North. Provinces of
    vincias de Tarapacá, Antofagasta,   Tarapacá, Antofagasta, Atacama
    Atacama y Coquimbo. n.d. xxiv,   and Coquimbo.
    389p. maps.   [TXU, BC, PRC, RPI
    .1-3   III. Nucleo Central I.   Central nucleus I. Provinces of
    Provincias de Aconcagua, Valpa-   Aconcagua, Valparaíso, Santiago,
    raíso, Santiago, O'Higgins y Col-   O'Higgins and Colchagua.
    chagua. n.d. xxxi, 866, [5]p.   [TXU, LC, PRC, RPI
    .1-4   IV. Nucleo Central II.   Central nucleus II. Provinces
    Provincias de Curicó, Talca,   of Curicó, Talca, Maule, Linares
    Maule, Linares y Ñuble. n.d.   and Ñuble.
    xxvii, 496, [5]p.   [TXU, BC, PRC, RPI
    .1-5   V. Concepción y la fron-   Concepción and the frontier.
    tera. Provincias de Concepción,   Provinces of Concepción, Arauco,
    Arauco, Bío-Bío, Malleco y Cau-   Bío-Bío, Malleco and Cautín.
    tín. n.d. xxiv, [2], 617p.   [BC, PRC, RPI
    .1-6   VI. Región de los Lagos,   Lake region, Canal region. Pro-
    Región de los Canales. Provin-   vinces of Valdivia, Osorno, Llan-
    cias de Valdivia, Osorno, Llan-   quihue, Chiloé, Aisén and Maga-
    quihue, Chiloé, Aisén y Maga-   llanes.
    llanes. n.d. xxvi, 468p. maps.   [TXU, BC, PRC, RPI

Chile. Dirección de Estadística
        y Censos.
    XIII censo de población, 29   Thirteenth census of population,
de noviembre de 1960. Santiago,   November 29, 1960.
1963-1965. Serie A-B in 26v.
1960.1-A   Resumen del país. n.d.   General summary.
    448, xv p.   [PRC, RPI
1960.1-B-1 through 1960.1-B-25. [One volume for each of the following areas.]
    1. Tarapacá. n.d. [8], 139p./2. Antofagasta. 1964. [4], 137p./
    3. Atacama. 1964. [4], 135, [3]p./4. Coquimbo. 1964. [3], 147p./

5. Aconcagua. 1965. [1], 140, [3]p./6. Valparaíso. 1965. [6], 141, [2]p./7. Santiago. 1964. [6], 174, [6]p./8. O'Higgins. 1965. [4], 141, [3]p./9. Colchagua. 1965. [1], 139, [2]p./10. Curicó. 1965. [1], 131, [2]p./11. Talca. 1965. [1], 133, [2]p./12. Maule. 1965. [v], 133p./13. Linares. 1965. [1], 129, [3]p./14. Ñuble. n.d. [4], 133, [3]p./15. Concepción. n.d. 123, [5]p./16. Arauco. 1964. 133, [5]p./17. Bío-Bío. n.d. 121, [5]p./18. Malleco. n.d. [6], 138, [2]p./19. Cautín. n.d. [6], 151, [4]p./20. Valdivia. n.d. [6], 138, [2]p./21. Osorno. n.d. [6], 130, [2]p./22. Llanquihue. n.d. [6], 134, [2]p./23. Chiloé. n.d. [6], 143, [2]p./24. Aisén. n.d. [6], 129, [2]p./25. Magallanes. n.d. [6], 136, [4]p. [PRC, RPI

Chile. Instituto Nacional de
      Estadística.
    XIV censo nacional de pobla-   Fourteenth national census of
ción y III de vivienda, abril   population and third of housing,
1970. Muestra de adelanto de   April 1970. Advance sample of
cifras censales. Santiago,   census figures.
1971. Vols. 1-14.
1970.1-1   Total país. vi, 75p.   General summary.
                                    [PRC
1970.1-2 through 1970.1-14. [One volume for each area or areas.] 2. Gran Santiago. xiv, 27p./3. Tarapacá. viii, 75p./4. Antofagasta. vii, 75p./5. Atacama, Coquimbo. vii, 75p./6. Aconcagua, Valparaíso. vii, 75p./7. Santiago. vii, 75p./8. O'Higgins, Colchagua. vii, 75p./9. Curicó, Talca, Linares, Maule. viii, 75p./10. Ñuble, Concepción, Arauco, Bío-Bío, Malleco. vii, 75p./11. Cautín. vii, 75p./12. Valdivia, Osorno. viii, 75p./13. Llanquihue, Chiloé, Aisén. viii, 75p./ 14. Magallanes. vii, 75p. [PRC

Chile. Instituto Nacional de
      Estadística.
    Características básicas de   Basic characteristics of the
la población (Censo 1970).   population (Census 1970).
Santiago, 1970-   . 26v.
  .2-1   Resumen país. n.d.   General summary.
      p.   [
1970.2-2 through 1970.2-26. [One volume for each area.] 2. Tarapacá. 32p./3. Antofagasta. 30p./4. Atacama. 27p./5. Coquimbo. 35p./ 6. Aconcagua. 34p./7. Valparaíso. 39p./8. Santiago. 68p./9. O' Higgins. 37p./10. Colchagua. 35p./11. Curicó. 28p./12. Talca. 28p./13. Maule. 24p./14. Linares. 28p./15. Ñuble. 38p./16. Concepción. 35p./17. Arauco. p./18. Bío-Bío. 28p./19. Malleco. 32p./20. Cautín. 37p./21. Valdivia. 32p./22. Osorno. 25p./23. Llanquihue. 29p./24. Chiloé. 34p./25. Aisén. 26p./26. Magallanes. 30p. [PRC

Chile. Instituto Nacional de
      Estadística.
    Censos '70. XIV censo de   Censuses '70. Fourteenth cen-
población y III de vivienda.   sus of population and third of
Viviendas, hogares y familias.   housing. Housing, households
Santiago, n.d. 26v.   and families.

.3-1   Resumen general.   General summary.
                                         [
1970.3-2 through 1970.3-26. [One volume for each state.] 2. Tarapacá.
    xvii, 60p./3. Antofagasta. xvii, 60p./4. Atacama. xvii, 60p./ 5.
    Coquimbo. xvii, 60p./6. Aconcagua. xvii, 60p./7. Valparaíso. xvii,
    60p./8. Santiago. xvii, 60p./9. O'Higgins. xvii, 60p./10. Colcha-
    gua. xvii, 60p./11. Curicó. xvii, 60p./12. Talca. xvii, 60p./13.
    Maule. xvii, 60p./14. Linares. xvii, 60p./15. Ñuble. xvii, 60p./
    16. Concepción. xvii, 60p./17. Arauco. xvii, 60p./18. Bío-Bío.
    xvii, 60p./19. Malleco. xvii, 60p./20. Cautín. xvii, 60p./21. Val-
    divia. xvii, 60p./22. Osorno. xvii, 60p./23. Llanquihue. xvii,
    60p./24. Chiloé. xvii, 60p./25. Aisén. xvii, 60p./26. Magallanes.
    xvii, 60p. [PRC

Chile. Instituto Nacional de
      Estadística.
    Población. Resultados defi-   Population. Final results of
    nitivos del XIV censo de pobla-   the Fourteenth census of popu-
    cion, 1970.   Santiago, 1977.   lation, 1970.
.4-1   Total país. v, 157p.   General summary.
    specimen forms.   [PRC, IASI, PSC
1970.4-2 through 1970.4-26. [One volume for each state.] 2. Tarapacá. v,
    156p./3. Antofagasta. v, 156p./4. Atacama. v, 156p./5. Coquimbo.
    v, 155p./6. Aconcagua. v, 155p./7. Valparaíso. v, 161p./8. Santiago.
    v, 163p./9. O'Higgins. v, 154p./10. Colchagua. v, 153p./11. Curicó.
          /12. Talca. v, 157p./13. Maule.   /14. Linares. v,
    157p./15. Ñuble. v, 155p./16. Concepción. v, 159p./17. Arauco. v,
    152p./18. Bío-Bío. v, 157p./19. Malleco.   /20. Cautín.
          /21. Valdivia.   /22. Osorno. v, 154p./23. Llanquihue.
          /24. Chiloé. v, 151p./25. Aisén.   /26. Magallanes.
    v, 157p. [PRC, IASI

CHINA, MAINLAND

People's Republic of China.   Capital: Peking
Statistical Agency: State Statistical Bureau
                     Kuo chia t'ung-chi chü
                     Peking,
Publications Distributor: Mail Order Dept.
                           Guozi Shudian
                           P.O. Box 399
                           Peking,

China. [Ministry of Interior. Census Bureau]
1947.1   [The 1947 population of China]. In: Chinese Journal (New York),
          August 16, 18, 19, and 20, 1947. (In Chinese). [Yale, Cornell

China. [Directorate General of
        Budgets, Accounts and Sta-
        tistics]
   .2   Chung hua min kuo t'ung chi   Statistical abstract of the Repub-
         t'i yao, 1947.   Nanking, 1947.   lic of China, 1947.
         140p. tables.   [Berkeley, PRC, RPI
   .3   Chung hua nien chien, 1948.   China yearbook, 1948.
         Nanking, 1948. Pp. 78-118.   [

China. American Embassy, Nan-
        king.
   .4   Official estimates of population... Nanking, n.d. 12p. [UN, RPI

China. Teng Hsiao-p'ing.
1953.1-1
                                            Census and general election com-
                                            pleted in China: population of
         In: New China News Agency, Pei-   China over 600 million.
         ping, June 19, 1954. [Translated [LC, TXU
         in: Survey of China Mainland
         Press, No. 832, June 19-21, 1954].

China. Kuo chia t'ung-chi chü.   State Statistical Bureau.
   .1-2 Kuan-yü ch'üan-kuo jen-ko   Communique of results of census
         tiao-ch'a teng-chi chieh-kuo ti   and registration of China's popu-
         king-pao. In: New China News   lation.
         Agency, Peiping, Nov. 1, 1954..   [LC, TXU, Berkeley, PRC, RPI
         [Translated in: Current Back-
         ground (Jong Kong), No. 301]

Hong Kong. American Conculate General.
   .1-3   Six hundred million. In: Survey of China Mainland Press, No.
         890. 1954. Pp. 31-33. [Berkeley, RPI

   .1-4 "The census results." China News Analysis (Hong Kong), No. 61, Nov.
         2, 1954. Pp. 2-5. [TXU, LC

   .1-5 "Our first scientific census." People's China (Peking), 1955, No. 7.
         Pp. 17-23. [TXU, LC

China. Kuo chia t'ung-chi chü.   State Statistical Bureau.
1953.1-6   1949-1956 nien wo kuo jen k'ou   1949-1956 statistical material
t'ung chi tzu liao. In: T'ung   on the population of our country.
chi kung tso (Peking), no. 11,   Statistical Work, no. 11.
June 14, 1957. Pp. 24-25.   [LC, TXU
[Translated in: Extracts of China
Mainland Magazines (Hong Kong).
no. 91, July 22, 1957. Pp. 22-25.

China. Ta Kung Pao (Publisher)   Ta Kung Newspaper.
.1-7 Jen min shou ts'e. Peking,   People's handbook, 1955 ed.
1955. 684p.   [LC, Harvard,

Tai, Shih Kuang.
.1-8 1953 population census of China.   Calcutta, Indian Statistical
Institute, 1956. 23p. [

Chen Ta.
.1-9 "New China's population census of 1953 and its relations to national reconstruction and demographic research." Bulletin of the International Statistical Institute (Stockholm), 36(2):255-271. (1956)
[LC,

China. Jen-min jih-pao she.   People's Daily Society.
.1-10   I chiu wu san nien (1953).   Documents of the population cen-
Ch'üan kuo jen kou tiao ch'a   sus of the whole country.
wen chien. In: Jen min jih   [
pao (Peiping), July 13, 1954.

Non-Mainland Chinese sources.

Krotevich, S.
1953.2-1 Vsekitaiskaia perepis' nase-   All-Chinese population census
leniia 1953g. Vestnik statis-   of 1953
tiki (Moskow), 1955, no. 5.   [TXU, NYPL, PRC, RPI
Pp. 31-50, schedules.

Pekshev, Iu. A and N.I. Shvetsov.
.2-2 Razvitie narodnogo khozia-   The growth of the national econ-
ĭstva Kitaĭskoĭ Narodnoĭ Repub-   omy of the Chinese People's Re-
like. Statisticheskie pokaza-   public. Statistical tables.
leli. Moscow, 1956. 51p.   [LC, Berkeley, PRC, RPI

Witthauer, Kurt.
.2-3 "China: Bevölkerung und   China: population and adminis-
Verwaltungsliederung." Peter-   trative divisions.
manns Geographische Mitteilungen   [TXU
(Gotha), 99(3):229-230.
Tables, map.

Skibbe, Bruno.
.2-4 "Die Veränderung der Volks-   Changes in China's population
dichte in China: zu einigen   density: some results of the

Ergebnissen der Volkszäh-
lung 1953." Petermanns
Geographische Mitteilungen
(Gotha), 99(4):299-302.

census of 1953.
[TXU

Chandrasekhar, Sripati.
.2-5 China's population, census and vital statistics. Hong King University Press, 1959. 69p. [TXU
    [Second edition, revised and enlarged, 1960. 73p.] [Princeton U.

U.S. Bureau of the Census.
    International population statistics reports. Washington, D.C.,
    1955-1965.
.2-6-1   The population of Communist China: 1953. 1955. 4p.
    tables. (P-90, no. 6) [Berkeley, PRC, RPI
.2-6-2   The size, composition, and growth of the population of Main-
    land China. 1961. 106p. (P-90, no. 15). [PRC
.2-6-3   Nonagricultural employment in Mainland China: 1949-1958.
    1965. 250p. (P-90, no. 21). [PRC

Henri, Louis.
.2-7 "La population de la Chine;   The population of China; the
la population de Formose." Popu-   population of Formosa.
lation (Paris), 9(4):744-746.   [TXU, Berkeley, PRC, RPI
(1954)

Mignet, Ch. (translator)
.2-8 "Le recensement de la Chine,   The census of China, method and
méthode et principaux résultats."   main results. (Translation of
Population (Paris), 11(4):725-736.   Krotevich, 1953.2-1)
(1956)   [TXU, Berkeley, PRC, RPI

Cressey, George.
.2-9 "The 1953 census of China." Far Eastern Quarterly, 14(3):387-388.
    (1955). [TXU, Berkeley, PRC, RPI

Kirby, E. Stuart.
.2-10 "The people of China, census results and population policies."
    Family Planning (London), July 1956. [Berkeley, Harvard, NYPL

Orleans, Leo A.
.2-11 "The 1953 Chinese census in perspective." Journal of Asian
    Studies, 16(4):565-573. (1957). [TXU

Shabad, Theodore.
.2-12 "The population of China's cities." Geographical Review, 49(1):
    32-42. (1959). [TXU

Li, Hiu min.
.2-13 "Population statistics of Chinese Mainland." Chinese Communist
    Affairs (Taipei), 4(2):46-59. (1968). [Yale, Princeton U.

Chen, Lin
.2-14 "A study of the Chinese Mainland population." Issues and Studies
    (Taipei), 5(2):17-25. (1968).   [U. Hawaii-Asian Coll.

Chen, Cheng-siang.
.2-15 "Population growth and urbanization in China, 1953-1970." Geo-
    graphical Review, 63(1):55-72. (1973). [TXU

Aird, John S.
.2-16 "Recent provincial population figures." The China Quarterly (Lon-
    don), no. 73. (March 1978). Pp. 1-42. [PRC

CHRISTMAS ISLAND

Territory of Christmas Island   Capital: Flying Fish Cove.
Statistical Agency: Central Statistics Office
       Flying Fish Cove,

       [See also Australia]
Publications Distributor: Department of Home Affairs
       P.O. Box 1252
       Canberra City,
       A.C.T. 2601, Australia

Malaya (Federation). Superintendent of Census.
1947.1 Malaya comprising the Federation of Malaya and the Colony of Singapore: a report on the 1947 census of population, by M.V. Del Tufo. London, Waterlow and Son, Ltd., 1949. 597p. maps. [Cited as part of the Colony of Singapore.] [PRC, BC, TXU, RPI

Singapore. Superintendent of Census.
1957.1 Report on the census of population, 1957. Singapore, Government Printing Office, 1964. 319p. [Cited in separate tables.] [PRC, UN, RPI

Australia. Commonwealth Bureau of Census and Statistics.
1961.1-7-5 Census of the Commonwealth of Australia, 30th June, 1961. Volume VII--Territories. Part V--External territories [Papua, New Guinea, Nauru, Norfolk Island, Christmas Island and Cocos (Keeling) Islands]: population and dwellings. Canberra, Government Printing Office, 1964. 59p. [PRC, RPI

Australia. Commonwealth Bureau of Census and Statistics.
1966.1-11-1 Census of the territory of Christmas Island, 30 June 1966. Summary of population. By K.M. Archer. [Canberra], 1968. 12p. (Census bulletin, No. 11-1). [PRC

[Australian Bureau of Statistics.]
1971.1 [1971 census of the Territory of Christmas Island] Canberra, n.d. [23]p. specimen form. [This is a copy of results by Collectors Districts forwarded by the Department of Home Affairs in August 1979.] [PRC

COCOS (KEELING) ISLANDS

Territory of Cocos (Keeling) Islands   Capital: West Island
Statistical Agency: See Australia.

Malaya (Federation). Superintendent of Census.
1947.1   Malaya comprising the Federation of Malaya and the Colony of Singapore: a report on the 1947 census of population, by M.V. Del Tufo.
London, Waterlow and Sons, Ltd., 1949. 597p. maps. [Cited as part
of the Colony of Singapore.] [PRC, BC, TXU, RPI

Singapore. Superintendent of Census.
1957.1   Report on the census of population, 1957. Singapore, Government
Printing Office, 1964. 319p. [Included in Singapore figures but not
separately cited.] [PRC, UN, RPI

Australia. Commonwealth Bureau of Census and Statistics.
1961.1-7-5   Census of the Commonwealth of Australia, 30th June, 1961.
Volume VII--Territories. Part V--External territories [Papua, New
Guinea, Nauru, Norfolk Island, Christmas Island and Cocos (Keeling)
Islands]: population and dwellings. Cenberra, Government Printer,
1964. 59p. [PRC, RPI

Australia. Commonwealth Bureau of Census and Statistics.
1966.1-12-1 Census of the territory of Cocos (Keeling) Islands, 30th June
1966. Summary of population. [Canberra], 1968. 12p. (Census bulletin, No. 12-1). [PRC

COLOMBIA

Republic of Colombia   Capital: Bogotá
Statistical Agency: National Administrative Bureau of Statistics
                     [Departamento Administrativo Nacional de Estadística]
                     (CAN) Via Eldorado/Via al Aeropuerto
                     Bogotá, D.E.,
Publications Distributor: same

     Colombia. Departament Adminis-
        trativo Nacional de Esta-
        dística (DANE)
        Censo de población de 1951.   Population census of 1951.
        Bogotá, 1954-1959. 17v.
1951.1-1   Resumen. 1954. 191p.   Summary.
                                  [PRC, JB-F, LC, RPI
1951.1-2 through 1951.1-17. [One volume for each area.] 2. Antioquía.
    1956. 347p./3. Atlántico. 1956. 171p./4. Bolívar. 1956. 251p./
    5. Boyacá. 1955. 340p./6. Caldas. 1959. 83p./7. Cauca. 1954.
    199p./8. Cundinamarca. 1954. 237p./9. Chocó. 1955. 142p./10.
    Huila. 1955. 191p./11. Magdalena. 1959. 76p./12. Nariño. 1956.
    234p./13. Norte de Santander. 1959. 77p./14. Santander. 1959.
    101p./15. Tolima. 1959. 81p./16. Valle del Cauca. 1959. 82p./
    17. Intendencias. n.d. 88p. [PRC, TXU, BC, JB-F, RPI

     Colombia. DANE.
        Censos nacionales. Bogotá,   National censuses.
        1952. 2v.
 .2-1   Clasificación ocupacional   Occupational classification for
    para los censos de 1951. 8, 36p.   the censuses of 1951.
                                  [PRC, BC, RPI
 .2-2   Definiciones de las pro-   Definitions of professions, occu-
    fesiones, ocupaciones y condi-   pations and conditions in the
    ciones en la "Clasificación..."   "Occupational classification..."
    3, 44p.   [PRC, RPI

     Colombia. DANE.
1964.1   XIII censo nacional de pob-   Thirteenth national census of
    lación, 15 de julio de 1964.   population, July 15, 1964.
    (Número de habitantes). Bogotá,   (Number of inhabitants).
    Multilith Estadinal, 1965. 25p.   [PRC, RPI

     Colombia. DANE.
        XIII censo nacional de pob-   Thirteenth national census of
    lación, y II censo nacional de   population and second national
    edificios y viviendas. (Julio   census of buildings and housing
    15 de 1964). Bogotá, D.E., 1967-   (July 15, 1964).
    1971. 23v.
 .2-1   Población. Resumen general.   Population. General summary.
    1967. 149p.   [PRC, JB-F, RPI
 .2-2   Edificios y viviendas. Re-   Buildings and housing. General
    sumen general. 1968. 236p.   summary.
                                    [PRC, RPI

1964.2-3-1 through 1964.2-21-2. ["P" - Población; "EV" - Edificios y Vivi-
    endas.] 3-1. Antioquía (P). 1969. 172p./3-2. Antioquía (EV). 1969.
    145p./4. Atlántico. 1969. 102p./5. Bogotá, D.E. 1969. 128p./6.
    Bolívar. 1969. 136p./7-1. Boyacá (P). 1970. 152p./7-2. Boyacá
    (EV). 1970. 139p./8. Caldas. 1969. 152p./9. Cauca. 1970. 124p./
    10. Cordoba. 1970. 102p./11-1. Cundinamarca (P). 1969. 138p./11-2.
    Cundinamarca (EV). 1970. 127p./12. Chocó. 1970. 96p./13. Huila.
    1970. 126p./14. Magdalena. 1970. 124p./15. Meta. 1970. 92p./16.
    Nariño. 1970. 156p./17. Norte de Santander. 1970. 124p./18. San-
    tander. 1970. 194p./19. Tolima. 1970. 150p./20. Valle del Cauca.
    1969. 156p./21-1. Intendencias (P). 1971. 209p./21-2. Intendencias
    (EV). 1971. 74p. [PRC, RPI

Colombia. DANE.
1973.0-1   Población total, número   Total population, number of
    de viviendas y promedio de per-   housing units and average per-
    sonal por vivienda, para las ca-   sons per unit, for the capital
    beceras municipales, según los   cities according to the censuses
    censos de 1951, 1964, 1973 (ta-   of 1951, 1964, 1973 (tabulated
    bulados del 26-I-1974). Bogotá,   on January 26, 1974).
    1974. 33p.   [PRC

Colombia. DANE.
.1   XIV censo nacional de pob-   Fourteenth national census of
    lación y III de vivienda. Mues-   population and third of housing.
    tra de avance. Población.   Advance sample. Population.
    Bogotá, 1975. 68p.   [BC, PRC, JB-F, NYPL

Colombia. DANE.
.2   XIV censo nacional de pob-   Fourteenth national census of
    lación y III de vivienda. Mues-   population and third of housing.
    tra de avance. Resumen de los   Advance sample. Summary of the
    departamentos. Bogotá, 1977.   departments.
    58p.   [BC, IASI

Colombia. DANE.
.3   La población en Colombia,   Population in Colombia, 1973.
    1973. XIV censo nacional de pob-   Fourteenth national census of
    lación y III de vivienda. Mues-   population and third of housing.
    tra de avance. Bogotá, 1978.   Advance sample.
    435p.   [NYPL, JB-F

Colombia. DANE.
.4   XIV censo nacional de pob-   Fourteenth national census of
    lación y III de vivienda, 1973:   population and third of housing,
    Medellín. Bogotá, 1976. [52]p.   1973: Medellín. [Final results].
    (Boletín mensual de estadística,   [NYPL
    26(301):5-56)

COMMONWEALTH CARIBBEAN

The censuses of 1943/1946, 1960 and 1970 are cited here to avoid the constant repetition in the entries for all the countries involved. The 1943 census is included to complete the West Indian set taken in 1946.

Jamaica. Central Bureau of Statistics.
1943.1   Eighth census of Jamaica and its dependencies, 1943: population, housing and agriculture. Kingston, Government Printer, 1945. "twenty-eight", cii, 571p. 4 folding maps. [TXU, NYPL, PRC, RPI

Jamaica. Central Bureau of Statistics.
West Indian census, 1946. Kingston, Government Printer, 1948-1950. Parts A-H.
1946.1-A   General report on the census of population. 1950. x, 122p. [TXU, NYPL, JB-F, PRC, RPI
.1-B   Census of agriculture in Barbados... [JB-F
.1-C   Census of the colony of Barbados, 9th April, 1946. 1950. 1v, 51p. [TXU, NYPL, JB-F, PRC, RPI
.1-D   Census of the colony of British Guiana, 9th April, 1946. 1949. lxviii, 88p. [TXU, NYPL, JB-F, PRC, RPI
.1-E   Census of British Honduras, 9th April, 1946. 1948. xlvi, 36p. [TXU, NYPL, JB-F, PRC, RPI
.1-F   Census of the Leeward Islands, 9th April, 1946. 1948. lx, 63p. [TXU, NYPL, JB-F, PRC, RPI
.1-G   Census of the colony of Trinidad and Tobago, 9th April, 1946. 1949. lxvi, 82p. [TXU, NYPL, JB-F, PRC, RPI
.1-H   Census of the Windward Islands: Dominica, Grenada, St. Lucia, St. Vincent, 9th April, 1946. 1950. lxxvi, 79p. [JB-F, RPI

Trinidad and Tobago. Central Statistical Office.
East Caribbean population census of 1960. Port of Spain, 1963-1970. Vols. I-III in 34v.
    I. Report on the 1960 census of the Eastern Caribbean. 1964-1967. Parts A-E and Supplement.
1960.1-1-A   Administrative report. 1967. vi, 78p. [TXU, PRC, RPI
.1-1-B   Boundaries of enumeration districts (Trinidad and Tobago). 1964. viii, 133p. [TXU, PRC, RPI
.1-1-C   Boundaries of enumeration districts (Barbados). 1965. v, 43p. [TXU, PRC, RPI
.1-1-D   Boundaries of enumeration districts (Windward Islands: Dominica, Grenada, St. Lucia, St. Vincent). 1965. vi, 45p. [TXU, PRC, RPI
.1-1-E   Boundaries of enumeration districts (British Guiana). 1965. vi, 74p. [TXU, PRC, RPI
.1-1-S   Supplement of maps (Trinidad and Tobago). 1964. 45 maps. [TXU, PRC, RPI
    II. Summary tables. 1963-1964. 6 parts.
.1-2-Ba   Barbados. Summary tables 1-19. 1963. xv, [158]p. [PRC, RPI
.1-2-W   Windward Islands. Summary tables 1-19. 1963. xv, [728]p. [PRC, RPI

[Separate volumes were also published for each area: Grenada. 1963.
xv, [156]p./Dominica. 1963. xv, [208]p./St. Lucia. 1963. xv,
[208]p./St. Vincent. 1963. xv. [156]p.] [PRC, RPI

            Trinidad and Tobago

1960.1-2-T-a   Part A - Summary tables 1-11. 1963. xiii, [722]p.
  [NYPL, PRC, RPI
 .1-2-T-b   Part B - Summary tables 12-19. 1963. xi, [366]p.
  [NYPL, PRC, RPI

            British Guiana.

 .1-2-BG-a   Part A - Summary tables 1-11. 1964. xiii, [410]p.
  [PRC, RPI
 .1-2-BG-b   Part B - Summary tables 12-19. 1964. xi, [272]p.
  [PRC, RPI

      III.   Detailed Cross-classification. 1965-1970. 19 parts.
          A - Individuals by type of household, internal and
             external migration.
          B - Marital status and union status.
          C - Fertility (not published).
          D - Age, ethnic origin and religion.
          E - Households and families.
          F - Educational attainment.
          G - Working population.
          H - Income distribution (not published).
          J - Miscellaneous (not published).

         Trinidad and Tobago.
 .1-3-T-1   Part A. 1965. vii, [29]p. [PRC, RPI
 .1-3-T-2   Part B. 1965. v, [48]p. [PRC, RPI
 .1-3-T-3
 .1-3-T-4   Part D. n.d. vi, [71]p. [PRC, RPI
 .1-3-T-5   Part E. 1966. vi, [73]p, [PRC, RPI
 .1-3-T-6   Part F. 1966. vi, [206]p. [PRC, RPI
 .1-3-T-7   Part G. 1965. viii, [221]p. [PRC, RPI
 .1-3-T-8
 .1-3-T-9

         Barbados.
 .1-3-Ba-1   Part A. 1970. ix, [22]p. [PRC, RPI
 .1-3-Ba-2   Parts B, D, F, G. 1967. xvi, [371]p. [PRC, RPI
 .1-3-Ba-3   Part E. 1968. vi, [48]p. [PRC, RPI
         Windward Islands: Dominica.
 .1-3-WD-1   Parts A, B, D, E, F, G. 1969. xx, [442]p. [PRC, RPI
         Windward Islands: Grenada.
 .1-3-WG-1   Part A. 1969. ix, [20]p. [PRC, RPI
 .1-3-WG-2   Parts B, D, E, F. 1967. xiv, [193]p. [PRC, RPI
         Windward Islands: St. Lucia.
 .1-3-WL-1   Parts A, F. 1969. xii, [131]p. [PRC, RPI
 .1-3-WL-2   Parts B, D, E, G. 1969. xiii, [293]p. [PRC, RPI
         Windward Islands: St. Vincent.
 .1-3-WV-1   Parts A, B, F. 1969. xiii, [176]p. [PRC, RPI
 .1-3-WV-2   Parts D, E, G. 1968. x, [289]p. [PRC, RPI
         British Guiana.
 .1-3-BG-1   Parts A, G. 1969. xi, [275]p. [PRC, RPI
 .1-3-BG-2   Parts B, D. 1967. ix, [130]p. [PRC, RPI
 .1-3-BG-3   Parts E, F. 1968. ix, [266]p. [PRC, RPI

Jamaica. Department of Statistics. Jamaica Tabulation Centre.
West Indies population census. Kingston, 1963-1964. 8 censuses
in 25 parts.
Census of Jamaica, 7th April, 1960. Vols. I-II in 17v.
    I. Administrative report and enumeration districts.
1960.2-J-la   Administrative report and enumeration district definitions. 1963. ii, 556p. [PRC, RPI
.2-J-lb   Enumeration district definitions (cont'd). 1963. ii,
four, pp. 557-1092. [PRC, RPI
.2-J-lc   Enumeration districts tables. 1963. ii, VIII, pp. 1093-
1497. [PRC, RPI
.2-J-ld   Enumeration districts tables (cont'd). 1963. ii, XXI,
pp. 1498-1992. [PRC, RPI
    II. Tables.
.2-J-2a-1   [General tables]. 1964. ix, XXVII, [387]p. [PRC, RPI
.2-J-2a-2   [General tables (cont'd)]. 1964. 323, 411p. [PRC, RPI
.2-J-2b   [Housing and households]. 1964. ii, XXVI, 308p. [PRC,
RPI
.2-J-2c   [Migration]. 1963. [435]p. [PRC, RPI
.2-J-2d   [Classifiable labour force]. (Not published).
.2-J-2e   [Classifiable labour force (cont'd)]. 1964. ix, 592p.
[PRC, RPI
.2-J-2f-1   [Classifiable labour force (cont'd)]. 1964. ix, 196p.
[PRC, RPI
.2-J-2f-2   [Classifiable labour force (cont'd)]. 1964. pp. 197-
815. [PRC, RPI
.2-J-2g   [Classifiable labour force (cont'd)]. 1964. v, 325p.
[PRC, RPI
.2-J-2g-2   [Classifiable labour force (cont'd)]. 1964. pp. 326-
780. [PRC, RPI
.2-J-2h   [Labour by industry and occupation]. 1963. [471]p.
[PRC, RPI
.2-J-2i   [Labour by industry]. 1964. vii, [507]p. [PRC, RPI
.2-J-2j   [Labour force and income]. 1964. viii, [685]p. [PRC
RPI
Census of British Honduras, 7th April, 1960. Vols. I-II.
.2-BH-1   I. xi, 208p. [Harvard, RPI
.2-BH-2   II. vii, 254p. [Harvard, RPI
Census of Cayman Islands, 7th April, 1960. Vols. I-II.
.2-C-1   I. (Not published).
.2-C-2   II. xxiii, 190p. [PRC, RPI
Census of Turks and Caicos Islands, 7th April, 1960. Vols.
I-II.
.2-TC-1   I. (Not published).
.2-TC-2   II. xix, 125p. [PRC, RPI
Census of Antigua, 7th April, 1960. Vols. I-II.
.2-A-1   I. (Not published).
.2-A-2   II. xviii, 168p. [PRC, UN, RPI
Census of British Virgin Islands, 7th April, 1960. Vols. I-II.
.2-BV-1   I. (Not published).
.2-BV-2   II. xxi, 197p. [UN, RPI

Census of Monserrat, 7th April, 1960. Vols. I-II.
.2-M-1   I. (Not published)
.2-M-2   II. xxii, 186p. [UN, PRC, RPI
Census of St. Kitts-Nevis-Anguilla, 7th April, 1960. Vols.
I-II.
.2-KNA-1   I. (Not published).
.2-KNA-2   II. x, 221p. [UN, RPI

West Indies. University. Census Research Programme.
    1970 population census of the Commonwealth Caribbean.   Kingston,
    Herald Limited, 1973-   . Vols. 1-10 in   v.
1970.1-1   1. Administrative volume.
            2. Enumeration district tabulations. Parts 1-
    .1-2-1

.1-3   3. Age tabulations. 1973. viii, 231p. [BC, PRC, PC
          4. Economic activity. Parts 1-16.
.1-4-1   Jamaica. 1973. x, 385p. [BC, PRC, PC
.1-4-2   Trinidad and Tobago. 1973. x, 361p. [BC, PRC, PC
.1-4-3   Guyana. 1973. x, 387p. [BC, PRC
.1-4-4   Barbados. 1973. x, 335p. [PC
.1-4-5   Belize. 1973. x, 257p. [PC
.1-4-6   St. Lucia. 1973. x, 361p. [PC
.1-4-7   Grenada. 1973. x, 257p. [PC
.1-4-8   St. Vincent. 1973. x, 387p. [PC
.1-4-9   Dominica. 1973. x, 335p. [PRC
.1-4-10   Bermuda. 1973. x, 265p. [PRC
.1-4-11   St. Kitts-Nevis. 1973. x, 439p. [PRC
.1-4-12   Montserrat. 1973. x, 153p. [PC
.1-4-13   Cayman Islands. 1973. x, 127p. [PC
.1-4-14   British Virgin Islands. 1973. x, 179p. [PC
.1-4-15   Turks and Caicos Islands. 1973. x, 205p. [PC
.1-4-16   Occupation by industry. 1976. x, 150p. [PRC, PC
.1-5   5. Internal migration - Jamaica, Trinidad and Tobago, Guyana,
    Barbados, British Honduras. 1975. xi, 295p. [BC, PRC, PC
          6. Education.
.1-6-1   Jamaica, Trinidad and Tobago, Guyana. 1975. viii, 377p.
    [BC, PRC, PC
.1-6-2   Barbados, Belize, St. Lucia, Grenada, St. Vincent. 1975.
    x, 327p. [BC, PRC, PC
.1-6-3   Dominica, Bermuda, St. Kitts-Nevis, Montserrat, Cayman
    Islands, British Virgin Islands, Turks and Caicos Islands. 1975.
    xii, 359p. [BC, PRC, PC

1970.1-7   7. Race and religion. 1976. vii, 182p. [PC
    .1-8-a   8a. Fertility. 1976. xv, 296p. [PC
    .1-8-b   8b. Union status. 1976. xvi, 321p. [PC
    .1-8-c   8c. Marital status. 1976. xi, 342p. [PC
              9. Housing and household.
    .1-9-1   Jamaica, Trinidad and Tobago, Guyana. 1975. xii, 390p.
        [BC, PRC, PC
    .1-9-2   Barbados, British Honduras, St. Lucia, Grenada. 1975. xiv,
        354p. [BC, IASI, PRC, PC
    .1-9-3   St. Vincent, Dominica, Bermuda. 1975. xii, 273p. [BC, PRC,
        PC
    .1-9-4   St. Kitts-Nevis, Montserrat, Cayman Islands, British Virgin
        Islands, Turks and Caicos Islands. 1975. xvi, 352p. [BC, PRC, PC
              10. Miscellaneous.
    .1-10-1   Income - Jamaica, Trinidad and Tobago, Guyana, Barbados,
        British Honduras. 1976. viii, 348p. [PRC, PC
    .1-10-2   Income - St. Lucia, Grenada, St. Vincent, Dominica, Bermuda,
        St. Kitts. 1976. viii, 408p. [PRC, PC
    .1-10-3   Income - Montserrat, Cayman, British Virgin Islands, Turks.
        1976. viii, 108p. [PRC, PC
    .1-10-4   Income - All members. 1976. viii, 120p. [PRC, OPR, PC

COMOROS

Republic of the Comoros   Capital: Moroni
Statistical Agency: Bureau of Statistical Studies and Surveys
                     [Bureau des Études et des Enquêtes Statistiques]
                     Commissariat au Plan et au Developpement
                     Moroni, Grande Comore,
Publications Distributor: same

The French overseas censuses of 1951 and 1956 were of non-indigenous
population only. The island of Mayotte has not yet joined the other
islands in independence.

France. INSEE.
1951   Le recensement de la population...
          [See French Overseas Territories, No. 1951.1]

France. INSEE.
1958.1   Recensement de la popula-   Census of population (1958),
          tion (1958) Comores.   Paris,   Comoro Islands.
          1959. [69]p.   [Berkeley

France. INSEE.
1966.1   Recensement de la population   Census of the population of the
          des Comores, 1966. Principaux   Comoro Islands, 1966. Main
          résultats. Résultats par vil-   results. Results by village,
          lage, sexe et groupes d'âge.   sex and age groups.
          1967. 43p.   [UN, BC, JB-F

France. INSEE.
  .2   Résultats statistiques du   Statistical results of the gen-
          recensement général de la popu-   eral census of the population of
          lation des Comores, effectué en   the Comoro Islands, taken in
          juillet-septembre 1966.   Paris,   July-September 1966.
          1968. 106p.   [NWU, NYPL

CONGO

People's Republic of the Congo   Capital: Brazzaville
Statistical Agency: National Center of Statistics and Economic Studies
                     [Centre National de Statistique et des Études
                        Économiques]
                     B.P. 2031
                     Brazzaville,
Publications Distributor: same

The French overseas censuses of 1946 and 1951 were of the non-indigenous population only. The first attempt at nation-wide coverage
was a demographic inquiry (1960-61) in all areas of the country except the two main cities which were censused in 1958 (Pointe Noire)
and 1961 (Brazzaville).

1946.
France. INSEE.
        Résultats du recensement...
        [See French Overseas Territories, Nos. 1946.1-1, 2, and 3.]

France. INSEE.
        Les français d'origine métropolitaine...
        [See French Overseas Territories, No. 1946.2]

1951
France. INSEE.
        Le recensement de la population...
        [See French Overseas Territories, No. 1951.1.]

Congo (Brazzaville). Service
        Statistique.
1958.1   Recensement démographique de   Demographic census of Pointe-
Pointe-Noire, décembre 1958.   Noire, December 1958. Final
Résultats définitifs. Par F.   results.
Ganon.   Paris, Impr. Servant-   [PRC, LC, JB-F, NWU, OPR, RPI
Crouzet, 1961. 104, xxii p.

Congo (Brazzaville). Service
        National de la Statistique,
        des Études Démographiques
        et Économiques.
1961.1   Enquête démographique 1960-61:   Demographic inquiry, 1960-61:
résultats définitifs.   Paris,   final results.
1965. 173p.   [JB-F, NWU

Congo (Brazzaville). Service
        National de la Statistique,
        ...
1961.1   Recensement de Brazzaville,   Census of Brazzaville, 1961:
1961: résultats définitifs.   final results.
Paris, 1965. 113p. maps.   [PRC, CU, RPI

Congo. Direction de la Statis-
        tique et de la Comptabilité
        Économique.

1974.1   Recensement général de la popu-   General population census of 1974.
lation de 1974. Repport général   General report of the census.
du recensement. Brazzaville,   [EB, UN, NWU
    p.

Congo. Direction de la Statis-
        tique...

.2   Recensement général de la popu-   General population census of 1974.
lation de 1974. Commune de Braz-   Commune of Brazzaville. Final
zaville. Résultats définitifs.   results.
Brazzaville, 1975. [3], 96p.   [PRC, NWU

Congo. Direction de la Statis-
        tique...
        Recensement général de la popu-   General population census of 1974.
lation de 1974. [Brazzaville],
1976-   . Vols. I-XV in 54v.
        I. Commune de Brazzaville.   Brazzaville.
1976. Parts 1-5.
.3-1-1   Structure démographique.   Demographic structure.
1976. 59p.   [PRC, UN, NWU
.3-1-2   Nuptialité--Mouvement   Nuptiality--Natural change.
naturel. 1976. 57p.   [PRC, UN, NWU
.3-1-3   Migrations. 1976. 61p.   Migrations.
                                            [PRC, UN, NWU
.3-1-4   Instruction et activité   Education and economic activity.
économique.   [EB
.3-1-5   Caractéristiques des ména-   Characteristics of households
ges et habitat. 1976. 103p.   and housing.
                                            [PRC, UN, NWU
        II. Commune de Pointe   Pointe-Noire.
Noire. 197 -   Parts 1-5.
.3-2-1   Structure démographique.   Demographic structure.
                                            [
.3-2-2   Nuptialité--Mouvement   Nuptiality--Natural change.
naturel.   [
.3-2-3   Migrations.   Migrations.
                                            [
.3-2-4   Instruction et activité   Education and economic activity.
économique.   p   [
.3-2-5   Caractéristiques des ména-   Characteristics of household
ges et habitat.   p.   and housing.
                                            [
        III. Communes de Loubomo et Nkayi. Parts 1-5.
        IV. Région de... Parts 1-4.
[Vols. V-XII are for the other regions.]
.3-13   XIII. Ensemble Congo.   Entire Congo.
                                            [
.3-14   XIV. Population des loca-   Population of places.
lités. 1975.   p.   [
.3-15   XV. Projections.   Projections.
                                            [

COOK ISLANDS

Capital: Rarotonga/Avarua

Statistical Agency: Statistics Office
                      Central Planning Bureau
                      Rarotonga,

                      [also see New Zealand]
Publications Distributor: same

New Zealand. Census and Statistics Department.
1945.1-2   Population census, 1945. Volume II. Island territories: Cook
    Islands and Niue, Tokelau Island, Western Samoa. Auckland, Leightons
    Ltd., 1947. 14p. [PRC

Note: From 1946 to 1966 the censuses were conducted by the Cook Island Administration. The only published results were summary tables
in the Annual Reports on the Cook Islands presented to the New Zealand
Parliament. However, total numbers of inhabitants were included in
the General Report (1951) and respective Volume I of the New Zealand
censuses of 1956, 1961, and 1966.

Cook Islands. Premier's Department. Census Supervisor.
1966.1   Population census, 1966. Wellington, New Zealand Government
    Printer, 1968. 78p. [PRC

Cook Islands. Central Planning Bureau. Statistics Office.
1976.0-1   1976 population census, preliminary results. Rarotonga, [1977].
    112p. map. (Quarterly statistical bulletin; special issue). [UN

Cook Islands. Central Planning Bureau. Statistics Office.
  .1   Census of population and housing, 1976. Rarotonga, 1977. [2],
    vii, 279p. [PRC, E-W, UN, OPR

COSTA RICA

Republic of Costa Rica   Capital: San José
Statistical Agency: General Bureau of Statistics and Censuses
                     [Dirección General de Estadística y Censos]
                     Apartado 10163
                     San José,
Publications Distributor: same

	Costa Rica. Dirección General de Estadística y Censos.	
1950.1	Censo de población de Costa Rica (22 de mayo de 1950). San José, 1953. v, 237p.	Population census of Costa Rica May 22, 1950). [PRC, JB-F, RPI
1963.1	Costa Rica. Dirección ... 1963 censo de población. San José, 1966. xliv, 633p.	1963 population census. [PRC, JB-F, RPI
.2	Costa Rica. Dirección... El area metropolitana de San José según los censos de 1963 y 1964. San José, 1967. xxxv, 256p.	The San José metropolitan area according to the censuses of 1963 and 1964 [economic]. [PRC, RPI
.3	Costa Rica. Dirección... Evaluación. Censos: población, vivienda, agropecuario, 1° de abril de 1963. San José, 1965. 49p.	Evaluation. Censuses: population, housing, agricultural, April 1, 1963. [PRC, RPI
	Costa Rica. Dirección... Censos nacionales de 1973. San José, 1973- . Nos. 1-	National censuses of 1973.
1973.1-1	Agropecuario. Aves de corral fuera de finca. 1973. 24p.	Agriculture. Non-farm chicken flocks. [PRC, JB-F
.1-2	Población: total, urbana y rural por provincias, cantones y distritos. 1974. 23p.	Population: total, urban and rural by province, canton and district. [PRC, BC, IASI, OPR, JB-F
.1-3	Agropecuario. 1974. 59, CR 187, P 286p.	Agriculture. [PRC, JB-F
.1-4	Vivienda. 1974. 447p.	Housing. [PRC, OPR, JB-F
.1-5	Población. Tomo I. 1974. xlix, 500p.	Population. Book I. [PRC, BC, IASI, OPR, JB-F
.1-6	Población. Tomo II. 1975. xlix, 631p.	Population. Book II. [PRC, BC, IASI, OPR, JB-F
.1-7	Agropecuario. Regiones agricolas. 1975. xliv, 432p.	Agriculture. Agricultural regions. [PRC, JB-F

1973.1-8   Vivienda. Area metro-
        politana. 1975. xxx, 65p.
    .1-9   Población. Area metro-
        politana. Tomo I. 1976. lii,
        88p.
    .1-10   Población. Area metro-
        politana. Tomo II. 1976. xv,
        198p.
    .1-11,12 Vivienda, Población.
        Ciudades capitales. n.d. xvi,
        219p.

Housing. Metropolitan area.
[BC, PRC
Population. Metropolitan area.
Book I.
[PRC, BC, IASI, OPR, JB-F
Population. Metropolitan area.
Book II.
[PRC, BC, IASI, OPR, JB-F
Housing, population. Capital
cities.
[PRC, BC, OPR, JB-F

        Costa Rica. Dirección... [and]
            CELADE.
    .2   Evaluación del censo de 1973
        y proyección de la población
        por sexo y grupos de edades,
        1950-2000. San José, 1976.
        105p.

Evaluation of the 1973 census
and population projection by
sex and age groups, 1950-2000.
[PRC

CUBA

Republic of Cuba   Capital: Havana
Statistical Agency: Central Bureau of Statistics
                      [Dirección Central de Estadística]
                      Junta Central de Planificación
                      20 de Mayo y Ayesteran
                      La Habana,
Publications Distributor: Director de Información y Relaciones Inter-
                           nacionales (of the above).

        Cuba. Oficina Nacional de los
          Censos Demográfico y
          Electoral
1953.1   Censo de población, vivien-   Census of population, housing
      das y electoral, enero 28 de   and the electorate, January 28,
      1953. Informe general. La   1953. General report.
      Habana, P. Fernández, 1955.   [TXU, LC, PRC, RPI
      xlviii, 325p.

        Cuba. Dirección Central de
          Estadística.
          Censo de población y vivien-   Census of population and housing
      das de 1970. La Habana, 1973-   of 1970.
      1974.
1970.1-1   Anticipo de datos por mues-   Advance results from sampling.
      treo. Análisis de las caracte-   Analysis of the demographic
      rísticas demográficas de la pob-   characteristics of the Cuban
      lación cubana. 76p.   Population.
                                               [OPR

   .1-2   Anticipo de datos por mues-   Advance results from sampling.
      treo. Análisis de las caracte-   Analysis of the labor force
      rísticas laborales de la pobla-   characteristics of the Cuban
      ción cubana. 86p.   population.
                                               [OPR

   .1-3   Datos fundamentales de la   Fundamental data of the popula-
      población en base a muestras.   tion based on sampling.
                                               [

   .1-4   Características diferen-   Differential characteristics of
      ciales de la población residente   the resident population of Matan-
      de Matanzas, zonas urbana y ru-   zas, urban and rural zones.
      ral. 1973. 71p.   [OPR, PRC

      [Note: There may be a report for each province, however, none but the
      above has been seen.]

   .1-5   Análisis de las caracte-   Analysis of the housing character-
      rísticas de las viviendas. 1974.   istics.
      xii, 89p.   [PRC

Cuba. Dirección Central de
  Estadística.
  Las provincias de Cuba en   The provinces of Cuba in the
el censo de 1970. ...: aná-   1970 census. ...: analysis of
lisis de las características   the demographic, labor force and
demográficas, laborales y de   housing characteristics.
las viviendas. La Habana,
1974
1970.2-1 through 1970.2-7. 1. Pinar del Río.   /2. Habana Metro.
    /3. Habana Interior.   /4. Matanzas.   /5.
Las Villas.   /6. Camagüey.   /7. Oriente.
[

Cuba. Junta Central de Plani-
  ficación.
.3   Censo de población y vivien-   Census of population and housing,
das, 1970. La Habana, Ed. ORBE,   1970.
1975. xix, 1035p.   [PRC, BC, UN

Cuba. Dirección Central de
  Estadística.
.4   Densidad de población y ur-   Population density and urbaniza-
banización; análisis de los re-   tion; analysis of the results of
sultados del censo de población   the population and housing census
y viviendas de 1970. La Haba-   of 1970.
na, Ed. ORBE, 1975. 85p.   [UN
maps.

Cuba has divided its former six provinces into fourteen new provinces:
Camagüey, Ciego de Ávila, Cienfuegos, Ciudad de Habana, Granma, Guan-
tánamo, Habana, Holbuín, Las Tunas, Matanzas, Pinar del Río, Sancti
Spíritus, Santiago de Cuba, Villa Clara. The Isle of Pines municipality is administered directly from Havana.

CYPRUS

Republic of Cyprus   Capital: Nicosia
Statistical Agency: Department of Statistics and Research
                     Ministry of Finance
                     Nicosia,
Publications Distributor: Printing Office
                           Republic of Cyprus
                           Nicosia,

Cyprus. Superintendent of Census.
    Census of Cyprus, 1946. [Nicosia], 1947. 3 parts.
1946.1-1   Brief summary of final population figures. 4p. [UN, PRC, RPI
   .1-2   Report on the civilian population of the six district towns.
    11, 7p. [UN, PRC, RPI
   .1-3   Tables of occupation (main occupation). 39p. [UN, PRC, RPI

Cyprus. Superintendent of Census.
   .2   Census of population, 1946. Nicosia, Government Printing Office,
    [1948]. 14p. (Sessional paper, No. 6 of 1948). [UN, PRC, RPI

Cyprus. Superintendent of Census.
    Census of population and agriculture, 1946.   London, O.F. Hodgson
and Son, Ltd., 1949. 2v.
   .3-1   Report. vii, 92p. [UN, PRC, RPI
   .3-2   Tables. unpaged. [UN, PRC, RPI

Note: The following registration did not include those twelve years
of age and under:

Cyprus. Statistics and Research Department.
1956.1   Registration of the population, 1956. Report and tables.   Nicosia,
    1958. ii, 111p. [OPR

Cyprus. Statistics and Research Department.
    Census of population and agriculture, 1960.   Nicosia, Government
Printing Office, 1962-1963. Vols. I-VI.
1960.1-1   Population by location, race and sex. 1962. ii, 26p. [PRC,
    UN, RPI
   .1-2   Housing. 1963. vi, 50p. [PRC, UN, RPI
   .1-3   Demographic characteristics. 1963. ii, 28p. [PRC, UN, RPI
   .1-4   Housing (supplement). 1963. ii, 39p. [PRC, UN, RPI
   .1-5   Employment and education. 1963. iv, 95p. [PRC, UN, RPI
   .1-6   Agriculture. 1963. iii, 50p. [PRC, UN, RPI

Cyprus. Statistics and Research Department.
    Household survey, 1971. Nicosia, 1972.
1971.1-1
   .1-2
   .1-3   Socio-demographic characteristics. ii, v, 39p. [OPR

There was a census in 1973 but no results have been released.

CZECHOSLOVAKIA

Czechoslovak Socialist Republic   Capital: Prague
Statistical Agency: Federal Statistical Office.
                   [Federální Statistický Úřad]
                   Sokolovská 142
                   18613 Prague 8 - Karlin,
Publications Distributor: same

Czechoslovakia. Státní Úřad
      Statistický.
      Soupis obyvatelstva ke dni
22. Května 1947. Prague,
1948. Parts 1-6. (Zprávy
státního úřadu statistického,
rada D, č. 7-22.)

1947.1-1   Přítommé obyvatelstvo,
domácnosti, počet obcí, výměra.
Pp. 219-230. (D, 7-8)

.1-2   Povolání obyvatelstva
podle tříd objektioního povolání a jeho sociální rozvrst-
vení. Pp. 231-264. (D, 9-12)

.1-3   Pohlaví, věk a rodinný
stav obyvatelstva. Pp. 309-
320. (D, 13-14)

.1-4   Obyvatelstvo podle místa
pobytu dne 1 knětna 1945. Pp.
353-360. (D, 15)

.1-5   Poměr obyvatelstva k povolání, skupiny objektivního
povolání. Pp. 361-390. (D,
16-19).

.1-6   Velikostní skupiny obcí.
Domácnosti soukromé a ústavní.
Objektivní povolání podle rodin-
ňeho stavu, věku, pohlaví a
velikostních skupin obcí. Pp.
103-105. (D, 20-22).

Czechoslovakia. Statní Úřad
      Statistický

.2   Soupisy obyvatelstva v Česko-
slovensku v letech 1946-1947.
Výsledky soupisu v Českých
zemích k 22 květnu 1947 a na
Slovensku ke 4. rijny 1946.
Prague, 1951. 38, 561p. (Čs.
statistika, sv. 184) (Řada IV,
š. 15)

Enumeration of the population
taken May 22, 1947. (Reports
of the National Statistical
Office, Series D, Nos. 7-22)

Present population, households,
number of localities, area.
[Berkeley, Harvard, NYPL

Population by occupation according to class of occupational
objective and its social status.
[Berkeley, Harvard, NYPL

Sex, age and marital status of
the population.
[Berkeley, Harvard, NYPL

Population according to residence on May 1, 1945.
[Berkeley, Harvard, NYPL

Population by occupation, occupation groups.
[Berkeley, Harvard, NYPL, RPI

Communities by size groups.
Private households and institutions. Occupation groups according to marital status, age,
sex and size of communities.
[Berkeley, Harvard, NYPL

Population enumerations of Czechoslovakia for the years 1946-
1947. Results of the enumeration of Bohemia taken May 22,
1947 and of Slovakia on October 4, 1946. [Czech. statistics, no. 184]
[Berkeley, Harvard, NYPL

Czechoslovakia. Státní Úřad
    Statistický.
    Sčítání lidu v republice Čes-
koslovenské ke dni 1. března 1950.
Prague, 1957-1958. (Československé statistiky, řada A, sv. 20,
21, 26 a 27.) Vols. I-IV.
1950.1-1   I. Nejdůležitější výsledky sčítání lidu a soupisu domů
a bytů za kraje, okresy a města.
1957. 36, 171p. (A, 20)
.1-2   II. Věkové složení a povolání obyvatelstva. 1958. 21,
315p. (A, 26)
.1-3   III. Plodnost žen. 1957.
204p. (A, 21)
.1-4   IV. Hospodářský lexikon
obcí. 1958. 345p. (A, 27)

Czechoslovakia. Státní Úřad
    Statistický.
    Sčítání lidu v Československé
republice ke dni 1. březnu 1950.
Prague, 1957-1958. (Československé statistiky, řada B, sv. 11,
44 a 45.)
.2-1   Podrobná data o přislus-
nosti obyvatelstva k hospodář-
skijm odvětvím za kraje, okresy
a krajská města. 1957. viii,
116p. (B, 11)
.2-2   A. Příslušnost obyvatelstva ke knupinám objektivních
povolání, hospodářská odvětví
podle velikostních skupin obcí
a vedlejší povolání zemědělců
podle krajů/ B. Stěhování obyvatelstva do krajských měst/ C.
Výsledky výběrového zpracování
dat o domácnostech/ D. Nabo-
ženské vyznání obyvatelstva v
krajích, okresech a krajských-
městech. 1958. 126p. (B, 44)
.2-3   Příslušnost obyvatelstva
k hospodářským odvětvím podle
pětiletých věkových skupin a
pohlaví. Data za kraje. 1957.
109p. (B, 45)

Czechoslovakia. Státní Úřad
    Statistichý.
.3   Statistický lexikon obcí
republiky Československé 1955.

Population census of the Czech-
oslovakian Republic taken March
1, 1950. (Czechoslovakian sta-
tistics, new series A, nos. 20,
21, 26 and 27.)
Main results of the population
and housing census for regions,
districts and towns.
[PRC, Berkeley, RPI
Age structure and occupation of
population.
[Mass, PRC, RPI
Fertility of women.
[PRC, RPI
Economic lexicon of communities.
[PRC, RPI

Population census of the Czechoslovakian Republic taken March 1,
1950. (Czechoslovakian statistics, series B, Nos. 11, 44 and
45).
Detailed data of the population
affiliation to the economic sectors [industries] for regions,
districts and regional centers.
[PRC, RPI
A. Affiliation of the popula
tion to occupational groups and
economic sectors according to
size of community and secondary
occupation of farmers by regions/
B. Population migration into
regional centers/ C. Results of
sampling data on households/ D.
Religious affiliation of the
population by regions, districts,
and regional centers.
[Mass, RPI
Population affiliation to economic sectors according to five-
year age groups and sex. Data
for regions.
[PRC, RPI

Statistical lexicon of communities of the Czechoslovakian

Podle správního rozdělení 1. ledna 1955, sčítání lidu a sčítání domů a bytů 1. března 1950. Prague, SEVT, 1955. 23, 574p.

Republic 1955. According to administrative division of January 1, 1955, and the censuses of population and of homes and multiple dwellings of March 1, 1950. [PRC, RPI

Czechoslovakia. Ústřední Komise Lidové Kontroly a Statistiky.
    Sčítání lidu, dom°a bytů v Československé Socialistické Republice k. 1 březnu 1961. Prague, 1965. (Československé statistike, nová řada A, sv. 35, 36, 37 a 41). Parts I-IV.

Census of population, homes and multiple dwellings of the Czechoslovakian Socialist Republic of March 1, 1961. (Czechoslovakian statistics, new series A, Nos. 35, 36, 37 and 41).

1961.1-1   I. Demografické charakteristiky obyvatelstva. 1965. 38, 350p. (A, 35)

Demographic characteristics of the population. [PRC, RPI

.1-2   II. Sociální, ekonomická a profesionélní skladba obyvatelstva. 1965. 18, 373p. (A, 36)

Social, economic and occupational composition of the population. [PRC, RPI

.1-3   III. Domy, byty, domácnosti a rodiny. 1965. 26, 283p. (A, 37)

Homes, multiple-dwellings, households and families. [PRC, UN, RPI

.1-4   IV. Dojížka do zaměstnání, věkové složení obyvatelstva za okresy a další doplňující data. 1965.   p. (A, 41)

Commuting to work, age composition of the population by district and further supplementary data. [Mass, RPI

Czechoslovakia. Ústřední Komise Lidové Kontroya a Statistiky.
    Rozbory výsledků sčítání lidu, domů a bytů k 1. březnu 1961. Prague, SEVT, 1963-1965. 12v.

Report of the results of the census of population and housing of March 1, 1961.

.2-1   ČSSR v číslech: vyvoj společnosti. 1965. 513p.

CSSR in figures: development of the society. [PRC, UN, RPI

1961.2-2 through 1961.2-12. [One volume for each region "in figures"]. 2. Praha (Prague). 1963. 319p./3. Středočeský kraj (Central Bohemian region). 1964. 398p./4. Západočeský kraj (West Bohemian region). 1963. 367p./5. Severočeský kraj (North Bohemian region). 1963. 319p./6. Jihočeský kraj (South Bohemian region). 1963. 356p./7. Východočeský kraj (East Bohemian region). 1964. 375p./8. Jihomoravský kraj (South Moravian region). 1964. 387p./9. Severomoravský kraj (North Moravian region). 1964. 387p./10. Západoslovenský kraj (West Slovakian region). 1964. 408p./11. Středoslovenslý kraj (Central Slovakian region). 1965. 358p./12. Východoslovenský kraj (East Slovakian region). 1965. 370p. [PRC, UN, RPI

Czechoslovakia. Ústřední Komise
    Lidové Kontroly a Statis-
    tiky.
.3   Statistický lexikon obcí ČSSR,   Statistical lexicon of the com-
1965.   Prague, SEVT, 1966.   munities of the ČSSR, 1965.
668p.   [BC

Czechoslovakia. Ústřední Komise
    Lidové Kontroly a Statis-
    tiky.
.4   CSSR in figures. Society development. Summary. Prague, 1965.
48, 448p. [In French and English. Translation of No. 1961.2-1].

Czechoslovakia. Federální
    Statistický Úrad.
    Výsledky sčítání lidu, domů   Results of the census of popula-
a bytů k 1.12.1970.   Prague,   tion and housing of Dec. 1, 1970.
SEVT, 1971-1972. Parts 1-3.
1970.1-1   Předběžné výsledky sčítané   Preliminary results of the census
lidu, domů a bytů k 1. prosinci   of population and housing, Dec.
1970 v ČSSR. 1971. 214p.   1, 1970, of the CSSR.
   [PRC
.1-2   Předběžné vysledky sčítání   Preliminary results... 2 percent
lidu, dom°a bytů k 1. prosinci   sample.
1970 v ČSSR. 2% výběrové šetři-   [PRC, OPR
ní. 1971. 253p.
.1-3   Mikrocensus 1970. 2% vý-   Microcensus 1970. 2 percent sam-
běrové šetřeni--příjmová část.   ple--income section.
1972. 228p.   [PRC, OPR

Czechoslovakia. Federální
    Statistický Úrad.
.2   Vývoj společnosti ČSSR podle   The development of the society
výsledků sčítání lidu, domů a   in CSSR according to the results
bytů 1970.   Prague, 1975.   of the census of population and
487p.   housing, 1970.
   [UN, PRC, OPR

There were a number of issues of <u>Reports and analyses</u> (Prague), series
"Other" (2 percent sample) with preliminary and final results of the
1970 census which were published by the Federal Statistical Office for
domestic use only.

DENMARK

Kingdom of Denmark
Statistical Agency: Statistics Denmark
[Danmarks Statistik]
Sejrøgade 11
DK 2100 Copenhagen,
Publications Distributor: same

Capital: Copenhagen

Denmark. Statistisk Departement.
1945.1 Folkemaengde og administratif inddeling 1945. Copenhagen, Bianco Lunos, 1946.
446p. (Statistiske meddelelser, 4de raekke, 128 bind,
1ste haefte.)

The population in administrative
divisions, 1945.
[UN, PRC, RPI

Denmark. Statistisk Departement.
.2 Befolkningens fordeling
efter køn og alder 1945.
Copenhagen, Bianco Lunos, 1946.
91p. (Statistiske meddelelser, 4de raekke, 128 bind,
2det haefte.)

The population according to sex
and age, 1945.
[UN, PRC, RPI

Denmark. Statistisk Departement.
1950.1 Folkemaengden 1950. Copenhagen, Bianco Lunos, 1952. 93,
124p. (Statistiske meddelelser, 4de raekke, 147 bind,
1ste haefte.)

Population 1950.
[UN, PRC, RPI

Denmark. Statistisk Departement.
[Folketaellingen 1950].
Copenhagen, Bianco Lunos, 1955-
1957. (Statistiske meddelelser, 4de raekke, 162 bind,
1ste-4de haefte.)
.2-1 Aldersfordelingen i 1950
og i de kommende ar. Køn,
alder og aegteskabelig stilling ved folketaellingen 1950.
1955. 155p. (4:162:1)
.2-2 Erhvervsgeografisk
materialesamling. Folketaellingen 1950. 1956. 207p.
(4:162:2)

Population census 1950.

Age distribution in 1950 and
the following decades. Sex,
age and marital status from
the 1950 population census.
[UN, PRC, RPI
Data of industrial geography
from the population census of
1950.
[BC, PRC, RPI

1950.2-3   Erhverv, fag og arbejds-   Industry, occupation, and social
     stilling ved folketaellingen   status, population census 1950.
     1950. 1957. 16, 105p. (4:   [BC, PRC, RPI
     162:3)
     .2-4   De private husstande ved   Non-institutional households,
     folketaellingen 1950. 1957.   from the population census 1950.
     35p. (4:162:4)   [BC, PRC, RPI

     Denmark. Statistisk Departe-
          ment.
1955.1   Folkemaengden 1. oktober   Population, October 1, 1955, in
     1955 og Danmarks administrative   administrative districts of Den-
     inddeling. Copenhagen, Bianco   mark.
     Lunos, 1957. 31, 482p. (Sta-   [BC, UN, PRC, RPI
     tistiske meddelelser, 4de raek-
     ke, 166 bind, 1ste haefte.)

     Denmark. Statistisk Departe-
          ment.
     .2   Folketaellingen 1955. (Sta-   Population census 1955.
     tistiske Efterretningen, 1959,   [
     no. 20)

     Denmark. Statistisk Departe-
          ment.
1960.1   Folkemaengden 26. september   Population, September 26, 1960,
     1960 og Danmarks administrative   in administrative districts of
     inddeling. Copenhagen, Aarhuus,   Denmark.
     1962. 305p. (Statistiske med-   [BC, PRC, RPI, RIR
     delelser 1962:13)

     Denmark. Statistisk Departe-
          ment.
     Folke- og boligtaellingen   Population and housing census,
     26. september 1960. Copenha-   September 26, 1960.
     gen, [publisher varies], 1963-
     1964. (Statistisk tabelvaerk.
     1963: I, III, V, VI. 1964:I,
     II, IV, V) Parts A-C in 8v.
     A. Folke- og boligtal i   A. Population and housing sta-
     kommuner og bymaessige bebyg-   tistics in municipalities and
     gelser 1960.   urban areas of rural districts.
1960.2-A-1   Øerne undtagen hoved-   The Islands except the capital.
     staden. Bianco Lunos, 1963.   [BC, PRC, RPI, RIR
     [6], 55, 55, 55p. (1963:I)
     .2-A-2   Jylland. Bianco   Jutland.
     Lunos, 1963. [6], 73, 73, 73p.   [BC, PRC, RPI, RIR
     (1963:III)
     .2-A-3   Hovedstaden med fors-   The capital with suburbs. Sum-
     taeder. Sammendrag. Aarhuus,   mary.
     1963. [6], 19, 19, 19, 19, 19p.   [BC, PRC, RPI, RIR
     (1963:V)

B. Fordelinger efter alder
og erhverv m.v.
1960.2-B-1   Køn, alder og aegteskabelig stilling. 1963. [2],
95p. (1963:VI)
.2-B-2   Erhverv og arbejdsstilling. 1964. 172p. (1964:I)

.2-B-3   Fag, arbejdsstilling
og erhverv. Andelsbogtrykkeriet
i Odense, 1964. 151p. (1964:V)
C. [Housing and households]
.2-C-1   Bolig- og husstands-
undersøgelse 1960.   Aarhuus,
1964. [2], 201p. (1964:II)
.2-C-2   Boligforholdene i byer
og bymaessige bebyggelser med
over 1000 indbyggere 1960.
1964. [2], 159, [2]p. (1964:IV)

Danmarks Statistik.
Folke- og boligtaellingen
27. september 1965. Copenhagen, 1969-1971. Parts A-C in
11v. (Statistisk Tabelvaerk)
A. Folke- og boligtal i kommuner og bymaessige bebyggelser.

1965.1-A-1   Hovedsadsområdet. Sam-
mendrag. 1969. 137p. (1969:
VII)
.1-A-2   Sjaelland undtagen ho-
vedstaden. 1969. 155p. (1969:
II)
.1-A-3   Bornholm, Lolland-Falster, Fyn. 1969. 127p. (1969:
I)
.1-A-4   Østlige Jylland. 1969.
105p. (1969:IV)
.1-A-5   Nordlige Jylland. 1969.
85p. (1969:V)
.1-A-6   Vestlige Jylland. 1969.
105p. (1969:VI)
.1-A-7   Sydlige Jylland. 1969.
71p. (1969:III)
B. Fordelinger efter alder
og erhverv, m.v.
.1-B-1   Køn, alder og aegteskabelig stilling. 1970. 127p.
(1970:III)
.1-B-2   Erhverv og arbejdsstilling. 1970. 204p. (1970:IV)

B. Distribution by age and in-
dustry, etc.
Sex, age and marital status.
[BC, PRC, RPI, RIR

Population by industry and social
status.
[BC, PRC, RPI, PRC
Occupation, social status and
industry.
[BC, PRC, RPI, RIR

Housing and households 1960.
[BC, PRC, RPI, RIR

Statistics on housing in towns
and urban areas of rural districts
with over 1000 inhabitants, 1960.
[BC, PRC, RPI, RIR

Population and housing census,
September 27, 1965.

A. Population and housing statistics in municipalities and
urban areas of rural districts.
Capital area. Summary.
PRC, RPI

Zealand except the capital.
[PRC, RPI

Bornholm, Lolland-Falster, Fyn.
[PRC, RPI

East Jutland.
[PRC, RPI
North Jutland.
[PRC, RPI
West Jutland.
[PRC, RPI
South Jutland.
[PRC, RPI
Distribution by age and industry,
etc.
Sex, age and marital status.
[PRC, RPI

Industry and social status.
[PRC, RPI

1965.1-B-3   Fag, arbejdsstilling   Occupation, social status and
   og erhverv. 1971. 197p.   industry.
   (1971:I)   [PRC, RPI
   .1-C   C. Bolig- og husstands-   C. Housing and households.
   undersøgelse. 1969. 131p.   [PRC, RPI
   (1969:VIII)

   Danmarks Statistik.
      Folke- og boligtaellingen   Population and housing census,
   9 november 1970.   Copenhagen,   November 9, 1970.
   1972-1977. (Statistisk Tabel-
   vaerk). Vols. A-C in 23v.
      A. Amtstabelvaerk.   A. Division tables. Population
   Folke- og boligtal i kommuner,   and housing in municipalities,
   sogne og bymaessige områder: parishes and urban areas.
1970.1-A-1   Bornholms amt. Bilag: Bornholms division. Annexes:
   cirkulaere, skemaer, kodeover-   circulars, questionnaires,
   sigter og oversaettelser. 127p.   codes, and translations.
   (1972:III)   [PRC
1970.1-A-2 through 1970.1-A-15. [One volume for each division. Translation
   in No. 1970.1-A-1 only.] 2. Ringkøbing. 107p. (1973:II)/3. Ribe.
   88p. (1973:III)/4. Viborg. 111p. (1973:V)/5. Sønderjyllands. 123p.
   (1973:VI)/6. Nordjyllands. 147p. (1973:VII)/7. Vejle. 99p. (1973:
   VIII)/8. Århus. 149p. (1973:IX)/9. Fyns. 158p. (1973:X)/10. Stor-
   strøms. 133p. (1973:XII)/11. Vestsjaellands. 124p. (1973:XIV)/12.
   Roskilde. 80p. (1973:XV)/13. Frederiksborg. 104p. (1973:XVI)/14.
   Københavns. 102p. (1973:XVII)/15. Københavns Kommune, Frederiksberg
   Kommune. 151p. (1974:II). [PRC
   .1-B-1   Pendling. Den aktive   Commuting. The economically
   befolknings fordeling efter   active population distributed
   arbejdssted og bopael. 307p.   by place of work and residence.
   (1974:IV)   [PRC
   .1-B-2   Folke- og boligtal i   Population and housing by trad-
   handelsområder og -distrikter.   ing areas and districts.
   155p. (1974:VIII).   [PRC
   .1-B-3   Danmarks administrative   Administrative divisions of Den-
   inddeling. Med areal-, Folke-   mark. Area, population and house-
   og husstandstal. 341p. (1975:   hold relationship.
   II)   [PRC
   .1-B-4   Danmarks byer. Folke-   Cities in Denmark. Population
   og boligtal i bymaessige områder   and housing in urban areas of
   med over 1000 indbyggere. 281p.   1000 plus inhabitants.
   (1975:VII)   [PRC
   .1-C-1   Beskaeftigelse og erh-   Occupations (trades) and indus-
   verv. Befolkningens fordeling   try. Population according to
   efter beskaeftigelsesforhold,   economic activity status, indus-
   erhverv og fag. 231p. (1974:   try and occupation.
   VII)   [PRC
   .1-C-2   Boligen. 285p. (1975:   Housing.
   VIII)   [PRC
   .1-C-3   Hele befolkningens erh-   Occupational distribution of the
   versfordeling. 159p. (1977:   whole population.
   II)   [PRC

1970.1-C-4   Uddannelse: oplysnin-
ger am skole- og erhvervsuddan-
nelse for de 14-49 årige. 122p.
(1977:VII)

Education: information on population aged 14-49 in school or
vocational training college.
[PRC

This is perhaps the last Danish census to be taken. They intend to
use only the vital registration system for future population statistics.

Denmark. Danmarks Statistik.
    Registerfolketaellingen, 1.
juli 1976.   Copenhagen, 1978.
Bind 1-5. (Statistisk tabelvaerk, 1978:VIII, 1979:I-   )

Population register count, July
1, 1976.

1976.1-1   Byer-Sogne. 1978. 420p.
(1978:VIII).

Cities-Parishes.
[OPR

.1-2   Kommuner. 1979. 399p.
(1979:I).

Municipalities.
[OPR

.1-3   Amtskommuner.

Municipalities by county.
[

.1-4   Hele landet-Bygrupper.

Whole country-Urban districts.
[

.1-5   Administrativ inddeling.

Administrative division.
[

DJIBOUTI

Republic of Djibouti   Capital: Djibouti
Statistical Agency:

Publications Distributor:

   To this date no census or nationwide demographic study has been taken.

           France. INSEE.
1946   Résultats du recensement...
              [See French Overseas Territories, Nos. 1946.1-1, 2, and 3.
                                                 1946.2]

           France. INSEE.
1951   Le recensement de la population...
              [See French Overseas Territories, No. 1951.1]

           France. Ministère de la France
                 d'Outre-Mer, Service des
                 Statistiques.
1951.2   Premiers résultats du recen-   First results of the census of
              sement de 1951 dans les terri-   1951 in the overseas territories
              toires d'outre-mer (population   (Non-indigenous population):
              non-originaire): 1re partie,   Part 1, Somaliland, French India,
              Côte des Somalis, Inde Française,   Saint Pierre and Miquelon.
              Saint-Pierre-et-Miquelon. Paris,   [PRC, RPI
              1952. 110, [2]p. (BMSOM, supplé-
              ment série "statistique," No. 14).

           France. INSEE.
1956.1   Recensement de la population   Census of the population of
              de la Côte Française de Somalis,   French Somaliland, 1956: non-
              1956: population non originaire,   indigenous population.
              1956.   Paris, 1961. 40p.   [PRC, RPI

DOMINICA

State of Dominica   Capital: Roseau
Statistical Agency:

Publications Distributor:

        Jamaica.   Central Bureau of Statistics.
1946   West Indian census, 1946...
                [See Commonwealth Caribbean, Nos. 1946.1-A
                                                 1946.1-H]

        Trinidad and Tobago.   Central Statistical Office
1960   Eastern Caribbean population census...
                [See Commonwealth Caribbean, Nos. 1960.1-1-A and D
                                                 1960.1-2-W
                                                 1960.1-3-WD]

        West Indies.   University.   Census Research Programme.
1970   1970 population census...
                [See Commonwealth Caribbean, Nos. 1970.1-1
                                                 1970.1-2-?
                                                 1970.1-3
                                                 1970.1-4-9 and 16
                                                 1970.1-6-3
                                                 1970.1-7
                                                 1970.1-8-a, b, and c
                                                 1970.1-9-3
                                                 1970.1-10-2 and 4]

DOMINICAN REPUBLIC

                                                Capital: Santo Domingo
Statistical Agency: National Statistics Office
                     [Oficina Nacional de Estadística]
                     Edificio para Oficinas Públicas
                     Apartado de correos, No. 1342
                     Santo Domingo,
Publications Distributor: same

        Dominican Republic. Dirección
            General de Estadística.
1950.1   Tercer censo nacional de pob-   Third national census of popula-
        lación: resumen general.   Ciu-   tion: general summary.
        dad Trujillo, 1953. xviii, 75p.   [TXU, PRC, RP]

        Dominican Republic. Dirección
            General de Estadística.
    .2   Población de la República   Population of the Dominican Repub-
        Dominicana censada en 1950.   lic enumerated in 1950. Distribu-
        Distribución según la división   tion according to the territorial
        territorial al 1° de julio de   division of July 1, 1954.
        1954. Ciudad Trujillo, 1954.   [TXU, PRC, RP]
        vi, 126p.

        Dominican Republic. Dirección
            General de Estadística.
    .3   Tercer censo nacional de pob-   Third national census of popula-
        lación, 1950.   Ciudad Trujillo,   tion, 1950.
        1958. 1v, 866p.   [TXU, PRC, JB-F, RP]

        Dominican Republic. Dirección
            General de Estadística.
    .4-1   Tercer censo nacional de   Third national census of popula-
        población, 1950. Común de San   tion, 1950. Commune of San Cris-
        Cristóbal.   Ciudad Trujillo,   tóbal.
        1952. xxxv, 170p.   [TXU, PRC, RP]

        [Note: This work was marked "Volume I" as if to imply other volumes
        to come. However, no further citations have been seen.]

        Dominican Republic. Dirección
            General de Estadística.
1960.1   División territorial de la   Territorial division of the Domin-
        República Dominicana. Provin-   ican Republic. Provinces, munici-
        cias, municipios, secciones,   palities, sections, parishes.
        parajes. Agosto de 1960.   August 1960.
        Ciudad Trujillo, 1961. iii, 433p.   [TXU, PRC, RP]

        Dominican Republic. Oficina
            Nacional de Estadística.
    .2   Cuarto censo nacional de pob-   Fourth national census of popu-

lación, 7 de agosto de 1960. Resumen general. Santo Domingo, 1966. 112p.

lation, August 7, 1960. General summary.
[PRC, JB-F, RPI

Dominican Republic. Oficina
   Nacional de Estadística.
   Censo nacional de población y habitación, 9 y 10 enero 1970. Boletín censal. Santo Domingo, 1969-   .

National census of population and housing, January 9 and 10, 1970. Census bulletin.

1970.0-1-1   [Algunas actividades para la preparación y empadronamiento del censo de población y habitación de 1970.] 1969. 56p.
  .0-1-2

[Some activities in the preparation and setting up of the 1970 census of population and housing.
[PRC

.0-1-3   Cifras oficiales preliminares. 1970. 33p.
.0-1-4   Normas de crítica para les informaciones de población. 1971. 38p.

Official preliminary figures.
[PRC
Criticism norms for population data.
[PRC

Dominican Republic. Oficina
   Nacional de Estadística.
.0-2 Censo nacional de población y habitación, 9-10 enero de 1970. Plan de tabulaciones de población (edición revisada). Santo Domingo, 1970. 34p.

National census of population and housing, January 9-10, 1970. Plan for the population tabulations (revised edition).
[PRC

Dominican Republic. Oficina
   Nacional de Estadística.
   Comentarios sobre los resultados definitivos del V censo nacional de población. Santo Domingo, 1971-1972.

Commentaries on the final results of the Fifth national census of population.

.0-3-1 [Primera parte]. 1971. [31]p.
.0-3-2 Segunda parte. 1972. 57p.

[First part]
[PRC
Second part.
[PRC

Dominican Republic. Oficina
   Nacional de Estadística.
.0-4 [Censo de población 1970. Tabulaciones 1 a 7, 10, 13, 14, 16-22, 24-27, 30, 34.] Santo Domingo, n.d. unpaged.

[Population census 1970. Tabulations...]
[PRC

Dominican Republic. Oficina
   Nacional de Estadística.
   V censo nacional de pobla-

Fifth national census of popula-

ción, 1970, 9 y 10 de enero de 1970.   Santo Domingo, 1976-
              .   Vol. I-IV.

1970.1-1   I. Caractéristicas generales de la población. 1976. xviii, 88p.

  .1-2   II. Caractéristicas educativas. 1978. xx, 534p.

  .1-3   III. Caractéristicas económicas.

  .1-4   IV. Fecundidad y migración.

tion, 1970, January 9 and 10, 1970.

General population characteristics. [PRC, IASI

Education characteristics. [PRC

Economic characteristics. [

Fertility and migration. [

ECUADOR

Republic of Ecuador   Capital: Quito
Statistical Agency: National Institute of Statistics and Censuses
                     [Instituto Nacional de Estadística y Censos.]
                     Junta Nacional de Planificación
                     Avda. 10 de Agosto, No. 229
                     Edificio "San Luis"
                     Quito,
Publications Distributor: same.

Ecuador. Dirección General de
          Estadística y Censos.
1950.1   El primer censo nacional de   The first national population
población del Ecuador.   Quito,   census of Ecuador.
Talleres Gráficos del Censo,   [JB-F, RPI
n.d. 17p.

Ecuador. Dirección General de
          Estadística y Censos.
.2   Resultados definitivos del   Final results of the national
censo nacional de población   population census taken Novem-
levantado en noviembre 29 de   ber 29, 1950.
1950.   Quito, 1952. 6p.   [BC, RPI

Ecuador. Dirección General de
          Estadística y Censos.
.3   Información censal. Resumen   Census information. Summary of
de los resultados definitivos del   the final results of the 1950
censo nacional de población de   national population census on:
1950 sobre: sexo, edad, estado   sex, age, marital status, lit-
civil, alfabetismo y población   eracy and economically active
económicamente activa e inactiva.   and inactive population.
Quito, Talleres Gráficos del   [PRC, BC, UN, JB-F, RPI
Censo, 1952. 61p.

Ecuador. Dirección General de
          Estadística y Censos.
    Boletín de información censal.   Bulletin of census information.
Resultados definitivos del censo   Final results of the national
nacional de población de 1950   census of population of 1950
sobre: edad y sexo, estado   on: age and sex, marital state,
civil, alfabetismo, población   literacy, economically active
económicamente activa y inactiva.   and inactive population.
Quito, 1951-1952. Boletines Nos.
1-17A.
1950.4-1 through 1950.4-17a. 1. carchi. 1951. 21p./2. Cañar. 1951. 17p./
    3. Bolívar. 1951. 17p./4. Cotopaxi. 1951. 25p./5. Imbabura. 1951.
    22p./6. Loja. 1952. 38p./7. Tungurahua. 1952. 21p./8. Chimborazo.
    1952. 30p./9. El Oro. 1952. 26p./10. Santiago-Zamora. 1952. 25p./
    11. Azuay. 1952. 30p./12. Napo Postaza. 1952. 25p./13. Esmeraldas.

1952. 13p./14. Los Ríos. n.d. 32p./15. Pichincha. 1952. 26p./
16. Manabí. 1952. 46p./17. Guayas. 1952. 34p./17a. Archipiélago
de Colón (Galápagos). 1952. 21p. [PRC, BC, RPI

Ecuador. Dirección General de
      Estadística y Censos.
    Primer censo nacional de pob-   First national population census
lación del Ecuador, 1950. Quito,   of Ecuador, 1950.
1953-   . Vols. I-X.
1950.5-1   Población por edad y sexo.   Population by age and sex.
  1954. 320p.   [TXU, PRC, RPI
 .5-2   Población urbana, suburbana   Urban, suburban and rural popu-
y rural. 1954. 133p.   lation.
                                         [TXU, PRC, BC, LC, RPI
 .5-3   Población por estado civil.   Population by marital status.
  1954. 137p.   [PRC, LC, RPI
 .5-4-1   Población por idiomas y   Population by languages and
dialectos. 1954. 152p.   dialects.
                                         [PRC, NYPL, Berkeley, RPI
 .5-4-2   [Never published].
      Población alfabeta y anal-   Literate and illiterate popula-
fabeta.   tion.
 .5-5-1   [República, provincias   [Republic, provinces of Azuay
de Azuay hasta Cotopaxi]. 1955.   through Cotopaxi.]
158p.   [PRC, TXU, RPI
 .5-5-2   [Provincias de Chimbo-   [Provinces of Chimborazo through
razo hasta Archipiélago de Colón].   Colon Archipelago.]
1955. 199p.   [PRC, RPI
 .5-6   [Never published]
 .5-7   [Never published]
 .5-8   [Never published]
 .5-9   [Never published]
 .5-10   [Never published]

Ecuador. Dirección General de
      Estadística y Censos.
    Primer censo nacional de pob-   First national population census,
lación, 29 de noviembre de 1950.   November 29, 1950. Final results.
Resultados definitivos. Quito,
Talleres Gráficos del Censo,
1953-
 .6-1-1   Provincia del Guayas.   Province of Guayas. Book I.
  Tomo I. 1953. 213p.   [PRC, BC, RPI
 .6-1-2   [Never published].
 .6-2-1   Provincia del Imbabura.   Province of Imbabura. Book I.
  Tomo I. 1953. 163p.   [PRC, TXU, RPI

[Note: The remaining provincial volumes seem never to have been
published.]

Ecuador. Dirección General de
    Estadística y Censos.
.7   Primer censo de población del   First population census of Ecua-
Ecuador, 1950. Resumen de carac-   dor, 1950. Summary of charac-
terísticas. Volumen único.   teristics. Unique volume.
Quito, Talleres Gráficos de la   [PRC, NYP:, TXU, RPI
Dirección, 1960. [Reimpreso
1965]. iv, 196p.

Ecuador. División de Estadís-
    tica y Censos.
    Segundo censo de población   Second population census and
y primer censo de vivienda, 25   first housing census, November
de noviembre de 1962. Quito,   25, 1962.
1964. Tomos I-IV.
1962.1-1   Población. [Tablas No.   Population. [Tables 1-21].
    1-21]. vi, 285p.   [PRC, JB-F, RPI
.1-2   Población. [Tablas No.   Population. [Tables 22-38].
    22-38]. vi, 325p.   [PRC, JB-F, RPI
.1-3   Población. [Tablas No.   Population. [Tables 39-53].
    39-53]. vi, 291p.   [PRC, JB-F, RPI
.1-4   [Vivienda]. vi, 155p.   Housing.
    [PRC, JB-F, RPI

Ecuador. División de Estadís-
    tica y Censos.
    Segundo censo de población   Second population census and
y primer censo de vivienda, 25   first housing census, November
de noviembre de 1962. Quito,   25, 1962.
1964. Vols. 1-16 in 18v.
1962.2-1 through 1962.2-16. 1. Carchi. xviii, 193p./2. Cañar. xviii,
198p./3. Esmeraldas. xviii, 205p./4. Pichincha. 297p./5. Azuay.
xviii, 338p./6. Bolívar. xviii, 191p./7. El Oro. xviii, 325p./
8. Imbabura. xviii, 243p./9. Loja. xviii, 424p./10. Los Ríos.
xviii, 369p./11. Región Oriental [Morona Santiago, Napo, Pastaza,
Zamora Chinchipe]. xviii, 263p./12-1. Guayas-Galápagos. xviii,
276p./12-2. Guayas-Galápagos. xviii, 270p./13-1. Manabí. xviii,
316p./13-2. Manabí. xviii, 268p./14. Tungurahua. xviii, 298p./
15. Chimborazo. xviii, 333p./16. Cotopaxi. xviii, 359p. [PRC,
BC, RPI

Ecuador. División de Estadís-
    tica y Censos.
.3   Resumen de los censos de pob-   Summary of the 1962 censuses
lación y vivienda de 1962.   of population and housing.
Quito, 1965. 96p.   [BC

Ecuador. Oficina de los Censos
    Nacionales.
1974.0-1 III censo de población; II   Third population census; second
de vivienda, 1974. Resultados   housing census, 1974. Provis-
provisionales. Quito, 1974.   ional results.
31p.   [PRC, BC, IASI

Ecuador.   Oficina de los Censos
      Nacionales.
1974.1   III censo de población; II
de vivienda, 1974.   Resultados
anticipados por muestreo.
Quito, 1975.   xvii, 66p.

Third population census; second
housing census, 1974.   Advanced
results through sampling.
[PRC, IASI, BC, UN

Ecuador.   Instituto Nacional de
      Estadística y Censos.
      III censo de población, 1974.
Resultados definitivos.   Quito,
1976-1978.   21 vols. in 37 v.
   .2-1   Resumen nacional.   1977.
xxii, 159, xi p.

Third population census, 1974.
Final results.

National summary.
[PRC, UN

1974.2-2-1 through 1974.2-21.   2-1. Azuay.   1976.   xxii, 408p./2-2. ...
1976.   pp. 409-683, xlviii p./3. Bolívar.   1977.   xxii, 488, xxxvp./
4. Cañar.   1977.   xxii, 400, xxviii p./5. Carchi.   1976.   xxii, 408,
xxviii p./6-1. Cotopaxi.   1977.   xxii, 403p./6-2. ...   pp. 404-583,
xli p./7-1. Chimborazo.   1976.   xxii, 403p./7-2. ...   pp. 404-678,
xlviii p./8-1. El Oro.   1976.   xxii, 393p./8-2. ...   pp. 394-668,
xlviii p./9. Esmeraldas.   1977.   xxii, 508, xxxv p./10. Galápagos.
1976.   xxii, 393, xxx p./11-1. Guayas.   1978.   xxii, 403p./11-2. ...
pp. 404-763./11-3. ...   pp. 764-1033./11-4. ...   pp. 1034-1213, xc p./
12. Imbabura.   1977.   xxi, 503, xxxiv p./13-1. Loja.   1978.   xxii,
398p./13-2. ...   pp. 399-763./13-3. ...   pp. 764-948, lxviii p./14-1.
Los Ríos.   1976.   xxii, 393p./14-2. ...   pp. 394-763, liv p./15-1.
Manabí.   1976.   xxii, 403p./15-2. ...   pp. 404-858./15-3. ...   pp.
859-1128./15-4. ...   pp. 1129-1312, xcv p./16-1. Morona Santiago.
1976.   xxii, 400p./16-2. ...   pp. 401-678, xlviii p./17-1. Napo. 1976.
xxii, 398p./17-2. ...   pp. 399-678, xlix p./18. Pastaza.   1976.   xxii,
308, xxii p./19-1. Pinchincha.   1976.   xxii, 418p./19-2. ...   pp. 419-
688, xlviii p./20-1. Tunguruhua.   1977.   xxii, 403p./20-2. ...   pp.
404-683, xlviii p./21. Zamora Chinchipe.   1976.   xxii, 398, xxviii p.
[PRC, OPR

EGYPT

Arab Republic of Egypt   Capital: Cairo
Statistical Agency: Central Agency for Public Mobilisation and Statistics.
                     Nasr City
                     Cairo,
Publications Distributor: same.

        Egypt. Statistics and Census Department.
            Population census of Egypt, 1947.   Cairo, 1951-1954. Vols. I-II
        in 19v. [In Arabic only].
1947.1-1-1 through 1947.1-1-18. Provinces. 1. Aswan. n.d.   [4], 163p./
        2. Gena. 1951. [5], 232p./3. Girga. 1952. [6], 271p./4. Asyat.
        1952. [7], 389p./5. Minya. 1952. [5], 292p./6. Beni Suef. 1951.
        [5], 211p./7. Faiyum. 1952. [5], 224p./8. Giza. 1952. [4], 227p./
        9. Beheira. 1952. [4], 277p./10. Daqahliya. 1952. [7], 355p./11.
        Sharqiya. 1953. [5], 372p./12. Gharbiya. 1953. [5], 519p./13.
        Qulyubiya. 1953. [6], 222p./14. Minufiya. 1953. [8], 296p./
        Governorates: 15. Cairo. 1952. [6], 242p./16. Alexandria. 1952.
        [8], 296p./17. Canal, Suez and Damietta. 1953. [5], 273p./18. Bar-
        dir. 1954. [6], 667p. [PRC, BC, RPI
    .1-2   General tables. 1954. v, 493p. [PRC, NYPL, JB-F, RPI

        Egypt. Department of Statistics and Census.
            1960 census of population. Cairo, 1962-1963. Vols. I-II in 23v.
        [In Arabic only].
1960.1-1-1 through 1960.1-1-22. Cities: 1. Alexandria. 1962. [24], 529,
        [1], 2p./2. Cairo. 1962. [24], 809, [1], 2p./3. Ismailia. 1962.
        [24], 323, [2]p./4. Port Said. 1962. [24], 297, [2]p./5. Suez.
        1962. [25], 259p./ Provinces of Lower Egypt: 6. Beheira. n.d.
        [24], 957, [2]p./7. Daqahliya. 1962. [24], 778, [1]p./8. Damietta.
        1962. [24], 222, [1]p./9. Gharbiya. 1962. [24], 734, [3]p./10.
        Kafr El Sheik. 1962. [24], 520, [1]p./11. Minufiya. n.d. [24],
        616, [1]p./12. Qealyubiya. 1962. [24], 607, [2]p./13. Sharqiya.
        n.d. [24], 956, [3]p./Provinces of Upper Egypt: 14. Aswan. n.d.
        [24], 463p./15. Asyût. n.d. [24], 757, [4]p./16. Beni Suef. n.d.
        [24], 553, [2]p./17. Faiyûm. 1962. [24], 460, [1]p./18. Giza. 1962.
        [24], 536, 2p./19. Minya. n.d. [24], 754, [3]p./20. Qena. n.d.
        [24], 551, [2]p./21. Souhag. 1962. [24], 668, [1]p./22. Frontier
        Districts: Red Sea, Western Desert, Southern Desert, Sinai. n.d.
        [22], 350, [1]p. [PRC, RPI
    .1-2   General tables. 1963. xviii, 319p. [PRC, RPI

        Although the 1966 census is called a "sample" there was a complete
        head count by sex, religion and nationality.

        Egypt. Central Agency for Public Mobilisation and Statistics.
            Final results of the sample census (microcensus) of population,
        1966.   Cairo, 1967. Vols. I-V. [In Arabic only].
1966.1-1   Method of taking the census and its stages. 48p. [PRC, NWU
    .1-2   Summary tables and urban governorates. 72p. [PRC, NWU

.1-3   Lower Egypt governorates. 254p. [PRC, NWU
.1-4   Upper Egypt governorates. 195p. [PRC, NWU
.1-5   Governorates of the frontiers. 48p. [PRC, NWU

Egypt. Central Agency for Public Mobilisation and Statistics.
1976.0-1   The preliminary results of the central population and housing
census, 22/23 November 1976, in Egypt. Cairo, 1976. 57p. [PRC,
BC, LC, NWU
.0-2   Preliminary results of the 1976 population and housing census
in Egypt. In: National Bank of Egypt, Economic bulletin (Cairo)
30(1):30-38. 1977. [JB-F

EL SALVADOR

Republic of El Salvador   Capital: San Salvador
Statistical Agency: General Bureau of Statistics and Censuses
                     [Dirección General de Estadística y Censos.]
                     Sección Punto Focal Nacional
                     Calle Arce, No. 953
                     San Salvador,
Publications Distributor: same

        El Salvador. Dirección General
            de Estadística y Censos.
1950.1   Segundo censo de población,   Second population census, June
        jujio 13 de 1950.   San Salvador,   13, 1950.
        1954. xxx, 621p.   [PRC, TXU, BC, JB-F, RPI

        El Salvador. Dirección General
            de Estadística y Censos.
   .2   Atlas censal de El Salvador.   Census atlas of El Salvador.
        San Salvador, Lud Dreikorn, 1955.   [PRC, BC, TXU, RPI
        110p.

        El Salvador. Dirección General
            de Estadística y Censos.
1961.1   Tercer censo nacional de pob-   Third national population cen-
        lación, 1961. Características   sus, 1961. Principal character-
        principales de la población ob-   istics of the population obtained
        tenidas por muestreo.   San Sal-   by sampling.
        vador, 1962. v, 85p.   [PRC, BC, JB-F, RPI

        El Salvador. Dirección General
            de Estadística y Censos.
   .2   Tercer censo nacional de pob-   Third national population cen-
        lación, 1961. Población por   sus, 1961. Population by area
        area y sexo, departamento, muni-   and sex by department, munici-
        cipio y canton.   San Salvador,   pality and canton.
        1965. vii, 61p.   [PRC, TXU, JB-F, RPI

        El Salvador. Dirección General
            de Estadística y Censos.
   .3   Tercer censo nacional de pob-   Third national population cen-
        lación, 1961.   San Salvador,   sus, 1961.
        1965. xxxiii, 833p.   [PRC, JB-F, RPI

        El Salvador. Dirección General
            de Estadística y Censos.
1971.0-1 Censos nacionales, 1971: mé-   National censuses, 1971: methods
        todos y procedimientos.   San   and procedures.
        Salvador, 1971.   [

        El Salvador. Dirección General
            de Estadística y Censos.
        Cuarto censo nacional de pob-   Fourth national census of popu-

lación, 1971.   San Salvador,
1974-1977. Vols. I-II.
1971.1-1   Características generales,
características educacionales,
fecundidad. 1974. xxxii, 477p.

    .1-2   Características económi-
cas. 1977. xxx, 592p.

lation, 1971.

General characteristics, educa-
tional characteristics, fertil-
ity.
[BC
Economic characteristics.
[PRC

ENGLAND AND WALES

	Capital: London
Statistical Agency:	Office of Population Censuses and Surveys.

St. Catherine's House
Kingsway
London WC2B 6JP,
        and
Central Statistical Office
Cabinet Office
Great George Street
London SW1P 3AQ,

Publications Distributor: Her Majesty's Stationery Office
Atlantic House
Holborn Viaduct
London EC1P 1BN,
        or
B.F. Stevens & Brown
Arden House, Mill Lane
Godalming, Surrey
GU7 1HA, England
        or
Pendragon House
2595 East Bayshore Road
Palo Alto, California, 94303, USA

Great Britain. General Register Office.
        Census 1951. England and Wales. London, HMSO, 1952-1959. 62v.
[Geographic divisions]
1951.1-1   Population of ecclesiastical areas [England]. 1955. viii,
        185p. [PRC, BC, RPI
    .1-2   Report on Greater London and five other conurbations. 1956.
        cxxxv, 351p. maps. [PRC, RPI
    .1-3   Wales (including Monmouthshire). Report on Welsh speaking
        population. 1955. xvi, 32p. [PRC, BC, RPI
                County reports [England]. 1953-1956. 42 counties in 37v.
1951.1-4-1 through 1951.1-4-37. 1. Bedfordshire. 1954. xli, 42p./2. Berk-
        shire. 1954. xliv, 54p./3. Buckinghamshire. 1954. xliii, 52p./
        4. Cambridgeshire & Huntingdonshire. 1954. xliv, 72p./5. Cheshire.
        1954. xlviii, 99p./6. Cornwall. 1955. xliii, 62p./7. Cumberland
        & Westmoreland. 1954. xliv, 64p./8. Derbyshire. 1954. xlvi, 72p./
        9. Devon. 1955. xlvi, 102p./10. Dorset. 1955. xlii, 52p./11.
        Durham. 1954. xlvi, 88p./12. Essex. 1954. xlviii, 117p./13. Glou-
        cestershire. 1954. xlvi, 70p./14. Hampshire. 1954. xlviii, 95p./
        15. Herefordshire & Shropshire. 1954. xlvii, 88p./16. Hertfordshire.
        1954. xlv, 74p./17. Kent. 1954. xlix, 110p./18. Lancashire. 1954.
        li, 218p./19. Leicestershire. 1954. xliii, 54p./20. Lincolnshire
        & Rutland. 1955. xlvii, 125p./21. London. 1953. xlix, 90p./22.
        Middlesex. 1953. xlvi, 69p./23. Norfolk. 1955. xlvi, 74p./24.
        Northamtonshire. 1954. xlvii, 68p./25. Northumberland. 1954. xliv,
        70p./26. Nottinghamshire. 1954. xlvi, 54p./27. Oxfordshire. 1954.
        xliv, 47p./28. Somerset. 1955. xlv, 82p./29. Staffordshire. 1954.

xlix, 92p./30. Suffolk. 1955. xlix, 82p./31. Surrey. 1954. xlvii, 78p./32. Sussex. 1954. liii, 95p./33. Warwickshire. 1954. xlv, 64p./34. Wiltshire. 1955. xliii, 58p./35. Worcestershire. 1954. xlvii, 60p./36. Yorkshire East & North Riding. 1954. xiii, 118p./ 37. Yorkshire West Riding. 1954. xlix, 177p.[PRC, RPI
County reports [Wales]. 1953-1956. 13 counties in 7v.
1951.1-5-1 through 1951.1-5-7. 1. Anglesey & Caernarvonshire. 1955. xliv, 60p./2. Brecknockshire & Carmarthenshire. 1954. xlvi, 62p./3. Cardiganshire & Pembrokeshire. 1955. xliv, 60p./4. Denbighshire & Flintshire. 1955. xlv, 62p./5. Glamorganshire. 1954. xlvi, 64p./ 6. Merionethshire, Montgomeryshire & Radnorshire. 1955. xlvi, 77p./ 7. Monmouthshire. 1954. xliv, 60p. [PRC, RPI
.1-6   Report on Isle of Man. 1956. xlvii, 42p. [PRC, RPI
[General]
.2   General report. 1958. vii, 224p. specimen forms. [PRC, BC, RPI
[Subject reports]
.3-1   Fertility report. 1959. cxi, 251p. [PRC, RPI
.3-2   Housing report. 1956. cxxix, 150p. [PRC, RPI
.3-3   Industry tables. 1957. xiii, 648p. [PRC, RPI
.3-4   Occupation tables. 1956. xv, 672p. [PRC, RPI
.3-5   Report on usual residence and workplace. 1956. xxxix, 288p. [PRC, RPI
[Other]
.4-1   Classification of industries. 1952. vi, 82p. [PRC, BC, RPI
.4-2   Classification of occupations. 1956. xvi, 317p. [PRC, RPI
        Index of place names. 1955. 2 parts.
.4-3-1   A-K. iv, 653p. [PRC, RPI
.4-3-2   L-Z. pp. 655-1377. [PRC, RPI

Note: For <u>One percent sample tables</u>, see Great Britain.

Great Britain. General Register Office.
    Census 1961. England and Wales.   London, HMSO, 1962-1966. 147 vols.
[Geographic divisions]
1961.1-1   Greater London tables. 1966. xvi, 68p. [PRC, RPI, RIR
        County reports [England]. 1963-1964. 49 parts.
1961.1-2-1 through 1961.1-2-49. 1. Bedfordshire. 1968. xxiii, 72p./2. Berkshire. 1964. xxiii, 94p./3. Buckinghamshire. 1964. xxiii,88p./ 4. Cambridgeshire. 1964. xxiii, 44p./5. Cheshire. 1964. xxiii, 172p./6. Cornwall & Isles of Scilly. 1964. xxiii, 85p./7. Cumberland. 1963. xxiii, 76p./8. Derbyshire. 1964. xxiii, 106p./9. Devon. 1964. xxiii, 143p./10. Dorset. 1963. xxii, 78p./11. Durham. 1963. xxiii, 169p./12. Isle of Ely. 1964. xxiii, 48p./13. Essex. 1963. xxiii, 247p./14. Gloucestershire. 1964. xxiii, 114p./15. Hampshire. 1963. xxiii, 141p./16. Herefordshire. 1964. xxiii, 61p./17. Hertfordshire. 1963. xxiii, 141p./18. Huntingdonshire. 1964. xxiii, 52p./19. Kent. 1963. xxiii, 193p./20. Lancashire. 1964. xxvi, 52p./ 21. Leicestershire. 1964. xxiii, 88p./22. Lincolnshire (Parts of Holland). 1964. xxii, 44p./23. Lincolnshire (Parts of Kesteven). 1964. xxiii, 52p./24. Lincolnshire (Parts of lindsey). 1964. xxiii,

108p./25. London. 1963. xxii, 269p./26. Middlesex. 1963. xxiii, 192p./27. Norfolk. 1964. xxiii, 113p./28. Northamptonshire. 1964. xxiii, 98p./29. Northumberland. 1963. xxiv, 122p./30. Nottingham-shire. 1964. xxiii, 104p./31. Oxfordshire. 1964. xxiii, 86p./32. Soke of Peterborough. 1964. xxiii, 42p./33. Rutland. 1964. xxii, 42p./34. Shropshire. 1964. xxiii, 76p./35. Somerset. 1964. xxiii, 115p./36. Staffordshire. 1963. xxiii, 177p./37. East Suffolk. 1964. xxiii, 88p./38. West Suffolk. 1964. xxiii, 55p./39. Surrey. 1963. xxiii, 189p./40. East Sussex. 1964. xxiii, 110p./41. West Sussex. 1964. xxiii, 84p./42. Warwickshire. 1963. xxiv, 135p./43. West-moreland. 1963. xxiii, 46p./44. Isle of Wight. 1963. xxiii, 44p./ 45. Wiltshire. 1964. xxiii, 82p./46. Worcestershire. 1963. xxiii, 108p./47. Yorkshire East Riding. 1964. xxiii, 88p./48. Yorkshire North Riding. 1964. xxiii, 110p./49. Yorkshire West Riding. 1963. xxiii, 300p. [PRC, BC, RPI, RIR

Country reports [Wales]. 1963-1964. 13 parts.
1961.1-3-1 through 1961.1-3-13. 1. Anglesey. 1963. xxii, 46p./2. Brecon-shire. 1963. xxiii, 50p./3. Caernarvonshire. 1963. xxiii, 58p./ 4. Cardiganshire. 1963. xxiii, 48p./5. Carmarthenshire. 1964. xxiii, 56p./6. Denbighshire. 1963. xxiii, 55p./7. Flintshire. 1963. xxiii, 50p./8. Glamorgan. 1963. xxiii, 124p./9. Merionethshire. 1963. xii, 46p./10. Monmouthshire. 1963. xxiii, 96p./11. Montgom-eryshire. 1963. xxii, 50p./12. Pembrokeshire. 1963. xxiii, 54p./ 13. Radnorshire. 1963. xxii, 46p. [PRC, BC, RPI, RIR
.1-4   Report on the Welsh speaking population. 1962. xii, 33p. [PRC, BC, RPI, RIR

Report on the Isle of Man. 1965-1966. Parts I-II.
.1-5-1   Population and housing. 1965. ix, 28p. [PRC, BC, RPI, RIR
.1-5-2   Migration, economic activity and other topics. 1966. x, pp. 29-48. [PRC, BC, RPI, RIR
[Subject reports - 100 percent tabulation].
.2-1   Age, marital condition and general tables. 1964. xv, 108p. [PRC, BC, RPI, RIR
.2-2   Birthplace and nationality tables. 1964. xi, 70p. specimen forms. [PRC, BC, RPI, RIR
.2-3   Fertility tables. 1966. xxii, 313p. [PRC, RPI, RIR

Housing tables. 1964-1965. Parts I-III.
.2-4-1   I. Buildings, dwellings and households. 1964. xv, 157p. [PRC, BC, RPI, RIR
.2-4-2   II. Tenure and household arrangements. 1965. xvi, 316p. [PRC, BC, RPI, RIR
.2-4-3   III. Local housing indices. 1965. xix, 353p. [PRC, BC, RPI, RIR
.2-5   Housing national summary tables. 1964. v, 14p. [PRC, BC, RPI, RIR
.2-6   Usual residence tables. 1964. xiii, 47p. [PRC, BC, RPI, RIR
[Subject reports - 10 percent sample]
.3-1   Commonwealth immigrants in the conurbations. 1965. xviii, 116p. [PRC, BC, RPI, RIR
.3-2   Education tables. 1966. xx, 11p. [PRC, BC, RPI, RIR
.3-3   Household composition tables. 1966. xxxiv, 352p. specimen forms. [PRC, BC, UN, RPI, RIR

.3–4   Household composition national summary tables. 1966. xv, 17p.
     [PRC, BC, RPI, RIR
                 Industry tables. 1966. Parts I–II.
.3–5–1   I. lii, 220p. [PRC, BC, RPI, RIR
.3–5–2   II. xxx, pp. 222–371. [PRC, BC, RPI, RIR
.3–6   Migration tables. 1966. xxix, 358p. [PRC, BC, RPI, RIR
                 Migration National summary tables. 1965. Parts I–II.
.3–7–1   I. ix, 34p. [PRC, BC, RPI, RIR
.3–7–2   II. x, 59p. [PRC, BC, RPI, RIR
.3–8   Occupational tables. 1966. xlv, 267p. [PRC, BC, RPI, RIR
.3–9   Occupation and industry national summary tables. 1965. xv, 9p.
     [PRC, RPI, RIR
                 Occupation and industry socio-economic groups. 1965–1966. 58
     parts.
1961.3–10–1 through 1961.3–10–45. 1. Bedfordshire. 1965. xi, 15p./2. Berk-
     shire. 1965. xi, 15p./3. Buckinghamshire. 1965. xi, 15p./4. Cam-
     bridgeshire. 1966. xi, 15p./5. Cheshire. 1966. xi, 29p./6. Corn-
     wall and Isle of Scilly. 1966. xi, 11p./7. Cumberland. 1966. xi,
     15p./8. Derbyshire. 1966. xi, 15p./9. Devon. 1966. xi, 19p./10.
     Dorset. 1966. xi, 15p./11. Durham. 1966. xi, 29p./12. Isle of Ely.
     1966. xi, 11p./13. Essex. 1965. xi, 51p./14. Gloucestershire. xi,
     17p./15. Hampshire. 1966. xi, 27p./16. Herefordshire. 1966. xi,
     11p./17. Hertfordshire. 1965. xi, 29p./18. Huntingdonshire. 1966.
     xi, iip./19. Kent. 1965. xi, 31p./20. Lancashire. 1966. xi, 69p./
     21. Leicestershire. 1966. xi, 15p./22. Lincolnshire. 1966. xi,
     29p./23. London. 1965. xi, 73p./24. Middlesex. 1965. xi, 49p./25.
     Norfolk. 1966. xi, 15p./26. Northamptonshire. 1966. xi, 11p./27.
     Northumberlandshire. 1966. xi, 17p./28. Nottinghamshire. 1966. xi,
     11p./29. Oxfordshire. 1966. xi, 15p./30. Soke of Peterborough.
     1966. xi, 15p./31 Rutland. 1966. xi, 11p./32. Shropshire. 1966.
     xi, 11p./33. Somerset. 1966. xi, 17p./34. Staffordshire. 1966. xi,
     31p./35. Suffolk. 1966. xi, 17p./36. Surrey. 1965. xi, 31p./37.
     Sussex. 1965. xi, 31p./38. Warwickshire. 1966. xi, 27p./39. West-
     moreland. 1966. xi, 11p./40. Isle of Wight. 1966. xi, 11p./41.
     Wiltshire. 1966. xi, 15p./42. Worcestershire. 1966. xi, 17p./43.
     Yorkshire East Riding. 1966. xi, 15p./44. Yorkshire North Riding.
     1966. xi, 17p./45. Yorkshire West Riding. 1966. xi, 47p. [PRC,
     BC, RPI, RIR
1961.3–11–1 through 1961.3–11–13. 1. Anglesey. 1966. xi, 11p./2. Brecon-
     shire. 1966. xi, 11p./3. Caernarvonshire. 1966. xi, 11p./4. Car-
     diganshire. 1966. xi, 11p./5. Carmarthenshire. 1966. xi, 11p./
     6. Denbighshire. 1966. xi, 11p./7. Flintshire. 1966. xi, 11p./8.
     Glamorgan. xi, 27p./9. Merionethshire. 1966. xi, 11p./10. Mon-
     mouthshire. 1966. xi, 15p./11. Montgomeryshire. 1966. xi, 11p./
     12. Pembrokeshire. 1966. xi, 11p./13. Radnorshire. 1966. xi, 11p.
     [PRC, RPI, RIR
.3–12   Socio-economic group tables. 1966. xxii, 109p. [PRC, BC,
     RPI, RIR
.3–13   Workplace tables. 1966. xviii, 307p. [PRC, BC, UN, RPI, RIR
[Other]
.4–1   Classification of occupations, 1960. 1960. xxxiv, 136p. [PRC,
     RPI, RIR

```
                    Index of place names.  1965.  Parts I-II.
.4-2-1        A-K.  iv, 624p.  [PRC, RPI, RIR
.4-2-2        L-Z.  pp. 625-1324.  [PRC, RPI, RIR
.4-3     Standard industrial classification, rev'd ed.  1958.
  [
```

Note: For <u>Scientific and technological qualifications</u>, <u>Summary re-</u>
<u>port</u>, and <u>Summary tables</u>, see Great Britain.

[Although entitled a "sample" the 1966 census was sufficiently broad in scope
and coverage to be included.]

Great Britain. General Register Office.
     Sample census, 1966. England and Wales.   London, HMSO, 1966-1969.
123 vols.
[Geographic divisions]
          County reports [England]. 1967. 46v.
1966.1-1-1 through 1966.1-1-46. All have specimen forms. 1. Bedfordshire.
     xxii, 33p./2. Berkshire. xxii, 35p./3. Buckinghamshire. xxii, 30p./4.
     Cambridgeshire and Isle of Ely. xxii, 26p./5. Cheshire. xxii, 72p./
     6. Cornwall and Isle of Scilly. xxii, 24p./7. Cumberland. xxii,
     30p./8. Derbyshire. xxii, 37p./9. Devon. xxii, 39p./10. Dorset.
     xxii, 26p./11. Durham. xxii, 71p./12. Essex. xxii, 26p./13. Glou-
     cestershire. xxii, 39p./14. Hampshire. xxii, 52p./15. Herefordshire.
     xxii, 19p./16. Hertfordshire. xxii, 57p./17. Huntingdon and Peter-
     borough. xxii, 24p./18. Kent. xxii, 54p./19. Lancashire. xxiii,
     140p./20. Leicestershire. xxii, 32p./21. Lincolnshire (Parts of Hol-
     land). xxii, 22p./22. Lincolnshire (Parts of Kesteven and Lincoln C.
     B). xxii, 35p./24. Greater London.   /25. Norfolk. xxii,
     35p./26. Northamptonshire. xxii, 35p./27. Northumberland. xxii, 35p./
     28. Nottinghamshire. xxii, 41p./29. Oxfordshire. xxi, 30p./30. Rut-
     land. xxii, 17p./31. Shropshire. xxii, 30p./32. 32. Somerset. xxii,
     32p./33. Staffordshire. xxii, 67p./34. East Suffolk. xxii, 30p./35.
     West Suffolk. xxii, 22p./36. Surrey. xxii, 52p./37. East Sussex.
     xxii, 41p./38. West Sussex. xxii, 35p./39. Warwickshire. xxii, 50p./
     40. Westmorland. xxii, 20p./41. Isle of Wight. xxi, 22p./42. Wilt-
     shire. xxii, 26p./43. Worcestershire. xxii, 39p./44. Yorkshire East
     Riding. xxii, 30p./45. Yorkshire North Riding. xxii, 30p./46. York-
     shire West Riding. xxii, 93p. [PRC, RPI
          County reports [Wales]. 1967. 13v.
1966.1-2-1 through 1966.1-2-13. All have specimen forms. 1. Anglesey.
     xxii, 17p./2. Breconshire. xxii, 17p./3. Caernarvonshire. xxii,
     21p./4. Cardiganshire. xxii, 17p./5. Carmarthenshire. xxii, 22p./
     6. Denbighshire. xxii, 22p./7. Flintshire. xxii, 22p./8. Glamorgan.
     xxii, 50p./9. Merionethshire. xxii, 17p./10. Monmouthshire. xxii,
     35p./11. Montgomeryshire. xxii, 17p./12. Pembrokeshire. xxii, 19p./
     13. Radnorshire. xxii, 17p. [PRC, RPI
[Subject reports]
          Economic activity county leaflets [England]. 1968. 42v.
1966.2-1-1 through 1966.2-1-42. [Same order as 1966.1-1 except Lincoln-
     shire, Suffolk and Sussex have only one volume each.] [PRC, RPI
          Economic activity county leaflets [Wales]. 1968. 13v.
1966.2-2-1 through 1966.2-2-13. [Same order as 1966.1-2.] [PRC, RPI

.2-3   Economic activity county leaflets. General explanatory notes.
          1966. xxiv, specimen forms. [PRC, RPI
.2-4   Household composition tables. 1968. xxxii, 316p. [PRC, RPI
          Housing tables. 1968. Parts I-II.
.2-5-1   I. xxvii, 232p. [PRC, RPI
.2-5-2   II. xxiv, pp. 233-281. [PRC, RPI
          Migration regional report. 1968. 9v.
.2-6-1   East Anglia. xxiii, 58p. [PRC, RPI
.2-6-2   East Midland. xxiii, 109p. [PRC, RPI
.2-6-3   North Western. xxiii, 158p. [PRC, RPI
.2-6-4   Northern. xxiii, 116p. [PRC, RPI
.2-6-5   South Eastern. xxiii, 438p. [PRC, RPI
.2-6-6   South Western. xxiii, 115p. [PRC, RPI
.2-6-7   Wales. xxiii, 94p. [PRC, RPI
.2-6-8   West Midland. xxiii, 114p. [PRC, RPI
.2-6-9   Yorkshire and Humberside. xxiii, 103p. [PRC, RPI
          Migration [summary] tables. 1968-1969. Parts I-II.
.2-7-1   I. 1968. xxiii, 202p. [PRC, RPI
.2-7-2   II. 1969. xxvi, 484p. [PRC, RPI
.2-8   Usual residence tables. 1969. xvi, 18p. [PRC, RPI
          Workplace and transport tables. 1968. Parts I-II.
.2-9-1   I. xxxiii, 364p. [PRC, RPI
.2-9-2   II. xxxiii, pp. 365-603. [PRC, RPI
[Other]
.3   Classification of occupations, 1966. 1966. xxiv, 148p. [PRC,
          UN, RPI

          Note: For Commonwealth immigrant tables, Economic activity sub-re-
          gional tables, Economic activity tables, Qualified manpower tables,
          Scientific and technological qualifications, and Summary tables, see
          Great Britain. For General and parliamentary constituency tables,
          see United Kingdom entry under Great Britain, 1966.

          Great Britain. Office of Population Censuses and Surveys.
             Census 1971. England and Wales.   London, HMSO, 1972-
          vols.
[Geographic Divisions]
             County reports [England]. 1972-1973. 138 vols.
1971.1-1-1a through 1971.1-1-46c. [Three volumes for each county. Same
          order as in 1966.1-1.] [PRC
             County reports [Wales]. 1972-1973. 39 vols.
1971.1-2-1a through 1971.1-2-13c. [Three volumes for each county. Same
          order as in 1966.1-2.] [PRC
.1-3   County reports. General explanatory notes. 1972. 32p. spec-
          imen forms. [PRC
             Report for the county of ... [England] as constituted on 1st
          April 1974. 1975-1977. 45 vols.
1971.1-4-1 through 1971.1-4-45. 1. Avon. 1976. viii, 83p./2. Bedfordshire.
          1975. viii, 62p./3. Berkshire. 1976. viii, 83p./4. Buckinghamshire.
          1976. viii, 68p./5. Cambridgeshire. 1975. viii, 83p./6. Cheshire.
          1976. viii, 105p./7. Cleveland. 1976. viii, 62p./8. Cornwall and
          Isles of Scilly. 1976. viii, 91p./9. Cumbria. 1975. viii, 83p./

10. Derbyshire. 1976. viii, 111p./11. Devon. 1976. viii, 123p./
12. Dorset. 1977. viii, 103p./13. Durham. 1976. viii, 103p./14.
Essex. 1976. viii, 160p./15 Gloucestershire. 1976. viii, 83p./
16. Hampshire. 1976. viii, 150p./17. Herefordshire & Worcestershire.
1977. viii, 113p./18. Hertfordshire. 1976. viii, 123p./19. Humberside. 1976. viii, 111p./20. Kent. 1976. viii, 160p./21. Lancashire. 1976. viii, 162p./22. Leicestershire. 1976. viii, 111p./
23. Lincolnshire. 1975. viii, 91p./24. Greater Manchester. 1975.
viii, 165p./25. Merseyside. 1975. viii, 92p./26. West Midlands.
1976. viii, 91p./27. Norfolk. 1976. viii, 91p./28. Northamptonshire. 1976. viii, 91p./29. Northumberland. 1976. viii, 83p./30.
Nottinghamshire. 1977. viii, 103p./31 Oxfordshire. 1975. viii,
70p./32. Salop. 1975. viii, 83p./33. Somerset. 1976. viii, 68p./
34. Staffordshire. 1976. viii, 111p./35. Suffolk. 1976. viii, 91p./
36. Surrey. 1976. viii, 127p./37. East Sussex. 1975. viii, 91p./
38. West Sussex. 1976. viii, 91p./39. Tyne & Wear. 1976. viii,
94p./40. Warwickshire. 1976. viii, 68p./41. Isle of Wight. 1975.
viii, 41p./42. Wiltshire. 1975. viii, 70p./43. North Yorkshire.
1976. viii, 107p./44. South Yorkshire. 1976. viii, 80p./45. West
Yorkshire. 1976. viii, 94p. [PRC

  Report for the county of ... [Wales] as constituted on 1st April
1974. 1975-1977. 8 vols.
1971.1-5-1 through 1971.1-5-8. 1. Clwyd. 1976. viii, 83p./2. Dyfed. 1975.
viii, 83p./3. Mid Glamorgan. 1976. viii, 83p./4. South Glamorgan.
1976. viii, 44p./5. West Glamorgan. 1975. viii, 62p./6. Gwent.
1976. viii, 68p./7. Gwynedd. 1976. viii, 70p./8. Powys. 1975.
viii, 51p. [PRC
 .1-6 Census 1971/Cyfrifiad 1971. Wales/Cymru. Summary tables/
Tablau Crynodeb. Cardiff, 1975. lxxix, 132p. specimen forms. [PRC
[Subject reports]
 .2-1 Availability of cars. 1973. xxv, 63p. [PRC
  Economic activity county leaflets [England]. 1975. 46 vols.
1971.2-2-1 through 1971.2-2-46. [Counties listed in the same order as 1966.
  1-1] [PRC
  Economic activity county leaflets [Wales]. 1975. 13 vols.
1971.2-3-1 through 1971.2-3-13. [Counties listed in the same order as 1966.
  1-2] [PRC
  Housing. 1974. Parts I-IV in 3v.
 .2-4-1 Households. xiii, 268p. [PRC
 .2-4-2&3 Amenities, and Dwellings. xxviii, 184p. [PRC
 .2-4-4 Density of occupation. xiii, 264p. plus correction to
table 11, South East Region. [PRC
 .2-5 Report on the Welsh language in Wales. Cardiff, 1973. vii,
83p. [PRC
 .2-6 Usual residence tables. 1974. xxvii, 59p. [PRC
[Subject reports - 10 percent sample]
 .3-1 Economic activity sub-regional tables. 1976. 1v, 411p. [PRC
  Household composition tables. 1975. Parts I-III.
 .3-2-1 I. xxx, 183p. [PRC
 .3-2-2 II. xxxi, 219p. [PRC
 .3-2-3 III. xxx, 247p. [PRC
  Migration regional report. 1975-1976. 27 vols.

1971.3-3-1a through 1971.3-3-9c. [Three parts for each region.] 1. East
      Anglia./2. East Midlands./3. North./4. North West./5. South East./
      6. South West./7. Wales./8. West Midlands./9. Yorkshire and Humber-
      side. [PRC
   .3-4   New towns. Economic activity, workplace and transport to work
      tables. 1976. xli, 107p. [PRC
              Workplace and transport to work tables. 1975. Parts I-II.
   .3-5-1   I. xvi, 432p. [PRC
   .3-5-2   II. xv, 232p. [PRC

      Note: For <u>Economic activity</u>; <u>Economic activity general explanatory
      notes</u>; <u>Age, marital condition and general tables</u>; <u>Country of birth
      tables</u>; <u>Household composition summary tables</u>; <u>Housing summary tables</u>;
      <u>Migration tables</u>; <u>Non-Private households</u>; <u>Persons of pensionable age</u>;
      <u>Qualified manpower tables</u>; <u>Summary tables</u>, see Great Britain.

EQUATORIAL GUINEA

Republic of Equatorial Guinea
Statistical Agency: General Secretariat
               [Secretaria General de la Presidencia de la República]
               Malabo,
Publications Distributor: same.

Capital: Malabo (former Santa
               Isabel)

Consists of Río Muni, Macías Nguema Biyogo (Fernando Póo), Pagalu (Annobón), Corisco, Elobey Grande and Elobey Chico.

Spain. Delegación Colonial de
      Estadística.

1950.1   Territorios españoles del Golfo de Guinea: resúmenes del censo general de la población efectuado con referencia al día 31 de diciembre de 1950. Madrid, Talleres Tipográficos-Gráficas Basagal, 1952. 166p.

Spanish territories of the Gulf of Guinea: summary of the general census of population taken December 31, 1950.
[PRC, LC, NWU, RPI

Spain. Instituto Nacional de
      Estadística.

.2   Censo de la población de España y territorios de su soberania y protectorado, según el empadronamiento realizado el 31 de diciembre de 1950. Tomo I. Madrid, 1952. 1v, 415p.

Census of the population of Spain and territories under its sovereignty and protectorship, according to the enumeration of December 31, 1950.
[TXU, RPI

Spain. Instituto Nacional de
      Estadística.

1960.1   Censo de la población y de las viviendas de España según la incripción realizado el 31 de diciembre de 1960. Tomo I, cifras generales de habitantes. Madrid, T.G. Victoria, 1962. xl, 404p.

Census of population and housing of Spain according to the enumeration taken December 31, 1960. Book I. General figures of inhabitants.
[TXU, PRC,

Equatorial Guinea. Gobierno
      General de la Región
      Equatorial

.2   Resumen general del censo de población de 31 de diciembre de 1960.   p.

General resumé of the population census of December 31, 1960.
[

Equatorial Guinea. Delegación
      de Estadística.

.3   Resultados definitivos del censo de población de 31 de

Final results of the population census of December 31, 1960, in

diciembre de 1960 en las pro-   the provinces of Fernando Po and
vincias de Fernando Póo y Río   Río Muni. General resumé.
Muni. Resumen general.   Santa   [PRC
Isabel, 1961. 1p.

Equatorial Guinea. Delegación
      Regional de Estadística.
   Nomenclator de población y   Population classification and
reseña demográfica de ...   demographic description of ...
Santa Isabel, 1966-1968.
1960.4-1   Fernando Póo. 1966.
             p.   [
   .4-2   Río Muni. 1968.
             p.   [

ETHIOPIA

Socialist State of Ethiopia   Capital: Addis Ababa
Statistical Agency: Central Statistical Office
                      P.O. Box 1143
                      Addis Ababa,
Publications Distributor: same

There have been censuses of the city of Addis Ababa but none of the
nation as a whole. National Sample Surveys (First round, 1964-67;
Second round, 1968-71), however, have been conducted.

Addis Ababa, Municipality.
1961.1   Report on the census of population, 10-11 September 1961.   Addis
Ababa, 1963. 66p. [PRC, NWU, RPI

[There was a census of Asmara, capital of Eritrea, in 1963 but no
publications have been located.]

Ethiopia. Central Statistical Office.
     Reports from the National Sample Survey. Urban survey report of...
Addis Ababa, 1966-1967.
1966.1-1 through 1966.1-9. 1. Adwa. 1966. 29p./2. Assab. 1966.   p./
3. Bahirdar. 1966. 29p./4. Debre Zeyt. 1967. 24p./5. Dessie.
1967. 29p./6. Gondar. 1966.   p./7. Harer. 1967. 29p./8. Jima.
1966. 24p./9. Soddo. 1967. 22p. [NWU

Ethiopia. Central Statistical Office.
     [Report from the National Sample Survey. Province of...]   Addis
Ababa, 1966-1968.
1966.2-1 through 1966.2-12. 1. Arussi. 1966. 47p./2. Begemdir. 1968.
59p./3. Gemu Gofa. 1967. 40p./4. Gojam. 1966. 35p./5. Hararge.
1968. 49p./6. Illubabar. 1968. 45p./7. Kefa. 1968. 46p./8. Shoa.
1966. 45p./9. Sidamo. 1968. 45p./10. Tigre. 1967. 37p./11. Wal-
lega. 1967. 44p./12. Wello. 1967. 46p. [NWU

Ethiopia. Central Statistical Office.
  .3   Population of Ethiopia (result from the National Sample Survey,
first round). Addis Ababa, 1971. 59p. (Statistical Bulletin, No.
6.) [NWU, OPR, PRC

Ethiopia. Central Statistical Office [and] Municipality of Addis
          Ababa.
1967.1   Population of Addis Ababa: results from the population sample
survey of October 1967. Addis Ababa, 1972. 84p. (Statistical
bulletin, No. 8). [NWU, PRC

Ethiopia. Central Statistical Office.
     Results of the National Sample Survey, second round.   Addis Ababa,
     1974. Vol. 1-5 in 3v. (Statistical bulletin, No. 10.)
1971.1-1   The demography of Ethiopia. 132p. [NWU

1968.1-2   Tables of demographic data by province.   245p.   [NWU
    .1-3   Livestock and poultry. 262p. [NWU
    .1-4   Indebtedness. 157p. [NWU
    .1-5   Land area and utilization. 180p. [NWU

    [Volumes 3-5, above, are bound together.]

    Ethiopia. Central Statistical Office.
    .2   Results of the 1968 population and housing censuses: population
    and housing characteristics of Asmara.   Addis Ababa, 1974.   iii, 86,
    [2]p. (Statistical bulletin, No. 12). [NWU, LC

    Ethiopia. Central Statistical Office.
    .3   Tables of demographic data for ninety-one towns: results of urban
    survey, second round.   Addis Ababa, 1975. 3v. (Statistical bulle-
    tin, No. 12). [UN, LC, NWU

    Work on the circa 1970 census has been suspended due to factors beyond
    the control of the statistical authorities.

FALKLAND ISLANDS

Colony of the Falkland Islands and Dependencies   Capital: Stanley
Statistical Agency: Colonial Secretary's Office
                     Stanley,
Publications Distributor: same.

        Falkland Islands. Registrar General.
1946.1   Report of the 1946 census: report of census taken on the night
        of the 31st March, 1946.   Stanley, Government Printing Office, 1946.
        20p. [PRC, BC, UN, RP]

        Falkland Islands. Registrar General.
1953.1   Report of the census taken on the night of the 28th March, 1953.
        Stanley, Government Printing Office, 1954. 9p. [PRC, BC, UN, RP]

        Falkland Islands. Census Supervisor's Office.
1962.1   Report of census 1962 [taken on the night of 18th March, 1962].
        Stanley, Government Printing Office, 1962. [2], 14p. [PRC, UN, RP]

        Falkland Islands. Census Office.
1972.1   Report of census 1972. Stanley, 1973. 12p. [PRC

FAROE ISLANDS

Capital: Thorshavn

Statistical Agency: See Denmark.
Publications Distributor: same.

Denmark. Statistiske Department
1945.1   Folkemaengde og administratif
inddeling 1945.   Copenhagen,
Bianco Lunos, 1946. 446p. (Statistiske meddelelser, 4de raekke,
128 bind, 1ste haefte).

The population in 1945 in administrative districts.
[TXU,

Denmark. Statistiske Department.
.2   Befolkningens fordeling efter
køn og alder 1945.   Copenhagen,
Bianco Lunos, 1946. 91p. (Statistiske meddelelser, 4de raekke,
128 bind, 2det haefte).

Population by sex and age, 1945.
[TXU, PRC, RPI

Denmark. Statistiske Department.
1950.1   Den faerøske befolknings fordeling efter køn, alder og civil-
stand m.v. ved folketaellingen
31. december 1950 samt aegteskaber, fødte og døde 1941-1955.
In: Statistiske efterretninger,
1956, No. 47. Pp. 403-407.

The Faroe Islands population by
sex, age and marital status, etc.,
according to the population census of December 31, 1950 with
marriages, births and deaths
1941-1955.
[BC, PRC, RPI

[Results for the 1950 census were also published in the following
work.]

Denmark. Statistiske Departement
1955.1   Faerøerne befolknings forhol-
dene 1941-55.   Copenhagen,
Bianco Lunos, 1959. 40p. (Statistiske meddelelser, 4de raekke,
173 bind, 3die haefte.)

The population of the Faroe
Islands, 1941-55.
[UN, BC, PRC, RPI

Denmark. Statistiske Departement.
1960.1   Faerøerne. Folketaellingen
1960. Aegteskaber, fødte og døde
1946-60.   Copenhagen, Andelsbogtrykkeriet i Odense, 1965. 44p.
(Statistik tabelvaerk, 1965:I)

Faroe Islands. Population census 1960. Marriages, births and
deaths 1946-60.
[PRC, BC, RPI, RIR

Danmarks Statistik.
1966.1   Faerøerne. Folke- og boligtaellingen 1. April 1966. Aegteskaber, fødte og døde 1961-65.
Copenhagen, Aarhuus, 1970. 92p.
(Statistik tabelvaerk, 1970:I)

Faroe Islands. Population and
housing census April 1, 1966.
Marriages, births and deaths
1961-65.
[PRC, UN, RPI

Danmarks Statistik.

1970.1   Faerøerne. Folke- og bolig-   Faroe Islands. Population and
           taellingen 16. november 1970.   housing census, November 16,
           Bilag: aegteskaber, fødte og   1970. Appendix: marriages,
           døde 1966-70.   Copenhagen,   births and deaths 1966-70.
           1975. 150p. (Statistik tabel-   [PRC, NYPL
           vaerk, 1975:I)

[Note: The 1970 census is intended to be the last one taken in Denmark, Greenland and the Faroe Islands. The vital registration system
only will be used.]

                              FIJI

Dominion of Fiji.   Capital: Suva
Statistical Agency: Bureau of Statistics
                      P.O. Box 2221, Government Buildings
                      Suva,
Publications Distributor: same

        Fiji. Census Commissioner's Office.
1946.1   A report on the results of the census of the population, 1946.
By John W. Gittens.   Suva, Government Printer, 1947. viii, 222p.
(Legislative Council paper, No. 35 of 1947). [PRC, EB, SU, E-W

        Fiji. Census Commissioner's Office.
1956.1   Report on the census of the population, 1956. By Norma McArthur.
Suva, Government Press, 1958. [4], 224p. specimen form, 2 folding
maps. (Legislative Council paper, No. 1 of 1958). [PRC, BC, PSC,
SU, Harvard, E-W, JB-F, UN, RPI

        Fiji. Census Commissioner's Office.
1966.1   Report on the census of the population, 1966. By F.H.A.G. Zwart.
Suva, Government Press, 1968. x, 240p. 10 maps. (Legislative Council paper, No. 9 of 1968). [PRC, EB, OPR, SU, Harvard, E-W, JB-F,
RPI

        Fiji. Census Department.
1976.0-1   Urban Fiji: boundaries used in the 1976 census of population.
A report to the Census Commissioner by M.L. Kakker and A.C. Walsh.
Suva, Government Printer, 1976. 244p. [E-W

        Fiji. Census Commissioner's Office.
        Report on the census of the population 1976.   Suva, EDP Services,
     1977. 2v. in 1. maps. (Parliamentary papers, No. 13 of 1977).
    .1-1   I. [Parts 1-3]. xi, 589p. [E-W, OPR, PRC, PSC
    .1-2   I. [Part 4]. 25 folding maps. [PRC, E-W, OPR, PSC

        Fiji. Bureau of Statistics.
        An analysis of data collected in the 1976 census.   Suva, 1978-
        . (Occasional paper, No. 1-).
    .2-1   Economic activity in Fiji. 1978. [4], ii, 57p. [PRC, E-W
    .2-2   Religion, school attendance and adult educational attainment,
    household and family size. 1978. [3], ii, 18p. [PRC, E-W

FINLAND

Republic of Finland   Capital: Helsinki
Statistical Agency: Central Statistical Office of Finland
                      P.O. 504
                      00101 Helsinki 10,
Publications Distributor: Government Printing Centre
                           Marketing Department
                           P.O. Box 516
                           SF-00101 Helsinki 10,

Finland. Tilastollinen Päätoi-
    misto.
    Vuoden 1950 yleinen väestö-   1950 population census.
laskenta. Helsinki, Valtion-   (Official statistics of Finland.
euvoston Kirjapaino, 1955-1958.   VI. Population statistics: C102)
Volumes I-IX. (Suomen viral-
linen tilasto. VI, Väestöti-
lastoa: C102). [In Finnish,
Swedish and English].
1950.1-1   Väkiluku, väestön ikä ja   Population, number, age and
kielisuhteet. 1956. 69p.   language.
                                         [PRC, UN, RPI
.1-2   Väestö elinkeinohaaran ja   Population by industry and in-
ammattiaseman mukaan. 1955.   dustrial status.
104p.   [PRC, UN, RPI
.1-3   Asuntokanta. 1956. 136p.   Housing.
                                         [PRC, UN, RPI
.1-4   Väestö elinkeinohaaran ja   Population by industry and in-
ammattiaseman mukaan. Yksityis-   dustrial status. Detailed clas-
kohtainen ryhmittely. 1956.   sification.
186p.   [PRC, UN, RPI
.1-5   Väestö ammatin sekä amma-   Population by occupation and
tillisen koulutuksen mukaan.   vocational training.
1956. 77p.   [PRC, UN, RPI
.1-6   Kiinteistö-ja rakennus-   Properties and buildings.
kanta. 1957. 83p. specimen   [PRC, UN, RPI
forms.
.1-7   Perhe ja ruokakunta.   Family and household.
1957. 95p.   [PRC, UN, RPI
.1-8   Väestön syntymäpaikka,   Population by birthplace, educa-
yleissivistys, kielitaito ja   tional level, knowledge of lan-
uskontokunta, ruotsinkielinen   guages, congregation, Swedish-
väestö ja ulkomaiden kansalai-   speaking population and aliens.
set. 1958. 69p.   [PRC, UN, RPI
.1-9   English summary. 1958.
10p.   [PRC, UN, RPI

Finland. Tilastollinen Päätoi-
    misto.
    Yleinen väestölaskenta 1960.   General census of population
Helsinki, Valtioneuvoston Kir-   1960.

japaino, 1962-1965. Vols. I-
XIII. (Suomen virallinen ti-
lasto VI, C:103). [In Finnish,
Swedish and English].

(Official statistics of Finland..
VI. Population statistics: C:103)

1960.1-1   Asuntokanta. 1962. 164p.

Housing.
[PRC, BC, RPI, RIR

.1-2   Väestön ikä, siviitisääty,
pääkieli ym. 1963. 134p. specimen forms.

Population by age, marital status,
main language, etc.
[PRC, BC, RPI, RIR

.1-3   Ammatissa toimivan väestön elinkeino ja ammattiasema.
1963. 73p.

Economically active population
by industry
[PRC, BC, RPI, RIR

.1-4   Väestön elinkeino ja ammattiasema. 1963. 191p. specimen forms.

Population by industry and industrial status.
[PRC, BC, RPI, RIR

.1-5   Perheet. 1964. 81p.

Families.
[PRC, BC, RPI, RIR

.1-6   Väestön sosio-ekonominen
asema. Ammatissa toimivan
väestön ikä. Työpaikan si-
jainti. 1963. 77p.

Population by socio-economic
status. Economically active
population by age. Place of
work.
[PRC, BC, RPI, RIR

.1-7   Ruokakunnat ja miiden
asuminen. 1963. 148p.

Households and their housing
conditions.
[PRC, BC, RPI, RIR

.1-8   Syntymäpaikka, koulusi-
vistys, siirtoväki ym. 1964.
21, 63p.

Population by birthplace and by
education, displaced population,
etc.
[PRC, BC, RPI, RIR

.1-9   Ammatti ja ammattikoulu-
tus. 1964. 155p.

Occupation and vocational training.
[PRC, BC, RPI, RIR

.1-10   Rakennuskanta. 1964.
320p. specimen forms.

Buildings.
[PRC, BC, RPI, RIR

.1-11   Taajamat ja miiden rajat,
ym. 1965. 127p.

Non-administrative urban settlements and their boundaries, etc.
[PRC, BC, RPI, RIR

.1-12   Täydennysosa. 1965. 26,
127p. specimen forms.

Supplementary volume.
[PRC, BC, RPI, RIR

.1-13   Taululuettelot. 1965.
19p.

Lists of tables.
[PRC, BC, RPI, RIR

Finland. Tilastokeskus.
   Väestölaskenta, 1970. Hel-
sinki, Valtion painatuskeskus,
1973-1976. Vols. I-XIX in 23v.
(Suomen virallinen tilasto. VI,
C:104) [In Finnish, Swedish and
English]

Population census 1970.

(Official statistics of Finland,
VI, Population statistics, C:104)

1970.1-1   Yleiset demografiset tie-
dot. 1973. 431p. specimen
forms.

General demographic data.
[PRC

	Elinkeino ja ammattiasema.	Industry and industrial status.
1973.	2v.	
1970.1-2-a	[Whole population].	
	461p.	[PRC
.1-2-b	[Economically active population]. 426p.	[PRC
.1-3	Työpaikan sijainti. 1974.	Place of work.
	400p.	[PRC
.1-4	Taajamat 1960-1970. 1976.	Localities 1960-1970.
	190p.	[PRC
.1-5	Asuntokanta. 1973. 408p.	Housing.
		[PRC
.1-6	Ruokakuntien rakenne.	Structure of households.
1974.	517p.	[PRC
	Koulutus. 1974. 2v.	
.1-7-a	[Whole population, 14 years & over, persons with university degrees]. 492p.	[PRC
.1-7-b	[Economically active population] 623p.	[PRC
.1-8	Perheet. 1973. 425p.	Families
		[PRC
.1-9	Ammatti ja sociaaliasema.	Occupation and social position.
1974.	611p.	[PRC
.1-10	Rakennuskanta, liike-yms. huoneistot. 1973. 398p.	Buildings, premises in commercial use, etc.
		[PRC
.1-11	Työvoima ja toimeentulon lähde. 1974. 469p.	Labour force and source of livelihood.
		[PRC
.1-12	Kesämökit. 1975. 313p.	Summer cottages.
		[PRC
.1-13	Tulot ammatin, koulutuksen ym. mukaan. 1975. 310p.	Incomes by occupation, education, etc.
		[PRC
.1-14	Ruokakuntien asunto-olot.	Housing conditions of households.
1974.	494p.	[PRC
.1-15	Tutkimus lasten lukumäärästä. 1975. 70p.	Fertility study.
		[PRC
.1-16	Tilastokartat. 1975.	Statistical maps.
	107p.	[PRC
	[Vähemmistöt]	Minorities.
.1-17-a	Ruotsinkielinen väestö.	Swedish-speaking population.
1974.	170p.	[PRC
.1-17-b	Mustalaiset. 1974.	Gipsies.
	92p.	[PRC
.1-17-c	Saamelaiset. 1974.	Lappish population.
	86p.	[PRC
.1-18	Väestöpyramidit. 1974.	Population pyramids.
	417p.	[PRC
.1-19	Taululuettelot. 1976.	List of tables.
	67p.	[PRC

Finland.   Tilastokeskus.
    Asunto- ja elinkeinotutkimus,   Population and housing census,
1975.   Helsinki, 1978.   Vols.I   1975.
VII.   (Suomen virallinen tilasto,
VI, C:105)
      I.   Ammatti ja elinkeino.   Occupation and industry.
1975.1-1-A   A.   650p.   [PRC, OPR
  .1-1-B   B.   566p.   specimen
  forms.   [PRC, OPR
  .1-2   II.   Asunnat ja asuminen.   Housing and housing conditions.
  504p.   [PRC, OPR
  .1-3   III.   Ruokakunnat ja per-   Households and families.
  heet.   382p.   [PRC, OPR
  .1-4   IV.   Koulutus.   777p.   Education.
                                                     [PRC
  .1-5   V.   Tulot.   548p.   Incomes.
                                                   [PRC, OPR
  .1-6   VI.   Alueittaiset taulut.   Regional tables.
  78p.   appendix.   [PRC, OPR
  .1-7   VII.   Asiahakemisto.   232p.   Tabulation programme.
                                                 [PRC, OPR

FRANCE

French Republic   Capital: Paris
Statistical Agency: National Institute of Statistics and Economic Studies
                     [Institut National de la Statistique et des Études
                        Économiques. INSEE]
                     18, Bd. Adolphe-Pinard
                     75675 Paris, Cedex 14,
Publications Distributor: Observatoire Économique de Paris (INSEE)
                     Tour Gamma A
                     195, rue de Bercy
                     75582 Paris, Cedex 12,

France. INSEE.
1946.1   Dénombrement de la population,   Enumeration of the population,
          1946.   Paris, Impr. Nationale,   1946.
          Presses Univ. de France, 1947.   [TXU, BC, PRC, RPI
          925p.

France. INSEE.
          Résultats statistiques du   Statistical results of the gen-
          recensement général de la popu-   eral population census taken
          lation effectué le 10 mars 1946.   March 10, 1946.
          Paris, Impr. Nationale, Presses
          Univ. de France, 1948-1953.
          Vols. I-VII in 10v.
.2-1   Population légale ou de   De jure or habitual resident
          résidence habituelle. Appendice: population. Appendix: popu-
          population des territoires fran-   lation of the French Overseas
          çais d'outre-mer et des pays   Territories and of foreign
          étrangers. 1948. 162p.   countries.
                                                  [TXU, UN, PRC, RPI
.2-2   Population présente total.   Total de facto population.
          1953. 434p. folding map.   [TXU, UN, PRC, RPI
          Population active: Economically active population:
.2-3-1   Ensemble de la popula-   Total.
          tion active. 1952. ii, 543p.   [TXU, UN, PRC, RPI
.2-3-2   Étrangers et naturalisés.   Aliens and naturalized citizens.
          1953. 142p.   [TXU, UN, PRC, RPI
.2-4   Familles. 1953. cxiv,   Families.
          157p.   [TXU, UN, PRC, RPI
.2-5   Infirmes. 1950. lxxi,   The disabled.
          38p.   [TXU, UN, PRC, RPI
.2-5s   Supplément. Les aveugles   Supplement. The blind and deaf-
          et les sourds-muets déclarés au   mutes declared in the general
          recensement général de la popu-   population census taken March
          lation effectué le 10 mars 1946.   10, 1946. Detailed results by
          Résultats détaillés par départe-   department.
          ment. 1950. 25p.   [TXU, UN, PRC, RPI
          Habitations: Dwellings:
.2-6-1   Immeubles. 1953. 74p.   Appartment buildings.
                                                  [TXU, UN, PRC, RPI

.2-6-2   Ménages et logements.   Households and housing.
   1949. xliii, 393p.   [TXU, UN, PRC, RPI
.2-7   Exploitations agricoles.   Agriculture.
   1950. lxiv, [4], cclvi, [2]p.   TXU, BC, UN, PRC, RPI

France. INSEE.
   Résultats statistiques du   Statistical results of the gen-
recensement général de la popu-   eral population census taken
lation effectué le 10 mars 1946.   March 10, 1946. De jure popula-
Population légale. État civil   tion. Marital status and pre-
et activité professionnelle de   sent occupation of the de facto
la population présente. Familles,   population. Families, appart-
immeubles, ménages et logements.   ments, households and housing.
Paris, Impr. Nationale et Presses
Univ. de France, 1951. Tomes I-
VI.
1946.3-1 through 1946.3-6. [All are variously paged.] 1. Ain à Cantal./
2. Charente à Gard./3. Haute-Garonne à Loiret./4. Lot à Oise./5. Orne
à Seine./6. Seine inférieure à Belfort. [TXU, BC, PRC, RPI

France. INSEE.
1954.1   Recensement de 1954. Popu-   Census of 1954. Population of
lation de la France: départe-   France: departments, arrondissements, arrondissements, cantons,   ments, cantons and communes.
et communes. (Metropole)   (Mother country).
Paris, Impr. Nationale, Presses   [NYPL, LC, UN, PRC, RPI
Univ. de France, 1954. [6],
985, [2]p.

France. INSEE.
.2   Villes et agglomérations ur-   Cities and urban agglomerations.
baines. Répartition de la popu-   Distribution of the population by
lation par catégories de communes   types of communes or agglomera-
ou d'agglomérations. Liste des   tions. List of cities and urban
villes et agglomérations urbaines   agglomerations having changed
ayant changé de catégorie entre   type between 1946 and 1954.
1946 et 1954.   Paris, Impr.   [TXU, PRC, RPI
Nationale, 1955. 115, 26p.

France. INSEE.
   Recensement général de la   General population census of May
population de mai 1954. Résul-   1954. Results of the one-in-
tats du sondage au 1/20ème: twenty sample: population, house-
Population, ménage, logements.   holds, dwellings.
Paris, Impre. Nationale, Presses
Univ. de France, 1955. 91 parts.
1954.3-1 through 1954.3-91. 1. Ain. 34p./2. Aisne. 38p./3. Allier. 37p./
4. Basses-Alpes. 31p./5. Hautes-Alpes. 33p./6. Alpes-Maritimes.
43p./7. Ardèche. 32p./8. Ardennes. 35p./9. Ariège. 31p./10. Aube.
39p./11. Aude. 35p./12. Aveyron. 36p./13. Bouches-du-Rhône. 42p./
14. Calvados. 44p./15. Cantal. 32p./16. Charente. 35p./17. Charente-Maritime. 38p./18. Cher. 35p./19. Corrèze. 35p./20. Corse.

[Not published]./21. Côte-d'Or. 37p./22. Côtes-du-Nord. 34p./23. Creuse. 31p./24. Dordogne. 36p./25. Doubs. 35p./26. Drôme. 35p./ 27. Eure. 34p./28. Eure-et-Loir. 33p./29. Finistère. 42p./30. Gard. 42p./31. Haute-Garonne. 37p./32. Gers. 33p./33. Gironde. 49p./34. Hérault. 42p./35. Ille-et-Vilaine. 39p./36. Indre. 33p./37. Indre-et-Loire. 41p./38. Isère. 44p./39. Jurs. 33p./40. Landes. 35p./ 41. Loir-et-Cher. 33p./42. Loire. 44p./43. Haute-Loire. 33p./44. Loire-Inférieure. 44p./45. Loiret. 43p./46. Lot. 33p./47. Lot-et-Garonne. 33p./48. Lozère. 31p./49. Maine-et-Loire. 40p./50. Manche. 34p./51. Marne. 41p./52. Haute-Marne. 35p./53. Mayenne. 33p./54. Meurthe-et-Moselle. 49p./55. Meuse. 33p./56. Morbihan. 35p./57. Moselle. 52./58. Nièvre. 33p./59. Nord. 106p./60. Oise. [2], 38p./ 61. Orne. 33p./62. Pas-de-Calais. 50p./63. Puy-de-Dôme. 42p./64. Basses-Pyrénées. 38p./65. Hautes-Pyrénées. 33p./66. Pyrénées-Orientales. 33p./67. Bas-Rhin. 46p./68. Haut-Rhin. 43p./69. Rhône. 57p./70. Haute-Saône. 31p./71. Saône-et-Loire. 40p./72. Sarthe. 37p./73. Savoie. 34p./74. Haute-Savoie. 33p./75. Seine. 180p./ 76. Seine-Maritime. 79p./77. Seine-et-Marne. 38p./78. Seine-et-Oise. 126p./79. Deux-Sèvres. 33p./80. Somme. 40p./81. Tarn. 38p./82. Tarn-et-Garonne. 33p./83. Var. 41p./84. Vaucluse. 33p./85. Vendée. 33p./86. Vienne. 35p./87. Haute-Vienne. 37p./88. Vosges. 36p./89. Yonne. 35p./90. Territoire de Belfort. 33p./91. (RP) Région de Paris. 135, [2]p, [TXU, PRC, RPI

France. INSEE.
Recensement général de la population de mai 1954. Résultats du sondage au 1/20ème: population, ménages, logements. Paris, Impr. Nationale, Presses Univ. de France, 1956. 2 parts.

General population census of May 1954. Results of the one-in-twenty sample: population, households, housing.

1954.4-1　France entière. 70p.

All France.
[BC, PRC

.4-2　Tableaux synoptiques. Départements, grandes agglomérations, grandes villes. 166p.

Synoptic tables. Departments, large agglomerations, large cities.
[TXU, UN, PRC, RPI

France. INSEE.
.5　Recensement général de la population de mai 1954. population légale (résultats statistiques). Population, superficie. Densité de population des principales circonscriptions administratives. Migration apparents, logements et maisons. Paris, Impr. Nationale, Presses Univ. de France, 1956. 307p.

General population census of May 1954. De jure population (statistical results). Population, area. Population density of principal administrative divisions. Apparent migration, dwellings and houses.
[TXU, UN, PRC, RPI

France. INSEE.
Recensement général de la population de mai 1954. Résultats du sondage au 1/20ème:

General population census of May 1954. Results of the one-in-twenty sample: economically

Population active.   Paris,
Impr. Nationale, Presses Univ.
de France, 1958-1960. 2 parts.
.6-1   Structure professionnelle.
(Activité collective, profession
individuelle, catégorie socio-
professionnelle, status).
France entière. Départements,
grandes agglomérations, grandes
villes. 1958. 424p.
.6-2   État civil et nationalité.
France entière. Départements,
grandes agglomérations, grandes
villes. 1960. 166p.

active population.

Occupational structure. (Collective activity, individual occupation, socio-occupational class,
status). All France. Departments, large agglomerations,
large cities.
[TXU, UN, PRC, RPI
Marital status and nationality.
All France. Departments, large
agglomerations, large cities.
[TXU, UN, PRC, RPI

France. INSEE.
Recensement général de la
population de mai 1954. Résultats statistiques: population,
ménages, logements, maisons.
Paris, Impr. Nationale, 1959-
1961. Parts 1-90, errata volume.

General population census of
May 1954. Statistical results:
population, households, dwellings,
houses.

1954.7-1 through 1954.7-91. [One volume for each Department and one "errata."
No volume for Ville de Paris.] 1. Ain. 1960. 61p./2. Aisne. 1959.
66p./3. Allier. 1960. 59p./4. Basses-Alpes. 1960. 46p./5. Hautes-
Alpes. 1960. 46p./6. Alpes-Maritimes. 1960. 68p./7. Ardèche.
1960. 58p./8. Ardennes. 1959. 61p./9. Ariège. 1960. 47p./10. Aube.
1959. 72p./11. Aude. 1960. 60p./12. Aveyron. 1960. 60p./13.
Bouches-du-Rhône. 1960. 67p./14. Calvados. 1959. 91p./15. Cantal.
1960. 47p./16. Charente. 1960. 59p./17. Charente-Maritime. 1960.
61p./18. Cher. 1960. 58p./19. Corrèze. 1960. 47p./20. Corse.
1961. 62p./21. Côte-d'Or. 1960. 76p./22. Côtes-du-Nord. 1959.
60p./23. Creuse. 1960. 46p./24. Dordogne. 1960. 63p./25. Doubs.
1960. 26p./26. Drôme. 1960. 59p./27. Eure. 1959. 64p./28. Eure-
et-Loir. 1960. 49p./29. Finistère. 1959. 78p./30. Gard. 1960.
71p./31. Haute-Garonne. 1960. 83p./32. Gers. 1960. 49p./33. Gironde. 1959. 93p./34. Hérault. 1960. 71p./35. Ille-et-Vilaine.
1959. 72p./36. Indre. 1960. 48p./37. Indre-et-Loire. 1960. 77p./
38. Isère. 1960. 91p./39. Jura. 1960. 39p./40. Landes. 1959.
48p./41. Loir-et-Cher. 1960. 47p./42. Loire. 1960. 82p./43. Haute-
Loire. 1960. 57p./44. Loire-Atlantique. 1960. 79p./45. Loiret.
1960. 78p./46. Lot. 1960. 47p./47. Lot-et-Garonne. 1959. 58p./
48. Lozère. 1960. 45p./49. Maine-et-Loire. 1960. 72p./50. Manche.
1959. 63p./51. Marne. 1959. 75p./52. Haute-Marne. 1959. 53p./
53. Mayenne. 1960. 47p./54. Meurthe-et-Moselle. 1960. 99p./55.
Meuse. 1960. 61p./56. Morbihan. 1959. 59p./57. Moselle. 1960.
106p./58. Nièvre. 1960. 56p./59. Nord. 1960. 185p./60. Oise.
1961. 73p./61. Orne. 1959. 61p./62. Pas-de-Calais. 1960. 99p./
63. Puy-de-Dôme. 1960. 88p./64. Basses-Pyrénées. 1959. 62p./65.
Hautes-Pyrénées. 1960. 50p./66. Pyrénées-Orientales. 1960. 46p./
67. Bas-Rhin. 1960. 91p./68. Haut-Rhin. 1960. 86p./69. Rhône.

1960. 97p./70. Haute-Saône. 1959. 58p./71. Saône-et-Loire. 1960.
72p./72. Sarthe. 1960. 72p./73. Savoie. 1960. 59p./74. Haute-
Savoie. 1960. 58p./75. Seine. 1961. 162p./76. Seine-Maritime.
1960.123p./77. Seine-et-Marne. 1961. 71p./78. Seine-et-Oise. 1961.
71p./79. Deux-Sèvres. 1959. 59p./80. Somme. 1959. 86p./81. Tarn.
1960. 82p./82p. Tarn-et-Garonne. 1960. 66p./83. Var. 1960. 68p./
84. Vaucluse. 1960. 65p./85. Vendée. 1960. 58p./86. Vienne. 1960.
57p./87. Haute-Vienne. 1960. 67p./88. Vosges. 1960. 61p./89. Yonne.
1960. 61p./90. Territoire de Belfort. 1960. 44p./91. Errata. n.d.
111p. [TXU, BC, PRC, RPI

France. INSEE.
.8   Les zones de peuplement in-   The zones of industrial or urban
      dustriel ou urbain. Paris,   settlement.
      Impr. Nationale, 1962. 170p.   [LC, PRC, RPI

France. INSEE.
.9   Code divers. Chiffrement   Divers codes. Encoding of indi-
      des bulletins individuels et   vidual lists and housing sched-
      feuilles de logement. (Recen-   ules (Population census of 1954).
      sement de la population de 1954).   [BC , RPI
      Paris, Impr. Nationale, 1954.
      29p.

France. INSEE.
      Recensement de 1962. Paris,   Census of 1962.
      Impr. des Journaux Officiels,
      1962-1964. 6 parts in 8v.
1962.1-1   Population de la France.   Population of France. Depart-
      Départements, arrondissements,   ments, districts, cantons, com-
      cantons, communes. 1962. xi,   munes.
      1141p.   [LC, BC, PRC, RPI, RIR
   .1-2   Villes de plus de 5.000   Cities of more than 5,000 inhab-
      habitants. 1962. 24p.   itants.
                                             [LC, PRC, RPI, RIR
             Population légale et sta-   De jure population and complimen-
      tistiques communales complémen-   tary communal statistics.
      taires. 1963. Vols. I-III.
1962.1-3-1 through 1962.1-3-3. [All are variously paged.] 1. Ain à Haute-
Garonne./2. Gers à Oise./3. Orne à Territoire de Belfort. [BC, PRC,
RPI, RIR
   .1-4   Population légale. Résul-   De jure population. Statistical
      tats statistiques. 1964. 150p.   results.
                                             [BC, PRC, RPI, RIR
   .1-5   Villes et agglomérations   Cities and urban agglomerations.
      urbaines. 1964. 216p.   [BC, UN, PRC, RPI, RIR
   .1-6   Les zones de peuplement   The zones of industrial or urban
      industriel ou urbain. 1964.   settlement.
      134p.   [BC, PRC, RPI, RIR

France. INSEE.
      Recensement de la population   Census of the population of March
      de mars 1962. Paris, 1964.   1962.
      2 parts in 4v.

Population, logements,
immeubles des communes rurales
classés par canton. Tomes I-II.
1962.2-1-1   Départements 01 à 44.
Variously paged.
.2-1-2   Départements 45 à 90.
Variously paged.
Population, logements,
immeubles des communes urbaines.
Tomes I-II.
.2-2-1   Départements 01 à 44.
Variously paged.
.2-2-2   Départements 45 à 90.
Variously paged.

Population, dwellings, housing of
rural communities classified by
canton.

[BC, PRC, RPI, RIR

[BC, PRC, RPI, RIR
Population, dwellings, housing of
urban communities.

[PRC, RPI, RIR

[PRC, RPI, RIR

France. INSEE.
Recensement de la population
de 1962. Exploitation exhaustive. Depouillement electroni-
que centralisé.   Paris, 1964-
1965. 2 parts.
.3-1   Codes. 1965. 236p.

.3-2   Programmes de tableaux.
1964. 301p.

Population census of 1962. Complete tabulation. Centralized
count by electronic means.

Codes.
[UN, RPI
Programs for tables.
[UN, RPI

France. INSEE.
Recensement de la population
de 1962. Sondage au 1/20.
Paris, 1963. 2 parts in 4v.
.4-1   Depouillement sur ordina-
teur. Procedure de depouillement. Dessins des bandes.
Codes. [6], 283p. (Document
no. 711)
Depouillement electroni-
que centralisé. Programme de
tableaux. 3 parts. (Document
no. 727)
.4-2-1   [4], 365p.
.4-2-2   [4], 295p.
.4-2-3   [6], 195p.

Population census of 1962. One-
in-twenty sample.

Computerized count. Method of
count. Outline of tapes. Codes.
[BC, RPI, RIR

Centralized electronic count.
Program of tables.

[BC, RPI
[BC, RPI
[BC, RPI

France. INSEE.
.5   Code no. 1 du recensement de
la population de 1962. Code geo-
graphique: départements, arrondissements, cantons, communes,
et agglomérations. France entière.
Paris, 1962. variously paged.

Code No. 1 of the population census of 1962. Geographic code:
departments, districts, cantons,
types of communes & agglomerations.
All France.
[UN, RPI

France. INSEE.
Recensement général de la
population de 1962. Résultats
du sondage au 1/20: population,
ménages, logements, immeubles.
Fascicules regionaux. Paris,
1964. 22v.

General population census, 1962.
Results of the one-in-twenty sample: population, households,
housing, buildings. Regional
fascicules.

.6-0   F.E. Récapitulation pour
la France entière. 1964. 32p.

F.E. Summary for all France.
[UN, PRC, RPI, RIR

1962.6-1.1 through 1962.6-9.2. 1.1 Région Parisienne. 76p./2.1 Champagne.
68p./2.2 Picardie. 60p./2.3 Haute-Normandie. 56p./2.4 Centre. 88p./
3.1 Nord. 75p./4.1 Lorraine. 80p./4.2 Alsace. 56p./4.3 Franche-
Comté. 68p./5.1 Basse-Normandie. 60p./5.2 Pays de la Loire. 83p./
5.3 Bretagne. 72p./6.1 Limousin. 59p./6.2 Auvergne. 67p./7.1 Poitou-
Charentes. 63p./7.2 Aquitaine. 75p./7.3 Midi-Pyrénées. 99p./8.1
Bourgogne. 67p./8.2 Rhône-Alpes. 108p./9.1 Languedoc. 80p./9.2 Provence-Côte d'Azur. 99p. [UN, PRC, RPI, RIR

France. INSEE.
Recensement général de la
population de 1962. Résultats
du sondage au 1/20 pour la France
entière. Paris, Impr. des Journaux Officiels, 1964-1968. 4
parts.

General population census, 1962.
Results of the one-in-twenty sample for all France.

.7-1   Population active. 1964.
183p.

Economically active population.
[PRC, BC, RPI, RIR

.7-2   Structure de population
totale. 1965. 130p.

Structure of the total population.
[LC, PRC, BC, RPI, RIR

.7-3   Logements, immeubles.
1965. 195p.

Housing, buildings.
[PRC, BC, RPI, RIR

.7-4   Ménages, familles. 1968.
241p.

Households and families.
[PRC, BC, RPI, RIR

France. INSEE.
.8   Recensement général de la
population de 1962. Résultats
du sondage au 1/20 et de l'exploitation exhaustive pour la
France entière. Migrations,
1954-1962. Paris, Direction
des Journaux Officiels, 1973.
355p.

General population census, 1962.
Results of the one-in-twenty sample and the complete tabulation
for all France. Migration, 1954-
1962.
[PRC, RPI

France. INSEE.
Recensement général de la
population de 1962. Résultats
du dépouillement exhaustif.
Population par région agricole.
Fascicules départementaux.
Paris, [pre-1964]. 78v.

General population census, 1962.
Results of the complete count.
Population by agricultural sec-
tion. Departmental fascicules.

1962.9-1 through 1962.9-90. 1. Ain. 45p./2. Aisne. [Not pub'd]/3. Aillier.
31p./4. Alpes (Basses). [Not pub'd]/5. Alpes (Hautes). [Not pub'd]/

6. Alpes-Maritimes. [Not pub'd]./7. Ardèche. 41p./8. Ardennes.
26p./9. Ariège. [45]p./10. Aube. 42p./11. Aude. 38p./12. Aveyron.
[71]p./13. Bouches-du-Rhône. [Not pub'd]./14. Calvados. 29p./15.
Cantal. 51p./16. Charente. 56p./17. Charente-Maritime. 44p./18.
Cher. 39p./19. Corrèze. 47p./20. Corse. [Not pub'd]./21. Côte-d'Or.
37p./22. Côtes-du-Nord. 32p./23. Creuse. 31p./24. Dordogne. 36p./
25. Doubs. [35]p./26. Drôme. 53p./27. Eure. 53p./28. Eure-et-Loire.
31p./29. Finistère. 48p./30. Gard. 46p./31. Garonne (Haute). [63]p./
32. Gers. [69]p./33. Gironde. 58p./34. Hérault. 42p./35. Ille-et-
Vilaine. 40p./36. Indre. 31p./37. Indre-et-Loire. 49p./38. Isère.
31p./39. Jura. 51p./40. Landes. 36p./41. Loir-et-Cher. 51p./42.
Loire. 53p./43. Loire (Haute). 43p./44. Loire-Atlantique. 45p./45.
Loiret. 47p./46. Lot. [66]p./47. Lot-et-Garonne. 40p./48. Lozère.
30p./49. Maine-et-Loire. 26p./50. Manche. 37p./51. Marne. 39p./52.
Marne (Haute). 42p./53. Mayenne. 23p./54. Meurthe-et-Moselle. 35p./
55. Meuse. 27p./56. Morbihan. 28p./57. Moselle. 31p./58. Nièvre.
28p./59. Nord. [Not pub'd]./60. Oise. [Not pub'd]./61. Orne. 33p./
62. Pas-de-Calais. [Not pub'd]./63. Puy-de-Dôme. 63p./64. Pyrénées
(Basses). 40p./65. Pyrénées (Hautes). [73]p./66. Pyrénées-Orientales.
46p./67. Rhin (Bas). 31p./68. Rhin (Haut). 43p./69. Rhône. 37p./
70. Saône (Haute). 43p./71. Saône-et-Loire. 43p./72. Sarthe. 45p./
73. Savoie. 57p./74. Savoie (Haute). 77p./75. Seine. [See Seine-et-
Oise]./76. Seine-Maritime. 33p./77. Seine-et-Marne. Région Parisienne
I. 61p./78. Seine-et-Oise; Seine. Région Parisienne II. 126p./79.
Sèvres (Deux). 56p./80. Somme. [Not pub'd]./81. Tarn. [69]p./82.
Tarn-et-Garonne. [89]p./83. Var. [Not pub'd]./84. Vaucluse. [Not
pub'd]./85. Vendée. 35p./86. Vienne. 48p./87. Vienne (Haute). 23p./
88. Vosges. 39p./89. Yonne. 37p./90. Belfort (Territoire de). 27p.
[PRC, RPI, RIR

France. INSEE.
    Recensement général de la   General population census, 1962.
population de 1962. Résultats   Results of the complete count.
du dépouillement exhaustif.
Paris, 1966-67. 2 parts in 96v.
1962.10-1-1 through 1962.10-1-°95. 1. Ain. 54p./2. Aisne. 82p./3. Allier.
64p./4. Basses-Alpes. 47p./5. Hautes-Alpes. 47p./6. Alpes-Maritimes.
75p./7. Ardèche. 49p./8. Ardennes. 63p./9. Ariège. 44p./10. Aube.
58p./11. Aude. 58p./12. Aveyron. 57p./13. Bouches-du-Rhône. 97p./
14. Calvados. 73p./15. Cantal. 48p./16. Charente. 62p./17. Charente-
Maritime. 71p./18. Cher. 60p./19. Corrèze. 56p./20. Corse. [Not
pub'd]./21. Côte-d'Or. 61p./22. Côtes-du-Nord. 58p./23. Creuse.
44p./24. Dordogne. 64p./25. Doubs. 68p./26. Drôme. 65p./27. Eure.
57p./28. Eure-et-Loure. 61p./29. Finistère. 72p./30. Gard. 72p./
31. Haute-Garonne. 60p./32. Gers. 54p./33. Gironde. 75p./34. Hérault. 69p./35. Ille-et-Vilaine. 65p./36. Indre. 55p./37. Indre-et-
Loire. 56p./38. Isère. 71p./39. Jura. 60p./40. Landes. 57p./41.
Loir-et-Cher. 52p./42. Loire. 80p./43. Haute-Loire. 52p./44. Loire-
Atlantique. 71p./45. Loiret. 61p./46. Lot. 49p./47. Lot-et-Garonne.
53p./48. Lozère. 43p./49. Maine-et-Loire. 65p./50. Manche. 64p./
51 Marne. 68p./53. Haute-Marne. 59p./53. Mayenne. 48p./54. Meurthe-
et-Moselle. 91p./55. Meuse. 59p./56. Morbihan. 60p./57. Moselle.
105p./58. Nièvre. 56p./59. Nord. 163p./60. Oise. 72p./61. Orne.

55p./62. Pas-de-Calais. 143p./63. Puy-de-Dôme. 66p./64. Basses-Pyrénées. 68p./65. Hautes-Pyrénées. 58p./66. Pyrénées-Orientales. 55p./67. Bas-Rhin. 70p./68. Haut-Rhin. 68p./69. Rhône. 71p./70. Haute-Saône. 51p./71. Saône-et-Loire. 83p./72. Sarthe. 57p./73. Savoie. 57p./74. Haute-Savoie. 60p./75. Seine. 84p./°75. Paris. 54p./76. Seine-Maritime. 85p./77. Seine-et-Marne. 70p./78. Seine-et-Oise. 94p./°78. Yvelines. 56p./79. Deux-Sèvres. 53p./80. Somme. 70p./81. Tarn. 65p./82. Tarn-et-Garonne. 47p./83. Var. 62p./84. Vaucluse. 58p./85. Vendée. 52p./86. Vienne. 60p./87. Haute-Vienne. 55p./88. Vosges. 62p./89. Yonne. 59p./90. Territoire de Belfort. 49p./°91. Essone. 48p./°92. Hauts-de-Seine. 42p./°93. Sein-Saint-Denis. 46p./°94. Val-de-Marne. 46p./°95. Val-d'Oise. 55p. [PRC, RPI, RIR

Note: In 1964, two departments were divided into seven.

.10-2 Population, ménages, logements. Tableaux synoptiques (départements, régions, grandes agglomérations, grandes villes).
1967. 93p.

Population, households, housing.
Synoptic tables (departments,
regions, large agglomerations,
large cities).
[RPI, RIR

France. INSEE.
.11 Les infirmes recensés en 1962.
Extrait des résultats du recensement général de la population du
7 mars 1962. Paris, Impr. Nationale, 1968. 51p.

The disabled enumerated in 1962.
Extract of the results of the
general population census of
March 7, 1962.
[PRC, RPI, RIR

France. INSEE.
Code des metiers. Paris,
Impr. Nationale, 1968. 2v.
1968.1-1 Code no. 2 du recensement
de la population de 1968. Index
alphabetique détaillé. 245p.

Occupations code.

Code no. 2 of the population census of 1968. Detailled alphabetical index.
[PRC

.1-2 Code no. 6 du recensement
de la population de 1968. Index
alphabetique des principales
designations de metiers. ix,
38p.

Code No. 6 of the population census of 1968. Alphabetical index
of major occupation groups.
[PRC

France. INSEE.
Recensement de 1968. Paris,
Dir. des Journaux Officiels,
1968-70. 5v.
.2-1 Tableaux statistiques de
population légale. Communes de
plus de 2.000 habitants. 1968.
100p.

Census of 1968.

Statistical tables of the de jure
population. Communes of 2,000
and more inhabitants.
[PRC

.2-2 Population de la France.
Départements, arrondissements,
cantons et communes. 1969.
1200p.

Population of France. Departments,
districts, cantons and communes.
[PRC

.2-3   Tableaux essentiels du   Essential tables of the one-in-
sondage au 1/20. 1969. 120p.   twenty sample.
(Collections de l'INSEE, Série   [
D3)
.2-4   Premièrs résultats d'en-   First total results.
semble. 1969.   p.   [
.2-5   Population née dans un   Population born in an overseas
département ou territoire d'   department or territory and resi-
outre-mer et résident en Metro-   dent in continental France.
pole. 1970. 142p.   [PRC

France. INSEE.
    Recensement de 1968. Popu-   Census of 1968. De jure popula-
lation légale et statistiques   tion and complementary community
communales complémentaires   statistics (demographic changes
(évolutions démographiques 1962-   1962-1968 and 1954-1962).
1968 et 1954-1962). Paris,
Impr. Nationale, 1969. Tomes
I-VI.
1968.3-1 through 1968.3-6. [All are variously paged.] 1. Ain à Charente./
2. Charente-Maritime à Gers./3. Gironde à Maine-et-Loire./4. Manche à
Orne./5. Pas-de-Calais à Seine-Maritime./6. Seine-et-Marne à Val-
d'Oise. [PRC

France. INSEE.
    Recensement général de la   General population census, 1968.
population 1968.   Paris, 1970.
2v.
.4-1   Villes et agglomérations   Cities and urban agglomerations.
urbaines. Délimitation 1968.   1968 boundaries. (Demographic
(Évolutions démographiques 1962-   changes 1962-1968 and 1954-1962).
1968 et 1954-1962). xxxi, 750p.   [PRC
.4-2   Les zones de peuplement   Zones of industrial and urban
industriel ou urbain. Délimi-   settlement. 1968 boundaries.
tation 1968. (Évolutions démo-   (Demographic changes 1962-1968
graphiques 1962-1968 et 1954-   and 1954-1962).
1962). xxxi, 925p.   [PRC

France. INSEE.
    Recensement général de la   General population census, 1968.
population de 1968. Résultats   Results of the one-in-twenty
du sondage au 1/20 pour la France   sample for all France.
entière. Paris, Impr. Nationale,
1971.   2v.
.5-1   Formation. 246p.   Formation.
                                             [PRC
.5-2   Population active. 217p.   Economically active population.
                                             [PRC

France. INSEE.
.6   Recensement général de la   General population census, 1968.
population de 1968. Résultats   Results of the one-in-twenty
du sondage au 1/20. Logements-   sample. Dwellings-buildings.

immeubles. Paris, Impr.   [PRC
Nationale, 1972. 325p.

France. INSEE.
  Recensement général de la   General population census, 1968.
population de 1968. Résultats   Results of the one-in-twenty and
des sondages au 1/20 et au 1/4.   one-in-four samples.
Paris, Impr. Nationale, 1972-
1973. 2v.
.7-1   Structure de la population   Structure of the total population.
totale. Sexe, âge, état matri-   Sex, age, marital status, nation-
monial, nationalité, catégorie   ality, category of population, etc.
de population, etc. 1972. 205p.   [PRC, UN
.7-2   Ménages-familles. 1973.   Households-families.
159p.   [PRC

France. INSEE.
  Recensement général de la   General population census, 1968.
population de 1968. Résultats   Results of the one-in-four sam-
du sondage au 1/4. Population-   ple. Population-households-
ménages-logements-immeubles.   housing-buildings. Departmental
Fascicules départementaux.   fascicules.
Paris, 1971. 96v.
.8-0   Agglomeration de Paris.   Metropolitan Paris.
186p.   [PRC
1968.8-1 through 1968.8-95. 1. Ain. 56p./2. Aisne. 68p./3. Allier. 37p./
4. Alpes-de-Haute-Provence. 48p./5. Hautes-Alpes. 52p./6. Alpes-
Maritimes. 112p./7. Ardèche. 56p./8. Ardennes. 60p./9. Ariège.
48p./10. Aube. 56p./11. Aude. 56p./12. Aveyron. 60p./13. Bouches-
du-Rhône. 106p./14. Calvados. 60p./15. Cantal. 52p./16. Charente.
56p./17. Charente-Maritime. 68p./18. Cher. 60p./19. Corrèze. 56p./
20. Corse. 48p./21. Côte-d'Or. 56p./22. Côtes-du-Nord. 56p./23.
Creuse. 48p./24. Dordogne. 56p./25. Doubs. 60p./26. Drôme. 64p./
27. Eure. 56p./28. Eure-et-Loire. 56p./29. Finistère. 64p./30. Gard.
68p./31. Haute-Garonne. 82p./32. Gers. 52p./33. Gironde. 90p./34.
Hérault. 64p./35. Ille-et-Vilaine. 64p./36. Indre. 52p./37. Indre-
et-Loire. 82p./38. Isère. 94p./39. Jura. 56p./40. Landes. 56p./
41. Loir-et-Cher. 52p./42. Loire. 94p./43. Haute-Loire. 52p./44.
Loire-Atlantique. 90p./45. Loiret. 60p./46. Lot. 48p./47. Lot-et-
Garonne. 56p./48. Lozère. 48p./49. Maine-et-Loire. 64p./50. Manche.
56p./51. Marne. 68p./52. Haute-Marne. 56p./53. Mayenne. 52p./54.
Meurthe-et-Moselle. 98p./55. Meuse. 52p./56. Morbihan. 60p./57. Moselle. 76p./58. Nièvre. 52p./59. Nord. 177p./60. Oise. 60p./61.
Orne. 56p./62. Pas-de-Calais. 106p./63. Puy-de-Dôme. 82p./64. Pyrénées-Atlantiques. 64p./65. Hautes-Pyrénées. 56p./66. Pyrénées-Orientales. 56p./67. Bas-Rhin. 86p./68. Haut-Rhin. 76p./69. Rhône. 94p./
70. Haute-Saône. 52p./71. Saône-et-Loire. 72p./72. Sarthe. 56p./73.
Savoie. 60p./74. Haute-Savoie. 68p./75. Ville de Paris. 132p./76.
Seine-Maritime. 128p./77. Seine-et-Marne. 68p./78. Yvelines. 68p./
79. Deux-Sèvres. 52p./80. Somme. 60p./81. Tarn. 64p./82. Tarn-et-
Garonne. 52p./83. Var. 86p./84. Vaucluse. 68p./85. Vendée. 56p./
86. Vienne. 60p./87. Haute-Vienne. 56p./88. Vosges. 56p./89. Yonne.
56p./90. Territoire de Belfort. 56p./91. Essone. 48p./92. Haute-de-
Seine. 100p./93. Seine-Saint-Denis. 72p./94. Val-de-Marne. 72p./95.
Val-d'Oise. 60p. [PRC

France.   INSEE.

Recensement général de la population de 1968. Résultats du sondage au 1/4. Population-ménages-logements-immeubles. Fascicules régionaux. Paris, Impr. Nationale, 1972. 23v.	General population census, 1968. Results of the one-in-four sample. Population-households-housing-buildings. Regional fascicules.

.9–0   Récapitulation pour la
France entière. 48p.

General population census, 1968.
Summary for all France.
[PRC

1968.9–1 through 1968.9–9.4. [All have 48 pages] 1.1 Parisienne./2.1 Champagne./2.2 Picardie./2.3 Haute-Normandie./2.4 Centre./2.5 Basse-Normandie./2.6 Bourgogne./3.1 Nord./4.1 Lorraine./4.2 Alsace./4.3 Franche-Comté./5.2 Pays de la Loire./5.3 Bretagne./5.4 Poitou-Charentes./7.2 Aquitaine./7.3 Midi-Pyrénées./7.4 Limousin./8.2 Rhône-Alpes./8.3 Auvergne./9.1 Languedoc-Roussillon./9.3 Provence-Côte./9.4 Corse. [PRC

France.   INSEE.

Code des metiers. (Code No. 64 du recensement de la population de 1975). Paris, 1975. 3v.	Occupations code. (Code No. 64 of the population census of 1975).

1975.0–1   Index alphabetique abrégé.
45p.

Abridged alphabetical index.
[

.0–2   Index alphabetique détaillé. 131p.

Detailed alphabetical index.
[PRC

.0–3   Index analytique. 145p.

Analytical index.
[PRC

France.   INSEE.

Recensement général de la population de 1975. Population du département de... Arrondissements, cantons, communes. Paris, [1976]. 95v.	General population census, 1975. Population of the department of ... Districts, cantons and communes.

1975.1–1 through 1975.1–95. [All are preceded by two unnumbered pages.] 1. Ain. 12p./2. Aisne. 20p./3. Allier. 8p./4. Alpes-de-Haute-Provence. 10p./5. Hautes-Alpes. 6p./6. Alpes-Maritimes. 6p./7. Ardèche. 9p./ 8. Ardennes. 14p./9. Ariège. 9p./10. Aube. 12p./11. Aude. 11p./12. Aveyron. 10p./13. Bouches-du-Rhône. 6p./14. Calvados. 19p./15. Cantal. 7p./16. Charente. 11p./17. Charente-Maritime. 13p./18. Cher. 8p./19. Corrèze. 8p./20. Corse. 11p./21. Côte-d'Or. 18p./22. Côtes-du-Nord. 11p./23. Creuse. 7p./24. Dordogne. 15p./25. Doubs. 17p./ 26. Drôme. 10p./27. Eure. 16p./28. Eure-et-Loir. 11p./29. Finistère. 10p./30. Gard. 10p./31. Haute-Garonne. 14p./32. Gers. 11p./33. Gironde. 13p./34. Hérault. 10p./35. Ille-et Vilaine. 11p./36. Indre. 7p./37. Indre-et-Loire. 8p./38. Isère. 14p./39. Jura. 15p./40. Landes 9p./41. Loir-et-Cher. 8p./42. Loire. 11p./43. Haute-Loire. 7p./44. Loire-Atlantique. 8p./45. Loiret. 11p./46. Lot. 9p./47. Lot-et-Garonne. 10p./48. Lozère. 6p./49. Maine-et-Loire. 11p./50. Manche. 17p./51. Marne. 16p./52. Haute-Marne. 20p./53. Mayenne. 8p./54. Meurthe-et-Moselle. 15p./55. Meuse. 17p./56. Morbihan. 8p./57. Moselle. 20p./58. Nièvre. 9p./59. Nord. 17p./60. Oise. 16p./61. Orne. 12p./62. Pas-de-Calais. 22p./63. Puy-de-Dôme. 12p./64. Pyrénées-Atlantiques. 15p./65. Hautes-Pyrénées. 11p./66. Pyrénées-Orientales. 8p./67. Bas-Rhin. 16p./68. Haut-Rhin. 11p./69. Rhône. 10p./70. Haute-Saône. 15p./71. Saône-et-Loire. 15p./72. Sarthe. 9p./73. Savoie. 9p./74. Haute-Savoie. 10p./75. Ville de Paris. 2p./76. Seine-Maritime. 18p./77. Seine-et-Marne. 13p./78. Yvelines. 9p./79. Deux-Sèvres. 12p./80. Somme. 19p./81. Tarn. 9p./82. Tarn-et-Garonne. 6p./83. Var. 7p./84. Vaucluse. 5p./85. Vendée. 9p./86. Vienne. 10p./87. Haute-Vienne. 8p./88. Vosges. 12p./89. Yonne. 14p./90. Territoire de Belfort. 4p./91. Essonne. 6p./92. Hauts-de-Seine. 5p./93. Seine-Saint-Denis. 4p./94. Val-de-Marne. 4p./95. Val-d'Oise. 6p. [PRC

France. INSEE.
.2   Recensement général de la population de 1975. Tableaux statistiques de population légale. Population légale des communes de plus de 2.000 habitants. Paris, Impr. Nationale, 1977. 99p.

General population census, 1975. Statistical tables of the de jure population. De jure population of communities of more than 2,000 inhabitants. [PRC

France. INSEE.
    Recensement général de la population de 1975. Population légale et statistiques communales complémentaires. (Évolutions démographiques 1968-1975 et 1962-1968). Paris, 1976. 94v.

General population census, 1975. De jure population and complementary communal statistics. (Demographic changes 1968-1975 and 1962-1968).

1975.3-1 through 1975.3-95. 1. Ain.   p./2. Aisne. 73p./3. Allier. 45p./ 4. Alpes-de-Haute-Provence.   p./5. Hautes-Alpes. 33p./6. Alpes-Maritimes. 37p./7. Ardèche. 45p./8. Ardennes. 53p./9. Ariège. 41p./ 10. Aube. 49p./11. Aude. 49p./12. Aveyron. 45p./13. Bouches-du-Rhône. 33p./14. Calvados.   p./15. Cantal. 37p./16. Charente. 49p./ 17. Charente-Maritime. 53p./18. Cher. 37p./19. Corrèze. 41p./20. Corse. [Not pub'd]./21. Côte-d'Or. 65p./22. Côtes-du-Nord. 45p./23. Creuse. 37p./24. Dordogne. 57p./25. Doubs. 57p./26. Drôme. 45p./ 27. Eure. 65p./28. Eure-et-Loir. 49p./29. Finistère. 45p./30. Gard. 49p./31. Haute-Garonne. 61p./32. Gers. 53p./33. Gironde. 61p./34. Hérault. 49p./35. Ille-et-Vilaine. 45p./36. Indre. 37p./37. Indre-et-Loire. 37p./38. Isère. 65p./39. Jura. 57p./40. Landes. 45p./ 41. Loir-et-Cher. 37p./42. Loire. 49p./43. Haute-Loire. 41p./44. Loire-Atlantique. 41p./45. Loiret. 45p./46. Lot. 45p./47. Lot-et-Garonne. 45p./48. Lozère. 33p./49. Maine-et-Loire. 45p./50. Manche. 57p./51. Marne. 61p./52. Haute-Marne. 49p./53. Mayenne. 41p./54. Meurthe-et-Moselle. 61p./55. Meuse. 53p./56. Morbihan. 41p./57. Moselle. 73p./58. Nièvre. 45p./59. Nord. 85p./60. Oise. 69p./61. Orne. 53p./62. Pas-de-Calais. 93p./63. Puy-de-Dôme. 57p./64. Pyrénées-Atlantiques. 61p./65. Hautes-Pyrénées. 49p./66. Pyrénées-Orientales. 33p./67. Bas-Rhin. 61p./68. Haut-Fhin. 53p./69. Rhône. 41p./70. Haute-Saône. 57p./71. Saône-et-Loire. 57p./72. Sarthe. 45p./73. Savoie. 49p./74. Haute-Savoie. 45p./75. Ville de Paris.   p./76. Seine-Maritime.   p./77. Seine-et-Marne. 61p./78. Yvelines. 49p./ 79. Deux-Sèvres. 45p./80. Somme. 73p./81. Tarn. 45p./82. Tarn-et-

Garonne.   33p./81. Var.   41p./84. Vaucluse.   29p./85. Vendée.   41p./
86. Vienne.   41p./87. Haute-Vienne.   37p./88. Vosges.   p./89. Yonne.
49p./90. Territoire de Belfort.   29p./91. Essonne.   37p./92. Haute-
de-Seine.   25p./93. Seine-Saint-Denis.   26p./94. Val-de-Marne.   25p./
95. Val-d'Oise.   37p.   [PRC, BC

France.   INSEE.
1975.4   30° recensement général de   30th general population census,
la population, 20 février/15   Feb. 20/March 15, 1975.   Cities
mars 1975.   Villes et agglomé-   and urban agglomerations: 1975
rations urbaines: délimitation   boundaries (demographic changes
1975 (évolutions démographiques   1968-1975 and 1962-1968).
1968-1975 et 1962-1968).   Paris,   [
1977.

France.   INSEE.
   .5   Principaux résultats du re-   Main results of the census of
censement de 1975.   Paris,   1975.
1977.   210p.   (Collections de   [UN, PRC
l'INSEE, Série D52).

France.   INSEE.
   Recensement général de la   General population census, 1975.
population de 1975.   Résultats   Results of the one-in-five sam-
du sondage au 1/5.   Population,   ple.   Population, households,
ménages, logements, immeubles.   dwellings, buildings.
Paris, [1978].   v.

FRENCH GUIANA

Department of French Guiana (France)   Capital: Cayenne
Statistical Agency: Ministry of Overseas Departments and Territories.
                      Guyane Delegation
                      (Ministère des Départements et Territoires d'Outre-Mer
                          Délégation de Guyane)
                      27, rue Oudinot
                      Paris 7e, France.
Publications Distributor: INSEE - Observatoire Économique de Paris
                           195, rue de Bercy--Tour Gamma A
                           75582 Paris, Cedex 12, France.

France. INSEE [and] Service
         Colonial des Statistiques.
1946.1   Résultats du recensement de   Results of the census of 1946,
         1946, territoires d'outre-mer   overseas territories (French of
         (Français d'origine métropoli-   metropolitan origin and foreigners)
         taine et étrangers): Guyane et   French Guiana and Inini.
         Inini.   Paris, 1948. 43p.   [Yale, PRC, RPI
         (BMSOM, supplément série "sta-
         tistique," No. 7).

France. INSEE [and] Ministère
         de la France d'Outre-Mer,
         Service des Statistiques.
   .2   Les français d'origine...
         [See French Overseas Territories, no. 1946.2.]

France. INSEE [and] Service des
         Départements d'Outre-Mer.
1954.1   Recensement de 1954: popula-   Census of 1954: population of
         tion des départements d'outre-   the overseas departments (Guade-
         mer (Guadeloupe, Guyane, Marti-   loupe, French Guiana, Martinique,
         nique, Réunion).   Paris, Impr.   Reunion).
         Nationale, 1954. 12p.   [LC, SU, Harvard, UN, PRC, RPI

France. INSEE.
   .2   Résultats statistiques du   Statistical results of the general
         recensement général de la popu-   census of population of the over-
         lation des départements d'outre-   seas departments taken July 1,
         mer effectué le 1er juillet 1954: 1954: French Guiana.
         Guyane.   Paris, Impr. Nationale, [UN, BC, PRC, RPI
         1957. 44p.

France. INSEE.
1961.1   Recensement de 1961. Popula-   Census of 1961. Population of the
         tion des départements d'outre-   overseas departments.
         mer.   Paris, Impr. des Journaux   [PRC, RPI
         Officiels, 1962. 12p.

France. INSEE.
   .2   Résultats statistiques du   Statistical results of the general
         recensement général de la popu-   census of the population of the

lation des départements d'outre-
mer, effectué le 9 octobre 1961.
3e volume: Guyane.   Paris,
1964. 67p.

overseas departments, taken Octo-
ber 9, 1961.   3d volume: French
Guiana.
[BC, PRC, RPI

France.   INSEE.
1967.1   Recensement de 1967.   Population des départements d'outre-
mer.   Paris, Impr. des Journaux
Officiels, 1968.   12p.

Census of 1967.   Population of
the overseas departments.
[PRC, RPI

France.   INSEE.
     Résultats statistiques du
recensement général de la population des départements d'outre-
mer, effectué le 16 octobre 1967:
Guyane.   Paris, Impr. Nationale,
n.d.   Partie 1-2.
 .2-1   Tableaux statistiques.
 n.d.   172p.
 .2-2

Statistical results of the general
census of the population of the
overseas departments, taken October 16, 1967: French Guiana.

Statistical tables.
[BC, PRC, RPI

France.   INSEE.
1974.1   Recensement de la population
des départements d'outre-mer,
1974.

Population census of the overseas
departments, 1974.

France.   INSEE.
 .2   Recensement général de la
population en 1974.   Population
de la France, départements d'
outre-mer: arrondissements,
communes.   Paris, 1976.   29p.

General population census, 1974.
Population of France, overseas
departments: districts, communes.
[

FRENCH OVERSEAS TERRITORIES

The censuses taken in 1946, 1951 and 1956 were of the non-indigenous population only. They are cited here to avoid the constant repitition in the
entries for all the countries involved.

France. INSEE [and] Service
Colonial des Statistiques.
Résultats du recensement de
1946 dans les territoires d'outre-
mer (Français d'origine métropolitaine et étrangers): Afrique Tro-
picale Française. (AOF, Togo,
Cameroun, AEF, Somalis). Paris,
1947-1948. (Bulletin mensuel de
statistique d'outre-mer, supplément série "statistique,", Nos.
3, 4, and 8).

Results of the census of 1946
in the overseas territories
(French of metropolitan origin
and foreigners): French Tropi-
cal Africa. (French West Africa,
Togo, Cameroon, French Equatorial Africa, French Somaliland).

1946.1-1   Répartition géographique.
1947. 23, [1]p. (No. 3)

Geographic distribution.
[Yale, PRC, RPI

.1-2   Répartition par âge et
nationalité. 1947. 51p.
(No. 4)

Distribution by age and nationality.
[Harvard, PRC, RPI

.1-3   État familial. 1948. 43p.
(No. 8)

Family status.
[Yale, PRC, RPI

France. INSEE [and] Service des
Statistiques.
.2   Les français d'origine métropolitaine et les étrangers dans
les territoires d'outre-mer au
recensement de 1946. Paris,
Presses Univ. de France, 1950.
li, 25p. (BMSOM, supplément
série "études," No. 18)

The French of metropolitan origin and foreigners in the overseas territories in the census
of 1946.
[BC, PRC, RPI

France. INSEE
1951.1   Le recensement de la population non originaire des territoires d'outre-mer en 1951.
Paris, Presses Univ. de France,
n.d. ii, 118, [2]p. (BMSOM,
supplément série "étude," No.
33)

Census of the non-indigenous
population of the overseas territories in 1951.
[Yale, PRC, RPI

French West Africa. Service de
la Statistique Générale.
.2   Recensement de la population
non autochtone de l'Afrique Occi-
dentale Français en juin 1951.
Dakar, 1955. [2], x, 69p.

Census of the non-native popu-
lation of French West Africa in
June 1951.
[PRC, RPI

French West Africa.   Haut-
    Commissariat Général.

1956.1   Premiers résultats définitifs   First final results of the cen-
du recensement de la population   sus of the non-indigenous popu-
non originaire de l'A.O.F. du 12   lation of French West Africa on
décembre 1956.   Dakar, 1959.   December 12, 1956.
13p.   [RPI

FRENCH POLYNESIA

Territory of French Polynesia (France)   Capital: Papeete, Tahiti
Statistical Agency: Service du Plan
                     Section d'Études Statistiques
                     Papeete,
Publications Distributor: same.

Called the Oceania Colony until 1946. Its 1946, 1951 and 1956 censuses
were of the total population.

France. INSEE.
    Résultats de recensement de   Results of the census of 1946 in
1946 dans les territoires d'outre-   the overseas territories: French
mer: Établissements français d'   Oceania settlements.
Océanie.   Paris, 1950. (BMSOM,
supplément série "statistique,"
nos. 11 & 12).
1946.1-1   Population océanienne.   Oceania population (native)
    x, 21, [2]p.   [PRC, BC, RPI
  .1-2   Français d'origine métro-   French of metropolitan origin and
politaine et étrangers. iii,   foreigners.
28, [2]p.   [PRC, BC, RPI

France. INSEE.
1951.1   Le recensement de la population...
    [See French Overseas Territories, no. 1951.1

France. INSEE.
  .2   Résultats de recensement de   Results of the census of 1951:
1951: Territoires d'outre-mer: Overseas territories: 4th part,
4e partie, Océanie (ensemble de   Oceania (the whole of the popula-
la population).   Paris, 1950?   tion).
xvii, 50p. (BMSOM, supplément   [PRC, BC, RPI
série "statistique," No. 17).

France.   INSEE [and] Ministère
          de la France d'Outre-Mer,
          Service des Statistiques.
1956.1   Recensement général de la   General population census, Decem-
population, décembre 1956 (Poly-   ber 1956 (French Polynesia).
nésie française). Résultats   Final results.
définitifs.   Paris, 1960. [4],   [UN, PRC, RPI
50, 125p.

France. INSEE.
1962.1   Résultats statistiques du   Statistical results of the general
recensement général de la popu-   census of the French Polynesian
lation de la Polynésie Française,   population, taken on November 9,
effectué le 9 novembre 1962.   1962.
[Paris, n.d.] 240p.   [UN, OPR, RPI

[France. INSEE]
  .2   Census 1962. [8]p.   [PRC, E-W, RPI

[France. INSEE]

.3   Census, 1962. Population de   Census 1962. Population of French
la Polynésie Française par cir-   Polynesia by district. Census of
conscription. Recensement du   November 9, 1962.
9 novembre 1962. n.p., n.d. 6p.   [PRC, E-W, RPI

Note: There was a "denombrement" made in 1967 that is referred to in
the following item. Indications are that it was an administrative type
census which did not give results satisfactory to the government.

French Polynesia. Centre ORSTOM
          de Papeete.   The population enumeration of
1967.1   Le denombrement de la popula-   1967 in the Leeward Islands area.
tion de 1967 dans la circonscrip-   [PRC
tion des Îles sous le Vent. Pre-
paré par Jean Fages. Papeete,
1970. 59p.

French Polynesia. Service du
          Plan. Statistique.   Census of February 8, 1971. Indi-
1971.0-1 Recensement du 8 février 1971. vidual data. (Provisional results).
Données individuelles. (Résul-   [PRC, Berkeley
tats provisoires). n.p., n.d.
v, 127p.

French Polynesia. Bureau d'
          Études Statistiques.   De jure population of the communes
.1   Population légale des communes   and districts of French Polynesia
et des districts de la Polynésie   according to the census of February
Française au recensement du 8   8, 1971.
février 1971. Papeete, 1970.   [PRC, Berkeley
(Bulletin de statistiques, 1970.
No. 5. Pp. 56-63).

France. INSEE.   Census of French Polynesia, April
1977.1   Recensement de la Polynésie   29, 1977: results of the census.
Française, 29 avril 1977: ré-   Population, housing and construc-
sultats du recensement. Popu-   tion, results by section of com-
lation, logements et construc-   mune.
tions, résultats par section de   [
commune. Paris, 1977.

GABON

Gabonese Republic   Capital: Libreville
Statistical Agency: National Service for Statistics and Economic Studies
                (Service de la Statistique et des Études Économiques)
                Ministère du Plan, du Developpement et la Statistique.
                B.P. 2081
                Libreville,
Publications Distributor: same

        France. INSEE [and] Service
              Colonial des Statistiques.
1946   Résultats du recensement...
              [See French Overseas Territories, Nos. 1946.1-1, 2, 3.
                                  1946.2]

        France. INSEE.
1951   Le recensement de la population...
              [See French Overseas Territories, No. 1951.1]

        Gabon. Service National de la
              Statistique.
1960.1   Recensement et enquête démo-   Demographic census and survey,
            graphiques, 1960-1961. Résul-   1960-1961. Results for Libreville.
            tats pour Libreville. Paris,   [PRC, LC, UN, RPI
            1962. 50p. specimen forms.

        Gabon. Service National de la
              Statistique.
            Recensement de la population,   Census of the population, 1960-
        1960-1961. Libreville, 1964.   1961.
            Parts 1-3.
        .2-1   Données d'ensemble. 62p.   Total population data.
                                                   [UN, BC, NWU, PRC, RPI
        .2-2   Tableaux par région: Regional tables: the Estuary,
            l'Estuaire, Haut-Ogooué, Moyen-   Upper Ogooué, Middle Ogooué,
        Ogooué, Ngounié, Nyanga. [155]p.   Ngounié, Nyanga.
                                                   [UN, NWU, PRC, RPI
        .2-3   Tableaux par région: Regional tables: Ogooué-Invido,
        Ogooué-Invido, Ogooué-Lolo,   Ogooué-Lolo, Maritime Ogooué,
        Ogooué-Maritime, Woleu-N'tem.   Woleu-N'tem.
        [117]p.   [UN, NWU, PRC, RPI

        Gabon. Service de Statistique.
        .3   Recensement et enquête démo-   Demographic census and survey,
            graphiques, 1960-1961. Ensemble   1960-1961. The whole of Gabon.
            du Gabon. Résultats définitifs.   Final results.
            Paris, 1965. 148p. specimen   [PRC, UN, NWU, JB-F, RPI
            forms.

        Gabon. Service National de la
              Statistique.
1969.1   Libreville: son expansion   Libreville: its dempgraphic ex-
        démographique, le recensement   pansion, census of June 1, 1969.

du 1er juin 1969.   Libreville,   [
1969. 18p.

Gabon. Service National de la
        Statistique.
1970.0-1 Recensement général de la   General census of the population,
        population, 1969-70. Méthodo-   1969-1970. Methodology.
        logie. Libreville, 1970. 59p.   [EB, IU, NWU, Harvard
        (Bull. mensuel de Statistique,
        supplément "études et enquêtes
        statistiques," No. 9).

Ganon. Service National de la
        Statistique.
    .1   Recensement général de la   General census of population,
        population, 1969-70. Denombre-   1969-70. Enumeration of the
        ment de la population Gabonaise   Gabonese population in the year
        année 1969.   Libreville,   1969.
                                                 [

THE GAMBIA

Republic of The Gambia.   Capital: Banjul
Statistical Agency: Central Statistics Division
                     Ministry of Economic Planning and Industrial Development
                     Wellington Street
                     Banjul,
Publications Distributor: same

Bathurst was a British Crown Colony and the rural areas were a protect-torate until independence (1965). It became a republic in 1970. The annual census of 1945 was of the protectorate only. That of 1951 was of Bathurst and Konbo St. Mary Division only.

Gambia. Census Controller's Office.
1963.1   Report on the census of population of the Gambia taken on 17/18 April, 1963, by H.A. Oliver. Bathurst, Government Printer, 1965. iv, 139p. map. (Sessional paper, No. 13 of 1965). [PRC, NWU, BC, CU, EB, IU, SU, Harvard, JB-F, RPI

Gambia. Central Statistics Division.
          Population census, 1973. Banjul, 1974-1976. Vols. I-III.
1973.1-1   I. Population: statistics for settlements and enumeration areas. unpaded. [PRC, BC, CPC, CU, EB, IU, NWU, PC, SU, Harvard, OPR
   .1-2   II. Housing: statistics for settlements and enumeration areas. unpaged. [PRC, BC, CPC, CU, EB, IU, NWU, PC, SU, Harvard
   .1-3   III. General report: statistics for local government areas and districts. 1976. [8], 714p. [PRC, BC, NWU, OPR

Gambia. Central Statistics Division.
   .2   Population census, 1973: recorded sample interviews. Banjul, 1974. 376p. [PRC, NWU

The next census will take place in 1983.

GAZA STRIP

"Except for Jammu and Kashmir, it is the world's only densely settled area not recognized as a de jure part of any extant country." (Encyclopedia Brittanica Yearbook, 1975). From 1949 to 1956 and again 1957 to 1967 the Gaza Strip was under Egyptian military rule. For the brief period 1956-1957 and then since 1967 it is under Israeli military administration.

No census was taken after 1931 until 1967.

Israel. Defence Forces and Central Bureau of Statistics. Census of population, 1967. Jerusalem, 1967-1970. Vols. 1-5.

1967.1-1   West Bank of the Jordan, Gaza Strip and Northern Sinai, Golan Heights. Data from full enumeration. 1967. xxxvii, 204p. maps. [PRC

.1-2   Housing conditions, household equipment, welfare assistance and farming in the Administered areas. 1968. xxxv, [34]p. [PRC

.1-3   Demographic characteristics of the population in the Administered areas. Data from sample enumeration. 1968. xxxiii, 76, [30]p. [PRC

.1-4   Labour force. Part 1. 1968. xxvi, 24, [26]p. [PRC

.1-5   The Administered territories. Additional data from the sample enumeration. 1970. xiii, 79, [12]p. [PRC

Note: Despite the lack of a "Labour force. Part 2" as implied by No. 1967.1-4 above, this set is considered complete by the Central Bureau of Statistics.

GERMANY, EAST

German Democratic Republic   Capital: East Berlin
Statistical Agency: National Central Office for Statistics
                    (Staatliche Zantralverwaltung für Statistik)
                    Hans Beimler Strasse 70/72
                    1026 Berlin,
Publications Distributor: Staatsverlag der DDR.

Germany. Statistisches Zentral-
     amt.
1945.1   Die Volkszählung vom 1 Dezem-   Population census of December 1,
ber 1945 in der sowjetischen   1945 in the Soviet occupation
Besatzungszone Deutschlands.   zone of Germany.
Berlin, Deutscher Zentralverlag   [
Gmbh., 1946. 46p.

Germany. Ausschuss der Deutschen
     Statistiker für die Volks-
     und Berufszählung 1946.
     Volks- und Berufszählung vom   Census of population and occupa-
29.Oktober 1946 in den vier Besat-   tions, October 29, 1946, in the
zungszonen und Gross-Berlin.   four occupation zones and Greater
Berlin-München, Duncker & Humblot,   Berlin.
1949-1953. 6v.
1946.1-1   Deutsches Gemeindeverzeich-   Register of German local areas.
nis. 1950. vi, 196p.   [PRC, BC, UN, RPI
.1-2   Volkszählung: Tabellen-   Population census: tables.
teil. 1949. vi, 165p.   [PRC, LC, UN, RPI
.1-3   Volkszählung: Textteil.   Population census: text.
1951. 71p.   [PRC, BC, UN, Berkeley, RPI
        Berufszählung: Tabellen-   Census of occupations: tables.
teil. 1950. Heft 1-2.
.1-4-1   Heft 1. vi, 153p.   [PRC, BC, UN, Berkeley, RPI
.1-4-2   Heft 2. v, 152p.   [PRC, BC, UN, Berleley, RPI
.1-5   Berufszählung: Textteil.   Census of occupations: text.
[1953]. viii, 120p.   [UN, RPI

Germany. Statistisches Amt des
     Vereinigten Wirtschafts-
     gebietes.
.2   Volkszählung vom 29. Oktober   Population census of October 29,
1946. Amtliches Gemeindever-   1946. Official list of communes
zeichnis für das vereinigte Wirt-   for the combined industrial regions.
schaftsgebeit. Stuttgart, W.   [UN, BC, PRC, RPI
Kohlhammer, [1949] 92p.

Germany. Statistisches Zentral-
     amt für die sowjetische
     Besatzungszone.
     Volks- und Berufszählung vom   Census of population and occupa-
29. Oktober 1946 in der sowje-   tions of October 29, 1946, in the
tischen Besatzungszone. Berlin,   Soviet Zone.

Deutscher Zentralverlag, 1948–
1949. Band I-IV in 12v.
.3-1   I. Amliches Gemeinde-   Official register of communes.
verzeichnis. 1948. 104p.   [PRC, LC, RPI
    II. Gemeindestatistik.   Local area statistics.
1948. Heft 1-5.
1946.3-2-1 through 1946.3-2-5. 1. Land Brandenburg. 40p./2. Land Mecklenburg.
43p./3. Land Sachsen-Anhalt. 73p./4. Land Thüringen. 42p./5. Land
Sachsen. 45p. [
    III. Landes- und Kreis-   State and district statistics.
statistik. 1949. Heft 1-5.
1946.3-3-1 through 1946.3-3-5. 1. Land Brandenburg. 146p./2. Land Mecklenburg. 146p./3. Land Sachsen-Anhalt. 167p./4. Land Thüringen. 150p./
5. Land Sachsen. 167p. [NYPL, PRC, RPI
    IV. Sowjetische Besat-   Soviet occupation zone.
zungszone. 1949. 243p.   [UN, PRC, RPI

German DR. Staatliche Zentral-
    verwaltung für Statistik.
1964.1   Volks- und Berufszählung: Census of population and occupa-
vorläufige Ergebnisse. Wohn-   tions: preliminary results. Resi-
bevölkerung nach Geschlecht,   dent population according to sex,
Alter und Gebiet am 31. Dezember   age and district as of December
1964. [Berlin], 1965. 305p.   31, 1964.
                                        [UN, PRC, OPR, RPI

German DR. Staatliche Zentral-
    verwaltung für Statistik.
.2   Verzeichnis der Gemeinden und   Register of communes and parts
Ortsteile der Deutschen Demokrat-   of communes of the German DR.
ischen Republik. (Strand vom   (According to the census of popu-
31. Dezember 1964, Volkszählung.)   lation, December 31, 1964).
Berlin, 1966. 642p.   [PSC,

German DR. Staatliche Zentral-
    verwaltung für Statistik.
.3   Ergebnisse der Volks- und   Results of the population and
Berufszählung am 31. Dezember   occupations census of December 31,
1964. [Berlin], 1967. 449p.   1964.
                                        [PRC, Harvard, RPI

German DR. Staatliche Zantral-
    verwaltung für Statistik.
    Die endgültigen Ergebnisse   Final results of the population
der Volks- und Berufszählung am   and occupations census of Decem-
31. Dezember 1964. Berlin,   ber 31, 1964.
1966-19 . 7v. (Schriften-
reihe der Volks- und Berufszählung am 31. Dezember 1964. Band
2-10/11).
.4-2   Haushalte nach Art, Grösse   Household according to type, size
und Gebiet. Wohnbevölkerung und   and district. Resident population
Haushalte in den Bezirken der DDR.   and household in the DDR regions.

Ergebnisse einer 2 prozentigen Stichprobenaufbereitung. 1966. 395p.

Results of a 2 percent sample.
[PSC

1964.4-3 Wohnbevölkerung nach Gemeinden mit Kreiskartogrammen der Bevölkerungsverteilung-- Einwohnerzahlen. 1965. 417p.

Resident population according to local areas with district cartograms of the population distribution--Total populations.
[OPR, UN

.4-4 Wohnbevölkerung nach Gemeinden mit Kreiskartogrammen der Bevölkerungsverteilung-- Personen im Arbeitsfähigen Alter. 1966. 451p.

Resident population according to local areas with district cartograms of the population distribution--Persons of working age.
[UN

.4-5 Ergebnisse über die Struktur der wirtschaftlich Tätigen Wohnbevölkerung. Ergebnisse einer zuanzigprozentigen Stichprobenaufbereitung. 1966. 298p.

Results on the composition of the economically active resident population. Results of a 20 percent sample.
[

.4-6/7 Wohnbevölkerung nach Alter, Familienstand, Hoch- und Fachschulabschluss, sozialer Gliederung und anderen Merkmalen Haushalte nach Art, Grösse und Zusammensetzung. 1967. 272p.

Resident population according to age, marital status, college and trade school education completed, social classification and other characteristics--Households according to type, size and composition.
[UN

.4-8/9 Wirtschaftlich Tätige und nicht wirtschaftlich Tätige Wohnbevölkerung. Wirtschaftlich Tätige Wohnbevölkerung nach Stellung im Betrieb, Wirtschaftszweig und Eigentumsform der Arbeitsstätte; Arbeitspendler. 1967. 234p.

Industrially employed and non-industrially employed resident population. Industrially employed resident population according to position in industry, industry and workplace property; commuting workers.
[

.4-10/11 Wirtschaftlich Tätige nach Berufen und Hoch- bzw. Fachschulabschluss. 1967. 379p.

Industrially employed according to occupation and college and trade school education completed.
[UN

German DR. Staatliche Zentralverwaltung für Statistik.

1971.1 Volks-, Berufs-, Wohnraum- und Gebäudezählung in der Deutschen Demokratischen Republik, 1.1.1971. [Berlin, 1975]. 147p. maps.

Census of population, occupations, housing and construction in the German Democratic Republic, Jan. 1, 1971.
[UN

GERMANY, WEST

Federal Republic of Germany   Capital: Bonn
Statistical Agency: Federal Statistical Office
                     (Statistisches Bundesamt)
                     Postfach 5528
                     6200 Wiesbaden,
Publications Distributor: Verlag W. Kohlhammer
                           Postfach 120
                           6500 Mainz 42,

Germany. Statistisches Amt
          von Gross-Berlin.
1945.1   Ergebnisse der Volks- und   Results of the census of popula-
          Berufszählung in Berlin am 12.   tion and occupations in Berlin,
          August 1945.   Berlin, 1948.   August 12, 1945.
          72p. (Berliner Statistik.   [PRC, RPI
          Sonderheft 5).

Germany. Ausschuss der Deutschen
          Statistiker für die Volks-
          und Berufszählung 1946.
          Volks- und Berufszählung vom   Census of population and occupa-
          29.Oktober 1946 in den vier Besat-   tions, October 29, 1946, in the
          zungszonen und Gross-Berlin.   four occupation zones and Greater
          Berlin-München, Duncker & Humblot,   Berlin.
          1949-1953. 6v.
1946.1-1   Deutsches Gemeindever-   Register of German local areas.
          zeichnis. 1950. vi, 196p.   [PRC, BC, UN, RPI
     .1-2   Volkszählung: Tabellen-   Population census: tables.
          teil. 1949. vi, 165p.   [PRC, LC, UN, RPI
     .1-3   Volkszählung: Textteil.   Population census: text.
          1951. 71p.   [PRC, BC, UN, RPI
             Berufszählung: Tabellen-   Census of occupations: tables.
          teil. 1950. Heft 1-2.
     .1-4-1   Heft 1. vi, 153p.   [PRC, BC, UN, RPI
     .1-4-2   Heft 2. v, 152p.   [PRC, BC, UN, RPI
     .1-5   Berufszählung: Textteil.   Census of occupations: text.
          [1953]. viii, 120p.   [UN, RPI

Germany. Statistisches Amt für
          die britische Besatzungs-
          zone.
          Volkszählung. Die Bevölkerung   Population census. The population
          der britischen Besatzungszone   of the British occupation zone
          nach den Ergebnissen der Volks-   according to the results of the
          aählung vom 29. 10. 1946.   Ham-   population census of October 29,
          burg, 1948-1949. (Statistik der   1946.
          britischen Besatzungszone.
          Band 1. Heft 1-6).
     .2-1   Amtliches Gemeindever-   Official register of local areas.
          zeichnis. Ortsanwesende Bevölk-   De facto population.
          erung. 1948. 40p.   [UN, RPI

1946.2-2   Wohnbevölkerung. 1948.   Resident population.
    43p.   [UN, LC, PRC, RPI
.2-3   Alphabetisches Verzeichnis.   Alphabetical register.
   1948. 27p.   [UN, LC, PRC, RPI
.2-4   Einführung in die Volks-   Introduction to the census of
und Berufszählung. 1949. 52p.   population and occupations.
   [UN, LC, PRC, RPI
.2-5   Tabellenteil. 1949.   Tables.
    140p.   [UN, LC, PRC, RPI
   Berufszählung: Tabellen-   Census of occupations: tables.
teil. 1950. 2 parts.
.2-6-1   I. 131p.   [UN
.2-6-2   II. 142p.   [UN

Germany. Ausschuss der Deutschen
        Statistiker für die Volks-
        und Berufszählung 1946.
.3   [Census of population, October 29, 1946: results for Bavaria and
other areas of the U.S. Zone and the British Zone.] [n.p., 1948?]
18 mimeographed tables. [BC, RPI

Germany. Statistisches Amt des
        Vereinigten Wirtschafts-
        gebietes.
.4   Volkszählung vom 29. Oktober   Population census of October 29,
1946. Amtliches Gemeindever-   1946. Official register of local
zeichnis für das vereinigte   areas for the combined occupation
Wirtschaftsgebiet. Stuttgart,   zones.
W. Kohlhammer, 1949. 92p.   [UN, RPI

Germany. Office of Military
        Government for Germany.
.5-1 The population of Germany. n.p., 1947. 10, x p. maps. (Special
report, 15 March 1947). [
.5-2 The population of the U.S. zone of Germany. Part 2. Some results
of the census of October 1946 in relation to economic, social and demographic policy. n.p., 1947. 113p. [
.5-3 Results of a census of the German population, 29 October 1946.
[Berlin], 1947. 2p. [UN, BC, PRC, RPI

Germany. Division de l'Econo-
        mie Générale et des
        Finances.
.6   Principaux résultats du   Main results of the demographic
recensement démographique de   census of October 29, 1946.
29 octobre 1946. Berlin, 1949.   [UN, LC, PRC, RPI
50p.

Note: The 1946 results issued by the German states were usually published in official state periodical series.

Baden. Statistisches Landesamt.
1946.BD-1   Gemeindestatistik des Landes Baden, Ausgabe 1946. [

1946.BAD-2-1 and .BAD-2-2   Endgültige Ergebnisse der Volkszählung./...Fort-
    setzung. 1948.
    .BAD-3-1 through .BAD-3-6 Statistische Zahlen aus Nordbaden, 1946 (No.3)/
    1947 (No. 7)/1948 (Nos. 24, 25)/1949 (No. 35).

    Bavaria. Bayerische Statistisches Landesamt.
    .BAV-1-1 through .BAV-1-5 Beiträge zur Statistik Bayerns, Heft 140-142,
    145, 146.

    Bremen. Statistisches Landesamt.
    .BR-1 Statistische Mitteilungen aus Bremen. Sonderheft 2.
    .BR-2-1/3, 9, 11, 12. Statistische Mitteilungen aus Bremen, Heft...

    Hamburg. Statistisches Landesamt.
    .HA-1-1 through .HA-1-5 Hamburg in Zahlen, Heft 3, 5, 11, 12, 13.

    Hesse. Hessisches Statistisches Landesamt.
    .HE-1 Beiträge zur Statistik Hessens, Heft 15.
    .HE-2 Amtliches Verzeichnis der Gemeinden in Hessen, Ausgabe Mai 1948.
    .HE-3-1 through .HE-3-12 Volks- und Berufszählung in Hessen am 29. Ok-
    tober 1946. Heft 1-12.

    Lower Saxony. Neidersächsisches Amtes für Landesplanung und Statistik.
    .LS-1 Veröffentlichen, Reihe F, Band 1.
    .LS-4-1 through .LS-4-3 Veröffentlichen, Reihe F, Band 4, Heft 1-3.

    North Rhine-Westphalia. Statistisches Landesamt.
    .NW-1-1 and .NW-1-2 Beiträge zur Statistik des Landes Nordrhein-West-
    falen. Heft 1-2.

    Rhineland-Pfalz. Statistisches Landesamt.
    .RP-1 Die Volks- und Berufszählung am 29. Oktober 1946 in Rheinland-
    Pfalz. Heft 1.
    .RP-2-1 through .RP-2-3 Statistik von Rheinland-Pfalz, Bände 1-3.
    .RP-3 Amtliches Gemeindeverzeichnis von Rheinland-Pfalz nach der Volks-
    zählung vom 29. Oktober 1946...

    Schleswig-Holstein. Statistisches Landesamt.
    .SH-1-1 and .SH-1-2 Statistische Monatshefte, 1 Jahrgang (1949), Sonder-
    heft A, C.

    Württemberg-Baden. Württembergisches Statistisches Landesamt.
    .WB-1 Statistischen Monatshefte Württemberg-Baden, Sonderheft zum Jahr-
    gang 1949.

    Württemberg-Hohenzollern. Statistisches Landesamt.
    .WH-1-1 through .WH-1-4 Württemberg-Hohenzollern in Zahlen. 2 Jahrgang
    (1947), Heft 3/4. 4 Jahrgang (1949), Heft 1/2, 3/4, 5.

    Greater Berlin. Hauptamt für Statistik.
    .GB-1 Berliner Statistik, Sonderheft 5. (Census of 1945).
    .GB-2 Berliner Statistik, Sonderheft 6/7. (Census of 1946).

    Saar. [Under control of France, 1945-1957].

Germany, FR. Statistisches
Bundesamt.
Zählung vom 13.9.1950.
Stuttgart-Köln, W. Kohlhammer,
1952-1956. (Statistik der
Bundesrepublik Deutschland,
Bände 31, 33-37, 41).

Census of September 13, 1950.

1950.1-31   Organisation und Technik
des Volksaählungswerkes 1950.
1956. 308p.

Organization and techniques of
the population census publications 1950.
[PRC, Harvard, RPI

.1-33   Amtliches Gemeindeverzeichnis für die Bundesrepublik
Deutschland (endgültige Ergebnisse nach der Volkszählung vom
13.9.1950). 1952. vi, 344p.
map.

Official register of local areas
for the German Federal Republic
(final results according to the
population census of September
13, 1950).
[PRC, BC, Harvard, RPI

.1-34   Einführung in die methodischen und systematischen Grund-
lagen der Volks- und Berufszählung vom 13.9.1950. 1955. 110p.

Introduction to the methodological and systematic foundation of
the population and occupations
census of September 13, 1950.
[PRC, BC, Harvard, RPI

Die Bevölkerung der Bundesrepublik Deutschland nach der
Zählung vom 13.9.1950. Heft 1-9.

The population of the German Federal Republic according to the
population census of September 13,
1950.

.1-35-1   Die Bevölkerung nach
Geschlect, Alter und Familienstand. 1952. 43p.

The population according to sex,
age and marital status.
[TXU, UN, Harvard, PRC, RPI

.1-35-2   Die Bevölkerung nach
der Religionszugehörigkeit.
1952. 27p. 2 maps.

The population according to religious affiliation.
[TXU, UN, Harvard, PRC, RPI

.1-35-3   Die Bevölkerung nach
dem Wohnort am 1.9.1939. 1953.
28p. map.

The population according to residence in September 1, 1939.
[PRC, BC, UN, Harvard, RPI

.1-35-4   Die Haushaltungen.
1954. xii, 97p. 2 maps.

Households.
[TXU, UN, Harvard, PRC, RPI

.1-35-5   Die verheirateten Frauen
nach Eheschliessungsjahren, Ge-
burtsjahren und Kinderzahl. 1953.
16p.

Women by years of marriage, year
of birth, and number of children.
[PRC, BC, UN, RPI

.1-35-6   Die Körperbehinderten.
1954. 80p.

The physically handicapped.
[PRC, BC, UN, RPI

.1-35-7   Fläche und Bevölkerung
der naturräumlichen Einheiten.
1954. 142p. 2 maps.

Area and population in natural
geographic units.
[PRC, BC, UN, RPI

.1-35-8   Die Struktur der Haushaltungen (Ergebnisse repräsen-
tativer Sonderauszählungen aus
dem Material der Volkszählung
vom 13.9.1950). 1954. 37p.

Household composition (results of
a special tabulation of the material from the population census of
September 13, 1950).
[TXU, UN, PRC, RPI

.1-35-9   Textheft. 1956. 117p.
5 maps.

Text.
[TXU, UN, PRC, RPI

Die berufliche und soziale Gliederung der Bevölkerung der Bundesrepublik Deutschland nach der Zählung vom 13.9.1950. Bände 36-37.

Occupational and social classifications of the population of the German Federal Republic according to the population census of September 13, 1950.

1950.1-36-1   Die Bevölkerung nach der Erwerbstätigkeit. 1953. 311p. 3 maps.

The population according to employment.
[PRC, BC, RP]

.1-36-2   Die Erwerbspersonen in der beruflichen Gliederung nach Alter und Familienstand. Die Selbständigen Beruflosen nach Altersgruppen. 1953. 212p.

Occupational classification of the gainfully employed by age and marital status. Self-supporting persons without occupation by age group.
[PRC, BC, RP]

.1-36-3   Textheft. 1956. 45p. 3 maps.

Text.
[PRC, BC, RP]

.1-37-1   Die Erwerbspersonen nach Berufen,Stellung in Beruf und Wirtschaftszweigen. 1953. 64p.

Gainfully employed by occupation, Employment status and industry.
[PRC, BC, RP]

.1-37-2   Die Erwerbspersonen nach Wirtschaftszweigen und Stellung in Beruf. 1953. 87p.

Gainfully employed by industry and employment status.
[PRC, BC, RP]

.1-37-3   Die Erwerbspersonen nach Berufsordnungen und der nebenberuflichen erwerbstätigkeit. 1953. 160p.

Gainfully employed by occupation group and incidental occupation employment.
[PRC, BC, RP]

.1-37-4   Die Erwerbspersonen und die Ehefrauen ohne Hauptberuf nach ihrer Sicherung bei Krankheit und nach der voraussichtlichen Altersversorgung. 1953. 21p.

Gainfully employed and married women without principal occupation according to their sickness (hospital) insurance and their expected old age pension scheme.
[PRC, BC, RP]

.1-37-5   Textheft. 1956. 36p. 1 map.

Text.
[BC, RP]

Germany, FR. Statistisches Bundesamt.

.2   Bibliographie zum Volkszählungswerk, 1950. 1956. 140p. (Statistik der Bundesrepublik Deutschland, Band 50).

Bibliography of population census publications, 1950.
[UN, RP]

Baden-Württemberg. Statistisches Landesamt.
.BAD-1-1 & 2 Beiträge zur Statistik von Württemberg-Baden, Nr. 13, 19.
.BAD-2 Statistik in Baden, Reihe: Volkszählung. Heft 2.
.BAD-3 Statistik in Baden, Reihe: Volkszählung. Sonderheft 1.
.BAD-4-2 through .BAD-4-5-2 Statistik von Baden-Württemberg, Bände 2, 3 (Teil 1-4), 4 (Teil 1-2).

Bavaria. Bayerisches Statistische Landesamt.
.BAV-1-1 through BAV-1-9 Beiträge zur Statistik Bayerns. Heft 169-172, 177, 185-188.

Bremen. Statistisches Landesamt.
1950.BR-1 Statistische Mitteilungen aus Bremen, Sonderheft 4.

Hamburg. Statistisches Landesamt.
.HA-1-1 through .HA-1-3-2 Statistik des Hamburgischen Staates. Heft 36,
37, 40 (Teil 1-2).

Hesse. Hessisches Statistisches Landesamt.
.HE-1-2 through .HE-1-4 Beiträge zur Statistik Hessens, Sonderreihe:
Volkszählung 1950. Heft 2-4.
.HE-2-1 through .HE-2-3 Beiträge zur Statistik Hessens, Sonderreihe:
Berufszählung 1950. Heft 1-3.
.HE-3-1 & .HE-3-2 Hessische Gemeindestatistik 1950. Nr. 48, Heft 1-2.

Lower Saxony. Niedersächsisches Amt für Landesplanung und Statistik.
.LS-1-1 through .LS-1-3 Veröffentlichungen des..., Folge 15, Heft 1, 2,
5.
.LS-2 Veröffentlichungen des..., Reihe F, Band 1, Heft 2.

North Rhine-Westphalia. Statistisches Landesamt.
.NW-1-1 through .NW-1-15, 17, 18. Beiträge zur Statistik des Landes
Nordrhein-Westfalen, Sonderreihe: Volkszählung 1950, Heft 1-15, 17,
18.
.NW-2-1 & .NW-2-2 Statistische Rundschau für das Land Nordrhein-Westfalen.
4 Jahrgang, Sonderheft 1-2.

Rhineland-Pfalz. Statistisches Landesamt.
.RP-1-1 through .RP-1-7 Statistik von Rheinland-Pfalz, Bände 12, 13, 17,
18, 21, 22, 28.

Schleswig-Holstein. Statistisches Landesamt.
.SH-1-1 through .SH-1-3 Statistik von Schleswig-Holstein. Heft 8, 9, 12.
.SH-2 Herausgegeben vom Statistischen Landesamt Schleswig-Holstein, 1953.

Württemberg-Hohenzollern. Statistisches Landesamt.
.WH-1-1 through .WH-1-3 Württemberg-Hohenzollern in Zahlen. Reihe:
Volkszählung. Heft 1-3.

Berlin. Statistisches Landesamt.
.B-1-1 through .B-1-6 Berliner Statistik, Sonderhefte 18, 24, 25, 30, 31,
39.

Saar. Statistisches Amt des Saarlandes.
1951.SA-1 Einzelschriften zur Statistik des Saarlandes, no. 10.
.SA-2-1 through .SA-2-6 Kurzbericht, 5 Jahrgang, Nr. II, Heft 1, 5, 6,
7, 8. 6 Jahrgang, Heft 1/4.

Germany, FR. Statistisches
    Bundesamt.
    Volks- und Berufszählung vom   Population and occupations census
6. Juni 1961. Stuttgart, W.   of June 6, 1961.
Kohlhammer, 1966-1968. (Bevölke-
rung und Kultur, Fachserie A-
Volkszählung, Heft 1-21).

1961.1-1   Die methodischen Grund-
lagen der Volks- und Berufszählung 1961. 1967. 267p.

Methodological bases of the population and occupations census 1961.
[PRC, BC, RPI, RIR

.1-2   Ausgewahlte Bevölkerungs-
gruppen. Deutsche Bevölkerung
und Ausländer. 1967. 122p.

Selected population groups. German population and foreigners.
[PRC, BC, RPI, RIR

.1-3   Bevölkerungsstand und
Bevölkerungsentwicklung. 1966.
144p.

Status and growth of the population.
[PRC, BC, RPI, RIR

.1-4   Bevölkerung nach Alter und
Familienstand. 1966. 274p.

Population by age and marital status.
[PRC, BC, RPI, RIR

.1-5   Bevölkerung nach der Religionszugehörigkeit. 1966. 92p.

Population by religious affiliation.
[PRC, BC, RPI, RIR

.1-6   Vertriebene und Deutsche
aus der SBZ--Verteilung und Struktur. 1967. 354p.

Refugees and Germans from the
Soviet Occupation Zone--distribu-
tion and composition.
[PRC, BC, RPI, RIR

.1-7   Ausländer--Verteilung und
Struktur. 1966. 232p.

Foreigners--distribution and composition.
[PRC, BC, RPI, RIR

.1-8   Bevölkerung in Anstalten.
1967. 98p.

Population in institutions.
[PRC, BC, RPI, RIR

.1-9   Pendler. 1967. 282p.
maps.

Commuters.
[PRC, BC, UN, RPI, RIR

.1-10   Bevölkerung nach Lebens-
unterhalt und Beteiligung am
Erwerbsleben. 1966. 111p.

Population by source of livelihood
and participation in the labor
force.
[PRC, BC, UN, RPI, RIR

.1-11   Bevölkerung und Erwerbspersonen mit überwiegendem Lebens-
unterhalt durch Angehörige bzw.
Rente u. dgl. 1967. 117p.

Population and the gainfully employed with principal source of
livelihood from relatives or pen-
sions, etc.
[PRC, BC, UN, RPI, RIR

.1-12   Erwerbspersonen in wirtschaftlicher und sozialer Gliederung. 1967. 195p.

The gainfully employed by industrial and social classification.
[PRC, UN, RPI, RIR

.1-13   Erwerbspersonen in beruf-
licher Gliederung. 1968. 376p.

The gainfully employed by occupational classification.
[PRC, BC, UN, RPI, RIR

.1-14   Erwerbstätige nach Wochen-
arbeitszeit und weiterer Tätig-
keit. 1967. 91p.

The employed by weeks worked time
and additional activity or occupation.
[PRC, BC, UN, RPI, RIR

.1-15   Personen mit einer abge-
schlossen Ausbildung an einer
Berufsfach- bzw. Fachschule
oder an einer Hochschule. 1968.
329p.

Persons with completed education
in vocational training, either in
a trade school or technical college.
[PRC, BC, UN, RPI, RIR

.1-16   Demographische und wirt-
schaftliche Struktur der Hous-
halte und Familien. (10 °/o Auf-
bereitung). 1968. 216p.

Demographic and industrial composition of households and families.
(10 °/o sample).
[PRC, BC, UN, RPI, RIR

1961.1-17   Erwerbstätigkeit von Frauen
      und Müttern. (10 °/o Aufbereitung). 1968. 116p.
  .1-18   Kinder und Jugendliche in
      Familien. (10 °/o Aufbereitung).
      1967. 94p.
  .1-19   Lebensverhältnisse der
      ältern Mitbürger. (10 °/o Auf-
      bereitung). 1967. 64p.
  .1-20   Religionszugehörigkeit in
      Familien. (10 °/o Aufbereitung).
      1967. 80p.
  .1-21   Untersuchungen zur Methode
      und Genauigkeit der Volks- und
      Berufszählung 1961.

Employment of women and mothers.
(10 °/o sample).
[PRC, BC, UN, RPI, RIR
Children and youth in families.
(10 °/o sample).
[PRC, BC, UN, RPI, RIR
Living conditions of older citi-
zens. (10 °/o sample).
[PRC, BC, UN, RPI, RIR
Religious affiliation in families.
(10 °/o sample).
[PRC, BC, UN, RPI, RIR
Report on the methods and accu-
racy of the 1961 census of popu-
lation and occupations.
[Never published.

Germany, FR. Statistisches
  .2   Amtliches Geneindeverzeichnis
      für die Bundesrepublik Deutsch-
      land--Ausgabe 1961--(Bevölker-
      ungs- und Gebietsstand 6. Juni
      1961). (Volkzählung). Mainz,
      W. Kohlhammer, 1963. 993p.

Official register of local areas
of the German Federal Republic--
1961 edition--(Status of population and territory, June 6, 1961)
(Population census).
[UN,

  Baden-Württemberg. Statistisches Landesamt.
.BAD-1-1 through .BAD-1-14 Statistik von Baden-Württemberg, Bände 83,
  90, 105 (Heft 1-11), 108.

  Bavaria. Bayerisches Statistisches Landesamt.
.BAV-1-1 through .BAV-1-10 Beiträge zur Statistik Bayerns, Bände 225,
  231, 236, 240, 245, 253, 254, 255, 260, 271.

  Bremen. Statistisches Landesamt.
.BR-1 Statistische Mitteilungen aus Bremen, Sonderheft 12.

  Hamburg. Statistisches Landesamt.
.HA-1-1 through .HA-1-4 Statistik des Hamburgischen Staates, Bände 71,
  72, 86, 87.

  Hesse. Hessisches Statistisches Landesamt.
.HE-1-1 through .HE-1-5 Beiträge zur Statistik Hessens, (Neue Folge).
  Nr. 5 (Heft 1-5).

  Lower Saxony. Niedersächsisches Landesverwaltungsamt--Abteilung
      Statistik.
.LS-1-1 through .LS-1-10 Statistik von Niedersachsen, Bände 27, 60-66,
  91, 92.

  North Rhine-Westphalia. Statistisches Landesamt.
.NW-1-1 through .NW-1-21. Beiträge zur Statistik des Landes Nordrhein-
  Westfalen, Sonderreihe Volkszählung 1961. Heft 1-21.

Rhineland-Pfalz. Statistisches Landesamt.
.RP-1-1 through .RP-1-7 Statistik von Rheinland-Pfalz, Bände 108, 109,
    112-116.

Saar. Statistisches Amt des Saarlandes.
.SA-1-1 through .SA-1-4 Einzelschriften zur Statistik des Saarlandes,
    Bände 22, 23, 30 (Teil I-II).

Schleswig-Holstein. Statistisches Landesamt.
.SH-1 Sammelband der Statistischen Berichte, AO/VZ 1961.
.SH-2 Gemeindestatistik Schleswig-Holstein, 1960/1961.

Berlin. Statistisches Landesamt.
.B-1-1 through .B-1-19 Berliner Statistik, Sonderhefte 98, 101-112, 119,
    126, 127, 131, 136, 138.

Cologne. Statistisches Amt.
.C-1 Die wichtigsten Ergebnisse der Volks-, Berufs- und Arbeitsstätten-
    zählung. Cologne, [1967], 164p.

Germany, FR. Statistisches
        Bundesamt.
    Volkszählung vom 27. Mai 1970.   Population census of May 27, 1970.
Stuttgart, W. Kohlhammer, 1972-
1978. (Bevölkerung und Kultur,
Fachserie A. Heft 1-26).
1970.1-1   Ausgewählte Strukturdaten   Selected characteristics for the
    für Bund und Länder. 1972. 27p.   Republic and States.
                                              [PRC

.1-2   Ausgewählte Strukturdaten   Selected characteristics for non-
    für nichtadministrative Gebiets-   administrative area units.
    einheiten. 1972. 245p.   [PRC
.1-3   Zusammengefasste Daten über   Summary data on population and
    Bevölkerung und Erwerbstätigkeit   employment for the Republic and
    für Bund und Länder. 1973. 29p.   States.
                                              [PRC
.1-4   Zusammengefasste Daten über   Summary data on population and
    Bevölkerung und Erwerbstätigkeit   employment for nonadministrative
    für nichtadministrative Gebiets-   area units.
    einheiten. 1973. 186p.   [PRC
.1-5   Bevölkerung und Bevölker-   Population and population change
    ungsentwicklung nach Alter und   according to age and marital sta-
    Familienstand. 1974. 411p.   tus.
                                              [PRC
.1-6   Bevölkerung nach der Reli-   Population according to religious
    gionszugehörigkeit. 1974. 79p.   affiliation.
                                              [PRC
.1-7   Geburten. 1974. 27p.   Births.
                                              [PRC
.1-8   Bevölkerung in Haushalten.   Population in households.
    1974. 95p.   [PRC
.1-9   Bevölkerung in Familien.   Population in families.
    1974. 55p.   [PRC

1970.1-10 Kinder und Jugendliche in Familien. 1974. 67p.	Children and youth in families. [PRC
.1-11 Bevölkerung in Anstalten. 1974. 39p.	Population in institutions. [PRC
.1-12 Ältere Mitbürger. 1974. 255p.	Older citizens. [PRC
.1-13 Bevölkerung nach den Ausbildungsstand, demographischen Merkmalen und Beteiligung am Erwerbsleben. 1974. 44p.	Population according to educational attainment, demographic characteristics and participation in the labor force. [PRC
.1-14 Bevölkerung nach dem Ausbildungsstand, ausgewählten Fachrichtungen und Nettoerwerbseinkommen. 1974. 340p.	Population according to educational attainment, selected programs of study and net earnings-income. [PRC
.1-15 Bevölkerung nach überwiegendem Lebensunterhalt und Beteiligung am Erwerbsleben. 1974. 151p.	Population according to main source of livelihood and labor force participation. [PRC
.1-16 Erwerbstätigkeit von Frauen und Müttern. 1974. 98p.	Employment of women and mothers. [PRC
.1-17 Erwerbstätige in wirtschaftlicher Gliederung nach Wochenarbeitszeit und weiterer Tätigkeit. 1974. 130p.	The employed by industrial classification according to weeks worked time and other activity. [PRC
.1-18 Erwerbstätige in wirtschaftlicher Gliederung und nach Nettoerwerbseinhommen. 1974. 52p.	The employed by industrial classification and according to net earning-income. [PRC
.1-19 Erwerbstätige in sozialer sozio-ökonomischer und beruflicher Gliederung. 1974. 403p.	The employed by social, socio-economic and occupational classification. [PRC
.1-20 Erwerbstätige nach Beruf und Alter. 1974. 319p.	The employed by occupation and age. [PRC
.1-21 Pendler. 1974. 131p.	Commuters. [PRC
.1-22 Vertriebene und Deutsche aus der D.D.R. 1974. 56p.	Refugees and Germans from the German Democratic Republic. [PRC
.1-23 Ausländer. 1974. 63p.	Foreigners. [PRC
.1-24 Zählungsergebnisse für den internationalen Vergleich. 1975. 279p.	Census results for international comparison. [PRC
.1-25 Methodische und praktische Vorbereitung sowie Durchführung der Volkszählung 1970. 1978. 390p.	Methodological and practical procedures for the carrying out of the population census of 1970. [PRC, OPR
.1-26 Untersuchungen zur Methode und Genauigkeit der Volkszählung 1970. 1978. 137p. (Bevölkerung und Erwerbstätigkeit, Fachserie 1).	Report on the methods and accuracy of the 1970 population census. [New serial publication]. [PRC, OPR

Germany, FR. Statistisches
    Bundesamt.
1970.2   Amtliches Gemeindeverzeichnis   Official register of local areas
für die Bundesrepublik Deutsch-   for the German Federal Republic.
land. Stuttgart, W. Kohlhammer,   [PRC
1972. 772p.

Germany, FR. Statistisches
    Bundesamt.
.3   Wohnbevölkerung in den Post-   Resident population in the postal
leiteinheiten und in ausgewähl-   areas and in selected administra-
ten administrativen Gebietsein-   tive districts as of May 27, 1970.
heiten am 27.5.1970. Stuttgart,   [PRC
W. Kohlhammer, 1973. 99p.

Baden-Württemberg. Statistisches Landesamt.
.BAD-1-1 through .BAD-1-12 Statistische Berichte, AO/VZ 1970, Nr. 1-12.

Bavaria. Statistisches Landesamt.
.BAV-1-1 through .BAV-1-13 Statistische Berichte, AO/VZ 1970, Nr. 1-13.

Bremen. Statistisches Landesamt.
.BR-1-1 through .BR-1-9 Statistische Berichte, AO/VZ 1970, Nr. 1-9.

Hamburg. Statistisches Landesamt der Freien und Hansestadt Hamburg.
.HA-1 Statistik des Hamburgischen Staats. Haft 101.
.HA-2 Hamburg in Zahlen,
.HA-3-1 through .HA-3- Statistische Berichte, AO/VZ 1970, Nr. 1-

Hesse. Hessisches Statistisches Landesamt.
.HE-1 Hessische Gemeindestatistik 1970. Band 2.
.HE-2-4 through .HE-2-10 Statistische Berichte, AO/VZ 1970, Nr. 4-10.

Lower Saxony. Niedersächsisches Landesverwaltungamt.
.LS-1-1 through .LS-1-14 Statistik von Neidersachsen, Nr. 186-194, 198-
202.

North Rhine-Westphalia. Statistisches Landesamt.
.NW-1-1 through .NW-1-16 (27v) Beiträge zur Statistik des Landes Nordrhein-Westfalen, Sonderreihe: Volkzählung 1970. Nr. 1-16 in 27v.

Rhineland-Pfalz. Statistisches Landesamt.
.RP-1-1 through .RP-1-7 Statistik von Rheinland-Pfalz. Bände 221, 228-
233.
.RP-2-2 Statistische Berichte, AO/VZ 1970, Nr. 2.

Saar. Statistisches Amt des Saarlandes.
.SA-1-1 through .SA-1-4 Einzelschriften zur Statistik des Saarlandes,
Nr. 35, 36, 40, 44.

Schleswig-Holstein. Statistisches Landesamt.
.SH-1-1 through .SH-1- Statistische Berichte, AO/VZ 1970, Nr.1-

Berlin. Statistisches Landesamt.
1970.B-1-1 through .B-1-4 Berliner Statistik, Sonderhefte 227-230.

GHANA

Republic of Ghana   Capital: Accra
Statistical Agency: Central Bureau of Statistics
                      P.O. Box 1098
                      Accra,
Publications Distributor: same

The former Gold Coast Colony and Protectorate (including Ashanti)
plus the former British Togoland became an independent republic in
1960.

Gold Coast. Census Office.
1948.1   The Gold Coast census of population, 1948: report and tables.
Accra, Government Printing Department, 1950. 422p. [TXU, BC, LC,
NWU, RPI

United Kingdom. Colonial Office.
.2   Census of 1948: population by sex, age, tribal divisions, occupation, and population of towns. In: Report by His Majesty's Government in the United Kingdom of Great Britain and Northern Ireland to
the General Assembly of the United Nations on the administration of
Togoland under United Kingdom trusteeship for the year 1949.   London,
1950. Appendix 1, pp. 145-149. [UN, RPI

Ghana. Census Office.
     1960 population census of Ghana.   Accra, 1962-1964. Vols. I-V.
1960.1-1   I. The gazetteer alphabetical list of localities with number of
population and houses. 1962. xxxiii, map, 405p. [PRC, TXU, BC, LC,
NWU, RPI
.1-2   II. Statistics of localities and enumeration areas: sex, age,
birthplace, school attendance and economic activity. 1962. xxvii,
map, 707p. [PRC, TXU, BC, LC, NWU, RPI
.1-3   III. Demographic characteristics of local authorities, regions
and total country: sex, age, school attendance and level of education
of total and foreign origin populations. 1964. xi, map, 160p. [PRC,
TXU, BC, LC, NWU, RPI
.1-4   IV. Economic characteristics of local authorities, regions and
total country: type of activity, industry, occupation and employment
status of total and foreign origin populations. 1964. xvi, map, 240,
A-20, B-10p. [PRC, TXU, BC, LC, NWU, RPI
.1-5   V. General report by B. Gil and K.T. de Graft-Johnson. 1964.
xvi, 410p. [PRC, TXU, BC, LC, NWU, RPI

Ghana. Census Office.
     1960 population census of Ghana. Special reports.   Accra, 1963-
     . Vol. A- .
.2-1   A. Statistics of towns with 10,000 population or more. 1964.
xv, map, 267p. [PRC, RPI
.2-2   B. Socio-economic indices of enumeration areas. [Not pub'd].
.2-3   C. Census data for new regions. [Not pub'd].
.2-4   D. List of localities by local authority, arranged in order of
geographic code number and showing the number of population and houses.
1963. 1144p. [BC, LC, RPI

.2-5   E. Tribes in Ghana, by B. Gil, A.F. Aryee, [and] D.K. Ghansah. 1964. cx, 128, [78]p. [PRC, TXU, BC, LC, RPI

.2-6   Demographic and economic characteristics of regions (based on a 10% sample): Adv. report of Vols. III and IV.   Accra, 1962. xxii, 122p.
[OPR

Ghana. Census Office.
.3   1960 Ghana population census maps. [Plan of enumeration areas]. Accra, Survey Dept., 1960. 6 maps. [PRC, LC, RPI

Ghana. Census Office.
     1970 population census of Ghana.   Accra, 1972-   . Vols. I-VI.
1970.1-1   I. The gazetteer, alphabetical list of localities with population, number of houses and main source of water supply. 1973. xli, 662p. [PRC, NWU

.1-2   II. Statistics of localities and enumeration areas: sex, age, birthplace, nationality, school attendance and economic activity. 1972. xliii, map, 971p. [PRC, BC, NWU

.1-3   III. Demographic characteristics of local authorities, regions and total country. 1975. xix, map, 345p. [PRC, BC

.1-4   IV. Detailed economic characteristics.

.1-5   V. General report.

.1-6   VI. The 1971 supplementary enquiry--a statistical summary.

Ghana. Census Office.
     1970 population census of Ghana. Special reports.   Accra, 1971-
     . Vol. A-D in 10 vols.
.2-1   A. Statistics of large towns.

.2-2   B. Socio-economic indices of enumeration areas.

.2-3   C. Census data for socio-economic regions.

         D. List of localities by local authority with population, number of houses and main source of water supply. 1971. 7 parts.
1970.2-4-1 through 1970.2-4-7. 1. Western region. iv, 183p./2. Central region. iv, 158p./3. Greater Accra and Eastern regions. iv, 213p./4. Volta region. iv, 197p./5. Ashanti region. iv, 411p./6. Brong Ahafo region. iv, 340p./7. Northern and Upper regions. iv, 197p. [PRC, NWU

Ghana. Census Office.
     1970 population census of Ghana. Maps.   Accra,   .
.3-1   A. Plan of enumeration areas.

.3-2   B. Statistical maps.

GIBRALTAR

Colony of Gibraltar   Capital: Gibraltar
Statistical Agency: Statistics Office
                      Government Secretariat
                      New Town, Gibraltar
Publications Distributor: same

        Gibraltar.   Census Office.
1951.1   Report on the census of Gibraltar taken on 3rd July, 1951. By K.
        L. Sanders, Census Commissioner.   Gibraltar, Garrison Library Print-
        ing Office, [1952].   39p. [PRC, BC, UN, RPI

        Gibraltar.   Census Office.
1961.1   Report on the census of Gibraltar taken 3rd October, 1961. By E.
        H. Davis, Census Commissioner.   Gibraltar, Garrison Library Printing
        Office, [1962].   49p. [TXU, PRC, RPI, RIR

        Gibraltar.   Census Office.
1970.1   Report on the census of Gibraltar, 1970.   Gibraltar, 1971. 96p.
        [PRC

GILBERT ISLANDS

Gilbert Islands Colony/Tuvalu   Capital: Bairiki, Tarawa
Statistical Agency: Central Government Office
                     P.O. Box 68
                     Bairiki, Tarawa,
Publications Distributor: Chief Publicity Officer
                           Broadcasting and Publications Division
                           P.O. Box 78
                           Bairiki, Tarawa,

Includes the Gilbert Islands, Phoenix Islands, Ocean Island, Line
Islands. Tuvalu, former Ellice Islands, was separated from Gilbert
Islands administration in 1976.

Gilbert and Ellice Islands Colony.
1947.1   A report on the results of the census of the population, 1947. By
          F.N.M. Pusinelli. Suva, Fiji, Government Press, 1951. ii, 103p.
          [PRC, Berkeley, Harvard, UN, RP]

Gilbert and Ellice Islands Colony.
1963.1   A report on the results of the census of population, 1963. Suva,
          Fiji, Government Press, 1964. 79p. 17 tables. [PRC, RP]

Gilbert and Ellice Islands Colony. Census Commissioner's Office.
1968.1   A report on the results of the census of the population, 1968. [By]
          F.H.A.G. Zwart [and] K. Groenewegen. New South Wales, Government
          Printer, 1970. 294p. [PRC

Gilbert and Ellice Islands Colony. Office of the Chief Minister.
          A report on the 1973 census of population. Bairiki, 1975-   .
          Vols. 1-2.
1973.1-1   Basic information. 1975. 217p. [PRC, E-W
     .1-2

GREAT BRITAIN

(Channel Islands, England & Wales, Scotland)   Capital: London
Statistical Agency: Office of Population Censuses and Surveys
                        [See England and Wales]
                        General Register Office
                        [See Scotland]
Publications Distributor: [See England and Wales]

     Great Britain. General Register Office.
        Census 1951. Great Britain. One per cent sample tables.   Lon-
     don, HMSO, 1952. Parts I-II.
1951.1-1   Ages and marital condition, occupations, industries, housing
     of private households. xix, 159p. [LC, UN, BC, NYPL, PRC, RPI
     .1-2   Characteristics and composition of private households, non-
     private households, education, birthplace, nationality, fertility,
     Welsh and Gaelic languages, conurbation supplement. vi, pp. 161-365,
     xix p. [LC, UN, BC, NYPL, PRC, RPI

     Great Britain. General Register Office
        Census 1961. Great Britain. London, HMSO, 1962-1968. 3 vols.
1961.1-1   General report. 1968. xi, 207p. specimen forms. [PRC, BC,
     RPI, RIR
     .1-2   Scientific and technological qualifications. 1962. xviii,
     18p. [PRC, BC, RPI, RIR
     .1-3   Summary tables. 1966. liii, 158p. specimen forms. [PRC, BC,
     RPI, RIR

     Great Britain. Office of Population Censuses and Surveys.
1966.0-1   Guide to census reports. Great Britain, 1801-1966.   London,
     HMSO, 1977. vii, 279p. [BC, PRC

     Great Britain. General Register Office.
        Sample census 1966. Great Britain. London, H,SO, 1967-1971.
     9 vols.
     .1-1   Commonwealth immigrant tables. 1969. xxxii, 253p. [PRC, RPI
     .1-2   Economic activity sub-regional tables. 1970. xxxvii, 387p.
     specimen forms. [PRC, RPI
        Economic activity tables. 1968-1969. Parts I-IV.
     .1-3-1   I. 1968. lxv, 199p. [PRC, RPI
     .1-3-2   II. 1968. lxxi, 325p. [PRC, RPI
     .1-3-3   III. 1969. xlix, pp. 325-447. [PRC, RPI
     .1-3-4   IV. 1969. xxi, pp. 448-494. [PRC, RPI
     .1-4   Qualified manpower tables. 1971. lxix, 175p. [PRC, RPI
     .1-5   Scientific and technological qualifications. 1971. xxxi, 55p.
     [PRC, RPI
     .1-6   Summary tables. 1967. xxxi, (viii), 93p. [PRC, RPI

     Great Britain. General Register Office.
1966.2   Census 1966. United Kingdom. General and parliamentary constit-
     uency tables. London, HMSO, 1969. viii, 277p. 12 folding maps.
     [PRC, RPI

Great Britain. Office of Population Censuses and Surveys; General
    Register Office.
        Census 1971. Great Britain. London, HMSO, 1973-1978. 23 vols.
1971.1-1   Age, marital condition and general tables. 1974. xxvi, 67p.
    [PRC
.1-2   Country of birth tables. 1974. xxxiii, 194p. [PRC
              Country of birth supplement tables (10% sample). 1978. 2v.
.1-3-1   Pt. 1. Housing and household composition. xxx, 411p. [PC
.1-3-2   Pt. 2. Migration and economic activity. xxxii, 276p. [PC
              Economic activity. 1973-1975. Parts I-V.
.1-4-1   I. (100%). 1973. xxvi, 102p. [PRC
.1-4-2   II. (10%). 1975. xliii, 215p. [PRC
.1-4-3   III. (10%). 1975. xliii, 319p. [PRC
.1-4-4   IV. (10%). 1975. xlvii, 261p. [PRC
.1-4-5   V. (10%). 1975. xvii, 156p. [PRC
.1-5   Economic activity county leaflets. General explanatory notes.
    1975. xxxix p. [PRC
.1-6   Household composition summary tables. (10%). 1975. vii, 111p.
    [PRC, OPR
.1-7   Housing summary tables. 1974. xiv, 43p. [PRC
              Migration tables. (10% sample). 1974-1978. Parts I-V in 7v.
.1-8-1   I. 1974. xxiii, 172p. [PRC
.1-8-2   II. 1976. xvii, 30p. [PRC
                  III.
.1-8-3-a   a. 1977. xxiv, 230p. [PRC
.1-8-3-b   b. 1977. xxiv, 174p. [PRC
.1-8-3-c   c. 1977. xxiv, 228p. [PRC
.1-8-4   IV. 1978. xxxvi, 120p. [
.1-8-5   V. (Data by areas reconstituted after 1974). 1978. xxiii,
    304p. [
.1-9   Non-private households. 1974. xxvii, 190p. [PRC
.1-10   Persons of pensionable age. 1974. xi, 329p. [PRC
.1-11   Qualified manpower tables. (10% sample). 1976. 162p. [PRC
.1-12   Summary tables. (1% sample). 1973. lii, 176p. specimen forms.
    [PRC, OPR

GREECE

Hellenic Republic   Capital: Athens
Statistical Agency: National Statistical Service
                     [Ethnikē Statistikē Ypēresia]
                     14, Lycourgou Street
                     Athens,
Publications Distributor: Publications and Information Division
                           (of the above).

Greece. Ethnikē Statistikē
     Ypēresia.
1947.1   Genikē apographē tou plēthys-   General population census of the
mou tēe Dodekanesou energētheisa   Dodecanese Islands taken October
tēn 19ēn oktōbriou 1947. Analy-   19, 1947. Analytical tables.
tikoi pinakes./Recensement géné-   [Note: The Dodecanese Islands
ral de la population du Dodeca-   were ceded to Greece by Italy in
neses effectué le 19 octubre   1947].
1947. Tableaux analytiques.   [
Athens, Ethnikōn Typographeion,
n.d. 186p.

Greece. Ethnikē Statistikē
     Ypēresia.
     Plēthysmos tēs Ellados kata   The population of Greece at the
tēn apographēn tēs 7ēs Apriliou   census of April 7, 1951.
1951./Population de la Grèce au
recensement du 7 avril 1951.
Athens, Ethnikōn Typographeion,
1955-1961.
1951.1-1   Pragmatikos plēthysmos   De facto population by depart-
kata nomous, eparchias, dēmous,   ments, provinces, municipalities,
koinotētas, poleis kai chōria./   communes, towns and villages.
Population de fait par départe-   [PRC, BC, UN, RPI
ments, municipalités, communes,
villes et villages. 1955.
194p.
   .1-2   Plēthysmos tēs Ellados   Population of Greece at the cen-
kata tēn apographēn tēs 7ēs   sus of April 7, 1951. [Supple-
Apriliou 1951. 1961. 62p.   ment].
                                                 [

Greece. Ethnikē Statistikē
     Ypēresia.
   .2   Lexikon tōn dēmōn koinotētōn   Directory of the municipalities,
kai synoikismōn tēs Ellados.   communes and places in Greece.
Athens, Ethnikōn Typographeion,   [
1956. [16], 245p.

Greece. Ethnikē Statistikē
     Ypēresia.
     Apotelesmata tēs apographēs   Results of the population census
tou plēthysmou tēs 7ēs Apriliou   taken April 7, 1951.
1951./Résultats du recensement

de la population effectué le 7
avril 1951.   Athens, Ethnikon
Typographeion, 1958-1961. Vol.
I-III.

.3-1   Istorikē episkopēsis.
Methodologikē ekthesis. Analysis tōn apotelesmatōn. Pinakes
kat epiphaneian kai ypsometron./
Aperçu historique. Rapport
methodologique. Analyse des résultats. Tableaux par superficie et altitude. 1961. cxcviii,
312p.

Historical note. Methodological
report. Analysis of findings.
Tables by area and altitude.
[PRC, BC, UN, PSC, RPI

.3-2   Pinakes dēmographikōn kai
koinōnikōn charaktēristikōn tou
plēthysmou./Tableaux des caractéristiques démographiques et
sociales de la population. 1958.
viii, 591p.

Tables of the demographic and
social characteristics of the
population.
[PRC, BC, UN, PSC, RPI

.3-3   Pinakes oikonomikōn charaktēristikōn tou plēthysmou./Tab-
leaux des caractéristiques économiques de la population. 1958.
vii, 385p.

Tables of the economic characteristics of the population.
[PRC, BC, UN, PSC, RPI

Greece. Ethnikē Statistikē
        Ypēresia.
    Plēthysmou tēs Ellados kata
tēn apographēn tēs 19ēs Martiou
1961./Population de la Grèce au
recensement 19 mars 1961.
Athens, Ethnikōn Typographeion,
1962. Parts 1-2.

The population of Greece at the
census of March 19, 1961.

1961.1-1   Pragmatikos plēthysmos
kata nomous, eparchias, dēmous,
koinotētas kai oikismous./Popu-
lation de fait par départements,
eparchies, communes-dèmes, communes et localités. 1962. 183p.

De facto population by departments, eparchies, cities, towns,
villages and rural communities.
[PRC, UN, RPI, RIR

.1-2   Nomimos plēthysmos kata
nomous, eparchias, dēmous kai
koinotētas. 1962. 60p.

Legal population according to
departments, eparchies, cities
and towns.
[PRC

Greece. Ethnikē Statistikē
        Ypēresia.
.2   Lexikon tōn dēmōn koinotētōn
kai oikismōn tēs Ellados.
Athens, Ethnikōn Typographeion,
1963. [23], 319p.

Directory of municipalities, communes and places in Greece.
[PRC, RPI

Greece. Ethnikē Statistikē
       Ypēresia.
     Apotelesmata tēs apographēs   Results of the population and
plēthysmou katoikiōn tēs 19ēs   housing census of March 19, 1961.
Martiou 1961. Deigmatolēptikē   Sample elaboration.
epexergasia. Athens, Ethnikōn
Typographeion, 1962-1963. Vol.
I-VII.

1961.3-1   Dēmographika charaktēris-   Demographic characteristics.
        tika. 1962. 31p.   [PRC, PSC, BC, RPI, RIR
  .3-2   Ekpaideusis (epipedon ge-   Education (general educational
        nikēs ekpaideuseōs epaggelmatikē level, professional training).
        ekpaideusis). 1962. 31p.   [PRC, PSC, BC, RPI, RIR
  .3-3   Apascholēsis (oikonomikōs   Employment (economically active
        energos plēthysmos apascholou-   population, employed and unem-
        menoi kai anepgoi, ōrai erga-   ployed, hours of work).
        sias). 1962. 63p.   [PRC, PSC, BC, RPI, RIR
  .3-4   Plēthysmos oikonomikōs mē   Economically non-active popula-
        energos. 1962. 29p.   tion.
                                          [PRC, PSC, BC, RPI, RIR
  .3-5   Esōterikē metanasteusis.   Internal migration.
        1963. 54p.   [PRC, PSC, BC, RPI, RIR
  .3-6   Synthēkai stegaseōs noiko-   Housing conditions.
        kyriōn. 1963. 31p.   [PRC, PSC, BC, RPI, RIR
  .3-7   Synthesis kai loipa cha-   Composition and other character-
        raktēristika tōn noikokyrtōn.   istics of households.
               p.   [

Greece. Ethnikē Statistikē
       Ypēresia.
     Apotelesmata tēs apographēs   Results of the census of popula-
plēthysmou katoikiōn tēs 19ēs   tion and housing taken March 19,
Martiou 1961./résultats du re-   1961.
censement de la population et
des habitations effectué le 19
mars 1961. Athens, Ethnikōn
Typographeion, 1963-1968. Vol.
I-III in 12v.

  .4-1   I. Plēthysmos kata geō-   Population by geographic and ad-
        graphikas kai dioikētikas ypo-   ministrative subdivisions.
        diaireseis./Population par sub-   [PRC, UN, RPI, RIR
        divisions géographiques et ad-
        ministratives. 1964. 70, 618p.
               II. Dēmographika koinō-   Demographic, social and economic
        nika kai oikonomika charaktēris- characteristics of the population;
        tika tou plēthysmou. Synthēkai   housing conditions of households.
        stagaseōs tōn noikokyriōn.   Data by cities, towns and villa-
        Stoicheia kata dmous kai koino-   ges.
        tētas./Caractéristiques démo-
        graphiques, sociales et écono-
        miques de la population; condi-
        tions de logement des ménages.
        Données par communes-dèmes et
        communes. 1963-1966. Parts 1-10.

1961.4-2-1   Synolon Ellados, peri-
         phereia prōteuouses poleodomika.
         Sygkrotēmata kai poleis 50.000
         katoikōn kai anō. 1966. 126,
         [6]p.

All Greece, region of Athens, urban agglomerations and cities of
50,000 inhabitants and over.
[PRC, UN, RPI, RIR

.4-2-2   Loipē sterea kai Eu-
         boia./Le reste de la Grèce cen-
         trale et Eubée. 1964. 199p.

The remainder of central Greece
and Euboea.
[UN, PRC, RPI, RIR

.4-2-3   Peloponnēsos./Pelopo-
         nèse. 1963. 239p.

Peloponesus.
[PRC, Berkeley, RPI, RIR

.4-2-4   Ionioi nēsoi./Iles
         Ioniènnes. 1964. [114]p.

Ionian Islands.
[PSC, UN, PRC, RPI, RIR

.4-2-5   Epeiros./Epire. 1963.
         [138]p.

Epirus.
[PSC, UN, PRC, RPI, RIR

.4-2-6   Thessalia./Thessalie.
         1963. 123p.

Thessaly.
[Berkeley, PRC, RPI, RIR

.4-2-7   Makedonia./Macédoine.
         1963. 311p.

Macedonia.
[UN, Berkeley, PRC, RPI, RIR

.4-2-8   Thrakē./Thrace. 1964.
         74p.

Thrace.
[UN, PRC, RPI, RIR

.4-2-9   Nēsoi Aigaiou./Iles de
         la mer Egée. 1966. 116p.

Aegean Islands.
[PRC, PSC, UN, RPI, RIR

.4-2-10   Krētē./Crète. 1964.
         139p.

Crete.
[UN, PRC, RPI, RIR

         III. Dēmographika, koinō-
nika kai oikonomika charaktēristika tou plēthysmou. Synthēkai
stegaseōs tōn noikokyriōn. Synolon Ellados geōgraphika diame-
rismata kata periochas astikas,
ēmiastikas kai agrotikas./Carac-
téristiques démographiques, sociales et économiques de la population. Conditions de logement
des ménages. Grèce entière;
région géographiques; circonscriptions urbaines; semi-urbaines et rurales. 1968. vii,
301p.

Demographic, social and economic
characteristics of the population.
Housing conditions of households.
Whole of Greece, geographic regions, urban, semi-urban and rural districts.
[PRC, BC, RPI, RIR

         Greece. Ethnikē Statistikē
                 Ypēresia.
1971.1   Plēthysmos tēs Ellados kata
         tēn apographēn tēs 14ēs Martiou
         1971. Pragmatikos plēthysmos
         kata nōmous, eparchias, dōmous,
         koinotōtas kai oikismous./Popu-
         lation de la Grèce au recense-
         ment du 14 mars 1971. Popula-
         tion de fait par départements,
         éparchies, commmunes-dèmes, com-
         munes et localités. Athens,
         1972. 180p.

Population of Greece according
to the census of March 14, 1971.
De facto population by departments,
eparchies, cities, towns, villages
and rural communities.
[PRC, OPR

Greece. Ethnikē Statistikē
      Ypēresia.
1971.2   Plēthysmos tēs Ellados kata
tēn apographēn tēs 14ēs Martiou
1971. Praghmadigòs plēthysmos
kata nōmous, eparchias, dōmous,
koinotōtas kai oikismous.
Athens, Ethnikōn Typographeion,
1972. 180p.

Population of Greece according
to the census of March 14, 1971.
De jure population by departments,
eparchies, cities, towns, villages
and rural communities.
⌊UN

Greece. Ethnikē Statistikē
      Ypēresia.
   Apotelesmata apographēs plē-
thysmou--katoikiōn tēs 14ēs
Martiou 1971. (Deigmatolēptikē
epechergasia). Athens, Ethnikōn Typographeion, 1973. Vol.
I-III.

Results of the population and
housing census of March 14, 1971.
(Sample elaboration).

.3-1   I. Stoicheia synolou chō-
ras, periochōn (astikōn-ēmiasti-
kōn-agrotikōn) kai kyriōn poleo-
domikōn synkrotēatōn. Dēmographika charaktēristika, ekpaideusis, apascholēsis, oikonomikōs
mē energos plēthysmos, synthēkai
stegaseōs noikokyrtōn kai esōterikē metanasteusis. xiii,
131p.

Data on the national level, areas
(urban, semi-urban, rural) and
main agglomerations. Demographic
characteristics, education, employment, economically non-active
population, housing conditions of
households and internal migration.
⌊PRC, OPR, RPI

.3-2   II. Stoicheia eis spipe-
don diamerismatos ē nomou meta
diakriseōs, entos autōn, tōn
periochōn eis astikas, ēmiastikas kai agrotikas. Dēmographika charaktēristika, ekpaideusis, apascholēsis, oikonomikōs mē energos plēthysmos.
vii, 498p.

Data on geographic region or department (nomos) level, with a
distinction of the areas within
them, into urban, semi-urban and
rural ones. Demographic characteristics, education, employment,
economically non-active population.
⌊PRC, OPR, RPI

.3-3   III. ... Stoicheia
esōterikēs metanasteuseōs tou
plēthysmou kai systhēkōn stegaseōs tōn noikokyrtōn. viii,
116p.

... Data on internal migration
and on housing conditions of households.
⌊PRC, OPR, RPI

Greece. Ethnikē Statistikē
      Ypēresia.
   Apotelesmata tēs apographēs
plēthysmou katoikōn tēs 14ēs
Martiou 1971./Résultats du recensement de la population et
des habitations effectué le 14
mars 1971. (Résultats de l'elaboration du sondage au 25 pour

Results of the census of population and housing taken March 14,
1971. (Results of the tabulation
of a 25 percent sample of the census questionnaires). Data on the
level of the whole of Greece, geographic region and department

cent des questionnaires du recensement). Données au niveau
de la Grèce entière, région géographique et département avec
subdifisions de chacun d'eaux,
en circonscriptions urbaines,
semi-urbaines et rurales.
Athens, 1975-1977. Vol. I-III.
1971.4-1   I.

with subdivisions of each, in
urban, semi-urban and rural
boundaries.

.4-2   II. Dēmographika kai
koinōnika charaktēristika tou
plēthysmou./Caractéristiques
démographiques et sociales de
la population. 1975. xxx, 478p.

Demographic and social characteristics of the population.
[PRC, RPI

.4-3   III. Oikonomika charaktēristika./Caractéristiques
économiques. 1977. xxii, 690p.

Economic characteristics of the
population.
[OPR, PRC, RPI

GREENLAND

Capital: Godthaab

Statistical Agency: Ministry for Greenland   Statistics of Denmark
                     [Ministeriet for Grønland]   [Danmarks Statistik]
                     Hausergade 3   Sejrøgade 11
                     1128 Copenhaben K,   DK 2100 Copenhagen,
Publications Distributor: Danmarks Statistik

Denmark. Statistiske Departe-
     ment.
1945.1   Folketaellingen i Grønland   Population census of Greenland
den 31 december 1945./Popula-   of December 31, 1945.
tion du Gröenland au 31 décem-   [PRC, LC, UN
bre 1945.   Copenhagen, Bianco
Lunos, 1950. 41p. (Statistiske meddelelser, 4th series,
134th volume, 5th part).

Denmark. Statistiske Departe-
     ment.
1951.1   Befolkningen i Grønland.   Population in Greenland by sex,
Fordelt efter kon, alder, ci-   age, marital status, etc., at the
vil stand m.v. ved folketael-   census of December 31, 1951. Popu-
lingen den 31. december 1951.   lation 1952-1954 and marriages,
Folketallet 1952-1954 samt   births and deaths 1946-1954.
aegteskaber, fødte og døde 1946-   [PRC, LC
1954.   Copenhagen, 1956. (Sta-
tistiske Efterretninger 1956,
no. 69).

Denmark. Statistiske Departe-
     ment.
1955.1   Folketaellingen i Grønland   Population census in Greenland,
1955.   Copenhagen, 1962. 1p.   1955.
(Statistiske Efterretninger   [PRC, LC
1962, no. 24).

Denmark. Statistiske Departe-
     ment.
1960.1   Grønland. Folketaellingen   Greenland. Population census
1960. Aegteskaber, fødte og   1960. Marriages, births and deaths
døde 1952-1960.   Copenhagen,   1952-1960.
1965. 85p. (Statistisk Ta-   [PRC, LC, RIR
belvaerk, 1965, II).

Denmark. Danmarks Statistik.
1965.1   Grønland. Folke- og bolig-   Greenland. Population and hous-
taellingen 31. december 1965.   ing census, December 31, 1965.
Aegteskaber, fødte og døde,   Marriages, births and deaths,
1961-65.   Copenhagen, 1969.   1961-65.
154p. (Statisitsk Tabelvaerk,   [PRC, LC
1969: IX).

Denmark. Danmarks Statistik.
1970.1   Grønland. Folke- og boligtaellingen 31. december 1970.
Bilag: aegteskaber, fødte og
døde 1966-70. Copenhagen,
1974. 224p. (Statistisk Tabelvaerk, 1974: VI).

Greenland. Population and housing census, December 31, 1970.
Appendix: marriages, births and
deaths 1966-70.
[PRC, LC

Denmark. Ministeriet for Grønland.
.2   Folke- og boligtaellingen i
Grønland, 31. december 1970.
Copenhagen, 1972. 13, [21]p.
plus supplementary insert.
(Meddelelser fra Økonomist-
statistisk Kontor, no. 25).

Population and housing census of
Greenland, December 31, 1970.
[PRC

Denmark. Danmarks Statistik.
1976.1   Folke- og boligtaellingen:
Grønland, 26. oktober 1976.
Copenhagen, 1978. 219p.

Population and housing census:
Greenland, October 26, 1976.
[BC

GRENADA

State of Grenada.   Capital: St. George's
Statistical Agency:

Publications Distributor: same

        Jamaica.   Central Bureau of Statistics.
1946   West Indian Census, ...
        [See Commonwealth Caribbean, Nos. 1946.1-A and H.]

        Trinidad and Tobago.   Central Statistical Office.
1960   Eastern Caribbean population census...
        [See Commonwealth Caribbean, Nos. 1960.1-1-A and D.
                                          1960.1-2-W
                                          1960.1-3-WG-1 and 2.]

        West Indies. University. Census Research Programme.
1970   1970 population census...
        [See Commonwealth Caribbean, Nos. 1970.1-1
                                          1970.1-2-?
                                          1970.1-3
                                          1970.1-4-7 and 16.
                                          1970.1-6-2
                                          1970.1-7
                                          1970.1-8-a, b, and c.
                                          1970.1-9-2
                                          1970.1-10-2 and 4.]

GUADELOUPE

Department of Guadeloupe (France)   Capital: Basse-Terre
Statistical Agency: INSEE, Departmental Service of Guadeloupe.
                     [INSEE, Service Départemental de la Guadeloupe]
                     B. P. 96
                     Basse-Terre,
Publications Distributor: same

France. Ministère de la France
         d'Outre-Mer. Service des
         Statistiques.
1946.1   État comparatif de la popu-   Comparative status of the popula-
lation du département recensée   tion of the Department enumerated
au 1er juillet 1936 et au 25   July 1, 1936 and April 25, 1946.
avril 1946. In: Journal Offi-   [UFL, PRC, RPI
ciel de la Guadeloupe, 20 sep-
tembre 1947. Paris, Impr.
Nationale, 1947. p. 975.

France. INSEE.
1954.1   Résultats statistiques du   Statistical results of the general
recensement général de la popu-   population census in the overseas
lation dans départements d'outre-   departments taken July 1, 1954:
mer effectué 1er juillet 1954:   French Antilles: Martinique and
Antilles françaises: Martinique   Guadeloupe.
et Guadeloupe. Paris, Impr.   [BC, PRC, RPI
Nationale, 1956. 300p.

France. INSEE.
1961.1   Résultats statistiques du   Statistical results of the general
recensement général de la popu-   population census of the overseas
lation des départements d'outre-   departments taken October 9, 1961:
mer effectué le 9 octobre 1961:   Guadeloupe.
Guadeloupe. Paris, Impr. Na-   [PRC, BC, UN, RPI
tionale, 1967. 183p.

France. INSEE.
1967.1   Résultats statistiques du   Statistical results of the general
recensement général de la popu-   population census of the overseas
lation des départements d'outre-   departments taken October 16, 1967:
mer effectué le 16 octobre 1967:   Guadeloupe. Part 1: statistical
Guadeloupe. 1re partie, tableaux   tables.
statistiques. Paris, Impr. Na-   [PRC
tionale, n.d. 106p.

[Part 2 had not been printed as of 1973 and no citation has been seen
up to the present.]

France. INSEE.
1974.1   Recensement de la population   Census of the overseas depart-
des départements d'outre-mer,   ments, 1974.
1974. Paris,   [

France.   INSEE.
1974.2   Recensement général de la   General population census of 1974.
         population en 1974.   Population   Population of France, overseas de-
         de la France, départements d'   partments: districts, communes.
         outre-mer: arrondissements,   [
         communes.   Paris, 1976.   29p.

GUAM

Capital: Agana.

Statistical Agency: U.S. Department of the Interior
Washington, D.C.   20240   USA

Publications Distributor: U.S. Government Printing Office
Washington, D.C.   20402   USA

U.S.   Bureau of the Census.
1950.1-2-51/54   Census of population: 1950.   A report of the seventeenth
decennial census of the United States.   Volume II.   Characteristics
of the population.   Part 51-54.   Territories and possessions (Alaska,
Hawaii, Puerto Rico, American Samoa, Canal Zone, Guam and Virgin Islands).   1953.   var. pag.   [PRC, TXU, RPI

Guam.   Office of the Chief Commissioner.
1955.1   Island-wide census as of June 30, 1955.   [Agana], n.d.   2p.
[PRC

Guam.   Office of the Chief Commissioner.
1958.1   Island-wide census as of June 30, 1958.   [Agana], n.d.   3p.
[PRC

U.S.   Bureau of the Census.
1960.1-1-54-57   Census of population: 1960.   The eighteenth decennial census
of the United States.   Volume I.   Characteristics of the population.
Part 54-57.   Outlying areas (Virgin Islands, Guam, American Samoa, and
Canal Zone).   1963.   [218]p.   [PRC, TXU, RPI

U.S.   Bureau of the Census.
1970.1-1-54/58   Census of population: 1970.   Volume I.   Characteristics of
the population.   Part 54-58.   Guam, Virgin Islands, American Samoa,
Canal Zone, Trust Territory of the Pacific Islands.   1973.   var. pag.
[PRC, TXU, RPI

GUATEMALA

Republic of Guatemala.   Capital: Guatemala, C.A.
Statistical Agency: General Bureau of Statistics.
                      [Dirección General de Estadística]
                      8ª, Calle 9-55, Zona 1
                      Guatemala, C.A.,
Publications Distributor: same

Guatemala. Dirección General
    de Estadística.
1950.0-1   Censos, abril 1950. Pob-   Censuses, April 1950. Popula-
lación, agropecuaria. Prepara-   tion, agriculture. Preparation,
ción, empadronamiento, elabora-   enumeration, processing.
ción. [Guatemala, Imprenta   [PRC, TXU, RPI
Iberia, n.d.] 48p.

Guatemala. Dirección General
    de Estadística.
.1   Sexto censo de población,   Sixth census of population, April
abril 18 de 1950. [Guatemala,   18, 1950.
Imprenta Universitaria, 1953].   [PRC, TXU, BC, RPI
244p.

Guatemala. Dirección General
    de Estadística.
.2   Sexto censo de población.   Sixth census of population.
[Guatemala, 1957]. lxvi, 304p.   [PRC, TXU, RPI

[Note: The introduction to No. 1950.2, above, cited the future publication of five regional volumes or two volumes of departmental results.
No citations have been seen of either set.]

Guatemala. Dirección General
    de Estadística.
1964.0-1   Censos de 1964: vivienda,   Censuses of 1964: housing, popu-
población, agropecuario y leyes   lation, agriculture and laws per-
alusivas a los censos. Manual   taining to the censuses. Manual
para el empadronador. Guate-   for the enumerator.
mala, 1964. 160p. specimen   [PRC, RPI
forms.

Guatemala. Dirección General
    de Estadística.
.0-2   Estudio post-enumerativo   Post-enumerative census study,
censal 1964. [Guatemala],   1964.
1965. 95p. map, specimen form.   [PRC, RPI

Guatemala. Dirección General
    de Estadística.
.1   Censo de población 1964.   Population census 1964. Results
Resultados de tabulación por   of the sampling tabulation.

muestreo.   Guatemala, 1966.   [UN, PRC, RPI
iv, 131p.

Guatemala.   Dirección General
        de Estadística.
1964.2   Población de la ciudad de   Population of Guatemala City.
Guatemala.   Censos 1964.   Resul-   Census of 1964.   Results of the
tados de tabulación por muestreo.   sampling tabulation.
[Guatemala, 1966].   xi, 175p.   [UN, PRC, RPI

Guatemala.   Dirección General
        de Estadística.
   .3   Censo de 1964.   Ajuste en la   Census of 1964.   Adjustment in
distribución de la población de   the population distribution of
la República de Guatemala por   the Republic of Guatemala by age.
edad.   [Guatemala], 1967.   [UN, PRC, RPI
[18]p.

Guatemala.   Dirección General
        de Estadística.
   .4   Algunas características de   Some population characteristics
la población de Guatemala, 1964.   of Guatemala, 1964.   Results of
Resultados de tabulación manual.   the manual tabulation.
[Guatemala], 1968.   [2], 37p.   [UN, PRC, RPI

Guatemala.   Dirección General
        de Estadística.
      VII censo de población, 1964.   Seventh population census, 1964.
Guatemala, 1971-1972.   Tomo I-III.
   .5-1   I.   Metodología.   Pobla-   Methodology.   Total population
ción total por sexo, edad, gru-   by sex, age, ethnic group, urban-
po étnico, urbano-rural y estado   rural and marital status.
civil.   1971.   529p.   [PRC, UFL, RPI
   .5-2   II.   Migración, ciudada-   Migration, citizenship, literacy,
nía, alfabetismo, asistencia   school enrollment, highest grade
escolar, último grado aprobado,   passed, other cultural character-
otras características culturales: istics: language, dress, foot-
lengua o idioma, traje, calzado   wear and religion.
y religión.   [1971].   823p.   [UN, PRC, RPI
   .5-3   III.   Ocupación principal,   Main occupation, branch of activ-
rama de actividad, y posición   ity and occupational position.
ocupacional.   Población econó-   Economically active population.
micamente activa.   Fecundidad.   Fertility.
1972.   477, [1]p.   [PRC, UN, RPI

Guatemala.   Dirección General
        de Estadística.
      Censos, VIII de población y   Censuses, 8th of population and
III de habitación, 26 de marzo--   3d of dwellings, March 26-April
7 de abril 1973.   Guatemala,   7, 1973.
1973-19   Series I-III in

Serie I. Cifras prelimi-
nares. No. 1-
1973.1-1-1   Población total de la
República: área urbana y rural,
sexo, departamento y municipio.
1973. 43p.
.1-1-2

Series I. Preliminary figures.

Total population of the Republic:
urban and rural area, sex, department and municipality.
[PRC, BC

Serie II. Resultados de
tabulación por muestreo.
.1-2-1   Población total--Repú-
blica-departamento-municipio de
Guatemala. Indígena--República-
departamento. 1974. xxxi,
463p.
.1-2-2

Series II. Sample tabulation
results.
Total population of the Republic,
department and municipality of
Guatemala. Native population of
the Republic and department.
[UN

Serie III. Cifras defi-
nitivas.
.1-3-1   República--población
total, población indígena.
1975. xliv, 587p.
.1-3-2   Ciudad Capital (Municipio de Guatemala), datos por
zona municipal, población total,
población indígena. 1977. xxv,
308p.
.1-3-3

Series III. Final figures.

The Republic--total population,
native population.
[PRC, BC, UN
Capital city (Municipality of
Guatemala), data by municipal
zone, total population, native
population.
[PSC, UN

Guatemala. Dirección General
de Estadística.
Censos nacionales 1973. Datos definitivos del VIII censo
nacional de población de 26 de
marzo de 1973. Población total
residente del departamento...
Guatemala, 1974. (Boletín informativo, 30.9.74/Informador
estadístico, Nos. 40-52).

National censuses of 1973. Final
data of the Eighth national population census of March 26, 1973.
Total resident population of the
department of...

1973.2-1 through 1973.2-14. 1. Guatemala (BI. 30.9.74) 4p./2. El Progresso,
Sacatepéques (IE, No. 40) 2p./3. Chimaltenango, Esquintla (IE, No.41)
2p./4. Santa Rosa, Sololá (IE, No.42) 2p./5. Tolonicapán, Quezaltenan-
go (IE, no. 43) 2p./6. Suchitepéquez (IE, No.44) 2p./7. Retalguleu,
San Marcos (IE, No.45) 2p./8. Huehuetenango (IE, No.46) 2p./9. Qui-
ché, Baja Verapaz (IE, No.47) 2p./10. Alta Verapaz, Petén (IE, No.48)

2p./11. Izabal, Zacapa (IE, No.49) 2p./12. Chiquimula, Jalapa (IE, No.50) 2p./13. Juliapa (IE, No.51) 2p./14. República de Guatemala (IE, No.52) 2p. [PRC

GUINEA

Republic of Guinea.   Capital: Conakry
Statistical Agency: Central Division of International Technical Cooperation.
                     [Division Centrale de Coopération Technique Internatio-
                        nale]
                     Presidence de la Republique de Guinée
                     B.P. 1210
                     Conakry,
Publications Distributor: same

         France. INSEE [and] Service Colonial des Statistiques.
1946   Résultats du recensement de 1946...
               [See French Overseas Territories, Nos. 1946.1-1, 2 & 3.
                                          1946.2]

         France. INSEE.
1951   Le recensement de la population...
               [See French Overseas Territories, No. 1951.1]

         French West Africa. Service de la Statistique Générale.
            Recensement de la population...
               [See French Overseas Territories, No. 1951.2]

         French West Africa. Service de
            la Statistique Générale.
1951.3   Population de l'A.O.F. en   Population of French West Africa
         1950-1951 par canton et groupe   in 1950-1951 by canton and ethnic
         éthnique, chiffres provisoires.   group, provisional figures.
         Dakar, 1952. [135]p.   [UN, PRC, RPI

         Guinea. Service des Statis-
               tiques.
            Étude démographique par son-   Demographic study by sample in
         dage en Guinée, 1954-1955.   Guinea, 1954-1955.
         Paris, 1956-[1961]. 3 parts.
1955.1-1   Technique d'enquête.   Technique of the survey.
         1956. [9], 109p.   [UFL, NWU, RPI
    .1-2   Résultats définitifs I.   Final results I. Individual da-
         Données individuelles: sexe,   ta: sex, age, ethnic group,
         âge, groupe éthnique, état ma-   marital status, fertility, mor-
         trimonial, fécontité, mortali-   tality.
         té. [1959]. iii, 209p.   [NWU, OPR, RPI
    .1-3   Résultats définitifs II.   Final results II. Individual
         Données individuelles: déplace-   data: geographic mobility, occu-
         ments, activité professionnelle,   pations, school attendance. Col-
         fréquentation scolaire. Données   lective data: households, con-
         collectives: ménages, conces-   cessions.
         sions. [1961]. [12], 211p.   [NWU, OPR, RPI

         France. INSEE.
1957.1   Enquête démographique de la   Demographic survey of the region

région du Konkoure (Guinée)
1957. Résultats définitifs.
Paris, 1962. [2], 71p.

of Konkoure (Guinea) 1957.
Final results.
[NWU, RPI

The next census was projected for 1978 but no publications have been
seen as yet.

GUINEA-BISSAU

Republic of Guinea-Bissau   Capital: Bissau
Statistical Agency: Statistical Service
                      [Serviços de Estatística]
                      Bissau,
Publications Distributor: same

The Cape Verde Islands, another former Portuguese possession, are expected to merge with Guinea-Bissau.

Portuguese Guinea.   Secção Téc-
     nica de Estatística.
     Provincia da Guiné. Censo   Province of Guinea.   Population
da população de 1950.   Lisboa,   census of 1950.
Junta de Investigações do Ultra-
mar, 1953-1959. (Estudos de
Ciências Políticas e Sociais,
No.25). Vol. I-II.
1950.1-1   I. População civilizada.   Civilized, [non-African], popula-
1959.   42, [11]p.   tion.
                                         [LC, PRC, NWU, Harvard
   .1-2   II. População não civi-   Non-civilized, [African], popula-
lizada. 1953. 602p.   tion.
                                         [LC, PRC, NWU, Harvard

Portuguese Guinea.
1952.1   Provincia da Guiné: recense- Province of Guinea: census of
amento da população indígena de   the indigenous population of 1952.
1952. In: Boletim cultural da   [NWU
Guiné Portuguesa, ano 8, No. 29).
[Bissau], 1953. Pp. 17-60.

Portuguese Guinea. Repartição
        Provincial do Serviços de
        Estatística.
1960.1   Censo de 1960. Estado da   Census of 1960.   State of the
população. [n.p., n.d.] 2   population.
folios (typed).   [PRC

[An official publication was never issued for the 1960 census.]

Portugal. Instituto Nacional de Estatística.
1970   [1970 recenseamento da população...
          [See Portugal 1970.3.]

The next census was scheduled for 1978 but no publications have been
seen as yet.

GUYANA

Cooperative Republic of Guyana   Capital: Georgetown
Statistical Agency: Statistical Bureau
                     Ministry of Economic Development
                     P.O. Box 542
                     Georgetown,
Publications Distributor: same

Jamaica. Central Bureau of Statistics.
1946   West Indian census, 1946...
          [See Commonwealth Caribbean, Nos. 1946.1-A & D]

Trinidad and Tobago. Central Statistical Office.
1960   East Caribbean population census of 1960...
          [See Commonwealth Caribbean, Nos. 1960.1-1-A & E
                                        1960.1-2-BG-1 & 2
                                        1960.1-3-BG-1, 2 & 3]

West Indies. University. Census Research Programme.
1970   1970 population census...
          [See Commonwealth Caribbean, Nos. 1970.1-1
                                        1970.1-2-?
                                        1970.1-3
                                        1970.1-4-3 & 16
                                        1970.1-5
                                        1970.1-6-1
                                        1970.1-7
                                        1970.1-8-a, b & c
                                        1970.1-9-1
                                        1970.1-10-1 & 4]

Guyana. Statistical Bureau.
1970.2   Population census, 1970: summary tables.   [Georgetown, 197?]
          29p. [

HAITI

Republic of Haiti.   Capital: Port-au-Prince
Statistical Agency: Haitian Institute of Statistics
                     [Institut Haïtien de Statistique]
                     Departement des Finances et des Affaires Économiques
                     Port-au-Prince,
Publications Distributor: same

Haiti. Bureau de Recensement.
1950.0-1   Recensement général de la   General census of the Republic
    République d'Haiti, août 1950...   of Haiti, August 1950... In-
    Instructions aux énumerateurs.   structions for the enumerators.
    Port-au-Prince, Impr. de l'État,   [Berkeley, PRC, RPI
    1950. 22p.

Haiti. Bureau de Recensement.
.0-2   Recensement de la Répub-   Census of the Republic of Haiti.
    lique d'Haiti. Premier dénom-   First enumeration of the popula-
    brement de la population.   tion.
    Port-au-Prince, n.d. 47p.   [BC, PRC, RPI

Haiti. Institut Haïtien de
      Statistique.
    Recensement général de la   General census of the Republic
    République d'Haiti, août 1950.   of Haiti, August 1950.
    Port-au-Prince, 1955-[1958?].
    Vol. I-V in 8v.
.1-1   I. Département du Nord-   Northwest department.
    ouest. 1955. 318p.   [UN, PRC, RPI
          II. Département du Nord.   North department.
    Tome 1-2.
.1-2-1   Démographie-économie.   Demography-economy.
    n.d. 531p.   [UN, PRC, RPI
.1-2-2   Famille et habitation-   Family and housing-agriculture
    agriculture et élevage. n.d.   and [animal] husbandry.
    235p.   [UN, PRC, RPI
.1-3   III. Département de l'   Artibunite department.
    Artibunite. n.d. 506p.   [UN, PRC, RPI
          IV. Département de l'   West department.
    Ouest. Tome 1-2.
.1-4-1   Démographie-économie.   Demography-economy.
    n.d. 529p.   [UN, PRC, RPI
.1-4-2   Famille et habitation-   Family and housing-agriculture
    agriculture et élevage. n.d.   and [animal] husbandry.
    260p.   [UN, PRC, RPI
          V. Département du Sud.   South department.
    Tome 1-2.
.1-5-1   Démographie-économie.   Demography-economy.
    n.d. 553p.   [UN, PRC, RPI
.1-5-2   Famille et habitation-   Family and housing-agriculture
    agriculture et élevage. n.d.   and [animal] husbandry.
    250p.   [UN, PRC, RPI

Haiti. Institut Haïtien de
Statistique.
.2   Dénombrement de la population de la République d'Haiti.
Résultats définitifs du recensement de 1950. Nouvelle édition-
avril, 1956. Port-au-Prince,
1956. 31p.

Enumeration of the population of
the Republic of Haiti. Final
results of the census of 1950.
New edition - April 1956.
[Berkeley, PRC, RPI

[Note: The following carry a logo, "Recensement Général, 1970."
This the date of the decree authorizing the census which was taken
in September 1971. The numbering will be that of the year the census
was taken; i.e., 1971.]

Haiti. Institut Haïtien de
Statistique.
1971.0-1   Recensement général 1970:
méthods et procedes. Port-au-
Prince, 1971.   p.

General census, 1970. Methods
and procedures.
[

Haiti. Institut Haïtien de
Statistique.
.0-2   Recensement général 1970:
résultats préliminaires du recensement général de la population, du logement et de l'agriculture (septembre 1971). Port-
au-Prince, 1973. vi, 49p. maps,
graphs.

General census, 1970. Preliminary results of the general census of the population, of housing and of agriculture (September 1971)
[PRC

Haiti. Institut Haïtien de
Statistique.
Résultats complémentaires du
recensement général de la population, du logement et de l'agriculture (septembre 1971): résultats préliminaires de l'enquête
démographique à passages répétés;
projections provisoires de population. Port-au-Prince, 1975.
2v.
.0-3-1   311p.
.0-3-2   190p.

Supplementary results of the
general census of the population,
of housing and of agriculture
(September 1971): preliminary
results of the demographic survey at repeated passages; provisional projections of the population.

[
[

HONDURAS

Republic of Honduras   Capital: Tegucigalpa, D.C.
Statistical Agency: General Bureau of Statistics and Censuses
                     [Dirección General de Estadística y Censos]
                     Secretaria de Economía
                     Tegucigalpa, D.C.,
Publications Distributor: Departamento de Estadísticas Continuas
                           (of the above).

Honduras. Dirección General de
        Estadística y Censos.
1945.1   Resumen del censo general de   Summary of the general population
          población levantado el 24 de   census taken June 24, 1945.
          junio de 1945. Tegucigalpa,   [TXU, JB-F,
          1947. [2], 191, ii p.

Honduras. Dirección General de
        Censos y Estadísticas.
1950.1   Resultados generales del cen-   General results of the general
          so general de la República le-   census of the Republic taken June
          vantado el 18 de junio de 1950.   18, 1950. [Cover title: General
          [Cover title: Resumen general   summary of the population census
          del censo de población...]   ...]
          Tegucigalpa, Talleres Tipográ-   [PRC, TXU, BC, RPI
          ficos Nacionales, 1952. 373,
          x p.

Honduras. Dirección General de
        Censos y Estadísticas.
        Detalle del censo de pobla-   Details of the population census
        ción por departamentos, levan-   by department, taken June 18,
        tado el 18 de junio de 1950.   1950.
        Tegucigalpa, 1952. Tomo I-II.
.2-1   I. [Departamentos de
        Atlántida, Colón, Comayagua,
        Copán, Cortés, Choluteca, El
        Paraíso, Francisco Morazán.]
        692p.   [PRC, TXU, UN, RPI
.2-2   II. [Departamentos de
        Intibucá, Islas de la Bahía,
        La Paz, Lempira, Octepeque,
        Olancho, Santa Bárbara, Valle,
        Yoro.] 840p.   [PRC, LC, UN, TXU, RPI

Honduras. Dirección General de
        Estadística y Censos.
1961.0-1-1 Manual de enumeración,   Enumeration manual, general cen-
        censo general de vivienda y   sus of housing and population,
        población, 1961. Tegucigal-   1961.
        pa, 1960. 30p.   [TXU, PRC, RPI

1961.0-1-2   Entrenamiento de delegados.
Tegucigalpa, 1961. 94p. speci-
men forms.

   Census workers' training manual.
[TXU, PRC, RPI

Honduras. Dirección General de
   Estadística y Censos.
.0-2-1   Censo experimental: vivienda, población, agropecuario,
municipio de Sabanagrande, sept.
1959. Tegucigalpa, 1960. [3],
53p.

   Experimental census: housing,
population, agriculture, municipality of Sabanagrande, Sept.
1959.
[TXU, PRC, RPI

.0-2-2   Censo experimental: vivienda, población, Barrio Buenos
Aires, [1959]. Tegucigalpa,
1960. 28p.

   Experimental census: housing,
population, Barrio Buenos Aires,
[1959].
[TXU, PRC, RPI

.0-2-3   Censo experimental: vivienda y población: Barrio el
Benque, San Pedro Sula, abril
1960. Tegucigalpa, 1960. 29p.

   Experimental census: housing
and population, Barrio el Benque,
San Pedro Sula, April 1960.
[PRC

.0-2-4   Censo experimental de vi-
vienda y población de Santa Rita,
Macuelizo, Azacualpa, abril 1960.
Tegucigalpa, 1961. iv, 89p.

   Experimental census of housing
and population of Santa Rita,
Macuelizo, Azacualpa, April 1960.
[PRC, RPI

Honduras. Dirección General de
   Estadística y Censos.
.0-3   Estudio de enumeración
post-censal del censo de población y viviendas de Honduras,
1961. Tegucigalpa, 1962. 29p.

   Study of the post-censal enumeration of the population and housing census of Honduras, 1961.
[LC

Honduras. Dirección General de
   Estadística y Censos.
.0-4-1   Censo nacional de vivienda
y población, abril 1961. Resumen preliminar. Tegucigalpa,
1961. 3, 1, 20p.

   National census of housing and
population, April 1961. Preliminary summary.
[BC, PRC, RPI

.0-4-2   Datos preliminares del
censo nacional de población,
abril 1961, obtenidos por medio
de muestra. Tegucigalpa, 1962.
xxv, 220p.

   Preliminary data from the national population census, April 1961,
obtained from a sample.
[BC, PRC, RPI

.0-4-3   Resumen preliminar: viviendas y población en cabeceras
municipales y en aldeas y caseríos, abril 1961. Tegucigalpa,
1962. 30p.

   Preliminary summary: housing and
population in municipal capitals
and in villages and small towns,
April 1961.
[BC, PRC, RPI

.0-4-4   Resultados preliminares
del censo de vivienda obtenidos
por muestra, abril 1961. Tegucigalpa, 1962. xi, 210p.

   Preliminary results of the hous-
ing census obtained from a sample,
April 1961.
[PRC

Honduras. Dirección General de
      Estadística y Censos.
   Población y vivienda, abril   Population and housing, April
1961. Departamento de...   Te-   1961. Department of...
gucigalpa, 1962–1964. 18v.
1961.1-1 through 1961.1-18 1. Atlántida. 1962. xxvi, 103p./2. Colón.
[1963]. xxiii, [2], 106p./3. Comayagua. [1963]. vi, [3], 119p./4.
Copán. 1963. vi, [3], 130p./5. Cortés. 1963. xxxii, [3], 121p./6.
Choluteca. n.d. xxi, [3], 119p./7. El Paraíso. 1963. v, [3], 119p./
8. Francisco Morazán. [1963]. xxi, [3], 132p./9. Gracias a Dios.
n.d. xx, [2], 75p./10. Intibucá. 1963. v, [3], 119p./11. Islas de
la Bahia. 1963. xxv, [2], 106p./12. La Paz. 1963. v, [3], 119p./
13. Lempira. 1963. v, [3], 130p./14. Ocotepeque. 1963. v, [3],
119p./15. Olancho. [1963]. vi, [3], 130p./16. Santa Bárbara. 1963.
v, [3], 130p./17. Valle. [1963]. xvi, [3], 106p./18. Yoro. [1963].
xv, [3], 119p. [BC, PRC, RPI

Honduras. Dirección General de
      Estadística y Censos.
.2   Censo nacional de población   National population and housing
y vivienda, abril 1961: cifras   census, April 1961: final figures
definitivas, población y vivien-   population and housing in munici-
das en cabeceras municipales y   pal capitals and in villages and
en aldeas y caseríos. Teguci-   small towns.
galpa, 1963. 24p.   [PRC, RPI

Honduras. Dirección General de
      Estadística y Censos.
.3   Principales poblaciones del   Principal population centers of
país. Tegucigalpa, 1963. vi,   the country.
158p.   [Berkeley, PRC, LC, RPI

Honduras. Dirección General de
      Estadística y Censos.
   Censo nacional de Honduras.   National census of Honduras.
Tegucigalpa, 1964. 2v.
.4-1   Características generales   General and educational character-
y educativas de la población.   istics of the population, April
Abril de 1961. 237p.   1961.
                                      [BC, PRC, RPI
.4-2   Características económi-   Economic characteristics of the
cas de la población, abril de   population, April 1961.
1961. 262p.   [BC, PRC, RPI

Honduras. Dirección General de
      Estadística y Censos.
   Censo de población y vivien-   Population and housing census.
da. Ciudad de..., abril 1961.   City of..., April 1961.
Tegucigalpa, 1965. 2v.
.5-1   San Pedro Sula. xx, 41p.   [PRC
.5-2   Tegucigalpa, D.C. xx,
43p.   [PRC

Honduras. Dirección General de
        Estadística y Censos.
.6   Segundo censo national de
vivienda de Honduras, abril 1961.
Tegucigalpa, 1964. xii, 135p.

Second national housing census of
Honduras, April 1961.
[Berkeley, PRC, RPI

Honduras. Dirección General de
        Estadística y Censos.
1974.1   Censo de poblacíon y vivienda, 1974. Resultados muestra.
Tegucigalpa, 1975. ii, 98p.

Census of population and housing,
1974. Sample results.
[PRC

Honduras. Dirección General de
        Estadística y Censos.
    Censo nacional de población.
Tegucigalpa, 1976-1977. Tomo I-
II.

National population census.

.2-1   I. Resumen por departamento y municipio. 1976. [v],
xxix, 256p.

Summary by department and municipality.
[BC, PRC, UN, NYPL

.2-2   II. Sumaria. 1977.
[v], 291p.

[General] summary.
[BC, PRC

Honduras. Dirección General de
        Estadística y Censos.
    Censo nacional de vivienda,
[1974]. Tegucigalpa, 1976.
Tomo I-III.

National housing census.

.3-1   I. [Resumen]. ii, 313p.

[Summary].
[PRC, UN, JB-F

.3-2   II. Cabeceras municipales.
i, 165p.

Municipal capitals.
[PRC, UN, JB-F

.3-3   III. Sumaria nacional.
iii, 157p.

National summary.
[PRC, UN, JB-F

Honduras. Dirección General de
        Estadística y Censos.
.4   [Informe general...]

HONG KONG

Colony of Hong Kong.
Statistical Agency: Census and Statistics Department
                     Kai Tak Commercial Building
                     317 Des Voeux Road, Central
                     Hong Kong.
Publications Distributor: Director of Information Services
                          Beaconsfield House, 6th Floor
                          Queen's Road, Central
                          Victoria, Hong Kong.

   Hong Kong. Census Commissioner's Office.
      Report on the census, 1961. By K.M.A. Barnett.   Hong Kong, Govern-
   ment Printer, [1962]. Vol. I-III.
1961.1-1   I. The preliminaries and the pilot censuses of 23 January and
      25 October, 1960. xli, 39p. specimen forms. 3 maps. [PRC, UN, RPI
   .1-2   II. The marine and land censuses, the household and personal
      tables. cxii, 91p. specimen forms. [PRC, UN, RPI
   .1-3   III. The economic tables, notes and comments. cxxxiv, 88p.
      [PRC, UN, RPI

   Hong Kong. Census Commissioner's Office.
      Report on the 1966 by-census. By K.M.A. Barnett.   Hong Kong,
   Government Printer, [1968]. Vol. I-II.
1966.1-1   I. Text, appendices and index. vii, LVp. 2 fold. maps. [PRC
      BC, RPI
   .1-2   II. Tables. iv, 202p. [PRC, BC, RPI

   Hong Kong. Census and Statistics Department.
1971.1   The 1971 census: a graphic guide.   Hong Kong, Government Printer,
      [1972]. iii, 25p. [PRC, BC

   Hong Kong. Census and Statistics Department.
      Hong Kong population and housing census, 1971.   Hong Kong, Govern-
   ment Printer, 1972-1974. 4v.
   .2-1   Basic tables. 1972. iii, 41p. [PRC, BC, UN
   .2-2   Main report. [1973]. v, 248p. 2 maps. [PRC, OPR, BC
   .2-3   Technical report. [1973]. [8], 303p. specimen forms. [PRC,
      BC
   .2-4   Transport characteristics. 1974. iii, 58p. [PRC

   Hong Kong. Census and Statistics Department.
1976.0-1   Coding manual, land by-census 1976.   Hong Kong, Government
      Printer, 1976. iv, 53p. [E-W, PRC

   Hong Kong. Census and Statistics Department.
      1976 population and housing by-census.   Hong Kong, Government
   Printer, 1977-   .
   .1-1   A graphic guide: 1976 by-census. 1977. v, 26p. [PRC, OPR
   .1-2   Basic tables. 1977. 55p. [E-W, PRC, PSC

```
                  Main report.   [1978].   2v.
1976.1-3-1          Analysis.   170p.   specimen form.   maps.   [OPR, E-W, PC
    .1-3-2          Tables.   272p.   [OPR, E-W, PC
```

HUNGARY

Hungarian People's Republic.   Capital: Budapest
Statistical Agency: Central Statistical Office
                      [Központi Statisztikai Hivatal]
                      Pf. 10/Keleti Károly u. 5-7
                      H-1525 Budapest II,
Publications Distributor: KULTURA
                      Hungarian Trading Company for Books & Newspapers
                      Pf. 149
                      H-1389 Budapest,

    Hungary.   Központi Statisztikai
         Hivatal.
         1949. évi népszámlálás.   1949 population census.
    Budapest, Allami, 1949-1952.
    Vol. 1-12 in 15v.
1949.1-1   Elözetes adatok. 1949.   Preliminary data.
    xvi, 103p.   [TXU, LC, NYPL, PRC, RPI
    .1-2   Mezögazdasági eredmények.   Agricultural data.
    1949. 63p.   [PRC, NYPL, RPI
    .1-3   Részletes mezögasdadági   Detailed agricultural data.
    eredmények. 1950. xvii, 539p.   [TXU, LC, NYPL, PRC, RPI
    .1-4   Épület- és lakásstatisz-   Building and housing census
    tikai eredmények. 1950. 66p.   statistical results.
    maps.   [PRC, LC, NYPL, RPI
    .1-5   Részletes épület- és lakás-   Building and housing census,
    statisztikai eredmények. 1950.   detailed results.
    xi, 455p.   [TXU, LC, NYPL, PRC, RPI
    .1-5a   Városias jellegü községek   Main data of the housing statis-
    föbb lakásstatisztikai adatai.   tics for communities of urban
    Kiegészités a részletes épület-   character. Supplement to the
    és lakásstatisztikai eredmények   publication...(1949.1-5).
    c. Kiadványhoz. 1950. 126p.   [PRC, LC, NYPL, RPI
    .1-6   Foglalkosásstatisztikai   Results of the occupation statis-
    eredmények. 1950. 108p.   tics.
                                                 [TXU, PRC, LC, NYPL, RPI
    .1-7   A foglalkozási statiszti-   Results of the occupation statis-
    ka országos eredményei. 1950.   tics for the whole country.
    xiv, 287p.   [TXU, LC, NYPL, PRC, RPI
    .1-7a   Munkanélküliek adatai.   Unemployment data. Supplement
    Kiegészités a foglalkozási sta-   to the publication...(1949.1-7).
    tisztika országos eredményei c.   [TXU, NYPL, PRC, RPI
    kiadványhoz. 1950. 28p.
    .1-8   A foglalkozási statistika   Detailed results of the occupa-
    részletes eredményei. 1950.   tion statistics.
    vii, 485p.   [TXU, LC, NYPL, PRC, RPI
    .1-8a   Nagyob városok foglalkozás-   Data of the occupation statistics
    statisztikai adatai. Kiegészites   in large towns. Supplement to
    a foglalkozási statisztika rés-   the publication...(1949.1-8).
    letes eredményei c. kiadványhoz.   [TXU, LC, NYPL, PRC, RPI
    1950. 56p.

.1-9   Demográfiai eredmények.
  1950. 71, 336p. map.
.1-10   Családstatisztikai eredmények. 1951. xxiv, 245p.
.1-11   A külterületi lakotthelyek
  föbb adatai. 1951. 115p.
.1-12   Összefoglaló föeredmények.
  1952. 61, 295, xxvi p.

Demographic results.
[TXU, LC, NYPL, PRC, RPI
Results of family statistics.
[TXU, LC, NYPL, PRC, RPI
Main data for suburban areas.
[TXU, LC, NYPL, PRC, RPI
Summary of final results.
[LC, NYPL, PRC, RPI

Hungary. Központi Statisztikai
    Hivatal.
    1960. évi népszámlálás.
Budapest, A Statisztikai Kiadó
Vállalat, 1960-1965. Vol. 1-
13 in 32v.

1960 population census.

1960.1-1   Elözetes adatok. 1960.
  304p.
.1-2   Személyi és családi adatok képuiseleti minta alapján.
  1960. 158p.
.1-2s   English supplement. 1960.
  56p.
    ...személyi és családi ada-
  tai. 1961-1962. 20v.

Preliminary data.
[TXU, PRC, BC, UN, RPI
Demographic and family data based
on a representative sample.
[TXU, PRC, BC, UN, RPI

[PRC, BC, UN, RPI
Demographic and family data of...
county.

1960.1-3-a through 1960.1-3-u. [All are for counties except where indicated].
a. Komárom. 1961. 237p./b. Fejér. 1961. 245p./c. Pest. 1961.
323p./d. Bács-Kiskun. 1961. 283p./e. Budapest (city). 1961. 539p./
f. Baranya and Pécs (city). 1961. 463p./g. Borsod-Abauj-Zemplén and
Miskolc (city). 1961. 503p./h. Györ-Sopron. 1962. 281p./i. Veszprém.
1962. 325p./j. Zala. 1962. 285p./k. Vas. 1962. 261, ix p./l. Somogy. 1962. 290, ix p./m. Tolna. 1962. 238, ix p./n. Nógrád. 1962.
237, ix p./o. Heves. 1962. 241, ix p./p. Szolnok. 1962. 241, ix p./
r. Szabolcs-Szatmér. 1962. 301, ix p./s. Hajdu-Bihar and Debrecen
(city). 1962. 341p./t. Békés. 1962. 237, ix p./u. Csongrád and
Szeged (city). 1962. 329, xii p. [PRC, BC, UN, RPI

.1-4   Lakásadatok I. Képviseleti minta és elözetes feldolgozás alapján. 1961. 119p.

Housing data I. Based on a representative sample and on preliminary processing.
[PRC, BC, UN, RPI

.1-5   Demográfiai adatok. 1962.
  200, xvi p.
.1-6   Foglalkozási adatok.
  1963. 322, xv p.
.1-7   A családok és háztartások
  adatai. 1963. 209, xii p.
.1-8   A lakások és lakóépületek
  adatai. 1963. 554p.

Demographic data.
[PRC, BC, UN, RPI
Occupational data.
[PRC, BC, UN, RPI
Family and household data.
[PRC, BC, UN, RPI
Data on housing and residential
buildings.
[PRC, BC, UN, RPI

.1-9   A keresök munkahelye. A
  népesség 1949 és 1960 évi lakó-
  helye. 1963. 368p.

Workplace and residence of gainfully employed. Residence in
1949 and 1960.
[PRC, BC, UN, RPI

.1-10   Foglalkozási adatok II.
1964. 335p.
.1-11   A lakott lakások és a
lakóházak adatai. 1964. 287p.

.1-12   A családok és háztartások
adatai II. 1964. 176p.
.1-13   Összefoglaló adatok 1964.
334p.

Occupational data II.
[PRC, BC, UN, RPI
Data on housing and residential
buildings.
[PRC, BC, UN, RPI
Family and household data II.
[PRC, BC, UN, RPI
Summary data.
[PRC, BC, UN, RPI

Hungary. Központi Statisztikai
Hivatal
.2   1960. évi népszámlálás. Az
adatfelvétel és feldolgozás.
Összefoglaló ismertetése. 1965.
120p.

1960 population census. Survey
of data and analysis. Summary
comments.
[PRC

Hungary. Központi Statisztikai
Hivatal.
1970. évi népszámlálás.
Budapest, Statisztikai Kiadó
Vállalat, 1970-1977. Vol. 1-
31 in 62v.
1970.1-1   Előzetes adatok. 1970.
376p.
.1-1a   Előzetes adatok. Az 1970.
julius 1--i államigazgatási
állapotnak megfelelöen. 1970.
151p.
.1-2   Részletes adatok az 1°/o
os képviseleti minta alapján.
1971. 238p.
     ...megye, számlálókörzeti
és külterületi adatai.

1970 population census.

Preliminary data.
[PRC
Preliminary data, July 1, 1970,
according to state administrative
areas.
[PRC
Detailed data from the one % representative sampling.
[PRC
...county, enumeration district
and suburb data. [Also city data.]

1970.1-3 through 1970.1-22a. [Three cities have no volume number and are
assigned "b" to the numeral used by the previous county cited.]
3. Györ-Sopron. 1971. 537, clvi p./3a. Györ-Sopron. 1971. 123p./
3b. Györ (town). 1972. 140p./4. Vas. 1971. 563, xlv p./4a. Vas.
1971. 107p./5. Tolna. 1971. 439, xliv p./5a. Tolna. 1971. 93p./
6-1. Csongrád I. 1971. 437, xlvi p./6-2. Csongrád and Szeged II.
1971. 313p./6a. Csongrád and Szeged. 1972. 119p./7. Fejér. 1971.
439, xliv p./7a. Fejér. 1972. 113p./7b. Székesfehérvár. 1972. 354p./
8. Békés. 1972. 487, xlvi p./8a. Békés. 1972. 143p./9-1. Baranya I.
1972. 663, xlv p./9-2. Baranya and Pécs II. 1972. 313p./9a. Baranya.
1972. 177p./10-1. Hajdu-Bihar I. 1972. 463, xlv p./10-2. Hajdu-
Bihar and Debrecen II. 1972. 313p./10a. Hajdu-Bihar. 1972. 137p./
11-1. Borsod-Abauj-Zemplén I. 1972. 711, xlvii p./11-2. Borsod-Abauj-
Zemplén and Miskolc II. 1972. 313p./11a. Borsod-Abauj-Zemplén. 1972.
227p./12. Heves. 1972. 463, xlv p./12a. Heves. 1972. 101p./13.
Veszprém. 1972. 685, il p./13a. Veszprém. 1972. 153p./14. Komárom.
1972. 511, xlvii p./14a. Komárom. 1972. 87p./15. Zala. 1972. 589,
xliv p./15a. Zala. 1972. 113p./16. Somogy. 1972. 589, xliv p./

16a. Somogy. 1972. 143p./17. Szabolcs-Szatmár. 1972. 563, xlv p./
17a. Szabolcs-Szatmár. 1972. 173p./18. Nógrád. 1972. 489, xliv p./
18a. Nógrád. 1972. 86p./19. Szolnok. 1972. 559, 1 p./19a. Szolnok.
1972. 134p./19b.-Szolnok. 1975. 368p./20. Bács-Kiskun. 1972. 511,
xlvii p./20a. Bács-Kiskun. 1972. 167p./21. Pest. 1972. 585, il p./
21a. Pest. 1972. 219p./22-1. Budapest I. 1973. 92, 470p./22-2.
Budapest II. 1973. 559p./22a. Budapest. 1973. 291p. [PRC

1970.1-23   Demográfiai adatok I.
            1973. 449p.

Demographic data I.
[PRC, OPR

.1-24   Foglalkozási adatok I.
            1973. 732p.

Occupational data I.
[PRC, OPR

.1-25   Háztartás és család adatok
            I. 1973. 213p.

Household and family data I.
[PRC, OPR

.1-26   Lakás és lakóépület adatok
            I. 1973. 178p.

Data on dwellings and buildings
I.
[PRC, OPR

.1-27   A Budapesti agglomeráció
            településeinek népességi jellem-
            zöi, a fövarosba dolgozni járók
            adatai. 1974. 111p.

Population characteristics of the
Budapest metropolitan area. Data
on workers traveling into the
capital.
[PRC

.1-28   A felsöfoku végzettségüek
            demográfiai adatai. 1976. 117p.

Demographic data of the population with third level education.
[PRC

.1-29   Foglalkozási adatok II.
            1977. 215p.

Occupational data II.
[PRC

.1-30   A keresök munkahelya a
            népesség. 1977. 42p.

Workplace and residence of gainfully employed population.
[

.1-[30a] ...[Tables]. 1976. 232p.

[

.1-31

The recapitulation of the data
collection and processing.
[

.1-31s   [English translation of 1970.1-31.] 1977. 231p. [PRC, OPR

ICELAND

Republic of Iceland.   Capital: Reykjavík.
Statistical Agency: Statistical Bureau of Iceland
                      [Hagstofu Íslands]
                      Reykjavík,
Publications Distributor: same

          Iceland. Hagstofu Íslands.
1950.1   Manntal á Íslandi 1. Desem-   Population census of Iceland on
          ber 1950.   Reykjavík, Ríkis-   December 1, 1950.
          prentsmidjunni Gutenberg, 1958.   [PRC, UN, RPI
          77, 196p. (Hagskÿrslur Íslands,
          II, 18).

          Iceland. Hagstofu Íslands.
1960.1   Manntal á Íslandi 1. Desem-   Population census of Iceland on
          ber 1960.   Reykjavík, Ríkis-   December 1, 1960.
          prentsmidjunni Gutenberg, 1969.   [PRC, BC, RPI
          56, 210p. (Hagskÿrslur Íslands,
          II, 47).

Note: Iceland has discontinued censuses and will rely on population
registers only.   It is not known if this practice began in 1970 or not.
The United Nations cites a "census" for Iceland in 1970 but the Statistical Bureau of Iceland says no.

INDIA

Republic of India.   Capital: New Delhi.
Statistical Agency: Office of the Registrar General
                     Ministry of Home Affairs
                     2-A, Man Singh Road
                     New Delhi, 110011,
Publications Distributor: same

   Note: Because of the great number and variety of publications stem-
   ming from Indian censuses, an attempt has been made to list only those
   reports that are strictly statistical results of the general population
   census. As a result, citations to Administrative Reports, Housing and
   Establishment Reports, Maps, Directories, District Census Handbooks,
   Village Survey Monographs, Ethnographic and Anthropological Studies
   have been left out or reduced to a minimum.

   India. Office of the Registrar General.
      Census of India, 1951. Census papers. Delhi, Manager of Publica-
      tions, 1952-1962. [e.g. 1951.1-52-1 is Paper No. 1 of 1952.]
1951.1-52-1 Final population totals - 1951 census. 1952. v, 25p. [TXU,
   RPI
   .1-52-2 Population zones, natural regions, subregions and divisions.
      1952. 152p. [TXU, RPI
   .1-53-1 Sample verification of the 1951 census. 1953.   25p. [BC, OPR
   .1-53-2 Religion. 1953. 37p. [TXU, BC, RPI
   .1-53-3 Summary of demographic and economic data. 1953. 157p. [TXU,
      BC, RPI
   .1-53-4 Special groups. 1953. 47p. [TXU, BC, RPI
   .1-53-5 Maternity data - 1951 census. 1953. 95p. [TXU, BC, RPI
   .1-54-1 Languages. 1954. 700p. [TXU, BC, RPI
   .1-54-2 Life tables - 1951 census. 1954. [6], 60p. [BC, RPI
   .1-54-3 Age tables - 1951 census. 1954. ii, 172p. [TXU, BC, RPI
   .1-54-4 Displaced persons - 1951 census. 1954. 176p. [TXU, BC, RPI
   .1-54-5 Literacy and educational standards - 1951. 1954. 296p. [TXU,
      BC, RPI
   .1-54-6 Estimation of birth and death rates in India during 1941-1950 -
      1951 census. 1954. 64p. [TXU, BC, RPI
   .1-54-7 Subsidiary tables - 1951 census. 1954. [ii], 270p. [TXU, BC,
      RPI
   .1-55-3 Economic classification by age groups - 1951 census: Uttar Pra-
      desh. 1956. [v], vii, 350p. [TXU, BC, RPI
   .1-55-4 Economic classification by age groups - 1951 census: Mysore.
      1956. [v], 200p. [TXU, BC, RPI
   .1-55-5 Economic classification by age groups - 1951 census: West Ben-
      gal. 1957. 309p. [TXU, RPI
   .1-55-6 Working population in Calcutta Industrial Region - distribution
      by industry, place of birth and educational attainment - 1951 census.
      1958. 677p. [TXU, BC, RPI
   .1-57-1 General population tables and summary figures by districts of
      re-organised states - 1951 census. 1957. 255p. [TXU, BC, RPI

1951.1-57-2 Livelihood, civil condition and literacy tables by age groups
        of sample population of re-organised states - 1951 census. 1957.
        265p. [TXU, BC, RPI
    .1-58-1 Characteristics of family households - 1951 census - West Bengal.
        1960. v, 535p. [TXU, BC, RPI
    .1-59-1 Religion and livelihood classes by educational standards of re-
        organised states - 1951 census. 1960. 49p. [TXU, BC, RPI
    .1-60-1 Economic tables of re-organised states - 1951 census. 1961.
        xxvi, 227p. [TXU, BC, RPI
    .1-60-2 Scheduled castes and scheduled tribes arranged in alphabetical
        order. 1960. 179p. [TXU, BC, RPI
    .1-60-3 Study of growth of towns between 1901-1951. 1962. v, 278p.
        [TXU, RPI

        India. Office of the Registrar General.
          Census of India, 1951.
          Vol. I-XVII.
              Volume I. India. Delhi, Manager of Publications, 1953-1955.
    .2-1-1-A   Report. 1953. xxxi, 234p. [TXU, BC, RPI
    .2-1-1-B   Appendices to the census report, 1951. 1955. v, 419p. [TXU,
        BC, RPI
    .2-1-2-A   Demographic tables. 1955. 412p. [TXU, BC, RPI
    .2-1-2-B   Economic tables (general population). 1954. xxvii, 466p.
        [TXU, BC, RPI
    .2-1-2-C   Economic tables (rural and urban population). 1954. 456p.
        [TXU, BC, RPI
              Volume II. Uttar Pradesh. Allahabad, Printing & Stationery,
        1952-1953.
    .2-2-1-A   Report. 1953. xxix, 497p. [TXU, BC, RPI
    .2-2-1-B   Subsidiary tables. 1952. x, 261p. [TXU, BC, RPI
    .2-2-2-A   General population tables. 1952. 189p. [TXU, BC, RPI
    .2-2-2-B   Economic tables. 1952. 701p. [TXU, BC, RPI
    .2-2-2-C   Age and social tables. 1953. 817p. [TXU, BC, RPI
              Volume III. Madras and Coorg. Madras, Government Press, 1953.
    .2-3-1   Report. 307p. [TXU, BC, RPI
    .2-3-2-A   Tables. 379p. [TXU, BC, RPI
    .2-3-2-B   Tables. 245p. [TXU, BC, RPI
              Volume IV. Bombay, Saurashtra and Kutch. Bombay, Government
        Central Press, 1953.
    .2-4-1   Report and subsidiary tables. ix, 333p. [TXU, RPI
    .2-4-2-A   General population tables, social and cultural tables and
        summary figures by talukas and petas. 403p. [TXU, RPI
    .2-4-2-B   Economic tables and household and age (sample) tables. 454p.
        [TXU, RPI
              Volume V. Bihar. Patna, Government Printer, 1953-1956.
    .2-5-1   Report. 1956. xvi, 219, xci, 20p. [TXU, RPI
    .2-5-2-A   Tables (A, E, C, and D series). 1953. 389, iv p. [TXU, RPI
    .2-5-2-B   Tables (economic tables). 1953. 319, vi p. [TXU, RPI
              Volume VI. West Bengal, Sikkim & Chandernagore. Delhi, Mana-
        ger of Publications, 1952-1954.
    .2-6-1-A   Report. 1953. xxi, 587p. [TXU, RPI
    .2-6-1-B   Vital statistics. West Bengal, 1941-50. 1952. ii, 75p.
        [TXU, RPI

1951.2-6-1-C   Report. 1953. xii, 517p. [TXU, RPI
  .2-6-2   Tables. 1953. iv, 535p. [TXU, RPI
  .2-6-3   Calcutta industrial region tables. 1954. vii, 438p. [TXU, RPI
  .2-6-4   Tables. 1954. vii, 438p. [TXU, RPI
          Volume VII. Madhya Pradesh. Nagpur, Government Printing, 1952-1953.
  .2-7-1-A   Report. 1953. xxx, 430p. [TXU, RPI
  .2-7-1-B   Subsidiary tables and notes thereon. 1953. v, 339p. [TXU, RPI
  .2-7-2-A   General population tables and summary figures for districts. 1952. 88p. [TXU, RPI
  .2-7-2-B   Economic tables. 1952. xx, 412p. [TXU, RPI
  .2-7-2-C   Household and age (sample) tables, and social and cultural tables. 1953. vi, 335p. [TXU, RPI
  .2-7-2-D   Maternity tables. 1953. 175p. [TXU, RPI
          Volume VIII. Punjab, PEPSU (Punjab and East Punjab States Union), Himachal Pradesh, Bilaspur & Delhi. Simla, Army Press, 1953.
  .2-8-1-A   Report. [d], xiii, 581, xcii p. [TXU, RPI
  .2-8-1-B   Subsidiary tables. iii, 201p. [TXU, RPI
  .2-8-2-A   General population, age and social tables. 427p. [TXU, RPI
  .2-8-2-B   Economic tables. xx, 233p. [TXU, RPI
          Volume IX. Hyderabad. Hyderabad-Deccan, Government Press, 1953-1954.
  .2-9-1-A   Report. n.d. xviii, 560p. [TXU, RPI
  .2-9-1-B   Subsidiary tables. 1954. iv, 214p. [TXU, RPI
  .2-9-2-A   Tables. 1953. 245p. [TXU, RPI
  .2-9-2-B   Tables. 1953. 361p. [TXU, RPI
          Volume X. Rajasthan and Ajmer. Jodhpur, Government Press, 1953.
  .2-10-1-A   Report. ix, vi, 422p. [TXU, RPI
  .2-10-1-B   Subsidiary tables and district index of non-agricultural occupations. iv, vi, 9, 463p. [TXU, RPI
  .2-10-1-C   Appendices. 210p. [TXU, RPI
  .2-10-2-A   Tables. 6, 461p. [TXU, RPI
  .2-10-2-B   Economic tables. 323p. [TXU, RPI
          Volume XI. Orissa. Cuttack, Orissa Government Press, 1953.
  .2-11-1   Report. xvi, 498p. [TXU, RPI
  .2-11-2-A   Tables. General population, social and cultural and land tables. [193]p. [TXU, RPI
  .2-11-2-B   Tables. Tables relating to economic classification, household and age. 297p. [TXU, RPI
          Volume XII. Assam, Manipur and Tripura. Shillong, Municipal Printing Press, 1953-1954.
  .2-12-1-A   Report. 1954. xxxviii, 431p. [TXU, RPI
  .2-12-1-B   Subsidiary tables. 1953. vi, 225p. [TXU, RPI
  .2-12-2-A   General population tables, summary figures for districts, social and cultural tables and land holdings of indigenous persons. 1953. 189p. [TXU, RPI
  .2-12-2-B   Economic tables and household and age (sample) tables. 1954. 306p. [TXU, RPI
          Volume XIII. Travancore-Cochin. Delhi, Manager of Publications, 1953.

.2-13-1-A   Report. ii, 81p. [TXU, RPI
.2-13-1-B   Subsidiary tables. iii, 79p. [TXU, RPI
.2-13-2   Tables. 303p. [TXU, RPI
      Volume XIV. Mysore Bangalore, Government Press, 1953-1954.
.2-14-1   Report. 1954. xiv, 448p. [TXU, RPI
.2-14-2   Tables. 1953. vi, 355p. [TXU, RPI
      Volume XV. Madhya Bharat & Bhopal. Gwalior, Government Central Press, 1953-1954.
.2-15-1-A   Report. 1954. iv, 75p. [TXU, RPI
.2-15-1-B   Subsidiary tables. 1954. 144p. [TXU, RPI
.2-15-2-A   Tables. General population tables, Household and age (sample) tables and Social and cultural tables. 1953. 307p. [TXU, RPI
.2-15-2-B   Economic tables. 1954. 207p. [TXU, RPI
      Volume XVI. Vindhya Pradesh. Delhi, Manager of Publications, 1953-1954.
.2-16-1   Report and subsidiary tables. 1953. x, 299p. [TXU, RPI
.2-16-2   General population, age, social and economic tables. 1954. v, 403p. [TXU, RPI
      Volume XVII. The Andaman and Nicobar Islands. Delhi, Manager of Publications, 1953.
.2-17-1&2   Report. Tables. lxxv, 53p. [TXU, RPI

India. Office of the Registrar General.
   Census of India, 1961. Census papers. Delhi, Manager of Publications, 1962-1968.
1961.1-62-1   Final population totals. 1962. ci, 454p. [TXU, RPI
.1-63-1   Religion. 1963. xxxvii, 49p. [TXU, RPI
.1-63-2   Age tables. 1963. ii, 64, 106p. [TXU, RPI
.1-66-1   Scientific and technical personnel tables. 1966. x, 223p. [TXU, RPI
.1-67-1   Workers from 1901/11 to 1961 by states and union territories and by cities. 1968. [v], iii, 145p. [TXU, RPI
.1-69-1   General population tables & Primary census abstract of reorganized states of Punjab & Haryana & Union Territory of Chandigarh & Himachal Pradesh. 1972. [4], 173p. [TXU

India. Office of the Registrar General
   Census of India, 1961. Vol. I-XXVII.
      Volume I. India. Delhi, Manager of Publications, 1963-1970.
.2-1-1-A(1)   General report. Text. Levels of regional development in India. 1965. 357, iv p. [PRC, TXU, RPI
.2-1-1-A(2)   General report. Tables. Levels of regional development in India. 1966. 892p. [PRC, TXU, RPI
.2-1-1-B   Vital statistics of the decade.
.2-1-1-C(1)   Subsidiary tables. [1968]. [2], viii, 617, 4, iv p. [PRC, TXU, RPI
.2-1-1-C(2)   Subsidiary tables. [1968]. [2], viii, [2], 527, [3], iv p. [PRC, TXU, RPI
.2-1-2-A(1)   General population tables. 1964. vi, 691, iv p. [PRC, TXU, RPI
.2-1-2-A(2)   Union primary census abstracts. 1963. lxxv, 185p. [PRC, TXU, RPI

1961.2-1-2-B(1)   General economic tables. 1965.   702, iv p. [PRC, TXU,
      RPI
  .2-1-2-B(2)   General economic tables. 1966. iv, 682p. [PRC, TXU, RPI
  .2-1-2-B(3)   General economic tables. 1965.   633, v p. [PRC, TXU, RPI
  .2-1-2-C(1)   Social and cultural tables. 1965. vi, 555, vii p. [PRC,
      TXU, RPI
  .2-1-2-C(2)   Language tables. 1964. ii, ccxliv, 534, iv p. [PRC, TXU,
      RPI
  .2-1-2-C(3)   Migration tables. [1966]. [4], vii, [1], 593, [1], iv p.
      [PRC, TXU, RPI
  .2-1-2-C(4)   Migration tables. [1967]. [4], vii, [1], 386, iv p.
      [PRC, TXU, RPI
  .2-1-3-1   Household economic tables. 1964. vi, 350p. [PRC, TXU,
      RPI
  .2-1-3-2   Household economic tables. [1964]. [2], 412, iv p. [PRC,
      TXU, RPI
  .2-1-5-A(1)   Special tables for scheduled castes. 1966. liii, 436p.
      [TXU, RPI
  .2-1-5-A(2)   Special tables for scheduled tribes. [1964]. [4], liii,
      [1], 518, vi p. [TXU, RPI
  .2-1-5-B(1)   Consolidated statement showing scheduled castes, scheduled
      tribes, denotified communities and other communities of similar status
      in different statutes and censuses starting from 1921. 1966. viii,
      601, vi p. [TXU, RPI
  .2-1-5-B(2)   [Same as above.] [1966]. viii, [2], 603, [1], vi p.
      [TXU, RPI
  .2-1-5-B(3)   [Same as above.] [1966]. viii, [2], 309, [1], vi p.
      [TXU, RPI
          Volume II. Andhra Pradesh. Delhi, Manager of Publications,
      1963-1967.
  .2-2-1-A(1)   General report. [Chapters I-V.] 1966. [2], xix, [1],
      LXXV, [5], 472, viii, [4]p. [TXU, RPI
  .2-2-1-A(2)   General report. [Chapters VI-IX.] 1967. [2], ix, [1],
      248, [6]p. [TXU, RPI
  .2-2-1-A(3)   General report. [Chapters X-XII.] 1967. [2], xiv, [22],
      741, iv, [1], 6p. [TXU, RPI
  .2-2-1-B   Report on vital statistics. 1968. 115p. [TXU, RPI
  .2-2-1-C   Subsidiary tables. 1965. iv, 608p. [TXU, RPI
  .2-2-2-A   General population tables. 1963. ii, viii, 299p. [TXU,
      RPI
  .2-2-2-B(1)   Economic tables. 1963. vi, 402p. [TXU, RPI
  .2-2-2-B(2)   Economic tables. 1964. 709p. [TXU, RPI
  .2-2-2-C   Cultural and migration tables. 1966. [2], v, [1], 693,
      [1], vi, [4]p. [TXU, RPI
  .2-2-3   Household economic tables. 1965. v, 593p. [TXU, RPI
  .2-2-5-A   Special tables for scheduled castes and scheduled tribes.
      1964. 327p. [TXU, RPI
          Volume III. Assam. Delhi, Manager of Publications, 1963-1966.
  .2-3-1-A   General report. [1965]. [4], xvii, [1], 466, [3]p.
      [TXU, RPI
  .2-3-1-B   Report on vital statistics. 1966. [8], 91p. [TXU, RPI
  .2-3-1-C   Subsidiary tables. 1965. [12], 425p. [TXU, RPI

1961.2-3-2-A   General population tables. [1964]. iv, 159, iv p. [TXU,
     RPI
    .2-3-2-B(1)   General economic tables. [1965]. x, 219, iv p. [TXU,
     RPI
    .2-3-2-B(2)   General economic tables. 1965. viii, 455p. [TXU, RPI
    .2-3-2-C   Cultural and migration tables. 1965. v, 475p. [TXU, RPI
    .2-3-3   Household economic tables. 1965. vii, 337p. [TXU, RPI
    .2-3-5-A   Scheduled tribes and scheduled castes. Reprints from old
     census reports and special tables. 1964. 147p. [TXU, RPI
              Volume IV. Bihar. Delhi, Manager of Publications, 1963-1969.
    .2-4-1-A(1)   General report. [Chapters I-IX.] [1967]. [1], xlii, [2],
     505, [1], vi p. [TXU, RPI
    .2-4-1-A(2)   General report. [Chapters X-XII.] [1969]. [1], xviii,
     495, [1], xxiii, [1], vi, [1]p. [TXU, RPI
    .2-4-1-B   Report on vital statistics. [Not published.]
    .2-4-1-C   Subsidiary tables. 1965. xxv, 651, iv p. [TXU, RPI
    .2-4-2-A   General population tables. 1963. viii, 652, v p. [TXU,
     RPI
    .2-4-2-B(1)   General economic tables (Tables B-I to B-IV & B-VII).
     1965. lxvi, 677, iv p. [TXU, RPI
    .2-4-2-B(2)   General economic tables (Tables B-V, B-VI, B-VIII & B-IX).
     1965. xii, 545, iv p. [TXU, RPI
    .2-4-2-C   Social and cultural tables. 1965. viii, 331, viii, v p.
     [TXU, RPI
    .2-4-2-D   Migration tables. 1965. iv, 539, vi p. [TXU, RPI
    .2-4-3-1   Household economic tables. 1965. x, 517, vi p. [TXU,
     RPI
    .2-4-3-2   Household economic tables. 1965. 429, v p. [TXU, RPI
    .2-4-5-A   Special tables for scheduled castes and scheduled tribes.
     1965. xxxiv, 413, v p. [TXU, RPI
    .2-4-10-1   Special migration tables relating to Dhanbad-Jharia-Sindri
     Town group. [1968]. [8], 284, vi, [1]p. [TXU, RPI
    .2-4-10-2   Special migration tables relating to Jamshedpur Town group.
     [1968]. [8], 260, vi, [2]p. [TXU, RPI
              Volume V. Gujarat. Delhi, Manager of Publications, 1963-1968.
    .2-5-1-A(1)   General report. 1965. xxiv, 643, vi p. [TXU, RPI
    .2-5-1-A(2a)   General report. 1965. xii, 259, vi p. [TXU, RPI
    .2-5-1-A(2b)   General report. 1965. xvi, pp. 261-936, vi p. [TXU, RPI
    .2-5-1-A(3)   General report. Economic trends and projections. 1965.
     ix, 201, vi p. [TXU, RPI
    .2-5-1-B   Report on vital statistics and fertility survey. 1966.
     ix, 73, vi p. [TXU, RPI
    .2-5-1-C   Subsidiary tables. 1965. 536, vi p. [TXU, RPI
    .2-5-2-A   General population tables. 1963. iv, 326, vi p. [TXU,
     RPI
    .2-5-2-B(1)   General economic tables. 1964. 361, vi p. [TXU, RPI
    .2-5-2-B(2)   General economic tables. 1964. 579, vi p. [TXU, RPI
    .2-5-2-C   Cultural and migration tables. 1964. 684, vi p. [TXU,
     RPI
    .2-5-3   Household economic tables. 1964. 517, vi p. [TXU, RPI
    .2-5-5-A   Tables on scheduled castes and scheduled tribes. 1964.
     385, vi p. [TXU, RPI

1961.2-5-10-A(1)   Special report on Ahmedabad City. [1967]. [1], xiii, [3], 295, [1], vi p. map. [TXU, RPI

.2-5-10-B   Special tables on cities and block directory. 1964. 678, vi p. [TXU, RPI

.2-5-10-C   Special migrant tables for Ahmedabad City. [1966]. vi, [2], 762, vi p. [TXU, RPI

        Volume VI. Jammu and Kashmir. Delhi, Manager of Publications, 1963-1970. [Only Indian part, after partition.]

.2-6-1-A(1)   General report. 1968. [3], xvi, 420, [2], viii p. [TXU, RPI

.2-6-1-A(2)   General report. 1968. [3], viii, 249, [3], viii p. [TXU, RPI

.2-6-1-A(3)   General report. 1970. [4], viii, 522, [2], viii p. [TXU, RPI

.2-6-1-B   Report on vital statistics of the decade. [Not published.]

.2-6-1-C   Subsidiary tables. 1966. iv, 366, viii p. [TXU, RPI

.2-6-2-A   General population tables. 1964. xxxii, 196, viii p. [TXU, RPI

.2-6-2-B   General economic tables. 1965. ii, 489, viii p. [TXU, RPI

.2-6-2-C   Cultural and migration tables. 1965. ix, 570, viii p. [TXU, RPI

.2-6-3   Household economic tables. 1964. 275, viii p. [TXU, RPI

.2-6-5-A   Tables on scheduled castes. 1964. 30, cxvi p. [TXU, RPI

        Volume VII. Kerala. Delhi, Manager of Publications, 1963-1970.

.2-7-1-A(1)   General report. 1965. [2], liv, 786, iv p. [TXU, RPI

.2-7-1-A(2)   General report. Appendices. 1965. [6], CCLVII, [1], iv p. [TXU, RPI

.2-7-1-B   Report on vital statistics. [1970]. vii, [3], 120, iv p. [TXU, RPI

.2-7-1-C   Subsidiary tables. 1968. viii, [2], 657, [3], iv p. [TXU, RPI

.2-7-2-A   General population tables. 1964. xiv, 222, iv p. [TXU, RPI

.2-7-2-B(1)   General economic tables. (Tables B-I to B-IV). 1965. [1], xvi, 193, [1], iv, [1]p. [TXU, RPI

.2-7-2-B(2)   General economic tables. (Tables B-V to B-IX). 1967. xvi, [2], 417, [2], iv p. [TXU, RPI

.2-7-2-C   Cultural and migration tables. 1965. [2], xiv, [2], 516, viii, [2], iv p. [TXU, RPI

.2-7-3   Household economic tables. 1965. xx, [2], 207, [3], iv p. [TXU, RPI

.2-7-5-A   Scheduled tribes and scheduled castes. 1967. [2], x, [1], 230, [2], iv p. [TXU, RPI

        Volume VIII. Madhya Pradesh. Delhi, Manager of Publications, 1963-1974.

.2-8-1-A   General report. 1974. [8], 753p. [TXU, RPI

.2-8-1-B   Report on vital statistics. [Not published.]

.2-8-1-C   Subsidiary tables. [1967], [6], iv, 999, [1], iv p. [TXU, RPI

1961.2-8-2-A   General population tables. 1963. xi, 393, iv p. [TXU,
    RPI
.2-8-2-B(1)   General economic tables. 1967. [8], xliv, 1072, iv p.
    [TXU, RPI
.2-8-2-B(2)   General economic tables. [1966]. [8], 783, [1], iv p.
    [TXU, RPI
.2-8-2-B(3)   General economic tables. 1965. [8], xliv, 353, [1], vi p.
    [TXU, RPI
.2-8-2-C(1)   Social and cultural tables. 1965. iv, 533, vi p. [TXU,
    RPI
.2-8-2-C(2)   Migration tables. 1967. [6], iii, [1], 387, [1], vi p.
    [TXU, RPI
.2-8-3-1   Household economic tables. 1966. [6], xliv, 468, vi p.
    [TXU, RPI
.2-8-3-2   Household economic tables. 1966. [6], xliv, 509, [1],
    vi p. [TXU, RPI
.2-8-5-A(1)   Special tables for scheduled castes. 1965. xxi, 488,
    vi p. [TXU, RPI
.2-8-5-A(2)   Special tables for scheduled tribes. 1966. [8], xxi,
    [1], 531, [1], vi p. [TXU, RPI
        Volume IX. Madras. Delhi, Manager of Publications, 1963–1973.
.2-9-1-A(1)   General report. 1966. v, 448p. [TXU, RPI
.2-9-1-A(2)   General report. 1968. [4], v, [1], 944p. [TXU, RPI
.2-9-1-B(1)   Demography and vital statistics. 1966. xi, 456p. [TXU,
    RPI
.2-9-1-B(2)   Demography and vital statistics. 1969. 595p. [TXU, RPI
.2-9-1-C   Subsidiary tables. 1964. iv, 695p. [TXU, RPI
.2-9-2-A   General population tables. 1963. ii, 442p. [TXU, RPI
.2-9-2-B(1)   General economic tables. 1964. ii, 597p. [TXU, RPI
.2-9-2-B(2)   General economic tables. 1964. ii, 651p. [TXU, RPI
.2-9-2-C(1)   Cultural tables. 1964. 479p. [TXU, RPI
.2-9-2-C(2a)   Migration tables. 1964. 665, viii p. [TXU, RPI
.2-9-2-C(2b)   Migration tables. 1965. [8], 311, [1], viii, [4]p. [TXU,
    RPI
.2-9-3   Household economic tables. 1964. vi, 575p. [TXU, RPI
.2-9-5-A(1)   Scheduled castes and tribes (report & tables). 1964.
    455p. [TXU, RPI
.2-9-5-A(2)   Scheduled castes and tribes (tables). 1965. [6], 363,
    [2]p. [TXU, RPI
.2-9-10-1   Madras City report. 1973. [10], 234, [1]p. [TXU, RPI
.2-9-10-2   Special migration tables. Madras City. 1965. xxi, 595p.
    [TXU, RPI
.2-9-10-3   Madras City. Census tables and primary census abstract.
    1966. [4], v, [1], 669, [8]p. [TXU, RPI
        Volume X. Maharashtra. Delhi, Manager of Publications, 1963–
    1966.
.2-10-1-A&B   General report. [Not published.]
.2-10-1-C   Subsidiary tables. 1965. xxiv, 614p. [TXU, RPI
.2-10-2-A   General population tables. 1963. 367, iii p. [TXU, RPI
.2-10-2-B(1)   General economic tables. Industrial classification. 1964.
    597, 2, iv p. [TXU, RPI

1961.2-10-2-B(2)   General economic tables. Occupational classification.
    1964. 511, iv p. [TXU, RPI
.2-10-2-C(1)   Social and cultural tables. 1965. ii, 316, iv, 2p.
    [TXU, RPI
.2-10-2-C(2)   Migration tables. 1966. 558, iv p. [TXU, RPI
.2-10-3   Household economic tables. 1964. 519, iv p. [TXU, RPI
.2-10-5-A   Scheduled castes and scheduled tribes in Maharashtra -
    tables. 1964. ii, 432, iv p. [TXU, RPI
.2-10-10-1   Greater Bombay census tables. 1964. iii, 333, 251, iv p.
    [TXU, RPI
.2-10-10-2   Cities of Maharashtra. 1968. [8], 650, 93, iv p. [TXU,
    RPI

            Volume XI. Mysore. Delhi, Manager of Publications, 1964-1969.
.2-11-1-A(1)   General report. [Chapters I to IX.] [1968]. [2], xxii,
    559p. [TXU, RPI
.2-11-1-A(2)   General report. [Chapter X.] [1968]. [2], 2, xxii, [1],
    pp. 560-1287p. [TXU, RPI
.2-11-1-B   Report on vital statistics. [Not published.]
.2-11-1-C   Subsidiary tables. [1969]. [6], iii, [3], 606, f p.
    [TXU, RPI
.2-11-2-A   General population tables. 1964. viii, 304, f p. [TXU,
    RPI
.2-11-2-B(1)   General economic tables. 1965. xi, 366, f p. [TXU, RPI
.2-11-2-B(2)   General economic tables. 1965. ii, 645, 4, f p. [TXU,
    RPI
.2-11-2-C(1)   Social and cultural tables. 1966. ix, 227p. [TXU, RPI
.2-11-2-C(2)   Migration tables. 1967. [6], vi, 484, f p. [TXU, RPI
.2-11-3   Household economic tables. 1965. xvi, 515, f p. [TXU,
    RPI
.2-11-5-A   Tables on scheduled castes and scheduled tribes. 1966.
    xviii, [2], 364, h p. [TXU, RPI
            Volume XII. Orissa. Delhi, Manager of Publications, 1963-1969.
.2-12-1-A(1)   General report. 1965. xxxviii, 394, ix p. [TXU, RPI
.2-12-1-A(2)   General report. 1965. pp. 395-847, ix, iv p. [TXU, RPI
.2-12-1-B   Report on vital statistics, and fertility survey. [1969].
    viii, 104, iv p. [TXU, RPI
.2-12-1-C   Subsidiary tables. 1966. viii, 395, iv p. [TXU, RPI
.2-12-2-A   General population tables. 1963. 220, iv p. [TXU, RPI
.2-12-2-B(1)   General economic tables. 1964. viii, 233, iv p. [TXU,
    RPI
.2-12-2-B(2)   General economic tables. 1964. viii, 251, iv p. [TXU,
    RPI
.2-12-2-C   Cultural and migration tables. 1965. 402, viii, iv p.
    [TXU, RPI
.2-12-3   Household economic tables. 1965. x, 677, iv p. [TXU,
    RPI
.2-12-5-A   Tables on scheduled castes and scheduled tribes. 1965.
    viii, 508, iv p. [TXU, RPI
            Volume XIII. Punjab. Delhi, Manager of Publications, 1963-
    1966.
.2-13-1-A(1)   General report. n.d. [2], xxviii, 438, vii p. [TXU, RPI
.2-13-1-A(2)   General report. xxviii, pp. 439-1076, vii p. [TXU, RPI

1961.2-13-1-B   Report on vital statistics. [Not published.]
 .2-13-1-C(1)   Subsidiary tables. 1965. vii, 477, vi p. [TXU, RPI
 .2-13-1-C(2)   Subsidiary tables. [1965]. viii, 391, [1], iv p. [TXU,
 RPI
 .2-13-2-A   General population tables. 1964. viii, 260, vi p. [TXU,
 RPI
 .2-13-2-B(1)   General economic tables. 1964. xxii, 437, iv p. [TXU,
 RPI
 .2-13-2-B(2)   General economic tables. 1965. vi, 538, vi p. [TXU, RPI
 .2-13-2-C(1)   Social and cultural tables. 1965. xii, 369, vi p. [TXU,
 RPI
 .2-13-2-C(2)   Migration tables. [1965]. viii, 636, iv p. [TXU, RPI
 .2-13-3   Household economic tables. 1965. xvi, 373, vi p. [TXU,
 RPI
 .2-13-5-A   Special tables on scheduled castes and scheduled tribes.
 1965. xii, 292, vi p. [TXU, RPI
  Volume XIV. Rajasthan. Delhi, Manager of Publications, 1964-
 1969.
 .2-14-1-A(1)   General report. [1968]. xxx, 301p. 16 maps. [TXU, RPI
 .2-14-1-A(2)   General report. [1968]. vii, [3], 576, x p. 18 maps.
 [TXU, RPI
 .2-14-1-B   Report on vital statistics. [Not published.]
 .2-14-1-C(1)   Subsidiary tables. 1968. ix, [1], 549, [1], vii p. [TXU,
 RPI
 .2-14-1-C(2)   Subsidiary tables. [1968]. viii, [2], 274, iv p. [TXU,
 RPI
 .2-14-2-A   General population tables. 1964. viii, xxii, 231, iv p.
 [TXU, RPI
 .2-14-2-B(1)   General economic tables. 1965. xiv, 453, vii p. [TXU,
 RPI
 .2-14-2-B(2)   General economic tables. 1965. 689, vi p. [TXU, RPI
 .2-14-2-C(1)   Social and cultural tables. [1965]. vii, [3], ix, [1],
 334, [2], viii, iv p. [TXU, RPI
 .2-14-2-C(2)   Migration tables. 1966. 509, vi p. [TXU, RPI
 .2-14-3   Household economic tables. 1965. xv, 632, vii p. [TXU,
 RPI
 .2-14-5-A   Special tables for scheduled castes and scheduled tribes.
 1965. xiv, 474, vi p. [TXU, RPI
  Volume XV. Uttar Pradesh. Delhi, Manager of Publications,
 1964-1970.
 .2-15-1-A(1)   General report. 1966. [2], xxi, [1], 560, vi p. [TXU,
 RPI
 .2-15-1-A(2)   General report. 1967. [2], xxi, [1], 640p. [TXU, RPI
 .2-15-1-B   Report on vital statistics. 1965. iv, 148, vi p. [TXU,
 RPI
 .2-15-1-C(1)   Subsidiary tables. 1970. [2], xi, [1], xi, [1], 631,
 [1], vi p. [TXU, RPI
 .2-15-1-C(2)   Subsidiary tables. 1967. [4], 333, [1], vi p. [TXU, RPI
 .2-15-1-C(3)   Subsidiary tables. 1967. [4], 165, [1], vi p. [TXU, RPI
 .2-15-2-A   General population tables. 1964. xix, 425, xi p. [TXU,
 RPI

1961.2-15-2-B(1)   General economic tables. 1965. viii, 683, vi p. [TXU,
        RPI
    .2-15-2-B(2)   General economic tables. 1965. [4], 644, vi p. [TXU,
        RPI
    .2-15-2-B(3)   General economic tables. 1966. [4], xv, [1[, 530, vi p.
        [TXU, RPI
    .2-15-2-B(4)   General economic tables. 1967. [4], xi, [3], pp. 531-
        1186, vi p. [TXU, RPI
    .2-15-2-B(5)   General economic tables. 1965. 501, vi p. [TXU, RPI
    .2-15-2-B(6)   General economic tables. 1965. iv, 373, [1], vi p.
        [TXU, RPI
    .2-15-2-C(1)   Cultural and migration tables. 1965. ii, 379, vi p.
        [TXU, RPI
    .2-15-2-C(2)   Cultural and migration tables. 1965. 543, vi p. [TXU,
        RPI
    .2-15-2-C(3)   Cultural and migration tables. 1966. [4], ii, 607, [1],
        vi p. [TXU, RPI
    .2-15-2-C(4)   Cultural and migration tables. 1966. [4], 287, [1], vi p.
        [TXU, RPI
    .2-15-2-C(5)   Cultural and migration tables. 1966. [6], 645, [1], vi p.
        [TXU, RPI
    .2-15-3-A   Household economic tables. 1966. [4], viii, 655, [1],
        vi p. [TXU, RPI
    .2-15-3-B   Household economic tables. 1970. [4], xiii, [1], 398,
        vi p. [TXU, RPI
    .2-15-5-A(1)   Special tables for scheduled castes. 1965. vi, 520, vi p.
        [TXU, RPI
    .2-15-5-A(2)   Special tables for scheduled castes. 1965. 611, vi p.
        [TXU, RPI
    .2-15-10   Special report on Kanpur City. 1965. vi, 105, vi p.
        [TXU, RPI
            Volume XVI. West Bengal & Sikkim.   Delhi, Manager of Publica-
        tions, 1963-1971.
    .2-16-1-A(1)   General report. Population progress. 1967. xiii, [11],
        396, [4]p. [TXU, RPI
    .2-16-1-A(2)   General report. Population and society. 1969. [18], 9
        plates, 516, [4]p. [TXU, RPI
    .2-16-1-B   Report on vital statistics. 1967. viii, 221p. [TXU, RPI
    .2-16-1-C   General report and subsidiary tables. 1967. viii, 471p.
        [TXU, RPI
    .2-16-2-A   General population tables. 1964. 377p. [TXU, RPI
    .2-16-2-B(1)   General economic tables. 1964. 428, iv p. [TXU, RPI
    .2-16-2-B(2)   General economic tables. 1966. 745p. [TXU, RPI
    .2-16-2-C(1)   Social and cultural tables. 1965. [6], 435, [1], iv p.
        [TXU, RPI
    .2-16-2-C(2)   Migration tables. 1966. [6], 2, 8 plates, pp. 3-273,
        iii p. [TXU, RPI
    .2-16-2-C(3)   Migration tables. 1966. [8], 515, [3]p. [TXU, RPI
    .2-16-3   Household economic tables. 1965. 703, iv p. [TXU, RPI
    .2-16-5-A(1)   Tables on scheduled castes. 1966. [2], lxviii, [2], 561,
        iii p. [TXU, RPI

1961.2-16-5-A(2)   Tables on scheduled tribes. 1967. [2], LXV, [3], 452,
     iii p. [TXU, RPI
  .2-16-10-A(1) Tables on the Calcutta industrial region. 1968. [2],
     XXXV, [1], 683p. [TXU, RPI
  .2-16-10-A(2) Tables on the Clacutta industrial region. 1969. XXXIV,
     585, [6]p. [TXU, RPI
          Volume XVII. Andaman and Nicobar Islands.   Sehore, Vijaya
     Printing Press, 1966.
  .2-17-1   General report. vii, [5], 585, [3], vi p. [TXU, RPI
  .2-17-2&3   General population tables, General economic tables, Cul-
     tural and migration tables, [and] Household economic tables. v, [3],
     481, vi p. (4 volumes in one) [TXU, RPI
  .2-17-4&5   Report and tables on housing and establishments [and]
     Report and tables on scheduled tribes. [4], vi, ii, ii, 294, [8],
     vi p. (2 volumes in one) [TXU, RPI
          Volume XVIII. Dadra and Nagar Haveli. n.p., 1967.
  .2-18-1-A   General report. [Not published.]
  .2-18-1-B   Report on vital statistics. [Not published.]
  .2-18-1-C through .2-18-5 Subsidiary tables, General population tables,
     General economic tables, Cultural and migration tables, Household eco-
     nomic tables, Housing and establishment tables, [and Special tables
     for scheduled castes and scheduled tribes. [12], xxxii, 261, [1],
     vii p. (7 volumes in one) [TXU, RPI
          Volume XIX. Delhi. Delhi, Manager of Publications, 1963-1966?
  .2-19-1   General report on the census. 1966. xv, 494, iv p.
     [TXU, RPI
  .2-19-2-A&B/.2-19-3 General population tables, General economic tables,
     [and] Household economic tables. n.d. [2], ii, [4], 595, [1], vi p.
     (3 volumes in one) [TXU, RPI
  .2-19-2-C   Cultural and migration tables. n.d. [4], ii, [2], 410,
     vi p. [TXU, RPI
  .2-19-5-A   Special tables on scheduled castes and scheduled tribes.
     n.d. [8], 180, vi p. [TXU, RPI
          Volume XX. Himachal Pradesh. Delhi, Manager of Publications,
     1963-1970.
  .2-20-1-A&B   General report [and] Report on vital statistics of the
     decade including reprints. [1970]. [2], viii, 750, [10]p. [TXU, RPI
  .2-20-1-C   Subsidiary tables. [1970]. [2], v, [1], 403, [3]p.
     [TXU, RPI
  .2-20-2-A   General population tables and primary census abstracts.
     1964. 107p. [TXU, RPI
  .2-20-2-B   Economic tables. 1965. xxii, 295p. [TXU, RPI
  .2-20-2-C   Cultural and migration tables. 1966. x, 533p. [TXU, RPI
  .2-20-3   Household economic tables. 1966. xviii, 132p. [TXU, RPI
  .2-20-5-A   Special tables on scheduled castes and scheduled tribes
     (including reprints). 1967. viii, 406p. [TXU, RPI
          Volume XXI. Laccadive, Minicoy and Amindivi Islands.   Ahmeda-
     bad, Nayan Printing Press, 1964-1967.
  .2-21-1-A&B   General report. [Not published.]
  .2-21-1-C through .2-21-5-A Subsidiary tables, General population tables,
     General economic tables, Cultural and migration tables, Household eco-
     nomic tables, Housing and establishment tables, [and] Special tables

for scheduled castes and scheduled tribes. 1967. xxxvii, [1], 462,
viii, [2], iv p. (6 volumes in one) [TXU, RPI
      Volume XXII. Manipur. Sehore, Vijaya Printing Press, 1966-
[1967].

1961.2-22-1   General report including subsidiary tables. 1966. x, ii,
[2], 346, vi p. [TXU, RPI
.2-22-2   General population tables, General economic tables, [and]
Social and cultural tables. 1968. ix, [1], xvii, [1], 671p. (3 volumes in one) [TXU, RPI
.2-22-3   Household economic tables, Housing and establishment
tables and report on housing, [and] Tables on scheduled castes and
scheduled tribes. [1967]. [4], iv, 313p. (3 volumes in one) [TXU,
RPI
      Volume XXIII. Nagaland. Calcutta, Government of India Press,
1967-1969.
.2-23-1   General report. [Not published.]
.2-23-2-A   General population tables. 1967. [4], v, [1], 77, iv p.
[TXU, RPI
.2-23-2-B   Economic tables. 1967. [8], 142, iv p. [TXU, RPI
.2-23-2-C   Cultural and migration tables. 1969. [8], 317, [3], xv,
[4]p. [TXU, RPI
.2-23-3   Household economic tables. [Not published.]
.2-23-5-A   Special tables for scheduled castes and scheduled tribes.
[1968]. [8], 120p. [TXU, RPI
      Volume XXIV. North-East Frontier Agency. Sehore, Vijaya Print-
ing Press, n.d.
.2-24-1   General report. [Not published.]
.2-24-2-A   General population tables and NEFA special tables. [8],
289, [3], vi p. [TXU, RPI
.2-24-2-B throuth .2-24-5 General economic tables, Cultural and migration tables, Household economic tables, Housing and establishment
tables, [and] Tables on scheduled castes and scheduled tribes. [2],
xxiv, 543, [1], iv p. (5 volumes in one) [TXU, RPI
      Volume XXV. Pondicherry State. Delhi, Manager of Publications,
1964.
.2-25-1   General report. 1964. ii, 704p. [TXU, RPI
.2-25-2-A&B   General population tables [and] General economic tables.
1964. 495p. [TXU, RPI
.2-25-2-C&D   Cultural tables [and] Migration tables. 1964. 251p.
[TXU, RPI
.2-25-3   Household economic tables, Housing and establishment tables,
[and] Scheduled castes tables. 1964. iii, 353p. (3 volumes in one)
[TXU, RPI
      Volume XXVI. Tripura. Delhi, Manager of Publications, 1965-
1967.
.2-26-1-1   General report. 1967. [10], xxxiv, 1046, [19]p. [TXU,
RPI
.2-26-1-C   Subsidiary tables. 1967. [4], viii, 678, iv p. [TXU, RPI
.2-26-2-1   General population tables and general economic tables.
1966. [4], 485, [1], 6, vii p. [TXU, RPI
.2-26-2-2   Cultural and migration tables. 1967. [4], 6, [2], 306,
vii p. [TXU, RPI

.2-26-3&5-A   Household economic tables, [and] Special tables on scheduled castes and scheduled tribes. 1967. [6], 404, vii p. (2 volumes
in one) [TXU, RPI
              Volume XXVII. Goa, Daman and Diu. n.p., n.d.
.2-27-2-A   General population tables. [6], 149, [1], iv p. [TXU,
RPI
.2-27-2-B   General economic tables, Social, cultural and migration
tables, Housing and establishment tables, [and] Subsidiary tables.
ii, [4], iii-ix, [7], 555p. (4 volumes in one) [TXU, RPI

India. Office of the Registrar General.
      Census of India, 1971. Census papers. Delhi, Manager of Publica-
tion, 1971-   .
1971.1-71-1   Provisional population totals. [iii], 57p. [BC, TXU
  .1-71-1s   Supplement. Provisional population totals. viii, 11, 229p.
[PRC, TXU
  .1-72-1   Final population totals. iii, 155p. map. [TXU
  .1-72-2   Religion. xv, 110p. map. [PRC, BC, TXU
  .1-72-3   Economic characteristics of the population (selected tables).
vi, 92p. [PRC, BC, TXU
  .1-74-1   Report on resurvey on economic questions--some results. 79p.
[TXU
  .1-74-2   Age and life tables (1 °/o sample). 16p. [TXU
  .1-75-1   Scheduled castes and scheduled tribes. (Table C-8, A & B).
xxi, 169p. [TXU
  .1-77-1   All India life tables. v, 41p. [TXU, BC
  .1-77-2   Fertility tables. [4], 77p. [TXU, E-W, BC
  .1-77-3
  .1-77-4

India. Office of the Registrar General.
      Census of India, 1971. Census centenary monographs. Delhi, Man-
ager of Publications, 1972-1973. No. 1-10.
.2-1   Indian census in perspective. By S.C. Srivastava. 1972. vi,
416p. [PRC, TXU
        Indian census through a hundred years. By D. Natarajan. 1973.
Parts 1-2.
.2-2-1   (Chapters I & II). xii, 706p. [PRC, TXU
.2-2-2   (Chapters II & IV). v, 550p. [PRC, TXU
.2-3   Intercensal growth of population. (Analysis of extracts from
all India census reports). By. D. Natarajan. 1972. xviii, 225p.
[PRC, TXU
.2-4   Civil registration system in India--a perspective. 1972. x,
213p. [PRC, TXU
.2-5   Bibliography of census publications in India. Compiled by C.G.
Jadhav. 1972. vi, 520p. [PRC, TXU
.2-6   Changes in sex ratio. By D. Natarajan. 1972. iv, 105p. [PRC
.2-7   Economic and socio-cultural dimensions of regionalisation. An
Indo-U.S.S.R. collaborative study. 1972. 4, lxii, 538p. [PRC, TXU
.2-8   Age and marital status. By D. Natarajan. 1972. 170p. [PRC
.2-9   Extracts from the all India census reports on literacy. By D.

Natarajan. 1972. [6], v, 118p. [PRC
1971.2-10   Language handbook on mother tongues in census. By R.C. Nigam.
1972. lxi, 340p. [PRC

India. Office of the Registrar General. Map Unit.
.3   Indian census centary atlas. [Compiled under the direction of] A.
Chandra Sekhar [and] B.K. Roy. New Delhi, 1977. 198p. maps. [UN

India. Office of the Registrar General.
Census of India, 1971. Delhi, Manager of Publications, 1972-   .
Series 1-30.
            Series 1. India.
.4-1-1   General report. [Not published yet.]
.4-1-2sp   Special. All-India census tables (estimated from 1 %
sample data). 1972. xii, 200p. [PRC, TXU
.4-1-2-A(1)   General population tables. 1975. vi, 564p. [PRC, TXU
.4-1-2-A(2)   Union primary census abstract. 1974. xlvii, 343p.
[PRC, TXU
.4-1-2-B(1)   General economic tables. 1977. lxxxviii, 553p. [TXU, PRC
.4-1-2-B(2)   General economic tables. 1978. xli, 548p. [TXU
.4-1-2-B(3)   General economic tables. 1977. xxxvi, 664p. [TXU, NYPL

.4-1-2-C(1)   Social and cultural tables. 1977. ii, 298p. [PRC, OPR
.4-1-2-C(2)   Social and cultural tables. 1977. iii, 211p. [TXU, OPR
.4-1-2-D   Migration tables.

.4-1-7-1   Special tables for degree holders and technical personnel
- 1971 census. (G-I through G-IV). 1974. xi, 673p. [PRC, TXU
.4-1-7-2   Special tables for degree holders and technical personnel
- 1971 census. (G-V through G-XII), 1974. xv, 641p. [PRC, TXU

            Series 2. Andhra Pradesh.
.4-2-1   General report. [Not published yet.]

.4-2-2-A   General population tables. 1972. vi, [8], 369p. [TXU

            Series 3. Assam.
.4-3-1   General report. [Not published yet.]

.4-3-2-A   General population tables. 1972. xxii, 212, lxviii p.
[TXU

1971.4-3-2-C(1)   Social and cultural tables. 1976. [4], 20p. [TXU

                Series 4. Bihar.
.4-4-1-A   General report. 1976.
.4-4-1-B
.4-4-1-C   Subsidiary tables.

.4-4-2-A   General population tables. 1976. viii, [2], 443p. [TXU
.4-4-2-As   General population tables, supplement. (Standard urban
   areas).

.4-4-2-B(1)   General economic tables. 1975. v, 127, vi p. [TXU
.4-4-2-B(2)   General economic tables.
.4-4-2-B(3)   General economic tables.
.4-4-2-C(1)   Social and cultural tables.
.4-4-2-C(2)   Social and cultural tables.
.4-4-2-D   Migration tables.

                Series 5. Gujarat.
.4-5-1   Portrait of population. 1975. xv, 280p. [LC, TXU

.4-5-2-A   General population totals. 1975. vi, 265p. [TXU
.4-5-2-As   General population totals, supplement. (Standard urban
   areas). 1975. vii, 63p. [TXU
.4-5-2-B(1)   General economic tables. 1975. xi, 107p. [LC, TXU, NYPL
.4-5-2-C(1)   Social and cultural tables. 1976. v, 115p. [TXU

                Series 6. Haryana.
.4-6-1

.4-6-2-A   General population tables. 1973. vi, [4], 169p. [TXU
.4-6-2-As   General population tables, supplement. (Standard urban
   areas). [1974]. vi, 77, viii p. [TXU

1971.4-6-2-B   Economic tables. 1972. [17], 469p. [TXU
   .4-6-2-C(1) & .4-6-5-A Social and cultural tables [and] Special tables
      on Scheduled Castes and Scheduled tribes. [1976]. [vi], [3], 161p.
      [TXU
   .4-6-2-D   Migration tables. [1977]. [vi], [9], 284p. [TXU

                Series 7. Himachal Pradesh.
   .4-7-1

   .4-7-2-A   General population tables. 1977. xxii, 190p. [TXU

                Series 8. Jammu & Kashmir.
   .4-8-1   Portrait of a population. By J.N. Zutshi. [1974]. ix,
      121p. [TXU

   .4-8-2-A   General population tables. [1972]. v, 206, x p. [TXU
   .4-8-2-B   General economic tables. 1976. vii, 739p. [TXU

   .4-8-2-D   Migration tables. 1976. 360p. [TXU

                Series 9. Kerala.
   .4-9-1   Portrait of population. By K. Narayanan. 1974. 195p.
      [TXU

   .4-9-2-A   General population tables. [1972]. [v], 242p. [TXU
   .4-9-2-B(1)   Economic tables. 1977. [8], 239p. [TXU
   .4-9-2-B(2)   Economic tables. 1977. [10], 443p. [TXU

   .4-9-2-C(1)   Social and cultural tables. 1976. vii, 288p. [TXU

                Series 10. Madhya Pradesh.
   .4-10-1

   .4-10-2-A   General population tables. 1974. [x], 509p. [TXU

1971.4-10-2-B(1)   General economic tables. 1974. lvii, 305, ix p. [TXU

.4-10-2-C(1)   Social and cultural tables. 1976. vii, 288p. [TXU

            Series 11. Maharastra.
.4-11-1

.4-11-2-A   General population tables. 1972. [4], ii, 363p. [TXU
.4-11-2-As   General population tables, supplement. (Standard urban
    areas). 1977. iii, 125p. [TXU
.4-11-2-B(1)   General economic tables. 1974. [6], 203p. [TXU
.4-11-2-C(1)   Social and cultural tables. 1976. [6], 392p. [TXU
.4-11-2-C(2)   Social and cultural tables. 1977. [4], ii, 367p. [TXU

            Series 12. Manipur.
.4-12-1

            Series 13. Meghalaya.
.4-13-1

.4-13-2-A   General population tables. 1974. [xii], 179p. [TXU

            Series 14. Mysore. (Now renamed Karnataka).
.4-14-1   Portrait of population. By P.Padmanobha. 1974. xx,
    214p. [TXU
.4-14-1-A(1)   General report. 1975. xii, 599p. [TXU, NYPL
.4-14-1-A(2)   General report. 1975. xv, [577]p. [TXU, NYPL

1971.4-14-2-A   General population tables. 1973. [10], 676p. [TXU

  .4-14-2-B(1)   General economic tables. 1974. viii, 843p. [TXU

        Series 15. Nagaland.
  .4-15-1

  .4-15-2-A   General population tables. 1975. vii, 164p. [TXU

        Series 16. Orissa.
  .4-16-1   Portrait of population. By B. Tripathi. 1973. xiv, [4],
    371p. [TXU

  .4-16-2-A   General population tables. [1973]. vii, [14], 375p.
    [TXU
  .4-16-2-As   General population tables, supplement. (Standard urban
    areas). 1975. vi, 88p. [TXU
  .4-16-2-B(1)   General economic tables. 1977. vi, [12], 268, vi p.
    [TXU

        Series 17. Punjab.
  .4-17-1

  .4-17-2-A   General population tables. [1973]. viii, 330p. [TXU
  .4-17-2-As   General population tables, supplement. (Standard urban
    areas). n.d. v, 105p. [TXU

  .4-17-2-C(1) and .4-17-5-A Distribution of population by religion and
    Scheduled Castes. 1977. v, 221p. [TXU

        Series 18. Rajasthan.
  .4-18-1

  .4-18-2-A   General population tables. 1973. lxii, 178, x p. [TXU
  .4-18-2-B(1)   General economic tables. 1975. xvii, 135p. [TXU, NYPL

  .4-18-2-C(1)   Social and cultural tables. 1978. xxi, 693p. [TXU

          Series 18A. Sikkim (will publish its own reports.)
          Series 19. Tamil Nadu (former Madras).
1971.4-19-1

.4-19-2-A   General population tables. 1973. viii, 650p. [TXU
.4-19-2-As   General population tables, supplement. (Standard urban
   areas). 1975. 217, ix p. [TXU
.4-19-2-B(1)   General economic tables. 1974. xxii, [3], 573p. [TXU
.4-19-5-A   Special tables on Scheduled Castes and Scheduled Tribes.
   1978. viii, 334p. [TXU
.4-19-9-A   Administrative atlas. [Madras], 1974. var. pag. [LC

          Series 20. Tripura.
.4-20-1   Portrait of a population. By A.K. Bhattacharya. 1974.
   ix, 200p. [TXU

          Series 21. Uttar Pradesh.
.4-21-1   Portrait of population. By D.M. Sinha. 1973. [8], viii,
   228p. [TXU

.4-21-2-A   General population tables. 1975. xl, 538p. [LC, TXU

.4-21-2-B(1)   General economic tables. 1973. [8], 459p. [TXU

.4-21-2-C(1)   Social and cultural tables. 1976. [10], 343p. [TXU

          Series 22. West Bengal.
.4-22-1

.4-22-2-A   General population tables. [1973]. x, 462p. [TXU

.4-22-2-B(1)   General economic tables. 1973. viii, 288p. [TXU

1971.4-22-11-1   Special monograph on age composititon of the population
    in the districts of West Bengal: 1872-1961. By S.B. Mukherjee. 1975.
    xv, 312p. [TXU

        Series 23. Andaman & Nicobar Islands.
.4-23-1   A portrait of population. 1978. lx, 219p. [TXU

.4-23-2-A   General population tables. [1973]. vi, 197p. [TXU

        Series 24. Arunachal Pradesh (former North East Frontier Agency).
.4-24-1   Portrait of a population. By J.K. Barthakur. [1975]. x,
    128p. [LC, TXU

.4-24-2-A   General population tables. 1973. xvi, 296p. [TXU
.4-24-2-B   Economic tables. 1973. xxiv, 531, 125p. [TXU
.4-24-2-C(1) Social and cultural tables. 1972. xxiv, 496p. [TXU

        Series 25. Chandigarh.
.4-25-1

        Series 26. Dadra and Nagar Haveli.
.4-26-1

.4-26-2   General population tables, Economic tables, Social and cul-
    tural tables, [and] Migration tables. 1977. ix, 378p. [TXU

            Series 27. Delhi.
1971.4-27-1

.4-27-2-A   General population tables. 1975. viii, 136, xi p. [TXU

            Series 28. Goa, Daman & Diu.
.4-28-1   Portrait of a population. By S.K. Gandhe. [1976]. iii,
    186p. [LC, TXU
.4-28-1-A   General report. 1977. x, 222p. [TXU

.4-28-2-A   General population tables. [1972]. vi, 142, viii p.
    [TXU
.4-28-2-B&D   Economic tables [and] Migration tables. 1977. [3], v,
    606p. [TXU
.4-28-2-C   Social and cultural tables. 1978. vi, 210p. [TXU

            Series 29. Laccadive, Minicoy and Amindivi Islands.
.4-29-1

.4-29-2-A   General population tables. [1973]. vi, 57p. [TXU
.4-29-2-B   Economic tables. 1978. [10], 254p. [TXU

.4-29-2-D   Migration tables. 1976. [10], 109p. [TXU

            Series 30. Pondicherry.
.4-30-1

.4-30-2-A   General population tables. 1973. viii, 167p. [TXU
.4-30-2-B   General economic tables. 1977. xxi, [12], 341p. [TXU
.4-30-2-C(1) and .4-30-5-A Social and cultural tables [and] Special
    tables on Scheduled Castes. 1978. [10], 108p. [TXU
.4-30-2-D   Migration tables. 1978. iii, 301p. [TXU

INDONESIA

Republic of Indonesia   Capital: Djakarta
Statistical Agency: Central Bureau of Statistics
                     [Biro Pusat Statistik]
                     P.O. Box 3
                     Djakarta,
Publications Distributor: same

        Indonesia. Biro Pusat Statistik.
1961.0-1   The future census (October 1961) of Indonesia. By J.N. Bhatta.
     Djakarta, 1961. 3, ii, 18p. Specimen forms. [UN, PRC, RPI

        Indonesia. Biro Pusat Statistik.
  .1   Sensus penduduk 1961. Re-   Population census 1961. Republic
     publik Indonesia. Djakarta,   of Indonesia.
     1962. 15p.   [PRC, UN, OPR, RPI

        Indonesia. Biro Pusat Statistik.
  .2   Sensus penduduk 1961. D.C.I.   Population census 1961. D,C,I,
     Djakarta Raya (angka-angka te-   Djakarta (final figures).
     tap). Djakarta, 1963. [ii],   [PRC, BC, RPI
     62, [1]p.

        Indonesia. Biro Pusat Statistik.
        Sensus penduduk 1961. Re-   Population census 1961. Republic
     publik Indonesia. Djakarta,   of Indonesia.
     1963. (SP-I-II).
  .3-1   Angka^2 sementara. viii,   Preliminary figures.
     13p.   [PRC, RPI
  .3-2   Seluruh Indonesia. Ang-   All Indonesia. Preliminary fig-
     ka^2 sementara hasil pengolahan   ures based on a 1º/o sample tabu-
     1 º/o sample--diperluas--. [8],   lation--extended.
     55, 37a-37i p.   [PRC, Yale, RPI

        Indonesia. Biro Pusat Statistik.
        Sensus penduduk 1961. Re-   Population census 1961. Republic
     publik Indonesia. Hasil pendaf-   of Indonesia. Results of house-
     taran rumahtangga bln. Maret   hold listing in March 1961.
     1961. Djakarta, 1965. (RT.I-
     II).
  .4-1   Djakarta Raya. 64p.   Djakarta Raya.
                                             [E-W
  .4-2   Seluruh Indonesia. [8],   All Indonesia.
     22p.   [PRC, BC, RPI

        Indonesia. Biro Pusat Statistik.
1971.0-1   Republic of Indonesia. 1971 population census. [Djakarta],
     n.d. 12, [19]p. [PRC

        Indonesia. Biro Pusat Statistik.
        Sensus penduduk 1971. Dja-   Population census 1971.
     karta, 1971-19 . Series A-L.

Series A.

.1-A-1   Djumlah blok sensus dan rumah tangga hasil pendaftaran rumah tangga, Juli/Agustus 1970. 1971. 91p.

Number of blocks and households, based on household listing July/August 1970.
[E-W, OPR

.1-A-2   Djumlah blok sensus dan rumah tangga dari tiap ketjamatan, disusun setjara abdjad. 1971 115p.

Number of census blocks and households by subdistrict, in alphabetical order.
[OPR, PRC

.1-A-3   Penggunaan bangunan menurut hasil pendaftaran rumah tangga, Juli/Agustus 1970. 1971. 292p.

Number of buildings by type, based on the household listing, July/August 1970.
[E-W, PRC

.1-A-4   Klasifikasi jenis pekerjaan/jabatan dan lapangan kerja untuk pengolohan sensus penduduk 1971. 1971. 80p.

ISCO and ISIC classifications for processing the 1971 population census.
[OPR

.1-A-5   Edit dan imputation untuk pengolahan sensus penduduk, 1971.

Editing and imputation for processing of the 1971 population census.
[Not published.

.1-A-6   Daftar nomor kode dan jumlah sampel blok sensus untuk pengolahan sensus penduduk 1971.

List of codes and samples of census blocks for processing population census result 1971
[Not published.

Series B. Angka sementara.

.1-B-1   Penduduk menurut propinsi dan kabupaten/kolamadya. 1972. xi, 302p.

Preliminary figures.
Population by province and regency/municipality.
[PRC, BC

.1-B-2   Penduduk menurut ketjamatan di Djawa-Madura. 1972. x, 105p.

Population by sub-district in Java-Madura.
[PRC, BC

.1-B-3   Penduduk menurut ketjamatan diluar Djawa-Madura. 1972. xi, 185p.

Population by sub-district in outer Java-Madura.
[PRC, BC

.1-C   Series C. Angka sementara. Tabel-tabel pendahuluan. 1972. xvi, 180p.

Preliminary figures. Advance tables.
[PRC, OPR

.1-D   Series D. Penduduk Indonesia. 1975. [14], xxx, 255p.

Population of Indonesia.
[PRC, NYPL, OPR

Series E. Penduduk... 1974. 26v.

Population of...(province).

1971.1-E-1 through 1971.1-E-26. [All have xxiv, 230p.] 1. D.I. Aceh./2. Sumatra Utara./3. Sumatra Barat./4. Riau./5. Jambi./6. Sumatra Selatan./7. Bengkulu./8. Lampung./9. D.K.I. Jakarta Raya./10. Jawa Barat./11. Jawa Tengah./12. D.I. Jogyakarta./12. Jawa Timur./14. Bali./15. Nusa Tenggara Barat./16. Nus Tenggara Timur./17. Kalimantan./18. Kalimantan Tangah./19. Kalimantan Selatan./20. Kalimantan Timur./21. Sulawesi Utara./22. Sulawesi Tangah./23. Sulawesi Selatan./24. Sulawesi Tanggara./25. Maluku./26. Irian Jaya. [PRC

.1-F   Series F. Keadaan tem-
pat tinggal di Indonesia. 1975.
xv, 108p.

Housing conditions in Indonesia.
[PRC

     Series G. Keadaan tem-
pat tinggal di... 1976. 26v.
1971.1-G-1 through 1971-G-26. 1. D.K.I. Jakarta Raya. 1976. xv, 108p./2.
Jawa Barat. 1976. xv, 108p./3. D.I. Yogyakarta. 1976. xv, 108p./
4. Jawa Tengah. 1976. xv, 108p./5. Jawa Timur. 1976. xv, 108p./6.
Sumatra. 1977. xv, 366p./

Housing conditions in...(province).

.1-H   Series H. Ulasan dari
poda hasil-hasil sensus penduduk 1971.

[PRC
Outline of the 1971 population
census results.

.1-I   Series I. Evaluasi dari
poda pelaporan umur.

[
Evaluation of age reporting.

     Series J. Perkiraan kelo-
hiran dan kematian.
.1-J-1

[
Estimates of birth and death
rates.

.1-J-2

     Series K. Proyeksi pen-
duduk menurut umur, kelamin dan
daerah (1971-2000). 1973-   .
3v.

Population projections by age,
sex and region (1971-2000).

.1-K-1   Proyeksi penduduk Indonesia, 1971-1981. Dibuat berdasarkan hasil sementara sensus
penduduk 1971. 1973. i, 34,
xxxix p.

Projection of the population of
Indonesia, 1971-1981. Based on
provisional results from the 1971
population census.
[PRC

.1-K-2   Proyeksi penduduk Indonesia, 1976-2001. 1978. [2],
12p.

Population projection, 1976-2001,
[and manpower].
[PRC

.1-K-3   Proyeksi angkatan kerja Indonesia selama Repelita III.
1979/80-1984/85. 1978. 49p.

Labour force projections for Indonesia during the Repelita III.
[PRC

     Series L.

[Analyses].

.1-L-1   Keadaan demografi di
Indonesia. 1976. xii, 63p.

Demographic situation of Indonesia.
[PRC

.1-L-2   Perkiraan angka kela-
hiran dan kematian di Indonesia,
berdasarkan sensus penduduk 1971.
1976. iv, 67p.

Estimates of fertility and mortality in Indonesia, based on the
1971 population census.
[PRC, UN, OPR

.1-L-3   Ulasan singkat sensus
penduduk 1971. 1976. ii, 14p.

A brief note on 1971 population
census.
[PRC, UN

Indonesia.   Central Bureau of Statistics.
        1976 intercensal population survey.   Technical report series.
     Monograph, No.1-   .   Jakarta, 1976-   .
1976.0-1   Organization and methods.   1976.   [5], 17, [36]p.   [PRC
   .0-2

Indonesia.   Biro Pusat Statis-
     tik.
        Survey penduduk antar sensus   1976 intercensal population sur-
     1976. Seri tabulasi nomor 1-4.   vey.
     Jakarta, 1978.
   .1-1   Keterangan angkatan kerja   Indonesian labor force.
     Indonesia. 174p.   [PRC, E-W
   .1-2   Keterangan fertilitas pen-   Fertility of the Indonesian popu-
     duduk Indonesia. 130p.   lation.
                                            [PRC, E-W
   .1-3   Keterangan demografi pen-   Demography of the Indonesian popu-
     duduk Indonesia. 78p.   lation.
                                            [PRC, E-W
   .1-4   Keterangan rumah tangga   Information on households in Indo-
     Indonesia. 67p.   nesia.
                                            [E-W

IRAN

Islamic Republic of Iran   Capital: Tehran
Statistical Agency: Statistical Centre of Iran
                      Plan and Budget Organization.
                      Iran Novin Ave.
                      Tehran,
Publications Distributor: Bureau of Supervision and International Relations
                            (of the above).

Iran. Ministry of Interior. Department of Public Statistics.
     Census districts statistics of the first national census of Iran,
     1956.   Tehran, 1957-1961. Vol. I-CX in 119v.
1956.1-1 through 1956.1-110. 1. Karaj. 1957. xi, 67p./2. Tehran. xiv,
     63p./3. Tabriz. 1958. xiv, 58p./4. Esfahan. 1958. xiv, 72p./5.
     Mashhad. 1959. xiv, 56p./6. Abadan. 1960. xiv, 45p./7. Shiraz.
     1960. xiv, 59p./8. Kermanshah. 1960. xiv, 56p./9. Ahvaz. 1960.
     xiv, 47p./10. Rasht. 1960. xiv, 49p./11. Hamedan. 1960. xiv, 56p./
     12. Ghom. 1960. xiv, 46p./13. Rezaeyeh. 1960. xiv, 50p./14. Yazd.
     1960. xiv, 62p./15. Ghazvin. 1960. xiv, 55p./16. Ardabil. 1960.
     xiv, 50p./17-1. Kerman. 1960. xiv, 51p./17-2. Zarand. 1960. xiv,
     48p./18. Arak. 1960. xiv, 50p./19. Dezfool. 1960. xiv, 48p./20.
     Boroojerd. 1960. xiv, 48p./21 Zanjan. 1960. xiv, 55p./22. Kashan.
     1960. xiv, 49p./23. Masjed-Soleiman. 1960. xiv, 48p./24-1. Korram-
     shahr. 1960. xiv, 44p./24-2. Shadekan. 1960. xiv, 48p./
     25-1. Sanandaj. 1960. xiv, 52p./25-2. Ghorveh. 1960. xiv, 42p./
     26. Khorramabad. 1960. xiv, 55p./27-1. Maragheh. 1960. xiv, 52p./
     27-2. Shahindezh. 1960. xiv, 40p./28. Babol. 1960. xiv, 53p./29.
     Khoy (Shanindezh). 1960. xiv, 40p./30. Bandar Pahlavi. 1960. xiv,
     43p./31. Kazeroon. 1960. xiv, 47p./32. Sabzevaran. 1961. xiv,
     47p./33. Najafabad. 1960. xiv, 48p./34. Behbahan. 1960. xiv, 46p./
     35. Shahreza. 1960. xiv, 48p./36. Jahrom. 1960. xiv, 44p./37.
     Semnan. 1960. xiv, 48p./38. Gorgan. 1960. xiv, 51p./39. Sari.
     1960. xiv, 48p./40. Neishaboor. 1960. xiv, 49p./41. Shahi. 1960.
     xiv, 48p./42. Amol. 1960. xiv, 46p./43. Ghoochan. 1960. xiv, 50p./
     44. Meyaneh. 1961. xiv, 44p./45. Malayer. 1961. xiv, 44p./46.
     Nahavand. 1960. xiv, 44p./47. Mahabad. 1961. xiv, 53p./48. Lahijan.
     1960. xiv, 49p./49. Arasbaran. 1961. xiv, 50p./
     50. Torbate Hydarieh. 1961. xiv, 48p./51. Bojnoord. 1961. xiv,
     46p./52. Shooshtar. 1961. xiv, 43p./53-1. Booshehr. 1961. xiv,
     42p./53-2. Kangan. 1961. xiv, 37p./54. Dashte Gorgan. 1961. xiv,
     48p./55-1. Bandar Abbas. 1961. xiv, 46p./55-2. Jask. 1961. xiv,
     38p./56. Zahedan. 1961. xiv, 49p./57. Shahrood. 1961. xiv, 44p./
     58. Ghasre Shirin. 1961. xiv, 46p./59. Behshahr. 1961. xiv, 43p./
     60. Bam. 1961. xiv, 45p./61. Chaharmahal. 1961. xiv, 55p./62.
     Saveh. 1961. xiv, 43p./63. Larestan. 1961. xiv, 49p./64-1. Birjand.
     1961. xiv, 54p./64-2. Ghaen. 1961. xiv, 43p./65. Marand. 1961.
     xiv, 42p./66. Kashmar. 1961. xiv, 43p./67. Sarab. 1961. xiv, 45p./
     68. Saghez. 1961. xiv, 45p./69. Nayriz. 1961. xiv, 46p./70. Gol-
     payegan. 1961. xiv, 46p./71. Zabol. 1961. xiv, 46p./72-1. Sirjan.
     1961. xiv, 48p./72-2. Baft. 1961. xiv, 47p./73. Fassa. 1961. xiv,
     41p./74. Tooyserkan. 1961. xiv, 45p./

75. Mahalat. 1961. xiv, 42p./76. Dashti va Dashtertan. 1961.
xiv, 43p./77. Aligoodarz. 1961. xiv, 43p./78. Rafsanjan. 1961. xiv,
43p./79. Darab. 1961. xiv, 43p./80. Garroos. 1961. xiv, 43p./81.
Damghan. 1961. xiv, 42p./82. Dargaz. 1961. xiv, 41p./83. Ilam.
1961. xiv, 42p./84. Abadeh. 1961. xiv, 47p./85. Shasavar. 1961.
xiv, 51p./86. Gonabad. 1961. xiv, 41p./87-1. Tabas. 1961. xiv,
45p./87-2. Ferdows. 1961. xiv, 40p./88. Ramhormoz. 1961. xiv, 46p./
89. Meshginshahr. 1961. xiv, 44p./90. Na'in. 1961. xiv, 44p./91.
Torbate. 1961. xiv, 44p./92. Foomenat. 1961. xiv, 47p./93. Kanga-
var. 1961. xiv, 45p./94. Dashte Mishan. 1961. xiv, 39p./95. Ardestan. 1961. xiv, 44p./96. Firoozabad. 1961. xiv, 43p./97. Khalkhal.
1961. xiv, 43p./98. Makoo. 1961. xiv, 43p./99. Bandar Langeh. 1961.
xiv, 42p./
100. Damavand. 1961. xiv, 42p./101. Shahabade Gharb. 1961. xiv,
46p./102. Minab. 1961. xiv, 42p./103. Saravan. 1961. xiv, 41p./
104. Iranshahr. 1961. xiv, 41p./105. Tavalesh. 1961. xiv, 43p./
106. Faridan. 1961. xiv, 41p./107. Hashtrood. 1961. xiv, 42p./108.
Nowshahr. 1961. xiv, 46p./33 [i.e., 109] Sabzevaran. 1961. xiv,
47p./110. Chahbahar. 1961. xiv, 41p. [UN, BC, LC, PRC, RPI

Iran. Ministry of Interior. Department of Public Statistics.
1956.2   [First national census of Iran]. Selected summary statistics for
the census districts of Iran: November 1956. Tehran, n.d. 117p.
[PSC

Iran. Ministry of Interior. Department of Public Statistics.
Results of the 1956 census of Iran. National and province statistics of the first census of Iran: November 1956. Tehran, 1961-1962.
Vol. I-II.
.3-1   I. Number and distribution of the inhabitants for Iran and the
census provinces. 1961. xxix, 526, [28]p. [UN, LC, BC, PRC, RPI
.3-2   II. Social and economic characteristics of the inhabitants, for
Iran and the census provinces. 1962. xxxvi, 477, [30]p. [UN, BC,
LC, PRC, RPI

Iran. Iranian Statistical Centre.
1966.0-1   Census of population and housing, Iran 1966; processing the data.
[Tehran], 1968. 16, [24]p. forms, tables. [BC

Iran. Iranian Statistical Centre.
National census of population and housing: November 1966. Advance
sample data for total country, urban and rural. Bulletin. [Tehran],
1966-1967. Nos. 1-4.
.1-1   [Preliminary census results. The total population of Iran.
Settled population only.] 1966.   p. [
.1-2   [... Unsettled population.] 1966.   p. [
.1-3   Demographic, social and economic characteristics of the population. 1967. [69]p. [PRC
.1-4   Household and housing characteristics. 1967. [21]p. [PRC, BC

Iran. Iranian Statistical Centre.
National census of population and housing: November 1966. Tehran,
1967-1968. Vol. I-CLXVIII.

1966.2-1 through 1966.2-168. 1. Karaj. 1967. 11, 12, 108p./2. Arak. 1967.
11, 12, 79p./3. Rey. 1967. 10, 11, 79p./4. Khomeyn. 1967. 10, 12,
76p./5. Tafresh. 1967. 10, 10, 76p./6. Damavand. 1967. 11, 12, 77p./
7. Mahallat. 1967. 11, 13, 105p./8. Garmsar. 1967. 10, 11, 76p./9.
Qom. 1967. 10, 11, 79p./10. Tehran. 1967. 11, 14, 322p./11. Saveh.
1967. 10, 12, 78p./12. Kashan. 1967. 10, 12, 94p./13. Shemiran.
1967. 9, 11, 79p./14. Qazvin. 1967. 11, 13, 124p./15. Natanz. 1967.
9, 11, 76p./16. Golpeyegan. 1967. 10, 13, 122p./17. Semirom. 1967.
10, 11, 75p./18. Nain. 1967. 10, 12, 77p./19. Shahreza. 1967. 10,
12, 122p./20. Najafabad. 1967. 11, 13, 136p./21. Ardestan. 1967.
10, 12, 77p./22. Yazd. 1967. 10, 15, 155p./23. Faridan. 1967. 10,
13, 93p./24. Esfahan. 1968. 12, 16, 361p./

25. Owramanat. 1967. 10, 11, 76p./26. Sonqor. 1967. 10, 11, 76p./
27. Qasr-e-shirin. 1967. 10, 13, 92p./28. Kermanshah. 1967. 10, 13,
137p./29. Shahabad. 1967. 10, 13, 120p./30. Jahrom. 1967. 11, 11,
78p./31. Abadeh. 1967. 10, 13, 135p./32. Estahbanat. 1967. 11, 12,
76p./33. Darab. 1967. 10, 14, 92p./34. Shiraz. 1968. 10, 13, 198p./
35. Fasa. 1967. 10, 13, 93p./36. Firuzabad. 1967. 10, 12, 76p./
37. Kazerun. 1967. 10, 11, 77p./38. Lar. 1968. 10, 13, 121p./39.
Mamasani. 1968. 10, 11, 76p./40. Neyriz. 1967. 11, 11, 76p./41 Arde-
bil. 1967. 10, 11, 78p./42. Arasbaran. 1967. 10, 12, 78p./43. Ta-
briz. 1968. 11, 15, 299p./44. Khalkhal. 1967. 9, 12, 76p./45. Sarab.
1967. 10, 11, 76p./46. Maragheh. 1967. 10, 13, 136p./47. Marand.
1967. 10, 13, 94p./48. Meshkinshahr. 1967. 10, 12, 76p./49. Miyaneh.
1967. 10, 12, 78p./

50. Hastrud. 1968. 10, 12, 77p./51. Khoy. 1968. 10, 12, 78p./
52. Rezaiyeh. 1968. 10, 12, 78p./53. Shahpur. 1968. 10, 11, 76p./
54. Maku. 1968. 9, 12, 75p./55. Mahabad. 1968. 10, 13, 93p./56.
Miyandoab. 1968. 10, 13, 121p./57. Naqadeh. 1968. 10, 11, 76p./
58. Khaneh. 1968. 9, 10, 75p./59. Sardasht. 1968. 9, 10, 75p./60.
Astara. 1967. 10, 12, 76p./61. Bandar-e-Pahlavi. 1967. 10, 11, 78p./
62. Rasht. 1967. 10, 12, 79p./63. Rudbar. 1967. 9, 11, 77p./64.
Rudsar. 1967. 10, 12, 93p./65. Zanjan. 1968. 11, 13, 136p./66.
Sowma'Ehsara. 1967. 9, 11, 77p./67. Tavalesh. 1967. 9, 12, 77p./
68. Fowman. 1967. 9, 12, 77p./69. Lahijan. 1968. 11, 13, 122p./
70. Langarud. 1967. 10, 12, 76p./71. Abadan. 1968. 10, 12, 79p./
72. Ahvaz. 1968. 10, 12, 79p./73. Izeh. 1968. 9, 11, 75p./74.
Bandar-e-Mahshahr (Ma'shur). 1968. 10, 12, 92p./

75. Behbehan. 1968. 10, 13, 136p./76. Khorramshahr. 1968. 10,
13, 94p./77. Dezful. 1968. 10, 14, 94p./78. Dasht-e-Mishan. 1968.
10, 12, 75p./79. Ramhormoz. 1968. 10, 12, 76p./80. Shustar. 1968.
10, 13, 93p./81. Masjed Soleyman. 1968. 10, 14, 94p./82. Tuiserkan.
1968. 10, 13, 92p./83. Malayer. 1968. 10, 12, 77p./84. Nahavand.
1968. 10, 12, 77p./85. Hamadan. 1968. 10, 12, 169p./86. Amol.
1968. 10, 12, 78p./87. Babol. 1968. 10, 14, 136p./88. Behshahr.
1968. 10, 13, 136p./89. Dasht-e-Gorgan(Gonbad-e-Qabus). 1968. 10,
12, 78p./90. Sari. 1968. 10, 11, 78p./91. Shahi. 1968. 10, 14,
94p./92. Shahsavar. 1968. 10, 12, 78p./93. Gorgan. 1968. 11, 14,
169p./94. Nur. 1968. 10, 11, 76p./95. Nowshahr. 1968. 10, 13, 94p./
96. Baft. 1968. 10, 12, 76p./97. Bam. 1968. 10, 12, 77p./98. Rafsanjan. 1968. Lo, 12, 93p./99. Jiroft. 1968. 10, 12, 77p./

100. Sirjan. 1968. 10, 12, 77p./101. Kerman. 1968. 10, 13,
154p./102. Esfarayen. 1968. 9, 11, 75p./103p. Bojnurd. 1968. 10,
12, 77p./104p. Birjand. 1968. 10, 13, 94p./105p. Torbat-e-Jam. 1968.
10, 12, 92p./106. Torbat-e-Heydariyeh. 1968. 10, 13, 94p./107. Dar-
1968. 10, 12, 87p./108. Sabzevar. 1968. 10, 12, 78p./109. Shirvan.
1968. 10, 12, 75p./110. Tabas. 1968. 10, 11, 76p./111. Ferdows.
1968. 10, 13, 91p./112. Quchan. 1968. 10, 12, 77p./113. Gorgan.
1968. 10, 14, 169p./114. Gonabad. 1968. 10, 12, 76p./115. Mashhad.
1968. 10, 13, 96p./116. Neyshabur. 1968. 10, 13, 94p./117. Iranshahr. 1968. 10, 12, 75p./118. Chahbahor. 1968. 10, 12, 65p./119.
Zabol. 1968. 10, 12, 77p./120. Zahedan. 1968. 10, 12, 78p./121.
Saravan. 1968. 10, 12, 75p./122. Baneh. 1968. 10, 11, 76p./123.
Bijar "Garus." 1968. 10, 12, 76p./124. Saqqez. 1968. 10, 12, 76p./
125. Sanandaj. 1968. 10, 12, 78p./126. Qorveth. 1968. 10, 12,
75p./127. Marivan. 1968. 9, 11, 75p./128. Borujen. 1968. 10, 13,
93p./129. Sharh-e-Kord. 1968. 10, 13, 195p./130. Aligudarz. 1968.
10, 12, 77p./131. Borujerd. 1968. 10, 13, 94p./132. Kashmar. 1968.
10, 12, 77p./133. Ilam. 1968. 10, 12, 79p./134. Badreh. 1968. 9,
11, 73p./135. Dehloran. 1968. 9, 11, 73p./136. Mehran. 1968. 9,
11, 73p./137. Boyer Ahmadi. 1968. 10, 11, 75p./138. Kohkiluyeh.
1968. 10, 13, 92p./139. Bandar-e-Bushehr. 1968. 10, 13, 122p./140.
Dashtestan. 1968. 10, 12, 77p./141. Bandar-e-Abbas. 1968. 10, 11,
78p./142. Bandar-e-Langeh. 1968. 10, 12, 92p./143. Minab. 1968.
10, 12, 76p./144. Damghan. 1968. 10, 12, 76p./145. Semnan. 1968.
10, 13, 93p./146. Shahrud. 1968. 10, 12, 78p./147. Central Ostan.
1968. 10, 14, 123p./148. Esfahan Ostan. 1968. 10, 13, 121p./149.
Kermanshahan. 1968. 10, 13, 115p./
150. Fars Ostan. 1968. 10, 13, 118p./151. East Azarbayjan Ostan.
1968. 10, 13, 122p./152. West Azarbayejan Ostan. 1968. 11, 13, 116p./
153. Gilan Ostan. 1968. 10, 13, 121p./154. Khuzestan Ostan. 1968.
11, 13, 120p./155. Hamadan Farmandarikol. 1968. 11, 14, 116p./156.
Mazandaran Ostan. 1968. 10, 13, 119p./157. Kerman Ostan. 1968. 10,
13, 115p./158. Khorasan Ostan. 1968. 11, 14, 121p./159. Sistan and
Bahichestan Ostan. 1968. 11, 14, 114p./160. Kordestan Ostan. 1968.
11, 14, 113p./161. Chahrmahal and Bakhtiryari Farmandarikol. 1968.
11, 13, 112p./162. Lorestan. 1968. 11, 14, 116p./163. Ilam Farmandarikol. 1968. 11, 13, 116p./164. Boyer Ahmad and Kohkiluyel Farmandarikol. 1968. 10, 13, 107p./165. Farmandarikol of ports and
islands of Persian Gulf. 1968. 10, 13, 113p./166. Farmandarikol
of ports and islands of Omman Sea. 1968. 11, 13, 114p./167. Samnan
Farmandarikol. 1968. 10, 13, 113p./168. Total country--settled population. 1968. 13, 20, 190p. [PRC, BC, RPI

Momeni, Djamchid. Translator.
1966.2-168a   National census of population and housing, 1966. Total coun-
try--settled population. Austin, Texas, Population Research Center,
1969. [56], 301p. [PRC

Iran. Iranian Statistical Center.
.3   [The population of Iranian Shahrestans on the basis of the 1966
census.] [Tehran], n.d. 22p. [PRC

Iran. Statistical Centre.
1966.4 Highlights of sex-age characteristics in Iran, 1956-1966: a socio-logical interpretation, by Jacquiline Rudolph-Touba. [Tehran], 1970. 5, 39p. [PRC

Iran. Statistical Centre.
[Current population sample survey in 1971 for urban areas and total country.] (Persian edition). Tehran, 1973-1974. 2v.
1971.1-1 [...urban areas]. 1973. vii, 196p. [PRC
.1-2 [Report of the results of the 1971 survey for the total country.] 1974. vi, 31p. [PRC

Iran. Statistical Centre.
.2 [The results of the current population sample survey conducted in rural areas in 1971.] Tehran, 1972. 199p. [

Iran. Statistical Centre.
1976.0-1 [Preliminary report of the census of population and housing, October 1976. Total country by provinces.] Tehran, 1977. 43p. (Publication, No. 1) (In Persian). [PSC

Iran. Statistical Centre.
National census of population and housing, November 1976. Based on 5% sample. Tehran, [1978]. 25v.
.1-1 Total country. [xx], 157, [13]p. [E-W, PC, BC, PRC
.1-2 Tehran Shahrestan. a-m, 51, [14]p. [PRC
1976.1-3-1 through 1976.1-3-23. Ostans. [All have 13, 51, 13 pages.] 1. Markazi./2. Gilan./3. Mazandaran./4. East Azarbayejan./5. West Azar-bayejan./6. Kermanshahan./7. Khuzestan./8. Fars./9. Kerman./10. Khor-asan./11. Esfahan./12. Sistan and Baluchestan./13. Kordestan./14. Ham-adan./15. Chaharmahal and Bakhtiyari./16. Lorestan./17. Ilam./18. Boyer Ahmad and Kohgiluyeh./19. Bushehr./20. Zanjan./21. Semnan./22. Yazd./23. Hormozgan. [BC, PSC

Iran. Statistical Centre.
National census of population and housing, November 1976. [Final results]. Tehran, 1978- . 186v.
.2-1 Total country.
1976.2-2-1 through 1976.2-2-23. Ostans.

1976.2-3-1 through 1976.2-3-162. Shahrestans.

IRAQ

Republic of Iraq.   Capital: Baghdad.
Statistical Agency: Central Statistical Organization
                     Ministry of Planning
                     P.O. Box 8001
                     Baghdad,
Publications Distributor: Department of Population and Public Relations.
                          (of the above.)

        Iraq. Directorate General of Census.
             Census of Iraq, 1947. Baghdad, 1954. Parts 1-3.
1947.1-1   Baghdad Liwa, Hillah Liwa, Dulaim Liwa, Karbala Liwa, Kut Liwa,
        Diyala Liwa. 313p. [LC, PRC,
    .1-2   Mosul Liwa, Kirkuk Liwa, Sulaimaniyah Liwa, Arbil Liwa. 260p.
        [LC, PRC
    .1-3   Basra Liwa, Muntafiq Liwa, Amara Liwa, Diwaniya Liwa. 239p.
        [LC, PRC

        Iraq. Directorate General of Census.
             Population census, 1957. Baghdad, 1962. Vol. I-X.
1957.1-1   I. General summary, figures for provinces and the country. xx,
        263, [2]p. [PRC
1957.1-2 through 1957.1-10. 2. Diala, Kirkuk, Arbil, Sulaimaniya, Mosul.
        394p./3. Basra, Nasiriya, Amara, Diwaniya, Ramadi, Kerbela, Kut, Hilla,
        Baghdad. 332p./4. Ramadi (Dulaim) and Baghdad. iv, 321, [6]p./5. Ar-
        bil and Mosul. iv, 334p./6. Hilla and Kerbela. iv, 243p./7. Nasiriya
        and Diwaniya. iv, 127, 4p./8. Basra and Amara. iv, 121, 149, [1]p./
        9. Kirkuk and Sulaimaniya. iv, 273, 2p./10. Kut and Diala. iv, 259,
        [1]p. [PRC, RPI

        Iraq. Directorate General of Census.
    .2   [Procedure and operation of the census of 1957.] Baghdad, n.d.
        [2], 400p. (Bulletin of the Ministry of Social Affairs. Vol. 3, no.
        1-2.) [UN, RPI

        Iraq. Directorate General of Census.
    .3   Abstract of the general census of 1957. Vol. 2, part (16). The
        summaries for Iraq. Baghdad, n.d. 31, [1]p. [RPI

        Iraq. Central Statistical Organization.
1965.1   General population census of 1965. Baghdad, 1973. x, 749p.
        [PRC

IRELAND

                                              Capital: Dublin.
Statistical Agency: Central Statistics Office
                      Ardee Road
                      Dublin 6,
Publications Distributor: Government Publications Sale Office
                           G.P.O. Arcade
                           Dublin 1,

Ireland. Central Statistics Office.
    Census of population of Ireland, 1946.   Dublin, The Stationery
Office, 1950-1954. Vol. I-X in 11v.
1946.1-1   I. Population, area and valuation of each district, electoral
    division and of each larger unit of area. 1950. vii, 139p. [PRC,
    TXU, UN, RPI
   .1-2   II. Occupation of males and females in each province, county,
    county borough, urban and rural districts. 1953. vii, 213p. [PRC,
    TXU, UN, RPI
   .1-3   III. Part 1. Religions. Part 2. Birthplaces. 1952. ix,
    131p. [PRC, TXU, UN, RPI
   .1-4   IV. Part 1. Housing. Part 2. Social amenities. 1954. x,
    222p. [PRC, TXU, UN, RPI
   .1-5-1   V. Part 1. Ages, orphanhood and conjugal conditions, classi-
    fied by areas only. 1950. vii, 257p. [PRC, TXU, UN, RPI
   .1-5-2   V. Part 2. Ages and conjugal conditions. Classified by occu-
    pations and industries. 1954. vi, 170p. [PRC, TXU, UN, RPI
   .1-6   VI. Industrial status. 1953. v, 103p. [PRC, TXU, UN, RPI
   .1-7   VII. Industries. 1952. vii, 114p. [PRC, TXU, UN, RPI
   .1-8   VIII. Irish language with special tables for the Gaeltacht
    areas. 1953. xi, 41p. [PRC, TXU, UN, RPI
   .1-9   IX. Fertility of marriage. 1953. viii, 248p. [PRC, TXU, UN,
    RPI
   .1-10   X. Dependency. 1952. v, 53p. [PRC, TXU, UN, RPI

Ireland. Central Statistical Office.
   .2   Censuses of population of Ireland, 1946 and 1951. General report.
    Dublin, The Stationery Office, 1958. vii, 274p. map. [PRC, TXU, UN,
    RPI

Ireland. Central Statistics Office.
    Census of population of Ireland, 1951.   Dublin, The Stationery
Office, 1952-1954. Vol. I-III in 5v.
1951.1-1   I. Population, area and valuation of each district, electoral
    division and of each larger unit of area. 1952. ix, 149p. [PRC, TXU,
    UN, RPI
   .1-2-1   II. Part 1. Ages and conjugal conditions. 1953. vi, 247p.
    [PRC, TXU, UN, RPI
   .1-2-2   II. Part 2. Ages and conjugal conditions classified by occu-
    pations. 1954. vi, 297p. [PRC, TXU, UN, RPI

.1-3-1   III.   Part 1.   Occupations of males and females in each province, county, couty borough, and each town of 5,000 and over population. 1954.   vii, 159p.   [PRC, TXU, UN, RPI
.1-3-2   III.   Part 2.   Industries and industrial status.   1954.   viii, 213p.   [PRC, TXU, UN, RPI

Ireland.   Central Statistics Office.
.2   Censuses of population of Ireland, 1946 and 1951.   General report. Dublin, The Stationery Office, 1958.   vii, 274p.   map.   [Same volume as 1946.2.]   [PRC, TXU, UN, RPI

Ireland.   Central Statistics Office.
1956.1   Census of the population of Ireland 1956.   Population, area and valuation of each district, electoral division and each larger unit of area.   Dublin, The Stationery Office, 1957.   xxii, 146p.   [PRC, TXU, UN, RPI

Ireland.   Central Statistics Office.
      Census of population of Ireland, 1961.   Dublin, The Stationery Office, 1963-1966.   Vol. I-IX.
1961.1-1   I.   Population, area and valuation of each district, electoral division and of each larger unit of area.   1963.   xi, 152p.   [PRC, TXU, RPI, RIR
.1-2   II.   Ages and conjugal conditions classified by areas only. 1963.   vi, 221p.   [PRC, TXU, RPI, RIR
.1-3   III.   Occupations of males and females in each province, county, county borough, and in each town of 5,000 and over population.   1963. vi, 172p.   [PRC, TXU, RPI, RIR
.1-4   IV.   Industries.   1964.   vii, 147p.   [PRC, TXU, RPI, RIR
.1-5   V.   Occupations, classified by ages and conjugal conditions. 1964.   vi, 205p.   [PRC, TXU, RPI, RIR
.1-6   VI.   Housing and social amenities.   1964.   vii, 165p.   [PRC, TXU, RPI, RIR
.1-7   VII.   Part 1.   Religions.   Part 2.   Birthplaces.   1965.   iv, 117p.   [PRC, TXU, RPI, RIR
.1-8   VIII.   Fertility of marriage.   1965.   iv, 215p.   [PRC, TXU, RPI
.1-9   IX.   Irish language with special tables for the Gaeltacht areas.   1966.   v, 35p.   [PRC, TXU, RPI, RIR

Ireland.   Central Statistics Office.
      Census of population of Ireland, 1966.   Dublin, The Stationery Office, 1967-1970.   Vol. I-VII.
1966.1-1   I.   Population of district electoral divisions, towns and larger units of area.   1967.   xx, 180p.   [PRC, RPI
.1-2   II.   Ages and conjugal conditions classified by areas.   1968. xx, 233p.   [PRC, RPI
.1-3   III.   Industries.   1968.   xx, 166p.   [PRC, RPI
.1-4   IV.   Occupations.   1969.   xx, 226p.   [PRC, RPI
.1-5   V.   Occupations and industries classified by ages and conjugal conditions.   1969.   xxvi, 247p.   [PRC, RPI
.1-6   VI.   Housing and households.   1969.   xvii, [3], 153p.   [PRC, RPI
.1-7   VII.   Education.   1970.   xv, 181p.   [PRC, RPI

Ireland. Central Statistics Office.
          Census of population of Ireland, 1971.   Dublin, The Stationery
          Office, 1972-   . Vol. I-XIII.
1971.1-1   I.   Population of district electoral divisions, towns, and larger
          units of area. 1972. xxv, 165p. [PRC
     .1-2   II. Ages and conjugal condition classified by areas only. 1973.
          xvii, 188p. [PRC
     .1-3   III. Industries. 1974. xiii, 155p. [PRC
     .1-4   IV. Occupations. 1975. xiv, 194p. [PRC
     .1-5   V.   Occupations and industries classified by ages and conjugal
          conditions. 1975. xvi, 167p. [PRC
     .1-6   VI. Housing. 1976. xiv, 170p. [PRC
     .1-7   VII. Household composition. 1976. xv, 44p. [PRC
     .1-8   VIII. Irish language. 1976. xiii, 37p. [PRC
     .1-9   IX. Religion. 1977. viii, 70p. [PRC, OPR
     .1-10   X.   Fertility of marriage. 1977. xiii, 125p. [PRC, OPR
     .1-11   XI. Usual residence, migration and birthplace. 1978. xvi,
          125p. [JB-F, PRC
     .1-12   XII. Part 1. Education. Part 2. Scientific and technological
          qualifications. 1978. xiv, 161p. [PRC
     .1-13   XIII. Transport and journey to work.

ISLE OF MAN

Capital: Douglas.

Statistical Agency: General Registry
                     Central Government Offices
                     Buck's Road
                     Douglas,
Publications Distributor: Central Reference Library (of the above)

        Great Britain. General Register Office.
1951.1   Report on Isle of Man.   London, HMSO, 1956. xlvii, 42p. [PRC, BC

        Great Britain. General Register Office.
        Report on Isle of Man.   London, HMSO, 1965-1966. 2 parts.
1961.1-1   Population and housing. 1965. ix, 28p. [PRC, OPR
    .1-2   Migration, economic activity and other topics. 1966. x, pp.29-
        48. [PRC

        Isle of Man. General Registry.
1966.1   Isle of Man. Census 1966 report.   Douglas, Island Development Co.,
        1966. ix, 21p. specimen form. [PRC

        Isle of Man. General Registry.
1971.1   Isle of Man. Census 1971. Interim report.   Douglas, Island Devel-
        opment Co., 1972. viii, 14p. specimen form. [PRC, OPR

        Isle of Man. General Registry.
    .2   Census 1971. Report on Isle of Man.   Castletown Press, 1975.
        xviii, 113p. [PRC

        Isle of Man. General Registry.
1976.1   Isle of Man. Census 1976 report.   [Douglas], Bridson & Horrox,
        1976. vii, 18p. [PRC, OPR

        Isle of Man. General Registry.
    .2   Isle of Man. Census 1976: further report.   Douglas, 1977. iii,
        7p. [OPR

ISRAEL

State of Israel.   Capital: Tel Aviv-Yafo
Statistical Agency: Central Bureau of Statistics
                     P.O. Box 13015
                     Jerusalem,
Publications Distributor: Publications Section (of the above).

    Israel. Central Bureau of Statistics.
      Registration of population (8 XI 1948).   Jerusalem, Government
    Printer, 1955-1956. Parts A and B.
1948.1-1   A. Towns, villages, and regions. By R. Bachi, G. Gil, H. Mühsam,
    and M. Sicron. 1955. xliv, 403, [42]p. (Special series, no. 36).
    [PRC, BC, OPR, RPI
  .1-2   B. Characteristics of the Jewish population and types of settle-
    ment. By B. Gil and M. Sicron. xcii, 63, [89]p. (Special series,
    no. 53). [PRC, BC, OPR, RPI

    Israel. Central Bureau of Statistics.
      Population and housing census 1961.   Jerusalem, 1961-1969. Publi-
    cations, no. 1-43.
1961.1-1   The geographical-statistical division of the urban settlements
    in Israel. 1962. xxviii, [2], 127, [56]p. [PRC, TXU, RPI
  .1-2   Classification of economic branches. 1961. viii, 74, [ ]p.
    [RPI
  .1-3   [Classification of occupations]. 1961. [v], 29, vii, 56p.
    [PRC, BC, LC, RPI
  .1-4   Population and housing census 1961. Provisional results. 1961.
    [12]p. [PRC, BC, LC, RPI
  .1-5   Statistics of population in settlements - provisional results.
    1962. xiv, 58, [8]p. [TXU, PSC, RPI
  .1-6   List of settlements, their population and code numbers. (Pro-
    visional data for 22 V 1961). 1962. 38, [14]p. [PSC, RPI
  .1-7   Demographic characteristics of the population. Part I. Data
    from Stage A of the census, general results. 1962. xlviii, 137,
    [52]p. [PRC, RPI
  .1-8   Demographic characteristics of the population. Part II. (Data
    from Stage A of the census by subdistricts, natural regions, types of
    settlements and municipal status). 1962. xlvii, 153, [52]p. [PRC,
    RPI
  .1-9   Labour force. Part I. Labour force characteristics (weekly)
    and employed persons, by economic branch, occupation and employment
    status. Data from Stage B of the census. 1963. ci, 237, [104]p.
    [PRC, RPI
  .1-10   The settlements of Israel. Part I. List of settlements. Geo-
    graphical information and population 1948-1961. 1963. xli, 133,
    [46]p. [PRC, RPI
  .1-11   The settlements of Israel. Part II. Sex, age, residence and
    population group. Data from Stage A of the census. 1963. xxix, 277,
    [32]p. [PRC, RPI
  .1-12   The settlements of Israel. Part III. Jewish population, by
    country of birth and period of immigration. Data from Stage A of the
    census. 1963. xxvii, 179, [50]p. [PRC, RPI

1961.1-13   Demographic characteristics of the population. Part III. First results from Stage B of the census. 1963. lix, 50, [58]p. [PRC, RPI

.1-14   Atlas of settlements in Israel, based on the findings of the census of population and housing 1961. 1963. [56]p. [PRC, RPI

.1-15   Languages, literacy and educational attainment. Part I. Data from Stage B of the census. 1963. lxvii, 86, [68]p. [PRC, RPI

.1-16   Housing. Part I. Data from Stage B of the census. 1964. liii, 29, [54]p. [PRC, RPI

.1-17   Moslems, Christians and Druzes in Israel 1961. Data from Stages A and B of the census. 1964. xci, 111, [182]p. [PRC, RPI

.1-18   The settlements of Israel. Part IV. Length of residence in settlement, number of years of study, extent of Hebrew speaking, labour force participation and economic branch of employed persons. Data from Stage B of the census. 1964. xlvii, 95, [62]p. [PRC, RPI

.1-19   Internal migration. Part I. Data from Stage B of the census. 1964. xxxiii, 25, [42]p. [PRC, RPI

.1-20   The division of the State of Israel into natural regions for statistical purposes. 1964. xxxvii, 126p. maps. [PRC, RPI

.1-21   Labour force. Part II. Labour force characteristics and employed persons, by educational attainment and literacy. Data from Stage B of the census. 1964. xxxv, 95, [36]p. diagrams. [PRC, RPI

.1-22   Demographic characteristics of the population. Part IV. Additional data from Stages A and B of the census. 1964. xxvii, 87, [26]p. maps. [PRC, RPI

.1-23   The settlements of Israel. Part V. Housing in settlements. Data from Stage B of the census. 1965. xxvi, 37, [22]p. [PRC, RPI

.1-24   Labour force. Part III. Additional data from Stage B of the census. 1965. xii, 143, [12]p. [PRC, RPI

.1-25   Procedures and definitions. Explanatory notes to the census publications. 1965. cvii, 91p. [PRC, BC, RPI

.1-26   Marriage and fertility. Part I. First data from Stage B of the census. 1965. xviii, 47, [30]p. diagrams. [PRC, RPI

.1-27   Labour force. Part IV. Occupation abroad. Additional data from Stage B of the census. 1965. xi, 59, [12]p. maps. [PRC, RPI

.1-28   The settlements of Israel. Part VI. Synoptic population data and statistics of settlements. Additional data from Stages A and B of the census. 1966. xix, 271, [52]p. [PRC, BC, RPI

.1-29   Languages, literacy and educational attainment. Part II. Additional data on languages spoken from Stage B of the census. 1966. vii, 101, [18]p. [PRC, BC, RPI

.1-30   Languages, literacy and educational attainment. Part III. Additional data on literacy and educational attainment from Stage B of the census. 1966. vii, 145, [18]p. [PRC, RPI

.1-31   Housing. Part II. Additional data from Stage B of the census. 1966. xviii, 44, [18]p. [PRC, RPI

.1-32   Marriage and fertility. Part II. Additional data from Stage B of the census. 1967. x, 76, [24]p. [PRC, BC, RPI

.1-33   Internal migration. Part II. Data from Stage B of the census. 1967. xii, 153, [20]p. [PRC, BC, RPI

.1-34   Survey of university graduates. Part I (1961). 1967. lvii, 35, [76]p. [PRC, BC, RPI

.1-35   Survey of university graduates. Part II (1961). 1967. xii, 39, [26]p. [PRC, RPI

.1-36   Families in Israel. Part I. Tables. 1968. xiii, 207, [23]p.
    [PRC, BC, RPI
.1-37   Working-life tables, by M. Hartmann. 1968. ii, 71p. [PRC, RPI
.1-38   Population in Jerusalem, Haifa and Tel Aviv-Yafo. 1968. xiii,
    121, [18]p. [PRC, BC, RPI
.1-39   Families in Israel (1961). Part II. [Analysis] by Judah Matras.
    1968. xii, 241p. [PRC, BC, RPI
         Evaluation of the census data. [By] Malka Kantorowitz. 1969.
    Vol. I-II.
.1-40-1   I. xv, 277, [7], 221, [18]p. [PRC, RPI
.1-40-2   II. xv, 165, [16]p. [PRC, RPI
.1-41   Fertility of married women in Israel.

.1-42   Main data of the census. Summary. Part I. Tables and diagrams.
    1969. xviii, 309, [14]p. [PRC, BC, RPI
.1-43   Main data of the census. Summary. Part II. Maps. 1969. vi,
    [6]p. plus 43 maps. [UN, RPI

    [Note: Demographic characteristics, Parts I-IV (see 1961.1-7, 8, 13,
    22); Families in Israel, Parts I-II (see 1961.1-36, 39); Housing, Parts
    I-II (see 1961.1-16, 31); Internal migration, Parts I-II (see 1961.1-
    19, 33); Labour force, Parts I-IV (see 1961.1-9, 21, 24, 27); Languages,
    literacy and educational attainment, Parts I-III (see 1961.1-15, 29, 30);
    Marriage and fertility, Parts I-II (see 1961.1-26, 32); Settlements of
    Israel, Parts I-VI (see 1961.1-10, 11, 12, 18, 23, 28); Survey of uni-
    versity graduates, Parts I-II (see 1961.1-34, 35).]

    Israel. Central Bureau of Statistics.
         Census of population, 1967. Jerusalem, 1967-1970. Vols. 1-5.
1967.1-1   West Bank of Jordan, Gaza Strip and Northern Sinai, Golan Heights.
    Data from full enumeration. 1967. xxxvii, 204p. maps. [PRC, RPI
    .1-2   Housing conditions, household equipment, welfare assistance and
    farming in the administered areas. 1968. xxxv, [34]p. [PRC, RPI
    .1-3   Demographic characteristics of the population in the administered
    areas. Data from sample enumeration. 1968. xxxiii, 76, [30]p. [PRC,
    RPI
    .1-4   Labour force. Part 1. 1968. xxvi, 24, [26]p. [PRC, RPI
    .1-5   The administered territories. Additional data from the sample
    enumeration. 1970. xiii, 79, [12]p. [PRC, RPI

    [Note: Despite the lack of a "Labour for, Part 2," implied by No.
    1967.1-4 above, this set is considered complete by the Central Bureau
    of Statistics.]

    Israel. Central Bureau of Statistics. Jerusalem Municipality.
         Census of population and housing 1967. East Jerusalem. Jerusalem,
    1968-1970. Parts I-II.
    .2-1   [I]. 1968. xlvi, 64, [48]p. 2 maps. [PRC, RPI
    .2-2   II. 1970. ix, 31, [10]p. [PRC, RPI

    Israel. Central Bureau of Statistics.
         Census of population and housing 1972. Jerusalem, 1972-   .
    (Population and housing census 1972 series, no. 1-   ).

1972.1-1   Population by natural region, type of locality and in large
       localities. Provisional results. 1972. ix, 41p. [PRC, BC
  .1-2   Population in conurbations, quarters and sub-quarters. Provi-
       sional results. 1972. xxv, 10, [24]p. 15 maps. [PRC, BC
  .1-3   The geographical-statistical division of urban localities in
       Israel. 1973. xxxvi, 244p. [PRC
  .1-4   Population and households for localities and statistical areas.
       1974. xxviii, 119, [26]p. [PRC
  .1-5   List of localities. Geographical information and population,
       1948, 1961, 1972. 1975. xiii, 193, [14]p. 3 maps. [PRC
  .1-6   Demographic characteristics of the population. Part I. Age,
       sex and marital status. Data from Stage A of the census. 1975.
       xxvii, 239, [66]p. [PRC
  .1-7   Housing, labour force and education. Provisional data from
       Stage B of the census. 1975. vii, 294, [30]p. map. [PRC
  .1-8   The division of the State of Israel into natural regions for
       statistical purposes. 1976. xxix, 158p. [PRC
  .1-9   Households in Israel. Demographic composition. Data from Stage
       A of the census. 1976. xxii, 275, [18]p. [PRC
  .1-9a   Households in Israel. Demographic composition. Data from Stage
       A of the census. (Additional data to Publication, no. 9). 1976. xi,
       87, [8]p. [PRC
  .1-10   Demographic characteristics of the population. Part II. Coun-
       try of birth, period of immigration and religion. Data from Stage A
       of the census. 1976. xiv, 337, [14]p. [PRC
  .1-11   Demographic characteristics of the population. Part III. Com-
       position of population in localities and statistical areas. Data
       from Stage A of the census. 1976. xxviii, 356, [28]p. [PRC

ITALY

Italian Republic   Capital: Rome
Statistical Agency: Central Statistical Institute
                      [Istituto Centrale di Statistica]
                      Via Cesare Balbo, 16
                      Roma,
Publications Distributor: Direzione Generale degli Affari Generali e del
                            Personale (of the above).

Italy. Istituto Centrale di
        Statistica.
1951.1   IX censimento generale della   Ninth general population census,
        popolazione, 4 Novembre 1951.   November 4, 1951. De jure popu-
        Popolazione legale dei comuni.   lation of communities.
        Roma, Istituto Poligrafico dello   [UN, PRC, RPI
        Stato, 1955.   233p.

Italy. Istituto Centrale di
        Statistica.
        IX censimento generale della   Ninth general population census,
        popolazione, 4 Novembre 1951.   November 4, 1951.
        Roma, [publisher varies], 1954-
        1958.   Vol. I-VIII in 101v.
           I.   Dati sommari per co-   Summary data for communities.
        mune. Provincia di... Roma,   Province of...
        Soc. ABETE, 1954-1956.   92 fasc.
1951.2-1-1 through 1951.2-1-92. 1. Alessandria. 1955. 75p./2. Asti. 1956.
    53p./3. Cuneo. 1956. 101p./4. Novara. 1956. 73p./5. Torino. 1955.
    119p./6. Vercelli. 1956. 73p./7. Valle d'Aosta. 1954. 49p./8. Ber-
    gamo. 1955. 93p./9. Brescia. 1956. 79p./10. Como. 1956. 91p./
    11. Cremona. 1954. 53p./12. Mantova. 1955. 39p./13. Milano. 1955.
    97p./14. Pavia. 1956. 77p./15. Sondrio. 1956. 49p./16. Varese.
    1955. 51p./17. Bolzano. 1955. 53p./18. Trento. 1955. 75p./19.
    Belluno. 1955. 37p./20. Padova. 1956. 55p./21. Rovigo. 1955. 35p./
    22. Treviso. 1954. 53p./23. Venizia. 1956. 35p./24. Verona. 1955.
    59p./
       25. Vicenza. 1956. 59p./26. Gorizia. 1955. 21p./27. Udine. 1955.
    83p./28. Territorio di Trieste. 1956. 19p./29. Genova. 1954. 37p./
    30. Imperia. 1955. 33p./31. La Spezia. 1955. 31p./32. Savona. 1956.
    35p./33. Bologna. 1955. 41p./34. Ferrara. 1954. 27p./35. Forli.
    1956. 35p./36. Modena. 1954. 39p./37. Parma. 1955. 41p./38. Pia-
    cenza. 1954. 39p./39. Ravenna. 1954. 23p./40. Reggio Nell'Emilia.
    1954. 37p./41. Arezzo. 1954. 37p./42. Firenze. 1956. 41p./43.
    Grosseto. 1954. 25p./44. Livorno. 1955. 23p./45. Lucca. 1955.
    39p./46. Massa-Carrara. 1954. 25p./47. Pisa. 1954. 33p./48. Pis-
    toia. 1954. 25p./49. Siena. 1955. 33p./
       50. Perugia. 1954. 43p./51. Terni. 1955. 31p./52. Ancona. 1954.
    33p./53. Ascoli Piceno. 1955. 35p./54. Macerata. 1955. 35p./55.
    Pesaro e Urbino. 1954. 37p./56. Frosinone. 1955. 51p./57. Latina.
    1955. 29p./58. Rieti. 1955. 25p./59. Roma. 1955. 51p./60. Viterbo.
    1955. 31p./61. Campobasso. 1956. 40p./62. Chieti. 1956. 49p./63.
    L'Aquila. 1955. 51p./64. Pescara. 1954. 31p./65. Teramo. 1955.

35p./66. Avellino. 1956. 49p./67. Benevento. 1955. 47p./68. Caserta. 1956. 49p./69. Napoli. 1955. 49p./70. Salerno. 1956. 69p./71. Bari. 1954. 28p./72. Brindisi. 1955. 21p./73. Foggia. 1955. 31p./74. Lecce. 1955. 47p./75. Taranto. 1955. 21p./76. Matera. 1954. 29p./ 77. Potenza. 1954. 47p./78. Catanzaro. 1955. 67p./79. Cosenza. 1956. 69p./80 Reggio de Calabria. 1956. 57p./81. Agrigento. 1955. 29p./82. Caltanissetta. 1955. 21p./83. Catania. 1955. 31p./84. Enna. 1954. 21p./85. Messina. 1955. 53p./86. Palermo. 1955. 47p./87. Ragusa. 1955. 19p./88. Siracusa. 1954. 21p./89. Trapani. 1955. 23p./ 90. Cagliari. 1955. 67p./91. Nuoro. 1955. 47p./92. Sassari. 1955. 47p. [PRC, BC, UN, RPI

1951.2-1-A   Appendice A. Dati rias-   Appendix A. Summary of provincial
suntivi provinciali. 1956. 41p.   data.
                                                [PRC, BC, LC, RPI
.2-1-B   Appendice B. Circoscri-   Appendix B. Ecclesiastical dis-
zioni ecclesiastiche. 1956.   tricts.
426p.   [PRC, BC, LC, RPI
.2-2   II. Famiglie e convivenze.   Families and households.
Tip. Fausto Failli, 1957. 524p.   [PRC, BC, TXU, RPI
.2-3   III. Sesso, età, stato   Sex, age, marital status and
civile, luogo di nascita. Soc.   place of birth.
ABETE, 1956. 440p.   [PRC, BC, TXU, RPI
.2-4   IV. Professioni. Tip.   Occupations.
Fausto Failli, 1957. 850p.   [PRC, BC, TXU, RPI
.2-5   V. Istruzione. Azienda   Education.
Beneventana Rip., 1957. 224p.   [PRC, BC, TXU, RPI
.2-6   VI. Abitazioni. Tip.   Housing.
Fausto Failli, 1957. 709p.   [PRC, BC, TXU, RPI
.2-7   VII. Dati generali rias-   General summary data.
suntivi. Azienda Beneventana   [PRC, BC, TXU, RPI
Tip., 1958. 454p.
.2-8   VIII. Atti del censimento.   Manual of the census.
Azienda Beneventana Tip., 1958.   [TXU, BC, RPI
624p.

Italy. Istituto Centrale di
    Statistica.
    IX censimento generale della   Ninth general population census.
popolazioni. III censimento   Third general census of industry
generale dell'industria e del   and commerce, November 4-5, 1951.
commercio, 4-5 Novembre 1951.   Demographic and economic charac-
Caratteristiche demografiche   teristics of large communities.
ed economiche dei grandi comuni.
Roma, 1959. Vol. I-III.
.3-1   I. Dati riassuntivi e dati   Summary data and data for commun-
dei comuni con oltre 100.000 abi-   ities of 100,000 inhabitants and
tanti. 441p.   over.
                                                [UN, RPI
.3-2   II. Comuni da 60.000 fino   Communities of 60,000 to 100,000
a 100.000 abitanti. 445p.   inhabitants.
                                                [UN, RPI

.3-3   III.   Comuni fino a 60.000   Communities of less than 60,000
abitanti. 448p.   inhabitants.
                                           [UN, RPI

Italy.   Istituto Centrale di
     Statistica.
.4   Comuni e loro popolazione al   Communities and their population
censimento del 1861 al 1951.   according to the censuses from
Roma, Tip. ABETE, 1960. 342,   1861 to 1951.
[4]p.   [PRC, TXU, BC, RPI

Italy.   Comune di Roma.   Ufficio
     di Statistica e Censimento.
.5   Roma.   Popolazione e terri-   Rome. Population and territory
torio dal 1860 al 1960, con la   from 1860 to 1960, with the ter-
distribuzione territoriale dei   ritorial distribution of the
risultati dei censimenti.   results of the censuses.
Roma, Tip. ABETE, 1960. viii,   [PRC, UN, Berkeley, RPI
432p.

Italy.   Istituto Centrale di
     Statistica.
1961.0-1   Disposizione e istruzioni   Arrangements and instructions for
per il 10° censimento della popo-   the Tenth population census and
lazione e il 4° censimento dell'   the Fourth census of industry and
industria e del commercio, 15-16   commerce, October 15-16, 1961.
ottobre 1961.   [Roma, Tip.   [PRC, TXU, BC, RPI
ABETE], 1961. vii, 237p.

Italy.   Istituto Centrale di
     Statistica.
.1   10° censimento generale della   Tenth general population census,
popolazione, 15 ottobre 1961.   October 15, 1961. Legal popula-
Popolazione legale dei comuni.   tion of communities.
Roma, Istituto Poligrafico dello   [PRC, UN, RPI
Stato, 1963. 241p.

Italy.   Istituto Centrale di
     Statistica.
.2   Popolazione e circoscrizioni   Population and administrative
amministrative dei comuni.   areas of communities.
Roma, Tip. Fausto Failli, 1963.   [PRC, UN, RPI
vii, 237p.

Italy.   Istituto Centrale di
     Statistica.
.3   Popolazione residente e pre-   De jure and de facto populations
sente dei comuni al censimenti   of communities according to the
dal 1861 al 1961. Circoscri-   censuses from 1861 to 1961. Ter-
zioni territoriali al 15 otto-   ritorial areas as of October 15,
bre 1961.   Roma, Tip. Fausto   1961.
Failli, 1967. ix, 419p.   [PRC

Italy. Istituto Centrale di
    Statistica.
    10° censimento generale della   Tenth general population census,
popolazione, 15 ottobre 1961.   October 15, 1961.
Roma, [publisher varies], 1963-
1970. Vol. I-X in 102v.
.4-1   I. Dati riassuntivi   Summary data by communities and
comunali e provinciali sulla   provinces on population and hous-
popolazione e sulle abitazioni.   ing.
Tip. ABETE, 1963. 156p.   [PRC, TXU, BC, RPI, RIR
.4-2   II. Dati riassuntivi   Summary data for communities and
comunali e provinciali sul al-   provinces on some principal struc-
cune principali caratteristiche   tural characteristics of the popu-
strutturali della popolazione;   lation; sex, age, schooling, eco-
sesso, età, istruzione, attivi-   nomic activity.
tà economica. Tip. ABETE, 1963.   [PRC, TXU, UN, RPI, RIR
533p.
    III. Dati sommari per   Summary data for communities.
comune. Provincia di ... Soc.   Province of ...
ABETE, 1964-1966. 93 fasc.
1961.4-3-1 through 1961.4-3-92. 1. Torino. 1966. 171p./2. Vercelli. 1965.
103p./3. Novara. 1966. 103p./4. Cuneo. 1966. 143p./5. Asti. 1964.
73p./6. Alessandria. 1966. 105p./7. Valle d'Aosta. 1964. 45p./8.
Imperia. 1964. 43p./9. Savona. 1964. 45p./10. Genova. 1966. 49p./
11. La Spezia. 1964. 43p./12. Varese. 1966. 71p./13. Como. 1966.
131p./14. Sondrio. 1966. 69p./15. Milano. 1966. 137p./16. Bergamo.
1966. 133p./17. Brescia. 1966. 133p./18. Pavia. 1966. 109p./19.
Cremona. 1966. 74p./20. Mantova. 1966. 51p./21. Bolzano. 1964.
229p./22. Trento. 1964. 133p./23. Verona. 1965. 81p./24. Vicenza.
1965. 81p./
    25. Belluno. 1964. 51p./26. Treviso. 1965. 75p./27. Venezia.
1965. 45p./28. Padova. 1965. 75p./29. Rovigo. 1964. 45p./30. Udine.
1965. 119p./31. Gorizia. 1964. 29p./32. Trieste. 1965. 31p./33.
Piacenza. 1964. 53p./34. Parma. 1964. 57p./35. Reggio Nell'Emilia.
1964. 49p./36. Modena. 1964. 53p./37. Bologna. 1965. 53p./38. Ferrara. 1964. 35p./39. Ravenna. 1965. 29p./40. Forli. 1965. 45p./
41. Pesaro e Urbino. 1964. 49p./42. Ancona. 1964. 47p./43. Macerata. 1964. 47p./44. Ascoli Piceno. 1965. 45p./45. Massa-Carrara.
1964. 33p./46. Lucca. 1964. 53p./47. Pistoia. 1964. 31p./48. Firenze. 1965. 53p./49. Livorno. 1964. 27p./
    50. Pisa. 1964. 45p./51. Arezzo. 1965. 51p./52. Siena. 1964.
45p./53. Grosseto. 1964. 33p./54. Perugia. 1965. 59p./55. Terni.
1965. 43p./56. Viterbo. 1965. 41p./57. Rieti. 1965. 49p./58.
Roma. 1966. 71p./59. Latina. 1965. 39p./60. Frosinone. 1965.
71p./61. Caserta. 1965. 69p./62. Benevento. 1966. 67p./63. Napoli.
1966. 69p./64. Avellino. 1966. 69p./65. Salerno. 1965. 101p./66.
L'Aquila. 1965. 73p./67. Teramo. 1966. 45p./68. Pescara. 1965.
41p./69. Chieti. 1965. 69p./70. Campobasso. 1965. 69p./71. Foggia.
1965. 41p./72. Bari. 1966. 39p./73. Taranto. 1966. 27p./74. Brindisi. 1965. 25p./
    75. Lecce. 1966. 65p./76. Potenza. 1965. 67p./77. Matera. 1964.

37p./78. Cosenza. 1966. 99p./79. Catanzaro. 1966. 97p./80. Reggio di Calabria. 1965. 71p./81. Trapani. 1966. 31p./82. Palermo. 1966. 67p./83. Messina. 1966. 73p./84. Agrigento. 1965. 39p./85. Caltanissetta. 1965. 27p./86. Enna. 1965. 25p./87. Catania. 1965. 41p./88. Ragusa. 1965. 25p./89. Siricusa. 1965. 27p./90. Sassari. 1965. 65p./91. Nuoro. 1966. 65p./92. Caligiari. 1966. 95p. [PRC, BC, RPI, RIR

.4-3-93   Appendice. Dati riassuntivi nazionali. Soc. ABETE, 1966. 95p.

Summary of national data. [PRC, BC, TXU, RPI, RIR

.4-4   IV. Famiglie e convivenze. Soc. ABETE, 1967. 677p.

Families and households. [PRC, BC, TXU, RPI, RIR

.4-5   V. Sesso, età, stato civile, luogo di nascita. Tip. STAGRAME, 1968. 735p.

Sex, age, marital status, birthplace. [PRC, BC, TXU, RPI, RIR

.4-6   VI. Professioni. Soc. ABETE, 1967. 1204p.

Occupations. [PRC, BC, TXU, RPI, RIR

.4-7   VII. Istruzione. Soc. ABETE, 1968. 722p.

Education. [PRC, BC, RPI,

.4-8   VIII. Abitazioni. Soc. ABETE, 1967. 907p.

Housing. [PRC, TXU, BC, RPI, RIR

.4-9   IX. Dati generali riassuntivi. Soc. ABETE, 1969. 584p.

General summary data. [PRC, UN, RPI, RIR

.4-10   X. Atti del censimento. Tip. Sagral, 1970. 333p.

Manual of the census. [PRC, BC, UN, RPI, RIR

Italy. Istituto Centrale di Statistica.

1971.1   11° censimento generale della popolazione, 24 ottobre 1971. Popolazione legale dei comuni. Roma, 1973. 241p.

Eleventh general population census, October 24, 1971. Legal population of communities. [PRC

Italy. Istituto Centrale di Statistica.
11° censimento generale della popolazione, 24 ottobre 1971. Roma, [publisher varies], 1972- . Vol. I-XI in   v.

Eleventh general population census, October 24, 1971.

.2-1   I. Primi risultati provinciali e comunali sulla popolazione e sulle abitazioni. Dati provisori. Roma, Tip. F. Failli, 1972. vii, 256p. specimen forms.

First provincial and community results on population and on housing. Provisional data. [PRC

II. Dati per comune sulle caratteristiche strutturali della popolazione e delle abitazioni. Provincia di... Roma, Soc. ABETE, 1972-1974. 94 fasc. e 2v.

Data for communities on the structural characteristics of the population and of housing. Province of... [Plus 2 volumes of national totals.]

1971.2-2-1 through 1971.2-2-94. 1. Torino. 1974. x, 193p./2. Vercelli.
1973. x, 145p./3. Novara. 1973. x, 145p./4. Cuneo. 1974. x, 193p./
5. Asti. 1972. x, 145p./6. Alessandria. 1973. x, 145p./7. Valle d'
Aosta. 1972. x, 49p./8. Varese. 1974. x, 97p./9. Como. 1974. x,
193p./10. Sondrio. 1972. x, 49p./11. Milano. 1974. x, 193p./12.
Bergamo. 1974. x, 193p./13. Brescia. 1974. x, 145p./14. Pavia.
1974. x, 145p./15. Cremona. 1973. x, 97p./16. Mantova. 1973. x,
49p./17. Bolzano. 1973. x, 457p./18. Trento. 1973. x, 145p./19.
Verona. 1973. x, 97p./20. Vicenza. 1973. x, 97p./21. Belluno.
1973. x, 49p./22. Treviso. 1974. x, 97p./23. Venezia. 1973. x,
49p./24. Padova. 1973. x, 97p./
        25. Rovigo. 1973. x, 49p./26. Pordenone. 1973. x, 49p./27. Udine.
1973. x, 97p./28. Gorizia. 1972. x, 49p./29. Trieste. 1973. x,
56p./30. Imperia. 1973. x, 49p./31. Savona. 1973. x, 49p./32. Genova. 1973. x, 49p./33. La Spezia. 1973. x, 49p./34. Piacenza.
1973. x, 49p./35. Parma. 1973. x, 49p./36. Reggio Nell'Emilia.
1973. x, 49p./37. Modena. 1974. x, 49p./38. Bologna. 1973. x,
49p./39. Ferrara. 1973. x, 29p./40. Ravenna. 1973. x, 23p./41.
Forli. 1973. x, 49p./42. Massa-Carrara. 1973. x, 23p./43. Lucca.
1974. x, 49p./44. Pistoia. 1973. x, 29p./45. Firenze. 1973. x,
49p./46. Livorno. 1973. x, 27p./47. Pisa. 1973. x, 49p./48. Arezzo.
1973. x, 49p./49. Siena. 1973. x, 49p./
        50. Grosseto. 1973. x, 27p./51. Perugia. 1973. x, 49p./52. Ter-
ni. 1973. x, 49p./53. Pesaro e Urbino. 1972. x, 49p./54. Ancona.
1973. x, 49p./55. Macerata. 1972. x, 49p./56. Ascoli Piceno. 1972.
x, 49p./57. Viterbo. 1973. x, 49p./58. Rieti. 1974. x, 49p./59.
Roma. 1974. x, 97p./60. Latina. 1973. x, 49p./61. Frosinone. 1973.
x, 97p./62. L'Aquila. 1973. x, 97p./63. Teramo. 1973. x, 49p./64.
Pescara. 1973. x, 49p./65. Chieti. 1973. x, 97p./66. Isernia.
1973. x, 49p./67. Campobasso. 1973. x, 97p./68. Caserta. 1974. x,
97p./69. Benevento. 1974. x, 97p./70. Napoli. 1974. x, 97p./71.
Avelino. 1974. x, 97p./72. Salerno. 1974. x, 99p./73. Foggia.
1974. x, 49p./74. Bari. 1973. x, 49p./
        75. Taranto. 1973. x, 27p./76. Brindisi. 1973. x, 27p./77. Lecce.
1974. x, 97p./78. Potenza. 1973. x, 97p./79. Matera. 1973. x, 49p./
80. Cosenza. 1974. x, 99p./81. Catanzaro. 1973. x, 99p./82. Reggio
di Calabria. 1974. x, 97p./83. Trapani. 1974. x, 27p./84. Palermo.
1974. x, 97p./85. Messina. 1974. x, 97p./86. Agrigento. 1973. x,
49p./87. Caltanissetta. 1973. x, 27p./88. Enna. 1973. x, 27p./89.
Catania. 1974. x, 49p./90. Ragusa. 1973. x, 23p./91. Siracusa.
1973. x, 23p./92. Sassari. 1974. x, 97p./93. Nuoro. 1973. x, 97p./
94. Cagliari. 1974. x, 145p. [PRC

.2-2-A   Italia. Dati riassun-   Italy. Summary data. Part 1.
tivi. Parte primera. 1974. x,   [PRC
97p.

.2-2-B   Italia. Dati riassun-   Italy. Summary data. Part 2.
tivi. Parte seconda. 1974. x,   [PRC
227p.

        III. Popolazione delle   Population of the geographic re-
frazioni geografiche e delle   gions and of the inhabited places
località abitate dei comuni.   of the communities. [Plus one
Roma, Soc. ABETE, 1973-1975.   Appendix: Summary volume.]
20 fasc. e lv.

1971.2-3-1 through 1971.2-3-20. 1. Piemonte. 1975. viii, 162p./2. Valle
   d'Aosta. 1973. vii, 12p./3. Lombardia. 1975. vii, 197p./4. Tren-
   tino-Alto Adige. 1974. vii, 46p./5. Veneto. 1974. vii, 113p./6.
   Friuli-Venezia Giulia. 1973. vii, 43p./7. Liguria. 1974. vii, 46p./
   8. Emilia-Romagna. 1973. vii, 106p./9. Toscana. 1974. vii, 102p./
   10. Umbria. 1973. vii, 31p./11. Marche. 1973. vii, 46p./12. Lazio.
   1975. vii, 58p./13. Abruzzi. 1974. vii, 50p./14. Molise. 1973.
   vii, 16p./15. Campania. 1975. vii, 65p./16. Puglia. 1974. vii,31p./
   17. Basilicata. 1974. vii, 14p./18. Calabria. 1975. vii, 52p./19.
   Sicilia. 1975. vii, 64p./20. Sardegna. 1975. vii, 36p. [PRC

.2-3-A   Appendice: tavoli rias-   Appendix: summary tables.
   suntivi.   [
.2-4   IV. Famiglie e convivenze.   Families and households.
   Roma, Grafiche Chicca, 1976. ix,   [PRC
   695p.
.2-5   V. Sesso, età, stato ci-   Sex, age, marital status.
   vile. Roma, Soc. ABETE, 1974.   [PRC
   vi, 1245p.
          VI. Professione e attivi-   Occupations and economic activity.
   tà economiche. Roma, Tipo-lito
   Sagraf, 1975-1977. Tomo 1 e 2.
.2-6-1   Attività economiche.   Economic activity.
   1975. viii, 658p.   [PRC
.2-6-2   Professione. 1977.   Occupations.
   xii, 536p.   [PRC
.2-7   VII. Istruzione. Roma,   Education.
   Soc. ABETE, 1975. ix, 502p.   [PRC
          VIII. Abitazioni. Roma,   Housing.
   Tipo-lito Sagraf, 1975. Tomo 1
   e 2.
.2-8-1   Caratteristiche strut-   Structural characteristics of oc-
   turali delle abitazioni occupa-   cupied and unoccupied dwellings.
   te e non occupate. ix, 382p.   [PRC
.2-8-2   Abitazione occupate   Occupied dwellings according to
   secondo la condizione del capo   the condition of the family head.
   famiglia. ix, 770p.   [PRC
          IX. Risultati degli spo-   Results of the sample selections.
   gli campionari. Roma, 1977.
   Tomo 1 e 2.
.2-9-1   Luogo di nascita -   Place of birth - place of resi-
   luogo di residencia al 1961 e   dence in 1961 and 1966.
   al 1966. ix, 375p.   [PRC
.2-9-2   Altri caratteri. xiii,   Other characteristics.
   397p.   [PRC
.2-10   X. Dati generali riassun-   General summary data.
   tivi. Roma, Panetto & Petrel-   [PRC
   li, 1976. xiii, 393p.
.2-11   XI. Atti del censimento.   Manual of the census.
   Roma, 1977. 357p. specimen   [PRC
   forms.

Italy.   Istituto Centrale di
            Statistica.
.3   Popolazioni residente e pre-   De jure and de facto populations
sente dei comuni, censimenti   of communes, censuses from 1961
dal 1961 al 1971.   Roma, 1977.   to 1971.
2v.
1971.3-1   viii, 403p.   [BC
  .3-2   vi, 540p.   [BC

IVORY COAST

Republic of the Ivory Coast.   Capital: Abidjan.
Statistical Agency: Statistical Office
                    [Direction de la Statistique]
                    Ministère de l'economie et des Finances
                    B.P.V. 55
                    Abidjan,
Publications Distributor: same.

          France. INSEE [and] Service Colonial des Statistiques.
1946   Résultats du recensement de 1946...
            [See French Overseas Territories, Nos. 1946.1-1, 2 & 3
                                                    1946.2]

          France. INSEE.
1951   Le recensement de la population...
            [See French Overseas Territories, No. 1951.1]

          French West Africa. Service de
              la Statistique Générale.
1951.2   Population de l'A.O.F. en 1950-   Population of French West Africa
          1951 par canton et groupe éthni-   in 1950-1951 by canton and ethnic
          que, chiffres provisoires. Da-   group, provisional figures.
          kar, 1952. [135]p.   [UN, PRC, RPI

          French West Africa. Service de
              la Statistique Générale.
  .3   Recensement de la population   Census of the non-native popula-
          non autochtone de l'Afrique Occi-   tion of French West Africa in
          dentale Français en juin 1951.   June 1951.
          Dakar, 1955. [2], x, 69p.   [PRC, RPI

          Ivory Coast. Service de la
              Statistique.
          Recensement de la commune   Census of the commune of Abidjan.
          d'Abidjan. Abidjan, 1956. 2v.
1955.1-1   Organisation, instruction,   Organization, instruction, docu-
          documents utilisés, résultats   ments used, provisional global
          provisoires globaux. 67p.   results.
                                                [NWU, RPI
  .1-2   Résultats par quartiers et   Results by sectors and by ethnic
          par groupes éthniques. Réparti-   groups. Distribution of family
          tion des chefs des familles par   heads by socio-occupational cate-
          catégorie socio-professionnele.   gory.
          57p.   [NWU, RPI

          Ivory Coast. Service de la
              Statistique.
  .2   Recensement d'Abidjan, 1955.   Census of Abidjan, 1955. Final
          Résultats définitifs. [Abid-   results.
          jan, 1960]. 105p.   [NWU, RPI

Ivory Coast. Direction de la
      Statistique et des Études
      Économiques et Démogra-
      phiques.

1957.1   Recensement des centres ur-   Census of the urban centers of
bains d'Abengourou, Agboville,   Abengourou, Agboville, Dimbokro
Dimbokro et Man, 1956-1957.   and Man, 1956-1957. Final re-
Résultats définitifs. Paris,   sults.
INSEE, 1960. 113p.   [NWU, RPI

Ivory Coast. Service de la
      Statistique et de la
      Mécanographie.

1958.1   Étude démographique du 1er Demographic study of the first
secteur agricole de la Côte d'   agriculture sector of the Ivory
Ivoire, 1957-1958. Paris,   Coast, 1957-1958.
1958. [4], 36, 88p.   [NWU, RPI

Ivory Coast. Direction de la
      Statistique et des Études
      Économiques et Démogra-
      phiques.

.2   Recensement démographique de   Demographic census of Boake,
Bouaké, juillet-août 1958. Ré-   July-August 1958. Final results.
sultats définitifs. Paris,   [NWU, RPI
INSEE, 1961. [61]p.

Ivory Coast. Direction de la
      Statistique et des Études
      Économiques et Démogra-
      phiques.

.3   Enquête démographique, 1957-   Demographic survey, 1957-1958.
1958. Résultats définitifs.   Final results.
      [

Ivory Coast. Ministère des
      Finances, des Affaires
      Économiques et du Plan.
      Villes de Côte d'Ivoire: Cities of the Ivory Coast: Man,
Man, Daloa, Gagnoa (1961).   Daloa, Gagnoa (1961).
Paris, SEDES, 1972. 2v.

1961.1-1   Enquête socio-économique.   Socio-economic survey.
1962. [61]p. charts, maps.   [NWU
.1-2   Annexes. 1962?. 176p.   Appendices.
      [NWU

Ivory Coast. Ministère des
      Finances, des Affaires
      Économiques et du Plan.

.2   Enquête socio-économique   Socio-economic survey of the city

sur la ville de Bouaké [1961].
Paris, SEDES, [1963?]. [2 appendices unpaged, tables only.]

of Bouake [1961].
[NWU

Ivory Coast. Direction de la
        Statistique et des Études
        Économiques et Démogra-
        phiques.
1963.1   Repertoire des localités
de la Côte d'Ivoire et population; classement par circonscrip-
tion administrative [1962-1963].
[Abidjan], 1965. 269p.

Directory of Ivory Coast places
and population, classed by administrative boundaries [1962-1963].
[NWU

Ivory Coast. Ministère des
        Finances, des Affaires
        Économiques et du Plan.
        Région du Sud-Est, Étude
socio-économique [1963-64].
Paris, SEDES, 1967. 8v. in 3.

South-east region, socio-economic
study [1963-64].

1964.1-1   La demographie. 163p.

Demography.
[NWU

.1-2   La sociologie. 144p.

Sociology.
[NWU

.1-3   L'agriculture I. 286p.

Agriculture, I.
[NWU

.1-4   L'agriculture II. 157p.

Agriculture, II.
[NWU

.1-5   Les budgets familiaux.
305p. 7 tables.

Family budgets.
[NWU

.1-6   Le commerce et les trans-
ports. 222p.

Business and transportation.
[NWU

.1-7   Les comptes économiques.
78p.

Economic reports.
[NWU

.1-8   Rapport de synthèse.
70p.

Synthesis report.
[NWU

[Volumes 1-2 are bound together; as are 3 and 4, and 5 through 8.]

Ivory Coast. Ministère des
        Finances, des Affaires
        Économiques et du Plan.
1965.1   Côte d'Ivoire, 1965: population, études regionales 1962-
1965. Synthèse.   Abidjan,
1967. 208p.

Ivory Coast, 1965: population,
regional studies 1962-1965. Synthesis.
[NWU

Ivory Coast. Ministère des
        Finances, des Affaires
        Économiques et du Plan.
        Étude socio-économique de la
zone urbaine d'Abidjan [1962-65].

Socio-economic study of the urban
zone of Abidjan [1962-65].

Paris, 1962-1965.   Vol. 1-9.
1965.2-1
                                                    [
.2-2   Méthodologie des enquêtes.   Survey methodology.
  1964. 64p.   [NWU
         État de la population   Condition of the population of
d'Abidjan en 1963. Tome 1-2.   Abidjan in 1963.
.2-3-1   Tableaux statistiques.   Statistical tables.
  1964. 127p.   [NWU
.2-3-2   Analyse des résultats.   Analysis of results.
  1964. 69p.   [NWU
.2-4   L'habitat en 1963. 1965.   Housing in 1963.
  95p. charts.   [NWU
.2-5
                                         [
.2-6   Structures et transforma-   Structure and change of domestic
tions des groupements domestiques   groups of Abidjan.
d'Abidjan. 1965. 92p.   [NWU
.2-7   La concession urbaine: The urban concession: ecology
ecologie et rapports sociaux pro-   and the relation between social
blemes fonciers et immobiliers.   and real property problems.
1965. 151p.   [NWU
.2-8
                                         [
.2-8   Les immigrants temporaires   Temporary migrants in Abidjan.
a Abidjan. 1965. 33p.   [NWU

Ivory Coast. Ministère des
        Finances, des Affaires
        Économiques et du Plan.
1966.1   Recensement de la ville de   Census of the city of Dabou, 1966.
Dabou, 1966. Données indivi-   Individual data.
duelles.   Abidjan, 1966.   [

Ivory Coast. Bureau du Recense-
        ment Général de la Popula-
        tion.
1975.0-1 Répertoire des localités de   Directory of Ivory Coast places
la Côte d'Ivoire et population   and population 1975: provision-
1975: tome provisoire.   Abid-   al volume.
jan, 1976. vii, 371p.   [PRC

Ivory Coast. Bureau du Recense-
        ment Général de la Popula-
        tion.
     Recensement général de la   General census of population,
population, 1975. Résultats   1975. Final results. Depart-
définitifs. Departement de...   ment of...
Abidjan, 1977. 26v.
1975.1-1 through 1975.1-26. 1. Abengourou. [153]p./2.

Ivory Coast. Bureau du Recense-
    ment Général de la Popula-
    tion.

1975.2   Recensement général de la
population, 1975. Résultats au
1/10ᵉ.   Abidjan, 1977. 80p.

General census of population,
1975. Results of the one-in-ten
[sample]
[PRC, PSC

Ivory Coast. Bureau du Recense-
    ment Général de la Popula-
    tion.

.3   Recensement général de la population, avril 1975: résultats
exploitation exhaustive disponi-
bles pour l'ensemble du pays.
Abidjan, 1978. 41p. (Document
No. 0-1).

General census of population,
April 1975: results of the complete enumeration available for
the whole country.
[UN

JAMAICA

                                        Capital: Kingston
Statistical Agency: Department of Statistics.
                     9 Swallowfield Road
                     Kingston 5,
Publications Distributor: same

     The 1943 census is included to complete the West Indian census taken
     in 1946.

     Jamaica. Central Bureau of Statistics.
1943.1   Eighth census of Jamaica and its dependencies, 1943: population,
     housing and agriculture. Kingston, Government Printer, 1945.
     "twenty-eight," cii, 571p. 4 folding maps. [TXU, NYPL, PRC, RPI

     Jamaica. Department of Statistics. Jamaica Tabulation Centre.
          West Indies population census. Census of Jamaica, 7th April, 1960.
     Kingston, 1963-1964. Vol. I-II in 17v.
          I. Administrative report... Parts A-D.
1960.2-1-A   Administrative report and enumeration districts definitions.
     1963. ii, 556p. [PRC, JB-F, RPI
     .2-1-B   Enumeration districts definitions (Cont'd). 1963. ii, four,
     pp. 557-1092. maps. [PRC, JB-F, RPI
     .2-1-C   Enumeration district tables. 1963. ii, VIII, pp. 1093-1497.
     [PRC, RPI
     .2-1-D   Enumeration district tables (Cont'd). 1963. ii, XXI, pp.
     1498-1992. [PRC, JB-F, RPI
          II. Tables. Parts A-J.
     .2-2-A-1   [General tables]. 1964. ix, xxvii, [387]p. [PRC, RPI
     .2-2-A-2   [General tables]. 1964. 323, 411p. [PRC, RPI
     .2-2-B   [Housing and households]. 1964. 11, XXVI, 308p. [PRC, RPI
     .2-2-C   [Migration]. 1963. [432]p. [PRC, RPI
     .2-2-D   [Classifiable labour force]. [Not published].
     .2-2-E   [Classifiable labour force]. 1964. ix, 592p. [PRC, JB-F,
     RPI
     .2-2-F-1   [Classifiable labour force]. 1964. ix, 196p. [PRC, RPI
     .2-2-F-2   [Classifiable labour force]. 1964. pp. 197-815. [PRC, RPI
     .2-2-G-1   [Classifiable labour force]. 1964. v, 325p. [PRC, JB-F, RPI
     .2-2-G-2   [Classifiable labour force]. 1964. pp. 326-780. [PRC, JB-F,
     RPI
     .2-2-H   [Labour by industry and occupation]. 1963. [471]p. [PRC,
     JB-F, RPI
     .2-2-I   [Labour by industry]. 1964. viii, [507]p. [PRC, JB-F, RPI
     .2-2-J   [Labour force and income]. 1964. viii, [685]p. [PRC, JB-F,
     RPI

     West Indies. University. Census Research Programme.
1970   1970 population census of the Commonwealth Caribbean.
          [See Commonwealth Caribbean, Nos. 1970.1-1
                                        1970.1-2-?

                                   1970.1-3
                                   1970.1-4-1 & 16
                                   1970.1-5
                                   1970.1-6-1
                                   1970.1-7
                                   1970.1-8-a, b, &. c
                                   1970.1-9-1
                                   1970.1-10-1 & 4

         Jamaica. Department of Statistics. Division of Censuses and Surveys.
              Commonwealth Caribbean population census, 1970. Jamaica. Kings-
           ton, 1974-   . Vol. I-VI in
1970.2-1   I. Administrative report.
              II. Subject matter tables at parish, constituency or special
           area levels. Parts A-
    .2-2-

              III. Subject matter tables at enumeration district levels.
           Parts A-
    .2-3-A   Age. 1977. ii, 315p. [
    .2-3-B
    .2-3-C
    .2-3-D
    .2-3-E-1
    .2-3-E-2   [Dwellings]. 1977. ii, 398p. [OPR
              IV. Enumeration district tables, by parishes. 1974. 14 parts.
1970.2-4-1 through 1970.2-4-14. 1. Kingston. 171p./2. St. Andrew. 393p./
           3. St. Thomas. 114p./4. Portland. 114p./5. St. Mary. 129p./6. St.
           Ann. 163p./7. Trelawny. 97p./8. St. James.   /9. Hanover. 79p./
           10. Westmorland. 145p./11. St. Elizabeth. 155p./12. Manchester.
              /13. Clarendon. 204p./14. St. Catherine. 234p. [PRC
              V. Enumeration district maps and descriptions.
1970.2-5-1 through 1970.2-5-14.

              VI. Demographic atlas of urban areas. 1977. Parts 1-
1970.2-6-1 through 1970.2-6-? 1. Kingston metropolitan area. 52p./2.

           [OPR

Jamaica.   Department of Statistics.   Division of Censuses and Surveys.
     Commonwealth Caribbean population census 1970.   Jamaica.   Kings-
     ton, 1973-1974.   5v.
1970.3-1   Population (provisional totals).   1973.   xix, 44p.   [BC, PRC
   .3-2   Dwellings (provisional totals).   1973.   viii, 80p.   [BC, PRC,
   JB-F
   .3-3   Education.   1974.   73p.   [BC, PRC, JB-F
   .3-4   Internal migrants.   1973.   33, iv p.   [BC, PRC
   .3-5   Economic activity.   1974.   vii, 68p.   [BC, PRC, JB-F

JAPAN

Capital: Tokyo

Statistical Agency: Bureau of Statistics
Office of the Prime Minister
95, Wakamatsucho, Shinjuju
Tokyo 162,

Publications Distributor: Government Publications Service Center
All Japan Official Gazette, Inc. - Agency
No. 2-1, Kasumigaseki 1-chome, Chiyoda-ku
Tokyo 100,

Japan. Bureau of Statistics.
      Special census of 1945: selected tables. [Tokyo, n.d.] 3 parts.
1945.1-1   Population of Japan proper, prefectures, cities and counties,
by sex. [1], 21p. [LC, PRC, RPI
 .1-2   Population by sex for ken, shi, gun, machi, mura. [1], 303p.
[LC, PRC, RPI
 .1-3   Population by sex and age, Japan, prefectures, six major cities.
[2], 53p. [LC, PRC, RPI

Japan. Bureau of Statistics.
1946.1   Population census, 26 April, 1946. In: Official gazette (English
edition), 25-27 July, 12-19 August, 1947. [

Japan. Bureau of Statistics.
 .2   [Summary of results of general census of 1940, population censuses
of 1944, 1945, 1946.] 1949. [2], 153p. [OPR

Japan. Bureau of Statistics.
      Shōwa nijūni-nen rinji koku-   1947 extraordinary population
sei chōsa... Tokyo, 1947. 2v.   census...
1947.0-1   ...ni mochiiru shokugyō   Classification of occupations.
bunruihyō. 6p.   [OPR
 .0-2   ...oyobi jingyōsho tōkei   Classification of industries for
chōsa ni mochiiru sangyō bun-   the 1947 extraordinary population
ruihyō. 14p.   census and the 1947 establishment
    census.
    [OPR

Japan. Bureau of Statistics.
      Shōwa nijūni-nen rinji koku-   Report of the 1947 extraordinary
sei chōsa kekka hōkoku. Tokyo,   population census.
1948-1949. Nos. 1-7.
 .1-1   Jinkō no gaiyō. 1948.   Summary of population.
  8p.   [PRC, OPR, RPI
 .1-2   Zenkoku to dō fu ken gun   Population by to, do, fu, ken,
shi ku chō son betsu jinkō.   gun, shi, ku, machi and mura.
1948. 120p.   [
 .1-3   Rōdōryoku jinkō ni kansu-   Summary of population in the
ru gaiyō. 1948. 39p.   labor force.
    [PRC, OPR, RPI

.1-4   Shusshin chiiki oyobi koku-   Summary of population by native
seki betsu jinkō no gaiyō. 1948.   origin and nationality.
5p.   [

.1-5   Mekura oshi oyobi tsunbo   Number of blind, deaf and mute.
no kazu. 1948. 6p.   [

.1-6   Setaisū no gaiyō. 1948.   Number of households.
4p.   [PRC, RPI

.1-7   Nenrei betsu jinkō. 1949.   Population by age.
301p.   [PRC, UN, RPI

Japan. Bureau of Statistics.
.2   Wagakuni jinkō no gaiyō: Summary report of the population
shōwa nijūni-nen rinji kokusei   of Japan: report of the results
chōsa kekka hōkoku.   Tokyo,   of the 1947 extraordinary popula-
1948. 74p.   tion census.
                                         [

Japan. Bureau of Statistics.
.2a   Summary report, population census of Japan, 1 October 1947. [Eng-
lish edition summarizing results of the Extraordinary population census carried out on October 1, 1947.]   Tokyo, 1949.   [4], 253p. [PRC,
TXU, BC, UN, RPI

United States. Department of State.
.3   Administrative subdivisions of Japan with appendix of 47 prefectur-
al maps.   Washington, D.C., [1946]. xv, 652p. [BC, PRC, RPI

Japan. Bureau of Statistics.
1948.1   Shōwa nijūsan-nen jōjū chōsa   Report on the 1948 resident popu-
hōkoku.   Tokyo, Nihon Hyoron-   lation census.
sha, 1949. 157p.   [

Japan. Bureau of Statistics.
   Report on the resident population census, 1948.   Tokyo, 1949.
Vol. 1-2.
.2-1   Resident population, ration population, self-supplying population, and number of households by prefecture. 93p. [UN, PRC, RPI
.2-2   Resident population and number of households by city, ward,
town and village, ration population or self-supplying population by
city. 226p. [UN, PRC, RPI

Japan. Bureau of Statistics.
   Shōwa nijūgo-nen kokusei   1950 population census...
chōsa:...   Tokyo, 1949-1950.
7 items.
1950.0-1   Chōsaku settei oyobi dō   Manual for designing enumeration
shi ku chō son chōsaku chizu   districts and preparation of maps
sakusei yōryō. 1949. 26p. 6   of enumeration districts for shi,
maps.   ku, machi and mura.
                                         [UN, RPI
.0-2   Chōsain hikkei. 1950.   Manual for enumerator.
88p.   [UN, RPI

.0-3   Shidōin hikkei. 1950   Manual for supervisor.
    98p.   [UN, RPI
.0-4   ...ni mochiiru sangyō bun-   Classification of industries for...
rui naiyō reiji. 1950. 63p.   [PRC, RPI
.0-5   ...yō shokugyō bunrui.   Classification of occupations for..
    1950. [1], 18, 181p.   [PRC, RPI
.0-6   ...shokugyō bunrui sangyō   Index of occupational and indus-
bunrui: shokugyōmei oyobi san-   trial titles for...
gyōmei sakuin. 1950. 42, 371p.   [PRC, RPI
.0-7   ...kankei hōkishū. 1950.   Laws and regulations concerning...
    28p.   [RPI

Japan. Bureau of Statistics.
.0-8   1950 population census training manual for enumerators and supervisors. [English edition]. 1958. [4], 91p. [PRC, RPI

Japan. Bureau of Statistics.
    Population census of 1950.   Tokyo, 1951-1955. Vol. I-VIII in 54v.
.1-1   I. Total population. 1951. [10], iv, 251p. [PRC, UN, RPI
.1-2   II. Results of one percent sample tabulation. 1952. [6], vi,
    84p. [PRC, UN, RPI
          III. Results of ten percent sample tabulation. 1952. Part 1-2.
.1-3-1   Sex, age, marital status, citizenship, education, household,
    housing, fertility. 1952. [8], iv, 206p. [PRC, UN, RPI
.1-3-2   Labor force status, occupation, industry, class of worker,
    hours worked. 1952. [9], vi, 450p. [PRC, UN, RPI
.1-4   IV. All Japan, 1. Sex, age, marital status, citizenship, birth-
    place, education, household, housing. 1954. [2], iv, 272p. [PRC,
    UN, RPI
.1-5   V. All Japan, 2. Labor force status, occupation, industry,
    class of worker. 1954. [2], ii, 591, [1]p. [PRC, UN, RPI
.1-6   VI. De jure population and de facto population. 1954. [2],
    ii, 455, [1]p. [PRC, UN, RPI
          VII. Report by prefecture. 1953-1954. Part 1-46.
1950.1-7-1 through 1950.1-7-46. [Nos. 1-35 were published in 1953; Nos. 36-
    46, in 1954.] 1. Hokkaido. [1], ii, 306p./2. Aomori-ken. [3], ii,
    202p./3. Iwate-ken. [3], ii, 240p./4. Miyagi-ken. [3], ii, 225p./
    5. Akita-ken. [3], ii, 236p./6. Tamagata-ken. [3], ii, 252p./7. Fu-
    kushima-ken. [3], ii, 335p./8. Ibaraki-ken. [3], ii, 323p./9. Tochi-
    gi-ken. [3], ii, 205p./10. Gumma-ken. [3], ii, 235p./11. Saitama-
    ken. [3], ii, 298p./12. Chiba-ken. [3], ii, 304p./13. Tokyo-to.
    [3], ii, 194p./14. Kanagawa-ken. [3], ii, 207p./15. Niigata-ken.
    [3], ii, 351p./16. Toyama-ken. [3], ii, 225p./17. Ishikawa-ken. [3],
    ii, 210p./18. Fukui-ken. [3], ii, 202p./19. Yamanashi-ken. [3], ii,
    215p./20. Nagano-ken. [3], ii, 338p./21. Gifu-ken. [3], ii, 287p./
    22. Shizouka-ken. [3], ii, 295p./23. Aichi-ken. [3], ii, 280p./24.
    Mie-ken. [3], ii, 296p./
        25. Shiga-ken. [3], ii, 206p./26. Kyoto-fu. [3], ii, 233p./27.
    Osaka-fu. [5], ii, 273p./28. Hyogo-ken. [3], ii, 357p./29. Nara-ken.
    [3], ii, 181p./30. Wakayama-ken. [3], ii, 222p./31. Tottori-ken. [3],
    ii, 199p./32. Shimane-ken. [3], ii, 243p./33. Okayama-ken. [3], ii,

341p./34. Hiroshima-ken.   [3], ii, 335p./35. Yamaguchi-ken.   [3], ii,
225p./36. Tokushima-ken.   [3], ii, 177p./37. Kagawa-ken.   [3], ii,
202p./38. Ehime-ken.   [3], ii, 262p./39. Kochi-ken.   [3], ii, 204p./
40. Fukuoka-ken.   [3], ii, 302p./41. Saga-ken.   [3], ii, 171p./42. Nagasaki-ken.   [3], ii, 216p./43. Kumamoto-ken.   [1], ii, 309p./44. Oita-
ken.   [2], iii, 252p./45. Miyazaki-ken.   [2], ii, 167p./46. Kagoshima-
ken.   [1], ii, 193p.   [BC, PRC, UN, RPI

.1-8   VIII.   Final report of the 1950 population census.   1955.   687,
27p.   [PRC, RPI

Japan.   Bureau of Statistics.
.2   Taishō tyū-nen naishi shōwa   On the comparison of the number
nijūgo-nen kokusei chōsa sangyō   of employed persons by industries
betsu shūgyōsha no hikaku.   in censuses from 1920 to 1950.
Tokyo, 1952.   [5], 35p.   [PRC, RPI

Japan.   Bureau of Statistics.
.3   Shōwa nijūgo-nen kokusei   On the comparison of the results
chōsa to rōdōryoku chōsa no rō-   on the labor force status of popu-
dōryoku jōtai ni kansuru sūji   lation between the 1950 population
no hikaku ni tsuiteno ichi kentō.   census and the monthly labor force
Tokyo, 1952.   34p.   survey.
                                           [

Japan.   Bureau of Statistics.
.4   Population census of 1950.   Special report: fertility of Japanese
women.   Tokyo, 1956.   251p.   [UN, PRC, RPI

Japan.   Bureau of Statistics.
    Population census of 1950.   Population maps of Japan.   Tokyo, 1956.
3 maps.
.5-1   Population density by shi, machi and mura.   3 sheets.   [PRC, RPI
.5-2   Population distribution.   1 sheet.   [
.5-3   Population density by isopleth.   1 sheet.   [PRC, RPI

Japan.   Bureau of Statistics.
1954.1   Report on the population census of the Amami Islands, June 1954.
n.p., 1954.   [3], iii, 19, 41, [1]p.   [BC, PRC, RPI

Japan.   Bureau of Statistics.
    Shōwa sanjū-nen kokusei   1955 population census...
shōsa:...   Tokyo, 1955.   8v.
1955.0-1   Kokusei chōsa no tebiki.   Manual for enumerator.
60p.   [BC, PRC
.0-2   Kokusei chōsa shidō yōryō.   Manual for supervisor.
60p.   [
.0-3   ...chōsuku settei yōryō.   Manual for designing enumeration
36p.   map.   districts.
                                          [
.0-4   ...sangyō bunrui.   7, 6,   Classification of industries...
125p.   [

1955.0-5   ...shokugyō bunrui. 7,   Classification of occupations...
       10, 190p.   [
    .0-6   ...sangyō bunrui sangyōmei   Index of industrial titles...
       sakūin. 6, 165p.   [
    .0-7   ...shokugyō bunrui shoku-   Index of occupational titles...
       gyōmei sakūin. 10, 208p.   [
    .0-8   ...shi chō son kankei shiji   Summary of instructions for shi,
       jikō tekiyō. Kokusei chōsa kan-   machi and mura. Laws and regula-
       dei hōreishu. 69p.   tions concerning...
                                           [

       Japan. Bureau of Statistics.
    .0-9   The numbers and names of shi, ku, machi and mura.   Tokyo, n.d.
       [2], 37p. [UN, PRC, RPI

       Japan. Bureau of Statistics.
    .0-10   Population census of Japan. 2nd ed.   Tokyo, 1958.   33p. spe-
       cimen forms. [PRC, RPI

       Japan. Bureau of Statistics.
    .1   Shōwa sanjū-nen kokusei chōsa   1955 population census: final
       zenkoku to dō fu ken gun shi ku   count of population by to, do,
       chō son betsu jinkō.   Kakuteisu.   fu, ken, gun, shi, ku, machi and
       Tokyo, 1956. 40p.   mura.
                                           [

       Japan. Bureau of Statistics.
          1955 population census of Japan.   Tokyo, [1958].
    .2-1   The numbers and names of shi, ku, machi and mura.   [2], 37p.
       [UN, RPI
    .2-2   Revision of area for all Japan, to, do, fu, ken, gun, shi, ku,
       machi and mura. [1], 12p. [UN, PRC, RPI

       Japan. Bureau of Statistics.
    .3   Shōwa sanjū-nen kokusei chōsa   Outline of the enumeration dis-
       chōsaku no gaiyō.   Tokyo, 1958.   tricts for the 1955 population
       79p.   census.
                                           [

       Japan. Bureau of Statistics.
          1955 population census of Japan.   Tokyo, 1956-1959. Vol. I-V in
       54v.
    .4-1   I. Total population. 1956. [8], iv, 370p. [BC, PRC, RPI
             II. One percent sample tabulation. 1957. Parts 1-3.
    .4-2-1   Sex, age marital status, nationality, household and housing.
       [9], viii, 192p. [BC, PRC, RPI
    .4-2-2   Labor force status, industry, class of worker, place of work
       and unemployment. [15], ix, 476p. [BC, PRC, RPI
    .4-2-3   Occupation. [7], vii, 458p. [BC, PRC, RPI
             III. Report for all Japan. 1959. Parts 1-2.
    .4-3-1   Sex, age, marital status, nationality, household and housing.
       [4], iv, 280p. [BC, PRC, RPI

.4-3-2   Labor force status, industry, occupation and class of worker.
[3], iv, 430p. [BC, PRC, RPI
                IV. Place of work. 1959. Parts 1-2.
.4-4-1   Place of work of employed persons. [3], vi, 761p. [BC, PRC,
RPI
.4-4-2   Industry of employed persons by place of work. [4], iv, 592p.
[BC, PRC, RPI
                V. Report by prefecture. 1957-1959. Parts 1-46.
1955.4-5-1 through 1955.4-5-46. 1. Hokkaido. 1959. [7], vi, 451p./2. Aomori-
ken. 1958. [5], vi, 243p./3. Iwate-ken. 1957. [5], vi, 267p./4. Miyagi-ken. 1958. [6], vi, 273p./5. Akita-ken. 1958. [6], vi, 277p./
6. Yamagata-ken. 1957. [6], vi, 235p./7. Fukushima-ken. 1958. [6],
vi, 333p./8. Ibaraki-ken. 1957. [6], vi, 311p./9. Tochigi-ken. 1959.
[6], vi, 241p./10. Gumma-ken. 1957. [5], vi, 277p./11. Saitama-ken.
1957. [6], vi, 313p./12. Chiba-ken. 1957. [6], vi, 295p./13. Tokyo-
to. 1959. [8], vi, 331p./14. Kanagawa-ken. 1957. [6], vi, 297p./
15. Niigata-ken. 1958. [6], vi, 380p./16. Toyama-ken. 1957. [8],
vi, 223p./17. Ishikawa-ken. 1958. [8], vi, 241p./18. Fukui-ken.
1957. [6], vi, 227p./19. Yamanashi-ken. 1957. [6], vi, 259p./20.
Nagano-ken. 1959. [6], vi, 438p./21. Gifu-ken. 1958. [6], vi,
329p./22. Shizuoka-ken. 1957. [6], vi, 347p./23. Aichi-ken. 1958.
[6], vi, 385p./24. Mie-ken. 1957. [6], vi, 287p./
        25. Shiga-ken. 1959. [6], vi, 241p./26. Kyoto-fu. 1959. [6], vi,
307p./27. Osaka-fu. 1958. [6], vi, 369p./28. Hyogo-ken. 1959. [6],
vi, 425p./29. Nara-ken. 1958. [6], vi, 279p./30. Wakayama-ken. 1959.
[6], vi, 289p./31. Tottori-ken. 1957. [6], vi, 189p./32. Shimane-ken.
1958. [7], vi, 273p./33. Okayama-ken. 1957. [6], vi, 305p./34. Hiroshima-ken. 1958. [6], vi, 369p./35. Yamaguchi-ken. 1958. [6], vi,
242p./36. Tokushima-ken. 1958. [6], vi, 241p./37. Kagawa-ken. 1958.
[6], vi, 249p./38. Ehime-ken. 1957. [6], vi, 281p./39. Kochi-ken.
1958. [6], vi, 271p./40. Fukuoka-ken. 1958. [6], vi, 333p./41. Saga-
ken. 1959. [4], vi, 233p./42. Nagasaki-ken. 1958. [6], vi, 283p./
43. Kumamoto-ken. 1958. [6], vi, 337p./44. Oita-ken. 1958. [5], vi,
243p./45. Miyazaki-ken. 1958. [5], vi, 237p./46. Kagoshima-ken.
1958. [7], vii, 293p. [BC, PRC, RPI

Japan. Bureau of Statistics.
.5   Summary of the results of the 1955 population census of Japan.
Tokyo, 1960. [2], ix, 604p. [BC, PRC, RPI

Japan. Bureau of Statistics.
.6   Shōwa sanjū-nen oyobi shōwa   On the comparison of the number
nijūgo-nen kokusei chōsa sangyō   of employed persons by industries
betsu shūggōsha no hikaku.   between the 1955 and 1950 popu-
Tokyo, 1958. 191p.   lation censuses.
                                        [

Japan. Bureau of Statistics.
      1955 population census: population maps of Japan.   Tokyo, 1959.
Parts 1-3 in 4v.
.7-1   Population distribution and density.   3 sheets.   [UN, RPI

.7-2   Population growth by districts. 3 sheets. [UN, RPI
.7-3   Population density by landform division. 3 sheets. [UN, RPI
.7-3a   Population density... Appendix. vi, 25p. [UN, RPI

Japan. Bureau of Statistics.
1960.0-1   Kokusei chōsa no shiori.   A guide to the 1960 population
Tokyo, 1960. 19p.   census.
                                              [PRC, RPI

Japan. Bureau of Statistics.
.0-2   Kokusei chōsa no tebiki.   1960 population census of Japan:
Tokyo, 1960. 76p.   manual for enumerator.
                                              [PRC, RPI

Japan. Bureau of Statistics.
.0-3   Kokusei chōsa shidō yōryō.   1960 population census: manual
Tokyo, 1960. 104p.   for supervisor.
                                              [

Japan. Bureau of Statistics.
   Shōwa sangūgo-nen kokusei   1960 population census.
chōsa...   Tokyo, 1960-1961.
6 items.
.0-4-1   ...chihō shūkei no tabiki.   ... manual for local tabulation.
1960. 44p.   [RPI
.0-4-2   ...chōsaku settei no ta-   ...manual for designing enumera-
biki. 1960. 31p. 4 maps.   tion districts.
                                              [RPI
.0-4-3   ...shokugyō bunrui. 1960.   Classification of occupations...
198p.   [RPI
.0-4-4   ...sangyō bunrui. 1961.   Classification of industries...
6, 184, 8p.   [RPI
.0-4-5   ...ni mochiiru sangyō bun-   Explanation of industrial and
rui shokugyō bunrui no kaisetsu.   occupational classification...
1961. vi, 54, x, 80p.   [RPI
.0-4-6   ...kankei hōkishū. 1960.   Laws and regulations concerning...
73p.   [RPI

Japan. Bureau of Statistics.
.0-5   Laws, cabinet orders, instructions and notifications concerning
the 1960 population census of Japan.   Tokyo, 1961. 46p. [

Japan. Bureau of Statistics.
   Shōwa 35-nen kokusei chōsa   1960 population census series.
shiryō.   Tokyo, 1962-1964. Nos.
1-3.
.1-1   Shōwa 35-nen oyobi shōwa   On the comparison of the number
30-nen kokusei chōsa ni yoru   of employed persons by industries
sangyō shokugyō betsu shugyōsha   and occupations between the 1960
no hikaku. 1962. 121p.   and 1955 population censuses.
                                              [

1960.1-2   Shōwa sanjūgo-nen kokusei   On the comparison of the number
        chōsa to shōwa, sanjūgo-nen jigy-   of employed persons between the
        ōsho tōkei chōsa no shūgyōsha   1960 population census and the
        jūgōsha-sū no hikaku. 1963.   1960 establishment census.
        60p.   [TXU, RPI
    .1-3   Shōwa sanjūgo-nen kokusei   On the comparison of the results
        chōsa to rōdōryoku chōsa no kek-   between the 1960 population cen-
        ka no hikaku. 1964. 66p.   sus and the monthly labor force
                                                 survey.
                                                 [TXU, RPI

        Japan. Bureau of Statistics.
    .2   Shōwa 35-nen kokusei chōsa   Outline of the enumeration dis-
        chōsaku no gaiyō narabini kan-   tricts for the 1960 population
        kei shiryō no riyō. 1963. 160p.   census and on the utilization of
                                                 the related materials.
                                                 [

        Japan. Bureau of Statistics.
            1960 population census:...   Tokyo, 1961.   4 items.
    .3-1   Densely inhabited districts: its population, area and map.
        [3], 40p. 71 maps. [PSC, BC, PRC, RPI
    .3-2   One percent sample tabulation advance report.   [2], viii, 566p.
        [UN, PRC, RPI
    .3-3   Final count of population.   49p. [PSC, RPI
    .3-4   Shōwa sanjūgo-nen kokusei   On the population by age, indus-
        chōsa ni yoru nenrei betsu jinkō   try and so forth, based on the
        sangyō betsu jinkō tō ni tsuite.   1960 population census.
        10p. 6 tables.   [

        Japan. Bureau of Statistics.
            1960 population census of Japan.   Tokyo, 1961-1964. Vol. 1-4 in
        56v.
    .4-1   1. Total population. 1961. [10], iv, 262p. [PRC, TXU, RPI
                2. One percent sample tabulation. 1962. Parts 1-6.
    .4-2-1   Age, marital status, legal nationality, education and fertil-
        ity. xi, 397p. [PRC, TXU, RPI
    .4-2-2   Migration. xi, 209p. [TXU, RPI
    .4-2-3   Labor force status, industry, employment status, hours worked
        and unemployment. xi, 598p. [TXU, RPI
    .4-2-4   Occupation. xi, 458p. [TXU, RPI
    .4-2-5   Household. xi, 517p. [TXU, RPI
    .4-2-6   Housing. xi, 245p. [TXU, RPI
                3. All Japan. 1964. Parts 1-3.
    .4-3-1   Age, marital status, legal nationality, migration, education,
        fertility, labor force status, industry, occupation, household, hous-
        ing. [2], xxi, 475p. 2 folding charts. [TXU, RPI
    .4-3-2   Industry and usual place of residence. [2], xvi, 876p. 2
        folding charts. [TXU, RPI
    .4-3-3   Usual place of residence and place of work or location of
        school. [4], xvi, 876p. 2 folding charts. [TXU, RPI

4. Complete counts by prefecture. 1962-1964. Parts 1-46.
1960.4-4-1 through 1960.4-4-46. [All have maps.] 1. Hokkaido. 1963. [2],
viii, 771p./2. Aomori-ken. 1962. [2], viii, 348p./3. Iwate-ken.
1962. [2], viii, 346p./4. Miyagi-ken. 1963. [2], viii, 374p./5.
Akita-ken. 1962. [2], viii, 362p./6. Yamagata-ken. 1962. [2], viii,
302p./7. Fukushima-ken. 1963. [2], viii, 512p./8. Ibaraki-ken. 1962.
[2], viii, 440p./9. Tochigi-ken. 1962. [2], viii, 322p./10. Gumma-
ken. 1963. [2], viii, 376p./11. Saitama-ken. 1962. [2], viii, 502p./
12 Chiba-ken. 1963. [2], viii, 474p./13. Tokyo-to. 1964. [2], viii,
463p./14. Kanagawa-ken. 1963. [2], viii, 363p./15. Niigata-ken.
1963. [2], viii, 544p./16. Toyama-ken. 1962. [2], viii, 268p./17.
Ishikawa-ken. 1963. [2], viii, 274p./18. Fukui-ken. 1962. [2],
viii, 268p./19. Yamanashi-ken. 1962. [2], viii, 320p./20. Nagano-ken.
1964. [2], viii, 532p./21. Gifu-ken. 1963. [2], viii, 472p./22.
Shizuoka-ken. 1963. [2], viii, 489p./23. Aichi-ken. 1963. [2],
viii, 613p./24. Mie-ken. 1963. [2], viii, 374p./
25. Shiga-ken. 1963. [2], viii, 296p./26. Kyoto-fu. 1963. [2],
viii, 324p./27. Osaka-fu. 1963. [2], viii, 525p./28. Hyogo-ken.
1963. [2], viii, 529p./29. Nara-ken. 1962. [2], viii, 284p./30.
Wakayama-ken. 1962. [2], viii, 302p./31. Tottori-ken. 1963. [2],
viii, 248p./32. Shimane-ken. 1963. [2], viii, 312p./33. Okayama-ken.
1963. [2], viii, 442p./34. Hiroshima-ken. 1963. [2], viii, 494p./
35. Yamaguchi-ken. 1963. [2], viii, 336p./36. Tokushima-ken. 1962.
[2], viii, 288p./37. Kagawa-ken. 1962. [2], viii, 270p./38. Ehime-
ken. 1962. [2], viii, 382p./39. Kochi-ken. 1963. [2], viii, 304p./
40. Fukuoka-ken. 1963. [2], viii, 549p./41. Saga-ken. 1963. [2],
viii, 292p./42. Nagasaki-ken. 1962. [2], viii, 386p./43. Kumamoto-
ken. 1963. [2], viii, 444p./44. Oita-ken. 1963. [2], viii, 348p./
45. Miyazaki-ken. 1962. [2], viii, 298p./46. Kagoshima-ken. 1963.
[2], viii, 442p. [TXU, RPI

Japan. Bureau of Statistics.
1960 population census of Japan: 10 percent sample tabulation.
Tokyo, 1964. Parts 1-4.
.5-1   Marital status and migration. 427p. [TXU, UN, PRC, RPI
.5-2   Industry and occupation. [2], ii, 428p. specimen forms. [TXU,
UN, PRC, RPI
.5-3   Fertility. [2], iv, 426p. specimen forms. [TXU, UN, PRC, RPI
.5-4   Household. 481p. [TXU, UN, PRC, RPI

Japan. Bureau of Statistics.
.6   Population of Japan, 1960: summary of the results of the 1960 population census of Japan. Tokyo, 1963. [2], xiii, 666p. 2 specimen
forms. [TXU

Japan. Bureau of Statistics.
1960 population census of Japan: abridged report for all Japan,
prefectures, cities, towns and villages. Tokyo, 1964-1965. Parts
1-7.
.7-1   All Japan. 1965. x, 420p. [TXU, PSC, PRC, Berkeley, RPI
.7-2   Hokkaido and Tohoku. 1964. iv, 349p. [TXU, PSC, UN, PRC, RPI

.7-3   Kanto. 1965. iv, 335p. [TXU, PSC, UN, PRC, RPI
.7-4   Chubu. 1965. iv, 423p. [TXU, PSC, UN, BC, PRC, RPI
.7-5   Kinki. 1965. iv, 319p. [TXU, PSC, UN, PRC, RPI
.7-6   Chugoku and Shikoku. 1965. iv, 383p. [TXU, PSC,
.7-7   Kyushu. 1965. iv, 327p. [TXU, PSC, RPI

Japan. Bureau of Statistics.
    1960 population census: population maps of Japan.   Tokyo, 1963-
    1965. Nos. 1-6.
.8-1   Population distribution by shi, ku, machi and mura. 1963. [4],
    36p. [UN, PRC, RPI
.8-2   Population change by shi, ku, machi and mura. 1963. 3 sheets.
    [UN, PRC, RPI
.8-3   Population density and densely inhabited districts by shi, ku,
    machi and mura. 1964. 3 sheets. [UN, PRC, RPI
.8-4   Percentage of workers employed in prime industry for shi, ku,
    machi and mura. 1965. 1 sheet. [UN, PRC, RPI
.8-5   Number of workers employed in manufacture, construction and min-
    ing for shi, machi and mura. 1965. 1 sheet. [UN, PRC, RPI
.8-6   Workers and students commuting to large cities. 1965. 4 sheets.
    [UN, PRC, RPI

Japan. Bureau of Statistics.
    Shōwa sanjūgo-nen kokusei   1960 population census...
chōsa...   Tokyo, 1960-1964.
2v.
.9-1   ...ni kansuru jigō chōsa   Manual for the Post-enumeration
no tebiki. 1960. 10p.   survey of ...
                                         [TXU, RPI

.9-2   ...jigō chōsa no kekka   Summary results of the Post-enu-
gaiyō. 1964. 182p.   meration survey of...
                                         [TXU, RPI

Japan. Bureau of Statistics.
    Shōwa yonjū-nen kokusei   1965 population census...
chōsa...   Tokyo, 1965. 6
items.
1965.0-1-1   ...no tebiki. 45p.   Manual for enumerator.
                                         [
.0-1-2   ...shidōin no tebiki.   Manual for supervisor.
    46p.   [
.0-1-3   ...sangyō bunrui. 185,   Classification of industries.
    8p.   [
.0-1-4   ...shokugyō bunrui. 198p.   Classification of occupations.
                                         [RPI
.0-1-5   ...ni mochiiru sangyō   Explanation of industrial and
    bunrui shokugyō bunrui no kai-   occupational classification.
    setsu. vi, 55, x, 80p.   [
.0-1-6   ...sangyō bunrui sakuin.   Index of industrial classifica-
    12, 301p.   tion.
                                         [

Japan. Bureau of Statistics.
   1965 population census of Japan. Tokyo, 1966-1969. Vol. 1-6 in
   104v.
.1-1   1. Total population. 1966. iv, 314p. [PRC, PSC, RPI
        2. One percent sample tabulation results. 1967. Parts 1-5.
.1-2-1   Age, sex, marital status, and legal nationality. xxv, 149p.
   appendices. [PRC, PSC, RPI
.1-2-2   Labor force status, industry and employment status. xxv,
   669p. appendices. [PRC, PSC, RPI
.1-2-3   Occupation. xxv, 671p. appendices. [PRC, PSC, RPI
.1-2-4   Households. xxv, 407p. appendices. [PRC, PSC, RPI
.1-2-5   Housing conditions. xxv, 371p. appendices. [PRC, PSC, RPI
        3. Reports for the Whole Japan (complete count). 1967. Parts
   1-3 in 4v.
.1-3-1   Age, sex, marital status, legal nationality, labor force
   status, industry, occupation, employment status and households.
   xxviii, 415p. [PRC, RPI
.1-3-2-1   Place of work and place of schooling. Division 1. var. paged.
   [PRC, PSC, RPI
.1-3-2-2   Place of work and place of schooling. Division 2. var. paged.
   [PRC, PSC, RPI
.1-3-3   Industry by place of work. var. paged. [PRC, PSC, RPI
        4. Reports for prefectures (complete count). 1966-1967. Parts
   1-46.
1965.1-4-1 through 1965.1-4-46. [All have maps and appendices.] 1. Hokkaido.
   1967. xviii, 828p./2. Aomori-ken. 1966. xviii, 266p./3. Iwate-ken.
   1966. xviii, 245p./4. Miyagi-ken. 1967. xviii, 298p./5. Akita-ken.
   1966. xviii, 279p./6. Yamagata-ken. 1966. xviii, 198p./7. Fukushima-
   ken. 1966. xviii, 388p./8. Ibaraki-ken. 1966. xviii, 346p./9. Tochigi-ken. 1966. xviii, 218p./10. Gumma-ken. 1966. xviii, 279p./
   11. Saitama-ken. 1966. xviii, 411p./12. Chiba-ken. xviii, 380p./13.
   Tokyo-to. 1967. xviii, 348p./14. Kanagawa-ken. 1966. xviii, 259p./
   15. Niigata-ken. 1966. xviii, 459p./16. Toyama-ken. 1966. xviii,
   171p./17. Ishikawa-ken. 1966. xviii, 178p./18. Fukui-ken. 1966.
   xviii, 169p./19. Yamanashi-ken. 1966. xviii, 241p./20. Ngano-ken.
   1966. xviii, 481p./21. Gifu-ken. 1966. xviii, 367p./22. Shizuoka-
   ken. 1966. xviii, 367p./23. Aichi-ken. 1966. xviii, 477p./24. Mie-
   ken. 1966. xviii, 276p./
      25. Shiga-ken. 1966. xviii, 209p./26. Kyoto-fu. 1966. xviii,
   241p./27. Osaka-fu. 1967. xviii, 394p./28. Hyogo-ken. 1966. xviii,
   426p./29. Nara-ken. 1966. xviii, 195p./30. Wakayama-ken. 1966.
   xviii, 209p./31. Tottori-ken. 1966. xviii, 152p./32. Shimane-ken.
   1966. xviii, 228p./33. Okayama-ken. 1966. xviii, 348p./34. Hiroshima-ken. 1966. xviii, 411p./35. Yamaguchi-ken. 1966. xviii, 241p./
   36. Yokushima-ken. 1966. xviii, 203p./37. Kagawa-ken. 1966. xviii,
   180p./38. Ehime-ken. 1966. xviii, 283p./39. Kochi-ken. 1966. xviii,
   215p./40. Fukuoka-ken. 1966. xviii, 451p./41. Saga-ken. 1966.
   xviii, 201p./42. Nagasaki-ken. 1966. xviii, 285p./43. Kumamoto-ken.
   1966. xviii, 352p./44. Oita-ken. 1966. xviii, 234p./45. Miyazaki-
   ken. 1966. xviii, 186p./46. Kagoshima-ken. 1966. xviii, 350p.
   [PRC, PSC, RPI

5. Twenty percent sample tabulation results for the Whole Japan.
1969. Parts 1-2.
.1-5-1   Age, month of birth, marital status, legal nationality, households, quasi-household members and housing condition. [8], xxvi, 333p.
appendices. [PRC, RPI
.1-5-2   Industry and occupations. [8], xxvi, 565p. appendices.
[PRC, RPI
6. Twenty percent sample tabulation results for prefectures.
1968. Parts 1-46.
1965.1-6-1 through 1965.1-6-46. 1. Hokkaido. [8], xxv, 433, 5, [2]p./2.
Aomori-ken. [8], xxv, 248, 5, [2]p./3. Iwate-ken. [8], xxv, 257,
[2]p./4. Miyagi-ken. [8], xxv, 254, 5, [2]p./5. Akita-ken. [8], xxv,
253, 5, [2]p./6. Yamagata-ken. [8], xxv, 246, 5, [2]p./7. Fukushima-
ken. [8], xxv, 257, 5, [2]p./8. Ibaraki-ken. [8], xxv, 291, 5, [2]p./
9. Tochigi-ken. [8], xxv, 242, 5, [2]p./10. Gumma-ken. [8], xxv, 259,
5, [2]p./11. Saitama-ken. [8], xxv, 319, 5, [2]p./12. Chiba-ken.
[8], xxv, 399, 5, [2]p./13. Tokyo-to. [8], xxv, 395, 5, [2]p./14. Kanagawa-ken. [8], xxv, 338, 5, [2]p./15. Niigata-ken. [8], xxv, 326, 5,
[2]p./16. Toyama-ken. [8], xxv, 285, 5, [2]p./17. Ishikawa-ken. [8],
xxv, 225, 5, [2]p./18. Fukui-ken. [8], xxv, 224, 5, [2]p./19. Yamanashi-ken. [8], xxv, 257, 5, [2]p./20. Nagano-ken. [8], xxv, 329, 5,
[2]p./21. Gifu-ken. [8], xxv, 291, 5, [2]p./22. Shizuoka-ken. [8],
xxv, 296, 5, [2]p./23. Aichi-ken. [8], xxv, 422, 5, [2]p./24. Mie-ken.
[8], xxv, 263, 5, [2]p./
25. Shiga-ken. [8], xxv, 229, 5, [2]p./26. Kyoto-fu. [8], xxv,
317, 5, [2]p./27. Osaka-fu. [8], xxv, 436, 5, [2]p./28. Hyogo-ken.
[8], xxv, 396,5, [2]p./29. Nara-ken. [8], xxv, 232, 5, [2]p./30. Wakayama-ken. [8], xxv, 231, 5, [2]p./31. Tottori-ken. [8], xxv, 213, 5,
[2]p./32. Shimane-ken. [8], xxv, 243, 5, [2]p./33. Okayama-ken. [8],
xxv, 284, 5, [2]p./34. Hiroshima-ken. [8], xxv, 254, 5, [2]p./35.
Yamaguchi-ken. [8], xxv, 254, 5, [2]p./36. Tokushima-ken. [8], xxv,
223, 5, [2]p./37. Kagawa-ken. [8], xxv, 221, 5, [2]p./38. Ehime-ken.
[8], xxv, 263, 5, [2]p./39. Kochi-ken. [8], xxv, 240, 5, [2]p./40.
Fukuoka-ken. [8], xxv, 372, 5, [2]p./41. Saga-ken. [8], xxv, 230,
5, [2]p./42. Nagasaki-ken. [8], xxv, 259, 5, [2]p./43. Kumamoto-ken.
[8], xxv, 285, 5, [2]p./44. Oita-ken. [8], xxv, 249, 5, [2]p./45.
Migazaki-ken. [8], xxv, 232, 5, [2]p./46. Kagoshima-ken. [8], xxv,
294, 5, [2]p. [PRC, PSC, RPI

Japan. Bureau of Statistics.
.2   1965 population census of Japan. Denseley inhabited districts.
Tokyo, 1966. var. paged. [PRC, PSC, RPI

Japan. Bureau of Statistics.
.3   1965 population census of Japan. Final count of population, October 1, 1965. Tokyo, 1966. [vi], 51p. [PSC, RPI

Japan. Bureau of Statistics.
.4   Summary of one-percent sample tabulation results. 1965 population
census of Japan. Tokyo, [1966?]. [8], xxix, 174, [2]p. [PSC, RPI

Japan. Bureau of Statistics.
  1965 population census of Japan. Abridged report, series 1.
[Whole Japan]. Tokyo, 1968-1970. Parts 1-2.
.5-1 Population of Japan. Summary of results. 1970. [xv], 870p.
[PSC, OPR, RP]
.5-2 Place of work and place of schooling. 1968. [6], 234, xiv,
C-20, [3]p. [PSC, RP]

Japan. Bureau of Statistics.
  1965 population census of Japan. Abridged report, series 2.
Tokyo, 1967. Parts 1-46.
1965.6-1 through 1965.6-46. [Same order as 1965.1-6-1 through 1965.1-6-46].

Japan. Bureau of Statistics.
.7 1965 population census of Japan. 20 percent tabulation results.
Industry and occupation by place of work. Tokyo, 1970. [6], xi,
600p. appendices. [PRC, PSC, RP]

Japan. Bureau of Statistics.
.8 Explanation of "Population maps of Japan." 1965 population census.
Tokyo, n.d. [4], 58, [10]p. [PSC, RP]

Japan. Bureau of Statistics.
  1965 population census. Population maps of Japan. Tokyo, 1969-
1970. Nos. 1-6. 2 appendices.
.9-1 Population distribution by shi, ku, machi and mura. 1969. 3
sheets. [UN, RP]
.9-2 Population change by shi, ku, machi and mura. 1969. 3 sheets.
[
.9-3 Percentages of workers employed in industries for shi, ku, machi
and mura. 1969. 3 sheets. [UN, RP]
.9-4 Workers and students commuting to large cities. 1969. [ii], 12
sheets. [PSC, RP]
.9-5 Households and housing by shi, ku, machi and mura. 1969. 4
sheets. [UN, RP]
.9-6 Sex and age compositions by shi, ku, machi and mura. 1970. 3
sheets. [UN, RP]
.9-7 Appendices 1-2. Shi, ku, machi and mura boundaries. 1:1,000,000
(3 sheets) and 1:1,500,000 (1 sheet). [1970]. [UN, RP]

Japan. Bureau of Statistics.
.10 Population census of Japan. Special tabulation results. Household and family [1955, 1960, 1965]. Tokyo, 1970. [8], 597, A-12p.
[PRC, RP]

Japan. Bureau of Statistics.
1970.0-1 Schema of the 1970 population census of Japan. 1971. 13p.
[BC

Japan. Bureau of Statistics.
  1970 population census of Japan. Advanced report series. Tokyo,

1971.   Nos. 1-4.
.1-1   Preliminary count of population. 122p. [
.1-2   Final count of population. 60p. [
.1-3   Prompt report of the basic findings (1 percent sample). xxiii,
   484p. [PRC, BC
.1-4   Advanced report of population of Densely Inhabited Districts.
   50p. [

Japan. Bureau of Statistics.
    1970 population census of Japan. Reference report series.   Tokyo,
1972-1974. Nos. 1-7.
.2-1   User's guide of census data and materials related to enumeration
   districts. [Japanese only]. 1972. 140p. [PRC, E-W, BC
.2-2   Supplement to the User's guide of census data and materials related to enumeration districts. [Japanese only]. 1973. 229p. [PRC,
   E-W
.2-3   Comparison of employed persons by industry in the population
   censuses, 1920 through 1970. 1973. 378p. [PRC, E-W, PSC
.2-4   Commuting population. 1973. 384, A-10p. [PRC
.2-5   Major metropolitan areas. 1973. 265p. [PRC, E-W, NYPL, PSC
.2-6   Results by population size of shi, machi and mura and of DIDs.
   1974. [x], xvi, 247p. [PRC
.2-7   Comparison of employed persons by occupation in the population
   censuses, 1930 through 1970. 1974. 414p. [E-W, PSC

Japan. Bureau of Statistics.
    1970 population census of Japan. Abridged report series.   Tokyo,
1972. Nos. 1-2 in 48v.
.3-1   1. Population of Japan. 1972. 142p. [BC
            2. Prefectures. 1972. Parts 1-47.
1970.3-2-1 through 1970.3-2-47. [Same order as Nos. 1970.5-3-1 through 1970.
   5-3-47 following.] [OPR

Japan. Bureau of Statistics.
    1970 population census of Japan. Special volumes.   Tokyo, 1971-
1973. 2v.
.4-1   Densely inhabited districts. 1971. viii, 47, [363]p. 3 sheets.
   [PRC, BC
.4-2   Atlas of census tract boundaries. 1973. v, 65, [1]p. fold.
   maps, tables. [BC

Japan. Bureau of Statistics.
    1970 population census of Japan.   Tokyo, 1971-1975. Vol. I-VIII
in 75v.
.5-1   I. Total population. 1971. xxx, 237p. [PRC, BC
.5-2   II. Whole Japan (Results of basic tabulation). 1972. xxviii,
   651, A-1 to C-10p. Specimen forms. [PRC, BC
            III. Prefectures and municipalities. 1971-1972. Parts 1-47.
1970.5-3-1 through 1970.5-3-47. [All have maps.] 1. Hokkaido. 1972. xviii,
   1238p./2. Aomori-ken. 1972. xviii, 444p./3. Iwate-ken. 1971. xviii,
   446p./4. Miyagi-ken. 1971. xviii, 500p./5. Akita-ken. 1971. xviii,
   458p./6. Yamagata-ken. 1971. xviii, 390p./7. Fukushima-ken. 1972.

xviii, 540p./8. Ibaraki-ken. 1971. xviii, 580p./9. Tochigi-ken.
1972. xviii, 395p./10. Gumma-ken. 1971. xviii, 466p./11. Saitama-
ken. 1971. xviii, 676p./12. Chiba-ken. 1971. xviii, 609p./13.
Tokyo-to. 1972. xviii, 714p./14. Kanagawa-ken. 1972. xviii, 564p./
15. Niigata-ken. 1971. xviii, 696p./16. Toyama-ken. 1971. xviii,
330p./17. Ishikawa-ken. 1971. xviii, 341p./18. Fukui-ken. 1972.
xviii, 321p./19. Yamanashi-ken. 1972. xviii, 419p./20. Nagano-ken.
1972. xviii, 716p./21. Gifu-ken. 1971. xviii, 594p./22. Shizuoka-
ken. 1972. xviii, 554p./23. Aichi-ken. 1972. xviii, 805p./24. Mie-
ken. 1971. xviii, 479p./
　　　25. Shiga-ken. 1971. xviii, 369p./26. Kyoto-fu. 1972. xviii,
465p./27. Osaka-fu. 1972. xviii, 785p./28. Hyogo-ken. 1972. xviii,
749p./29. Nara-ken. 1971. xviii, 375p./30. Wakayama-ken. 1971.
xviii, 375p./31. Tottori-ken. 1972. xviii, 309p./32. Shimane-ken.
1972. xviii, 405p./33. Okayama-ken. 1971. xviii, 541p./34. Hiroshima-ken. 1972. xviii, 637p./35. Yamaguchi-ken. 1971. xviii, 430p./
36. Tokushima-ken. 1971. xviii, 349p./37. Kagawa-ken. 1971. xviii,
339p./38. Ehime-ken. 1971. xviii, 475p./39. Kochi-ken. 1972. xviii,
397p./40. Fukuoka-ken. 1972. xviii, 717p./41. Saga-ken. 1971.
xviii, 371p./42. Nagasaki-ken. 1971. xviii, 483p./43. Kumamoto-ken.
1971. xviii, 573p./44. Oita-ken. 1971. xviii, 413p./45. Miyazaki-
ken. 1971. xviii, 349p./46. Kagoshima-ken. 1971. xviii, 577p./47.
Okinawa. 1971. xxix, 401p. [PRC, BC

1970.5-4　　IV.　Census tracts. 1973. xix, 617, A-1 to C-21p. [PRC, BC
　　　　　　V.　Results of detailed tabulation. 1973. Parts 1-2 in 8v.
.5-5-1-1　　Whole Japan. Division 1. 1973. xxviii, 803, A-1 to G-3.
[PRC, BC
.5-5-1-2　　Whole Japan. Division 2. 1973. xxviii, 455, A-1 to G-3.
[PRC, BC
.5-5-2-1　　Prefectures. Division 1. Hokkaido and Tohoku. 1973.
xxxviii, var. paged. [PRC
.5-5-2-2　　Prefectures. Division 2. Kanto. 1973. var. paged. [PRC
.5-5-2-3　　Prefectures. Division 3. Chubu. 1973. var. paged. [PRC
.5-5-2-4　　Prefectures. Division 4. Kinki. 1973. var. paged. [PRC
.5-5-2-5　　Prefectures. Division 5. Chugoku and Shikoku. 1973. var.
paged. [PRC
.5-5-2-6　　Prefectures. Division 6. Kyushu. 1973. var. paged. [PRC
　　　　　　VI.　Commutation. 1972. Parts 1-4 in 10v.
　　　　　　Part 1.　Population, age, sex, industry and occupation by
　place of work or locality of schooling. Divisions 1-6.
.5-6-1-1　　　Division 1. Hokkaido and Tohoku. xxi, 726, A-1 to C-10p.
[PRC, BC
.5-6-1-2　　　Division 2. Kanto. xxi, 823, A-1 to C-10p. [PRC, BC
.5-6-1-3　　　Division 3. Chubu. xxi, 906, A-1 to C-10p. [PRC, BC
.5-6-1-4　　　Division 4. Kinki. xxi, 707, A-1 to C-10p. [PRC, BC
.5-6-1-5　　　Division 5. Chugoku and Shikoku. xxi, 672, A-1 to C-10p.
[PRC, BC
.5-6-1-6　　　Division 6. Kyushu. xxi, 708, A-1 to C-10p. [PRC, BC
　　　　　　Part 2.　Place of work or locality of schooling. Divisions
　1-2.
.5-6-2-1　　　Division 1. East Japan. xv, 885, A-1 to R-18p. [PRC, BC
.5-6-2-2　　　Division 2. West Japan. xv, 718, A-1 to R-18p. [PRC, BC

1970.5-6-3   Part 3. Means of transportation to work or to attend school.
          xiv, 426, A-1 to R-18p. [PRC, BC
     .5-6-4   Part 4. Industry and occupation by place of work and usual
          place of residence. xvi, 563, A-1 to R-18p. [PRC, BC
                         VII. Internal migration. 1973. Parts 1-4.
     .5-7-1   Hokkaido-Tohoku. var. paged. [PRC, BC
     .5-7-2   Kanto-Chubu. var. paged. [PRC, BC
     .5-7-3   Kinki-Chogoku. var. paged. [PRC, BC
     .5-7-4   Shikoku-Kyushu. var. paged. [PRC, BC
                         VIII. Special tabulation results (one percent sample tabulation).
          1973-1975. Parts 1-3.
     .5-8-1   Household and family. 1975. xxi, 363p. [PRC, BC
     .5-8-2   Fertility of women. 1975. xvii, 203p. [PRC, BC
     .5-8-3   Means of transportation to work or to attend school. 1973.
          65, A-10, B-13, C-15p. [PRC, BC

          Japan. Bureau of Statistics.
     .6   Population of Japan. Summary of the results of the 1970 population
          census of Japan.   Tokyo, 1975. xx, 818p. [PRC, E-W

          Japan. Bureau of Statistics.
               Population maps of Japan.   Tokyo, 1971-1974. Parts 1-24 & 1v.
     .7-1   Population distribution by landforms. 1973. 3 sheets. [BC
     .7-2   Population density by shi, ku, machi and mura. 1973. 1 sheet.
          [BC
     .7-3   Rate of population change by shi, ku, machi and mura. 1973. 3
          sheets. [PRC, BC
     .7-4   Percent working age population by shi, ku, machi and mura. 1973.
          1 sheet. [PRC, BC
     .7-5   Ratio of aged population by shi, ku, machi and mura. 1973. 1
          sheet. [PRC, BC
     .7-6   Percent population moved after 1965. 1973. 1 sheet. [BC
     .7-7   Number of persons per household by shi, ku, machi and mura.
          1973. 1 sheet. [BC
     .7-8   Percent family nuclei by shi, ku, machi and mura. 1973. 1 sheet.
          [BC
     .7-9   Percent employed households by shi, ku, machi and mura. 1973.
          1 sheet. [BC
     .7-10   Percent agricultural households by shi, ku, machi and mura.
          1973. 1 sheet. [BC
     .7-11   Number of dwelling rooms per household by shi, ku, machi and
          mura. 1973. 1 sheet. [BC
     .7-12   Number of tatami per household member by shi, ku, machi and mura.
          1973. 1 sheet. [BC
     .7-13   Percent owned houses by shi, ku, machi and mura. 1973. 1 sheet.
          [BC
     .7-14   Percent persons completed elementary school or junior high school
          by shi, ku, machi and mura. 1973. 1 sheet. [BC
     .7-15   Percent persons completed junior high school or university by
          shi, ku, machi and mura. 1973. 1 sheet. [BC
     .7-16   Percent workers employed in primary industries by shi, ku, machi
          and mura. 1973. 1 sheet. [BC

.7-17   Percent workers employed in secondary industries by shi, ku, machi and mura. 1973. 1 sheet. [BC

.7-18   Percent workers employed in tertiary industries by shi, ku, machi and mura. 1973. 1 sheet. [BC

.7-19   Percent workers in production and transport occupations by shi, ku, machi and mura. 1973. 1 sheet. [BC

.7-20   Percent workers in sales and service occupations by shi, ku, machi and mura. 1973. 1 sheet. [BC

.7-21   Percent workers in clerical, technical and managerial occupations by shi, ku, machi and mura. 1973. 1 sheet. [BC

.7-22   Workers and students commuting to large cities. 1974. 21 sheets. [BC

.7-23   Distribution of commuting persons by means of transportation. 1974. 1 sheet. [BC

.7-24   Ratio of day and night-time population. 1974. 1 sheet. [BC

.7-Ex   Explanation of "Population maps of Japan," 1970 population census. [1975]. pp. 13-20. [PRC, BC

Japan. Bureau of Statistics.
    1975 population census of Japan. Advanced report series. Tokyo, 1975-1977. Nos. 1-6 in 51v.

1975.1-1   Preliminary count of population, October 1, 1975. 1975. 105p. [PRC, BC, E-W

.1-2   Population counts based on lists of households, October 1, 1975. 1976. [53]p. [PRC, BC, UN

.1-3   Final count of population and households, October 1, 1975. 1977. iv, 50p. [PRC, BC

.1-4   Prompt report of the basic findings. (Result for 1 percent tabulation), October 1, 1975. 1975. xxi, 651p. [PRC, UN

    Prompt report of the basic findings for prefectures and municipalities. (Result for twenty percent tabulation). 1976. Parts 1-47.

1975.1-5-1 through 1975.1-5-47. 1. Hokkaido. viii, 191p./2. Aomori-ken. viii, 68p./3. Iwate-ken. viii, 67p./4. Miyagi-ken. viii, 81p./5. Akita-ken. viii, 68p./6. Yamagata-ken. viii, 57p./7. Fukushima-ken. viii, 87p./8. Ibaraki-ken. viii, 92p./9. Tochigi-ken. viii, 59p./10. Gumma-ken. viii, 72p./11. Saitama-ken. viii, 101p./12. Chiba-ken. viii, 92p./13. Tokyo-to. viii, 94p./14. Kanagawa-ken. viii, 84p./15. Niigata-ken. viii, 105p./16. Toyama-ken. viii, 49p./17. Ishikawa-ken. viii, 52p./18. Fukui-ken. viii, 47p./19. Yamanashi-ken. viii, 67p./ 20. Nagano-ken. viii, 110p./21. Gifu-ken. viii, 95p./22. Shizuoka-ken. viii, 81p./23. Aichi-ken. viii, 117p./24. Mie-ken. viii, 70p./ 25. Shiga-ken. viii, 57p./26. Kyoto-fu. viii, 70p./27. Osaka-fu. viii, 109p./28. Hyogo-ken. viii, 112p./29. Nara-ken. viii, 55p./30. Wakayama-ken. viii, 57p./31. Tottori-ken. viii, 47p./32. Shimane-ken. viii, 62p./33. Okayama-ken. viii, 85p./34. Hiroshima-ken. viii, 93p./ 35. Yamaguchi-ken. viii, 64p./36. Tokushima-ken. viii, 55p./37. Kagawa-ken. viii, 52p./38. Ehime-ken. viii, 72p./39. Kochi-ken. viii, 62p./40. Fukuoka-ken. viii, 119p./41. Saga-ken. viii, 57p./42. Nagasaki-ken. viii, 77p./43. Kumamoto-ken. viii, 92p./44. Oita-ken. viii, 62p./45. Miyazaki-ken. viii, 54p./46. Kagoshima-ken. viii, 90p./47. Okinawa-ken. viii, 62p. [PRC, BC, UN

.1-6   [Advanced report of population of Densely inhabited districts.] 1977. 48p. [PRC

Japan. Bureau of Statistics.
    1975 population census of Japan. Abridged report series. Tokyo,
1976-1979. Parts 1-3 in 49v.
.2-1   Population of Japan. 1977. 125p. [PRC
         Population of prefectures. 1976-1977. Parts 1-47.
1975.2-2-1 through 1975.2-2-47. [Same order as Nos. 1975.4-3-1 through 1975.
4-3-47, following.] [
.2-3   Population of Japan. 1979.   p. [

Japan. Bureau of Statistics.
    1975 population census of Japan. Enumeration districts series.
Tokyo, 1976-1977. Nos. 1-4 in 5v.
.3-1   [User's guide of census data and materials related to enumeration districts.] [Japanese only]. 1976. 142p. [
.3-2   [Supplement to the User's guide of census data and materials
related to enumeration.] [Japanese only]. 1977. 120p. [
.3-3   Densely inhabited districts. 1977. 560p. [
         Census tracts. 1977. Parts 1-2.
.3-4-1   Results of tabulation by census tracts.

.3-4-2   Boundary maps of census tracts.

Japan. Bureau of Statistics.
    1975 population census of Japan. Tokyo, 1977-19 . Vol. 1-6 in
    v.
.4-1   1. Total population. 1977. xxxii, 282p. [PRC
.4-2   2. Whole Japan. (Results of complete count tabulation). 1977.
xiv, 806, A-9, B-10, C-12p. specimen forms. [PRC
        3. Prefectures and municipalities. 1977. Parts 1-47.
1975.4-3-1 through 1975.4-3-47. [All have maps.] 1. Hokkaido. xiv, 1317p./
2. Aomori-ken. xiv, 438p./3. Iwate-ken. xiv, 427p./4. Miyagi-ken.
xiv, 489p./5. Akita-ken. xiv, 452p./6. Yamagata-ken. xiv, 342p./7.
Fukushima-ken. xiv, 550p./8. Ibaraki-ken. xiv, 589p./9. Tochigi-ken.
xiv, 359p./10. Gumma-ken. xiv, 463p./11. Saitama-ken. xiv, 679p./
12. Chiba-ken. xiv, 565p./13. Tokyo-to. xiv, 580p./14. Kanagawa-ken.
xiv, 496p./15. Niigata-ken. xiv, 708p./16. Toyama-ken. xiv, 289p./
17. Ishikawa-ken. xiv, 314p./18. Fukui-ken. xiv, 280p./19. Yamanashi-ken. xiv, 418p./20. Nagano-ken. xiv, 739p./21. Gifu-ken. xiv,
617p./22. Shizuoka-ken. xiv, 535p./23. Aichi-ken. xiv, 772p./24.
Mie-ken. xiv, 472p./
    25. Shiga-ken. xiv, 348p./26. Kyoto-fu. xiv, 412p./27. Osaka-fu.
xiv, 634p./28. Hyogo-ken. xiv, 679p./29. Nara-ken. xiv, 344p./30.
Wakayama-ken. xiv, 352p./31. Tottori-ken. xiv, 278p./32. Shimane-
ken. xiv, 398p./33. Okayama-ken. xiv, 490p./34. Hiroshima-ken. xiv,
550p./35. Yamaguchi-ken. xiv, 400p./36. Tokushima-ken. xiv, 330p./
37. Kagawa-ken. xiv, 300p./38. Ehime-ken. xiv, 462p./39. Kochi-ken.
xiv, 368p./40. Fukuoka-ken. xiv, 746p./41. Saga-ken. xiv, 342p./42.
Nagasaki-ken. xiv, 488p./43. Kumamoto-ken. xiv, 593p./44. Oita-ken.
xiv, 398p./45. Miyazaki-ken. xiv, 318p./46. Kagoshima-ken. xiv,
590p./47. Okinawa-ken. xiv, 374p. [PRC

4. Commutation. 1978. Parts 1-2 in 53v.
   Part 1. Results of complete count tabulation. Population, age, sex and industry by place of work or locality of schooling. 1978. Nos. 1-47.
1975.4-4-1-1 through 1975.4-4-1-47. 1. Hokkaido. vi, 375, [18]p./2. Aomori-ken. vi, 113, [18]p./3. Iwate-ken. vi, 106, [18]p./4. Miyagi-ken. vi, 133, [18]p./5. Akita-ken. vi, 117, [18]p./6. Yamagata-ken. vi, 76 , [18]p./7. Fukushima-ken. vi, 157, [18]p./8. Ibaraki-ken. vi, 175, [18]p./9. Tochigi-ken. vi, 99, [18]p./10. Gumma-ken. vi, 128, [18]p./11. Saitama-ken. vi, 225, [18]p./12. Chiba-ken. vi, 181, [18]p./13. Tokyo-to. vi, 363, [18]p./14. Kanagawa-ken. vi, 243, [18]p./15. Niigata-ken. vi, 193, [18]p./16. Toyama-ken. vi, 63, [18]p./17. Ishikawa-ken. vi, 77, [18]p./18. Fukui-ken. vi, 61, [18]p./19. Yamanashi-ken. vi, 113, [18]p./20. Nagano-ken. vi, 209, [18]p./21. Gifu-ken. vi, 187, [18]p./22. Shizuoka-ken. vi, 147, [18]p./23. Aichi-ken. vi, 297, [18]p./24. Mie-ken. vi, 128, [18]p./
   25. Shiga-ken. vi, 100, [18]p./26. Kyoto-fu. vi, 155, [18]p./27. Osaka-fu. vi, 363, [18]p./28. Hyogo-ken. vi, 253, [18]p./29. Nara-ken. vi, 97, [18]p./30. Wakayama-ken. vi, 95, [18]p./31. Tottori-ken. vi, 69, [18]p./32. Shimane-ken. vi, 99, [18]p./33. Okayama-ken. vi, 145, [18]p./34. Hiroshima-ken. vi, 159, [18]p./35. Yamaguchi-ken. vi, 101, [18]p./36. Tokushima-ken. vi, 89, [18]p./37. Kagawa-ken. vi, 79, [18]p./38. Ehime-ken. vi, 123, [18]p./39. Kochi-ken. vi, 89, [18]p./40. Fukuoka-ken. vi, 255, [18]p./41. Saga-ken. vi, 89, [18]p./42. Nagasaki-ken. vi, 137, [18]p./43. Kumamoto-ken. vi, 169, [18]p./44. Oita-ken. vi, 105, [18]p./45. Miyazaki-ken. vi, 76, [18]p./46. Kagoshima-ken. vi, 163, [18]p./47. Okinawa-ken. vi, 89, [18]p. [PRC

   Part 2. Results of twenty percent sample tabulation. Indus-try, occupation, employment status, family type of household, economic type of household and tenure by place of work or usual place of resi-dence. 1978. Divisions 1-6.
.4-4-2-1   Division 1. Hokkaido and Tohoku. var. paging. [PRC
.4-4-2-2   Division 2. Kanto. var. paging. [PRC
.4-4-2-3   Division 3. Chubu. var. paging. [PRC
.4-4-2-4   Division 4. Kinki. var. paging. [PRC
.4-4-2-5   Division 5. Chugoku and Shikoku. var. paging. [PRC
.4-4-2-6   Division 6. Kyushu. var. paging. [PRC
   5. Results of detailed tabulation. 1978. Parts 1-2 in 48v.
      Whole Japan. 1978. Parts 1 and 2.
.4-5-1-1   1. xxvi, 1176p. [
.4-5-1-2   2. xxvi, 1081p. [
1975.4-5-2-1 through 1975.4-5-2-47. [Same order as 1975.4-4-1 set above.]
   [
   6. Results of special tabulation.

Japan. Bureau of Statistics.
    1975 population census of Japan. Reference report series. 1978–
1979. Parts 1-3.
1975.5-1   Commuting population. 1978. viii, 443, A-15, B-9, C-8p.
    [OPR
  .5-2   Population of metropolitan areas. 1979. xviii, 301p. [OPR
  .5-3   Results by population size of shi, machi, mura and of DID's.

Japan. Bureau of Statistics.
    1975 population census of Japan. Population maps of Japan.
Tokyo, 1976-19 . Nos. 1- .
  .6-1   Population distribution by landforms. 1977. 3 sheets. [OPR
  .6-2   Population density. 1976. 1 sheet. [PSC, OPR
  .6-3   Rate of population change. 1977. 1 sheet. [PSC, OPR
  .6-4   Percent working age population. 1976. 1 sheet. [PSC, OPR
  .6-5   Ratio of aged population. 1978. 1 sheet. [PSC, OPR
  .6-6   Ratio of children and aged population. 1978. 1 sheet. [PSC,
  OPR
  .6-7   Number of persons per household. 1978. 1 sheet. [PSC, OPR
  .6-8   Percent family nuclei. 1978. 1 sheet. [PSC, OPR
  .6-9   Percent employed households. 1978. 1 sheet. [PSC, OPR
  .6-10   Number of tatami per household member. 1978. 1 sheet. [PSC,
  OPR
  .6-11   Number and change rate of workers employed in primary industries.
  1978. 3 sheets. [PSC, OPR
  .6-12   Number and change rate of workers employed in secondary industries. 1978. 3 sheets. [PSC, OPR
  .6-13   Number and change rate of workers employed in tertiary industries. 1978. 3 sheets. [PSC, OPR
  .6-14   Percent workers employed in industries (3 sectors). 1978. 1
  sheet. [PSC, OPR
  .6-15   Ratio of workers in clerical, technical and managerial occupations and workers in production and transport occupations by shi, ku,
  machi and mura. 1978. 1 sheet. [PSC, OPR
  .6-16   Ratio of day- and night-time population by shi, ku, machi and
  mura. 1978. 1 sheet. [PSC, OPR
  .6-17   Workers and students commuting to large cities. 1978. 37p.
  [PSC, OPR

JOHNSTON ISLAND

[United States Unincorporated Territory]   Capital: [Administered from
                                                       Washington, D.C.]

The U.S. censuses for 1950, 1960 and 1970 carry only total number of
inhabitants in Table 1 of the U.S. Summary volume for those years.

JORDAN

The Hashemite Kingdom of Jordan.   Capital: Amman
Statistical Agency: Department of Statistics
                     P.O. Box 2015
                     Amman,
Publications Distributor: same.

    Jordan.   Department of Statistics.
      First census of population and housing, 18 November, 1961.   Interim
    report, no. 1-10.   Amman, 1962-1963. [Arabic and English].
1961.1-1   Number and characteristics of structures in municipalities.
    1962. xi, [3], 34, [6]p. [PRC
      Distribution and characteristics of population of ... district.
    9v.
1961.1-2 through 1961.1-10. 2. Ma'an. 1962. xiv, 77, [5]p./3. Al-Karak.
    1963. xii, [2], 102, [5]p./4. Al-Balqa. 1963. xii, [1], 78, [5]p./
    5. Hebron. 1963. [2], xii, [1], 93, [9]p./6. Amman. 1963. [2], xiv,
    [1], 122, [7]p./7. Jerusalem. 1963. xvii, [1], 141, [23]p./8. Nablus.
    1963. xvii, [1], 173, [22]p./9. Ajloun. 1963. xvii, [1], 196, [22]p./
    10. Scattered tents. 1963. xviii, [1], 109, [22]p. [PRC, TXU, BC

    Jordan.   Department of Statistics.
      First census of population and housing, 18 November, 1961.   Amman,
    1964-1965. Vol. I-IV. [Arabic and English].
  .2-1   I. Final tables. General characteristics of the population.
    Geographic location, personal and cultural characteristics, educational
    characteristics, fertility, Jordanians abroad. 1964. xxvi, 341,
    [30]p. 4 maps. [PRC, OPR
  .2-2   II. Final tables. Economic characteristics of the population.
    1964. xx, 70, [25]p. [PRC, OPR
  .2-3   III. Final tables. Household and housing characteristics.
    1964. xxii, 73, [27]p. [PRC, OPR
  .2-4   IV. Methods report. 1965. 113, xxp. [PRC, OPR

    Note: The West Bank of Jordan and East Jerusalem was censused in
    1967 by the Israelis. See Israel 1967.1-1 through 1967.1-5 and 1967.
    2-1 and 1967.2-2.

KENYA

Republic of Kenya.   Capital: Nairobi.
Statistical Agency: Central Bureau of Statistics
                     Ministry of Finance and Planning
                     P.O. Box 30266
                     Nairobi,
Publications Distributor: same

Kenya. Census Office.
1948.1   Report on the census of the non-native population of Kenya Colony
and Protectorate taken on the night of 25th February 1948. Nairobi,
Government Printer, 1953. [5], 133p. [Includes Africans in non-
native premises.] [PRC, LC, BC, TXU, NWU, RPI

British East Africa. High Commission. Statistical Department.
   .2   African population of Kenya Colony and Protectorate. Geographical
and tribal studies. (Source: East African population census, 1948).
Nairobi, 1950. [Reprinted 1953]. 58p. [PRC, TXU, LC, NWU, RPI

Kenya. Ministry of Finance and Economic Planning. Economics and
        Statistics Division.
1962.1   Kenya population census, 1962. Tables. Advance report of Volumes
I and II. Nairobi, 1964. 94p. [Note: Some tables are not dupli-
cated in Vols. I-II.] [PRC, BC, UN, NWU, RPI

Kenya. Ministry of Economic Planning and Development. Statistics
        Division.
          Kenya population census, 1962. Nairobi, 1964-1966. Vol. I-IV.
   .2-1   I. Populations of census areas by sex and age group. 1964.
   125p. [PRC, UN, NWU, RPI
   .2-2   II. Population of locations and county council wards by race,
   tribe and sex. 1965. 208p. [PRC, UN, NWU, RPI
   .2-3   III. African population. 1966. iii, 119p. [PRC, UN, NWU, RPI
   .2-4   IV. Non-African population. 1966. 95p. [PRC, UN, NWU, RPI

Kenya. Ministry of Finance and Economic Planning. Statistics Divi-
        sion.
          Kenya population census, 1969. Nairobi, 1970-1977. Vol. I-IV.
1969.1-1   I. [Age, sex, area, density, tribe or nationality.] 1970.
   ii, 123p. map. [PRC, BC, NWU
   .1-2   II. Data on urban population. 1971. v, 82p. [PRC, BC, NWU
   .1-3   III. Data on education, relationship to head of household,
   birthplace and marital status. 1971. iii, 73p. [PRC, BC, NWU
   .1-4   IV. Analytical report. 1977. (iii), 89p. [PRC, NWU

Kenya. Central Bureau of Statistics.
1976.0-1 Demographic survey, 1973-1976. Methodological report. Nairobi,
   1977. 75p. [NWU

The next census is proposed for 1979.

KOREA, NORTH

Democratic People's Republic of Korea   Capital: Pyongyang.
Statistical Agency: Central statistical Office
                        P'yŏngyang,
Publications Distributor: same

The last census was taken May 1, 1944. The following are some sources
cited as having population statistics:

Chosŏn Chung'ang T'ongsinsa.
1961.1   Chosŏn chung'ang yŏngam,
           1961. Pyongyang, 1962. (JPRS:
           17,890. Translations of por-
           tions of Chosŏn Chung'ang Yŏn-
           gam, 1961. Feb. 28, 1963.
           SPTS 773).

Korean Central News Agency.
Korean Central yearbook, 1961.
[JPRS - U.S. Department of Commerce. Joint Publications Research Service].
[

Chosŏn Chung'ang T'ongsinsa.
1965.1   Chosŏn chung'ang yŏngam,
           1965. Pyongyang, 1965. (JPRS:
           35,146. Information from the
           1965 Korean yearbook. Transla-
           tions of selected portions of
           Chosŏn Chung'ang Yŏngam, 1965.
           Asia/II A, B, D, E, H.)

Korean Central yearbook, 1965.
[

Korea (Republic) Kingsankwŏn-
           munje Yŏnguso.
1958.1   Pukhan ch'ŏnggam, 1945-1958.
           Seoul, 1968.   p.

General survey of North Korea,
1945-1958.
[

Korea (Republic). Ministry of
           Public Information.
1967.1   Pukhan yoram.   Seoul, 1968.
                p.

Survey of North Korea.
[

Korea (Republic). Tōitsu
           Chōsen Shimbunsha.
1968.1   Tōitsu chōsen nenkan, 1967-
           1968. Tokyo, 1967.   p.

One-Korea yearbook, 1967-1968.
[

KOREA, SOUTH

Republic of Korea   Capital: Seoul
Statistical Agency: Bureau of Statistics
                     Economic Planning Board
                     Seoul,
Publications Distributor: The Government Publication Center
                           Jung Ku, 1-ka, Taepyung-Ro
                           Seoul,

U.S. Army Military Government (Korea).
1946.1   Population of South Korea, by geographic divisions and sex, September 1946.   [Seoul], 1946. 5, 7, 70p. [OPR

Korea (Republic). Bureau of
        Statistics.
1949.1   Daehan minguk Je'ilhoe Chong   Advanced report of the First General census result, Korea 1949.
ingu chōsa Kyo'lgwa sog'bo.
Seoul, 1949.   p.   [UH-A

Note: Only the advanced report was published. The remaining data was destroyed during the Korean War. Results were also printed in the following:

Korea (Republic). Bureau of Statistics.
.2   Korea statistical yearbook, 1952. Vol. 1.   Seoul, 1953.   p.
[LC

Korea (Republic). Bureau of Statistics.
    Republic of Korea, statistical summation.   Seoul, 1949. Nos. 8, 9, 11, 12...
.3-8   Marital status of Koreans fifteen years of age and over, Republic of Korea [and] Educational level of Koreans fifteen years of age and over, by sex. P.4. [
.3-9/10 Population of Republic of Korea, by province and sex, as of 1 May 1949. P. 1./Population of cities and towns in Republic of Korea with populations over 40,000 by sex. P. 2./Foreigners in Republic of Korea, by province and sex. P. 3. [
.3-11   Population density of Korea, by zones and provinces. P. 3.
    [
.3-12   Population of Republic of Korea, by sex and age distribution as of 1 May 1949. P. 10. [

U.S. Economic Cooperation Administration, Mission to Korea.
.4   Special report on general population survey, Republic of Korea, 1 May 1949. n.p., n.d. 27p. [

Korea (Republic). Bureau of Statistics.
    Report of the simplified general population census, Republic of Korea.   Seoul, 1959. Vol. I-X.
1955.1-1   I. Whole country. 181p. [E-W, PRC, RPI

1955.1-2 through 1955.1-10. 2. Special city of Seoul. 205p./3. Kyonggi-Do.
      627p./4. Chungchungbug-Do. 345p./5. Chungchungnam-Do. 503p./6. Ky-
      ongsangbug-Do. [and Kyongsangnam-Do]. 795p./7. Chollabug-Do. 531p./
      8. Chollanam-Do. 745p./9. Kangwon-Do. 561p./10. Cheju-Do. 107p.
      [

      Korea (Republic). Economic Planning Board. Bureau of Statistics.
         1960 population and housing census of Korea. Seoul, 1963-1964.
      Vol. 1-2 in 14v.
            1. Complete tabulation report. 1963.
1960.1-1-1   Whole country. 216p. specimen forms. [PRC, RPI
1960.1-1-2 through 1960.1-1-11. [All have specimen forms.] 2. Seoul special
      city. x, 135p./3. Gyeonggi-Do. x, 173p./4. Chungcheongbug-Do. x,
      137p./5. Chungcheongnam-Do. x, 161p./6&7. Jeonlabug-Do and Jeonla-
      nam-Do. 273p./8,9&10. Gyeongsangbug-Do, Gyeongsangnam-Do and Gang-
      weon-Do. 431p./11. Jeju-Do. x, 97p. [PRC, BC, RPI
            2. 20 percent sample tabulation report. 1963-1964.
       .1-2-1   Whole country. 1963. [2], 414p. specimen forms. [PRC, BC,
      RPI
1960.1-2-2 through 1960.1-2-10&11. 2&3. Seoul special city and Gyeonggi-Do.
      1964. 285p./4&5. Chungcheongbug-Do and Chungcheongnam-Do. 1964.
      407p./6&7. Jeonlabug-Do and Jeonlanam-Do. 1964. 407p./8&9. Gyeong-
      sangbug-Do and Gyeongsangnam-Do. 1964. 407p./10&11. Gangweon-Do and
      Jeju-Do. 1964. 407p. [PRC, BC, RPI

      Korea (Republic). Bureau of Statistics.
         1960 census monograph series. Seoul, 1966. 2v.
       .2-1   An evaluation study for the accuracy of the 1960 population and
      housing census of Korea, by Jay Soo Park. 1966. 120p. [OPR
       .2-2   Population distribution and internal migration in Korea, by Ehn
      Hyun Choe. 1966. 133, [22], 26p. [OPR

      Korea (Republic). Economic Planning Board. Bureau of Statistics.
         1966 population census report of Korea. Seoul, 1968-1969. 12v.
1966.1-1   Whole country. 1969. 497p. [PRC
1966.1-2 through 1966.1-12. 2. Seoul special city. 1968. 187p./3. Busan
      City. 1968. 163p./4. Gyeonggi-Do. 1968. 375p./5. Gangweon-Do.
      1968. 355p./6. Chungcheongbug-Do. 1968. 337p./7. Chungcheongnam-Do.
      1968. 359p./8. Jeonlabug-Do. 1968. 355p./9. Jeonlanam-Do. 1969.
      401p./10. Gyeongsangbug-Do. 1969. 411p./11. Gyeongsangnam-Do. 1969.
      397p./12. Jeju-Do. 1968. 303p. [PRC

      Korea (Republic). Bureau of Statistics.
1970.1   [Revised tables of the results of the general population and hous-
      ing census, Aug. 31, 1970]. Seoul, 1970. 73p. tables. [Korean
      only]. [BC

      Korea (Republic). Economic Planning Board. Bureau of Statistics.
         1970 population and housing census report. Seoul, 1972-1973.
      Vol. I-II in 16v.
            I. Complete enumation. 1972.
       .2-1-1   Republic of Korea. 1972. [vi], 416, [iv]p. [Harvard

1970.2-1-2 through 1970.2-1-12. 2. City of Seoul. 1972.   p./3. Busan
        City. 1972. 126p./4. Gyeong-gi-Do. 1972. 310p./5. Gang-weon Do.
        1972. 236p./6. Chungcheong Bug Do. 1972. 202p./7. Chungcheong Nam
        Do. 1972. 262p./8. Jeonra Bug Do. 1972. 250p./9. Jeonra Nam Do.
        1972. 354p./10. Gyeongsang Bug Do. 1972. 398p./11. Gyeongsang Nam
        Do. 1972. 360p./12. Jeju Do. 1972. 120p. [PRC, E-W, OPR
                II. 10 percent sample survey. 1973.
    .2-2-1   Economic activity. iv, 391p. [E-W, OPR
    .2-2-2   Fertility. iv, 258p. [E-W, OPR
    .2-2-3   Internal migration. iv, 217p. [E-W, OPR
    .2-2-4   Housing. 219p. [E-W, OPR

        Korea (Republic). Bureau of Statistics.
1975.0-1   Preliminary count of population and housing census, as of Oct.
        1, 1975. [Seoul], 1976. 179p. [UN, BC, NYPL

        Korea (Republic). Bureau of Statistics.
    .1   Advance report of the 1975 population and housing census (based on
        a five percent sample survey). 1976. 322p. [E-W, NYPL

        Korea (Republic). National Bureau of Statistics.
        1975 population and housing census report. Seoul, 1977-1978.
        Vol. I-II in 15v.
                I. Complete enumeration. 1977.
    .2-1-1   Whole country. 1977. 368p. [E-W, OPR
1975.2-1-2 through 1975.2-1-12. 2. City of Seoul. 158p./3. Busan City. 99p./
        4. Gyeonggi Do. 222p./5. Gangweon Do. 161p./6. Chungcheongbug Do.
        134p./7. Chungcheongnam Do. 181p./8. Jeonlabug Do. 167p./9. Jeonla-
        nam Do. 228p./10. Gyeongsangbug Do. 267p./11. Gyeongsangnam Do.
        228p./12. Jeju Do. 85p. [E-W
                II. 5 percent sample survey. 1978.
    .2-2-1   Economic activity. 1978. 331p. specimen form. [OPR
    .2-2-2   Fertility. 1978. 351p. specimen form. [OPR
    .2-2-3   Internal migration and housing. 1978. 209p. specimen form.
        [OPR

KUWAIT

                                                    Capital: Kuwait City
State of Kuwait
Statistical Agency: Central Statistical Office
                     The Planning Board
                     P.O. Box 15
                     Kuwait City,
Publications Distributor: same

        Kuwait. Department of Social Affairs.
1957.1   [Population census, 1957]. [Arabic only].   Kuwait City, Govern-
        ment Printing Office, [1959?]. 364p. [UN

        Kuwait. Department of Social Affiars and Labour.
    .1a   Population census, 1957. [English version].   Kuwait City, Aueleia,
        1960. 364p. [PRC, BC, RPI

        Kuwait. Department of Social Affairs.
    .2   [Population census, 1957. Selected tables.] [Arabic only]. Ku-
        wait City, Government Printer, 1959. 7 tables. [UN

        Kuwait. Ministry of Social Affairs and Labour.
1961.0-1 [Population census, 21st of May 1961. Preliminary results.]   Ku-
        wait City, Government Press?, 1961. 112p. [UN

        Kuwait. Ministry of Social Affairs and Labour.
            Kuwait, census, 1961. General population census.   Kuwait City,
        1961. 2v.
    .1-1   I.

    .1-2   II.

        Kuwait. Central Statistical Office.
1965.1   [Results of the population census in Kuwait, 1965].   [Arabic only].
        Kuwait City, 1966. 368p. [

        Kuwait. Central Statistical Office.
            [Population census, 1970]. [Arabic only].   Kuwait City, 1972.
        2v.
1970.1-1   [National level]. [10], 455p. map. specimen forms. [PRC, UN
    .1-2   [Governates]. [8], 170p. [PRC, UN

        Kuwait. Central Statistical Office.
    .2   Population census, 1970. [English version].   Kuwait City, 1972.
        is, [2], 111p. specimen forms. [PRC, UN, PC, BC

        Kuwait. Central Statistical Office. Census Division.
            [Population census, 1975]. Kuwait City, 1976-1977. Vol. I-III.
        [Arabic only].
1975.1-1   I. [General tabulations]. 1976. [34], 543p. [PRC
    .1-2   II. [General tabulations]. 1976. [32], 357p. [PRC
    .1-3   III. [Detailed and general tabulations]. 1977. [23], 609p.
        [PRC

Kuwait. Central Statistical Office. Census Division.
.2   Population census, 1975. Kuwait City, 1977. ix, [4], 301p. specimen forms. [English translation and abstract of 3 volume Arabic version]. [PRC

LAOS

Lao People's Democratic Republic.   Capital: Vientiane.
Statistical Agency: National Statistical Service
                     [Service National de la Statistique]
                     Ministère du Plan et de la Coopération
                     Vientiane,
Publications Distributor: same

France. Direction de la Statis-
         tique Générale.
1946.1   "Superficie, population et   Area, population and population
          densité de la population des   density of the French Union coun-
          pays de l'Union française vers   tries around 1946. In: Statis-
          1946." In: Résultats statis-   tical results of the general
          tiques du recensement général   population census taken March 10,
          de la population effectué le 10   1946. Vol. I, De jure population.
          mars 1946. Vol. I, Population   [TXU, PRC, RPI
          légale.   Paris, 1948. Appen-
          dix, pp. 145-147.

France. Ministère de la France d'Outre-Mer. Service des Statistiques.
  .2   Les français d'origine métropolitaine...
          [See French Overseas Territories, No. 1946.2]

U.S. International Cooperation Administration.
1953.1   Census of population. Vientiane, U.S.O.M., 1956. 22p. [

Laos. Direction de la Statis-
       tique.
1959.1   Note sur la population du   Note on the population of Laos.
          Laos. [Vientiane], n.d. 5p.   [PRC

Laos. Direction de la Statis-
       tique.
          Estimation de la population   Population estiamtes in adminis-
          dans la circonscription adminis-   trative boundaries. Province of
          trative. Province de... [Vien-   ...
          tiane], 1956-1958. 5v.
1959.2-1 through 1959.2-5. 1. Attropeu. 1956. 12p./2. Saravane. 1956.
          21p./3. Savannakhet. 1956. 29p./4. Sayaboury. 1958. 14p./5. Xg
          Khouang. 1956. 26p. [PRC, RPI

Laos. Direction de la Statis-
       tique.
          Population officielle du   Official population of Laos.
          Laos. Province de... [Vien-   Province of...
          tiane], 1959-1960. 4v.
1959.3-1 through 1959.3-4. 1. Champassak. 1959. [1], 17p./2. Khammouane.
          1960. [23]p./3. Luang Prabang. 1960. [51]p./4. Vientiane. 1959.
          [1], 21p. [PRC, RPI

Laos.   Service de la Statistique.
1960.1   Estimation de la population
du Laos en 1960.   [Vientiane],
1961? 2p.

Population estimate of Laos in
1960.
[PRC

Laos.   Service de la Statistique.
1961.1   Population du Laos en 1961.
[Vientiane], 1962? 1p.

Population of Laos in 1961.
[PRC, RPI

Laos.   Service de la Statistique.
1962.1   Population officielle en Mai
1962.   [Vientiane], n.d. 1p.

Official population in May 1962.
[PRC, RPI

Laos.   Service National de la
          Statistique.
1967.1   Résultats provisoire du recensement de la population de la
ville de Luang Prabang en 1967.
Vientiane, 1968. 5p.

Provisional results of the population census of the city of Luang
Prabang in 1967.
[

Laos.   Service National de la
          Statistique.
.2   Recensement de la population
de la ville de Khammouane [and
other cities of Laos].   Vientiane, 1968. 23p.

Population census of the city of
Khammouane [and other cities of
Laos].
[

LEBANON

Republic of Lebanon.   Capital: Beirut.
Statistical Agency: Central Statistical Bureau
                      [Direction Central de la Statistique]
                      Ministère du Plan
                      Beirut,
Publications Distributor: same

The government has not taken a regular census since 1932.   There was
a partial census in 1942 for rationing purposes.   A study was made in
1958-59 by a demographic specialist from Princeton University.   The
latest sample survey, cited below, includes demographic data but ex-
cludes the Palestinians in refugee camps.

Lebanon.   Direction Central de
      la Statistique.
      L'enquête par sondage sur la   Sample survey of the economically
population active au Liban,   active population of Lebanon,
Novembre 1970.   Beirut, 1972.   November 1970.
Vol. 1-2.
1970.1-1   Méthodes, analyse et pre-   Methods, analysis and presenta-
sentation des résultats.   1972.   tion of the results.
203p.   map.   [OPR
.1-2   Tableaux des résultats.   Result tables.
580p.   [OPR

Lebanon.   Direction Central de
      la Statistique.
      Les movements migratoires au   Migratory movements in Lebanon.
Liban.   (Résultats d'une enquête   (Results of a survey on migrants
sur les migrants effectuée en   taken in 1971).
1971).   Beirut, 1974.   Parts I-
II in 4v.
1971.1-1   I.   Méthodes.   27p.   Methods.
                                            [OPR
          II.   Résultats.   Results.
.1-2-1   Caractéristiques des   Characteristics of migrants.
migrants.   30p.   [OPR
.1-2-2   Chronologie et itiné-   Chronology and itinerary of migra-
raire des migrations dans la vie   tions in the life of the migrants.
du migrants.   36p.   [OPR
.1-2-3   Les aspects socio-éco-   Socio-economic aspects of migra-
nomiques de la migration.   49p.   tion.
                                            [OPR

LESOTHO

Kingdom of Lesotho.   Capital: Maseru.
Statistical Agency: Bureau of Statistics
                     P.O. Box MS 455
                     Maseru,
Publications Distributor: same

        Basutoland Government.
1946.1   Basutoland census, 7th May 1946. Morija, Morija Printing Works,
        1951. 38p. [PRC, LC, NWU, RPI

        Basutoland. Census and Social Survey Office.
1956.1   1956 population census, 8th April 1956. Reported by D.H. Taylor,
        Census Officer. Maseru, 1958. vi, 118p. [PRC, LC, NWU, JB-F, RPI

        Lesotho. Bureau of Statistics.
          1966 population census report. Maseru, Government Printer, 1969-
          . Parts I-IV in Vol. I-III.
1966.1-1   I. Part I. Administrative, methodological and financial report.
        Pp. 1-81. Part II. Census tables. 1969. pp. 83-216. [PRC, NWU, RPI
  .1-2   II. Part III. Village lists, village populations and enumera-
        tion area population densities. 1971. 149p. [PRC, NWU, RPI
  .1-3   III. Part IV. Analytical report. [Not yet published].

        Lesotho. Bureau of Statistics.
          1976 population census reports. Maseru, Government Printer, 1977-
          . Vol. I-   in   v.
1976.1-1   I.

        II. Village list--Populations.
  .1-2-1   Alphabetical list and enumeration area population densities.
        1977. ix, 409p. map. [PRC

LIBERIA

Republic of Liberia.   Capital: Monrovia.
Statistical Agency: Bureau of Statistics
                      Ministry of Planning and Economic Affairs
                      P.O. Box 9016
                      Monrovia,
Publications Distributor: same

      Liberia. Bureau of Statistics.
         1962 population census of Liberia. Population characteristics of
      major areas.   Monrovia, 1964. Parts A and B in 13v.
             A. Area reports. Nos. A1–A12.
1962.1-A-1 through 1962.1-A-12. 1. Grand Bassa County. ii, xiii, 47p./2.
      Grand Cape Mount County. ii, xiii, 31p./3. Maryland County. ii,
      xiii, 37p./4. Montserrado County. ii, xiii, 57p./5. Sinoe County.
      ii, xiii, 26p./6. Central Province. ii, xiii, 66p./7. Eastern Pro-
      vince. ii, xiii, 26p./8. Western Province. ii, xiii, 46p./9. Kru
      Coast Territory. ii, xiii, 18p./10. Marshall Territory. ii, xiii,
      19p./11. River Cess Territory. ii, xiii, 18p./12. Sasstown Terri-
      tory. ii, xiii, 18p. [PRC, NWU, RPI
   .1-B   B. Summary report for Liberia. xvi, 31p. [PRC, NWU, RPI

      Liberia. Ministry of Planning and Economic Affairs.
1974.0-1   Administrative report of the 1974 census of population and
      housing. Monrovia, 1974. 68p. [NWU

      Liberia. Ministry of Planning and Economic Affairs.
         1974 census of population and housing. Population bulletins.
      Monrovia, 1975-   . Nos. 1-
   .1-1   Provisional population totals and demographic indices. 1975.
      a-c, xiii, 54p. [PRC, LC, NWU, OPR
   .1-2   Final population totals and related percentages with some sali-
      ent demographic characteristics. 1976. lxviii, 217p. maps. [PRC,
      PSC, UN, NWU, PC

      The next census may be taken in 1984.

LIBYA

Socialist People's Libyan Arab Jamahiriya. Capital: Tripoli
Statistical Agency: Census and Statistical Department
                    Ministry of Planning and Development
                    Tripoli,
Publications Distributor: same

Libya. Department of Census and Statistics.
1954.1   General population census of Libya, 1954. Report and tables.
Tripoli, 1959. 234p. [PRC, UN, RP]

Libya. Department of Census and Statistics.
.2   General population census of Libya, 1954. Final results--summary
tables. Tripoli, 1959. 114, 3p. [PRC, UN, RP]

Libya. Census and Statistical Department.
General population census, 1964. Tripoli, 1965. [Arabic only].
10v.
1964.1-1 through 1964.1-10. [One for each Muqata.] 1. Tripoli.   /
2. Benghazi.   /3. Sebha.   [4. Gebel Gharbi.
        /5. Zawia.   /6. Homs.   /7.
Misurata.   /8. Derna.   [/9. Gebel Akhdar.
        /10. Ubari.   [

Libya. Census and Statistical Department.
.2   General population census, 1964. Tripoli, [1965]. 86, xxxv p.
[PRC, NWU, RP]

Libya. Census and Statistical Department.
Population census papers. Tripoli, n.d. Nos. 1-3.
.3-1   Literacy in Libya. 4, 15, 2, 8p. [PRC, RP]
.3-2
.3-3   The labour force of Libya. 4, 32, 2, 18p. [PRC, RP]

Libya. Census and Statistical Department.
1973.0-1   [Preliminary results. Population.] [Arabic only].

.0-1a   Population census. [English version of 1973.0-1]. Tripoli,
1973. iv, 11p. [PRC, NWU
.0-2   [Preliminary results. Housing and establishments.] [Arabic
only].
.0-2a   Housing and establishment census. [English version of 1973.0-2]
[Tripoli], 1973. vi, [11]p. [PRC, NWU

Libya. Census and Statistical Department
.1   Population census, summary data. Tripoli, 1977. v, 32p. [

Libya. Census and Statistical Department.
[Census of population and housing. Results for Mohafadas.]
[Arabic only]. Tripoli,   . Nos. 1-10.

1973.2-1 through 1973.2-10.   1. Derna.   /2. Giabel El-Akhdar.
                    /3. Benghazi.   /4. El-Khalig.   /
   5. Misurata.   /6. Homs.   /7. Tripoli.
              /8. Zawia.   /9. Gharian.   /10.
   Sebha.   [

   Libya.   Census and Statistical Department.
       [Census of population and housing. Subject reports.] [Arabic only]
   Tripoli,
   .3-1

LIECHTENSTEIN

Principality of Leichtenstein.   Capital: Vaduz.
Statistical Agency: Statistical Office of the Principality of Liechtenstein
              [Amt für Statistik des Fürstentums Liechtenstein]
              FL-9490 Vaduz,
Publications Distributor: same

Liechtensteinisches Amt für Statistik. 1950.1 Volkszählung: 1. Dezember 1950. Vaduz, Fürstliche Regie- rung, 1953. xii, 51p.	Population census: December 1, 1950. [PRC, RPI
Liechtensteinisches Amt für Statistik. 1960.1 Liechtensteinische Volks- zählung, 1. Dezember 1960. Vaduz, Verlag Fürstliche Regie- rung, 1963. unpaged.	Liechtenstein population census, December 1, 1960. PRC, RPI, RIR
Liechtensteinisches Amt für Statistik. .2 Liechtensteinische Volks- zählung, 1. Dezember 1960. Haushaltungstatistik. Vaduz, Fürstliche Regierung, 1966. iv, 436p.	Liechtenstein population census, December 1, 1960. Household sta- tistics. [TXU

Liechtenstein. Amt für Statis-
     tik.
     Liechtensteinische Volks-
zählung. Vaduz, 1972-1975.
Bände 1-8.
	Liechtenstein population census.

1970.1-1 Gemeinden. Demographische Merkmale, Wirtschaftssektoren, Haushaltungen. 1972. 191p.	Communities. Demographic charac- teristics, Industrial sectors, Households. [PRC
.1-2 Familiennamen leichten- steinischer Staatsbürger mit Wohnsitz im Fürstentum Liechten- stein. Gebäude, Haushaltungen, Wohnungen und Personen nach Ortschaften. Pendelwanderung. 1972. 67p.	Family names of Liechtenstein citizens residing in the Princi- pality. Buildings, households, dwellings, and persons according to locality. Commuting. [PRC, LC
.1-3 Gebäude und Wohnungen. 1973. 68p.	Buildings and dwellings. [PRC
.1-4 Erwerb und Beruf. Sozio- ökonomische Gruppen. Gemeinden, Zählkreistabellen. 1974. 185p.	Earnings and occupation. Socio- economic groups. Communities, Census district tables. [PRC

1970.1-5   Heimat, Geburtsort. Wohn-   Homeland, birthplace. Place of
    ort vor 1, vor 5 Jahren (Binnen-   residence one and five years be-
    wanderung), Schulbildung. Ehe-   fore (Internal migration). Level
    frauen, Kinderzahl. 1975. 71p.   of education. Married women,
                                          number of children.
                                          [PRC

.1-6   Pendler, Arbeitsweg, Ver-   Commuter, journey to work, means
    kehrsmittel. 1975. 62p.   of transportation.
                                          [PRC

.1-7   Gebäude und Wohnungen.   Buildings and dwellings.
    1975. 65p.   [PRC
.1-8   Haushaltungen. 1975.   Households.
    151p.   [PRC

LUXEMBOURG

Grand Duchy of Luxembourg.   Capital: Luxembourg.
Statistical Agency: Central Office of Statistics and Economic Studies
                      [Service Central de la Statistique et des Études
                         Économiques (STATEC)]
                      Case Postale, No. 304
                      Luxembourg.
Publications Distributor: same.

Luxembourg. Office de la Sta-
    tistique Générale.
1947.1   Recensement de la population   Population census of December 31,
du 31 décembre 1947. Premiers   1947. First results and alpha-
résultats et liste alphabétique   betical list of places.
des localités. Esch-sur-Al-   [TXU
zette, Impr.-Relieur Henry Ney-
Etcher, [1948]. 90p. (Publication, fasc. 78).

Luxembourg. Office de la Sta-
    tistique Générale.
.2   Les activités au Grand-Duché   Economic activity in the Grand
de Luxembourg d'après le recen-   Duchy of Luxembourg according to
sement de la population du 31   the population census of December
décembre 1947. In: Bulletin   31, 1947.
du Service d'Études et de l'   [BC, PRC, RPI
Office de Statistique Générale,
Vol. I, no. 1-2, annexe. Luxembourg, 1950. Pp. 119-135.

Luxembourg. Office de la Sta-
    tistique Générale.
.3   La structure de la population   Composition of the population of
du Grand-Duché de Luxembourg d'   the Grand Duchy of Luxembourg
après le recensement de la popu-   according to the population cen-
lation du 31 décembre 1947.   sus of December 31, 1947. Sex,
Sexe, état civil, âge, natio-   marital status, age, nationality,
nalité, pays de naissance et   birthplace and religion.
culte. In: Bulletin du Service   [BC, PRC, RPI
d'Études et de l'Office de Sta-
tistique Générale, Vol. I, no.
4, annexe. Luxembourg, 1950.
pp. 331-370.

Luxembourg. STATEC.
    Recensement de la population   Population census of December 31,
du 31 décembre 1960. Luxem-   1960.
bourg, Impr. Bourg-Bourger,
1966-1968. (Bulletin Statistique, RP. 60). Vol. I-VI in 5v.

1960.1-1   I. Population, maisons
et ménages au 31.12.1960 par
communes, sections et localités
et tableaux rétrospectifs.
[1962]. 85p. (RP.60-I)

Population, houses and households
as of December 31, 1960, by communities, sections and places,
and retrospective tables.
[PRC, BC, RPI, RIR

.1-2   II. Caractéristiques per-
sonnelles de la population (sexe,
âge, état matrimonial, nationalité, lieu de naissance, culte).
1966. 47p. (RP.60-II)

Personal characteristics of the
population (sex, age, marital
status, nationality, birthplace,
religion).
[PRC, BC, RPI, RIR

.1-3   III. Caractéristiques
économiques de la population
(statut professionnel, activité,
profession principale, profession
accessoire, catégorie socio-économique). 1967. 124p. (RP.60-
III).

Economic characteristics of the
population (professional status,
industry, main occupation, secondary occupation, socio-economic
category).
[PRC, BC, RPI, RIR

.1-4   IV. Ménages et familles.
1967. 24p. (RP.60-IV).

Households and families.
[PRC, BC, RPI, RIR

.1-5&6   V. Maisons et logements.
VI. Méthodologie et législation.
1968. 103p. (RP.60-V-VI).

Houses and lodgings.
Methodology and legislation.
[PRC, BC, RPI, RIR

Luxembourg. STATEC.
1966.1   Recensement de la population
au 31 décembre 1966.   Luxembourg, 1968. 189p.

Population census of December 31,
1966.
[PRC

Luxembourg. STATEC.
     Recensement de la population
au 31 décembre 1970.   Luxembourg, 1974-1977. Vol. I-VI in
8v.

Population census of December 31,
1970.

1970.1-1   I. Caractéristiques per-
sonnelles de la population.
1974. 7, 155p.

Personal characteristics of the
population.
[PRC

.1-2   II. Caractéristiques
socio-économiques de la population. 1975. 16, 180p.

Socio-economic characteristics
of the population.
[PRC

.1-3&4   III. Ménages et familles.
IV. Logements et maisons. 1976.
118, 40p.

Households and families.
Lodgings and houses.
[PRC

.1-5   V. Rapports techniques.
Méthodologie et législation. Dépouillement mécanographique.
1976. iv, 115p.

Technical reports. Methodology
and legislation. Mechanical tabulation.
[PRC

     VI. Résultats par subdi-
vision territoriale. Fasc. A-D.

Results by territorial subdivi-
sion.

.1-6-A   Principaux résultats
et nomenclature des subdivisions
territoriales. 1976. 8, 49p.

Main results and list of territorial subdivisions.
[PRC

1970.1-6-B   Caractéristiques per-
        sonnelles et socio-economiques
        de la population. Ménages et
        familles. Logements et maisons.
        1976. 8, 106p.
  .1-6-C   Navetteurs (mobilité
        géographique de la main-d'oeuvre).
        1976. 9, 36p.
  .1-6-D   Statistiques autres
        que celles du recensement de la
        population. (Territoire et cli-
        mat, population, statistiques
        économiques, autres statistiques).
        1977. ix, 127p.

Personal and socio-economic
characteristics of the popula-
tion. Households and families.
Lodgings and houses.
[PRC
Commuters (geographic mobility
of the labor force).
[PRC

Statistics other than those of
the population census. (Territory and climate, population,
economic and other statistics).
[PRC

MACAO

Province of Macao (Portugal)   Capital: Macao.
Statistical Agency: Department of Statistical Services
                     [Repartição dos Serviços de Estatística]
                     Caixa Postal, No. 471
                     Macao,
Publications Distributor: same

Portugal. Instituto Nacional
    de Estatística.
1950.1   Censo da população do ultra-   Census of the overseas territories
mar de 1950: 5, Província de   of 1950: 5, Province of Macao.
Macau./Recensement des terri-   [
toires d'outre-mer de 1950: 5,
Province de Macao. In: Boletim mensal do INE, ano 23, No.
11.   Lisboa, 1961. Pp. 1–4.

Macao. Repartição Central dos
        Serviços de Administração
        Civil.
.2   Censo da população relativo   Census of population relative to
ao ano de 1950.   Macao, Impren-   the year 1950.
sa Nacional, 1953. viii, 75p.   [PRC, RPI

Macao. Repartição Provincial
        dos Serviços de Economia
        e Estatística Geral. Sec-
        ção de Estatística.
1960.1   X recenseamento geral da po-   Tenth general population census
pulação em Macau, Taipa e Colo-   in Macao, Taipa and Colombo (on
ane (em 15 de dezembro de 1960).   December 15, 1960).
Macao, Imprensa Nacional, 1962.   [PRC, BC, RPI
105p.

Portugal. Instituto Nacional
        de Estatística.
.2   A população de Macau segundo   The population of Macao according
o recenseamento de 1960 (nume-   to the census of 1960 (final num-
ros definitivos). In: Le bul-   bers).
letin mensuel, No. 1 de 1963.   [Harvard, RPI
[Lisboa], 1963. Pp. 1–4.

Portugal. INE. [and] Macao.
        Repartição Provincial
        dos Serviços de Estatís-
        tica.
1970.1   XI recenseamento geral da   Eleventh general population cen-
população e I recenseamento da   sus and first housing census, 1970.
habitação, 1970.   Portugal.   Portugal. Province of Macao.
Provincia de Macau.   Macao,   [PRC, JB-F, BC
Impr. Nacional, 1972. 84p.

MADAGASCAR

Democratic Republic of Madagascar.   Capital: Antananarivo.
Statistical Agency: National Institute of Statistics and Economic Research.
             [Institut National de la Statistique et de la Recherche
                Économique (INSRE)].
             Ministère des Finances
             B.P. No. 485
             Antananarivo,
Publications Distributor: same.

France. INSEE.
1946.1   Résultats du recensement de   Results of the 1946 census in
           1946 dans les territoires d'   the overseas territories (French
           outre-mer (français d'origine   of metropolitan origin and for-
           métropolitaine et étrangers):   eigners): Madagascar.
           Madagascar.   Paris, 1949. 56p.   [PRC, RPI
           (BMSOM, supplément série "sta-
           tistique," No. 9)

France. INSEE.
  .2   Les français d'origine métropolitaine...
         [See French Overseas Territories, no. 1946.2].

France. INSEE.
1951.1   Le recensement de la population non originaire...
         [See French Overseas Territories, No. 1951.1].

Madagascar. Service de Statis-
        tique Générale.
  .2   Résultats du recensement de   Results of the census of the non-
         la population non autochtone de   native population of Madagascar
         Madagascar et dépendances en   and dependancies in October 1951.
         octobre 1951.   Tananarive, 1955.   [PRC, RPI
         [2], vii, 46p.

Madagascar. Service de Statis-
        tique.
1960.1   Résultats globaux des recense-   Global results of the population
         ments de la population des six   censuses of six cities, provincial
         villes, chefs-lieux de province.   capitals.
         Tananarive, 1960.   p.   [
         (Bulletin mensuel de statistique,
         no. 63)

Madagascar. INSRE.
  .2   Recensements urbains. Chefs-   Urban censuses. Provincial capi-
         lieux de provinces: Tananarive--   tals: Tananarive--Majunga--Tama-
         Majunga--Tamatave--Diego Suarez--   tave--Diego Suarez--Fianarantsoa--
         Fianarantsoa--Tuléar.   Paris,   Tuléar.
         INSEE, 1966. 193p.   [PRC, NWU, RPI

Madagascar. INSRE.
    Recensements urbains. Tana-   Urban censuses.
narive, Impr. Nationale, 1965-
1966. 3v.
1964.1-1   Antsirabe--Ambatolampy--   (Province of Tananarive).
Arivonimamo. 1965. 59p.   [PRC, NWU, RPI
  .1-2   Ambositra--Ambalavao--   (Province of Fianarantsoa).
Monanjary--Manakara--Farafangana.   [PRC, RPI
1966. 75p.
  .1-3   Ambatondrazaka--Fénérive--   (Provinces of Tamatave, Tuléar,
Maroantsetra--Moramanga--Fort   Majunga and Diego Suarez).
Dauphin--Morombe--Morondava--   [PRC, NWU, RPI
Antalaha--Hell Ville--Sambava--
Marovoay. 1966. 176p.

Madagascar. INSRE.
1966.1   Enquête démographique, Mada-   Demographic survey, Madagascar,
gascar, 1966.   Tananarive, 1967.   1966.
169p.   [PRC, NWU

Madagascar. INSRE.
1970.1   Recensement des communes de   Census of the communes of Belazao,
Belazao, Ambano, Faratsiho (Pré-   Ambano, Faratsiho (prefecture of
fecture du Vakinankaratra): Re-   Vakinankaratra): test census for
censement-pilote en vue de la   the methodology conceived for the
mise au point de la méthodolo-   general census of the population
gie conçue pour le recensement   of Madagascar.
général de la population de Ma-   [NWU
dagascar.   Tananarive, 1972.
48p.

Publications from the 1975 census have not been seen as yet.

MALAWI

Republic of Malawi.   Capital: Lilongwe.
Statistical Agency: National Statistical Office
                     P.O. Box 333
                     Zomba,
Publications Distribution: same

Nyasaland. Superintendent of Census.
1945.1   Report on the census of 1945. Zomba, Government Printer, 1946.
18, [34]p. [PRC, LC, UN, NWU, RPI

Nyasaland and Rhodesia. Federation.
1956.1   Census of population, 1956. Salisbury, 1960. [3], 167p. 2 fold.
tables. specimen forms. [TXU, UN, RPI

Nyasaland and Rhodesia. Federation. Central Statistical Office.
     Preliminary results of the federal censuses of population, 1961,
employees. [Salisbury], 1962. 3v.
1961.0-1   Industrial and racial distribution of employees. 15p. [NWU,
     RPI
  .0-2   Detailed geographical distribution of the non-African population.
     27p. [NWU
  .0-3   Results of a 10 percent sample of the non-African census forms.
     [2], 13p. [NWU, RPI

Malawi. National Statistical Office.
1966.0-1   Malawi population census 1966. A methodological report, by G.T.
     Ngubola Kamwambe. Zomba, Government Printer, 1971. [PRC, NWU, RPI
  .0-2   Malawi population census 1966. Provisional report. Zomba,
     Government Printer, [1966]. [1], [95]p. 2 maps. [PRC, NWU, RPI

Malawi. Department of Census and Statistics.
  .1   Malawi population census 1966. Final report. Zomba, Government
     Printer, 1969. [iii], xviii, 142p. 3 maps. [PRC, NWU, RPI

Malawi. National Statistical Office.
     Malawi population census, 1966: ...district. Village population
by sex, age, race and education. Zomba, Government Printer, 1967.
22v.
1966.2-1 through 1966.2-22. 1. Chikwawa. 26p./2. Chiradzulu. 59p./3. Chi-
     tipa. 12p./4. Cholo. 30p./5. Dedza. 61p./6. Dowa. 60p./7. Fort
     Johnston. 60p./8. Lilongwe. 88p./9. Karonga. 13p./10. Kasungu. 38p./
     11. Kasupe. 65p./12. Mchinji. 27p./13. Mlanje. 58p./14. Mzimba.
     75p./15. Ncheu. 41p./16. Nkhata Bay. p./17. Nkhotakota. 18p./18.
     Nsange. 33p./19. Ntchisi. 30p./20. Rumpi. 19p./21. Salima. 27p./
     22. Zomba. 84p. [PRC, NWU

Malawi. National Statistical Office.
1972.1   Blantyre City population sample census, September 11-October 11,
     1972. Zomba, Government Printer, 1974. vi, 117p. [TXU, BC, JB-F,
     NWU

Malawi.   National Statistical Office.
  .2   Malawi population change survey, February 1970-January 1972.
     Zomba, Government Printer, 1973.   83p.   [NWU

Malawi.   National Statistical Office.
1973.0-1   Chiradzulu population pilot census, August 1973.   Zomba, Govern-
     ment Printer, 1974.   38p.   [NWU

Malawi.   [Department of the Registrar General]
1977.0-1   A guide to the population census, 1977.   [Zomba, Government
     Printer, 1977].   10p.   [

MALAYSIA

                                        Capital: Kuala Lumpur.
Statistical Agency: Department of Statistics.
                    [Jabatan Perangkaan]
                    Young Road
                    Kuala Lumpur 10-01,
Publications Distributor: Publication Section (of the above).

Malaya. [Superintendent of Census Office].
1947.1   A report on the 1947 census of population: comprising the Federation of Malaya [Malay Peninsula] and the Colony of Singapore. By M.
V. Del Tufo. Kuala Lumpur, Government Printer, 1949. 597p. maps.
[UN, PRC, OPR, E-W, RPI]

Sarawak. [Superintendent of Census Office].
.2   A report on the 1947 census. By J.L. Noakes. Kuching, 1950.
282p. [UN, PRC, TXU, RPI]

North Borneo [Sabah]. [Superintendent of Census Office].
1951.1   A report on the census of population held on 4th June, 1951. London, 1953. 237p. map. [UN, PRC, RPI]

Malaya. Department of Statistics.
1957.0-1   1957 population census of the Federation of Malaya. Manual of
enumeration procedure. [Kuala Lumpur], n.d. 49p. [UN, PRC, RPI]

Malaya. Superintendent of Census Office.
.0-2   The 1957 census. A preliminary report based on "first count
total" returns. By T.E. Smith. Kuala Lumpur, Government Printer,
1957. [2], 57p. [UN, PRC, RPI]

Malaya. Department of Statistics.
    1957 population census of the Federation of Malaya [Malay Peninsula].
By J.M.N.H. Fell, Superintendent of Census. Kuala Lumpur, 1958-1960.
14 reports.
.1-1   Distribution of population by race and sex for states, mukims,
municipalities, town boards, local councils, etc. 1958. ii, 61p.
[UN, PRC, TXU, RPI]
1957.1-2 through 1957.1-12. 2. Selangor. 1959. [viii], 83p./3. Penang.
1959. [viii], 79p./4. Kedah. 1959. [vii], 86p./5. Malacca. 1959.
[vii], 74p./6. Jahore. 1959. [vii], 89p./7. Negri Sembilan. 1959.
[vi], 77p./8. Perak. 1959. [vi], 95p./9. Pahang. 1959. [vii], 77p./
10. Kelantan. 1959. [vi], 83p./11. Trengganu. 1959. [vi], 75p./12.
Perlis. 1959. [vi], 66p. [UN, PRC, TXU, RPI]
.1-13   Administrative report. n.d. [ii], 237p. [UN, PRC, RPI]
.1-14   Final report. (Summary tables for the Federation, with general
comments on the census). 1960. [5], 181p. [UN, PRC, TXU, RPI]

North Borneo [Sabah]. Superintendent of Census Office.
1960.0-1   Census of population, 1960. Manual of enumeration procedure.
By L.W. Jones. [Kuching], n.d. 29p. specimen forms. [PRC, RPI]

North Borneo [Sabah]. Superintendent of Census Office.
.1-1   Report on the census of population taken on 10th August, 1960.
By L.W. Jones.   Kuching, Government Printing Office, 1962.   iii, 305p.
2 maps. [PRC, RPI
.1-2   Additional tables.   n.d.   35p.   [PRC, RPI

Sarawak. Superintendent of Census Office.
.2-1   Report on the census of population taken on 15th June, 1960.
By L.W. Jones.   Kuching, Government Printing Office, 1962.   iii, 337p.
2 maps. [PRC, RPI
.2-2   Additional tables.   1962.   56p.   [PRC, RPI

Malaysia. Jabatan Perangkaan.
    Banchi pendudok dan perumahan   1970 population and housing cen-
Malaysia 1970.   Kuala Lumpur,   sus of Malaysia.
1971-1973.
1970.1-1   Rengkasun kiraan luar.   Field count summary.
1971. vi, 109p. maps.   [PRC, BC
.1-2   Kawasan bandaran gabungan   Urban conurbations--population and
--penduduk dan isirumah dolam   household in ten gazetted towns
sepuluh buah bandar yang diwarta-   and their adjoining built-up
kan dan kawasan-kawasan tepubina   areas.
bergabung dengannya. 1971. vi,   [BC
30p. 10 maps.
.1-3   Gulongan masharakan. 1972.   Community groups.
vi, 292p. map.   [PRC, BC
.1-4   Pembahagian umur. 1973.   Age distributions.
viii, 198p. maps.   [PRC, BC, LC

Malaysia. Jabatan Perangkaan.
    Banci penduduk dan perumahan   1970 population and housing cen-
Malaysia, 1970. Jilid I. Jadual-   sus of Malaysia. Vol. I. Basic
jadual asas penduduk.   Kuala   population tables.
Lumpur, 1974-1976. 13 parts.
1970.2-1 through 1970.2-13. [All have maps.] 1. Perlis. 1978. ix, 313 p./
2. Penang & Province Wellesley. 1975. ix, 435p./3. Malacca. 1977.
ix, 435 p./4. Negri Sembilan. 1977. ix, 435p./5. Selangor. 1975.
ix, 437p./6. Pahang. 1976. ix, 377p./7. Trengganu. 1977. ix, 377p./
8. Kelantan. 1976. ix, 375p./9. Kedah. 1977. ix, 375 p./10. Perak.
1975. ix, 437p./11. Johore. 1976. viii, 435p./12. Sabah. 1976.
viii, 527p./13. Sarawak. 1976. x, 547p. [BC, OPR, PRC

Malaysia. Jabatan Perangkaan.
    Lapuran am. Banci penduduk   General report. Population cen-
Malaysia, 1970. Kuala Lumpur,   sus of Malaysia.
1975-1977. Vol. I-II.
.3-1   I. 1977. xliii, 518p.   [PRC, JB-F
.3-2   II. 1975. ix, 430p.
maps. specimen forms.   [PRC, JB-F

Malaysia. Jabatan Perangkaan.
Banchi pendudok dan perumahan
Malaysia, 1970.   Kuala Lumpur,
1971-1973. Vo. I-II in 25v.

1970 population and housing census of Malaysia.

I. Jadual^2 'am perumahan.
1971-1972. 11 parts.

General housing tables. [The 11
West Malaysian states.]

1970.4-1-1 through 1970.4-1-11. [All have maps.] 1. Perlis. 1971. viii,
74p./2. Penang and Province Wellesley. 1972. viii, 109p./3. Malacca.
1972. viii, 109p./4. Negri Sembilan. 1972. viii, 113p./5. Selangor.
1972. viii, 117p./6. Pahang. 1972. viii, 105p./7. Trengganu. 1972.
viii, 101p./8. Kelantan. 1972. viii, 103p./9. Perak. 1972. viii,
116p./10. Kedah. 1972. viii, 105p./11. Johore. 1972. viii, 111p./
[PRC, BC

II. Jadual^2 'am perumahan,
bandar^2, kampang^2 dan kawasan^2
majlis tempatan. 1972-1973. 13
parts in 14v.

General housing tables, towns,
villages, and local council areas.
[The 11 West Malaysian states and
the 2 East Malaysian states].

1970.4-2-1 through 1970.4-2-12. [All have maps.] 1. Perlis. 1972. viii,
85p./2. Penang and Province Wellesley. 1972. xx, 413p./3. Malacca.
1972. xiv, 249p./4. Negri Sembilan. 1972. xxiv, 495p./5. Selangor.
1972. xxiv, 567p./6. Pahang. 1972. xx, 413p./7. Trengganu. 1972.
xviii, 331p./8. Kelantan. 1972. xx, 413p./9-1. Perak. 1973. xxx,
320p./9-2. Perak. pp. 323-731./10. Kedah. 1973. xxiv, 495p./11.
Johore. 1973. xxiv, 567p./13-1. Sarawak. 1973. viii, 198p./13-2.
Sabah. 1973. viii, 113p. [PRC, BC

Malaysia. Jabatan Perangkaan.
.5   Banchi perumahan 1970. Malaysia barat laporan akhir.   Kuala
Lumpur, 1973. viii, 183p. maps.

West Malaysia census of housing,
1970. Final report.
[PRC, BC

Malaysia. Jabatan Perangkaan.
.6   Lapuran perantaraan mengenui
penyiasatan selepas banci. Kuala
Lumpur, 1973. vi, 8p.

An interim report on the Post
Enumeration Survey.
[PRC, BC

Malaysia. Jabatan Perangkaan.
[Special reports].

.7-1

Internal migration

.7-2

Manpower

.7-3

Fertility and mortality

.7-4

Census map atlas.

Malaysia. Jabatan Perangkaan.
Kertas penyelidekan.   Kuala
Lumpur, 19754-   . No. 1-   .

Research reports.

1970.8–1   Unjuran penduduk dalam tahun setahun Malaysia, 1970–1990. 1975. xvii, 91p.

Population projections in single years, 1970–1990.
[PRC

.8–2

.8–3

.8–4

.8–5

.8–6

.8–7

.8–8   Jangkaan hidup bekerja di semenanjung Malaysia, 1970. 1974. ix, 55p.

The expectation of working life in Peninsula Malaysia, 1970.
[TXU, BC

.8–9

.8–10

.8–11

.8–12

.8–13   Punca-punca Penawaren tenaga Buruh-Sekarang dan masa hadapan. 1978. viii, 115p.

Sources of labour supply--present and future.
[OPR

.8–14   Corak kegunaan tenaga buruh di semenanjung Malaysia. 1978. v, 83p.

The pattern of labour utilization in Peninsular Malaysia.
[OPR

MALDIVE ISLANDS

Republic of Maldives   Capital: Malé
Statistical Agency: Department of Information, Broadcasting and Tourism
                          Malé,
Publications Distributor: same

Ceylon. Superintendent of Census.
1946.1   Census of the Maldive Islands, 1946. [Provisional results]. In: Ceylon Government gazette, No. 9612, October 11, 1946. [Colombo], 1946. 1p. [UN

Note: From 1955-1974 there were Annual reports of population. [EB

[Maldives].
1966.1   Population statistics of the Maldive Islands. n.p., 1967. 31p. [Contains population totals in year groups, 1962-1966]. [UN, PRC, RPI

The Population and Housing Census of Maldives was taken 30 December 1977/1 January 1978. No publications have been seen as yet.

MALI

Republic of Mali.   Capital: Bamako
Statistical Agency: Division of Statistics and National Accounts.
                    [Division de la Statistique et de la Comptabilité
                        Nationale]
                    Ministère de l'Économie Rurale et du Plan
                    Bamako-Koulouba,
Publications Distributor: same

        France. INSEE [and] Service Colonial des Statistiques.
1946   Résultats du recensement de 1946...
            [See French Overseas Territories, Nos. 1946.1-1, 2 and 3.]

        France. INSEE [and] Ministère de la France d'Outre-Mer.
1946   Les français d'origine métropolitaine...
            [See French Overseas Territories, No. 1946.2]

        France. INSEE.
1951   Le recensement de la population...
            [See French Overseas Territories, No. 1951.1.]

        French West Africa. Service de la Statistique Générale.
1951   Recensement de la population non autochtone...
            [See French Overseas Territories, No. 1951.2.]

        French West Africa. Haut-Commissariat Général.
1956   Premiers résultats définitifs du recensement...
            [See French Overseas Territories, No. 1956.1.]

        Mali. Direction de la Statis-
                tique.
            Enquête démographique dans   Demographic survey in the Central
        le Delta Central Nigérien.   Nigerian Delta.
        Paris, 1963. Fasc. 1-2.
1958.1-1   Résultats sommaires. 45p.   Summary results.
                                                 [NWU, RPI
    .1-2   Résultats détaillés.   Detailed results.
        203p.   [NWU, RPI

        French West Africa. Service de
                la Statistique Générale
    .2   Enquête démographique, 1957-   Demographic survey, 1957-1958.
        1958. Paris, 1958. 38p.   [OPR

        France. INSEE.
1961.1   Bamako. Recensement, 1958.   Bamako. Census, 1958. Demogra-
        Enquête démographique, 1960-61.   phic survey, 1960-61. Final
        Résultats définitifs. Paris,   results.
        1969. [12], 48, [4], 49p.   [NWU, RPI

Mali.   Service de la Statistique
          Générale et de la Mecano-
          graphie.
1961.2   Enquête démographique au Mali,   Demographic survey in Mali, 1960-
          1960-1961.   Paris, INSEE, 1969.   1961.
          349p.   [NWU, OPR, RPI

Mali.   Service de la Statistique
          et de la Comptabilité Eco-
          nomique Nationale.
1966.0-1 Recensement, Ville de Bamako,   Census, City of Bamako, 1965-1966:
          1965-1966: rapport provisoire.   provisional report.
          Bamako, 1967.   p.   [

Mali.   Bureau Central de Recense-
          ment.
1976.0-1 Recensement général de la   General population census of Mali
          population du Mali (1er au 16   (December 1-16, 1976): provision-
          décembre 1976): résultats pro-   al results.
          visoires.   Koubouba, 1977.   [
                p.

MALTA

Republic of Malta.   Capital: Valletta
Statistical Agency: Central Office of Statistics and Electoral Office
                     Auberge de Castille
                     Valletta,
Publications Distributor: Department of Information
                          (of the above).

Malta. Office of Statistics.
1948.1   Eleventh census of the Maltese Islands, 1948, taken on Monday, 14th
     June 1948 under the authority of Act LL of 1948. Valletta, Progress
     Press Co., 1949. [7], xxiv, 447p. [PRC, BC, RPI

Malta. Central Office of Statistics.
          Census of 1957, the Maltese Islands. Valletta, 1959. 3v.
1957.1-1   Report on population and housing. [3], xcviii, [1], 276p. [BC,
     PRC, RPI, RIR
  .1-2   Report on economic activities. [8], cvii, 318p. [BC, PRC, RPI
     RIR
  .1-3   General report. [Never published.]

Malta. Central Office of Statistics.
  .2   1957 census silhouette of the Maltese Islands. Valletta, 1959.
     [9], 30p. [TXU, BC, RPI, RIR

Malta. Census Office.
          Malta census, 1967. Census of population, housing and employment
     taken on 26th November 1967. Valletta, 1969-   . 3 parts in 4v.
1967.1-1   Report on housing characteristics. 1969. [vi], 500p. maps.
     [PRC, UN, RPI
          Report on economic activities. n.d. Vol. I-II.
  .1-2-1   I. lxxix, 471p. [PRC
  .1-2-2   II. 461p. [PRC
  .1-3   Report on population. [Never published.]

MARTINIQUE

Department of Martinique (France)   Capital: Fort-de-France.
Statistical Agency: INSEE - Departmental Service of Martinique.
                     [INSEE - Service Départemental de la Martinique.]
                     B.P. No. 605
                     Fort-de-France,
Publications Distributor: INSEE - Observatoire Economique de Paris
                           195, rue de Bercy--Tour Gamma A
                           75582 Paris, Cedex 12, FRANCE

Martinique. Service de la
          Statistique.
1946.1   Les tableaux de la population   Population tables of Martinique
de la Martinique en 1946. In: in 1946.
Journal Officiel de la Martini-   [UFL, PRC, RPI
que, 17 octobre 1946. Pp. 955-
962.

France. INSEE [and] Ministère de la France d'Outre-Mer.
  .2   Les français d'origine métropolitaine...
         [See French Overseas Territories, No. 1946.2.]

France. INSEE [and] Service
          Colonial des Statistiques.
  .3   Recensement de la population   Census of the population of Mar-
de la Martinique en 1946. Paris,   tinique in 1946.
1947. 34p. (Bulletin mensuel   [Yale, PRC, RPI
des statistiques coloniales,
supplément série "études,", No.
13).

France. INSEE [and] Service
          Colonial des Statistiques.
  .4   Résultats du recensement de   Results of the census of 1946 in
1946 dans les territories d'   the overseas territories (French
outre-mer (français d'origine   of metropolitan origin and for-
métropolitaine et étrangers):   eigners): Martinique.
Martinique.   Paris, 1948. 34,   [Yale, PRC, RPI
[2]p. (BMSOM, supplément série
"statistique," No. 5).

France. INSEE.
1954.1   Résultats statistiques du   Statistical results of the general
recensement général de la popu-   census of the population of the
lation des départements d'outre-   overseas departments taken July 1,
mer effectué le 1er juillet 1954:   1954: French Antilles: Martini-
Antilles françaises: Martinique   que and Guadeloupe.
et Guadeloupe.   Paris, Impre.   [UN, PRC, RPI
Nationale, 1956. 300p.

France.   INSEE.
1961.1   Résultats statistiques du
recensement général de la population des départements d'outre-
mer effectué le 9 octobre 1961:
Martinique.   Paris, Impr. Nationale, 1965.   182p.

Statistical results of the general
census of the population of the
overseas departments taken October
9, 1961: Martinique.
[BC, PRC, RPI

France.   INSEE.
1967.1   Population des départements
d'outre-mer d'après le recensement de 1967.   Répartititon par
commune de la population.
Paris, 1968.   p.

Population of the overseas departments according to the census of
1967.   Distribution by commune of
the population.
[

France.   INSEE.
.2   Résultats statistiques du
recensement général de la population des départements d'outre-
mer effectué le 16 octobre 1967.
1re partie: tableaux statistiques: Martinique.   Paris, Impr.
nationale, 1970.   134p.

Statistical results of the general
census of the population of the
overseas departments taken October
16, 1967.   1st part: statistical
tables: Martinique.
[UN, PRC, RPI

France.   INSEE.
1974.1   Recensement général de la
population en 1974 des départements d'outre-mer.   Paris,   .
          p.

General census of the population
in 1974 of the overseas departments.
[

France.   INSEE.
.2   Résultats définitifs de la
population des départements d'
outre-mer d'après le recensement de 1974.   Paris,   .
          p.

Final results of the population
of the overseas departments according to the census of 1974.
[

France.   INSEE.
.3   Recensement général de la
population de la France, départements d'outre-mer: arrondissements, communes.   Paris, 1976.
29p.

General census of population of
France, overseas departments:
districts, communes.
[

MAURITANIA

Islamic Republic of Mauritania.   Capital: Nouakchott.
Statistical Agency: Bureau of Statistics and Economic Studies
                     [Direction de la Statistique et des Études Économiques]
                     B.P. No. 240
                     Nouakchott,
Publications Distributor: same

1946   France. INSEE [and] Service Colonial des Statistiques.
        Résultats du recensement de 1946...
        [See French Overseas Territories, Nos. 1946.1-1, 2 and 3.]

1946   France. INSEE [and] Ministère de la France d'Outre-Mer.
        Les français d'origine métropolitaine...
        [See French Overseas Territories, No. 1946.2.]

1951   France. INSEE.
        Le recensement de la population non originaire...
        [See French Overseas Territories, No. 1951.1.]

1951   French West Africa. Service de la Statistique Générale.
        Recensement de la population non autochtone...
        [See French Overseas Territories, No. 1951.2.]

        French West Africa. Service de
           la Statistique Générale.
1954.0-1   Mauritanie: population   Mauritania: population in 1954
        en 1954 par canton et groupe   by canton and ethnic group (pro-
        éthnique (chiffres provisoires).   visional figures).
        Dakar, 1954. 19p.   [

        Mauritania. Service de la Sta-
           tistique.
1962.1   Démographie des principales   Demography of main cities in 1961-
        villes en 1961-62. Nouakchott,   1962.
        1963. In: Bulletin de statis-   [
        tique et économique, No. 1.
        Pp. 4-13.

        Mauritania. Service de la Sta-
           tistique.
  .2   Recensement démographique des   Demographic census of the agglo-
        agglomerations (27 principaux   merations (27 principal centers
        centres de la République Islami-   of the Islamic Republic of Mauri-
        que de Mauritanie) enquête 1961-   tania), survey 1961-62.
        62. Nouakchott, 1964. 91p.   [
        (Bulletin statistique et écono-
        mique, No. 3).

Mauritania. Ministère des Fi-
        nances, du Plan et de la
        Fonction Publique.
1965.0-1   Enquête démographique,   Demographic survey, 1964-1965:
    1964-1965: généralités--métho-   generalities--methodology, pro-
    dologie, résultats provisoires.   visional results.
    [Edited by] J. Branez.   Paris,   [NWU
    SEDES, 1966. 240p. specimen
    forms.

Mauritania. Ministère des Fi-
        nances, du Plan et de la
        Fonction Publique.
    Enquête démographique en   Demographic survey in Mauritania,
Mauritanie, 1964-1965.   Paris,   1964-1965.
INSEE & SEDES, 1972. 2v.
    .1-1   Méthodologie. 165p.   Methodology.
                                       [NWU
    .1-2   Résultats définitifs. Final results.
        327p.   [NWU

Mauritania. Bureau Central du
        Recensement de la Popula-
        tion.
1976.0-1   Résultats provisoires Provisional general results of
    généraux du recensement général   the general census of population.
    de la population.   Nouakchott,   [
    [1977]. 23p.

Mauritania. Bureau Central du
        Recensement de la Popula-
        tion.
    .0-2   Seconds résultats provi-   Second provisional results of
    soires du recensement général   the general census of population.
    de la population.   Nouakchott,   [
    1977. 54p.

MAURITIUS

Capital: Port Louis.
Statistical Agency: Central Statistical Office.
                    Rose Hill,
Publications Distributor: Government Printing Office
                          Elizabeth II Avenue
                          Port Louis,

Mauritius. Central Statistical Office.
     Census 1952 of Mauritius and its dependencies. Port Louis, H.F.
Kelly, Acting Government Printer, 1953. Parts I-III.
1952.1-1   I. Population: density, urban and rural distribution, ethnical
     constitution, sex distribution, ages, marital status, birthplaces,
     nationalities, religions, villages and hamlets population, dependen-
     cies. 39p. [PRC, LC, NWU, RPI
  .1-2   II. Population: languages, education, occupations and activi-
     ties, industrial distribution and status, households, fertility. 40p.
     [PRC, LC, NWU, RPI
  .1-3   III. Housing of private households; buildings in relation to
     economic activity; establishments and enterprises. 21p. [PRC, LC,
     NWU, RPI

Mauritius. Central Statistical Office.
     1962 population census of Mauritius and its dependencies. Port
Louis, Government Press, 1964. Vol. I-II.
1962.1-1   I. [Demographic, social and economic characteristics of Mauri-
     tius and Rodrigues.] 66p. forms. [NWU, PRC
  .1-2   II. [Population by localities, households and families, build-
     ings, dwellings and housing conditions.] [3], 75, 4p. [NWU, PRC

Mauritius. Central Statistical Office.
     1972 housing and population census of Mauritius. [Port Louis],
Government Printer, 1974-1976. Vol. I-VI.
1972.1-1   I. 1972 population census of Mauritius. Preliminary report.
     1974. viii, 58p. specimen form. [PRC, NWU
  .1-2   II. 1972 housing census of Mauritius. Preliminary report.
     1974. 38p. [NWU
  .1-3   III. 1972 housing and population census of Mauritius--Island
     of Rodrigues. [Final results]. 1975. 91p. [NWU
  .1-4   IV. 1972 housing and population census of Mauritius--Island of
     Mauritius. Housing [Final results]. 1975. v, 231p. [PRC
  .1-5   V. 1972 housing and population census of Mauritius--Island of
     Mauritius. Population--General tables. [Final results]. 1976. ix,
     196p. specimen forms. [PRC, NWU
  .1-6   VI. 1972 housing and population census of Mauritius. Popula-
     tion. Population in constituencies. 1976. ii, 22p. [PRC, NWU

     The next census is proposed for 1982.

MEXICO

United Mexican States   Capital: Mexico, D.F.
Statistical Agency: General Bureau of Statistics
                     [Dirección General de Estadística (DGE)]
                     Secretaria de Programación y Presupuesto
                     Balderal 71/Agencia de Correos 245
                     México, D.F. 1,
Publications Distributor: same.

Mexico. Dirección General de
    Estadística.
1950.1   Integración territorial de   Territorial division of Mexico:
los Estados Unidos Mexicanos: Seventh general population cen-
Séptimo censo general de pob-   sus.
lación. México, 1950. 734p.   [TXU, PRC, UN, RPI

Mexico. DGE.
 .2   Memoria de los censos gene-   Report of the general censuses
rales de población, agrícola,   of population, agriculture, live-
ganadero y ejidal, 1950.   stock and public land, 1950.
México, 1952. 542p.   [TXU, PRC, Yale, RPI

Mexico. DGE.
    Séptimo censo general de   Seventh general population cen-
población, 6 de junio de 1950.   sus, June 6, 1960.
Mexico, Talleres Gráficos de
la Nación, 1952-1953. 33v.
1950.3-1 through 1950.3-32. [All are Estados except where noted.] 1. Aguascalientes. 1952. 51p./2. Baja California Territorio Norte. 1952.
44p./3. Baja California Territorio Sur. 1952. 54p./4. Campeche. 1952.
54p./5. Coahuila. 1952. 116p./6. Colima. 1952. 57p./7. Chiapas.
1952. 274p./8. Chihuahua. 1952. 189p./9. Distrito Federal. 1953.
92p./10. Durango. 1952. 128p./11. Guanajuato. 1952. 159p./12. Guerrero. 1952. 191p./13. Hidalgo. 1952. 195p./14. Jalisco. 1952.
332p./15. México. 1953. 257p./16. Michoacan. 1952. 264p./17. Morelos. 1953. 93p./18. Nayarit. 1953. 73p./19. Nuevo Leon. 1953.
166p./20. Oaxaca. 1953. 810p./21. Puebla. 1953. 404p./22. Querétaro.
1952. 69p./23. Territorio de Quintana Roo. 1953. 43p./24. San Luis
Potosí. 1953. 156p./25. Sinaloa. 1952. 100p./26. Sonora. 1953.
171p./27. Tabasco. 1952. 121p./28. Tamaulipas. 1953. 138p./29.
Tlaxcala. 1953. 101p./30. Veracruz. 1953. 427p./31. Yucatán. 1953.
226p./32. Zacatecas. 1953. 155p. [PRC, TXU, BC, RPI
 .3-33   Resumen general. 1953.   General resume.
264p.   [PRC, TXU, RPI

Mexico. DGE.
 .4   Séptimo censo general de pob-   Seventh general population cen-
lación, 6 de junio de 1950.   sus, June 6, 1950. Special part.
Parte especial. [Tables 35-43].   [BC, PRC, RPI
n.p., n.d. Pp. [3]-303, [1]p.

Mexico. DGE.
1960.1 VIII censo general de población, 1960, 8 de junio de 1960.
Resumen general. Mexico, 1962.
li, 652, [2]p.
.1a Población económicamente
activa. (Rectificación a los
cuadros 25, 26 and 27 del Resumen general ya publicado). 1964.
iii, 74p.

Eighth general population census,
1960. June 8, 1960. General
resume.
[PRC, TXU, RPI
Economically active population.
(Correction to Tables 25, 26 and
27 of the General resume, already
published).
[PRC, RPI

Mexico. DGE.
VIII censo general de pobla-
ción, 1960. 8 de junio de 1960.
México, Talleres Gráficos de la
Nación, 1963-1964. 32 parts in
35v.

Eighth general population census,
1960. June 8, 1960.

1960.2-1 through 1960.2-32. [All are Estados except where noted.] 1. Aguascalientes. 1963. xix, 105p./2. Baja California [Norte]. 1963.
120p./3. Baja California Territorio [Sur]. 1964. 147p./4. Campeche.
1963. 145p./5. Coahuila. 1963. 384p./6. Colima. 1963. 148p./7.
Chiapas. 1963. 905p./8. Chihuahua. 1963. 615p./9. Distrito Federal. 1963. 297p./10. Durango. 1963. xix, 353p./11. Guanajuato.
1963. 448p./12. Guerrero. 1963. 646p./13. Hidalgo. 1964. 502p./
14. Jalisco. 1963. xix, 1005p./15. México. 1963. 1007p./16. Michoacan. 1963. xix, 892p./17. Morelos. 1963. xix, 268p./18. Nayarit.
1963. xix, 186p./19. Nuevo Leon. 1964. 492p./20-1. Oaxaca. 1963.
xxvi, 1192p./20-2. Oaxaca. 1963. xxvi, pp. 1193-2384./21-1. Puebla.
1963. xix, 842p./21-2. Puebla. 1963. xxiii, pp. 843-1540./22. Querétaro. 1963. xix, 183p./23. Quintana Roo, Territorio. 1963. xix,
63p./24. San Luis Potosí. 1963. xx, 461p./25. Sinaloa. 1964. 240p./
26. Sonora. 1963. xxi, 585p./27. Tabasco. 1963. 378p./28. Tamaulipas. 1963. xx, 380p./29. Tlaxcala. 1963. 377p./30-1. Veracruz.
1964. 840p./30-2. Veracruz. 1964. 701p./31. Yucatán. 1963. xix,
779p./32. Zacatecas. 1963. xx, 451p. [PRC, TXU, BC, RPI

Mexico. DGE.
VIII censo general de población, 1960. Localidades de la
República par entidades federa-
tivas y municipios. Mexico,
1963. Tomo I-II.
.3-1 I. [Aguascalientes through
Nayarit.] 788p.
.3-2 II. [Nuevo Leon through
Zacatecas.] 801p.

Eighth general population census,
1960. Localities of the Republic
by federal entities and municipalities (counties).

[PRC, TXU, UN, RPI

[PRC, TXU, UN, RPI

Mexico. DGE.
.4 Ingresos por trabajo de la
población económicamente activa
y jefes de familia (VIII censo
de población de 1960). Mexico,
1964. [6], 40p.

Income from work of the economically active population and heads
of families. (Eighth population
census, 1960).
[UN, PRC, RPI

Mexico. DGE.
.5   Memoria de los censos nacio-   Report on the national censuses,
nales, 1960-61. Mexico, 1965.   1960-61.
297p.   [PRC, RPI

Mexico. DGE.
1970.0-1   IX censo general de pobla-   Ninth general population census.
ción. Manual de empadronamiento.   Enumerator's manual. Housing
Cuestionario para una vivienda.   schedule.
México, D.F., 1969. 61p. spe-   [PRC
cimen forms.
.0-2   ... Catálogo mexicano de   ... Mexican catalog of occupa-
ocupaciones. (C-4-0). México,   tions.
D.F., 1970.   p.   [IASI
.0-3   ..., 28 de enero de 1970.   ..., January 28, 1970. Prelimi-
Datos preliminares sujetos a   nary data subject to correction.
rectificación. México, D.F.,   [TXU
1970. 55p.

Mexico. DGE.
.1   IX censo general de población,   Ninth general population census,
con datos sobre la vivienda, 28   with data on housing, January 28,
de enero de 1970. Resumen de   1970. Summary of the main char-
las principales características   acteristics by federal entity.
por entidad federativa. Mexico,   [PRC
1970. xxx, 448p.

Mexico. DGE.
.2   IX censo general de población,   Ninth general population census,
(28 de enero 1970). Resumen   1970. (January 28, 1970). Abre-
general abreviado. México, D.   viated general resume.
F., 1972. xxxv, 327, [19]p.   [PRC

Mexico. DGE.
IX censo general de población,   Ninth general population census,
1970. (28 de enero de 1970).   1970. (January 28, 1970). State
Estado de... México, D.F.,   of...
1971. 32 parts in 33v.
1970.3-1 through 1970.3-32. [All are Estados except where noted.] 1. Aguascalientes. lxxxiii, 170, [19]p./2. Baja California. lxxxiii, 149,
[19]p./3. Baja California, Territorio de. lxxxiii, 166, [19]p./4.
Campeche. lxxxiii, 166, [19]p./5. Coahuila. lxxxiii, 308, [19]p./6.
Colima. lxxxiii, 176, [19]p./7. Chiapas. lxxxiii, 659, [19]p./8.
Chihuahua. lxxxiii, 447, [19]p./9. Distrito Federal. lxxxiii, 247,
[19]p./10. Durango. lxxxiii, 312, [19]p./11. Guanajuato. lxxxiii,
361, [19]p./12. Guerrero. lxxxiii, 478, [19]p./13. Hidalgo. lxxxiii,
534, [19]p./14. Jalisco. lxxxiii, 740, [19]p./15. México. lxxxiii,
721, [19]p./16. Michoacan. lxxxiii, 685, [19]p./17. Morelos. lxxxiii,
285, [19]p./18. Nayarit. lxxxiii, 214, [19]p./19. Nuevo Leon. lxxxiii, 368, [19]p./20-1. Oaxaca. lxxxiii, 267p./20-2. Oaxaca. xli,
611p./21. Puebla. lxxxiii, 1157, [19]p./22. Querétaro. lxxxiii, 214,
[19]p./23. Quintana Roo, Territorio de. lxxxiii, 149, [19]p./24. San

Luis Potosí. lxxxiii, 397, [19]p./25. Sinaloa. lxxxiii, 208, [19]p./
26. Sonora. lxxxiii, 447, [19]p./27. Tabasco. lxxxiii, 206, [19]p./
28. Tamaulipas. lxxxiii, 325, [19]p./29. Tlaxcala. lxxxiii, 321,
[19]p./30. Veracruz. lxxxiii, 1122, [19]p./31. Yucatán. lxxxiii, 608,
[19]p./32. Zacatecas. lxxxiii, 405, [19]p. [PRC, TXU

Mexico. DGE.

1970.4   IX censo general de población,   Ninth general population census,
1970. (28 de enero de 1970).   1970. (January 28, 1970). Gen-
Resumen general. México, D.F.,   eral resume.
1972. xci, 1121, [19]p.   [PRC, TXU

Mexico. DGE.
IX censo general de población,   Ninth general population census,
1970. (28 de enero de 1970).   1970. (January 28, 1970). Lo-
Localidades por entidad federa-   calities by federal entity and
tiva y municipio con algunas   municipality (county) with some
características de su población   characteristics of their popula-
y vivienda. México, D.F.,   tion and housing.
1973. Vol. I-III in 4v.
.5-1   I. Aguascalientes a Gue-
rrero. xxiv, 809p.   [PRC, IASI
.5-1a   I (anexo). Planos, Distri-   Maps, Federal District.
to Federal. 26 maps.   [PRC, IASI
.5-2   II. Hidalgo a Oaxaca.
xxviii, 804p.   [PRC, IASI
.5-3   III. Puebla a Zacatecas.
xxviii, 891p.   [PRC, IASI

MIDWAY ISLAND

United States Unincorporated Territory   Capital: Administered from
                                                         Washington, D.C.

The U.S. censuses for 1950, 1960 and 1970 carry only total number of
inhabitants in Table 1 of the U.S. Summary volume for those years.

MONACO

Principality of Monaco.   Capital: Monaco-Ville.
Statistical Agency: Statistical and Economic Studies Service
                     [Service des Statistiques et des Études Économiques
                     (SSEE)]
                     4, rue des Iris
                     Monaco,
Publications Distributor: same

       Monaco. Mairie de Monaco.
             Recensement du 31 janvier   Census of January 31, 1961.
       1961. Monaco, 1961. 2v.
1961.1-1   Population de passage.   Population in transit.
       12p.   [PRC, RPI
    .1-2   Population fixée habitant   Permanent residents of the prin-
       la principauté. 18p.   cipality.
                                               [PRC, RPI

       Monaco. SSEE.
1962.1   Recensement de la population,   Census of the population, 1962.
       1962. Monaco, n.d. [28]p.   [PRC, RPI

       Monaco. SSEE.
1968.1   Recensement de la population,   Census of the population, 1968.
       1968. Monaco, n.d. [28]p.   [PRC, OPR, RPI

       Monaco. SSEE.
    .2   Recensement de la population,   Census of the population, 1968/
       1968/1962, étude comparative.   1962, a comparative study.
       Monaco, n.d. 88p.   [PRC, RPI

                              MONGOLIA

Mongolian People's Republic.   Capital: Ulan Bator
Statistical Agency: Central Statistical Board
                      Council of Ministers
                      Ulan Bator,
Publications Distributor: same

      Censuses were taken in 1956, 1963, and 1969 but no citation of publi-
      cations has been seen. Mongolia plans to conduct a nationwide Census
      of Population and Housing in 1979.

MONTSERRAT

Colony of Montserrat.   Capital: Plymouth
Statistical Agency: Statistics Office
                     Chief Minister's Office/P.O. Box 292
                     Plymouth,
Publications Distributor: same [and] University of West Indies
                                       Census Research Programme
                                       Mona
                                       Kingston 7, Jamaica

1946
        Jamaica. Central Bureau of Statistics.
           West Indian census, 1946...
             [See Commonwealth Caribbean, Nos. 1946.1-A and F.]

1960
        Jamaica. Department of Statistics. Jamaica Tabulation Centre.
           West Indies population census. Census of Montserrat...
             [See Commonwealth Caribbean, Nos. 1960.8-1 and 2.]

1970
        West Indies. University. Census Research Programme.
           1970 population census of the Commonwealth Caribbean...
             [See Commonwealth Caribbean, Nos. 1970.1-1
                                       1970.1-2-?
                                       1970.1-3
                                       1970.1-4-12 and 16.
                                       1970.1-6-3
                                       1970.1-7
                                       1970.1-8-a, b, and c
                                       1970.1-9-4
                                       1970.1-10-3 and 4.]

        Montserrat. Statistics Office.
   .2   Digest of statistics, 1973. Plymouth, 1973. Tables 5-8. [PRC

MOROCCO

Kingdom of Morocco.   Capital: Rabat
Statistical Agency: Bureau of Statistics
                     [Direction de la Statistique]
                     Secretariat d'État au Plan et au Developpement Regional
                     Premier Ministre/B.P. 178
                     Rabat,

                     National Institute of Statistics and Applied Economy
                     [Institut National de Statistique et l'Economie
                            Appliquée (INSEA)]
Publications Distributor: same.

Until 1956, Morocco was divided in three zones: the North zone (Provinces of Al Hoceima, de Nador and de Tétouan) was administered by Spain, Tangier was under international administration, and the rest of the country which formed the South zone was a French Protectorate. The enclaves of Tarfaya and of Ifni were governed by Spain.

Morocco (French). Service des
       Statistiques.
     Dénombrement général de la
population de la zone française
de l'Empire Chérifien effectué
le 1er mars 1947.   Rabat, 1949.
Fasc. 1–4.

1947.1-1   Population non marocaine.
       xxix, [2], 53p.
   .1-2   Population marocaine.
       xxvii, 75p.
   .1-3   Ensemble de la population.
       10, 16p.
   .1-4   Population active. xi,
       49p.

General enumeration of the population in the French zone of the Sherifian Empire taken March 1, 1947.

Non-Moroccan population.
[BC, PRC, RPI
Moroccan population.
[LC, PRC, RPI
Total population.
[LC, PRC, RPI
Economically active population.
[LC, PRC, RPI

Morocco (Spanish). Junta Central del Censo.
     Censo general de la población
y estadística de edificaciones y
viviendas, para aduares, fracciones, cabilas y nucleos urbanos.
Tetuán, 1952. 3v. (Boletín
oficial de la zona de protectorado español en Marruecos, año
40, Nos. 4, 30, 36).

General census of the population and statistics of buildings and housing, by villages, fracciones, cabilas and urban centers.

1950.1-1   [Territory of Yebola, cabilas of Beni Hozmar, Beni Hassan, Beni Lait, urban center of Rincon del Medik; Territory of Rif, cabilas of Beni Bunsar, Tarquist, Beni Jennus; Territory of Lucas, cabilas of Beni Issef, Beni Scar, Amar, Bdava, Msora, Garbia.] (Bull. No. 4) Pp. 69-76. [
   .1-2   [Territory of Lucas, cabila of Jolat; Territory of Yebala, Tetuán urban center.] (Bull. No. 30). Pp. 844-849. [

.1-3   [Territory of Quert, cabila of Beni Bugafar.] (Bull. No. 36).
Pp. 1005-1006. [

Spain. Instituto Nacional de
        Estadística.
.2   Censo de la población de   Census of the population of Spain
España y territorios de su sobe-   and territories under its govern-
ranía y protectorado, según el   ance and protection according to
empadronamiento realizado el 31   the enumeration taken December 31,
de diciembre de 1950. Tomo I.   1950.
Madrid, 1952. Pp. 343-344.   [TXU, LC, RPI

[Note: The results of the 1950 enumeration of Spanish Morocco also
was published in Vols. I and III of the Moroccan census of 1960.]

Morocco (French). Service Cen-
        tral des Statistiques.
1952.1-1   Recensement général de la   General census of the population
population de la zone française   in the French zone of the Sheri-
de l'Empire Chérifien effectué   fien Empire taken April 15, 1951.
le 15 avril 1951. Fascicule 1.   Part 1. Non-Moroccan population.
Population non marocaine. Résul-   General results.
tats généraux.   Rabat, 1953.   [PRC, RPI
17p.
        [Title change.]
        Recensement général de la   General census of the population
population en 1951-1952.   Rabat,   in 1951-1952.
1953-1955. Vol. II-IV.
.1-2   II. Population non maro-   Non-Moroccan population. [De-
caine. [Résultats détaillés.]   tailled results.]
1954. 1v, 185, [5]p.   [PRC, RPI
.1-3   III. Population marocaine   Moroccan Moslem population.
musulmane. 1955. xlix, 59,   [PRC, RPI
[3]p.
.1-4   IV. Population marocaine   Moroccan Israelite population.
israélite. 1953. 113, [2]p.   [PRC, RPI

Morocco. Service Central des
        Statistiques.
1960.1   Recensement démographique   Demographic census (June 1960):
(juin 1960): population légale   resident population of Morocco.
du Maroc.   Rabat, Impr. Arissala,   [PRC, BC, NWU, RPI
1961. 143p. 16 maps.

Morocco. Service Central des
        Statistiques.
.2   Recensement démographique   Demographic census (June 1960):
(juin 1960): population rurale   rural population of Morocco.
du Maroc.   Casablanca, Impr.   [PRC, NWU, RPI
et Papeterie Universitaire, 1962.
843p.

Morocco.   Service Central des
       Statistiques.
    Résultats du recensement de   Results of the census of 1960.
1960.   Rabat, 1965-1972.   Vol.
I-IV.
.3-1   I. Nationalité--sexe--   Nationality--sex--age.
âge. 1965. 159p.   [PRC, NWU, RPI
.3-2   II. Population active.   Economically active population.
1965. Pp. 165-514.   [PRC, NWU, RPI
.3-3   III. État matrimonial,   Marital status, level of educa-
niveau d'instruction, evolution   tion, evolution of the urban popu-
de la population urbaine, lieu   lation, birthplace, and duration
de naissance et durée de resi-   of residence.
dence. 1972. [2], Pp. [515]-   [PRC, NWU, RPI
939.
.3-4   IV. Ménages--caractéris-   Households--socio-economic charac-
tiques socio-économiques des   teristics of households, dwellings,
ménages, logements, perspectives   demographic perspectives, method-
démographiques, rapport méthodo-   ological report.
logique. 1972. [4], pp. 942-   [PRC, NWU, RPI
1095.

Morocco.   Direction de la Sta-
       tistique.
    Recensement général de la   General census of the population
population et de l'habitat.   and of housing. Series "S".
Série "S". Résultats de l'ex-   Results of the sample tabulation
ploitation du sondage au 1/10.   of 1 in 10.
Rabat, 1972-   . 6v.
1971.1-1   Résultats du sondage au   Results of the 1 in 10 sample.
1/10. 1972. 125p.   [PRC, NWU
.1-2   Population active. 1973.   Economically active population.
167p.   [PRC, NWU
.1-3   Caractéristiques culturel-   Cultural characteristics of the
les de la population. 1973.   population.
39p.   [PRC, NWU
.1-4   Habitat. 1974. 58p.   Housing.
                                         [PRC, NWU
.1-5   Résultats du sondage au   Results of the 1 in 10 sample by
1/10 par provinces et régions.   provinces and regions.
       .   p.   [
.1-6   Travaux d'analyse entre-   Analytical works based on the 1
pris sur le sondage au 1/10.   in 10 sample.
       .   p.   [

Morocco.   Direction de la Sta-
       tistique.
    Recensement général de la   General census of population and
population et de l'habitat, 1971.   housing, 1971. Series "E".
Série "E". Résultats de l'ex-   Results of the complete tabula-
ploitation exhaustive.   Rabat,   tion.
1971-   . Vol. I-VIII in   v.

.2-1   I.   Population légale du
Maroc. 1971. xvii, 176p.
        II.   Population rurale
(par région). 1973. Nos. 1-7.
1971.2-2-1 through 1971.2-2-7. 1. Centre.
3. Nordouest. v, 215p./4. Sud.
ental. v, 88p./7. Centre Sud.
.2-3   III. Recueil de données
par province. 1977. 243p.
        IV.   Données communales.
Région du... 1977. Nos. 1-7.
1971.2-4-1 through 1971.2-4-7. 1. Centre.
Nordouest. 103p./4. Sud. 84p./5. Tensift.
7. Centre Sud. 60p. [PRC

Legal population of Morocco.
[PRC, NWU
Rural population (by region).

v, 226p./2. Centre Nord. v, 203p./
v, 323p./5. Tensift. v, 262p./6. Ori-
[PRC, NWU
Collection of data by province.
[PRC
Community data. Region of...

110p./2. Centre Nord. 78p./3.
79p./6. Oriental. 54p./

There are eight volumes proposed in Series E.

MOZAMBIQUE

People's Republic of Mozambique.   Capital: Maputo (former
Statistical Agency: National Bureau of Statistics   Lourenço Marques)
                     [Direcção Nacional de Estatística]
                     Caixa Postal 493
                     Maputo,
Publications Distributor: same.

      Mozambique. Repartição Técnica
         de Estatística.
1945.1   Recenseamento da população   Census of the non-indigenous popu-
não indígena, em 12 de junho de   lation, on June 12, 1945.
1945. Lourenço Marques, Impr.   [PRC, LC, NWU, RPI
Nacional, 1947. xxx, 235p.

      Mozambique. Repartição Técnica
         de Estatística.
   .2   Inventario das edificações   Inventory of buildings of the
da Colônia em 12 de junho de   Colony on June 12, 1945.
1945. Lourenço Marques, Impr.   [PRC
Nacional, 1949. xiii, 254p.

      Portugal. Instituto Nacional
         de Estatística.
1950.1   Censos da população do ultra-   1950 censuses of overseas popula-
mar de 1950. 3: Províncias de   tion. 3: Provinces of Angola
Angola e Moçambique./Recensement   and Mozambique。
de la population dans les terri-   [
toires d'outre-mer en 1950. 3:
Angola et Mozambique. In: Boletim mensal do I.N.E., ano 23,
No. 6, pp. 4-14. Lisboa, 1951.

      Mozambique. Repartição Técnica
         de Estatística.
      Recenseamento geral da popu-   General census of population,
lação em 1950. Lourenço Mar-   1950.
ques, Imprensa Nacional, 1953-
1955. Vol. I-III.
   .2-1   I. População civilizada.   Civilized population.
   1953. xxxvi, 682p.   [PRC, LC, NWU, JB-F, RPI
   .2-2   II. Inventario das edi-   Inventory of buildings and dwell-
   ficações e fogos. 1954. 39p.   ings.
                                             [PRC, LC, NWU, JB-F, RPI
   .2-3   III. População não civi-   Non-civilized (African) population.
   lizada. 1955. xli, 419, A-16p.   [PRC, LC, NWU, JB-F, RPI

      Mozambique. Direcção dos Ser-
         viços de Economia e de
         Estatística Geral.
1955.1   Recenseamento geral da popu-   General census of the civilized

lação civilizada em 1955.
Lourenço Marques, Imprensa Nacional, 1958. 1199, A-7p.

population in 1955.
[PRC, LC, JB-F, NWU, RPI

Mozambique. Repartição de
Estatística Geral.
1960.1 Alguns aspectos do IV (sic)
recenseamento geral da população do Moçambique (1960). In:
Boletim mensal de estatística,
ano 4, no. 3. Lourenço Marques, 1963. Pp. 55-56.

Some aspects of the Fourth (Third)
general census of population of
Mozambique (1960).
[PRC, RPI

Mozambique. Direcção Provincial
dos Serviços de Estatística
Geral.
III recenseamento geral da
população no provincia de Moçam-
bique, 1960. Distrito de...
Lourenço Marques, 1967-1969.
Vol. 1-9.

Third general population census
of the province of Mozambique,
1960. District of...

1960.2-1 through 1960.2-9. 1. Lourenço Marques. 196?. 293p./2. Gaza. 1967.
301p./3. Inhambane. . p./4. Manica e Sofala. 1967. 458p./5.
Tete. 1968. 292p./6. Zambésia. 1968. 455p./7. Moçambique. 1968.
499p./8. Cabo Delgado. 1969. 309p./9. Niassa. 1969. 181p. [NWU

Mozambique. Direcção Provincial
dos Serviços de Estatística
Geral.
.3 III recenseamento geral da
população no provincia de Moçambique, 1960. Resumo geral.
Lourenço Marques, 1969. 79p.

Third general population census
of the province of Mozambique,
1960. General resume.
[NWU

Portugal. INE [and] Mozambique.
Direcção Provincial dos
Serviços de Estatística.
IV recenseamento geral da
população, 1970. Distrito de...
Lourenço Marques, 1973-1974.
Vol. 1-9.

Fourth general census of population, 1970. District of...

1970.1-1 through 1970.1-9. 1. Lourenço Marques. 1973. xxxvii, 497p./2.
Manica e Sofala. 1973. xxxvii, 559p./3. Tete. 1973. xxxvii, 515p./
4. Niassa. 1973. xxxvii, 515p./5. Gaza. 1973. xxxvii, 508p./6. Cabo
Delgado. 1973. xxxvii, 525p./7. Inhambane. 1974. xxxvii, 530p./8.
Zambésia. 1974. xxxvii, 544p./9. Moçambique. 1974. xxxvii, 559p.
[PRC, NWU, CPC

Portugal. INE [and] Mozambique.
Direcção Provincial dos
Serviços de Estatística.
.2 IV recenseamento geral de

Fourth general census of popula-

população, 1970. Resumo geral.   tion, 1970. General resume.
Lourenço Marques, 1974. xxxv,   [PRC, NWU, CPC
146p.

Note: In addition to Maputo (Lourenço Marques), other cities renamed
are Pemba (Porto Amélia), Chicualacuala (Malvérnia), Xai-Xai (Vila de
João Belo), Chimoio (Vila Pery), Angoche (António Enes), Lichinga (Vila
Cabral), Lupidichi (Olivença), Mavago (Valadim), Catandica (Vila Gou-
veia), Cuamba (Novo Freixo).

        Ten provinces were formed from nine districts: Cabo Delgado,
Gaza, Inhambane, Manica, Maputo, Nampula, Niassa, Sofala, Tete, Zam-
bézia.

The next census is proposed for 1980.

NAMIBIA

Capital: Windhoek

Statistical Agency: Department of Statistics
Private Bag 44
Pretoria, Republic of South Africa

Central Statistical Office
Windhoek,
Publications Distributor: The Government Printer
Private Bag X85
Pretoria, Republic of South Africa

Data for Walvis Bay is included with South West Africa in 1951 and 1960 census reports.

South Africa. Bureau of Census and Statistics.
1946.1   Summaries of 1921, 1925, 1936, 1946 and 1951 censuses. In: Official yearbook of the Union and of Basutoland, Bechuanaland and Swaziland.   Pretoria, [annual].   [NWU

South Africa. Bureau of Census and Statistics.
1951.1   South West Africa: population census, 8th May, 1951.   Pretoria, The Government Printer, 1958.   [2], 133p. [PRC, NWU, RPI

South Africa. Bureau of Census and Statistics.
1960.1   First results of the population census, 6 September, 1960. Part I, Union of South Africa. Part II, Territory of South West Africa. In: Special report, no. 234. Geographical distribution of the population. Pretoria, Government Printer, 1960. viii, 36p. [UN, PRC, RPI

NAURU

Republic of Nauru.   Capital: Yaren.
Statistical Agency: Department of Island Development and Housing.
                     Yaren,
Publications Distributor: same

        The censuses of 1947 and 1954 were for non-indigenous populations
only.

        Australia. Commonwealth Bureau of Census and Statistics.
1947.CB-7   Census of the Commonwealth of Australia, 30th June, 1947. Cen-
        sus bulletin 7. Summary for the territory of Nauru. Canberra,
        Government Printer, 1948. 7, [1]p. [PRC, RPI

        Australia. Ceommonwealth Bureau of Census and Statistics.
           Census of the Commonwealth of Australia, 30th June 1947. Can-
        berra, Government Printer, n.d. Vol. I & III.
     .1-1   I. Part VII. Analysis of population in local government areas:
        Papua-New Guinea, Norfolk Island, Nauru. Pp. 465-492. [TXU, RPI
     .1-3   III. Part XXVI. Analysis of dwellings: Papua-New Guinea, Nor-
        folk Island, Nauru. Pp. 1927-1946. [TXU, RPI

        Australia. Commonwealth Bureau of Census and Statistics.
1954.1-7-5   Census of the Commonwealth of Australia. Volume VII. Terri-
        tories. Part V. External territories (Papua, New Guinea, Norfolk
        Island and Nauru). Canberra, Government Printer, 1958. 30p. [PRC,
        RPI

        Australia. Commonwealth Bureau of Census and Statistics.
1961.CB-24   Census of the Commonwealth of Australia, 30th June, 1961. Cen-
        sus bulletin 24. Summary of population and dwellings for the terri-
        tory of Nauru. Canberra, Government Printer, 1963.   p. [RPI

        Australia. Commonwealth Bureau of Census and Statistics.
     .1-7-5   Census of the Commonwealth of Australia. Volume VII. Terri-
        tories. Part V. External territories (Papua, New Guinea, Nauru, Nor-
        folk Island, Christmas Island and Cocos (Keeling) Islands): Popula-
        tion and dwellings. Canberra, Government Printer, 1965. 59p. [PRC,
        RPI

        Australia. Commonwealth Bureau of Census and Statistics.
1966.FC-2   Census of the Commonwealth of Australia, 30th June 1966. Field
        count statement, no. 2. Population: Nauru, Norfolk Island, Christ-
        mas Island and Cocos (Keeling) Islands. Canberra, Government Printer,
        1966. 1p. [RPI

        Australia. Commonwealth Bureau of Census and Statistics.
     .1-13-1 Census of Nauru, 30 June 1966. Census bulletin no. 13-1. Sum-
        mary of population. Canberra, Government Printer, 1968. 12p. [PRC,
        RPI

Nauru.   Department of Island Development and Housing.
1977.0-1   Preliminary report, census 1977 in the Republic of Nauru.
      Yaren, 1977.   p. [

NEPAL

Kingdom of Nepal.   Capital: Kathmandu
Statistical Agency: Central Bureau of Statistics
                     National Planning Commission Secretariat
                     Ram Shah Path, Thapathali
                     Kathmandu,
Publications Distributor: same.

        Nepal. Department of Statistics.
1952.1   Population interim report. Kathmandu, 1956. [120]p. [PRC, Har-
       vard, RPI

        Nepal. Department of Statistics.
   .2   Census of population, Nepal 1952/54 A.D.   Kathmandu, 1958. xx,
       81p. [PRC, TXU, E-W, RPI

        Nepal. Department of Statistics.
1961.0-1   Preliminary report of the national population census, 1961:
       provisional figures. Kathmandu, 1962. 10 p. [PRC, RPI

        Nepal. Department of Statistics.
   .1   National population census, 1961. Kathmandu, 1965?.   p.
       [

        Nepal. Census Bureau of Statistics.
1971.1   Census of population of Nepal by zone and district, 1971: final
       [compiled tabulations]. Kathmandu, 1973? 4p. [

        Nepal. Central Bureau of Statistics.
   .2   Population census, 1971: abstracts. Kathmandu, 1975. 85p. [PRC,
       UN, LC, BC, E-W

        Nepal. Central Bureau of Statistics.
          Population census - 1971. Kathmandu, 1975. Vol. I-V in 7v.
   .3-1   I. General characteristics tables. var. paging. [PRC, E-W,
       InU, Berkeley, UN
             II. Social characteristic tables.
   .3-2-1   Part 1. var. paging. [PRC, E-W, InU, Berkeley, UN
   .3-2-2   Part 2. var. paging. [PRC, E-W, InU, Berkeley, UN
             III. Economic characteristics.
   .3-3-1   Part 1. var. paging. [PRC, E-W, InU, Berkeley, UN
   .3-3-2   Part 2. var. paging. [PRC, E-W, InU, Berkeley, UN
   .3-4   IV. Female fertility characteristics. var. paging. [PRC, E-W,
       InU, Berkeley, UN
   .3-5   V. Selected locality tables--major urban. var. paging. [PRC,
       E-W, InU, Berkeley, UN

NETHERLANDS

Kingdom of the Netherlands.   Capital: Amsterdam/The Hague.
Statistical Agency: Central Statistical Bureau
                     [Centraal Bureau voor de Statistiek]
                     Prinses Beatrixlaan, 428
                     Voorburg,
Publications Distributor: same.

Netherlands. Centraal Bureau
        voor de Statistiek.
        12e Volkstelling, 31 Mei 1947,   Twelfth census of population and
annex Woningtelling.   The Hague,   housing, May 31, 1947.
1947. 3v.
1947.0-1   Handleiding voor de Gemeen-   Manual for the local authorities.
tebesturen. 79p.   [PRC, RPI
    .0-2   Handleiding voor de Gemeen-   Manual for local authorities.
tebesturen. Aanvulling betref-   Concerning the checking of the
fende de Registercontrole. 7p.   population registers.
                                         [PRC, RPI
    .0-3   [Model A-B (of housing enumerator's forms.] [10]p. [PRC, RPI

Netherlands. Centraal Bureau
        voor de Statistiek.
1947.1   Uitkomsten van de Volks- en   Results of the population and
Beroepstelling, 31 Mei 1947.   occupation census, May 31, 1947.
Nederland.   [The Hague], n.d.   Netherlands.
32p.   [PRC, UN, RPI

Netherlands. Centraal Bureau
        voor de Statistiek.
        12e Volkstelling, annex   Twelfth census of population and
Woningtelling, 31 Mei 1947.   housing, May 31, 1947.
Utrecht/Zeist, Uitgeversmaat-
schappij W. De Haan N.V., 1949-
1957. Series A-B in 13v.
        A. Bijks- en provinciale   A. Data for the Kingdom and the
cijfers. Deel 1-5 in 7v.   provinces.
    .2-A-1   Belangrijkste uitkoms-   Main results of the population
ten der eigenlijke Volkstelling.   census.
1954. 130p.   [PRC, BC, UN, RPI
    .2-A-1a   Bijlage. Organisatie   Annex. Administrative report.
van de telling. n.d. 30p.   [PRC, BC, UN, RPI
tables.
    .2-A-2   Beroepstelling. 1952.   Census of occupations.
211p.   [PRC, BC, UN, RPI
    .2-A-2a   Bijlage. Beroepstel-   Annex. Census of occupations:
ling: Systematische beroepsin-   systematic classification of occu-
deling. 1952. 53p.   pations.
                                         [PRC, BC, UN, RPI
    .2-A-3   Woning- en gezinstel-   Housing and family census.
ling. 1951. 127p.   [PRC, BC, UN, RPI

.2-A-4   Statistiek der bestaande   Statistics of existing marriages
huwelijken en van de vruchtbaar-   and marital fertility.
heid dezer huwelijken. 1951.   [PRC, BC, UN, RPI
144p.
.2-A-5   Statistiek der acade-   Statistics of university graduates.
misch-gevormden. 1950. 77p.   [PRC, BC, UN, RPI
        B. Voornaamste cijfers   B. Principal data for each munici-
per gemeente. Deel 1-6.   pality.
.2-B-1   Plaatselijke indeling.   Population data for municipalities
1950. 198p.   and clusters.
                                             [PRC, BC, UN, RPI
.2-B-2   Woning- en gezinstel-   Housing and family census.
ling. 1949. 71p.   [PRC, BC, UN, RPI
.2-B-3   Gestichtsbevolking.   Population living in institutions.
1949. 81p.   [PRC, BC, UN, RPI
.2-B-4   Varende en rijdende   Population in vessels, houseboats
bevolking. 1953. 30p.   and caravans.
                                             [PRC, BC, RPI
.2-B-5   Kerkelijke gezindten.   Religious affiliations.
1950. 68p.   [PRC, BC, UN, RPI
.2-B-6   Beroepsbevolking naar   Economically active population by
woon-, werk- en geboortegemeente.   place of residence, place of work,
1952. 157, 8p.   and place of birth.
                                             [PRC, BC, UN, RPI

Netherlands. Centraal Bureau
      voor de Statistiek.
      13e algemene volkstelling,   Thirteenth general population cen-
31 Mei 1960. Handleiding voor   sus, May 31, 1960. Manual for the
de gemeentebesturen.   The Hague,   local authorities.
Deel 1-3.
1960.0-1-1   1. 26p.   [PRC, RPI
.0-1-2   2. A. Telling van de be-   A. Enumeration of the population
volking in gestichten, instellin-   in private institutions, public
gen en tehuizen. B. Telling   nursing homes. B. Enumeration
van de bevolking op varende sche-   of the population on houseboats
pen en in woonwagens. 18, 12p.   and in mobile homes.
specimen forms.   [PRC, RPI
.0-1-3   3. Aanwijzingen voor de   Instructions for the checking of
registercontrole. 16p.   population registers.
                                             [PRC, RPI

Netherlands. Centraal Bureau
      voor de Statistiek.
.0-2 13e algemene volkstelling,   Thirteenth general population cen-
31 mei 1960. Instructie voor   sus, May 31, 1960. Instructions
het tellen van de bevolking in   for the enumeration of the popula-
woningen en bewoonde andere ruim-   tion living in conventional dwel-
ten.   The Hague, 1960. 32p.   lings or other housing units.
specimen forms.   [PRC, RPI

Netherlands. Centraal Bureau
 voor de Statistiek.
  Uitkomsten van de 13de algemene volkstelling, 31 mei 1960.
The Hague, n.d. 3v.

Results from the Thirteenth general population census, May 31,
1960.

1960.1-1   [Tables 1-27A]. [102]p.   [BC, RPI
 .1-2   Tables 25A, B, C, D and
Table 26A. [54]p.   [BC, RPI
 .1-3   [Tables 1-27A]. [266]p.   [BC, RPI

Netherlands. Centraal Bureau
 voor de Statistiek.
  13e algemene volkstelling,
31 mei 1960. Zeist/Hilversum,
De Haan, 1963-1972. Deel 1-14
in 20v.

Thirteenth general population
census, May 31, 1960.

 .2-1   1. Inleiding tot de voornaamste onderwerpen van de telling. [Not published.]

Introduction to the main items
of the census.
[Not published.]

 .2-1a   1a. Bijlage. Begrippen
en definities. [Not published].

Annex. Concepts and definitions.
[Not published.]

 .2-2   2. Bevolking van gemeenten en onderdelen van gemeenten.
1964. 196p.

Population of municipalities and
their territorial subdivisions.
[PRC, UN, RPI, RIR

 .2-3   3. Geboortegemeente en
periode van vestiging in de gemeente. 1966. 61p.

Municipality of birth and duration of residence in present municipality.
[PRC, RPI, RIR

 .2-4   4. Geslacht, leeftijd en
burgerlijke staat. 1965. 117p.
     5. Huishoudens, gezinnen
en woningen.

Sex, age and marital status.
[PRC, BC, RPI, RIR
Households, families and housing.

 .2-5-A   Algemene inleiding.
1972. 96p.

General introduction.
[PRC, RPI

 .2-5-B   Voornaamste cijfers per
gemeente. 1964. 97p.

Principal data for each municipality.
[PRC, BC, RPI, RIR

 .2-6   6. Bestaande huwelijken
en vruchtbaarheid van deze huwelijken. 1969. 57p.
     7. Kerkelijke gezindte.

Existing marriages and marital
fertility.
[PRC, BC, RPI, RIR
Religious affiliation.

 .2-7-A   Algemene inleiding.
1968. 106p.

General introduction.
[PRC, RPI, RIR

 .2-7-B   Voornaamste cijfers per
gemeente. 1963. 93p.

Principal data for each municipality.
[PRC, BC, RPI, RIR

     8. Genoten onderwijs en
opleidingsniveau.

Type of education received and
overall level of education.

 .2-8-A   Algemene inleiding.
1969. 87p.

General introduction.
[PRC, BC, RPI, RIR

.2-8-B   Voornaamste cijfers   Principal data for each municipal-
per gemeente. 1964. 117p.   ity.
                                          [PRC, BC, RPI, RIR
.2-9   9. Academisch gevormden.   University graduates.
1964. 93p.   [PRC, BC, RPI, RIR
       10. Beroepsbevolking.   Economically active population.
.2-10-A   Algemene inleiding.   General introduction.
1967. 151, [2]p.   [PRC, RPI, RIR
.2-10-B   Voornaamste cijfers   Principal data for each municipal-
per gemeente. 1964. 163p.   ity.
                                          [PRC, BC, RPI, RIR
.2-10-C   Vergelijking van de   Comparison of the results of the
uitkomsten van de beroepstel-   general population censuses of
lingen 1849-1960. 1966. 52p.   1849-1960--economically active
                                          population.
                                          [PRC, BC, RPI, RIR
.2-11   11. Buiten de woongemeente   Economically active population
werkenden. 1965. 105p.   working outside their municipal-
                                          ity of residence.
                                          [PRC, BC, RPI, RIR
.2-12   12. Bevolking in inrich-   Population living in institutions.
tingen en tehuizen. 1966. 79p.   [PRC, BC, RPI, RIR
.2-13   13. Varende en rijdende   Population permanently living on
bevolking. 1965. 40p.   inland vessels and in caravans.
                                          [PRC, BC, RPI, RIR
.2-14   14. Voornaamste kenge-   Principal key figures for each
tallen per gemeente. 1966.   municipality.
99p.   [PRC, RPI, RIR

Netherlands. Centraal Bureau
    voor de Statistiek.
.3   13e algemene volkstelling,   Thirteenth general population
31 mei 1960. Beroepstelling: census, May 31, 1960. Census of
1. Systematische beroepsindel-   occupations: 1. Systematic clas-
ing. 2. Alfabetische index.   sification of occupations. 2.
The Hague, 1964? 24p.   Alphabetical index.
                                          [PRC

Netherlands. Centraal Bureau
    voor de Statistiek.
1971.0-1 14e algemene volkstelling,   Fourteenth general population
annex woningtelling. Voorlopige   census, and housing census. Pre-
uitkomsten. The Hague, n.d.   liminary results.
[9]p.   [PRC

Netherlands. Centraal Bureau
    voor de Statistiek.
.0-2 14e algemene volkstelling,   Fourteenth general population
28 februari 1971. Systematische   census, February 28, 1971. Sys-
beroepsindeling. The Hague,   tematic list of occupations.
1971. 38p. (Werkexemplaar).   (Working paper).
                                          [PRC

Netherlands. Centraal Bureau
  voor de Statistiek.
1971.1 14e algemene volkstelling,
28 februari 1971. Steekproef
1 op 10 [x10]. Uitkomsten voor
Nederland. (Serie S). Voorburg, n.d. 62p.

Fourteenth general population
census, February 28, 1971. One-
in-ten sample. Results for the
Netherlands.
[PRC

Netherlands. Centraal Bureau
  voor de Statistiek.
14e algemene volkstelling,
28 februari 1971. Systematische classificaties. (Serie C)
Voorburg, n.d. Vol. 1-3.

Fourteenth general population
census, February 28, 1971. Classification schemes.

.2-1 1. Bedrijfsclassificatie.
 n.d. 18p.

Classification of enterprises.
[PRC

.2-2 2. Beroepsclassificatie.
 n.d. 58p.

Classification of occupations.
[PRC

.2-3 3. Onderwijsclassificatie.
 n.d. 41p.

Classification of education.
[PRC

Netherlands. Centraal Bureau
  voor de Statistiek.
14e algemene volkstelling,
annex woningtelling, 28 februi-
ari 1971. The Hague-Voorburg,
1978- . Series A-B in v.
 A.

Fourteenth general population
census, and housing census, Feb-
uary 28, 1971.

.3-A-1A

.3-A-1B Niet-nederlandse natio-
 naliteiten. 1978. 70p.

Aliens.
[PRC

Netherlands. Centraal Bureau
    voor de Statistiek.
  14e algemene volkstelling,   Fourteenth general population
annex woningtelling, 28 februari   census, and housing census, Feb-
1971. Definitieve uitkomsten.   ruary 28, 1971. Final results.
Voorburg, 1977? 12v. (Serie I)
.4-1   Nederland. [63]p.   Whole country.
  [Set is missing Table 23.1]   [PRC
1971.4-2 through 1971.4-12. [All are variously paged, unbound, and missing
  Table 23.1]. 2. Groningen./3. Friesland./4. Drenthe./5. Overijssel./
  6. Gelderland./7. Utrecht./8. Noord-Holland./9. Zuid-Holland./10. Zee-
land./11. Noord-Brabant./12. Limburg. [PRC

Note: There are also Final results for small areas, i.e. 40 COROP
areas and 873 communities. [All variously paged and unbound.] [PRC

Netherlands. Centraal Bureau
    voor de Statistiek.
  Monografieën volkstelling   1971 census monographs.
1971. Voorburg, 1978-1979.
Nos. 1-18.
.5-1   Huisvestingssituatie in   Housing situation in the Nether-
Nederland. 1978. xix, 109p.   lands.
                       [PRC

.5-2   Geboorte-intervallen.   Rate of fertility.
1978. xx, 82p.   [PRC
.5-3   Gescheidenen en verweduw-   Divorced and widowed persons.
den. 1978. xx, 121p.   [PRC
.5-4   Wederzijdse kenmerken van   Mutual characteristics of married
huwelijkspartners. 1979. xx,   persons.
62p.   [PRC, OPR
.5-5   Laagstgeklasseerden in   Households with low incomes.
Nederland. 1978. xxii, 139p.   [OPR
.5-6   Een sociaal-demografische   A social and economic analysis of
analyse van de huwelijkssluiting   nuptiality in the Netherlands.
in Nederland. 1979. xxi, 206p.   [PRC
.5-7   Beroepsarbeid door vrouwen   Economic activity of women in the
in Nederland. 1979. xxiv, 165p.   Netherlands.
                       [PRC
.5-8   Vergrijzing.

                       [

.5-9   Ontwikkelingsfasen van het
gezin.   [
.5-10   De positie van jongeren ten   Pre-adults in relation to their
opzichte van het ouderlijk gezin.   families.
1979. xx, 67p.   [OPR
.5-11   Huishoudenssamenstelling
en samenlevingsvormen.

                       [
.5-12   Onderwijs in Nederland.

                       [

1971.5-13   Kerkelijke gezindten.

[

.5-14   Groeiende in kwijnende
plattelandskernen.

[

.5-15   Typologieën van Nederlandse gemeenten naar stedelijk-
heidsgraad en bevolkingsgroei.

[

.5-16   Regionale arbeidsmarkten.

[

.5-17   Opleiding, beroepen- en
werkgelegenheidsstructur.

[

.5-18   Huishouden, huwelijk en
gezin.

[

NETHERLANDS ANTILLES

                                              Capital: Willemstad.
Statistical Agency: Statistical Bureau
                      [Bureau voor de Statistiek]
                      Departement Sociale & Economische Zaken
                      Fort Amsterdam
                      Curaçao,
Publications Distributor: same.

Netherlands Antilles. Bureau
        voor de Statistiek.
1960.1   Volkstelling 1960: Curaçao,   Population census 1960: Curaçao,
Bonaire, St. Maarten, St. Eusta-   Bonaire [and Windward Islands],
tius en Saba.   Willemstad, 1961.   St. Maarten, St. Eustatius and
40, 110, 39, 47p. [Deel A-D in   Saba.
lv.]   [TXU, BC, PRC, RPI

Netherlands Antilles. Office of Vital Statistics and Census (Aruba).
  .2   The population of Aruba: a report based on the census of 1960, by
Amos H. Hawley.   [Oranjested], Lago Oil and Transport Co., n.d.   [3],
41, [125]p. [PRC, RPI

Netherlands Antilles. Bureau
        voor de Statistiek.
1966.1   Volkstelling Bovenwindse Ei-   Population census of the Wind-
landen, 20 Februari 1966.   Fort   ward Islands, February 20, 1966.
Amsterdam, Curaçao, n.d. [19]p.   [PRC, BC

Netherlands Antilles. Bureau
        voor de Statistiek.
    Eerste algemene volks- en   First general population and hous-
woningtelling Nederlandse Antil-   ing census of the Netherlands
len.   Fort Amsterdam, 1974.   Antilles.
Vol. A1-A10.
1972.1-A1   Handleiding voor het raad-   Manual for the use of the tables.
plegen van de tabellen. 78p.   [PRC
10 charts. specimen forms.
  .1-A2   Uitkomsten Nederlandse   Results for the Netherlands Antil-
Antillen totaal. [129]p.   les in total.
                                             [PRC
1972.1-A3 through 1972.1-A10. Uitkomsten [Results for...].   3. Leeward Islands
group. [129]p./4. Aruba. [129]p./5. Bonaire. [129]p./6. Curaçao.
[129]p./7. Windward Islands group. [125]p./8. St. Maarten. [125]p./
9. St. Eustatius. [135]p./10. Saba. [125]p. [PRC

NEW CALEDONIA

Territory of New Caledonia (France).   Capital: Nouméa.
Statistical Agency: South Pacific Commission
                     P.O. Box D5
                     Noumea,
                        and
                     Statistical Service
                     [Service de la Statistique]
                     B.P. 823
                     Noumea Cedex,
Publications Distributor: same (for non-INSEE publications)
                             or
                     INSEE - Observatoire Économique de Paris
                     195, rue de Bercy - Tour Gamma A
                     75582 Paris, Cedex 12, France

France.   Service Colonial des
          Statistiques.
1946.1   Résultats du recensement de   Results of the census of 1946.
          1946.   Territoires d'outre-mer.   Overseas territories.   New Cale-
          Nouvelle-Calédonie.   Paris,   donia.
          1948. 47p. (Bulletin mensuel   [Yale, RPI
          de statistique d'outre-mer,
          supplément série "statistique,"
          no. 6).

France. INSEE [and] Service des Statistiques.
  .2   Les français d'origine métropolitaine...
          [See French Overseas Territories, No. 1946.2]

France. INSEE.
1951.1   Le recensement de la population non originaire...
          [See French Overseas Territories, No. 1951.1]

France. INSEE.
  .2   Premiers résultats du recense-   First results of the census of
          ment de 1951 dans les territoires   1951 in the overseas territories.
          d'outre-mer.   Population non ori-   Non-indigenous population: Part
          ginaire: 3ème partie, Nouvelle-   3, New Caledonia.
          Calédonie.   Paris, n.d. xii,   [Berkeley, RPI
          [2], 43p. (BMSOM, supplément
          série "statistiques," no. 16).

France. INSEE.
1956.1   Recensement général de la   General census of the population
          population de la Nouvelle Calé-   of New Caledonia 1956. Statisti-
          donie 1956. Tableaux statisti-   cal tables.
          ques.   Paris, 1962. v, 210p.   [PRC, OPR, RPI

France. INSEE.
1963.1   Analyse des résultats du
recensement de la population
de Nouvelle-Calédonie (provisoire), 2 Mai 1963.   Paris,
1965. 70p.

Analysis of the results of the
population census of New Caledonia (provisional), May 2, 1963.
[PRC, OPR, RPI

France. INSEE.
  .2   Résultats statistiques du
recensement général de la population de la Nouvelle-Calédonie
effectué le 2 mai 1963.   Paris,
1966. 119p.

Statistical results of the general
census of the population of New
Caledonia, May 2, 1963.
[UN, RPI

France. INSEE.
1969.1   Résultats statistiques du
recensement général de la population de la Nouvelle-Calédonie
effectué en mars 1969.   Paris,
1972? 148p. specimen forms.

Statistical results of the general
census of the population of New
Caledonia taken March 1969.
[E-W, OPR

France. INSEE.
1974.1   Dénombrement de la population
de Nouvelle-Calédonie, Avril
1974.   Paris, n.d. 119p.

Enumeration of the population of
New Caledonia, April 1974.
[PRC, UN

France. INSEE.
  .2   Recensement de la population
de Nouvelle-Calédonie, 23 avril
1974.   Paris, 1974. 86p. (Its:
Service Statistique de N.C., no.
1).

Census of the population of New
Caledonia, April 23, 1974.
[E-W

France. INSEE.
1976.1   Résultats statistiques du
recensement général de la population de la Nouvelle-Calédonie,
 23 avril 1976.   Paris, [1977].
54p.

Statistical results of the general
census of the population of New
Caledonia, April 23, 1976.
[E-W, OPR

France. INSEE.
     Résultats du recensement de
la population de la Nouvelle Calé-
donie, 23 avril 1976.   Paris,
1977?. 2v.
 .2-1   Text. 183p.

 .2-2   Annexes. 78 tables. specimen forms.

Results of the census of population of New Caledonia, April 23,
1976.

Text.
[OPR, E-W
Appendices.
[OPR, E-W

NEW HEBRIDES

New Hebrides Condominium (British and French)   Capital: Port-Vila.
Statistical Agency: Condominium Bureau of Statistics.
                    Vila,
Publications Distributor: same (for non-INSEE publications).

                    Observatoire Économique de Paris (for INSEE pubns.)
                    195, rue de Bercy, Tour Gamma A
                    75582 Paris, Cedex 12, FRANCE

France. INSEE.
1957.1   Recensement de la population   Census of the population of New
           des Nouvelles Hébrides (popula-   Hebrides (non native population),
           tion non originaire), 1957.   1957.
           Paris, 1961. 50p.   [LC

France. INSEE.
1967.1   Le recensement du Condominium   The census of the New Hebrides
           des Nouvelles-Hébrides, 1967.   Condominium, 1967. Principal
           Principaux résultats.   [Paris,   results.
           n.d.] 49p.   [PRC, BC, RPI

           New Hebrides. Director of Census.
    .2   Condominium of the New Hebrides. A report on the first census of
           the population, 1967. By Norma McArthur and J.F. Yaxley.   Sidney,
           Australian Government Printer, 1968. viii, 488p. specimen form.
           [PRC, LC, UN, RPI

           New Hebrides. Condominium Bureau
              of Statistics.
           Recensement de la population   Census of population and housing
           et de l'habitat, Port-Vila et   [Greater] Vila and Santo [Town],
           Luganville, 29 octobre 1972.   October 29, 1972.
           Port-Vila, 1973. Parts 1-3.
1972.1-1   Données sur l'habitat.   Housing data.
     .1-1   43p. maps.   [PRC
    .1-2   Données sur la population.   Population data.
           95p. maps.   [PRC, LC
    .1-3   [Never produced.]

NEW ZEALAND

Dominion of New Zealand   Capital: Wellington.
Statistical Agency: Department of Statistics
                         Private Bag
                         Wellington C.1,
Publications Distributor: Government Printing Office
                         Private Bag
                         Wellington,

New Zealand. Census and Statistics Department.
1945.1   Population census, 1945. Interim returns of ages, marital status,
          religious professions, birthplaces, duration of residence of overseas-
          born, race, war service, industries, occupations, occupational status,
          travelling time. Wellington, The Gisborne Herald Co., 1948. [2],
          26p. [PRC, LC, RPI

New Zealand. Census and Statistics Department.
          Population census, 1945. Wellington, Government Printer and others,
          1947-1952. Vol. I-XI, Appendices A-C.
   .2-1   I. Increase and location of population. Auckland, Leightons,
          Ltd., 1947. [4], xiii, 68p. [PRC, LC, RPI
   .2-2   II. Island territories: Cook Islands and Niue, Tokelau Island,
          Western Samoa. Auckland, Leightons, Ltd., 1947. [4], 14p. [PRC,
          LC, RPI
   .2-3   III. Maori census. Wellington, Gisborne Herald Co., 1950.
          [4], v, 58p. [PRC, LC, RPI
   .2-4   IV. Ages and marital status. Wellington, Gisborne Herald Co.,
          1949. [2], 78p. [PRC, LC, RPI
   .2-5   V. Dependent children. Wellington, Government Printer, 1952.
          52p. [PRC, LC, RPI
   .2-6   VI. Religious professions. Wellington, Government Printer,
          1952. [3], iii, 24p. [PRC, LC, RPI
   .2-7   VII. Birthplaces and duration of residence of overseas-born.
          Wellington, Government Printer, 1952. v, 47p. [PRC, LC, RPI
   .2-8   VIII. Race. Wellington, Government Printer, 1951. [4], v,
          33p. [PRC, LC, RPI
   .2-9   IX. Industries and occupations. Wellington, Gisborne Herald
          Co., 1951. [4], vii, 108p. [PRC, LC, RPI
   .2-10   X. Incomes. Wellington, Southland Times Co., 1952. [4], ii,
          110p. [PRC, LC, RPI
   .2-11   XI. Dwellings and households. Wellington, Government Printer,
          1952. [4], ii, 81p. [PRC, LC, RPI
   .2-12-A   Census of poultry.
   .2-12-B   War service. Wellington, Government Printer, 1950. 20p.
          [PRC, LC, RPI
   .2-12-C   Usual place of residence. Wellington, Government Printer,
          1952. 8p. [PRC, LC, RPI

New Zealand. Census and Statistics Department.
1951.1   Census of 17th April, 1951. Interim returns of population and
          dwellings. Wellington, Government Printer, 1951. 36p. [PRC, LC,
          RPI

New Zealand. Census and Statistics Department.
    Population census, 1951. Wellington, Government Printer, 1953-1956. Vol. I-VIII and Appendices A-B.
.2-1   I. Increase and location of population. 1953. 112, [5]p. [PRC, LC, RPI
.2-2   II. Ages and marital status. 1953. 84p. [PRC, LC, RPI
.2-3   III. Religious professions (including summaries for dependent children, race and war service). 1953. 28p. [PRC, LC, RPI
.2-4   IV. Industries, occupations and incomes. 1954. 112p. [PRC, LC, RPI
.2-5   V. Birthplaces and duration of residence of overseas-born. 1954. 23p. [PRC, LC, RPI
.2-6   VI. Maori census. 1954. 56p. [PRC, LC, RPI
.2-7   VII. Dwellings and households. 1954. 31p. [PRC, LC, RPI
.2-8   VIII. General report. 1956. 195p. [PRC, LC, RPI
.2-9-A   Census of poultry.
.2-9-B   Life tables, 1950-52, and values of annuities. 1954. 31p. [PRC, RPI

New Zealand. Census and Statistics Department.
    Population census, 1951. New Zealand life tables, 1950-52. Expectations of life. Chances of living and dying at each age. Wellington, 1953. 2v.
.3-1   Non-Maori lives. 17p. [UN, RPI
.3-2   Maori lives. 12p. [PRC, BC, RPI

New Zealand. Census and Statistics Department.
.4   Maps of urban areas. Wellington, Government Printer, 1952. 15 maps. [PRC, RPI

New Zealand. Department of Statistics.
1956.1   Census of 17 April, 1956. Interim returns of population and dwellings. Wellington, Government Printer, 1956. 27p. [PRC, LC, RPI

New Zealand. Department of Statistics.
    Population census, 1956. Wellington, Government Printer, 1957-1961. Vol. I-X and Appendices A-B.
.2-1   I. Increase and location of population. 1957. 124p. [PRC, LC, BC, RPI
.2-2   II. Ages and marital status. 1958. 130p. [PRC, LC, BC, RPI
.2-3   III. Religious professions. 1958. 36p. [PRC, LC, BC, RPI
.2-4   IV. Industries and occupations. 1959. 148p. [PRC, LC, BC, RPI
.2-5   V. Incomes. 1959. 39p. [PRC, LC, BC, RPI
.2-6   VI. Birthplaces and duration of residence of overseas-born. 1959. 32p. [PRC, LC, BC, RPI
.2-7   VII. Race. 1959. 40p. [PRC, LC, BC, RPI
.2-8   VIII. Maori population and dwellings. 1960. 102p. [PRC, LC, BC, RPI
.2-9   IX. Dwellings and households. 1959. 92p. [PRC, LC, BC, RPI
.2-10   X. General report. 1960. 133p. [PRC, LC, BC, RPI

.2-11-A   Census of poultry.
.2-11-B   New Zealand life tables, 1955-1957. 1961. 24p. [PRC, LC,
   BC, RPI

New Zealand. Department of Statistics.
1961.1   Population census, 1961: Interim returns of population and dwellings. Wellington, Government Printer, 1961. 34p. [LC, RPI

New Zealand. Department of Statistics.
   Population census, 1961. Wellington, Government Printer, 1962-
   1965. Vol. 1-10 and Appendices A-B.
.2-1   Increase and location of population. 1962. 97, [4]p. [PRC,
   TXU, LC, RPI
.2-2   Ages and marital status. 1963. 92p. [PRC, TXU, LC, RPI
.2-3   Religious professions. 1964. 27p. [PRC, TXU, LC, RPI
.2-4   Industries and occupations. 1965. 120p. [PRC, TXU, LC, RPI
.2-5   Incomes. 1965. 48p. [PRC, TXU, LC, RPI
.2-6   Birthplaces and duration of residence of persons born overseas.
   1964. 26p. [PRC, TXU, LC, RPI
.2-7   Race. 1963. 39p. [PRC, TXU, LC, RPI
.2-8   Maori population and dwellings. 1965. 88p. [PRC, TXU, LC,
   RPI
.2-9   Dwellings and households. 1964. 104p. [PRC, TXU, LC, RPI
.2-10   The New Zealand people 1961. General report on the 1961 population census. 1965. 119p. [PRC, TXU, LC, RPI
.2-11-A   Census of poultry.
.2-11-B   New Zealand life tables, 1960-1962. 1965. 21p. [LC, RPI

New Zealand. Department of Statistics.
.3   Census of population 1961: Summary results. Wellington, Government Printer, 1963. 12p. [

New Zealand. Department of Statistics.
.4   Census of population 1961: Incomes and dwellings of Maoris.
   Wellington, Government Printer, 1964. 4p. [

New Zealand. Department of Statistics.
   1966 census of population and dwellings. Supplement. Wellington,
   Government Printer, 1967. Nos. 1-9.
1966.1-1 through 1966.1-9. 1. Northland Statistical Area. 9p./2. Central
   Auckland S.A. 9p./3. South Auckland-Bay of Plenty S.A. 17p./4. East
   Coast and Hawke's Bay S.A. 9p./5. Taranaki S.A. 9p./6. Wellington
   S.A. 17p./7. Marlborough, Nelson and Westland S.A's. 9p./8. Canter-
   bury S.A. 16p./9. Otago and Southland S.A's. 17p. [PRC

New Zealand. Department of Statistics.
   New Zealand Census of population and dwellings, 1966. City subdivisions. Wellington, 1968. 4 parts.
1966.2-1 through 1966.2-4. 1. Auckland. 17p./2. Dunedin. 7p./3. Christ-
   church. 10p./4. Wellington and Lower Hutt. 17p. [PRC

New Zealand. Department of Statistics.
.3   New Zealand census of population and dwellings, 1966. Summary
results. Wellington, Government Printer, 1968. 25p. [PRC, RPI

New Zealand. Department of Statistics.
New Zealand census of population and dwellings, 1966. Wellington,
Government Printer, 1968-1971. Vol. 1-10 in 11v.
.4-1   Increase and location of population. 1967. 83, [9]p. [PRC,
LC, RPI
.4-2   Ages and marital status. 1968. 92p. [PRC, LC, RPI
.4-3   Religious professions. 1968. 28p. [PRC, LC, RPI
.4-4   Industries and occupations. 1969. [2], 172p. [PRC, LC, RPI
.4-5   Incomes. 1969. 52, [2]p. [PRC, LC, RPI
.4-6   Education and birthplaces. 1969. 52p. [PRC, LC, RPI
.4-7   Race. 1969. 40p. [PRC, LC, RPI
.4-8   Maori population and dwellings. 1969. 132p. [PRC, LC, RPI
Dwellings and households. Parts A-B.
.4-9-A   Dwellings. 1969. 79p. [PRC, LC, RPI
.4-9-B   Households. 1970. 128p. [PRC, LC, RPI
.4-10   The New Zealand people. General report on the census of population and dwellings 1966. 1971. 140p. [PRC, LC, BC, RPI

New Zealand. Department of Statistics.
New Zealand census of population and dwellings, 1971. Supplements
(Summaries for territorial areas). Wellington, Government Printer,
1973-1974. Parts 1-9 in 10v.
1971.1-1 through 1971.1-9. 1. Northland Statistical Area. 1973. 26p./2.
Central Auckland S.A. 1973. 25p./2a. Auckland urban areas. 1973.
111p./3. South Auckland-Bay of Plenty S.A. 1973. 75p./4. East Coast
and Hawke's Bay S.A's. 1973. 49p./5. Taranaki S.A. 1973. 26p./6.
Wellington S.A. 1974. 126p./7. Marlborough, Nelson and Westland S.
A's. 1974. 32p./8. Canterbury S.A. 1974. 72p./9. Otago and Southland S.A's. 1974. 75p. [PRC, LC

New Zealand. Department of Statistics.
New Zealand census of population and dwellings, 1971. Wellington,
Government Printer, 1972-1977. Vol. 1-12.
.2-1   Increase and location of population. 1972. 104p. 3 maps.
[PRC, LC, BC
.2-2   Ages and marital status. 1974. 76p. [PRC, BC
.2-3   Religious professions. 1974. 38p. [PRC, LC, BC
.2-4   Industries and occupations. 1974. 147p. [PRC, LC, BC
.2-5   Incomes. 1975. 88p. [PRC, LC, BC
.2-6   Education. 1975. 117p. [PRC, LC, BC
.2-7   Birthplaces and ethnic origin. 1975. 84p. [PRC, LC, BC
.2-8   Maori population and dwellings. 1975. 179p. [PRC, LC, BC
.2-9   Dwellings. 1975. 108p. [PRC, LC, BC
.2-10   Households, families, and fertility. 1976. 123p. [PRC, LC, BC
.2-11   Internal migration. 1976. 113p. [PRC, LC, BC
.2-12   The New Zealand people, 1971. [General report.] 1977. 164p.
[PRC, LC, BC

New Zealand.   Department of Statistics.
    1976 census of population and dwellings.   Bulletins.   Wellington,
Government Printer, 1976-1978.   Nos. 1-14.
1976.1-1   Provisional population and dwellings statistics.   1976.   52p.
[PRC, UN
 .1-2   Provisional national statistics.   1976.   34p.   [PRC, LC, BC
1976.1-3 through 1971.1-11.   3. Northland Statistical Area.   1977.   29p. /4.
Central Auckland S.A.   1977.   81p./5. South Auckland-Bay of Plenty S.
A.   1977.   55p./6. East Coase and Hawke's Bay S.A's.   1977.   29p./7.
Taranaki S.A.   1977.   29p./8. Wellington S.A.   1977.   81p./9. Marlborough, Nelson, and Westland S.A's.   1977.   29p./10. Canterbury S.A.
1977.   55p./11. Otago and Southland S.A's.   1977.   55p.   [PRC
 .1-12   New Zealand regional summary.   1977.   29p.   [PRC, LC
 .1-13   New Zealand national statistics.   (Replacing sample-based statistics published in 'Provisional national statistics' in December
1976).   [See 1976.1-1 above].   1978.   31p.   [PRC
 .1-14   Ages and marital status.   1978.   16p.   [

New Zealand.   Department of Statistics.
    1976 census of population and dwellings.   Wellington, Government
Printer, 1977-   .   Vol. 1-12 in   v.
    1. Location and increase of population.   3 parts.
 .2-1-A   A.   1977.   48p.   [PRC, BC
 .2-1-B   B.   1977.   72p.   [PRC
 .2-1-C

NICARAGUA

Republic of Nicaragua.   Capital: Managua.
Statistical Agency: Executive Office of Investigations and Censuses
[Oficina Ejecutiva de Encuestas y Censos]
Apartado 4031
Managua, D.N.,
        and
Dirección General de Estadística y Censos
Ministerio de Economía, Industria y Comercio
Apartado postal 59
Managua, D.N.,
Publication Distributor: same

    Nicaragua. Dirección General
       de Estadística y Censos.
1950.1   Resultados del censo nacional   Results of the national popula-
de población de 1950 (avance de   tion census of 1950 (advance re-
las cifras definitivas). Mana-   port of the final figures).
gua, 1952. 20p.   [PRC, TXU, LC, RPI

    Nicaragua. Dirección General
       de Estadística y Censos.
     Censo general de población   General population census of the
de la República de Nicaragua,   Republic of Nicaragua, 1950.
1950. Informe general y cifras   General report and figures for
del departamento de... Mana-   the department of...
gua, Talleres Nacionales, 1952-
1954. Vol. I-XVII.
1950.2-1 through 1950.2-16. [Nos. 5-9, 11-16 apparently never published].
   1. Boaco. 1951. viii, 362p./2. Carazo. 1952. viii, 407p./3. Chi-
nandega. 1952. xi, 635p./4. Chontales. 1953. ix, 425p./5. Estelí.
        /6. Granada.   /7. Jinotega.
     /8. León.   /9. Madriz.   /
   10. Managua. 1952. vii, 367p./11. Masaya.   /12.
   Matagalpa.   /13. Nueva Segovia.   /
   14. Rio San Juan.   /15. Rivas.   /16.
   Zelaya.   [PRC, LC, RPI
  .2-17   La República de Nicaragua.   The Republic of Nicaragua.
   1954. vi, 472, [3]p.   [PRC, LC, RPI

    Nicaragua. Dirección General
       de Estadística.
     Censos 1963. Managua, Depto.   Censuses 1963.
de Publicaciones, 1963-1964.
Boletín 1-3 in 4v.
1963.1-1   Cifras provisionales.   Provisional figures.
   1963. [3], 17, [1]p.   [LC
  .1-1a   Anexo. 1964.   p.   Annex.
                          [

.1-2   Viviendas (resultados de
tabulación por muestreo). 1964.
[2], vii, [1], 11, [2]p.

Housing (results from the sample
tabulation).
[PRC, LC, RPI

.1-3   Población (resultados de
tabulatión por muestreo). 1964.
[2], xviii, 18p.

Population (results from the sample tabulation).
[PRC, LC, RPI

Nicaragua. Dirección General
      de Estadística.
.2   Censos 1963. Población y
viviendas por municipios y co-
marcas. Resumen. Managua,
Dept° de Publicaciones, 1964.
104p.

Censuses 1963. Population and
housing by municipalities and districts. Summary.
[PRC

Nicaragua. Dirección General
      de Estadística.
      Censos nacionales, 1963, pob-
lación. Managua, Dept° de Publicaciones, 1964-1967. Vol. I-
V.

National censuses, 1963. Population.

.3-1   I. Características generales por departamentos y municipios. 1964. xxxvii, 118p.
folding maps.

General characteristics by department and municipalities.
[PRC, TXU, BC, LC, RPI

.3-2   II. Características educacionales por departamentos y
municipios. 1965. [6], xvi,
[2], 239p.

Educational characteristics by
department and municipalities.
[PRC, TXU, LC, RPI

.3-3   III. Características
económicas de la población por
departamentos y municipios.
1967. [4], xiii, [3], 137p.

Economic characteristics of the
population by department and
municipalities.
[LC, RPI

.3-4   IV. Características
demográficas detalladas de la
población por departamentos y
ciudades principales. 1967.
[4], xxiv, [2], 160p.

Detailed demographic characteristics of the population by department and principal cities.
[LC, RPI

.3-5   V. Características económicas detalladas de la población por departamentos y ciudades principales. 1967. [2],
xiv, [2], 414p.

Detailed economic characteristics
of the population by department
and principal cities.
[LC, RPI

Nicaragua. Oficina Ejecutiva
      de los Censos.
1971.0-1 Manual del enumerador. Censos nacionales 1971: vivienda,
población, agropecuario. Managua, D.N., Gurdian, S.A., 1971.
96, [2]p.

Enumerator's manual. National
censuses 1971: housing, population, agriculture.
[PRC

Nicaragua. Oficina Ejecutiva
de los Censos.
1971.0-2 Guía de administración censal para la enumeración.
Managua, D.N., 1971. 10, [1],
2p. specimen forms.

Census administration guide for
the enumeration.
[PRC

Nicaragua. Oficina Ejecutiva
de los Censos.
Censos nacionales, 20 abril
1971. Boletín. Managua, 1971-
1972. Nos. 1-4.

National censuses, April 20, 1971.
Bulletin.

.1-1   Población, vivienda. Cifras preliminares (recuento
manual). 1971. xi, 27p.

Population, housing. Preliminary
figures (manual count).
[PRC, BC

.1-2   Agropecuario. Cifras
preliminares (recuento manual).

Agriculture. Preliminary figures
(manual count).

.1-3   Población. Tabulaciones
preliminares a base de muestra.
1972.   p.

Population. Preliminary tabulations based on sampling.
[

.1-4   Vivienda. Tabulaciones
preliminares a base de muestra.
1972.   p.

Housing. Preliminary tabulations
based on sampling.
[

Nicaragua. Oficina Ejecutiva
de los Censos.
Censos nacionales, 20 de
abril de 1971: población.
Managua, D.N., 1974-   . Vol.
I-

National censuses, April 20, 1971:
population.

.2-1   I. Población. Características generales. 1974. xxix,
384p.

Population. General characteristics.
[PRC, LC, BC

.2-2   II. Población. Características educacionales. 1974.
205p.

Population. Educational characteristics.
[PRC, LC, BC

.2-3   III. Población. Características económicas. 1974.
414p.

Population. Economic characteristics.
[PRC, LC, BC

IV. Población por muni-
cipios. Vol. I- .

Population by municipalities.

.2-4-1   I. Características
generales. 1975. ix, 304p.
.2-4-2

General characteristics.
[PRC

NIGER

Republic of Niger.   Capital: Niamey.
Statistical Agency: Statistical and Data Processing Service
                     [Service de la Statistique et de la Mécanographie]
                     Commissariat Général au Developpement.
                     Niamey,
Publications Distributor: same

         France. INSEE [and] Service Colonial des Statistiques.
1946   Résultats du recensement de 1946...
            [See French Overseas Territories, Nos. 1946.1-1, 2 and 3.]

         France. INSEE [and] Ministère de la France d'Outre-Mer.
1946   Les français d'origine métropolitaine...
            [See French Overseas Territories, No. 1946.2]

         France. INSEE.
1951   Le recensement de la population...
            [See French Overseas Territories, No. 1951.1]

         French West Africa. Service de la Statistique Générale.
1951   Recensement de la population non autochtone...
            [See French Overseas Territories, No. 1951.2]

         French West Africa. Service de
               la Statistique Générale.
1951.3   Population de l'A.O.F. en   Population of French West Africa
            1950-51 par canton et groupe   in 1950-1951 by canton and ethnic
            éthnique, chiffres provisoires.   group, provisional figures.
            Dakar, 1952. [135]p.   [UN, PRC, RPI

         France. SEAE.
1960.0-1   La situation démographi-   The demographic situation of the
            que de la République de Niger.   Republic of Niger.
            Paris, 1960.   p.   [

         Niger. Service de la Statis-
               tique.
   .0-2   Résultats provisoires du   Provisional results of the census
            recensement de Niamey, 1960.   of Niamey, 1960.
            In: Bulletin trimestriel de   [
            statistique, 1960, No. 7.   Paris,
            INSEE, 1960. pp. 23-30.

         Niger. Service de la Statis-
               tique.
            Étude démographique du Niger.   Demographic survey of Niger.
            Paris, INSEE, 1962-1963. Fasc.
            1-2.
   .1-1   Données collectives. Ré-   Collective data. Final results.
            sultats définitifs. 1962. 81p. [NWU, PRC, LC, RPI

.1-2   Données individuelles.   Individual data.   Final results.
Résultats définitifs. 1963.   [NWU, PRC, LC, RPI
[2], 88p.

Niger. Service de la Statis-
       tique.
1963.1   Étude démographique et éco-   Demographic and economic study in
nomique en milieu nomade. 2.   the nomadic environment. Demo-
Démographie, budgets et consom-   graphy, budgets and expenditure.
mation. Paris, INSEE, 1966.   [PRC, NWU, RPI
[4], 201p. map.

Niger. Service de la Statis-
       tique.
1977.0-1 Recensement général de la   General census of the population,
population, 1977. [Note on   1977.
the pilot census].   [Niamey],   [
1977. 26p.

NIGERIA

Republic of Nigeria.   Capital: Lagos.
Statistical Agency: The Chief Statistician
                     Federal Office of Statistics
                     P.M. Bag 12528
                     Lagos,
Publications Distributor: same

   Nigeria. Department of Statis-
     tics.
1950.1 Population census of Lagos, 1950. Census bulletins.   Lagos, Government Printer, 1955. Nos. 1-8 in 1v. [LC

   Nigeria. Department of Statistics.
 .2 Population census of Lagos, 1950. Administrative report, analysis
and summary tables, detailed tables, copies of schedules, forms, instructions, etc., census map of Lagos.   Kaduna, Government Printer,
1951. ii, 114p. 2 maps. [PRC, NWU, LC, RPI

   Nigeria. Department of Statistics.
   Census of Nigeria, 1952(-1953).   Lagos, Government Printer, 1952.
   2v.
1953.0-1 Census officer's handbook. 18p. [LC, RPI
 .0-2 Supervisors' and enumerators' instructions. 16p. [LC, PRC, RPI

   Nigeria. Department of Statistics.
   Population census of the Western Region of Nigeria, 1952.   Lagos,
Government Printer, 1955-1956. 10v.
     Bulletins, No. 1-9. 1955.
1953.1-1-1 through 1953.1-1-9. 1. Main figures for the region. [1], 14p./
 2. Ijebu Province. 11p./3. Ondo Province. 18p./4. Oyo Province. 10p./
 5. The Colony. 16p./6. Benin Province. 32p./7. Ibadan Province. 32p./
 8. Abeokuta Province. 26p./9. Delta Province. 28p. [NWU, RPI
 .1-2 Census report and tables; the Western Region of Nigeria (a short
 description of the region and its people); schedules and instructions;
 map of the region. 1956. v, 49p. [NWU, LC, PRC, RPI

   Nigeria. Department of Statistics.
   Population census of the Northern Region of Nigeria, 1952.   Zaria,
Gaskiya Corp., 1952-195? 14v.
1953.2-1-1 through 1953.2-1-13. 1. Main figures for the region. 1952. [2],
 46p./2. Benue Province. 1954. 28p./3. Katsina Province. 1954. 10p./
 4. Zaria Province. 1954. 12p./5. Niger Province. 1954. 12p./6. Pla-
 teau Province. 1954. 21p./7. Bornu Province. 1954. 19p./8. Kano
 Province. 1954. 41p./9. Bauchi Province. 1954. 13p./10. Adamawa
 Province. 1954. 27p./11. Sokota Province. 1954. 23p./12. Iloren
 Province. 1954. 14p./13. Kabba Province. 1954. 15p. [NWU, LC, RPI
 .2-2 Census report and tables. The Northern region of Nigeria (a
 short description of the region and its people); schedules and instructions; map of the region. 195? v, 58, [2]p. [NWU, LC, PRC, RPI

Nigeria. Department of Statistics.
    Population census of the Eastern region of Nigeria, 1953. Port
Harcourt, C,M,S, Niger Press, 1953-1955. 10v.
1953.3-1-1 through 1953.3-1-9. 1. Main figures of the region. 1953. [1],
    20p./2. Bamenda Province. 1955. 15p./3. Rivers Province. 1955. 36p./
    4. Ogoja Province. 1955. 60p./5. Cameroons Province. 1955. 31p./6.
    Calabar Province. 1955. 84p./7. Onitsha Province. 1955. 26p./8.
    Owerri Province. 1955. 46p./9. Corrigendum. 1955. 5p. [NWU, LC,
    PRC, OPR, RPI
  .3-2   Census report and tables; the Eastern region of Nigeria (a short
    description of the region and its people); schedules and instructions;
    map of the region. 1955. v, 72p. [NWU, LC, PRC, OPR, RPI

Nigeria. Department of Statistics.
  .4   Population census of Nigeria, 1952-53. Lagos, n.d. 13p. [OPR

Nigeria. Department of Statistics.
    Population census of Suru-Lere (Suru-Lere, Idi-Oro and Idi-Araba).
    [Lagos], 1957. 2v.
1957.1-1   Administrative report. 2p. [
  .1-2   14 tables. 16p. [

Nigeria. Federal Census Office.
    Population census of Nigeria, 1963. Lagos, n.d. Vol. I-III in
    11v.
          I.
1963.1-1-1   Federal Territory of Lagos. 1964. 15p. [LC, OPR, NWU
  .1-1-2   Northern Region. 1964. 260p. [NWU
  .1-1-3   Western Region. 1964. 2, 124p. [NWU, LC, RPI
  .1-1-4   Eastern Region. 1964. 4, 211p. [NWU, LC, RPI
  .1-1-5   Mid-West Region. 1964. 47p. [NWU
          II.
  .1-2-1   Federal Territory of Lagos. iii, 41p. [NWU, OPR, RPI
  .1-2-2   Northern Region. xi, 678p. [NWU, RPI
  .1-2-3   Western Region. vi, 296p. [NWU, RPI
  .1-2-4   Eastern Region. vii, 369p. [NWU, RPI
  .1-2-5   Mid-West Region.   [
  .1-3   III. Combined national figures. [1968]. 4, 109p. [BC, NWU,
    RPI

Nigeria. Federal Office of Statistics.
1966.1   Rural demographic sample survey, 1965-66. Lagos, 1968. [50]p.
    [OPR

The results of the 1973 census were cancelled.

NIUE

(New Zealand Associated State)   Capital: Alofi
Statistical Agency: Secretary to the Government
                     Government of Niue
                     Alofi,
Publications Distributor: same

        New Zealand. Census and Statistics Department.
1945.2-2 Population census, 1945. Volume II, Island territories: Cook
        Islands and Niue, Tokelau Island, Western Samoa. Auckland, Leightons
        Ltd., 1947. [4], 14p. [PRC, RPI

        New Zealand. Department of Island Territories.
1951.1   "Niue, population census, September 1951, by Europeans and Niueans,
        by villages, and by ages, by sex, compared with results of census of
        September 1945." In: Cook Islands annual report, 1952. Wellington,
        Government Printer, 1952. p. 59. [Yale, RPI

        New Zealand. Department of Island Territories.
1956.1

        New Zealand. Department of Island Territories.
1965.1   "Niue population, census March 1965, by sexes compared with results
        of census of September 1961." In: Cook, Niue, and Tokelau Islands
        annual report, 1965. Wellington, Government Printer, 1965. p. 63.
        [E-W

        Niue Island. Census Officer.
1971.1   Census of population and dwellings, Niue Island, 1971. Wellington,
        Government Printer, 1974. 48p. [PRC, LC

        Note: See also New Zealand censuses of 1951 (Vol. 8), 1956 (Vol.1),
        1961 (Vol. 1), 1966 (Vol. 1) and 1971 (Vol. 1) for number of inhabi-
        tants by sex only.

        Niue Island. Department of Justice.
        1976 census of population and housing. Report. Alofi, 1978.
        Vol. 1-
1976.1-1   1. Basic information. 1978.   p. [E-W

NORFOLK

Territory of Norfolk Island (Australia).   Capital: Kingston.
Statistical Agency: Australian Bureau of Statistics
                     P.O. Box 10
                     Belconnen (ACT) 2616, AUSTRALIA
Publications Distributor: Government Printing Office
                           Box 17
                           Canberra (ACY) 2600, AUSTRALIA

Australia. Commonwealth Bureau of Census and Statistics.
1947.CB-5   Census of the Commonwealth of Australia, 30th June, 1947. Census bulletin 5. Summary for the Norfolk Island. Canberra, Government Printer, 1948. 8p. [NYPL, RPI

Australia. Commonwealth Bureau of Census and Statistics.
       Census of the Commonwealth of Australia, 30th June, 1947.   Can-
berra, Government Printer, n.d.
.1-1   (Vol. I, Part VII). Analysis of population in local government
       areas: Papua-New Guinea, Norfolk Island, Nauru. pp. 465-492. [TXU, LC
.1-3   (Vol. III, Part XXVI). Analysis of dwellings: Papua-New Guinea,
       Norfolk Island, Nauru. pp. 1927-1946. [TXU, PRC, LC

Australia. Commonwealth Bureau of Census and Statistics.
1954.1-7-5   Census of the Commonwealth of Australia. Volume VII. Terri-
       tories. Part V. External territories (Papua, New Guinea, Norfolk
       Island and Nauru). Canberra, Government Printer, 1958. 30p. [PRC,
       LC, RPI

Australia. Commonwealth Bureau of Census and Statistics.
1961.CB-7   Census of the Commonwealth, 30th June, 1961. Census bulletin
       No. 7. Summary of population and dwellings for the territory of Nor-
       folk Island. Canberra, Government Printer, 1962. 12p. [LC, RPI

Australia. Commonwealth Bureau of Census and Statistics.
.1-7-5   Census of the Commonwealth of Australia. Volume VII. Terri-
       tories. Part V. External territories (Papua, New Guinea, Nauru,
       Norfolk Island, Christmas Island and Cocos (Keeling) Islands). Can-
       berra, Government Printer, 1965. 59p. [PRC, LC, RPI

Australia. Commonwealth Bureau of Census and Statistics.
1966.FC-2   Census of the Commonwealth of Australia, 30th June 1966. Field
       count statements. No. 2. Population: Nauru, Norfolk Island, Christ-
       mas Island and Cocos (Keeling) Islands. Canberra, Government Printer,
       1966. 1p. [LC, RPI

Australia. Commonwealth Bureau of Census and Statistics.
.1-10-1 Census of population and housing, 30 June 1966. Bulletin, No.
       10-1. Census of the Territory of Norfolk Island. Summary of popula-
       tion. Canberra, Government Printer, 1968. 12p. [PRC, LC, RPI

Norfolk Island Administration.
1971.1   [Census 1966 and 1971].   [Kingston, n.d.] 14p.   [PRC

NORTHERN IRELAND

Capital: Belfast

Statistical Agency: General Register Office
                     Fermanagh House
                     Ormeau Avenue
                     Belfast BT2 8HX,
Publications Distributor: Government Bookshop
                           80 Chicester Street
                           Belfast BT1 4JY

Northern Ireland. General Register Office.
    Census of population of Northern Ireland, 1951. Belfast, HMSO,
    1952-1955. 8 parts.
1951.1-1-1 through 1951.1-1-7. County reports. 1. Antrim. 1954. xxviii,
    87p./2. Armagh. 1954. xxvii, 59p./3. Belfast county borough. 1953.
    xxviii, 44p./4. Down. 1954. xxvii, 83p./5. Fermanagh. 1954. xxv,
    77p./6. County and county borough of Londonderry. 1954. xxvii, 84p./
    7. Tyrone. 1954. xxvii, 87p. [PRC, LC, RPI
  .1-2   General report. 1955. xlix, iii, 95p. maps, specimen forms.
    [PRC, LC, RPI

Northern Ireland. General Register Office.
    Census of population of Northern Ireland, 1961. Belfast, HMSO,
    1962-1965. 10 parts.
1961.1-1   Topographical index. 1962. x, 189p. [PRC, RPI, RIR
1961.1-2-1 through 1961.1-2-7. County reports. 1. Antrim. 1963. xxxiv,
    64p./2. Armagh. 1963. xxxiv, 56p./3. Belfast county borough. 1963.
    xxxiv, 64p./4. Down. 1963. xxv, 77p./5. Fermanagh. 1964. xxxii,
    49p./6. County and county borough of Londonderry. 1964. xxxvi, 92p./
    7. Tyrone. 1964. xxxii, 65p. [PRC, LC, RPI, RIR
  .1-3   General report. 1964. lxi, 84p. specimen forms. [PRC, RPI,
    RIR
  .1-4   Fertility report. 1965. x, 50p. [PRC, RPI, RIR

Northern Ireland. General Register Office.
1966.1   Census of population of Northern Ireland, 1966. General report.
    Belfast, HMSO, 1968. xxiv, 1, 177p. folding table. specimen form.
    [PRC, LC, RPI

Note: For General and parliamentary constituency tables, see under
Great Britain, No. 1966.2.

Northern Ireland. General Register Office.
    Census of population 1971. Northern Ireland. Belfast, HMSO,
    1972-1977. 15 parts.
1971.1-1-1 through 1971.1-1-7. County reports. 1. Antrim. xi, 87p./2. Ar-
    magh. xi, 54p./3. Belfast county borough. xi, 75p./4. Down. xi,
    98p./5. Fermanagh. xi, 35p./6. County and county borough of London-
    derry. xi, 62p./7. Tyrone. xi, 60p. [PRC, LC
  .1-2   Economic activity tables. 1977. xiii, 303p. specimen forms.
    [PRC, LC

1971.1-3   Education tables. 1975. xii, 78p. specimen forms. [PRC, LC
     .1-4   Fertility tables. 1976. ix, 89p. maps. specimen forms. [PRC,
          BC, UN, LC
     .1-5   Housing and household composition tables. 1975. xiv, 118p.
          [PRC, UN, LC
     .1-6   Migration tables. 1976. x, 49p. [PRC, LC, UN
     .1-7   Religion tables. 1975. x, 56p. appendix. [PRC, LC
     .1-8   Workplace and transport to work tables. 1975. ix, 42p. [PRC,
          UN, LC
     .1-9   Summary tables. 1975. xii, 149p. [PRC, BC, UN, LC

NORWAY

Kingdom of Norway.   Capital: Oslo.
Statistical Agency: Central Bureau of Statistics
                     [Statistisk Sentralbyrå]
                     Dronningens Gate, 16
                     P.B. No. 8131 Dep.
                     Oslo 1,
Publications Distributor: same

Norway. Statistisk Sentralbyrå.
  Folktellingen i Norge 3. de-   Population census of Norway,
sember 1946/Recensement de la   December 3, 1946.
population 3 décembre 1946.
Oslo, H. Aschehoug & Co., 1950-
1954. Vol. I-VI. (Norges Officielle Statistikk, rekke XI:
2, 31, 41, 50, 99, 155)
1946.1-1   I. Folkemengde og areal   Population and area of administra-
i de forskjellige deler av lan-   tive divisions. Inhabited islands.
det. Bebodde øyer. Hussamlin-   Agglomerations.
ger./Population et superficie   [PRC, TXU, LC, BC, RPI
des divisions administratives,
etc. Iles habitées. Agglomérations. 1950. 22, 179p.
(NOS XI: 2)
.1-2   II. Trossamfunn./Popula-   De jure population by religion.
tion de droit classée par con-   [PRC, TXU, LC, RPI
fession. 1950. 32p. (NOS XI:
31)
.1-3   III. Folkemengden etter   Population by sex, age and mari-
kjønn, alder og ekteskapelig   tal status, by occupations, and
stilling, etter levevei og etter   by place of birth in rural com-
fødested i de enkelte herreder   munes and cities.
og byer./Population par sexe,   [PRC, TXU, LC, BC, RPI
âge et état civil, par profes-
sions et par lieu de naissance
dans les communes rurales et
les villes. 1951. 12, 317p.
(NOS XI: 41)
.1-4   IV. Folkemengden etter   Population by sex, age and mari-
kjønn, alder og ekteskapelig   tal status. The kingdom and coun-
stilling. Riket og Fylkene.   ties. Resident aliens.
Fremmede statsborgere./Popula-   [PRC, TXU, LC, BC, RPI
tion par sexe, âge et état
civil. Royaume et préfectures.
Sujets étrangers. 1951. 27,
76p. (NOS XI: 50).
.1-5   V. Boligstatistikk./Sta-   Housing statistics.
tistique d'habitation. 1952.   [PRC, TXU, LC, BC, RPI
viii, 47, 230p. (NOS XI: 99)

.1-6   VI. Yrkesstatistikk./Sta-   Occupational statistics.
tistique de professions. 1954.   [PRC, TXU, LC, BC, RPI
379p. (NOS XI: 155)

Norway. Statistisk Sentralbyrå.
   Folketellingen 1. desember   Population census, December 1,
1950.   Oslo, H. Aschehoug & Co.,   1950.
1953-1959. Vol. I-X. (NOS, rek-
ke XI: 145, 146, 153, 221, 236,
258, 271, 303, 323).
1950.1-1   I. Folkemengde og areal   Population and area of the vari-
i de ymse administrative innde-   ous administrative divisions of
linger av landet. Hussamlinger   the country. Agglomerations in
i herredene. 1953. 24, 234p.   rural municipalities.
(NOS XI: 145)   [PRC, LC, RPI
.1-2   II. Folkemengden etter   Population by sex, age, and mari-
kjønn, alder og ekteskapelig   tal status. The whole country,
stilling. Riket, fylkene og de   counties, rural municipalities
enkelte herreder og byer. 1953.   and towns.
19, 190p. (NOS XI: 146)   [PRC, LC, RPI
.1-3   III. Folkemengden etter   Population by principal occupa-
hovedyrke i de enkelte kommuner   tion in the rural and town muni-
og fylker. 1956. 236p. (NOS   cipalities and counties.
XI: 221)   [PRC, LC, RPI
.1-4   IV. Oversikt over yrkes-   A survey of statistics on occu-
statistikken. Detaljoppgaver   pation. Detailed figures for
for riket. 1959. 387p. (NOS   the whole country.
XI: 323)   [PRC, RPI
.1-5   V. Barnetallet i norske   Fertility of marriages.
ekteskap. 1957. 92, 223p.   [PRC, LC, RPI
(NOS XI: 271)
.1-6   VI. Personer 15 år og mer   Persons 15 years of age or more
etter utdanning. 1957. 209p.   by education.
(NOS XI: 258)   [PRC, LC, RPI
.1-7   VII. Trossamfunn. 1954.   Religious denominations.
42p. (NOS XI: 153)   [PRC, LC, RPI
.1-8   VIII. Personer født i   Persons born abroad. Aliens liv-
utlandet. Fremmede statsbor-   ing in Norway. Use of Lappish
gere. Bruken av samisk og kvensk.   and Quainish.
1956. 66p. (NOS XI: 236)   [PRC, LC, RPI
.1-9   IX. Husholdningenes sam-   Composition of households.
mensetning. 1958. 92p. (NOS   [PRC, LC, RPI
XI: 303)
.1-10   X. Boligstatistikk. 1957.   Housing statistics.
156p. (NOS XI: 253)   [PRC, LC, RPI

Norway. Statistisk Sentralbyrå.
   Folketelling 1960.   Oslo, H.   Population census 1960.
Aschehoug & Co., 1963-1964.
Vol. I-VIII. (NOS, rekke XII,
Nos. 108, 117, 129, 133, 140,
151, 157, 158)

1960.1-1   I. Folkemengde og areal etter administrative inndelinger. Tettbygde strøk i herredene. Bebodde øyer. 1963. 236p. (NOS XII: 108)
Population and area by administrative divisions. Densely populated areas in rural municipalities. Inhabited islands.
[PRC, LC, RPI, RIR

.1-2   II. Folkemengden etter kjønn, alder og ekteskapelig status. 1963. 167p. (NOS XII: 117)
Population by sex, age and marital status.
[PRC, LC, RPI, RIR

.1-3   III. Folkemengden etter naering, stilling og sosial status. 1964. 287p. (NOS XII: 129)
Population by industry, occupation and status.
[PRC, RPI, RIR

.1-4   IV. Utdanning. 1964. 129p. (NOS XII: 133)
Education.
[PRC, RPI, RIR

.1-5   V. Husholdninger og familiekjerner. 1964. 115p. (NOS XII: 151)
Households and family nuclei.
[PRC, RPI, RIR

.1-6   VI. Boliger. 1964. 77p. (NOS XII: 157)
Housing.
[PRC, RPI, RIR

.1-7   VII. Barnetallet i ekteskap. 1964. 97p. (NOS XII: 158)
Fertility of marriages.
[PRC, RPI, RIR

.1-8   VIII. Trossamfunn. Fødested. Statsborgerskap. Eiere av personbil. Leiligheter med telefon. 1964. 85p. (NOS XII: 140)
Religious denomination. Place of birth. Citizenship. Private car owners. Dwelling units with telephone.
[PRC, RPI, RIR

Note: There was a separate volume published for each of 734 municipalities.

Norway. Statistisk Sentralbyrå.
1970.1   Markedstall: folke- og boligtelling, 1970.   Oslo, 1974. 139p. maps. (NOS, A659)
Market data: population and housing census, 1970.
[UN

Norway. Statistisk Sentralbyrå.
Folke- og boligtelling 1970. Oslo, H. Aschehoug & Co., 1974-1976. (NOS A679, 693, 708, 739, 730, 823). Vol. I-VI.
Population and housing census, 1970.

.2-1   I. Folkemengden etter geografiske inndelinger. 1974. 195p. (NOS A679)
Population by geographical divisions.
[PRC, LC

.2-2   II. Naering, yrke og arbeidstid m.v. 1975. 327p. (NOS A693)
Industry, occupation, working hours, etc.
[PRC, LC

.2-3   III. Utdanning. 1975. 225p. (NOS A708)
Education.
[PRC, LC

.2-4   IV. Familier og husholdninger. 1975. 105p. (NOS A739)
Families and households.
[PRC, LC

1970.2-5   V. Boligstatistikk. 1975.   Housing statistics.
        155p. (NOS A730)   [PRC, LC
    .2-6   VI. Kontrollundersøkelse.   Evaluation survey.
        1976. 89p. (NOS A823)   [PRC, LC

    Note: There was a separate volume published for each of 451 munici-
    palities.

    Norway. Statistisk Sentralbyrå.
    .3   Folkemengden etter alder og   Population by age and marital
    ekteskapelig status, 31. desember   status, 31 December 1970. ["This
    1970.   Oslo, H. Aschehoug & Co.,   publication corresponds with Vol.
    1971. 149p.   II, Population Census 1960,...
                                              The figures may be considered as
                                              the first results of the Popula-
                                              tion Census 1970."]
                                              [PRC

OMAN

Sultanate of Oman   Capital: Muscat.
Statistical Agency: National Statistical Department
                     Development Council, Technical Section
                     P.O. Box 881
                     Muscat,
Publications Distributor: same.

Reference has been made to a census of cities in 1975 but no citations have been seen.

PACIFIC ISLANDS

Trust Territory of the Pacific Islands (U.S.)   Capital: Saipan
Statistical Agency: High Commissioner's Office
                           Trust Territory of the Pacific Islands
                           Saipan, Mariana Islands 96950
                                    and
                           U.S. Department of the Interior
                           Washington, D.C. 20240
Publications Distributor: High Commissioner's Office
                                    and
                           U.S. Government Printing Office
                           Washington, D.C. 20402

United States. Department of the Navy.
1950.1   Report on the administration of the Trust Territory of the Pacific
Islands for the period July 1, 1949 to June 30, 1950. Washington,
D.C., GPO, 1950. P. 63. [NYPL, RPI

Pacific Islands. Trust Territory. High Commissioner's Office.
1958.1   Census report 1958, Trust Territory of the Pacific Islands. Agana,
Guam, Office of the High Commissioner, 1959. 39p. maps. [PRC, LC

United States. Bureau of the Census.
1970.1-1-54/58   Census of population: 1970. Volume I. Characteristics
of the population. Part 54-58. Guam, Virgin Islands, American Samoa,
Canal Zone, Trust Territory of the Pacific Islands. 1973. var. pag.
[PRC, LC, RPI

Pacific Islands. Trust Territory. High Commissioner's Office.
1973.1   1973 population of the Trust Territory of the Pacific Islands.
Saipan, Mariana Islands, 1975. 292p. [PRC, UN

Note: Mariana Islands (name changed to Northern Mariana Islands) will
become a U.S. commonwealth in 1981.

PAKISTAN

Islamic Republic of Pakistan.   Capital: Islamabad.
Statistical Agency: Statistics Division/Census Organization
                     Government of Pakistan
                     I-S.M.C.H. Society
                     Karachi-3,
Publications Distributor: Manager of Publications
                          Central Publications Branch
                          Block No. 44, Shahrah-i-Iraq
                          Karachi,
                                    and
                          University Book Service
                          K-35, Notomal Garden
                          New Town, Karachi 5,

Pakistan. Office of the Census Commissioner.
     Census of Pakistan, 1951. Karachi, Manager of Publications, 1951-
   1956. Vol. I-IX.
1951.1-1   I. Pakistan. Reports and tables. n.d. var. pag. [PRC, RPI
   .1-2   II. Baluchistan. Report and tables. n.d. var. pag. [PRC,
   BC, RPI
   .1-3   III. East Bengal. Report and tables. n.d. var. pag. [TXU,
   RPI
   .1-4   IV. North-West Frontier Province. Report and tables. n.d.
   var. pag. [TXU, RPI
   .1-5   V. Punjab and Bahawalpur States. Report and tables. n.d. var.
   pag. [TXU, RPI
   .1-6   VI. Sind and Khairpur State. Report and tables. n.d. var.
   pag. [TXU, RPI
   .1-7   VII. West Pakistan. Tables of economic characteristics. n.d.
   var. pag. [TXU, RPI
   .1-8   VIII. East Pakistan. Tables. n.d. var. pag. [TXU, RPI
   .1-9   IX. Administrative report. Part 1. The census commissioner's
   report. Part 2. The report of the provincial superintendents of
   census operation... 1953. x, 237p. [PRC, BC, RPI

Pakistan. Office of the Census Commissioner.
     Census of Pakistan, 1951. Census bulletins. Karachi, 1951-1957.
   Nos. 1-6.
   .2-1   Provisional tables of population. 1951. ii, 6p. [PRC, BC, RPI
   .2-2   Population according to religion. 1951. ii, 39, [2]p. 2 maps.
   [PRC, BC, RPI
   .2-3   Urban and rural population and area. 1952. 44p. 2 maps.
   [PRC, BC, RPI
   .2-4   Population according to economic status. 1953. [3], xi, 69,
   [1]p. [PRC, BC, RPI
   .2-5   Part 1, Detailed age tables in 5-year age groups. Part 2, East
   Bengal, detailed age tables. n.d. 241, 131p. [PRC, BC, RPI
   .2-6   Demographic miscellany. 1957. [2], i, 74, [2]p. [PRC, BC, LC

Pakistan. Office of the Census Commissioner.
     Census of Pakistan, 1951. Village lists.   Karachi, 1952.   59v.
1951.3-1-1 through 1951.3-1-4. [One for each District in Bahawalpur State].
    [PRC, BC
1951.3-2-1 through 1951.3-2-17. [One for each District in East Bengal].
    [PRC, BC
1951.3-3-1 through 1951.3-3-7. [One for each state in North-West Frontier
    Province]. [PRC, BC
1951.3-4-1 through 1951.3-4-6. [One for each District in North-West Frontier
    Province]. [PRC, BC
1951.3-5-1 through 1951.3-5-16. [One for each District in Punjab]. [PRC, BC
1951.3-6-1 through 1951.3-6-9. [One for each District in Sind and Khairpur
    State]. [PRC, BC

Pakistan. Office of the Census Commissioner.
     1961 census of Pakistan. Census bulletins.   Karachi, Manager of
    Publications, 1961-1963. Nos. 1-7.
1961.1-1   Provisional tables of population by sex and literacy. 1961.
    15p. [BC, RPI
  .1-2   Final tables of population by sex, urban-rural, religion, non-
    Pakistanis. 1961. 210p. [TXU, BC, RPI
  .1-3   Age, sex, and marital status. 1962. xxvi, 416, [3]p. [PRC,
    TXU, BC, RPI
  .1-4   Literacy and education. 1962. xxiii, 331, [3]p. [TXU, RPI
  .1-5   Economic characteristics. 1963. xxii, 125, [3]p. [TXU, BC,
    RPI
  .1-6   Cottage industry. 1963. 105p. [TXU, RPI
  .1-7   Population projections of Pakistan, 1961-81.   .   p.
    [

Pakistan. Office of the Census Commissioner.
     1961 census of Pakistan. Karachi and Islamabad, Manager of Publi-
    cations, 1963-1964. Vol. I-X in 12v.
  .2-1   I. Pakistan. Tables and report. By A. Rashid.   Karachi, 1963.
    xii, [422]p. [PRC, TXU, RPI
  .2-2   II. East Pakistan. Tables and report. By H.H. Nomani.   Kara-
    chi, 1964. v, [1054]p. [PRC, TXU, RPI
  .2-3   III. West Pakistan. Tables and report. By A.A. Khan.   Kara-
    chi, 1964. xi, [1443], [34]p. [PRC, TXU, RPI
  .2-4   IV. Pakistan. Non-agricultural labor force, 1961.   Islamabad,
    1964. [4], iv, ii, 287, v p. [PRC, TXU, RPI
  .2-5   V. Economic characteristics. Tables for East Pakistan.   Kara-
    chi, 1964. [8], 1231p. appendices. [PRC, RPI
     VI. West Pakistan. Non-agricultural labour force. Part 1-2.
  .2-6-1   1. Islamabad, 1964. 2, 2, v, [1], 1191p. [PRC, TXU, RPI
  .2-6-2   2. Islamabad, 1964. [5], pp. 1192-2374. App. A-D. [PRC,
    TXU, RPI
  .2-7   VII. Administrative report. (For Official Use Only). [Not
    available].
  .2-8   VIII. Housing, 1960. Pakistan. Karachi, 1963. iii, [161],
    xi p. [PRC, TXU, RPI

1961.2-9   IX. Housing, 1960. East Pakistan. Karachi, 1963. 567, [9]p.
      [PRC, TXU, RPI
     .2-10   X. Housing, 1960. West Pakistan. Karachi, 1963. [10], vi,
      1313, [16]p. [PRC, TXU, RPI

      Pakistan. Office of the Census Commissioner.
           Population census of Pakistan, 1961. District census reports: 1.
      General description; 2. General tables; 3. Housing tables; 4. Popula-
      tion tables; 5. Village statistics. Karachi, Manager of Publications,
      n.d. 67v.
1961.3-1-1 through 1961.3-1-49. [One for each District in West Pakistan].
      [TXU, RPI
     .3-2   Census report of tribal agencies. Parts I-III: General des-
      cription, population tables and village statistics. n.d. var. pag.
      [TXU, RPI
1961.3-3-1 through 1961.3-3-17. [One for each District in East Pakistan].
      [TXU, RPI

      Pakistan. Census Organization.
           Population census of Pakistan, 1972. Islamabad and Karachi, Mana-
      ger of Publications, 1973-   . 58v.
1972.1-1   Provisional tables. Islamabad, 1973. [2], 4p. (Census bulle-
      tin, No. 1). [PRC, BC, UN
1972.1-2-1 through 1972.1-2-50. District Census Reports. [All have App. I-IV
      and 1 map]. 1. Bahawalnagar. 1978. vii, 170p./2. Bahawalpur. 1977.
      viii, 225p./3. Bannu. 1975. vii, 86p./4. Campbelpur. 1977. vii,
      154p./5. Chagai. 1976. vii, 59p./6. Chitral. 1976. vii, 57p./7.
      Dadu. 1976. ix, 151p./8. D.G. Khan. 1977. ix, 178p./9. D.I. Khan.
      1975. vii, 106p./10. Dir. 1976. vii, 90p./11. Gujranwala. 1977.
      ix, 201p./12 Gujrat. 1977. viii, 211p./13. Hazara. 1976. ix, 229p./
      14. Hyderabad. 1977. viii, 213p./15. Jacobabad. 1976. ix, 118p./
      16. Jhang. 1977. ix, 178p./17. Jhelum. 1977. ix, 173p./18. Kachhi.
      1976. viii, 141p./19. Kalat. 1976. ix, 148p./20. Karachi. 1977.
      ix, 148p./21. Khairpur. 1976. vii, 128p./22. Kharan. 1976. vii,
      56p./23. Kohat. 1975. vii, 91p./24. Lahore. 1978. ix, 215p./
           25. Larkana. 1976. ix, 152p./26. Lasbela. 1976. ix, 99p./
      27. Loralai. 1976. vii, 101p./28. Lyallpur. 1977. ix, 210p./29.
      Malakand Protected Area. 1976. vii, 60p./30. Mardan. 1975. ix,
      112p./31. Mekran. 1976. ix, 126p./32. Mianwali. 1977. ix, 186p./
      33. Multan. 1977. ix, 341p./34. Muzaffargarh. 1977. viii, 225p./
      35. Nawabshah. 1977. viii, 181p./36. Peshawar. 1975. ix, 185p./37.
      Quetta-Peshin. 1976. vii, 97p./38. Rahimyar Khan. 1977. ix, 189p./
      39. Rawalpindi. 1977. viii, 175p./40. Sahiwal. 1978. ix, 268p./41.
      Sanghar. 1976. ix, 127p./42. Sargodha. 1977. ix, 271p./43. Sheik-
      hupura. 1977. ix, 191p./44. Sialkot. 1977. viii, 326p./45. Sibi.
      1976. ix, 147p./46. Sukkur. 1977. ix, 184p./47. Swat. 1975. vii,
      86p./48. Tharparker. 1977. ix, 205p./49. Thatta. 1975. ix, 163p./
      50. Zhob. 1976. vii, 80p. [PRC, UN, LC, OPR, E-W
     .1-3   Census report, Federally Administered Tribal Areas.   .
           [
     .1-4   Census report, Islamabad Federal Capital. 1978. vii, 51p. App.
      I-IV. map. [PRC

             Provincial census report.   . 4v.
1972.1-5-1 through 1972.1-5-4. 1. Baluchistan.   /2. North-
    West Frontier Province.   /3. Punjab.   /
    4. Sind.
  .1-6   Pakistan census report.
  .1-7   Administrative report. (For Official Use Only). [Not avail-
    able].

    [Note: The census of 1972 is only one of the three censuses that was
    conducted in two parts. The following is the second part].

    Pakistan. Census Organization.
        Housing, economic and demographic survey, 1973.   Islamabad, n.d.
    Vol. I-II in 6v.
1973.1-1   I.

             II. Statistical tables. Nos. I-V.
  .1-2-1   I. Pakistan. xi, 384p. [OPR
  .1-2-2   II. N.W.F.P. xii, 337p. [OPR
  .1-2-3   III. Punjab. xvi, 484p. [OPR
  .1-2-4   IV. Baluchistan. xii, 312p. [OPR
  .1-2-5   V. Sind. xii, 382p. [OPR

PANAMA

Republic of Panama.   Capital: Panama
Statistical Agency: Bureau of Statistics and Census
                      [Dirección de Estadística y Censo (DEC)]
                      Contraloría General de la República
                      Apartado 5213
                      Panama 5,
Publications Distributor: same

Panama.   Dirección de Estadís-
          tica y Censo.
1950.0-1   Panamá, censos 1950.   Panama, censuses 1950.
          Panama, Imprenta Nacional, 1950.   [PRC, TXU, RPI
          70, [2]p.

Panama.   DEC.
          Censos nacionales de 1950.   National censuses of 1950.
          Panama, Imprenta Nacional, 1950-
          1954.   2v.
.0-2-1   Quinto censo nacional de   Fifth national census of popula-
          población y vivienda, 10 de di-   tion and housing, December 10,
          ciembre de 1950.   Instrucciones   1950.   Instructions for the enu-
          a los empadronadores.   1950.   merators.
          53p.   [PRC, RPI
.0-2-2   Informe general sobre pre-   Report on the preparation and
          paración y ejecución de los cen-   execution of the censuses.
          sos.   1954.   xvi, 139, [1]p.   [PRC, RPI

Panama.   DEC.
          Quinto censo nacional de pob-   Fifth national census of popula-
          lación y vivienda, 10 de diciem-   tion and housing, December 10,
          bre de 1950.   Panama, Imprenta   1950.
          nacional, 1951-1954.   2v.
.0-3-1   Procedimiento para cuatro   Procedure for four basic tabula-
          tabulaciones básicas de pobla-   tions of population.
          ción.   1951.   vi, 29p.   [PRC, RPI
.0-3-2   Definiciones adoptadas   Definitions adopted for the 1950
          para el censo de 1950.   1954.   census.
          [15]p.   [PRC, RPI

Panama.   DEC.
.0-4   Discrepancias de los lí-   Discrepancies of district boun-
          mites de distrito... Censos de   daries... Censuses of 1950.
          1950.   Panama, Imprenta Nacio-   [PRC, RPI
          nal, 1953.   v, 79p.

Panama.   DEC.
          Quinto censo nacional de   Fifth national census of popula-
          población y vivienda, 10 de   tion and housing, December 10,
          diciembre de 1950.   Boletín   1950.   Information bulletins.

informativo.   Panama, Imprenta
Nacional, 1951-1956.   Nos. 1-7.
.1-1   Cifras preliminares.   1951.   Preliminary figures.
ix, 25p.   [PRC, TXU, LC, RPI
.1-2   Población total; cifras   Total population; official figures.
oficiales.   1952.   22p.   [PRC, TXU, RPI
.1-3   Densidad de población por   Population density by square kilo-
kilómetro cuadrado de la Repúb-   meter of the Republic by province,
lica por provincia, censo de   census 1950.
1950.   1952.   xi, 91p.   [PRC, TXU, RPI
.1-4   Número de viviendas, ma-   Number of dwellings, construction
terial de construcción.   1952.   material.
iv, 18p.   [PRC, TXU, RPI
.1-5   Lugares poblados.   1954.   Populated places.
xi, 168p.   [PRC, TXU, RPI
.1-6   Viviendas por manzana,   Dwellings by block, cities of
ciudades de Panamá y Colón.   Panama and Colon.
1956.   iii, [1], 21p.   [PRC, TXU, RPI
.1-7   Nomenclatura y localiza-   Nomenclature and location of popu-
ción de los lugares poblados.   lated places.
1956.   ix, 83p.   [PRC, TXU, RPI

Panama.   DEC.
   Censos nacionales de 1950.   National censuses of 1950.   Fifth
Quinto censo de población.   Pa-   census of population.
nama, Imprenta Nacional, 1954-
1959.   Vol. I-VI.
.2-1   I.   Características gene-   General characteristics.
rales.   1954.   xxxvi, 331p.   [PRC, TXU, LC, RPI
.2-2   II.   Características edu-   Educational characteristics.
cativas.   1954.   xx, 299p.   [PRC, TXU, LC, RPI
.2-3   III.   Características   Economic characteristics.
económicas.   1954.   xxxiv, 247p.   [PRC, TXU, LC, RPI
.2-4   IV.   Población indígena.   Indigenous [Indian] population.
1954.   xxvii, 83p.   [PRC, TXU, LC, RPI
.2-5   V.   Población urbana.   Urban population.
1956.   xxv, 227p.   [PRC, TXU, LC, RPI
.2-6   VI.   Características de   Characteristics of the family.
la familia.   1957.   xxxii, 212p.   [PRC, TXU, LC, RPI

Panama.   DEC.
   Censos nacionales de 1960.   National censuses of 1960.
Panama, Imprenta Nacional, 1962.
2v.
1960.0-1-1   Algunas características   Some important characteristics of
importantes de la población, 11   the population, December 11, 1960.
de diciembre de 1960.   [7]p.   [PRC, BC, RPI
.0-1-2   Algunas características   Some important characteristics of
importantes de la vivienda pana-   the Panamanian housing, December
meña, 11 de diciembre de 1960.   11, 1960.
[27]p.   [PRC

Panama. DEC.
Informe general sobre el levantamiento de los censos nationales, 1960-1962. Panama, Imprenta Nacional, 1962-1964.
Parts 1-7 in 8v.

General report on the execution
of the national censuses, 1960-
1962.

1960.0-2-1   Ensayos censales (población, vivienda y agropecuario).
1962. xiii, 152p.

Census essays (population, housing, agriculture).
[PRC, BC, RPI

.0-2-2   Cartografía censal. 1962.
vi, 32p.

Census cartography.
[PRC, BC, RPI

.0-2-3   Sexto censo de población
y segundo de vivienda, 11 de
diciembre de 1960. 1962. xii,
150p.

Sixth census of population and
second of housing, December 11,
1960.
[PRC, TXU, BC, RPI

.0-2-4   Segundo censo agropecuario,
16 de abril de 1961. 1962. x,
104p.

Second agricultural census, April
16, 1961.
[PRC, TXU, BC, RPI

.0-2-5   Primer censo nacional industrial, comercial y de servicios, abril-julio de 1962.
1963. x, 74p.

First national industrial, com-
mercial and services census,
April-July 1962.
[PRC, TXU, BC, RPI

.0-2-5s   Suplemento. Primer censo
de construcción y electricidad,
segundo semestre de 1963. [1964].
vi, 34p.

Supplement. First census of construction and electricity, second
half of 1963.
[PRC, BC, RPI

.0-2-6   Tabulación. 1964. viii,
98p.

Tabulation.
[PRC, TXU, BC, RPI

.0-2-7   Resumen. [1964]. xii,
69p.

Summary.
[PRC, UN, RPI

Panama. DEC.
Censos nacionales de 1960.
Sexto censo de población y se-
gundo de vivienda. Panama,
Imprenta Nacional, 1962-1965.
Vol. I-IX in 10v.

National censuses of 1960. Sixth
census of population and second
of housing.

.1-1   I. Lugares poblados de
la República. 1962. xiv, 313p.

Populated places of the Republic.
[PRC, TXU, UN, LC, RPI

.1-2   II. Ciudad de Panamá.
1963. xviii, 396p.

City of Panama.
[PRC, TXU, LC, RPI

.1-3   III. Ciudad de Colón.
1963. xviii, 294p.

City of Colon.
[PRC, LC, RPI

.1-3s   Suplemento. Sectoriza-
ción censal. Ciudades de Panamá y Colón. 1964. xv, 98p.

Supplement. Census division.
Cities of Panama and Colon.
[LC, RPI

.1-4   IV. Características generales. 1963. xxxii, 175p.

General characteristics.
[PRC, TXU, LC, RPI

.1-5   V. Características económicas. 1964. xxxiii, 446p.

Economic characteristics.
[PRC, TXU, LC, RPI

.1-6   VI.   Características educativas. 1964. ix, 208p.

Educational characteristics.
[PRC, TXU, LC, RPI

.1-7   VII. Características de
la familia. 1964. xxviii, 317p.

Characteristics of the family.
[PRC, TXU, LC, RPI

.1-8   VIII. Migración internal.
1965. xxviii, 75p.

Internal migration.
[PRC, TXU, LC, RPI

.1-9   IX.   Población indígena.
1964. ix, 127p.

Indigenous [Indian] population.
[PRC, TXU, LC, RPI

Panama. DEC.
.2   Censos nacionales de 1960.
Sexto censo de población y
segundo de vivienda. Compendio general de población. Panama, Imprenta Nacional, 1965.
xxii, 149p.

National censuses of 1960. Sixth
census of population and second
of housing. General compendium
of population.
[PRC, TXU, LC, RPI

Panama. DEC.
     Censos nacionales de 1970.
Ensayos censales. 1971. Vol.
I-II.

National censuses of 1970.
Census essays.

1970.0-1-1   I. Población y vivienda.
vi, 43p.

Population and housing.
[PRC

.0-1-2   II. Censo agropecuariol
v, 34p.

Agricultural census.
[PRC

Panama. DEC.
     Censos nacionales de 1970.
Informe methodológico sobre el
levantamiento de los censos nacionales de 1970-1972.   Panama,
1973-   . Vol. I-IV.

National censuses of 1970. Methodological report on the execution
of the national censuses of 1970-
1972.

.0-2-1   I. Séptimo censo de población y tercero de vivienda.
1973. 147p.

Seventh census of population and
third of housing.
[PRC, BC, IASI

.0-2-2   II. III censo agropecuario, 16 de mayo de 1972.   .

Third census of agriculture, May
16, 1972.
[BC

.0-2-3   III. [Industrial, comercial, de servicios, electricidad y construcción.]

[Industrial, commercial, services,
electricity and construction censuses.]
[

.0-2-4   IV. [Procesamiento de
datos.]

[Data processing.]
[

Panama. DEC
     Censos nacionales de 1970:
VII de población; III de vivienda, 10 de mayo de 1970.   Panama, 1970-1971. 4v.

National censuses of 1970: VII
of population; III of housing,
May 10, 1970.

.1-1   Cifras preliminares. 1970.
xi, 28p.

Preliminary figures.
[PRC, BC, LC

1970.1-2   Algunas características importantes de la población. (Avance de tabulaciones finales). 1971.

Some important characteristics of the population. (Advance of final tabulations).
[

.1-3   Algunas características importantes de la vivienda. (Avance de tabulaciones finales). 1971. viii, 23p.

Some important characteristics of housing. (Advance of final tabulations).
[PRC

.1-4   Resultados generales. Panama, 1971. ix, 50p.

General results.
[PRC, BC, OPR, LC

Panama. DEC.

.2   Censos nacionales de 1970: VII censo nacional de población y III censo de vivienda, 10 de mayo de 1970. Resúmenes de tabulaciones finales. Panama, 1973. 8p.

National censuses of 1970: VII national census of population and III census of housing, May 10, 1970. Summaries of final tabulations.
[PRC

Panama. DEC.
Censos nacionales de 1970: séptimo censo de población; tercer censo de vivienda, 10 de mayo de 1970. Panama, 1972-1976. Vol. I-VI in 7v.

National censuses of 1970: seventh census of population; third census of housing, May 10, 1970.

.3-1   I. Lugares poblados de la República. 1972. xiii, 423p.

Populated places of the Republic.
[PRC, BC, LC

.3-1a   Anexo. Nomenclatura y localización de los lugares poblados de la República. 1972. pp. 424-542.

Annex. Nomenclature and localization of the populated places of the Republic. [Appears both separate and included in Vol. I]
[PRC, LC

.3-2   II. Características de la vivienda. 1973. xii, 481p.

Housing characteristics.
[PRC

.3-3   III. Compendio general de población. 1975. xv, 404p.

General compendium of population.
[PRC, IASI, BC, LC

.3-4   IV. Características generales, educativas, migración interna, fecundidad y hogares. 1975. xii, 215p.

General, educational, internal migration, fertility and household characteristics.
[PRC, BC, LC

.3-5   V. Características económicas. 1976. xv, 505p.

Economic characteristics.
[PRC, IASI, BC, LC

.3-6   VI. Sectores censales de los distritos de Panamá, San Miguelito y Colón. 1976. xviii, 121p.

Census divisions of the metropolitan areas of Panama, San Miguelito and Colon.
[PRC, IASI

Note: "The plan for the publication of provincial volumes was modified in view of the fact that the Dirección de Estadística y Censo edited in 1973 provincial volumes with data from the various censuses and continuous statistics."

Panama. DEC.
    Compendio estadístico. Pro-   Statistical compendium. Province
vincia de...   Panama, 1973.   of...
9v.
1970.4-1 through 1970.4-9. 1. Bocas del Toro. 66p./2. Coclé.   p./3. Colón.
99p./4. Chiriquí.   p./5. Darién. 76p./6. Herrera. 91p./7. Los
Santos. 102p./8. Panamá. 135p./9. Veraguas.   p. [LC, PRC

Panama. DEC.
    Censos nacionales de 1970:   National censuses of 1970: ...
... Monografías. Panama,   Monographs.
197 -197 . Nos. 1-10.
.5-1

PANAMA CANAL ZONE

Capital: Balboa Heights.
Statistical Agency: U.S. Bureau of the Census.
Washington, D.C. 20233
Publications Distributor: U.S. Government Printing Office
Washington, D.C. 20402

The treaty returning the Zone to Panamá was signed 1978.

U.S. Bureau of the Census.
1950.1-2-51/54 Census of population: 1950. A report of the seventeenth
decennial census of the United States. Volume II. Characteristics
of the population. Part 51-54. Territories and possessions (Alaska,
Hawaii, Puerto Rico, American Samoa, Canal Zone, Guam, and Virgin
Islands). 1953. var. pag. [PRC, LC, RPI

U.S. Bureau of the Census.
1960.1-1-54/57 Census of population: 1960. The eighteenth decennial census
of the United States. Volume I. Characteristics of the population.
Part 54-57. Outlying areas (Virgin Islands, Guam, American Samoa, and
Canal Zone). 1963. [218]p. [PRC, LC, RPI

U.S. Bureau of the Census.
1970.1-1-54/58 Census of population: 1970. Volume I. Characteristics of
the population. Part 54-58. Guam, Virgin Islands, American Samoa,
Canal Zone, Trust Territory of the Pacific Islands. 1973. var. pag.
[PRC, LC, RPI

PAPUA NEW GUINEA

Capital: Port Moresby.

Statistical Agency: Bureau of Statistics.
P.O. Wards Strip
Port Moresby,
Publications Distributor: same

Australia. Commonwealth Bureau of Census and Statistics.
1947.CG-6   Census of the Commonwealth of Australia. Bulletin no. 6. Summary for the territory of Papua-New Guinea. Canberra, Government Printer, 1950. 10p. [Non-indigenous population only.] [LC, RPI

Australia. Commonwealth Bureau of Census and Statistics.
   Census of the Commonwealth of Australia, 30th June 1947. Canberra, Government Printer, n.d. Vol. I & III.
.1-1   I, Part VII. Analysis of population in local government areas: Papua-New Guinea, Norfolk Island, Nauru. Pp. 465-492. [TXU, RPI
.1-3   III, Part XXVI. Analysis of dwellings: Papua-New Guinea. Pp. 1927-1946. [TXU, RPI

Australia. Commonwealth Bureau of Census and Statistics.
1954.1-7-5   Census of the Commonwealth of Australia. Volume VII. Territories. Part V. External territories (Papua, New Guinea, Norfolk Island and Nauru): Population and dwellings. Canberra, Government Printer, 1958. 30p. [Non-indigenous population only.] [PRC, RPI

Australia. Commonwealth Bureau of Census and Statistics.
1961.CB-16   Census of the Commonwealth, 30th June 1961. Census bulletin, no. 16. Summary of non-indigenous population and dwellings for the territory of Papua and New Guinea. Canberra, Government Printer, 1962. 26p. [TXU, RPI

Australia. Commonwealth Bureau of Census and Statistics.
.1-7-5   Census of the Commonwealth of Australia. Volume VII. Territories. Part V. External territories (Papua, New Guinea, Nauru, Norfolk Island, Christmas Islands and Cocos(Keeling) Islands). Canberra, Government Printer, 1965. 59p. [Non-indigenous population only.] [PRC, RPI

Papua New Guinea. Bureau of Statistics.
   Census of Papua and New Guinea, 1966. Preliminary bulletins. Konedobu, Government Printer, 1966-1970. Nos. 1-38.
      (First) Preliminary bulletins, Nos. 1-19. 1966.
1966.1-1 through 1966.1-18. [Districts] 1. West Sepik. 4p./2. Northern. 4p./3. New Ireland. 4p./4. Central. 5p./5. Morobe. 5p./6. Western. 4p./7. Southern Highlands. 4p./8. Chimbu. 4p./9. East Sepik. 4p./ 10. Manus. 3p./11. Madang. 5p./12. East New Britain. 5p./13. West New Britain. 4p./14. Bougainville. 4p./15. Eastern Highlands. 4p./ 16. Western Highlands. 4p./17. Milne Bay. 4p./18. Gulf. 4p. [PRC, BC, LC, RPI
.1-19   Population of Papua and New Guinea. 1966. 7p. map. [PRC, BC, RPI

.1-20   Summary of population. 1970. [2], 70p. map. [PRC, BC, LC,
RPI

Preliminary bulletins. 1969. Nos. 21-38.
1966.1-21 through 1966.1-38. [Districts]. 21. Western. 36p./22. Gulf.
36p./23. Central district and Port Moresby urban area. 58p./24. Milne
Bay. 36p./25. Northern. 36p./26. Southern Highlands. 36p./27. Eastern Highlands district and Goroka urban area. 58p./28. Chimbu. 36p./
29. Western Highlands district and Mount Hagen urban area. 57p./30.
West Sepik. 36p./31. East Sepik district and Wewak urban area. 58p./
32. Madang district and Madang urban area. 58p./33. Morobe district
and Lae urban area. 58p./34. West New Britain. 36p./35. East New
Britain and Rabaul urban area. 58p./36. New Ireland. 36p./37. Bougainville. 36p./38. Manus. 36p. [PRC, BC, LC, RPI

Note: "The Preliminary bulletins numbers 1-38 may be taken as the
final figures."

Papua New Guinea. Bureau of Statistics.
1971.0-1   Population census - July 1971. Preliminary bulletin no. 1 -
Urban centres. Konedobu, Government Printer, 1972. 3p. [PRC

Papua New Guinea. Bureau of Statistics.
.0-2   1971 census - Interim bulletin. Konedobu, 1973. 15p. [

Papua New Guinea. Bureau of Statistics.
Population census - 1971. Summary of population estimates (pre-
release). Konedobu, 1973-1974. 2v.
.1-1   Population distribution. 1973. 7p. [PRC, BC, LC
.1-2   Population characteristics. 1974. 17p. [PRC, BC, LC

Papua New Guinea. Bureau of Statistics.
1971 census. Characteristics of the population. Konedobu, 1974.
Bulletins Nos. 1-27.
.2-1   Papua New Guinea. 16p. [PRC, JB-F, BC
1971.2-2 through 1971.2-19. [Districts]. 2. Western. 16p./3. Gulf. 16p./
4. Central. 16p./5. Milne Bay. 16p./6. Northern. 16p./7. Southern
Highlands. 16p./8. Western Highlands. 16p./9. Chimbu. 16p./10. Eastern Highlands. 16p./11. Morobe. 16p./12. Madang. 16p./13. East Sepik.
16p./14. West Sepik. 16p./15. Manus. 16p./16. New Ireland. 16p./17.
West New Britain. 16p./18. East New Britain. 16p./19. Bougainville.
16p. [PRC, JB-F, BC, LC
1971.2-20 through 1971.2-27. [Major urban areas.] 20. Port Moresby. 16p./
21. Mount Hagen. 16p./22. Goroka. 16p./23. Lae. 16p./24. Madang
urban. 16p./25. Wewak. 16p./26. Rabaul. 16p./27. Arawa-Kieta-Pangun.
16p. [PRC, JB-F, BC

Papua New Guinea. Bureau of Statistics.
Population census 1971. Census monographs. Port Moresby, Government Printer, 1976- . No. 1- .
.3-1   The determinants of labour force participation rates in Papua
New Guinea. 1976. viii, 79p. [PRC, UN

PARAGUAY

Republic of Paraguay.   Capital: Asunción.
Statistical Agency: General Bureau of Statistics and Censuses
                     [Dirección General de Estadística y Censos (DGEC)]
                     Humaita 463--Casilla de Correo, no. 1118
                     Asunción,
Publications Distributor: same.

Paraguay. Dirección General de
     Estadística.
     Censo nacional de población   National census of population
y viviendas, 28 octubre 1950.   and housing, October 28, 1950.
Departamento de...   Asunción,   Department of ...
1953-1955.   17v.
1950.1-1 through 1950.1-17. 1. Concepción. 1953. 24p./2. San Pedro. 1953.
    26p./3. Las Cordilleras. 1953. 26p./4. Guaira. 1953. 22p./5. Caa-
    guazú. 1954. 24p./6. Caazapú. 1954. 24p./7. Itapúa. 1954. 26p./
    8. Misiones. 1954. 26p./9. Paraquari. 1954. 27p./10. Alto Paraná.
    1954. 23p./11. Central. 1954. 23p./12. Neembucu. 1955. 23p./13.
    Amambay. 1955. 23p./14. Presidente Hayes. 1954. 23p./15. Boquerón.
    1955. 23p./16. Olimpo. 1954. 23p./17. Ciudad de Asunción. 1955.
    26p. [PRC, RPI   (Numbers 1, 4, and 11, above, not available).

Paraguay. Dirección General de
     Estadística.
.2   Censo de población y vivienda,   Census of population and housing,
1950. [Cuadros referentes al   1950. [Tables referring to the
país en su totalidad.] In: country in total.] . . . Chap-
Anuario estadístico de la Repú-   ter II. Population and housing.
lica del Paraguay, 1948-1953.   [PRC, RPI
Cap. II. Población y viviendas.
Asunción, El Arte, S.A., 1955.
Pp. 20-38.

Paraguay. Dirección General de
     Estadística.
.3   Censo de población y vivienda,   Census of population and housing,
1950. Cuadros generales, comen-   1950. General tables, analytical
tario analítico.   Asunción, 1962.   commentary.
19, [2]p.   [PRC, RPI

Paraguay. DGEC.
1962.0-1   Censo de población y   Census of population and housing,
vivienda de 1962: cifras pro-   1962: provisional figures.
visionales.   Asunción, [1963].   [PRC, RPI
2p.

Paraguay. DGEC.
.0-2   Cuadro 3. Población y   Table 3. Urban and rural popula-
vivienda urbana y rural en 1962   tion and housing in 1962 and inter-

y variación intercensal urbana
(cifras provisionales). [Asun-
ción[, 1963. 6p.

censal urban variation (provisional figures).
[PRC, BC, RP]

Paraguay. DGEC.
.0-3   Datos preliminares del
censo de población y vivienda
de 1962 obtenidos por medio de
muestra. Asunción, 1964. 23p.

Preliminary data from the census
of population and housing of 1962
taken by means of sample.
[PRC, BC, RP]

Paraguay. DGEC.
     Censo de población y vivien-
da, 14 de octubre de 1962. [De-
partamento de...] Asunción,
1964-1965. 17v.
1962.1-1 through 1962.1-17. 1. Concepción.

Census of population and housing,
October 14, 1962. [Department of
...]

/2. San Pedro.
     /3. Cordillera.   /4. Guaira.   /5. Caa-
guazú.   /6. Caazapú.   /7. Itapúa.
     /8. Misiones.   /9. Paraquarí.   /
10. Alto Paraná.   /11. Central.   /12. Ñeembucu.
     /13. Amambay.   /14. Presidente Hays.
     /15. Boquerón.   /16. Olimpo.   /17. Asun-
ción. 1965. 85p. [PRC, TXU

Paraguay. DGEC.
.2   Censo de población y vivienda,
14 octubre de 1962. [Total país]
Asunción, 1966. [59]p.

Census of population and housing,
October 14, 1962. [Whole country]
[PRC, TXU, BC

Paraguay. DGEC.
1972.0-1   Censo nacional de población y viviendas, 1972. (Cifras provisionales). Asunción,
1973. 32p.

National census of population and
housing, 1972. (Provisional figures).
[PRC, BC, LC

Paraguay. DGEC.
.1   Censo nacional de población
y viviendas, 1972. Muestra del
10 por ciento. Asunción, 1974.
56p.

National census of population and
housing, 1972. Ten percent sample.
[PRC, OPR, BC, LC

Paraguay. DGEC.
     Censo nacional de población
y viviendas, 1972. Asunción,
1975-1976. 2v. maps.
.2-1   ... 1975. xxiii, 561p.
.2-2   De acuerdo a los departamentos creados en la nueva división territorial. 1976. iii,
290p.

National census of population and
housing, 1972.

[UN, PRC, LC
In accord with the departments
created in the new territorial
division.
[UN

PERU

Republic of Peru   Capital: Lima
Statistical Agency: National Institute of Statistics
                     [Instituto Nacional de Estadística (INE)]
                     Avenida 28 de julio, 1056/Apartado 2095
                     Lima,
Publications Distributor: same

Peru. Dirección Nacional de
       Estadística y Censos.
1961.0-1 Resultados preliminares del   Preliminary results of the popu-
censo de población de 1961.   lation census of 1961.
[Lima, 1962]. [8], 101p.   [PRC, LC, RPI

Peru. Dirección Nacional de
       Estadística y Censos.
.1   Sexto censo nacional de pob-   Sixth national census of popula-
lación y primero de vivienda,   tion and first of housing, July
2 de julio de 1961: princi-   2, 1961: main results obtained
pales resultados obtenidos por   by sample.
muestreo.   Lima, 1963. 39p.   [PRC, RPI

Peru. Dirección Nacional de
       Estadística y Censos.
.2   Sexto censo nacional de pob-   Sixth national census of popula-
lación levantado el 2 julio de   tion taken July 2, 1961: final
1961: resultados finales de   results of first priority.
primera prioridad.   Lima,   [PRC, LC, RPI
Talleres Gráficos de la DNEC,
1964. xxviii, 4, 331, [2]p.
2 maps.

Peru. Dirección Nacional de
       Estadística y Censos.
    VI censo nacional de pobla-   Sixth national census of popula-
ción.   Lima, Ingeniero Numa   tion [and first of housing].
Leon de Vivero, 1962-1973. Vol.
I-VI in 33v.
    I. Resultados del VI   Results of the Sixth national cen-
censo nacional de población.   sus of population.
Tomo I-V.
.3-1-1   T.I. Cuadros compara-   Comparative tables, geographic
tivos, distribución geográfica,   distribution, age and sex, birth-
edad y sexo, lugar de nacimiento.   place.
1965. 289p.   [PRC, BC, RPI
.3-1-2   T.II. Migración, na-   Migration, citizenship, marital
cionalidad legal, estado conyu-   status, religion, fertility.
gal, religion, fecundidad.   [PRC, BC, RPI
1965. 162p.
.3-1-3   T.III. Idiomas, alfa-   Languages, literacy, school attend-
betismo, asistencia escolar, ni-   ance, educational level.
vel de educación. 1966. 286p.   [PRC, BC, RPI

.3-1-4   T.IV. Características económicas. 1966. 350p.

Economic characteristics.
[PRC, RPI

.3-1-5   T.V. Usos y costumbres locales, incapacidades físicas y mentales, algunas características de la familia. 1966. 126p.

Local customs and practices, physical and mental infirmities, some characteristics of the family.
[PRC, BC, RPI

II. Resultados del primer censo nacional de vivienda. Tomo I-II.

Results of the first national census of housing.

.3-2-1   T.I. Condición de ocupación, tipo de vivienda, número de ocupantes, tenencia, número de cuartos, material de construcción. 1964. 306p.

Use and type of housing, number of occupants, tenants, number of rooms, construction material
[PRC, TXU, RPI

.3-2-2   T.II. Servicios: de agua, higiénicos, baño y alumbrado; combustible de cocina, artefactos del hogar, alquileres, viviendas colectivas. 1964. 343p.

Services of water, sanitation, bath and electricity; fuel, artefacts in the home, renters, collective housing.
[PRC, TXU, RPI

.3-3   III. Resultados del premer censo nacional agropecuario. n.d. xxvii, 145, [1]p.

Results of the first national census of agriculture.
[TXU, RPI

IV. Censos nacionales de población, vivienda y agropecuario, 1961. Departamento de... Vol. I-XXIII.

National censuses of population, housing and agriculture, 1961. Department of...

1961.3-4-1 through 1961.3-4-23. 1. Amazonas. 1968. [10], 226, [3]p./2. Ancash. 1968. [14], 360, [7]p./3. Apurimac. 1968. [10], 212, [4]p./ 4. Arequipa. 1969. [12], 272, [2]p./5. Ayacucho. 1969. [12], 250, [3]p./6. Cajamarca. 1969.   /7. Cuzco. 1970. [12], 308p./8. Huancavelica. 1970. [12], 224p./9. Huanuco. 1970. [12], 239p./10. Ica. 1970. [10], 176, [3]p./11. Junin. 1970. [12], 254, [4]p./12. La Libertad. 1971. [12], 231p./13. Lambayeque. 1972. [12], 160, [3]p./14. Loreto. 1972. [10], 212, [3]p./15. Madre de Diós. 1973. [12], 146, [3]p./16. Moquegua. 1973. [14], 142p./17. Pasco. 1973. [14], 154p./18. Piura. 1974. [12], 222p./19. Puno. /20. San Martin.   /21. Tacna. /22. Tumbes.   /23. Lima y Provincia Constitucional del Callao. 1973. [40], 312, [6], 313- 431p. [PRC, LC, RPI

.3-5   V. Análisis de los resultados censales. [Not published].

Analysis of the census results.

.3-6   VI. Normas y metodología seguida en los censos de 1961. [Not published].

Norms and methodology followed in the 1961 censuses.

Peru. Dirección Nacional de Estadística y Censos. Sexto censo national de población y primer censo nacional

Sixth national census of population and first national census

de vivienda, 2 de julio de 1961.   of housing, July 2, 1961. Popu-
Centros poblados.   Lima, 1966–   lated centers.
1968. Tomo I–IV.
1961.4-1   I.   Amazonas, Ancash, Apurimac, Arequipa, Ayacucho.   1966.
ix, 472p.   [PRC, LC, RPI
  .4-2   II. Cajamarca. Prov. Constitucional del Callao, Cuzco,
Huancavelica, Huanuco. 1966.
ix, 481p.   [PRC, LC, RPI
  .4-3   III. Ica, Junin, La Liber-
tad, Lambayeque, Loreto, Lima,
Madre de Diós, Moquegua. 1966.
ix, 375p.   [PRC, LC, RPI
  .4-4   IV. Pasco, Piura, Puno,
San Martín, Tacna, Tumbres.
1968. ix, 415p.   [PRC, LC, RPI

Peru. Oficina Nacional de Desa-
       rrollo de Pueblos Jóvenes.
1970.0-1 Resultados preliminares del   Preliminary results of the census
censo de pueblos jóvenes.   Lima,   of new towns.
1971.   p.   [

Peru. Sistema Nacional de Apoyo
       a la Movilización Social.
  .1   Censo de pueblos jóvenes.   Census of New Towns. Vol. I.
Vol. I. Viviendas.   Lima, 1972.   Housing.
     p.   [

Peru. Oficina Nacional de
       Estadística y Censos.
       Censo de pueblos jóvenes.   Census of New Towns.
Lima, 1973-   . Vols. II–III.
  .2   II. Datos de población.   Population data. School attend-
Asistencia escolar, nivel de   ance, educational level.
educación. 1973. x, 335p.   [PRC
  .3   III. Datos de población.   Population data. [Marital or con-
[Estado civil o conyugal, pob-   jugal status, economically active
lación económicamente activa.]   population.]
Lima,   .   p.   [

Peru. ONEC.
1972.0-1   Censo nacional, 1972. Mapa National census, 1972. Demogra-
demográfico.   Lima, Instº Geo-   phic map.
gráfico Militar, n.d. 76x106cm.   [PRC

Peru. ONEC.
  .0-2   VII censo de población, II   Seventh population census, second
censo de vivienda. Plan censal   housing census. Census plans for
de 1972: informe final.   Lima,   1972: final report.
1977. iii, 80p.   [IASI

Peru. ONEC.

Censos nacionales: VII de población, II de vivienda, 4 de junio de 1972. Resultados definitivos. Nivel nacional. Lima, 1974. Tomo I-II.

National censuses: seventh of population, second of housing, June 4, 1972. Final results. National level.

.1-1   I. xxii, 630p.

[PRC

.1-2   II. xxiii, 631-1280, xxiii-xxiv p.

[PRC

Peru. ONEC.

Censos nacionales: VII de población, II de vivienda, 4 de junio de 1972. Departamento de ... Lima, 1974-1975. 24 parts in 47v.

National censuses: seventh of population, second of housing, June 4, 1972. Department of...

1972.2-1-1 through 1972.2-24. 1-1. Amazonas. 1974. vi, VIII, 440p./1-2. Amazonas. vi, 441-896p. App. (IX-XX)/2-1. Ancash. 1974. vi, VIII, 490p./2-2. Ancash. vi, 491-1048p./2-3. Ancash. vi, 1049-1594p./2-4. Ancash. vi, 1595-2105p./3-1. Apurimac. 1974. vi, VIII, 492p./3-2. Apurimac. vi, 493-1018p. App. (IX-XX)/4-1. Arequipa. 1974. XX, 656p./4-2. Arequipa. XII, 657-1324p. App. (XXI-XXXII)/5-1. Aycucho. 1974. XX, 574p./5-2. Ayacucho. XX, 575-1230p. App. (XXI-XXXII)/ 6-1. Cajamarca. 1974. XX, 736p./6-2. Cajamarca. XX, 737-1525p./7. Callao. XXX, 233p. App. (XXXI-XLVIII)/8-1. Cuzco. 1974. XX, 550p./ 8-2. Cuzco. XII, 551-1118p./8-3. Cuzco. XII, 1119-1620p. App. (XXI-XXXII)/9-1. Huancavelica. 1974. XX, 494p./9-2. Huancavelica. XII, 495-1012p. App. (XXI-XXXII)/10-1. Huanuco. 1974. v, VII, 520p./ 10-2. Huanuco. vi, 521-1048p. App. (IX-XX)/11-1. Ica. 1974. XX, 394p./11-2. Ica. XII, 395-787p. App. (XXI-XXXII)/12-1. Junin. 1975. /12-2. Junin. /13-1. La Libertad. 1974. vi, VIII, 548p./13-2. La Libertad. vi, 549-1098p. App. (IX-XX)/14. Lambayeque. 1974. XX, 621p. App. (XXI-XXXII)/15-1. Lima. 1974. vi, VIII, 577p./15-2. Lima. vi, 578-1171p./15-3. Lima. vi, 1172-1727p. App. (IX-XX)/16-1. Loreto. 1974. XX, 416p./16-2. Loreto. XX, 417-900p. App. (XXI-XXXII)/17. Madre de Diós. 1974. v, VIII, 351p. App. (IX-XX)/18. Moquegua. 1974. XX, 486p. App. (XXI-XXXII)/19. Pasco. XX, 560p. App. (XXI-XXXII)/20-1. Piura. 1974. XX, 532p./20-2. Piura. XII, 533-1043p. App. (XXI-XXXII)/21-1. Puno. 1974. XX, 676p./21-2. Puno. XII, 677-1378p. App. (XXI-XXXII)/22-1. San Martín. 1974. XX, 448p./22-2. San Martín. XII, 449-892p. App. (XXI-XXXII)/23. Tacna.   /
24. Tumbes. XX, 436p. App. (XXI-XXXII). [PRC, LC

PHILIPPINES

Republic of the Philippines.   Capital: Manila.
Statistical Agency: National Census and Statistics Office
                     National Economics and Development Authority
                     P.O. Box 779
                     Manila,
Publications Distributor: Publications Division (of the above).

Philippines. Bureau of the Census and Statistics.
    Census of the Philippines, October 1, 1948. Population of the
    Philippines, October 1, 1948. Special bulletins. Manila, Bureau of
    Printing, 1948. 2v.
1948.1-1   No. 1. 84p. [PRC, UN, RPI
   .1-2   Supplement. 32p. [PRC, UN, RPI

Philippines. Bureau of the Census and Statistics.
   .2   Census of the Philippines: 1948. Population classified by pro-
    vince, by city, municipality, and by municipal district and barrio.
    Manila, Bureau of Printing, 1951. 258p. [TXU, LC, RPI

Philippines. Bureau of the Census and Statistics.
    Census of the Philippines, 1948. Manila, Bureau of Printing, 1952-
    1954. Vol. I-IV in 9v.
          I. Report by province for census of population. 1954. 2v.
   .3-1-1   Abra to Bohol. xiv, 1105p. [TXU, LC, RPI
   .3-1-2   Bukidnon to Cavite. xiii, Pp. 1111-2289. [PRC, LC, RPI
          II. Report by province for census of agriculture. 1953. 3v.
   .3-2-1   Abra to Cebu. ix, 627p. [PRC, LC, RPI
   .3-2-2   Cotabato to Mountain Province. ix, Pp. 633-1246. [PRC, LC
   RPI
   .3-2-3   Negros Occidental to Zamboanga. ix, Pp. 1247-1841. [PRC,
   LC, RPI
          III. Summary and general report on the 1948 census of popula-
    tion and agriculture. 3v.
   .3-3-1   Population. 1954. xxvi, 2325p. [PRC, TXU, LC, RPI
   .3-3-2   Agriculture. 1954. ix, Pp. 2327-3117. [PRC, TXU, RPI
   .3-3-3   Summary report on the 1948 census of agriculture. 1952.
    xiii, 1174p. [PRC, RPI
   .3-4   IV. Economic census report: forestry, transportation, private
    schools and hospitals, professions, mines and quarries, electric light
    and power, fisheries, commerce, manufactures. 1953. [ii], 627p.
    [PRC, LC, RPI

Philippines. Bureau of the Census and Statistics.
   1960.0-1   Enumeration manual: 1960 census, Philippines. Manila, n.d.
      103p. [

Philippines. Bureau of the Census and Statistics.
   .1   Bulletin no. 1. Population of the Philippines by province and
    municipality, February 15, 1960. Manila, n.d. 56p. [LC, RPI

Philippines. Bureau of the Census and Statistics.
.2 Population of the Philippines by provinces and cities, February
15th, 1960. In: Journal of Philippine Statistics, Vol. 13, no. 1-3,
July-September, 1960. [LC

Philippines. Bureau of the Census and Statistics.
Census of the Philippines, 1960: population and housing. Final
reports. Manila, Bureau of Printing, 1962-1963. Vol. I-II in 56v.
I. Report by provinces. n.d. 55v.
1960.3-1-1 through 1960.3-1-55. 1. Abra. xiii, 17p./2. Agusan. xiii, 18p./
3. Aklan. xiii, 16p./4. Albay. xiii, 18p./5. Antique. xvi, 18p./6.
Bataan. xiii, 14p./7. Batanes. xiii, 11p./8. Batangas. xiii, 21p./
9. Bohol. xiii, 24p./10. Bukidnon. xiii, 16p./11. Bulacan. xiii,
18p./12. Cagayan. xiii, 21p./13. Camarines Norte. xiii, 14p./14.
Camarines Sur. xv, 23p./15. Capiz. xii, 16p./16. Catanduanes. xiii,
14p./17. Cavite. xiii, 16p./18. Cebu. xiv, 29p./19. Cotabato. xv,
24p./20. Davao. xiv, 23p./21. Ilocos Norte. xiii, 17p./22. Ilocos
Sur. xiv, 19p./23. Iloilo. xv, 28p./24. Isabela. xiv, 21p./
25. Laguna. xiii, 21p./26. Lanao del Norte. xiii, 16p./27. Lanao
del Sur. xiii, 19p./28. La Union. xiii, 18p./29. Leyte. xiv, 35p./
30. Manila. xiii, [1], 14p./31. Martinduque. xiii, 11p./32. Masbate.
xiii, 18p./33. Misamis Occidental. xiii, 16p./34. Misamis Oriental.
xiii, 17p./35. Mountain Province. xiii, 22p./36. Negros Occidental.
xiii, 21p./37. Negros Oriental. xiv, 21p./38. Nueva Ecija. xiii,
22p./39. Nueva Vizcaya. xiii, 16p./40. Mindoro Occidental. xiii,
12p./41. Oriental Mindoro. xiii, 18p./42. Palawan. xv, 16p./43. Pampanga. xiii, 188p./44. Pangasinan. xv, 26p./45. Quezon. xii, [4],
26p./46. Rizal. xii, 19p./47. Romblon. xiii, 14p./48. Samar. xv,
33p./49. Sorsogon. xiii, 16p./
50. Sulu. xvi, 16p./51. Surigao. xiv, 21p./52. Tarlac. xiii,
18p./53. Zambales. xiii, 16p./54. Zamboanga del Norte. xiii, 16p./
55. Zamboanga del Sur. xiv, 20p. [TXU, BC, LC, RPI
.3-2 II. Summary report. Population and housing. 1963. xxviii,
26p. [TXU, BC, LC, RPI
.3-2a Appendix. Migration statistics. 1963. 11p. [LC

Philippines. Bureau of the Census and Statistics.
Census of the Philippines: 1960. Population and housing. Special
report. Manila, Bureau of Printing, [1965]- .
.4-1 Fertility and labor force characteristics. [1965]. x, 32p.
[LC, RPI

Philippines. Bureau of the Census and Statistics.
1970.0-1 1970 census of population and housing. Advance report. Manila,
1971. 67v. [Issued as separates and also in one volume. See listing
in Final reports below.] [PRC, BC, LC

Philippines. Bureau of the Census and Statistics.
1970 census of population and housing. Special report. Manila,
1971-1973. Nos. 1-4.
.1-1 Total population of the Philippines and each province, city, municipality and municipal district--1970. 1971. 96p. [PRC, OPR, BC, LC

.1-2   Urban population of the Philippines by category, region, province, city and municipality: 1970. (Based on the new definition).
1972. iv, 38p. [OPR
.1-3   Population, land area, density and percent change in three censal years 1948, 1960 and 1970: Philippines. 1972. [viii], 44p.
[PRC, E-W
.1-4   New population projections by age, sex and province for the
Philippines: 1970-2000. 1973. [vi], xvi, 425p. [

Philippines. National Census and Statistical Office.
    1970 census of population and housing. Final reports.   Manila,
1972-1974. Vol. I-II in 68v.
        I. [Report by province.] 67v.
1970.2-1-1 through 1970.2-1-67. 1. Abra. 1974. xxvii, 534p./2. Agusan del
Norte. 1974. xxviii, 423p./3. Agusan del Sur. 1974. xxvii, 439p./
4. Aklan. 1972. xxvii, 599p./5. Albay. 1974. xxviii, 507p./6. Antique. 1974. xxviii, 491p./7. Bataan. 1974. xxvii, 456p./8. Batanes.
1974. xxvii, 169p./9. Batangas. 1974. xxvii, 599p./10. Benguet.
1974. xxvii, 414p./11. Bohol. 1972. xxvii, 677p./12. Bukidnon. 1974.
xxviii, 489p./13. Bulacan. 1972. xxvii, 566p./14. Cagayan. 1974.
xxix, 553p./15. Camarines Norte. 1974. xxvii, 432p./16. Camarines
Sur. 1974. xxviii, 632p./17. Camiguin. 1974. xxvi, 384p./18. Capiz.
1974. xxviii, 491p./19. Cataduanes. 1974. xxviii, 430p./20. Cavite.
1974. xxviii, 536p./21. Cebu. 1972. xxix, 821p./22. Cotabato. 1974.
xxix, 605p./23. Davao del Norte. 1974. xxix, 487p./24. Davao del
Sur. 1974. xxix, 449p./
        25. Davao Oriental. 1974. xxviii, 443p./26. Eastern Samar. 1974.
xxix, 523p./27. Ifugao. 1974. xxix, 408p./28. Ilocos Norte. 1974.
xxvii, 488p./29. Ilocos Sur. 1974. xxviii, 579p./30. Iloilo. 1974.
xviii, [11], 674p./31. Isabela. 1974. xxix, 600p./32. Kalinga-Apayao.
1974. xxviii, 437p./33. La Union. 1974. xxviii, 496p./34. Laguna.
1974. xxi, [xxii-xxvii], 561p./35. Lanao del Norte. 1974. xxvii,
485p./36. Lanao del Sur. 1974. xxviii, 540p./37. Leyte. 1974.
xxviii, 707p./38. Manila. 1974. xxvii, 198p./39. Marinduque. 1974.
xxvii, 397p./40. Masbate. 1972. xxvii, 516p./41. Misamis Occidental.
1974. xxviii, 461p./42. Misamis Oriental. 1974. xxvii, 551p./43.
Mountain Province. 1974. xxvii, 426p./44. Negros Occidental. 1974.
xxix, 589p./45. Negros Oriental. 1974. xxviii, 572p./46. Northern
Samar. 1974. xxviii, 488p./47. Nueva Ecija. 1974. xxvii, 594p./
48. Nueva Vizcaya. 1974. xxvii, 477p./49. Occidental Mindoro. 1974.
xxvii, 423p./
        50. Oriental Mindoro. 1974. xxviii, 480p./51. Palawan. 1974.
xxix, 493p./52. Pampanga. 1974. xxviii, 516p./53. Pangasinan. 1974.
xxviii, 710p./54. Quezon. 1974. xxx, 714p./55. Rizal. 1974. xxix,
508p./56. Romblon. 1974. xxvii, 475p./57. Samar (Western). 1974.
xxvii, 490p./58. Sorsogon. 1974. xxviii, 478p./59. South Cotabato.
1974. xxvii, 457p./60. Southern Leyte. 1974. xxvii, 471p./61. Sulu.
1974. xxx, 489p./62. Surigao del Norte. 1974. xxvii, 517p./63. Surigao del Sur. 1974. xxviii, 474p./64. Tarlac. 1972. xxvii, 508p./
65. Zambales. 1974. xxviii, 464p./66. Zamboanga del Norte. 1974.
xxix, 500p./67. Zamboanga del Sur. 1974. xxix, 584p. [PRC, BC, LC
.3-2   II. National Summary. 1974. xxxi, 962p. [PRC, BC, LC

Philippines. National Census and Statistics Office.
    1975 integrated census of the population and its economic activi-
ties. Final report. Population. Phase I [100 percent enumeration].
Manila, 1975. Vol. I-II in 74v.
        I. [Report by province]. 73v.
1975.1-1-1 through 1975.1-1-73. 1. Abra.   p./2. Agusan del Norte.
    xxix, 165p./3. Agusan del Sur. xxix, 171p./4. Aklan. xxix, 184p./5.
    Albay. xxix, 190p./6. Antique. xxix, 191p./7. Basilan. xxix, 164p./
    8. Bataan. xxix, 168p./9. Batanes. xxix, 64p./10. Batangas. xxix,
    243p./11. Benguet. xxix, 175p./12. Bohol. xxix, 279p./13. Bukidnon.
    xxix, 197p./14. Bulacan. xxix, 205p./15. Cagayan. xxix, 224p./16.
    Camarines Norte. xxix, 168p./17. Camarines Sur. xxix, 249p./18. Cami-
    guin. xxix, 145p./19. Capiz. xxix, 185p./20. Catanduanes. xxix,
    166p./21. Cavite. xxix, 199p./22. Cebu. xxix, 299p./23. Davao (Davao
    del Norte). xxix, 189p./24. Davao del Sur. xxix, 176p./
        25. Davao Oriental. xxix, 165p./26. Eastern Samar. xxix, 203p./
    27. Ifugao. xxix, 151p./28. Ilocos Norte. xxix, 204p./29. Ilocos Sur.
    xxix, 240p./30. Iloilo. xxix, 290p./31. Isabela. xxix, 250p./32. Ka-
    linga-Apayao. xxix, 178p./33. La Union. xxix, 196p./34. Laguna.
    xxix, 227p./35. Lanao del Norte. xxix, 196p./36. Lanao del Sur. xxix,
    236p./37. Leyte. xxix, 299p./38. Metro Manila.   /39. Maguin-
    danao. xxix, 176p./40. Marinduque. xxix, 150p./41. Masbate.
        /42. Misamis Occidental. xxix, 183p./43. Misamis Oriental. xxix,
    213p./44. Mountain Province. xxix, 161p./45. Negros Occidental. xxix,
    227p./46. Negros Oriental. xxix, 209p./47. North Cotabato. xxix, 176p./
    48. Northern Samar. xxix, 202p./49. Nueva Ecija. xxix, 233p./
        50. Nueva Vizcaya. xxix, 173p./51. Occidental Mindoro. xxix, 164p./
    52. Oriental Mindoro. xxix, 177p./53. Palawan. xxix, 194p./54. Pam-
    panga. xxix, 200p./55. Pangasinan. xxix, 283p./56. Quezon. xxix,
    290p./57. Quirino. xxix, 146p./58. Rizal. xxix, 225p./59. Romblon.
    xxix, 182p./60. Samar (Western). xxix, 206p./61. Siquijor. xxix,
    149p./62. Sorsogon. xxix, 182p./63. South Cotabato. xxix, 182p./64.
    Southern Leyte. xxix, 187p./65. Sulu. xxix, 176p./66. Sultan Kudarat.
    xxix, 165p./67. Surigao del Norte. xxix, 213p./68. Surigao del Sur.
    xxix, 189p./69. Tarlac. xxix, 184p./70. Tawi-Tawi. xxix, 155p./74.
    Zambales. xxix, 174p./72. Zamboanga del Norte. xxix, 194p./73. Zam-
    boanga del Sur. xxix, 234p. [PRC, LC
.1-2   II. National summary. 1978. xxxii, 161p. specimen forms.
    [PRC

Philippines. National Census and Statistics Office.
    1975 integrated census of the population and its economic activi-
ties. Final report. Economic activities. Phase II [Sample]. Manila,
197 . Vol. I-II in 74v.
        I. [Report by province]. 73v.
1975.2-1-1 through 1975.2-1-73. [Same order as 1975.1-1 above.] [
.2-2   II. National summary.
    [

Philippines. National Census and Statistics Office.
    Philippines, 1975. Special report. Manila, 1978-   . No. 1-
.3-1   Total population of the Philippines by region, province, city,
    municipality and municipal district: 1975. Manila, 1978. vi, 97p.
    [PRC

PITCAIRN

(British Colony)   Capital: Adamstown
Statistical Agency: Secretary
                      Pitcairn Island Council
                      Adamstown,
                           and
                      South Pacific Office
                      Government House Grounds
                      Suva, FIJI
Publications Distributor: same

Although the island is administered from Fiji, it is not included in
any of Fiji's censuses. Annual censuses (begun 1952) are taken on
December 31 by the Secretary to the Pitcairn Island Council for the
annual report to the Secretary-General of the United Nations.

POLAND

Polish People's Republic.   Capital: Warsaw.
Statistical Agency: Central Statistical Office
                  [Główny Urzad Statystyczny (GUS)]
                  Al. Niepodległości 208
                  Warszawa 00-925,
Publications Distributor: Ars Polona-Ruch
                  Foreign Trade Enterprise
                  Krakowskie Przedmiescie 7
                  Warszawa,

Poland. Główny Urzad Statys-
      tyczny.

1946.1   Powszechny sumaryscny spis   General summary of the population
ludności z dnia 14.II.1946r.   census of February 14, 1946.
Warsaw, 1946. xvi, 108p.   [PRC, LC, RPI
(Statystyka Polski, Seria D,
Zeszyt 1).

Poland. GUS.
    Narodowy spis powszechny z   National general census of Decem-
dn. 3.XII.1950. Struktura za-   ber 3, 1950. Occupational and
wodowi i demograficzna ludności.   demographic structure of the popu-
Indywidualne gospodarstwa rolne.   lation. Individual farms.
Warsaw, 1954. Tom I-XX.

1950.1-1   I. Polska. [8], 139p.   All Poland.
                                         [BC

1950.1-2 through 1950.1-20. [Provinces, except where noted.] 2. Białystok.
    [2], 110p./3. Bydgoszcz. [2], 128p./4. Gdańskie. 116p./5. Kielce.
    [2], 112p./6. Koszalin. [2], 112p./7. Kraków. [2], 122p./8. Lublin.
    [2], 118p./9. Łódz. [2], 118p./10. City of Łódz. [2], 36p./11. Olsz-
    tyn. [2], 124p./12. Opole. [2], 120p./13. Poznań. [2], 143p./14.
    Rzeszów. [2], 122p./15. Stalingrad [now Katowice]. 149p./16. Szcze-
    cin. [2], 110p./17. Warsaw. [2], 130p./18. City of Warsaw. [2],
    60p./19. Wrocław. 141p./20. Zielona Góra. [2], 122p. [RPI

Poland. GUS.
    Narodowy spis powszechny z   National general census of Decem-
dnia 3.XII.1950r. Warsaw, 1952-   ber 3, 1950.
1956. 4v.

.2-1   Wyniki spisu opracowane   Results of the census based on
metoda reprezentacyjna. 1952.   the sampling process.
xx, 210p.   [BC

.2-2   Miejsce zamieszkania lud-   Place of residence of the popu-
ności w sierpniu 1939r. 1955.   lation in August, 1939.
xi, 198p.   [BC

.2-3   Praca uboczna. 1955. xi,   Supplementary employment.
128p.   [BC

.2-4   Gospodarstwa domowe w mias-   Households in towns.
tach. 1956. x, 67p.   [BC

Poland. GUS.
   Spis powezechny z dnia 6   General census of December 6,
grudnia 1960r. Lucność. Gos-   1960. Population. Households.
podarstwa domowe. Mieszkania.   Dwellings. Results of a sampling
Wyniki opracowane metoda repre-   process.
zentacyjna. Warsaw, 1962.
25v.

1960.1-1   Uwagi wstępne. [ii],   Introductory remarks.
     26p.   [Harvard, PRC, RPI

1960.1-2 through 1960.1-23. [Provinces, except where noted.] 2. Białystok.
    38p./3. Bydgoszcz. 42p./4. Gdansk. 38p./5. Katowice. 44p./6. Kielce.
    42p./7. Koszalin. 36p./8. City of Kraków. 21p./9. Kraków. 38p./10.
    Lublin. 42p./11. City of Łódz. 21p./12. Łódz. 38p./13. Olsztyn.
    38p./14. Opole. 38p./15. City of Poznań. 21p./16. Poznań. 46p./17.
    Rzeszów. 42p./18. Szczecin. 36p./19. City of Warsaw. 21p./20. War-
    saw. 44p./21. City of Wrocław. 21p./22. Wrocław. 44p./23. Zielona
    Góra. 38p. [Harvard, PRC, RPI
  .1-24   Polska. 29p.   All Poland.
                                 [

  .1-25   [Special supplement.]
     1962. x, 20p.   [BC

Poland. GUS.
   Spis powszechny z dnia 6   General census of December 6,
grudnia 1960r. Ludność. Gospo-   1960. Population. Households.
darstwa domowe. Wyniki ostatec-   Final results.
zne. Warsaw, 1963-1965. (Biu-
letyn statystyczny, Seria L, Nos.
1-23).

1960.2-1 through 1960.2-22. [Provinces, except where noted.] 1. City of
    Kraków. 23p./2. Kraków. 43p./3. Rzeszów. 43p./4. Olsztyn. 43p./
    5. City of Warsaw. 23p./6. Warsaw. 43p./7. Kielce. 43p./8. Zielona
    Góra. 43p./9. City of Poznań. 23p./10. Poznań. 43p./11. City of
    Łódz. 23p./12. Łódz. 43p./13. City of Wrocław. 23p./14. Wrocław.
    43p./15. Lublin. 43p./16. Koszalin. 43p./17. Katowice. 43p./18.
    Białystok. 43p./19. Szczecin. 43p./20. Opole. 43p./21. Bydgoszcz.
    43p./22. Gdansk. 43p. [LC, BC, Berkeley, PRC, RPI
  .2-23   Polska. 1964. [1], 51p.   All Poland.
                                   [LC, Berkeley, PRC, RPI

Poland. GUS.
   Spis powszechny z dnia 6   General census of December 6,
grudnia 1960r. Ludność. Gospo-   1960. Population. Households.
darstwa domowe. Wyniki ostatecz-   Final results.
ne. Warsaw, 1963-1965. Vol. 1-
23 in 57v. (Statystyka Polski,
Seris "L").

1960.3-1 through 1960.3-22-2B. [Provinces, except where noted. Part I -
    Province tables, Parts II A&B - District tables.] 1. City of Kraków.
    1964. 143p./2-1. Kraków. 1965. 119p./2-2A. Kraków. 139p./2-2B.
    Kraków. 209p./3-1. Rzeszów. 1965. 119p./3-2A. Rzeszów. 160p./3-2B.

Rzeszów. 241p./4-1. Olsztyn. 1964. 119p./4-2A. Olsztyn. 132p./
4-2B. Olsztyn. 193p./5. City of Warsaw. 1965. 149p./6-1. Warsaw.
1965. 121p./6-2A. Warsaw. 217p./6-2B. Warsaw. 327p./7-1. Kielce.
1965. 117p./7-2A. Kielce. 163p./7-2B. Kielce. 239p./8-1. Zielona
Góra. 1965. 119p./8-2A. Zielona Góra. 122p./8-2B. Zielona Góra.
181p./9. City of Poznań. 1965. 125p./10-1. Poznań. 1965. 121p./
10-2A. Poznań. 226p./10-2B. Poznań. 337p./11. City of Łódz. 1965.
125p./12-1. Łódz. 1965. 119p./12-2A. Łódz. 135p./12-2B. Łódz.
207p./13. City of Wrocław. 1965. 123p./14-1. Wrocław. 1965. 121p./
14-2A. Wrocław. 206p./14-2B. Wrocław. 309p./15-1. Lublin. 1965.
119p./15-2A. Lublin. 147p./15-2B. Lublin. 223p./16-1. Koszalin.
1965. 119p./16-2A. Koszalin. 102p./16-2B. Koszalin. 153p./17-1.
Katowice. 1965. 121p./17-2A. Katowice. 197p./17-2B. Katowice.
313p./18-1. Białystok. 1965. 119p./18-2A. Białystok. 135p./18-2B.
Białystok. 201p./19-1. Szczecin. 1965. 119p./19-2A. Szczecin.
96p./19-2B. Szczecin. 143p./20-1. Opole. 1965. 119p./20-2A. Opole.
116p./20-2B. Opole. 177p./21-1. Bydgoszcz. 1965. 119p./21-2A. Bydgoszcz. 172p./21-2B. Bydgoszcz. 259p./22-1. Gdansk. 1965. 119p./
22-2A. Gdansk. 116p./22-2B. Gdansk. 179p. [UN, LC, PRC, RPI

.3-23   Polska. 1965. 119p.   All Poland.
                                           [BC, UN, LC, PRC, RPI

Poland. GUS.
.4   Spis powszechny z dnia 6   General census of December 6,
grudnia 1960r. Wyniki Wstepne: 1960. Summary of results: popu-
ludność, mieszkania, budynki   lation, dwellings, buildings to-
oraz gospodarstwa rolne. Wyda-   gether with agriculture. Second
nie II, według podziału adminis-   edition, according to administra-
tracyjnego z dnia 1.I.1962.   tive divisions of January 1, 1962.
Polska. Warsaw, 1964. viii,   All Poland.
17p.   [BC, LC, RPI

Poland. GUS. Biuro Spisów.
Narodowy spis powszechny 8.   National general census of Decem-
XII.1970. Wyniki ostateczne.   ber 8, 1970. Final results.
Warsaw, 1971-1973. Vol. 1-47
in 65v. 3 sections.
Struktura demograficzna   Demographic and economic structure
i zawodowa ludności. Gospodar-   of the population. Households.
stwa domowe. 1971-1972. (Lud-
ność, zeszyt, no. 1-23). 40v.
1970.1-1 through 1970.1-22A. [Provinces, except where noted. Part A - District tables.] 1. Olsztyn. 1971. xxxi, 490p./1A. Olsztyn. 1971.
294p./2. Warsaw. 1972. xxxi, 498p./2A. Warsaw. 1972. 505p./3. City
of Warsaw. 1972. xxxi, 266p./4. Katowice. 1972. xxxi, 496p./4A.
Katowice. 1972. 482p./5. Wrocław. 1972. xxxi, 498p./5A. Wrocław.
1972. 477p./6. City of Wrocław. 1972. xxxi, 241p./7. Krakow. 1972.
xxxi, 490p./7A. Krakow. 1972. 321p./8. City of Krakow. 1972. xxxi,
253p./9. Łódz. 1972. xxxi, 490p./9A. Łódz. 1972. 318p./10. City of
Łódz. 1972. xxxi, 241p./11. Poznań. 1972. xxxi, 498p./11A. Poznań.
1972. 517p./12. City of Poznań. 1972. xxxi, 241p./13. Opole. 1972.

xxxi, 490p./13A. Opole. 1972. 273p./14. Szczecin. 1972. xxxi,
486p./14A. Szczecin. 1972. 225p./15. Gdansk. 1972. xxxi, 490p./
15A. Gdansk. 1972. 276p./16. Rzeszow. 1972. xxxi, 494p./16A. Rzeszow. 1972. 368p./17. Bydgoszcz. 1972. xxxi, 494p./17A. Bydgoszcz.
1972. 393p./18. Bialostok. 1972. xxxi, 490p./18A. Bialostok. 1972.
306p./19. Kielce. 1972. xxxi, 494p./19A. Kielce. 1972. 360p./20.
Koszalin. 1972. xxxi, 486p./20A. Koszalin. 1972. 229p./21. Lublin.
1972. xxxi, 490p./21A. Lublin. 1972. 334p./22. Zielona Góra. 1972.
xxxi, 490p./22A. Zielona Góra. 1972. 280p. [PRC

.1-23   Polska. 1972. xlv,   All Poland.
508p.   [PRC
         Dzietność kobiet. 1971.   Fertility of women.
.1-24   Część I. xi, 314p.   [UN, OPR, RPI
.1-24-A   Część II. Tablice Woje-
wódzkie. 495p.   [OPR

         Migracje ludności. 1972-   Migration of the population.
1973. (Ludność, zeszyt, no. 25-
47).
1970.1-25 through 1970.1-46. [Provinces, except where noted.] 25. Olsztyn.
1972. xxiii, 210p./26. Warsaw. 1972. xxiv, 97p./27. City of Warsaw.
1972. xviii, 31p./28. Katowice. 1973. xv, 218p./29. Wrocław. 1973.
xv, 121p./30. City of Wrocław. 1973. xv, 35p./31. Krakow. 1973. xv,
102p./32. City of Krakow. 1973. xv, 35p./33. Lódz. 1973. xv, 102p./
34. City of Lódz. 1973. xv, 35p./35. Poznan. 1973. xv, 220p./36.
City of Poznan. 1973. xv, 35p./37. Opole. 1973. xv, 115p./38. Szczecin. 1972. xxiv, 93p./39. Gdansk. 1972. xv, 207p./40. Rzeszow.
1972. xv, 103p./41. Bydogoszcz. 1973. xv, 103p./42. Bialostok. 1973.
xv, 216p./43. Kielce. 1973. xv, 102p./44. Koszalin. 1973. xv, 117p./
45. Lublin. 1973. xv, 102p./46. Zielona Góra. 1973. xv, 178p. [PRC

.1-47   Polska. 1973. xvi,   All Poland.
317p.   [PRC

Poland. GUS. Biuro Spisów.
.2   Narodowy spis powszechny   National general census 1970.
1970. Statystyczna charakter-   Statistical characteristics of
ystyka miejscowości. Polska.   municipalities. Poland.
Warsaw, 1971. xviii, 222p.   [PRC

Poland. GUS. Biuro Spisów.
.3   Metodologia i organizacja   Methodology and organization of
Narodowego spisu powszechnego   the National general census of
1970.   Warsaw, 1972.   p.   1970.
                                      [

Note: Poland has divided its former 22 provinces into 49 provinces.

Poland. GUS.
1978.0-1   Wstępne wyniki Narodowego   Preliminary results of the nation-
Spisu Powszechnego: stan na 7.   al population census of December
XII:1978r. Warsaw, 1979. In: 7, 1978.
Wiadomości statystycene 24(3):1-6.   [

PORTUGAL

Portuguese Republic.   Capital: Lisbon.
Statistical Agency: National Statistical Institute
                          [Instituto Nacional de Estatística (INE)]
                          Avenida Antonio José de Almeida
                          Lisboa 1,
Publications Distributor: Imprensa Nacional -- Casa da Moeda
                                 Direcção Comercial
                                 Rua D. Francisco Manuel de Melo, 5
                                 Lisboa 1,

Portugal.   Instituto Nacional
de Estatística.
     IX recenseamento geral da
população no continente e ilhas
adjacentes em 15 de dezembro de
1950.   Lisboa, 1952-1954.
Tomos 1-3 & Anexo in 5v.

Ninth general population census
of the mainland and adjacent islands on December 15, 1950.

1950.1-1   População residente e
presente, familias, casais,
mulheres casadas, convivências, estrangeiros, cegos,
surdos-mudos e orfãos.   1952.
798p.

De jure and de facto population,
families, married couples, married
women, households, foreigners, the
blind, deaf-mutes and orphans.
[PRC, TXU, UN, LC, RPI

.1-2   Idade e instrução.   1952.
468p.

Age and education.
[PRC, TXU, UN, LC, RPI

.1-3-1   Condições perante o trabalho, encargos de familia e
meio de vida.   1953.   595p.

Employment status, heads of families, and means of livelihood.
[PRC, TXU, UN, LC, RPI

.1-3-2   População agrícola.   1953.
218p.

Agricultural population.
[PRC, TXU, UN, LC, RPI

.1-4   Anexo.   Inquérito as condições de habitação da familia.
1954.   233p.

Supplement.   Survey of family
housing conditions.
[PRC, TXU, UN, LC, RPI

Portugal.   INE.
1960.0-1   X recenseamento geral da
população.   Listas alfabéticas
dos concelhos e freguesias.
(Atualizadas em 31/12/62).
Lisboa, n.d.   49p.

Tenth general population census.
Alphabetical lists of councils
and parishes.   (Established Dec.
31, 1962).
[BC, PRC, RPI

Portugal.   INE.
     X recenseamento geral da popu-
lação no continente e ilhas adjacentes (As 0 horas de 15 de dezembro de 1960).   Lisboa, [pub-
lisher varies], 1961-1964.   Tomos I-VI & Anexo in 11v.

Tenth general population census
of the mainland and adjacent islands (as of midnight, December
15, 1960).

     I.   Prédios e fogos; popu-
lação.   1964.   Vol. I-II.

Buildings and dwellings; population.

.1-1-1   Dados retrospectivos
(distritos, concelhos e freguesias). 260p. maps.
.1-1-2   Dados retrospectivos
(lugares). viii, 1164p. maps.
.1-2   II. Familias, convivências e população residente e
presente, por freguesias, concelhos, distritos e centros urbanos. 1963. vi, 662p. maps.
.1-3-1   III, Vol. I.   Idade.
1963. viii, 180p.
.1-3-2   Vol. II.   Instrução.
[1964]. 195p.
.1-4   IV.   Estrangeiros; orfãos;
cegos e surdos-mudos. 1963.
xiv, 173p.
            V. Condições perante o
trabalho e meio de vida. 1964.
Vol. I-III.
.1-5-1   Vol. I.   Total geral;
totais dos centros urbanos e
das zonas rurais. xxv, 323p.
.1-5-2   Vol. II.   Distritos.
424p. maps.
.1-5-3   Vol. III.   Concelhos
e centros urbanos. xxii, 176p.
maps.
.1-6   VI.   Condições de habitação dos agregados domésticos.
1964. x, 500p. maps.
.1-7   Anexo.   Inventário de prédios e fogos (em julho de 1960).
1962. 284p. maps.

Portugal. INE.
1970.0-1   11º recenseamento da população, continente e ilhas adjacentes, 1970. Lista alfabética
de concelhos e freguesias.
Lisboa, 1971. 50p.

.0-2   11º recenseamento da população, continente e ilhas adjacentes, 1970. Conversão das
classificações de actividades
(CITA) e profissões (CITP) utili-
zadas nos recenseamentos de 1970
e 1960.   Lisboa, 1973. 151p.

Retrospective data (districts,
councils and parishes).
[PRC, TXU, BC, LC, RPI, RIR
Retrospective data (places).
[PRC, TXU, BC, LC, RPI, RIR
Families, households, de jure and
de facto population by parishes,
councils, districts and urban
centers.
[PRC, TXU, BC, LC, RPI, RIR
Age.
[PRC, TXU, BC, LC, RPI. RIR
Education.
[PRC, TXU, BC, LC, RPI, RIR
Foreigners; orphans; the blind
and deaf-mutes.
[PRC, TXU, BC, RPI, RIR
Employment status, and means of
livelihood.

General total; totals for urban
centers and rural zones.
[PRC, TXU, BC, LC, RPI, RIR
Districts.
[PRC, TXU, BC, LC, RPI, RIR
Councils and urban centers.
[PRC, TXU, BC, LC, RPI, RIR

Housing conditions of domestic
aggregates.
[PRC, TXU, BC, LC, RPI, RIR
Supplement. Inventory of build-
ings and dwellings. (July, 1960).
[PRC, TXU, BC, LC, RPI, RIR

Eleventh population census, mainland and adjacent islands, 1970.
Alphabetical list of councils and
parishes.
[PRC, LC

Eleventh population census, mainland and adjacent islands, 1970.
Conversion of the classifications
of economic activities (CITA) and
occupations (CITP) used in the
censuses of 1970 and 1960.
[PRC

Portugal. INE.
1970.0-3   11 recenseamento da população, continente e ilhas adjacentes, 1970: dados preliminares. [Lisboa, 1971]. 106p.

Eleventh population census, mainland and adjacent islands, 1970:
preliminary data.
[UN

Portugal. INE
.1   11° recenseamento da população, continente e ilhas adjacentes, 1970. (Estimativa a 5%).
Alguns quadros de apuramentos
consideros prioritários. Lis,
boa, 1973. [48], 111, 9p.

Eleventh population census, mainland and adjacent islands, 1970.
(Five percent sample). Some tables of verifications considered
priority.
[OPR

Portugal. INE.
     11° recenseamento da popula-
ção, continente e ilhas adjacentes, 1970. Estimativa a 20%.
Lisboa, 1973. Vol. 1-2.
.2-1   [Características gerais].
[18], [363]p.
.2-2   [Características econômi-
cas e sociais]. [14], [236]p.

Eleventh population census, mainland and adjacent islands, 1970.
Twenty percent sample.

General characteristics.
[PRC, UN, LC
Economic and social characteris-
tics.
[PRC, UN, LC

Portugal. INE.
.3   [1970 recenseamento da população, provincias do ultramar.
Lisboa, 1973?]. 1 folder.

1970 population census, overseas
provinces. (Includes: Angola,
Cape Verde, Guinea-Bissau, Macao,
São Tome & Principe, Mozambique,
Portuguese Timor).
[UN

PUERTO RICO

Commonwealth of Puerto Rico.   Capital: San Juan
Statistical Agency: Bureau of Economic Planning
                     Planning Board
                     P.O. Box 9447
                     Santurce, Puerto Rico 00908
                         and
                     U.S. Bureau of the Census
                     Washington, D.C. 20233
Publications Distributor: U.S. Government Printing Office
                           Washington, D.C. 20402

    U.S. Bureau of the Census.
1950.1-2-51/54   Census of population: 1950. A report of the seventeenth
    decennial census of the United States. Volume II. Characteristics of
    the population. Part 51-54. Territories and possessions (Alaska,
    Hawaii, Puerto Rico, American Samoa, Canal Zone, Guam, and Virgin
    Islands). Washington, D.C., GPO, 1953. var. pag. [PRC, LC, RP]

    U.S. Bureau of the Census.
   .2-14-21   Census of population: 1950. Advance report. PC-14:
    Summary reports of population characteristics (various areas). No. 21.
    Fertility by social and economic status, for Puerto Rico: 1950.
    Washington, D.C., 1954. 28p. [LC, BC

    U.S. Bureau of the Census.
   .3-4   Puerto Rico censo de población: 1950. Indice alfabético de
    ocupaciones e industrias. Washington, D.C., GPO, 1951. xxxii, 81p.
    [LC, BC, RP]

    U.S. Bureau of the Census.
1960.1-1-53   Census of population: 1960. The eighteenth decennial
    census of the United States. Volume I. Characteristics of the popu-
    lation. Part 53. Puerto Rico. Washington, D.C., GPO, 1964. lxxv,
    400p. [PRC, LC, RP]

    U.S. Bureau of the Census.
        Censuses of population and housing: 1960. Final reports. PHC(1).
    Census tracts. Washington, D.C., GPO, 1962. 3v.
   .2-1-178   Mayaguez. 44p. [LC, BC, RP]
   .2-1-179   Ponce. 50p. [LC, BC, RP]
   .2-1-180   San Juan. 115p. [LC, BC, RP]

    U.S. Bureau of the Census.
1970.1-1-53   Census of population: 1970. Volume I. Characteristics
    of the population. Part 53. Puerto Rico. Washington, D.C., GPO,
    1974. x, 1341, A-87p. [Also published as separate parts A, B, C, &
    D]. [PRC, BC, LC, RP]

U.S.   Bureau of the Census.
Census of population and housing: 1970. PHC(1). Census tracts.
Washington, D.C., GPO, 1972. 3v.
1970.3-1-239   Mayaguez. x, P-41, H-20, A-38p. [BC, LC, TXU, RPI
  .3-1-240   Ponce. x, P-45, H-22, A-38p. [BC, LC, TXU, RPI
  .3-1-241   San Juan. x, P-192, H-100, A-38p. [PRC, BC, LC, RPI

QATAR

State of Qatar.   Capital: Doha
Statistical Agency: Ministry of Information.
                      Government of Qatar
                      P.O. Box 1836
                      Doha,
Publications Distributor: same

The 1970 census was "a simple head-count." No citations or publication have been seen.

REUNION

Department of Réunion (France)   Capital: Saint-Denis
Statistical Agency: INSEE - Departmental Statistical Service of Reunion
                     [INSEE - Service Départemental de Statistique de la
                        Réunion]
                     95, rue Jules Auber/B.P. 52
                     Saint-Denis,
Publications Distributor: same, or Observatoire Économique de Paris
                                195, rue de Bercy--Tour Gamma A
                                75582 Paris, Cedex 12, France

Réunion chose to administer both the regular census and the non-indigenous census in 1946.

France. Service des Statisti-
            ques.
1946.1   Résultats du recensement de   Results of the census of 1946 in
          1946 dans les territoires d'ou-   the overseas territories (French
          tre-mer (français d'origine mé-   of metropolitan origin and for-
          tropolitaine et étrangers):   eigners): Reunion.
          Réunion.   Paris, 1949. 28p.   [PRC, Harvard, UN, RPI
          (Bulletin mensuel de statisti-
          que d'outre-mer, supplément
          série "statistique," No. 10).

France. Service des Statisti-
            ques.
    .2   Le recensement de 1946 a la   The census of 1946 in Reunion,
          Réunion (2e partie: Population   (2d part: Population of Reunion
          d'origine réunionnaire.) Paris,   origin).
          1950. xii, 17p. (BMSOM, sup-   [PRC, BC, UN, RPI
          plément série "statistique," no.
          13).

France. Service des Statistiques.
1946   Les français d'origine métropolitaine...
          [See French Overseas Territories, no. 1946.2].

France. INSEE.
1954.1   Recensement de 1954. Popula-   Census of 1954. Population of
          tion des départements d'outre-   the overseas departments.
          mer.   Paris, Impr. Nationale,   [PRC, UN, RPI
          1954. 12p.

France. INSEE.
    .2   Résultats statistiques du   Statistical results of the general
          recensement général de la popula- population census of the overseas
          tion des départements d'outre-   departments taken July 1, 1954:
          mer effectué le 1er juillet   Reunion.
          1954: Réunion.   Paris, Impr.   [UN, PRC, RPI
          Nationale, 1956. 174p.

France. INSEE.
1961.1   Recensement de 1961. Popu-   Census of 1961. Population of
lation des départements d'outre-   the overseas departments.
mer.   Paris, Impr. des Journaux   [PRC, UN, RPI
Officiels, 1962. 12p.

France. INSEE.
 .2   Résultats statistiques du   Statistical results of the general
recensement général de la popu-   population census of the overseas
lation des départements d'outre-   departments taken October 9, 1961:
mer effectué le 9 octobre 1961:   Reunion.
Réunion.   Paris, Impr. Nationale,   [UN, PRC, RPI
n.d.   222p.

France. INSEE.
1967.1   Recensement de 1967. Popu-   Census of 1967. Population of
lation des départements d'outre-   the overseas departments.
mer.   Paris, Impr. des Journaux   [PRC
Officiels, 1968. 12p.

France. INSEE.
Résultats statistiques du   Statistical results of the general
recensement général de la popu-   population census of the overseas
lation des départements d'outre-   departments taken October 16, 1967:
mer, effectué le 16 octobre 1967:   Reunion.
Réunion.   Paris, 1971-
.2-1   Tableaux statistiques.   Statistical tables.
1971. [2], 117p.   [PRC, UN, OPR, NWU, LC
.2-2   [Analyses des résultats].
                                              [

Reunion.   INSEE - Service Départe-
mental de Statistique.
1974.1   Recensement général de la popu-   General population census of Octo-
lation du 16 octobre 1974. Répar-   ber 16, 1974. Geographical dis-
tition géographique de la popula-   tribution of the population and of
tion et des logements.   Saint-   housing.
Denis, 1976. 64p.   [PRC, NWU

France. INSEE.
 .2   Recensement général de la popu-   General population census of
lation de la France; départements   France; overseas departments:
d'outre-mer: arrondissements,   districts, communes.
communes.   Paris, 1976. 29p.   [NWU

RHODESIA

Zimbabwe-Rhodesia   Capital: Salisbury
Statistical Agency: Central Statistical Office
                     P.O. Box 8063, Causeway
                     Salisbury,
Publications Distributor: same

1946.1   Rhodesia. Central Statistical Office.
          Report on the census of population of Southern Rhodesia held on
          7th May, 1946. Salisbury, 1949. [4], 340p. specimen forms. [UN,
          NWU, TXU, LC, RPI

1948.1   Rhodesia. Central Statistical Office.
          Report on the demographic sample survey of the African population
          of Southern Rhodesia (1948). Salisbury, 1951. 26p. specimen forms.
          [UN, LC, PRC, RPI

1951.1   Rhodesia. Central Statistical Office.
          Census of population, 1951. Salisbury, 1953. 122p. [UN, NWU, LC,
          PRC, RPI

1955.1   Rhodesia. Central Statistical Office.
          The 1953-55 demographic sample survey of the indigenous African
          population of Southern Rhodesia. Salisbury, 1959. 32p. [TXU

1956.1   Rhodesia. Central Statistical Office.
          Census of population, 1956. Salisbury, 1960. [6], 167p. speci-
          men forms. [BC, LC, NWU, PRC, RPI

1958.1   Rhodesia. Central Statistical Office.
          Second report on the Salisbury African demographic survey, August/
          September, 1958. Salisbury, 1959. 30p. [RPI

1959.1   Rhodesia. Central Statistical Office.
          Report on the Bulawayo African demographic survey held in May 1959.
          Salisbury, 1960. [2], 48p. [TXU, LC, RPI

     .2   Rhodesia. Central Statistical Office.
          Report on Umtali and Gwelo African demographic surveys held in Aug-
          ust and September, 1959. Salisbury, 1960. [2], 58p. [TXU, Boston U.,
          RPI

1960.1   Rhodesia. Central Statistical Office.
          Report on Wankie African demographic survey held in April/May, 1960.
          Salisbury, 1961. 15p. [UN, RPI

1961.1   Rhodesia. Central Statistical Office.
          Final report on the September, 1961, census of employees. Salis-
          bury, 1965. [2], 53p. specimen form. [NWU, LC, RPI

Rhodesia.   Central Statistical Office.
.2   1961 census of the European, Asian and Coloured population.   Salisbury, Government Printer, 1966.   114p.   map, forms.   [UN, RPI

Rhodesia.   Central Statistical Office.
1962.1   Final report of the April/May, 1962, census of Africans in Southern
Rhodesia.   Salisbury, 1964.   91p.   [TXU, NWU, BC, LC, PRC, RPI

Rhodesia.   Central Statistical Office.
1969 population census.   Interim reports.   Salisbury, 1971.   Vol.
I-II.
1969.1-1   I.   The European, Asian and Coloured population.   ii, 38p.   [PRC,
BC, LC, NWU
.1-2   II.   The African population.   ii, 40p.   [PRC, BC, LC, NWU

Rhodesia.   Central Statistical Office.
.2   Census of population, 1969.   Salisbury, 1971.   [8], 210p.   [BC

ROMANIA

Socialist Republic of Romania.   Capital: Bucharest
Statistical Agency: Central Statistical Bureau
                    [Direcţia Centrală de Statistică (DCS)]
                    Str. Stavropoleos, nr. 6
                    Bucharest, Sectorul 4,
Publications Distributor: LIBRI
                    Serviciul I 1/Export
                    Calea Victoriei, nr. 126
                    Bucharest, Sectorul 1,

Romania. Institutul Central de
    Statistică.
1948.0-1 Populaţia şi clădirile muni-
    cipuili Bucureşti in 1948: re-
    zultatele provisorii ale recen-
    sământului dela 25 Ianuarie.
    [Bucureşti], 1948. 107p.

Population and buildings of the
municipality of Bucharest in 1948:
provisional results of the census
of January 25.
[BC, PRC, RPI

Romania. Institutul Central de
    Statistică.
.0-2 "Populaţia Republicii Popu-
    lare Române la 25 Ianuarie 1948.
    Rezultate provisorii ale recen-
    sământului." [By] Dr. A. Golo-
    pentia and Dr. D.C. Georgescu.
    In: Probleme economice, no. 2,
    Martie 1948. Buchurest, 1948.
    48p.

"Population of the People's Repub-
lic of Romania on January 25, 1948.
Provisional results of the census.
[UN, PRC, RPI

[See Note after 1966 census entry.]

Romania. Direcţia Centrală de
    Statistică.
    Recensămîntul populaţiei din
    21 februarie 1956. Bucharest,
    1959-1961. 4v.
1956.1-1   Rezultate generale. 1959.
    xxxiii, 1081p.
        Structura social-economică
    a populaţiei. 2 parts.
.1-2-1   Populaţia activă, popu-
    laţia pasivă; grupe sociale;
    ramuri, subramuri de activitate.
    1960. cxx, 1021p.
.1-2-2   Ocupaţii. 1961. lxxi,
    1469p.
.1-3   Structura demografică a
    populaţiei. Numărul şi reparti-
    zarea teritorială a populaţiei;

Population census of February 21,
1956.

General results.
[UN, PRC, TXU, LC, RPI

Active and inactive population;
social groups; branches and sub-
branches of activity.
[UN, PRC, TXU, LC, RPI
Occupations.
[UN, PRC, TXU, LC, RPI
Demographic structure of the population. Number and territorial
distribution of the population;

starea civilě; naţionalitate;   marital status; nationality;
limbă maternă; nivel de instru-   mother tongue; educational level;
ire; familie. 1961. lii, 693p.   families.
                                         [UN, PRC, TXU, LC, RPI

Romania. Central Statistical Office.
.2   Population census of February 21, 1956. General results. [English
translation of Contents, Text and Table Headings.]   Bucharest, 1959.
74, [1]p. [UN, PRC, RPI

Romania. DCS.
     Recensămîntul populaţiei si   Census of the population and hous-
locuinţelor din 15 martie 1966.   ing of March 15, 1966.
Bucharest, 1969–1970. Vol. I–
VIII in   v.
       I. Rezultate generale.   General results.
1966.1-1-1   Populaţie. 1969. lxxx-   Population.
   viii, 941p.   [PRC, OPR
   .1-1-2

Note: There are comparisons of statistics from the 1948, 1956 and
1966 censuses in: Anuarul Demografic al R.S.R., 1974. Bucharest,
1974. Pp. 1–129. [PRC

Romania. Comisia Centrală pen-
     tru Recensămîntul popula-
     ţiei şi al locuinţelor.
1977.0-1 Comunicat privind rezultatele   Communiqué on the preliminary

preliminare ale recensămîntului populaţiei şi al locuinţelor din 5 ianuarie 1977. In: Revista de statistica (Bucharest) 26(6): 4-13. June 1977.

results of the population and housing census of January 5, 1977. [

RWANDA

Republic of Rwanda.   Capital: Kigali
Statistical Agency: Official Bureau of Documentation and General Statistics.
                      [Direction Générale de la Documentation et de la Statis-
                          tique Générale]
                      Ministère du Plan et des Ressources Naturelles
                      Kigali,
Publications Distributor: same

        Note: No full census has been taken.

        Belgian Congo. Gouvernement Gé-
            néral. Section Statistique.
1952.1   Résultats du recensement gé-   Results of the general census of
            néral de la population non-indi-   the non-indigenous population of
            gène du Congo Belge et du Ruanda-   the Belgian Congo and of Ruanda-
            Urundi du 3 janvier 1952./Resul-   Urundi of January 3, 1952.
            taten van de algememe telling   [UN, PRC, RPI
            van de niet-inlandse bevolking
            van Belgisch-Kongo en Ruanda-
            Urundi op 3 januari 1952.   [Leo-
            poldville], 1952. 87p. (Bulle-
            tin mensuel des statistiques du
            Congo Belge et du Ruanda-Urundi,
            3ème année, no. 21).

        Belgian Congo. Direction de la
            Statistique.
            Résultats du recensement de   Results of the census of the non-
        la population non-indigène au   indigenous population of January
        3-1-58./Uitslagen van de telling   3, 1958.
        van de niet-inlandse bevolking
        op 3-1-58.   [Leopoldville],
        1959-1960. Fasc. A-F. (Bulle-
        tin mensuel des statistiques
        générales du Congo Belge et du
        Ruanda-Urundi, série speciale,
        no. 1).
            A. Race blanche./Blanke   A. White race.
        ras.
1958.1-1   a. Population par na-   Population by nationality and oc-
            tionalité et groupe profession-   cupational group.
            nel. 1959. [2], 136p.   [BC, PRC, RPI
    .1-2   b. Population... Mis-   Population... Missionaries.
        sionnaires. 1959. 9, pp. 137-   [BC, PRC, RPI
        255.
    .1-3   c. Population par âge.   Population by age... Population
        ... Population suivant durée   according to duration of resi-
        du séjour... 1959. 12, pp.   dence.
        259-351.   [BC, PRC, RPI

.1-4   d.   Population active
... Agents d'entreprise...
1959. 14, pp. 349-488.
.1-5   e.   Chefs de ménage...
1960. 14, pp. 490-646.
.1-6   B. Population totale des
autres races. 1960. 14, pp.
650-700.

Economically active population...
Business agents...
[BC, PRC, RPI
Household heads...
[BC, PRC, RPI
Total population of other races.
[BC, PRC, RPI

Rwanda.   Office Générale des
Statistiques.
Enquête démographique, 1970.
Paris, SEAE, 1973.   Tome 1-2.
1970.1-1   Présentation--Résultats
d'enquête--Méthodologie--Anne-
xes. 129p.
.1-2   Domaine d'etude--Base de
sondage--Stratification--Echan-
tillon--Calendrier. 280p.

Demographic survey, 1970.

Presentation--results--methodol-
ogy--appendices.
[OPR, NWU
Area of study--sample basis--stra-
ticiation--tabulation--calender.
[OPR, NWU

The next census was proposed for 1978 but no publications have been
seen as yet.

RYUKYU ISLANDS

Prefecture of Japan (since 1972).   Capital: Naha, Okinawa.
Statistical Agency: Bureau of Statistics
                     Office of the Prime Minister
                     95, Wakamatsucho, Shinjuku
                     Tokyo 162, Japan
Publications Distributor: Government Publications Service Center
                           All Japan Official Gazette, Inc. - Agency
                           No. 2-1, Kasumigaseki 1-chome, Chiyoda-ku
                           Tokyo 100, Japan

Ryukyu Islands (U.S. Military Government). Programs and Statistics
        Section.
     Population census, 1 December 1950.   [Naha, 1951-195?]. Books
  100-700 in 93v.
1950.1-100   All Ryukyus. [1951]. ii, 50p. [BC, PRC, RPI
   .1-200   Okinawa Gunto. ii, 50p. [BC, PRC, RPI
1950.1-2-01 through 1950.1-2-56. Administrative ficisions of Okinawa Gunto.
     [All have ii, 50p.] 1. Kunigami./2. Ogimi./3. Higashi./4. Haneji./5.
     Nakijun./6. Kami Motobu./7. Motobu./8. Yabu./9. Nago Cho./10. Onna./
     11. Kushi./12. Ginoza./13. Kin./14. Ie./15. Ishikawa Shi./16. Misato./
     17. Yonagusuku./18. Katsuren./19. Gushikawa./20. Golku./21. Yomitan./
     22. Kadena./23. Chatan./24. Kitanakagusuku./25. Nakagusuku./26. Gino-
     wan./27. Nishibara./28. Urasoe./29. Shuri Shi./30. Naha Shi./31. Mawa-
     shi./32. Oroku./33. Tamagusuku./34. Itoman./35. Kanegusuku./36. Miwa./
     37. Takamine./38. Kochinda./39. Gushichan./40. Tomigusuku./41. Chinen./
     42. Sashiki./43. Yonabaru./44. Ozato./45. Haebaru./46. Nakazato./47.
     Gushikawa Kume-Jima./48. Tokashiki./49. Zamami./50. Iheya./51. Izena./
     52. Azuni./53. Tonaki./54. Minami Daito./55. Kita Daito./56. Zaniji.
     [BC, RPI
   .1-300   Amami Gunto. ii, 50p. [BC, PRC, RPI
1950.1-1-60 through 1950.1-3-79. Administrative divisions of Amami Gunto.
     [All have ii, 50p.] 60. Nase Shi./61. Mikata./62. Yamoto./63. Uken./
     64. Nishikata./65. Saneku./66. Chinzei./67. Koniya Cho./68. Sumiko./
     69. Tatsugo./70. Kasari./71. Kikai Cho./72. Somachi./73. Kametsu Cho./
     74. Higashi Amagi./75. Amagi./76. Isen./77. Wadomari Cho./78. China
     Cho./79. Yoron. [BC, RPI
   .1-400   Miyako Gunto. ii, 50p. [BC, PRC, RPI
1950.1-4-80 through 1950.1-4-85. Administrative divisions of Miyako Gunto.
     [All have ii, 50p.] 80. Hirara Shi./81. Gusukube Cho./82. Shimoji
     Cho./83. Ueno./84. Irabu./85. Tarama. [BC, RPI
   .1-500   Yaeyama Gunto. ii, 50p. [BC, RPI
1950.1-5-90 through 1950.1-5-93. Administrative divisions of Yaeyama Gunto.
     [All have ii, 50p.] 90. Ishigaki Shi./91. Ohama Cho./92. Taketomi
     Cho./93. Yonaguni Cho. [BC, RPI
   .1-600   Northern Okinawa. ii, 50p. [BC, RPI
   .1-700   Southern Okinawa. ii, 50p. [BC, RPI

Ryukyu Islands. Ryukyu seifu
        gyosei shuseki tōkei-kyoku.
   .2   Ryukyu tōkei hōkoku. 1950-   Monthly statistics of the Ryukyu

nen kokusei chōsa tokusho go.
Naha, 1952. 132p.

Islands. Special edition on the
1950 national census.
[

Sōri-fu. Tōkei-kyoku.
.3   Amami gunto jinkō chōsa kekka hōkoku. Tokyo, 1954. iii,
19, 41p.

Report on the population census
of the Amami Islands.
[PRC, RPI

Ryukyu Islands. Statistics Bureau.
     Report on 1955 provisional census. Keigi Makiya, 1957. Vol. 1-2
     in 5v.
1955.1-1   1. Summary. xi, 179p. [PRC, RPI
   .1-2-1   2-1. Northern Okinawa. [2], 170p. [PRC, RPI
   .1-2-2   2-2. Central Okinawa. [2], 140p. [PRC, RPI
   .1-2-3   2-3. Southern Okinawa. [2], 260p. [PRC, RPI
   .1-2-4   2-4. Miyako, Yaeyama. [2], 100p. [PRC, RPI

Ryukyu Islands. Statistics Agency.
     Report on 1960 census: population. Kokichi Shinjo, 1964. Vol.
     1-2 in 6v.
1960.1-1-1   1-1. Summary no. 1. 490, 12p. [BC, PRC, RPI
   .1-1-2   1-2. Summary no. 2. 581p. [PRC, RPI
              2. Cities, towns and villages. Nos. 1-4.
   .1-2-1   Northern Okinawa. 396p. [PRC, RPI
   .1-2-2   Central Okinawa. 326p. [PRC, RPI
   .1-2-3   Southern Okinawa. 582p. [PRC, RPI
   .1-2-4   Miyako and Yaeyama. 232p. [PRC, RPI

Ryukyu Islands. Statistics Agency.
     Report on the 1965 provisional census. n.p., 1967-1968. Vol. 1-2
     in 5v.
1965.1-1   1. Summary for Okinawa.   p. [
              2. Districts. Parts 1-4.
   .1-2-1   Northern.   p. [
   .1-2-2   Central.   p. [
   .1-2-3   Southern.   p. [
   .1-2-4   Miyako and Yaeyama.   p. [

Ryukyu Islands. Statistics Agency.
1970.1   1970 population census report. Final tabulated population by city,
     town and village. [Naha], 1970.   p. [

Ryukyu Islands. Statistics Agency.
.2   1970 population census of Japan. Okinawa. Naha, 1971. [9], xxix,
     401p. map. [PRC

Japan. Bureau of Statistics.
1975.1-5-47   1975 population census of Japan. Prompt report of the basic
     findings for prefectures and municipalities. (Result for twenty-per-
     cent tabulation). Part 47. Okinawa-ken. Tokyo, 1976. [8], viii,
     62p. [PRC

Japan.   Bureau of Statistics.
1975.4-3-47   1975 population census of Japan.   Volume 3.   Prefectures and
municipalities.   Part 47.   Okinawa-ken.   Tokyo, 1977.   [10], xiv,
374p.   maps.   [PRC

ST. HELENA AND ASCENSION

Colony of St. Helena (Great Britain)   Capital: Jamestown, St. Helena.
Statistical Agency: Census Supervisor
                      Government of St. Helena
                      The Castle, St. Helena,
Publications Distributor: same

1946.1   St. Helena.   Census Supervisor's Office.
        Census of population, St. Helena Island and Ascension Island, 1946.
        St. Helena, Government Printing Office, 1946.   [12]p.   [BC, LC, RPI

1956.1   St. Helena.   Census Supervisor's Office.
        Census of the Island of St. Helena and Ascension Island in 1956.
        St. Helena, Government Printer, 1957.   [10]p.   [PRC, RPI

1966.1   St. Helena.   Census Supervisor's Office.
        Census of the population of St. Helena Island and Ascension Island,
        1966.   St. Helena, Government Printing Office, 1966.   [20]p.   [PRC,
        RPI

ST. KITTS-NEVIS-ANGUILLA

State of St. Kitts-Nevis-Anguilla.   Capital: Basseterre.
Statistical Agency: Ministry of Trade, Development, Industry and Tourism
                     Government Headquarters
                     P.O. Box 186
                     St. Kitts, W.I.
Publications Distributor: same.

        Jamaica. Central Bureau of Statistics.
1946   West Indian census, 1946.   Kingston, Government Printer, 1948-
        1950.
             [See Commonwealth Caribbean, Nos. 1946.1-A and 1946.1-F].

        Jamaica. Department of Statistics. Jamaica Tabulation Centre.
1960   West Indies population census. [Leeward Islands]. Census of St.
        Kitts-Nevis-Anguilla, 7th April, 1960.   Kingston, n.d.
             [See Commonwealth Caribbean, Nos. 1960.2-KNA-1 and 1960.2-KNA-2]

        Note: Anguilla was not included in the following census but was to
        have been enumerated in 1974. No citation, however, has been seen.

        West Indies. University. Census Research Programme.
1970   1970 population census of the Commonwealth Caribbean.   Kingston,
        Herald Ltd., 1973-   .
             [See Commonwealth Caribbean, Nos. 1970.1-1
                                               1970.1-2-?
                                               1970.1-3
                                               1970.1-4-11 and 16
                                               1970.1-6-3
                                               1970.1-7
                                               1970.1-8-a, b, and c.
                                               1970.1-9-4
                                               1970.1-10-2 and 4]

ST. LUCIA

State of St. Lucia   Capital: Castries
Statistical Agency: Central Statistical Unit
                     Statistical Department
                     Bridge Street
                     Castries, St. Lucia, W.I.
Publications Distributor: same

1946   Jamaica. Central Bureau of Statistics.
           West Indian census, 1946.   Kingston, Government Printer, 1948-
        1950.
              [See Commonwealth Caribbean, Nos. 1946.1-A and 1946.1-H.]

1960   Trinidad and Tobago. Central Statistical Office.
           Eastern Caribbean population census of 1960.   Port of Spain, 1963-
        197 .
              [See Commonwealth Caribbean, Nos. 1960.1-1-A and D
                                             1960.1-2-W
                                             1960.1-3-WL-1 and 2]

1970   West Indies. University. Census Research Programme.
           1970 population census of the Commonwealth Caribbean.
              [See Commonwealth Caribbean, Nos. 1970.1-1
                                             1970.1-2-?
                                             1970.1-3
                                             1970.1-4-6 and 16
                                             1970.1-6-2
                                             1970.1-7
                                             1970.1-8-a, b, and c.
                                             1970.1-9-2
                                             1970.1-10-2 and 4]

ST. PIERRE AND MIQUELON

Department of St. Pierre and Miquelon (France)   Capital: St.-Pierre.
Statistical Agency: INSEE
                      18, Blvd. Adolphe-Pinard
                      75675 Paris, Cedex 14, FRANCE
Publications Distributor: Observatoire Economique de Paris
                           195, rue de Bercy--Tour Gamma A
                           75582 Paris, Cedex 12, FRANCE

Note: Unlike the other French overseas territories, the non-indigenous
population censuses taken here were of the TOTAL population.

France. INSEE.
1951   Le recensement de la population non originaire...
          [See French Overseas Territories, No. 1951.1]

France. INSEE.
1951.2   Résultats du recensement de   Results of the census of 1951,
          1951, territoires d'outre-met: overseas territories: Part 1,
          1re partie, Côte Français de   French Coast of the Somalis,
          Somalis, Inde Française, Saint-   French India, St. Pierre and Mi-
          Pierre-et-Miquelon. Paris,   quelon.
          1952. 110p. (Bulletin mensuel   [BC, UN, PRC, RPI
          de statistique d'outre-mer,
          supplément série "statistique,"
          no. 14).

France. INSEE.
1957.1   Recensement de la population   Census of the population of St.
          de Saint-Pierre et Miquelon.   Pierre and Miquelon.
          Paris, 1962. 50p.   [BC, LC, PRC, RPI

France. INSEE.
1962.1   Saint Pierre et Miquelon: St. Pierre and Miquelon: census
          Recensement de la population,   of the population, April 1962.
          avril 1962. Paris, 1962. 36p.   [BC, LC, PRC, RPI

France. INSEE.
1967.1   Recensement de la population   Census of the population of the
          du territoire de Saint-Pierre   St. Pierre and Miquelon territory,
          et Miquelon, 1967. Paris,   1967.
          1967. 93p.   [UN, LC, PRC, RPI

France. INSEE.
1974.1   Recensement de la population   Census of the population of the
          du territoire de Saint-Pierre   St. Pierre and Miquelon territory,
          et Miquelon, 1974. Paris,   1974.
          1974. 51p.   [PRC, UN, BC, LC, JB-F

ST. VINCENT

State of St. Vincent   Capital: Kingstown
Statistical Agency: Statistical Unit
                     Kingstown,
Publications Distributor: same

1946   Jamaica. Central Bureau of Statistics.
             West Indian census, 1946. Kingston, Government Printer, 1948-
          1950.
                 [See Commonwealth Caribbean, Nos. 1946.1-A and 1946.1-H]

1960   Trinidad and Tobago. Central Statistical Office.
             Eastern Caribbean population census of 1960.   Port of Spain, 1963-
          197 .
                 [See Commonwealth Caribbean, Nos. 1960.1-1-A and D
                                                 1960.1-2-W
                                                 1960.1-3-WV-1 and 2]

1970   West Indies. University. Census Research Programme.
             1970 population census of the Commonwealth Caribbean.
                [See Commonwealth Caribbean, Nos. 1970.1-1
                                                 1970.1-2-?
                                                 1970.1-3
                                                 1970.1-4-8 and 16
                                                 1970.1-6-2
                                                 1970.1-7
                                                 1970.1-8-a, b, and c.
                                                 1970.1-9-3
                                                 1970.1-10-2 and 4]

SAN MARINO

Republic of San Marino.   Capital: San Marino
Statistical Agency: State Statistical Service
                     [Servizio Statale di Statistica]
                     San Marino,
Publications Distributor: same

    The seem to be no official census publications. Results are released
theough statistical annuals. The 1947 census is their Fourth.

    San Marino. Ufficio Statale di
        Statistica.
1947.1   Censimento di 1947. In: Census of 1947.
    Analisi statistica socio-econo-   [PRC
    mica, anno I, no. 1 (Giugno 1971)

    San Marino. Ufficio Statale di
        Statistica.
1974.1   Dinamica demografica ed evo-   Demographic dynamics and social
    luzione sociale nella Repubblica   evolution in the Republic of
    di San Marino.   San Marino,   San Marino.
    1975. ix, 137p.   [PRC

SÃO TOMÉ AND PRINCIPE

Democratic Republic of São Tomé and Principe. Capital: São Tomé.
Statistical Agency: Statistic Services
              [Serviços de Estatística]
              São Tomé,
Publications Distributor: same

Portugal. Instituto Nacional
    de Estatística.

1950.1   Censos de população do ultra-   Censuses of population of the
mar de 1950. 6, Provincia de   overseas territories in 1950.
S. Tomé e Principe. In: Bole-   No. 6, Province of São Tomé and
tim mensal do I.N.E. Ano 23,   Principe.
no. 11, Nov. 1951. Pp. 4-7.   [UN, RPI

São Tomé e Principe. Repartição
    Provincial dos Serviços de
    Economia. Secção de Esta-
    tística Geral.

1960.1   Censo da população de 1960.   Census of population of 1960.
n.p., 1963. 2p.   [PRC, RPI

São Tomé e Principe. Repartição
    Provincial dos Serviços de
    Estatística.

1970.1   Censo da população, 1970.   Census of population, 1970.
Concelho do Principe. [São   Council of Principe.
Tomé], 197 . 8p.   [LC

Portugal. Instituto Nacional de Estatística.
1970   [1970 recenseamento da população...
    [See Portugal 1970.3.]

SAUDI ARABIA

Kingdom of Saudi Arabia.   Capital: Riyadh
Statistical Agency: Central Statistical Department
                      Ministry of Finance and National Economy
                      Riyadh,
Publications Distributor: same

There was a census of 1962-1963 but the count was incomplete; no
publications have appeared.

SCOTLAND

Capital: Edinburgh

Statistical Agency: General Register Office
New Register House
Edinburgh, EH1 3YT,
Publications Distributor: See England and Wales.

Scotland. General Registry Office.
Census 1951. Report on the fifteenth census of Scotland. Edinburgh, HMSO, 1952-1956. Vols. I-V in 39v.
I. [Cities and counties]. 1952-1954.
1951.1-1-1 through 1951.1-1-35. 1. City of Edinburgh. 1952. 47p./2. City of Glasgow. 1952. 57p./3. City of Aberdeen. 1953. 36p./4. City of Dundee. 1953. 46p./5. Aberdeen. 1953. 48p./6. Angus. 1953. 46p./ 7. Argyll. 1953. 44p./8. Ayr. 1953. 58p./9. Banff. 1953. 39p./ 10. Berwick. 1953. 32p./11. Bute. 1953. 32p./12. Caithness. 1953. 30p./13. Clackmannan. 1953. 32p./14. Dumfries. 1953. 45p./15. Dumbarton. 1953. 47p./16. East Lothian. 1953. 37p./17. Fife. 1954. 64p./18. Inverness. 1954. 42p./19. Kincardine. 1954. 34p./20. Kircudbright. 1954. 38p./21. Lanark. 1954. 54p./22. Midlothian. 1954. 42p./23. Moray and Nairn. 1954. 66p./24. Orkney. 1954. 37p./25. Peebles. 1954. 32p./26. Perth and Kinross. 1954. 78p./ 27. Renfrew. 1954. 53p./28. Ross and Cromarty. 1954. 44p./29. Roxburgh. 1954. 40p./30. Selkirk. 1954. 34p./31. Stirling. 1954. 47p./32. Sutherland. 1954. 31p./33. West Lothian. 1954. 39p./34. Wigtown. 1954. 32p./35. Zetland. 1954. 34p. [PRC, BC, UN, RP]
.1-2   II. Population of towns and larger villages (excluding burghs) and of urban and rural areas. 1952. 26p. [PRC, UN, BC, RP]
.1-3   III. General volume. Population, age, sex and conjugal condition, birthplace and nationality, Gaelic-speaking population and housing (houses, households and household conveniences). 1954. lxx, 135p. [PRC, UN, BC, RP]
.1-4   IV. Occupations and industries (with some particulars of (a) the extent to which people live in ove area but work in another, and (b) occupations in relation to school leaving age). 1956. xlvi, 658p. [PRC, UN, BC, RP]
.1-5   V. Fertility of marriage. 1956. xvi, 87p. [PRC, UN, BC, RP]

Note: For the One percent sample tables, see Great Britain.

Scotland. General Registry Office.
Census 1961. Scotland. Population, dwellings, households. Edinburgh, HMSO, 1962-1966. Leaflet Nos. 1-27.
1961.1-1 through 1961.1-9. 1. City of Edinburgh. 1962. 2p./2. Counties of West Lothian, Midlothian, East Lothian. 1962. 7p./3. Cities of Glasgow, Edinburgh, Aberdeen, Dundee. 1963. 7p./4. Crofting counties: Argyll, Caithness, Inverness, Orkney, Ross and Cromarty, Sutherland, Zetland. 1963. 11p./5. North-eastern counties: Aberdeen, Banff, Kincardine, Moray, Nairn. 1963. 10p./6. East and central counties: Angus, Clackmannan, Fife, Kinross, Perth, Stirling.

1963. 11p./7. West and central counties: Ayr, Bute, Dunbarton,
Lanark, Renfrew. 1963. 11p./8. Southern countries: Berwick, Dumfries, Kirkcudbright, Peebles, Roxburgh, Selkirk, Wigtown. 1963.
10p./9. [Not published]. [PRC, RPI
.1-10   Housing. National summary tables. 1964. 19p. [PRC, RPI
.1-11   Population. Age by marital condition. Totals for Scotland as
enumerated 23rd April, 1961. 1964. 3p. [PRC, RPI
.1-12   Local housing indices. 1965. 22p. [PRC, RPI
         Occupation and Industry.
.1-13   National summary tables. 1965. 17p. [PRC, RPI
1961.1-14 through 1961.1-25. 14. Edinburgh and the Lothians. 1966. xx,
29p./15. Glasgow and Lanark. 1966. xx, 29p./16. Stirling. 1966.
xx, 19p./17. Dunbarton. 1966. xx, 29p./18. Renfrew. 1966. xx,
29p./19. Ayr and Bute. 1966. xxii, 29p./20. Dundee, Clackmannan
and Fife. 1966. xx, 29p./21. Angus, Kinross and Perth. 1966. xx,
29p./22. Aberdeen city, Aberdeen county, Banff, Kincardine, Moray
and Perth. 1966. xx, 33p./23. Crofting counties. 1966. xx, 33p./
24. Border counties. 1966. xx, 29p./25. Dumfries, Kirkcudbright
and Wigtown. 1966. xx, 19p. [PRC, RPI
.1-26   Internal migration. National and local summary tables. 1966.
xv, 22p. [PRC, BC, RPI
.1-27   Gaelic. Supplementary leaflet. 1966. [1], 8p. [, RPI

Scotland. General Registry Office.
    Census 1961. Scotland. Edinburgh, HMSO, 1963-1966. Vols. I-
X in 47v.
        I. County reports. 1963-1964. 35v.
1961.2-1-1 through 1961.2-1-35. 1. City of Edinburgh. 1963. 80p./2. City
of Glasgow. 1963. 109p./3. City of Aberdeen. 1963. 62p./4. City
of Dundee. 1963. 58p./5. Aberdeen. 1963. 103p./6. Angus. 1963.
110p./7. Argyll. 1964. 84p./8. Ayr. 1964. 148p./9. Banff. 1963.
80p./10. Berwick. 1964. 68p./11. Bute. 1964. 64p./12. Caithness.
1963. 66p./13. Clackmannan. 1964. 72p./14. Dumfries. 1964. 102p./
15. Dunbarton. 1964. 124p./16. East Lothian. 1963. 74p./17. Fife.
1964. 150p./18. Inverness. 1963. 98p./19. Kincardine. 1963. 68p./
20. Kirkcudbright. 1964. 72p./21. Lanark. 1964. 141p./22. Midlothian. 1963. 84p./23. Moray and Nairn. 1963. 122p./24. Orkney.
1963. 76p./25. Peebles. 1964. 66p./26. Perth and Kinross. 1964.
148p./27. Renfrew. 1964. 130p./28. Ross and Cromarty. 1963. 82p./
29. Roxburgh. 1964. 76p./30. Selkirk. 1964. 72p./31. Stirling.
1964. 114p./32. Sutherland. 1963. 64p./33. West Lothian. 1963.
88p./34. Wigtown. 1964. 66p./35. Zetland. 1963. 74p. [PRC, BC,
RPI, RIR
.2-2   II. Usual residence. 1965. xvi, 17p. [PRC, BC, RPI, RIR
.2-3   III. Age, marital condition and general tables. 1965. lxx,
109p. [PRC, BC, RPI, RIR
        IV. Housing and households. Part I-II.
.2-4-1   I. 1966. lxv, 193p. [PRC, BC, RPI, RIR
.2-4-2   II. Household composition tables. 1966. 234p. [PRC, BC,
RPI, RIR
.2-5   V. Birthplace and nationality. 1966. xxv, 39p. [PRC, BC,
RPI, RIR

```
            VI.  Occupation, industry and workplace.  Part I-III.
.2-6-1      I.  Occupation tables.  1966.  xiv, 199p.  [PRC, BC, RPI, RIR
.2-6-2      II.  Industry tables.  1966.  237p.  [PRC, BC, RPI, RIR
.2-6-3      III.  Workplace tables.  1966.  61p.  [PRC, BC, RPI, RIR
.2-7    VII. Gaelic.  1966.  xxiii, 28p.  [PRC, RPI, RIR
.2-8    VIII.  Internal migration.  1966.  127p.  [PRC, BC, RPI, RIR
.2-9    IX.  Terminal education age.  1966.  xix, 23p.  [PRC, BC, RPI, RIR
.2-10   X.  Fertility.  1966.  289p.  [PRC, BC, RPI, RIR
```

Scotland. General Registry Office.
.3   Place names and population, Scotland: an alphabetical list of populated places derived from the Census of Scotland. Edinburgh, HMSO, 1967. 190p. [

Note: For <u>Scientific and technological qualifications</u>, <u>Summary report</u>, and <u>Summary tables</u>, see Great Britain.

Scotland. General Register Office.
    Sample census 1966. Scotland. County reports. Edinburgh, HMSO, 1967-1968. 10v.
1966.1-1 through 1966.1-10. 1. Edinburgh, East Lothian, Midlothian, Stirling and West Lothian. 1967. xxvii, 39p./2. Clackmannan, Fife and Kinross. 1967. xxv, 38p./3. Glasgow and Lanark. 1967. xxiv, 33p./4. Dunbarton and Renfrew. 1967. xxiv, 41p./5. Dundee, Angus and Perth. 1967. xxv, 31p./6. Ayr and Bute. 1967. xxiv, 24p./7. Dumfries, Kirkcudbright and Wigtown. 1967. xxv, 27p./8. Argyll, Caithness, Inverness, Orkney, Ross and Cromarty, Sutherland and Zetland. 1967. xxx, 46p./9. Berwick, Peebles, Roxburgh and Selkirk. 1967. xxvi, 27p./10. Aberdeen city, Aberdeen county, Banff, Kincardine, Moray and Nairn. 1967. xxviii, 35p. [PRC, RPI

Scotland. General Register Office.
    Sample census 1966. Scotland. Edinburgh, HMSO, 1968-1969. 6v. in 7.
.2-1   Household composition tables. 1968. xxviii, 111p. [PRC, RPI
.2-2   Housing tables. 1968. xxviii, 111p. [PRC, RPI
        Migration tables. Part I-II.
.2-3-1   I. 1968. xxiv, 209p. [PRC, RPI
.2-3-2   II. 1969. xxviii, 134p. [PRC, RPI
.2-4   Report on the special study areas. 1968. xix, 345p. [PRC, BC, RPI
.2-5   Usual residence and birthplace tables. 1969. xix, 15p. [PRC, RPI
.2-6   Workplace and transport tables. 1968. xiv, 140p. [PRC, RPI
        Economic activity. Leaflets Nos. 1-10 (plus 1).
.2-7-0   General explanatory notes for the county tables in leaflets Nos. 1-10. 1968. 35p. [Harvard, PRC, RPI
1966.2-7-1 through 1966.2-7-10. 1. Edinburgh, East Lothian, Midlothian, Stirling and West Lothian. 37p./2. Clackmannan, Fife and Kinross. 36p./3. Glasgow and Lanark. 45p/4. Dunbarton and Renfrew. 36p./5. Ayr and Bute. 16p./6. Dundee, Angus and Perth. 26p./7. Aberdeen

city, Aberdeen county, Banff, Kincardine, Moray and Nairn.   27p./8.
Argyll, Caithness, Inverness, Orkney, Ross and Cromarty, Sutherland
and Zetland.   38p./9. Berwick, Peebles, Roxburgh and Selkirk.   26p./
10. Dumfries, Kirkcudbright and Wigtown.   26p. [Harvard, PRC, RPI

Note: For Commonwealth immigrant tables, Economic activity sub-
regional tables, Economic activity tables, Qualified manpower tables,
Scientific and technological qualifications, and Summary tables, see
Great Britain.   For General and parliamentary constituency tables,
Great Britain 1966.2.

Scotland. General Register Office.
     Census 1971. Scotland. County report.   Edinburgh, HMSO, 1972-
1973.   38v.
1971.1-1 through 1971.1-38. 1. Edinburgh city. 1973. xxii, 146p./2. Glasgow city. 1973. xii, 231p./3. Aberdeen city. 1973. xii, 93p./4.
Dundee city. 1972. xii, 92p./5. New towns: Cumbernauld, East Kil-
bride, Glenrothes, Irvine, Livingston. 1973. xx, 91p./6. Aberdeen.
1973. xii, 146p./7. Angus. 1972. xii, 140p./8. Argyll. 1973. xii,
135p./9. Ayr. 1973. xii, 241p./10. Banff. 1973. xii, 141p./11.
Berwick. 1972. xii, 82p./12. Bute. 1972. xi, 70p./13. Caithness.
1972. xii, 75p./14. Clackmannan. 1972. xii, 75p./15. Dumfries.
1973. xii, 149p./16. Dunbarton. 1972. xii, 159p./17. East Lothian.
1972. xi, 108p./18. Fife. 1973. xii, 275p./19. Inverness. 1973.
xii, 134p./20. Kincardine. 1973. xii, 88p./21. Kinross. 1972. xi,
40p./22. Kirkcudbright. 1972. xii, 102p./23. Lanark. 1973. xii,
230p./24. Midlothian. 1973. xii, 116p./25. Moray. 1973. xii,
107p./26. Nairn. 1972. xi, 40p./27. Orkney. 1973. xii, 107p./
28. Peebles. 1973. xii, 74p./29. Perth. 1973. xii, 163p./30.
Renfrew. 1972. xii, 166p./31. Ross and Cromarty. 1973. xii, 141p./
32. Roxburgh. 1972. xi, 86p./33. Selkirk. 1973. xii, 64p./34.
Stirling. 1972. xii, 169p./35. Sutherland. 1972. xi, 74p./36.
West Lothian. 1973. xii, 113p./37. Wigtown. 1972. xii, 74p./38.
Zetland. 1972. xi, 118p. [PRC

Scotland. General Register Office.
 .2   1971 census statistics. New local government areas as constituted
16 May 1975.   Edinburgh, HMSO, 1976. viii, 75p. [PRC

Scotland. General Register Office.
     Census 1971. Scotland. Report for ... region as constituted on
16th May 1975.   Edinburgh, HMSO, 1976. 9v.
1971.3-1 through 1971.3-9. 1. Borders. xi, 81p./2. Central. xi, 69p./3.
Dumfries and Galloway. xi, 82p./4. Fife. xi, 69p./5. Grampian. xi,
96p./6. Highland, and Orkney, Shetland, and Western Isles Islands
areas. xvii, 175p./7. Lothian. xi, 82p./8. Strathclyde. xi, 272p./
9. Tayside. xi, 73p. [PRC

Scotland. General Register Office.
     Census 1971. Scotland.   Edinburgh, HMSO, 1973-1978. 14v. in
23v.
          Economic activity. County tables. (10 percent sample). Part
I-IV.

1971.4-1-1   I.   v, 87p.   [PRC
  .4-1-2   II. v, 91p.   [PRC
  .4-1-3   III. v, 150p. [PRC
  .4-1-4   IV. v, 55p.   [PRC
  .4-2   Economic activity tables (100 percent). 1978. xiv, 126p.
    [PRC

        Fertility tables. Part I-II.
  .4-3-1   I. (100 percent). 1975. xvii, 257p. [PRC
  .4-3-2   II. (10 percent). 1976. xxi, 230p. [PRC
  .4-4   Gaelic report. 1975. xxiv, 22p. [PRC, BC, UN
  .4-5   Household composition tables (10 percent sample). 1975. xxxiv,
    354p. [PRC
  .4-6   Household composition tables (100 percent). 1978. xxiv, 69p.
    [PRC
  .4-7   Housing report. 1975. xliv, 255p. [PRC, BC, UN
        Migration tables. (10 percent sample). 1974-1977. Parts I-VI.
  .4-8-1   I. 1974. xxi, 173p. [PRC
  .4-8-2   II. 1976. xxv, 107p. [PRC
  .4-8-3   III. 1976. xxi, 183p. [PRC
  .4-8-4   IV. 1977. xxv, 286p. [PRC
  .4-8-5   V. 1977. xviii, 138p. [PRC
  .4-8-6   VI. 1977. xviii, 88p. [PRC
  .4-9   Migration tables (100 percent). 1978. xxviii, 154p. [PRC
  .4-10   Population tables. 1974. yxii, 206p. [PRC
  .4-11   Qualified manpower tables (100 percent). 1978. xli, 30p.
    [PRC
  .4-12   Scottish population summary. Area populations, economic activity, households. 1973. viii, 11p. appendix. [PRC
  .4-13   Usual residence and birthplace tables. 1974. xxi, 129p. [PRC
  .4-14   Workplace and transport tables. (10 percent sample). 1975.
  xxv, 142p. [PRC

  Scotland. General Register Office.
.5   Index of Scottish place names from 1971 census with location and
  population (over 100 persons.) Edinburgh, HMSO, 1975. xi, 186p.
  [PRC

  Note: For Economic activity; Economic activity general explanatory
  notes; Age, marital condition and general tables; Country of birth
  tables; Household composition summary tables; Housing summary tables;
  Migration tables; Manpower tables; Summary tables, see Great Britain.

SENEGAL

Republic of Senegal.   Capital: Dakar
Statistical Agency: Statistics and Data Processing Service
                     [Service de la Statistique et de la Mécanographie]
                     Ministère des Finances et des Études Économiques.
                     B. P. No. 116
                     Dakar,
Publications Distributor: Bureau du Commerce Extérieur
                           (of the above).

          France. INSEE [and] Service Colonial des Statistiques.
1946   Résultats du recensement de 1946 ...
              [See French Overseas Territories, No. 1946.1-1, 2 and 3].

          France. INSEE [and] Ministère de la France d'Outre-Mer.
              Les français d'origine métropolitaine...
              [See French Overseas Territories, No. 1946.2]

          France. INSEE.
1951   Le recensement de la population non originaire...
              [See French Overseas Territories, No. 1951.1]

          French West Africa. Service de la Statistique Générale.
              Recensement de la population non autochtone...
              [See French Overseas Territories, No. 1951.2]

          French West Africa. Service de
              la Statistique Générale.
1951.3   Population de l'A.O.F. en   Population of French West Africa
          1950-1951 par canton et groupe   in 1950-1951 by canton and ethnic
          éthnique, chiffres provisoires.   group, provisional figures.
          Dakar, 1952. [135]p.   [UN, PRC, RPI

          French West Africa. Service de
              la Statistique Générale.
              Recensement de 1951. Commune   Census of 1951. Mixed communes
          mixte de...   Dakar, 1952-1954.   of...
          3v.
.4-1   ...Diourbel. 1952. 27p.
          map.   [UN, OPR, RPI
.4-2   ...Zinquinchor. 1953.
          43p. map.   [LC, UN, OPR, RPI
.4-3   ...Thiès. 1954. 42p.
          map.   [NYPL, UN

          French West Africa. Service de
              la Statistique Générale.
              Recensement démographique de   Demographic census of Dakar (1955):
          Dakar (1955): résultats défini-   Final results.
          tifs.   Paris, 1958-1962. Fasc.
          1-2

1955.1-1 État civil, groupes éthniques, religion, nationalité et lieu de naissance, degré d'instruction, activité professionnelle de la population recensée. Résultats du sondage complementaire: âge au premier mariage, fécondité des femmes et mortalité de leurs enfants; enfants à chargé des hommes. 1958. 126p.

Marital status, ethnic groups, religion, nationality and birthplace, level of education, occupational activity of the enumerated population. Results of the complementary sample: age at first marriage, fertility of females and mortality of their children; children in the charge of males.
[NWU, LC, PRC, RPI

.1-2 Étude socio-démographique de la ville de Dakar. 1962. 143, vi, 69p. map.

Socio-demographic study of the city of Dakar.
[NWU, LC, OPR, RPI

France. INSEE.
1957.0-1 Enquête démographique 1957 au Sénégal: Résultats provisoires. Paris, 1957. [4], 29p. map.

Demographic survey 1957 in Senegal: provisional results.
[UN, OPR, RPI

Senegal. Service de la Statistique et de la Mécanographie.
1961.1 La population du Sénégal en 1960-61. Dakar, 1965. p.

The population of Senegal in 1960-1961.
[

Senegal. Direction de la Statistique.
Enquête démographique nationale, 1970-71. Dakar, 1971-1973. 3v.
1971.0-1 Résultats provisoires du 1er passage. 1971. [iii], 68p.

National demographic survey, 1970-71.

Provisional results from the first passage.
[NWU, LC, OPR

.0-2 Répertoire des villages. 1972. var. pag.

Village directory.
[NWU

.0-3 Méthodologie et documents annexes. 1973. 183p. specimen forms.

Methodology and annexed documents.
[NWU, LC

Senegal. Direction de la Statistique.
Enquête démographique nationale, 1970-1971: résultats définitifs. Dakar, 1974- .
Série A: données de structure.
1971.1-1 Pyramide des âges. 1974. 69p.

National demographic survey, 1970-1971: final results.

Series A: structure data.

Age pyramids.
[NWU, UN, LC, JB-F, NYPL

.1-2 Situation matrimoniale. 1974. 52p.

Marital situation.
[NWU, UN, LC, JB-F, NYPL

Senegal.   Bureau National du
      Recensement.
1976.0-1 Résultats provisoires du   Provisional results of the general
      recensement général de la popu-   census of the population of April
      lation d'avril 1976.   Dakar,   1976.
      1976. 13p.   [BC, NWU

Senegal.   Bureau du Recensements.
  .0-2 Sénégal--résultats provisoires   Senegal--provisional results of
      du recensement général de la   the general census of population.
      population. In: Bulletin de   [
      liaison: démographie Africaine,
      no. 24.   Paris, 1977. pp. 70-
      71.

SEYCHELLES

Republic of Seychelles.   Capital: Victoria, Mahé
Statistical Agency: Office of the Chief Statistician
                     P.O. Box 206
                     Victoria, Mahé,
Publications Distributor: same

       Seychelles. Office of the Census Commissioner.
1947.1   Census report for the year 1947.   Victoria, Government Printing
       Office, 1948. 15p. [BC, UN, PRC, RPI

       Seychelles. Office of the Census Commissioner.
1960.1   Population census of the Seychelles colony. Report and tables
       for 1960 by A.W.T. Webb.   [Kenya, Government Printer, 1960]. [2],
       68p. maps. [PRC, NWU, LC, RPI

       Seychelles. Office of the Census Commissioner.
1971.1   Population census, 1971: draft final report.   Victoria, 1977.
       xii, 47p. [

       Seychelles. Office of the Census Commissioner.
1977.1   1977 census report.   [Victoria], Government Press, 1978. [iv],
       215p. [PRC

       Seychelles. Census Office.
   .2   The Republic of Seychelles census 1977; summary of results, 31
       October 1977.   [Victoria, 1977]. 12p. [UN

SIERRA LEONE

Republic of Sierra Leone   Capital: Freetown
Statistical Agency: Central Statistics Office
                      Tower Hill
                      Freetown,
Publications Distributor: same

Sierra Leone.   Census Office.
1948.1   Census of the colony and protectorate of Sierra Leone, 1948.
Freetown, 1949.   2p.   [UN, RPI

Sierra Leone.   Central Statistics Office.
    1963 census of population, Sierra Leone.   Advance reports.   Free-
town, n.d.   Nos. 1–14.
1963.1-1 through 1963.1-14.   1. Port Loko./2. Kambia./3. Karene./4. Bombali./
    5. Koinadagu./6. Moyamba./7. Bonthe./8. Pujehun./9. Bo./10. Kenema./
    11. Kailahun./12. Kono./13. Sherbro Urban./14. Western Area.   [UN, RPI

Sierra Leone.   Central Statistics Office.
    1963 population census of Sierra Leone.   Freetown, Government
Printing Department, 1965.   Vol. 1–3.
    .2-1   Number of inhabitants.   [6], xxi, 178p.   maps, forms.   [BC, PRC,
    NWU, LC
    .2-2   Social characteristics.   [6], xxi, 370p.   maps, forms.   [BC, PRC,
    NWU, LC
    .2-3   Economic characteristics.   [6], xxi, 152p.   maps, forms.   [BC,
    NWU, LC

Sierra Leone.   Central Statistics Office.
    Household survey of the ... urban areas, March 1968–December 1969.
Freetown, 1969–1971.   4v in 6.
              Northern province.
1969.1-1-1   1969.   77p.   [JB-F
    .1-1-2   1971.   104p.   [JB-F
              Southern province.
    .1-2-1   1970.   82p.   [JB-F
    .1-2-2   1971.   99p.   [JB-F
    .1-3   Eastern province.   1971.   88, 119p.   [JB-F
    .1-4   Western area.   1967-68.   39, 71p.   [JB-F

Sierra Leone.   Central Statistics Office.
    Household survey of the rural areas of the provinces.   Freetown,
    1972.   2v.
1970.1-1   Household characteristics and housing conditions.   88p.   [JB-F
    .1-2   Final report: household expenditure and income and economic
    characteristics, July 1969-Jan. 1970.   126p.   [JB-F

The provisional results of the 1973 cansus have been released but citation to the publication has not been seen as yet.

SINGAPORE

Republic of Singapore   Capital: Singapore
Statistical Agency: Department of Statistics
                     P.O. Box 3010
                     Singapore 1,
Publications Distributor: Singapore National Printers (Private), Ltd.
                           303, Upper Serangoon Rd./P.O. Box 485
                           Singapore 13,

    Malaya. [Superintendent of Census Office].
1947.1   A report on the 1947 census of population: comprising the Federation of Malaya [Malay Peninsula] and the Colony of Singapore. By M.V.
del Tufo. Kuala Lumpur, Government Printer, 1949. 597p. maps.
[UN, PRC, OPR, E-W, RPI

    Singapore. Chief Statistician and Superintendent of Census Office.
1957.1   Report on the census of population, 1957. Singapore, Government
Printing Office, 1964. [5], vii, [2], 319p. [PRC, LC, E-W, RPI

    Singapore. Ministry of National Development and Economic Research
        Centre.
    Singapore sample household survey, 1966. [Singapore, Government
Printer, 1967-1970]. Report 1-2.
1966.1-1   Tables relating to population and housing. 1967. [5], vi, 303p.
    [PRC, RPI
  .1-2   Administrative report, by Ruth Daroesman. 1970. var. pag.
    [PRC

    Singapore. Housing and Development Board. Statistics and Research
        Department.
1968.1   Report on the census of resettlement areas, 1968. By Stephen H.K.
Yeh and the Statistics and Research Development Board. Singapore,
Government Printing Office, 1971? 310p. maps. [PRC, LC

    Singapore. Department of Statistics.
1970.0-1   Census of population, 1970, Singapore; interim release, by P.
Arumainathan. Singapore, 1970. 78p. tables. [PRC

    Singapore. Department of Statistics.
    Report on the census of population 1970, Singapore, by P. Arumai-
nathan. Singapore, 1973. 2v.
  .1-1   xiii, 302p. [PRC, LC
  .1-2   viii, 573p. [PRC, LC

SOLOMON ISLANDS

Solomon Islands (1978)   Capital: Honiara
Statistical Agency: Government Statistician
                      Ministry of Finance
                      G.P.O. Box 26
                      Honiara,
Publications Distributor: Government Printing Office
                      Honiara,

        Solomon Islands (British). Western Pacific High Commission.
1959.1   Report on the population census of 1959. By Norma McArthur.
        Honiara, 1961. ii, 102p. 21 maps. [PRC

        Note: The above census is "a census of selected areas..."

        Solomon Islands (British). Western Pacific High Commission.
1970.1   Report on the census of the population, 1970. By K. Groenewegen.
        Southampton, England, Hobbs the Printers, Ltd., n.d. viii, 370p. 27
        maps. [PRC, LC, BC

        Solomon Islands (British). Statistical Office.
1976.0-1   Population census, February 1976: provisional results.   Honiara,
        1976. [14]p. map. [PRC, UN

        Solomon Islands (British). Statistics Office.
   .0-2   Population census, 1976: preliminary results.   Honiara, 1977.
        [12]p. (Statistical bulletin, No. 3/77). [PRC, OPR

SOMALIA

Somali Democratic Republic   Capital: Mogadishu
Statistical Agency: Central Statistical Department
                  State Planning Commission
                  Ministry of Planning and Co-ordination
                  Mogadishu,
Publications Distributor: same.

British Somaliland may have been included in the East African Population Census, 1948, but no specific citations have been seen. Italian
Somalia was included in the census below.

Italy.   Instituto Centrale di
        Statistica.
1953.1   Censimento della popolazione   Census of the Italian and foreign
Italia e straniera della Somalia,   population of Somalia, November 4,
4 nov. 1953.   Roma, Fausto   1953.
Failli, 1958.   170, [1]p.   [UN, NWU, PRC, RPI

Somalia.   Statistical Service.
     A multi-purpose statistical survey of the ... town, 1962-1963.
Mogadiscio, 1963-1964.   10v.
1963.1-1 through 1963.1-10.   1. Berbera Town.   1964.   32p./2. Burao Town.
1964.   30p./3. Hargeisa Town.   1964.   42p./4. Borama Town (Hargeisa
Region).   1964.   21p./5. Erigavo Town (Burao Region).   1964.   19p./
6. Gebileh Town (Hargeisa Region).   1964.   21p./7. Las Anod Town (Burao Region).   1964.   19p./8. Laskoreh Town.   1964.   24p./9. Odweins
Town (Burao Region).   1964.   19p./10. Zeila Town (Hargeisa Region).
1964.   22p.   [NWU, OPR

Somalia.   Statistical Department.
1964.1   A multi-purpose survey of Afgoi municipality, [1964].   Mogadiscio,
1966.   36p.   [NWU

Somalia.   Statistical Department.
     The multi-purpose survey of ... District, [1968].   Mogadiscio,
1969.
1968.1-1 through 1968.1-4.   1. Afmedou.   32p./2. Gelib.   27p./3. Giamama.
30p./4. Coriolei.   23p.   [NWU

Processing of data from the 1975 census has been reactivated recently.

SOUTH AFRICA

Republic of South Africa.   Capital: Pretoria & Cape Town
Statistical Agency: Department of Statistics
                     Private Bag X44
                     Pretoria,
Publications Distributor: The Government Printer
                           Private Bag X85
                           Pretoria,

South Africa. Kantoor van
      Sensus en Statistiek.
   Sewende Bevolkingsensus van   Seventh census of the population
die Unie van Suid-Africa, opge-   of the Union of South Africa,
neem 7 mei 1946. Pretoria,   enumerated 7th May, 1946.
Government Printer, 1949-1955.
Vol. I-V.
1946.1-1   I. Geografiese verspreid- Geographical distribution of the
     ing van die Bevolking van die   population of the Union of South
     Unie van Suid-Africa. 1949.   Africa.
     iv, 105p. 2 maps.   [UN, BC, NWU, LC, PRC, RPI
  .1-2   II. Leeftye van die Blanke-, Ages of the European, Coloured,
     Kleurling-, Asiatiese- en Natur-   Asiatic and Native population.
     elle-Bevolking. 1950. v, 297p.   [UN, BC, NWU, LC, PRC, RPI
  .1-3   III. Suid-Afrikaanse Le-   South African life tables, Nos.
     wenstabelle. Nos. E.4 (Blankes)   E.4 (Europeans) and C.2 (Mixed
     en C.2 (Gemengdes en ander Kleur- and other Coloured).
     linge). 1951. xxiv, 14p.   [UN, BC, NWU, LC, PRC, RPI
  .1-4   IV. Tale en Geletterd-   Language and literacy.
     heid. 1953. v, 155p.   [UN, BC, NWU, LC, PRC, RPI
  .1-5   V. Beroepe en Bedrywe van   Occupations and industries of the
     die Blanke-, Asiate-, Kleurling-   European, Asiatic, Coloured and
     en Naturellebevolking. 1955.   Native population.
     x, 219p.   [UN, BC, NWU, LC, PRC, RPI

South Africa. Buro van Sensus
      en Statistiek.
   Bevolkingsensus, 8 Mei 1951.   Population census, 8th May 1951.
Pretoria, The Government Printer,
1954-1960. Vol. I-VIII.
1951.1-1   I. Geografiese verspreid- Geographical distribution of the
     ing van die Bevolking. n.d.   population.
     vi, 121p.   [UN, NWU, TXU, PRC, LC, RPI
  .1-2   II. Huwelikstaat van die   Marital status of the white popu-
     Blanke Bevolking van die Unie   lation of the Union of South Africa
     van Suid-Afrika tesame met 1946-   together with 1946 census figures
     sensussyfers vir alle Rasse van   for all races of the population.
     die Bevolking. 1954. ix, 154p.   [UN, NWU, PRC, LC, RPI
  .1-3   III. Godsdiens van die   Religions of the white population
     Blanke Bevolking van die Unie   of the Union of South Africa, to-
     van Suid-Afrika tesame met 1946-   gether with 1946 census figures

sensussyfers vir alle Rasse van die Bevolking. 1954. vi, 77p.

.1-4   IV. Geboorteplekke, Jaar van Aankoms en Burgerskap: (1) 1951-Sensus-Slegs Blankes; (2) 1946-Sensus-Alle Rasse. 1954. viii, 89p.

.1-5   V. Leeftye - Alle Rasse. 1958. 131p.

.1-6   VI. Tale en Geletterdheid: (1) Amptelike Tale (Blankes, Kleurlinge en Asiate) en Tale gebesig (Naturelle); (2) Huistale (Alle Rasse); (3) Geletterdheid (Naturelle). 1958. ix, 203p.

.1-7   VII. Huwelikstaat, Godsdiens en Geboorteplekke van Kleurlinge, Asiate en Naturelle. 1951. viii, 107p.

.1-8   VIII. Suid-Afrikaanse Lewenstabelle vir Blankes, Kleurlinge en Asiate. 1960. [2], 32p.

for all races of the population. [UN, NWU, PRC, LC, RPI
Birthplace, year of arrival and nationality: (1) 1951 census, white population only; (2) 1946 census, all races. [UN, NWU, PRC, LC, RPI
Ages - all races. [UN, NWU, TXU, PRC, LC, RPI
Languages and literacy: (1) Official languages (white, coloureds and asiatics) and languages spoken (natives); (2) Home languages (all races); (3) Literacy (natives). [UN, NWU, TXU, PRC, LC, RPI
Marital status, religions and birthplaces of coloureds, asiatics and natives. [UN, NWU, TXU, PRC, LC, RPI
South African life tables for whites, coloureds and asiatics. [UN, NWU, PRC, LC, RPI

South Africa. Bureau of Census and Statistics.
   Population census, 8 May 1951. Special reports. Pretoria, The Government Printer, n.d. 3v.

.2-1   Classification and status of urban and rural areas. xiii, 34p. (No. 197). [UN, RPI

.2-2   Geographical distribution of the population. 24p. (No. 200). [UN, NWU, RPI

.2-3   Home and official languages of the white population. 25p. (No. 204) [UN, RPI

South Africa. Buro van Sensus en Statistiek.
1960.1   Eerste Resultate van die Bevolkingsensus, 6 September 1960. Deel I - Unie van Suid Afrika, Deel II - Gebied van Suidwes-Afrika. Geografiese indeling van die Bevolking. Pretoria, Government Printer, 1960-1961. viii, 36p. (Special report, No. 234)

First results of the population census, September 6, 1960. Part I - Union of South Africa. Part II - Territory of South West Africa. Geographical distribution of the population. [UN, PRC, RPI

South Africa. Buro van Sensus en Statistiek.
   Bevolkingsensus, 1960. Steekproeftabellasie. Pretoria, 1962-1965. Nos. 1-8.

Population census, 1960. Sample tabulation.

.2-1   Nywerheidsafdelings, Ou-   Industry divisions, age groups,
derdomsgroepe, Huistale. Blankes.   home languages. Whites.
1962. viii, [3], 57p.   [UN, LC, PRC, RPI
.2-2   Nywerheidsafdelings, Ou-   Industry divisions, age groups,
derdomsgroepe, Huistale. Kleur-   home languages. Coloureds and
linge en Asiate. 1962. ix, [3],   asiatics.
66p.   [UN, LC, PRC, RPI
.2-3   Hoofberoepsgroepe. Blankes,   Major occupational groups. Whites,
Kleurlinge en Asiate. 1962. xi,   coloureds and asiatics.
[3], 56p.   [UN, LC, PRC, RPI
.2-4   Inkomste. Blankes, Kleur-   Income. Whites, coloureds and
linge en Asiate. 1962. xi, [3],   asiatics.
78p.   [UN, LC, PRC, RPI
.2-5   Nywerheidsafdelings, Ouder-   Industry divisions, age groups,
domsgroepe, Hoofberoepsgroepe.   major occupational groups. Bantu.
Bantoes. 1963. xi, [3], 75p.   [UN, LC, PRC, RPI
.2-6   Godsdiens. Alle Rasse.   Religions. All races.
1963. vii, [3], 38p.   [UN, LC, PRC, RPI
.2-7   Onderwyspeil. Alle Rasse.   Level of education. All races.
1964. xii, 97p.   [UN, LC, PRC, RPI
.2-8   Diverse. 1965. xviii,   Miscellaneous. [Contains infor-
108p.   mation for whites, coloureds, asi-
                                            atics and bantu on industry divi-
                                            sions, income and occupational
                                            groups, age group, birthplace,
                                            identity of employer, nationality,
                                            area of domicile and home language.
                                            [UN, LC, PRC, RPI

      South Africa. Buro vir Statis-
            tiek.
         Bevolkingsensus, 6 September   Population census, September 6,
      1960. Pretoria, Government   1960.
      Printer, 1963-1970. Vol. 1-11
      in 28v.
.3-1   Geografiese indeling van   Geographical distribution of the
die Bevolking. 1963. viii,   population.
95p. map.   [PRC, NWU, LC, RPI
         Verslag oor die metropoli-   Report on the metropolitan area
taanse Gebied van... 1966. Nos.   of...
1-14
1960.3-2-1 through 1960.3-2-14. 1. Cape Town. xvii, 161p./2. East London.
      xviii, 157p./3. Kimberley. xvii, 153p./4. Port Elizabeth. xviii,
      158p./5. Durban. xvii, 165p./6. Pietermaritzburg. xviii, 160p./7.
      East Rand (excluding Germiston). xviii, 161p./8. Germiston. xviii,
      158p./9. Johannesburg. xviii, 166p./10. Pretoria. xviii, 162p./11.
      Vereeniging-Vanderbijlpark. xviii, 159p./12. West Rand. xviii, 160p./
      13. Bloemfontein. xviii, 135p./14. The gold field area of the Orange
      Free State. xviii, 136p. [PRC, NWU, LC, RPI
.3-3   Kerverband. 1966. vi,   Religion.
176p.   [PRC, NWU, LC, RPI

.3-4   Onderwys. 1967. x, 518p.   Education.
                                                       [PRC, NWU, LC, RPI
.3-5   Persoonlike Inkomste.   Personal income.
   1967. xi, 213p.   [PRC, NWU, LC, RPI
.3-6   Nywerheid. 1967. vi,   Industry.
   356p.   [PRC, NWU, LC, RPI
         Eienskappe van die Bevolk-   Characteristics of the population
ing in elke Landdrosdistrik en   in each magisterial district and
ekonomiese Streek. 1968. Nos.   economic region.
1-3.
.3-7-1   Ouderdom, Huwelikstaat   Age, marital status and home
en Huistaal. xiii, 502p.   language.
                                                       [PRC, NWU, LC, RPI
.3-7-2   Beroep, Nywerheid en   Occupation, industry and type of
Tipe woning. xv, 350p.   abode.
                                                       [PRC, NWU, LC, RPI
.3-7-3   Inkomste volgens Werk-   Income by work status.
status. xv, 386p.   [PRC, NWU, LC, RPI
         Beroepe. 1969. Nos. 1-   Occupations.
2.
.3-8-1   Volgens Inkomste, Werk-   By income, work status, industry
status, Nywerheid, en Identiteit   and identity of employer.
van Werkgewer. xii, 497p.   [NWU, LC, RPI
.3-8-2   Volgens Ouderdom, Onder-   By age, level of education, home
wyspeil, Huistaal, Huwelikstaat,   language, marital status, citizen-
Bergerskap en Geboorteplek. xi,   ship and birthplace.
400p.   [PRC, NWU, LC, RPI
.3-9   Diverse Eienskappe volgens   Miscellaneous characteristics ac-
Ouderdom. Alle Rasse. 1968.   cording to age. All races.
x, 531p.   [PRC, NWU, LC, RPI
.3-10   Fertiliteit. 1969. viii,   Fertility.
433p.   [PRC, NWU, LC, RPI
         Gesinne. 1970. Nos. 1-2.   Families.
.3-11-1   Blanke Gesinne. xii,   White families.
231p.   [PRC, NWU, RPI
.3-11-2   Gesinne: Inkomste, Tipe   Families: income, type of dwel-
woning. Kleurlinge en Asiate.   ling. Coloureds and asiatics.
xii, 381p.   [LC, NWU, RPI

South Africa. Department of
     Statistics.
1970.0-1 Bevolkingsensus, 6 mei 1970.   Population census, 6 May 1970.
Republiek van Suid-Afrika. Be-   Republic of South Africa. Popu-
volking van Stede, Dorpe en nie-   lation of cities, towns and rural
stedelike Gebiede. Pretoria,   areas.
Government Printer, 1970. v,   [PRC, BC, NWU, JB-F
59p. (No. 02-05-01).

South Africa. Department of
     Statistics.
     Bevolkingsensus, 6 mei 1970.   Population census, 6 May 1970.
Steekproeftabellasie. Pretoria,   Sample tabulation.

Government Printer, 1971-1973.
7v.

1970.1-1   Ouderdomme - Blankes.   Ages - Whites.
            1971. xiv, 27p. (No. 02-01-01)   [PRC, BC, NWU, LC, JB-F
    .1-2   Ouderdomme - Kleurlinge   Ages - Coloureds and Asiatics.
            en Asiërs. xii, 26p. (No. 02-   [PRC, BC, NWU, LC, JB-F
            01-02)
    .1-3   Onderwys - Blankes, Kleur-   Education - Whites, Coloureds
            linge en Asiërs. 1971. xiv,   and Asiatics.
            180p. (No. 02-01-03)   [PRC, BC, NWU, LC, JB-F
    .1-4   Nywerheid - Blankes, Kleur-   Industry - Whites, Coloureds and
            linge en Asiërs. 1972. xii,   Asiatics.
            165p. (No. 02-01-04)   [PRC, BC, NWU, LC, JB-F
    .1-5   Beroepe - Blankes, Kleur-   Occupations - Whites, Coloureds
            linge en Asiërs. 1972. xii,   and Asiatics.
            43p. (No. 02-01-05)   [PRC, BC, NWU, LC, JB-F
    .1-6   Persoonlike Inkomste -   Personal income - Whites, Coloureds
            Blankes, Kleurlinge en Asiërs.   and Asiatics.
            1972. xiv, 80p. (No. 02-01-06) [PRC, BC, NWU, LC, JB-F
    .1-7   Bantoes - Ouderdom, Beroep,   Bantus. Age, occupation, indus-
            Nywerheid, Skoolstanderd, Geboor- try, level of education, birth-
            teplek. 1973. xiv, 184p. (No. place.
            02-02-02).   [PRC, BC, NWU, LC, JB-F

South Afica. Department of
       Statistics.
    Bevolkingsensus, 6 mei 1970.   Population census, 6th May 1970.
    [Final results].   Pretoria, Gov-   [Final results].
    ernment Printer, 1974-1977. 40v.
    .2-1   Gesinne - Geografiese Ver-   Families - Geographical distri-
            spreiding. 1974. xviii, 292p. bution.
            (No. 02-03-01)   [PRC, BC, NWU, LC, JB-F
    .2-2   Gesinne - Provinsies en   Families - Provinces and metro-
            metropolitaanse Gebiede. 1974. politan areas.
            xxiii, 223p. (No. 02-03-02).   [PRC, BC, NWU, LC, JB-F
    .2-3   Wonings - Geografiese Ver-   Dwellings - Geographical distri-
            spreiding. 1974. xvii, 264p.   bution.
            (No. 02-03-03).   [PRC, BC, NWU, LC, JB-F
    .2-4   Wonings - Provinsies en   Dwellings - Provinces and metro-
            metropolitaanse Gebiede. 1975. politan areas.
            xxxii, 142p. (No. 02-03-04).   [PRC, BC, NWU, JB-F
    .2-5   Inkomste en Werkstatus -   Income and work status. District
            Distrik en ekonomiese Streek.   and economic region.
            1975. xvi, 384p. (No. 02-01-   [PRC, BC, NWU, LC, JB-F
            02).
    .2-6   Aard van Onderwys. 1975.   Nature of education.
            xvi, 316p. (No. 02-05-02). [PRC, BC, NWU, LC, JB-F
    .2-7   Persoonlike Inkomste. 1975. Personal income.
            xvi, 312p. (No. 02-01-08). [PRC, BC, NWU, LC, JB-F
    .2-8   Kerkverband. 1975. xxii,   Religion.
            107p. (No. 02-05-03).   [PRC, BC, NWU, LC, JB-F

.2-9 Beroepe - (Inkomste, Nywerheid en Identiteit). 1975. xvii, 360p. (No. 02-05-04).

Occupations - (Income, industry and identity). [PRC, BC, NWU, LC, JB-F

.2-10 Enkelouderdomme 1941 tot 1970. 1976. xvi, 240p. (No. 02-05-05).

Single ages 1941 to 1970. [PRC, BC, NWU, LC, JB-F

.2-11 Beroep en Nywerheid volgens Distrik en ekonomiese Streek. 1976. xix, 230p. (No. 02-05-06).

Occupation and industry by district and economic region. [PRC, BC, NWU, LC, JB-F

.2-12 Onderwyspeil. 1976. xvii, 396p. (No. 02-05-07).

Level of education. [PRC, BC, NWU, LC, JB-F

.2-13 Ouderdom, Huwelikstaat en Tipe Woning volgens Distrik en ekonomiese Streek. 1976. xix, 540p. (No. 02-05-08).

Age, marital status, type of dwelling by district and economic region. [PRC, BC, NWU, LC, JB-F

.2-14 Nywerheid. 1976. xviii, 552p. (No. 02-05-09).

Industry. [PRC, BC, NWU, LC, JB-F

.2-15 Geografiese Verspreiding van die Bevolking. 1976. ix, 87p. (No. 02-05-10).

Geographic distribution of the population. [PRC, BC, NWU, LC, JB-F

.2-16 Beroepe (Ouderdom, Onderwyspeil, Huwelikstaat, Bergerskap, Geboorteplek, Volkseenheid). 1976. xviii, 302p. (No. 02-05-11).

Occupations (age, level of education, marital status, citizenship, birthplace, national unit). [PRC, BC, NWU, LC, JB-F

.2-17 Bevolking van Suid-Afrika 1904-1970. 1976. xviii, 436p. (No. 02-05-12).

Population of South Africa, 1904-1970. [PRC, BC, NWU, LC, JB-F

.2-18 Huistaal. 1977. xvi, 526p. (No. 02-01-09).

Home language. [PRC

[Bantoevolkseenhede]. 1976. 12v.

[Bantu National Units]

1970.2-19-1 through 1970.2-19-12. 1. Xhosa. xvii, 99p./2. South Ndebele. xvi, 90p./3. Seshoeshoe. xvi, 92p./4. Tswana. xvi, 103p./5. Shangaan. xvi, 98p./6. Venda. xvi, 96p./7. Zulu. xvi, 110p./8. Sepedi. xvi, 102p./9. Swazi. xvi, 92p./10. North Ndebele. xviii, 92p./11. Other S.A. Bantu. xvi, 98p./12. Foreign Bantus. xvi, 107p. [PRC, BC, NWU, LC, JB-F

[Metropolitaanse Gebied]. 1977. 13v.

[Metropolitan areas].

1970.2-20-1 through 1970.2-20-13. 1. Cape Town. xxii, 424p./2. East London. xxiii, 190p./3. Kimberley. xxiv, 164p./4. Port Elizabeth. xxii, 242p./5. Durban. xxiv, 216p./6. Pietermaritzburg. xxiv, 164p./7. Johannesburg. xxiv, 606p./8. East Rand. xxii, 528p./9. West Rand. xxii, 372p./10. Pretoria. xxiv, 294p./11. Vereeniging-Vanderbijlpark-Sasolburg. xxii, 190p./12. Bloemfontein. xxii, 166p./13. O.F.S. Goldfields. xxii, 126p. [PRC

SPAIN

Spanish State   Capital: Madrid.
Statistical Agency: National Statistical Institute
                     [Instituto Nacional de Estadística (INE)]
                     Avenida Generalísimo, 91
                     Madrid 16,
Publications Distributor: Administración de Publicaciones
                           (of the above)

Spain. Instituto Nacional de
    Estadística
        Censo de la población de   Census of the population of Spain
España y territorios de su sobe-   and territories under its sover-
rania y protectorado, según el   eignty and protectorship, accord-
empadronamiento realizado el 31   ing to the enumeration of Decem-
de diciembre de 1950.   Madrid,   ber 31, 1950.
1952-1959. Tomo I-III.
1950.1-1   I. Cifras generales de   General data on inhabitants.
    habitantes. 1952. 1v, 415p.   [PRC, BC, UN, LC, RPI
    .1-2   II. Clasificaciones de   Classification of the de facto
    la población de hecho de la pe-   population of the peninsula and
    nínsula e islas adyacentes, ob-   adjacent islands based on a 10
    tenida mediante una muestra de   per cent sample.
    10 por 100. 1954. x, 493p.   [PRC, UN, LC, RPI
    .1-3   III. Clasificaciones de   Classification of the de facto
    la población de hecho de la   population of the peninsula and
    península e islas adyacentes,   adjacent islands based on a 10
    obtenida mediante una muestra   per cent sample.
    de 10 por 100. 1959. 867p.   [PRC, UN, LC, RPI

Spain. INE.
        Censo de población de España   Census of the population of Spain
de 1950: nomenclator de las   of 1950: nomenclature of cities,
ciudades, villas, lugares, al-   towns, villages and other popu-
deas y demás entidades de pob-   lated places of Spain.
lación de España.   Madrid,
1954. Tomo I-V.
    .2-1   I. Alava a Córdoba.   549p.   [BC, PRC, RPI
    .2-2   II. La Coruña a Jaen.
    702p.   [BC, PRC, RPI
    .2-3   III. León a Navarra.
    685p.   [BC, PRC, RPI
    .2-4   IV. Orense a Pontevedra.
    696p.   [BC, PRC, RPI
    .2-5   V. Salamanca-Zaragoza,   ..., summaries and appendix.
    resúmenes y apendice. 621, [15]p.   [BC, PRC, RPI

Spain. INE.
        Indice general alfabético de   General alphabetical list of popu-
las entidades de población de   lated places in Spain: summary

España: resumen del nomenclator de las ciudades, villas, lugares, aldeas y demás entidades,
correspondiente al censo de la
población de 1950. [Madrid,
1956[. Tomo I-II.

.3-1   I. A-LL. viii, 584p.   of the nomenclature of cities,
.3-2   II. M-Z. [ii], 590, [1]p.   towns, villages, etc., according
                                             to the population census of 1950.

[UN, PRC, RPI
[UN, PRC, RPI

Spain. INE.
1960.0-1   Proyecto del censo de la   Plan of the census of population
población y de las viviendas de   and housing of Spain, 1960.
España de 1960.   Madrid, 1960.   [UN, RPI, RIR
69p.

Spain. INE.
.0-2   Censo de la población y   Census of population and housing,
de las viviendas, 1960: avance   1960: advance of population clas-
de la clasificaciones de la pob-   sifications according to a 1 per
lación obtenido mediante una mues-   cent sample.
tra del 1 por 100.   Madrid, 1962.   [PRC, BC, RPI
xiii, 26p.

Spain. INE.
.1   Censo de la población y de   Census of population and housing,
las viviendas 1960. Población   1960. De jure and de facto popu-
de derecho y hecho de los muni-   lation in the municipalities.
cipios de la nación.   Madrid,   [PRC, BC, RPI
Artes Gráficas, 1962. xx, 104p.

Spain. INE.
Censo de la población y de   Census of population and housing
las viviendas de España, según   in Spain, according to the enumer-
la inscripción realizada el 31   ation of December 31, 1960.
de diciembre de 1960.   Madrid,
T.G. Victoria-Regueras, 1962-
1969. Tomo I-IV in 6v.

.2-1   I. Cifras generales de   General data on the inhabitants.
habitantes. 1962. xl, 404p.   [PRC, BC, UN, LC, RPI, RIR
.2-2   II. Cifras generales de   General data on housing.
viviendas. 1964. viii, 207p.   [PRC, BC, UN, LC, RPI, RIR
        III. Población. Vol. 1-   Population.
3.
.2-3-1   Resumen nacional y pro-   National summary and provinces of
vincias de Alava a la Coruña.   Alava to La Coruña.
1969. var. pag.   [UN, PRC, RPI, RIR
.2-3-2   Provincias de Cuenca a   Provinces of Cuenca to Oviedo.
Oviedo. 1969. var. pag.   [UN, PRC, RPI, RIR
.2-3-3   Provincias de Palencia   Provinces of Palencia to Zaragoza
a Zaragoza y municipios de Ceuta   and the municipalities of Ceuta
y Melilla. [1969]. var. pag.   and Melilla.
                                             [UN, PRC, RPI, RIR

.2-4   IV. Clasificaciones de
las viviendas. [1969]. var.
pag.

Housing classifications.
[UN, PRC, RPI, RIR

Spain. INE.
    Censo de la población y de
las viviendas de España de 1960.
Nomenclátor de las ciudades,
villas, lugares, aldeas y demás
entidades de población.   Madrid, Ernesto Giménez, 1963.
Vol. I-V.

Census of population and housing
of Spain of 1960. Nomenclature
of the cities, towns, hamlets
and other populated places.

.3-1   I. Provincias de Alava
a Córdoba. 563p.
.3-2   II. Provincias de La
Coruña a Jaen. 699p.
.3-3   III. Provincias de León
a Navarra. 699p.
.3-4   IV. Provincias de Orense
a Pontevedra. 629p.
.3-5   V. Provincias de Salamanca a Zaragoza. Plazas de
soberania en el norte de Africa,
resúmenes generales y apendice
de variaciones. 663p.

Provinces of Alava to Córdoba.
[PRC, TXU, UN, RPI, RIR
Provinces of La Coruña to Jaen.
[PRC, TXU, BC, RPI, RIR
Provinces of León to Navarra.
[PRC, TXU, BC, RPI, RIR
Provinces of Orense to Pontevedra.
[PRC, TXU, BC, RPI, RIR
Provinces of Salamanca to Zara-
goza. Colonies in North Africa,
general summaries and appendix
of variations.
[PRC, TXU, BC, LC, RPI, RIR

Spain. INE.
.4   Indice general alfabético de
las entidades de población de
España: resumen del nomenclátor de las ciudades, villas,
lugares, aldeas y demás entidades, correspondiente al censo
de población de 1960.   Madrid,
1966. viii, 620p.

General alphabetical index of
populated places of Spain: summary of the nomenclature of cities,
towns, villages, hamlets, and
other places, according to the
population census of 1960.
[Berkeley, PRC, RPI

Spain. Dirección General de
          Urbanismo.
.5   Áreas metropolitanas de
España en 1960.   Madrid, 1965.
55p.

Metropolitan areas of Spain in
1960.
[PRC

Spain. INE.
1970.0-1   Proyecto para la realiza-
ción de los censos de 1970.
Madrid, 1970. 208p.

Project for the realization of
the 1970 censuses.
[BC, PRC

Spain. INE.
.1   Censo de la población de España, año 1970. Poblaciones de
derecho y de hecho de los municipios.   Madrid, 1971. vii,
126p.

Population census of Spain, 1970.
De jure and de facto populations
of the municipalities.
[PRC, LC

Spain. INE.

.2   Censo de la población de España según la inscripción realizada el 31 de diciembre de 1970.
Avance de resultados obtenidos
mediante una muestra del 2 por
100. Características de la población. Madrid, 1972. 40p.

Population census of Spain according to the enumeration taken December 31, 1970. Advance report
of the results obtained from a 2
per cent sample. Population characteristics.
[PRC, LC

Spain. INE.

    Censo de la población de Es-
paña según la inscripción realizada el 31 de diciembre de 1970.
Madrid, 1973-1974. Tomo I-V in
105v.

Population census of Spain according to the enumeration taken December 31, 1970.

.3-1   I. Número de habitantes
por municipio. 1972. xxxvi,
217p.
    II. Características de
la población. 1973. No. 1-51.

Number of inhabitants by munici-
pality.
[PRC, BC, JB-F, IASI, LC
Population characteristics.

1970.3-2-1 through 1970.3-2-51. 1. Alava. xviii, 48p./2. Albacete. xviii,
48p./3. Alicante. xviii, 67p./4. Almería. xviii, 49p./5. Ávila. xviii,
47p./6. Badajoz. xviii, 51p./7. Baleares. xviii, 48p./8. Barcelona.
xviii, 108p./9. Burgos. xviii, 48p./10. Cáceres. xviii, 48p./11. Cadiz.
xviii, 81p./12. Castellón. xviii, 48p./13. Ciudad Real. xviii, 60p./
14. Córdoba. xviii, 51p./15. La Coruña. xviii, 68p./16. Cuenca. xviii,
47p./17. Gerona. xviii, 51p./18. Granada. xviii, 51p./19. Guadalajara.
xviii, 47p./20. Guipuzcoa. xviii, 52p./21. Huelva. xviii, 48p./22.
Huesca. xviii, 50p./23. Jaén. xviii, 61p./24. León. xviii, 50p./25.
Lérida. xviii, 48p./26. Logroño. xviii, 48p./27. Lugo. xviii, 49p./
28. Madrid. xviii, 73p./29. Málaga. xviii, 51p./30. Murcia. xviii,
67p./31. Navarra. xviii, 48p./32. Orense. xviii, 48p./33. Oviedo.
xviii, 81p./34. Palencia. xviii, 46p./35. Las Palmas. xviii, 51p./36.
Pontevedra. xviii, 62p./37. Salamanca. xviii, 48p./38. Sta. Cruz de
Tenerife. xviii, 59p./39. Santander. xviii, 48p./40. Segovia. xviii,
47p./41. Sevilla. xviii, 54p./42. Soria. xviii, 46p./43. Tarragona.
xviii, 54p./44. Teruel. xviii, 48p./45. Toledo. xviii, 50p./46. Valencia. xviii, 56p./47. Valladolid. xviii, 48p./48. Vizcaya. xviii,
60p./49. Zamora. xviii, 48p./50. Zaragoza. xviii, 48p./51&52. Ceuta
and Melilla. xviii, 52p. [PRC, BC, JB-F, IASI

.3-3   III. Características de
la población. Total nacional.
1974. xxii, 185p.
    IV. Nomenclátor de las
ciudades, villas, lugares, aldeas y demás entidades de población. 1973. No. 1-51.

Population characteristics. National total.
[PRC
Nomenclature of cities, towns,
places, villages and other populated areas.

1970.3-4-1 through 1970.3-4-51. 1. Alava. 32p./2. Albacete. 32p./3. Alicante.
38p./4. Almería. 53p./5. Ávila. 56p./6. Badajoz. 42p./7. Baleares.
26p./8. Barcelona. 76p./9. Burgos. 114p./10. Cáceres. 50p./11. Cadiz.
26p./12. Castellón. 51p./13. Ciudad Real. 29p./14. Córdoba. 37p./15.
La Coruña. 442p./16. Cuenca. 58p./17. Gerona. 86p./18. Granada.

57p./19. Guadalajara. 69p./20. Guipuzcoa. 32p./21. Huelva. 28p./
22. Huesca. 70p./23. Jaén. 39p./24. León. 91p./25. Lérida. 75p./
26. Logroño. 44p./27. Lugo. 404p./28. Madrid. 46p./29. Málaga. 36p./
30. Murcia. 61p./31. Navarra. 79p./32. Orense. 194p./33. Oviedo.
283p./34. Palencia. 57p./35. Las Palmas. 30p./36. Pontevedra. 251p./
37. Salamanca. 89p./38. Sta. Cruz de Tenerife. 39p./39. Santander.
59p./40. Segovia. 54p./41. Sevilla. 34p./42. Soria. 57p./43. Tarragona. 48p./44. Teruel. 56p./45. Toledo. 46p./46. Valencia. 60p./
47. Valladolid. 54p./48. Vizcaya. 45p./49. Zamora. 63p./50. Zaragoza.
64p./51&52. Ceuta and Melilla. 15p. [PRC, LC

1970.3-5   V. Nomenclátor de las
ciudades, villas, lugares, aldeas y demás entidades de población. Indice general alfabético. 1974. [4], 483p.

Nomenclature of cities, towns,
places, villages and other populated areas. General alphabetical index.
[PRC, BC, LC

SRI LANKA

Republic of Sri Lanka.   Capital: Colombo
Statistical Agency: Department of Census and Statistics (DCS)
                     P.O. Box 563
                     Colombo 7,
Publications Distributor: Superintendent
                           Government Publications Bureau
                           P.O. Box 500
                           Colombo 1,

    Ceylon. Department of Census and Statistics.
        Census of Ceylon, 1946. Colombo, Government Press, 1950-1952.
    Vol. I-IV in 7v.
1946.1-1-1   I, Part 1. General report. 1950. [17], 340p. [PRC, TXU, LC,
    RPI
    .1-1-2   Part 2. Statistical digest. 1951. [11], 424p. [PRC, TXU,
    LC, RPI
    .1-2   II. Ages, conjugal condition and birthplace. 1952. [8], 398p.
    [PRC, RPI
    .1-3   III. Fertility. 1952. [5], 738p. [PRC, TXU, RPI
    .1-4   IV. Race, religion and literacy. 1952. xiii, 815p. [PRC, RPI

    Ceylon. DCS.
        Census of Ceylon, 1953. Colombo, Government Press, 1957-1962.
    Vol. I-IV in 10v.
1953.1-1   I. General report. 1957. viii, 215p. [TXU, PRC, LC, RPI
    .1-2-1   II, Part 1. Growth of population, place of birth, movement and
    nationality. 1958. viii, 326p. [TXU, PRC, LC, RPI
    .1-2-2   Part 2. Age. 1959. viii, 666p. [TXU, PRC, LC, RPI
    .1-2-3   Part 3. Conjugal condition and orphanhood. 1959. viii,
    311p. [TXU, PRC, LC, RPI
    .1-3-1   III, Part 1. Race and literacy. 1960. xii, 928p. [TXU, UN,
    LC, RPI
    .1-3-2   Part 2. Literacy and religion. 1960. ix, 1077p. [TXU,
    UN, LC, RPI
    .1-4-1   IV, Part 1. The gainfully employed population. 1960. viii,
    624p. [TXU, UN, LC, RPI
    .1-4-2-8A   Part 2, Section 8(A). income. (Ten percent sample). 1962.
    vii, 897p. [TXU, UN, RPI
    .1-4-2-8B   Section 8(B). Income. (Ten percent sample). 1962.
    vii, 949p. [TXU, PRC, UN, RPI
    .1-4-2-8C   Section 8(C). Income. (Ten percent sample). 1962.
    vii, 943p. [TXU, PRC, UN, RPI

    Ceylon. DCS.
        Census of Ceylon, 1953. Monographs. Colombo, Government Press,
    1954-1956. Nos. 1, 2, 3, 7, 8. [Others are non-population topics].
    .2-1   Post-enumeration survey, 1953. 1953. 24p. [LC, OPR
    .2-2   Demographic study of the city of Colombo. 1954. [5], 52p. maps.
    [TXU, PRC, LC, RPI

.2-3   Fertility trends in Ceylon. 1954.   p. [LC
.2-7   Sinhalese population growth, 1911–1946. 1955. 52p. [LC
.2-8   Fertility trends in Ceylon. 1953 census, (one percent sample).
     1956. 36p. [UN, PRC, RPI

Ceylon. DCS.
     Census of population, Ceylon, 1963.   Colombo, Government Press,
     1967-   . Vol. I-   in   v.
             I. Tables based on a ten percent sample. 1967.   Part I-II.
1963.1-1-1   Part I. General characteristics. xiii, 98p. [UN, PRC, LC,
     RPI
.1-1-2   Part II. The gainfully employed population. xi, 44p. [UN,
     PRC, RPI

Note: The reminder was not published.

Sri Lanka. DCS.
1971.0-1   1971 census of population and housing. An outline of the scope
     and content of the census.   Colombo, Government Press, 1969. 20p.
     [

Sri Lanka. DCS.
     Census of population, 1971. Preliminary releases.   Colombo, 1972.
     No. 1-3.
.0-2-1 Population of districts, towns and D.R.O. divisions by sex, age
     (under 18 years and 18 and over), ethnic group and religion. iv, 35p.
     [BC, LC
.0-2-2 Population of electorates by sex, age (under 18 years and 18 and
     over), ethnic group and religion. 15p. [BC
.0-2-3 Population for wards of towns and Grama Sevaka (village headmen)
     divisions by sex, age...   p. [

Sri Lanka. DCS.
.0-3   Census of population 1971. Preliminary report.   Colombo, 1974.
     103p. [PRC

Sri Lanka. DCS.
     Census of population, 1971. Colombo, 1975-   . Vol. I-   in
     v.
             I. [Districts]. 22v.
1971.1-1-1 through 1971.1-1-22.

II. All islands tables. 1975-   . Parts 1-2.
1971.1-2-1   Part 1. General characteristics of the population. 1975.
   vi, 62p. [UN, PRC
.1-2-2   Part 2. The economically active population.

.1-3   III. General report. [1978]. xv, [1], 153p. appendices.
   [UN, PRC, PC, E-W

SUDAN

Democratic Republic of the Sudan.   Capital: Khartoum
Statistical Agency: Department of Statistics.
                     Ministry of National Planning
                     P.O. Box 700
                     Khartoum,
Publications Distributor: same

      Sudan. Population Census Office.
1956.0-1   The 1953 pilot population census for the first population census
      of Sudan.   Khartoum, 1955. 183p. maps, illus., charts. [BC, TXU,
      PRC, NWU, LC, RPI

      Sudan. Population Census Office.
         First population census of Sudan 1955–1956: methods reports.
      Khartoum, 1958–1960. Vol. I–II.
      .0-2-1   I.   1960.   [7], 224p. [TXU, PRC, RPI
      .0-2-2   II. [Appendices and charts]   1958.   353p. maps. [PRC, NWU,
         RPI

      Sudan. Population Census Office.
         First population census of Sudan, 1955–1956: interim reports.
      Khartoum, 1956–1958. Nos. 1–9 in 10v.
      .0-3-1   First interim report. n.d.   52p. [BC, UN, NWU, LC, PRC, RPI
      .0-3-2   Second interim report. n.s.   55, [1]p. [BC, UN, NWU, LC, PRC,
         RPI
      .0-3-3   Third interim report. 1957. 59p. [BC, UN, NWU, LC, PRC, RPI
      .0-3-4   Fourth interim report. 1957. 62p. [BC, UN, NWU, LC, PRC, RPI
      .0-3-5   Fifth interim report. 1957. 57p. map. [BC, UN, NWU, LC, PRC,
         RPI
      .0-3-6   Sixth interim report. 1957. 59p. map. [BC, UN, NWU, LC, PRC,
         RPI
      .0-3-7   Seventh interim report. 1957. 61p. map. [BC, UN, NWU, LC,
         PRC, RPI
      .0-3-8   Eighth interim report. 1957. 52p. map. [BC, UN, NWU, LC, PRC,
         RPI
      .0-3-9   Last (ninth) interim report. 1958. 67p. [UN, NWU, LC, PRC,
         RPI
      .0-3-10 Supplement to interim reports. 1956. [1], 37p. maps. [BC, UN,
         NWU, LC, PRC, RPI

      Sudan. Population Census Office.
      .0-4   First population census of Sudan 1955–56: notes on Omodia map.
      Khartoum, 1958. 76p. map. [BC, NWU, LC, PRC, OPR

      Sudan. Population Census Office.
      .1   First population census of Sudan, 1955–56: 21 facts about the
      Sudanese, by Karol Jozef Krotki.   Salzburg, Austria, R. Kiesel, 1958.
      60p. maps, illus. [UN, PRC, NWU, TXU, RPI

Sudan. Population Census Office.
.2   Population census in Wadi Halfa rural area and town.   Khartoum,
      [1960]. 151p. [UN, RPI

Sudan. Population Census Office.
      First population census of Sudan, 1955-56: town planner's supple-
      ment. Khartoum, 1960. Vol. I-II.
.3-1   I. Prepared by D.B. Climenhaga. 323p. [PRC, NWU, LC, RPI
.3-2   II. Prepared by Zein M. Omar. 149p. [NWU, LC, RPI

Sudan. Population Census Office.
      First population census of Sudan, 1955-56: final reports.   Khar-
      toum, 1961-1962. Vol. I-III.
.4-1   I. 1961. xx, 141p. map. [TXU, LC, RPI
.4-2   II. 1962. 467p. [PRC, LC, RPI
.4-3   III. 1962. [2], xx, 478p. [PRC, LC, RPI

Sudan. Department of Statistics.
1966.0-1   Demographic and housing survey of the three towns area, 1964/65.
      Survey plan. I. Khartoum.   Khartoum, 1964. [2], 21, [5], 27p.
      specimen forms. [UN, RPI

Sudan. Department of Statistics.
      Population and housing survey, 1964/65.   Khartoum, 1965-1968.
      14v.
1966.1-1 through 1966.1-14. 1. Atbara. 1966. [1], 59p./2. El Fasher. 1966.
      [1], 58p. map./3. El Gedaref. 1967. [1], 51, [1]p. map./4. El Gen-
      eina. 1966. [1], 51p. map./5. Kassala. 1966. [1], 58p. map./6.
      Khartoum. 1965. [1], 110p. map./7. Khartoum North. 1966. [1], 61p.
      map./8. Kosti. 1967. [1], 53p. map./9. En Naboud. 1967. [1], 52p.
      map./10. Nyala. 1966. [1], 51p. map./11. El Obeid. 1966. [1], 59p.
      map./12. Omdurman. 1966. [1], 78p. map./13. Port Sudan. 1966.
      [67]p. map./14. Wad Medani. 1966. [1], 61p. map. [NWU, LC, RPI

Sudan. Department of Statistics.
      Population and housing survey, 1964/65. Urban areas.   Khartoum,
      1968. 6v.
1966.2-1 through 1966.2-6. 1. Blue Nile Province. [1], xiii, 107p./2. Dar-
      fur Province. [1], xiii, 38p./3. Kassala Province. [1], xiii, 63p./
      4. Khartoum Province. [1], xiii, 39p./5. Kordofan Province. [1],
      xiii, 78p./6. Northern Province. [1], xiii, 55p. [LC, RPI

Sudan. Department of Statistics.
  .3   Population and housing survey, 1964/65. General survey of the ur-
      ban area.   Khartoum, 1968. [3], xv, 89p. [UN, RPI

Sudan. Population Census Office.
1973.0-1   1973 population census: enumerator's manual.   [Khartoum],
      1973. 33, 44, 5p. [LC

Sudan. Population Census Office.
        Second population census, 1973. Khartoum, 1976-   . Vol. I-
    in   v.
.1-1   I. Socio-economic characteristics. 1977. [309]p. [PSC
.1-2   II.
.1-3   III. Characteristics of the nomadic population. 1977. 203p.
    [PSC
.1-4-1   IV, Part 1. Housing characteristics of urban areas (35 selected
    towns). 1977.   151p. [PSC
.1-4-2   Part 2. Socio-economic characteristics of urban areas (35
    selected towns). 1977. [299]p. [PSC

        Complete census by province.
1973.2-1 through 1973.2-10. 1. Bahr el Gazal. 1976. [121]p./2. Blue Nile.
    1977. [126]p./3. Darfur. 1977. [122]p./4. Equatoria. 1976. [121]p./
    5. Kassala. 1976. [122]p./6. Khartoum. 1977. [122]p./7. Kordofan.
    1977. [123]p./8. Northern. 1977. [123]p./9. Red Sea. 1977. [122]p./
    10. Upper Nile. 1976. [121]p. [PSC

SURINAME

Republic of Suriname   Capital: Paramaribo
Statistical Agency: General Statistical Office
                     [Algemeen Bureau voor de Statistiek (ABS)]
                     P.O. Box 244
                     Paramaribo,
Publications Distributor: same

Surinam. Welvaartsfonds.	
Tweede algemeen volkstelling	Second general population census
Suriname, 1950. Paramaribo,	of Suriname, 1950.
1954-1956. Series A (II-VIII,X),	
Series E (XXIII, XXIV) in 11v.	

1950.1-1   I. Algemeen gedeelte.   General volume.
          [Not published].   [
              Serie A: Aantal, landaard   Series A: Number, racial origin,
          en geslacht, geographische sprei- and sex; geographical distribu-
          ding, leeftijdsopbouw en herkomst tion, age composition and nati-
          der getelde Woonbevolking. Vol.   vity of the enumerated resident
          II-VIII, X)   population.
1950.1-2 through 1950.1-8. 2. Paramaribo city and district. 1954. 107p./
          3. Suriname district. 1954. viii, 128, vi, [2]p./4. Saramacca dis-
          trict. 1955. [3], 80, [2], vi, [5]p./5. Commwijne district. 1955.
          [3], vi, 82, [8]p./6. Coronie district. 1955. 56, vii p./7. Nicke-
          rie district. 1955. 76, [94]p./8. Marowijne district. 1955. vi,
          80, [3]p. [PRC, BC, RP]
    .1-9   IX. De sampling: India-   Sample: Amerindians and bush-
          en boschnegers in stamverband. negroes in tribes.
          [Not published].   [
    .1-10   X. Geheel Suriname, inclu- All Suriname, including lepers
          sief de leprozen en vreemdelin- and foreigners, and supplement,
          gen en supplement, inhoudende: contents: a. List of places and
          a. Lijst van plaats en planta-   plantations. b. Summary charts.
          genamen. b. Overzichtskaarten. [PRC, BC, RP]
          1954. 80, [56], vi, [2]p.

Note: Evidently Series B, C, and D were never published.

          Serie E: Woning- en gezins-   Census of housing and households.
          telling. Vol. XXIII-XXIV.
    .1-23   XXIII. Woningtelling.   Housing census. Number, distri-
          Aantal, spreiding, soort en be- bution, type and occupancy of
          zetting der woningen. 1956.   dwellings.
          76, [1]p.   [PRC, BC, RP]
    .1-24   XXIV. Gezinstelling. Sa-   Household census. Summary and
          menstelling en inkomens der huis- income of households; persons in
          houdingen; huishoudelijk perso- households.
          neel. 1956. 88, [1]p.   [PRC, BC, RP]

Suriname. Algemeen Bureau voor
        de Statistiek.
      Derde Surinamse volkstelling,   Third Suriname population census,
1964.   Paramaribo, 1964-1967.   1964.
(Suriname in cijfers, No. 33,
parts 1-9).
1964.1-1 through 1964.1-8. [Districts]. 1. Coronie. 1964.   p./2. Suriname. 1964.   p./3. Nickerie. 1965.   p./4. Commewijne. 1965.
    p./5. Paramaribo. 1965.   p./6. Saramacca. 1965.   p./7. Maro-
wijne. 1965.   p./8. Brokopondo. 1965.   p. [UN
  .1-9   Geheel Surinam. Inclu-   All Suriname. Including limited
sief beperkte telling. 1967.   count.
74p.   [UN, BC, RPI

Suriname. Bureau voor de
        Statistiek.
1972.0-1 Voorlopig resultaat vierde   Preliminary results of the fourth
algemene volkstelling, 1972.   general population census, 1972.
Paramaribo, 1972. 24p. (Suri-   [BC, JB-F, LC
name in cijfers, No. 60, part ?).

SWAZILAND

Kingdom of Swaziland.   Capital: Mbabane; Lobamba.
Statistical Agency: Central Statistical Office
                     P.O. Box 456
                     Mbabane,
Publications Distributor: same

       Swaziland. Office of the Government Secretary.
1946.1   Swaziland census, 1946.   Mbabane, 1950. [2], xvi, 59p. [UN, NWU,
       LC, PRC, RPI

       Swaziland. Office of the Government Secretary.
1956.1   Swaziland census, 1956. Territory of Swaziland.   Mbabane, 1958?
       47p. [LC, NWU, PRC, RPI

       Swaziland. Census Commissioner's Office.
          Report on the 1966 Swaziland population census. [By] H.B. Jones.
       Mbabane, 1968. 2v.
1966.1-1   Report. [2], xiii, [2], 723p. [PRC, NWU, LC, RPI
    .1-2   Distribution and density maps. 2 fold. maps. [PRC, LC, RPI

       The next census was taken in 1976 but no publications have been seen
       as yet.

SWEDEN

Kingdom of Sweden.   Capital: Stockholm.
Statistical Agency: Central Bureau of Statistics.
                      [Statistiska Centralbyrån]
                      Fack
                      S-102 50 Stockholm 27,
Publications Distributor: Government Publishing House
                           Box 23 116
                           S-104 35 Stockholm 23,

Sweden.   Statistiska Centralbyrån.
    Folkräkningen den 31 december   Population census of December 31,
1945./Recensement de la popula-   1945.
tion en 1945.   Stockholm, P.A.
Norstedt & Söner, 1947-1954.
Vol. I-XI in 18v.
1945.1-1   I.   Areal och folkmängd   Area and population of various
inom särskilda förvaltningsom-   administrative divisions, etc.
råden m.m. Befolkningsagglo-   Populated places of urban charac-
merationer./Superficie et popu-   ter in the countryside.
lation dans les différents di-   [LC, UN, PRC, RPI
visions administratives, etc.
Agglomérations de population de
caractère urbain à la campagne.
1947. ix, 49, 299, [4]p.
    II.   Partiella undersök-   Sample survey (eight percent sam-
ningar (tolvtedelssamplingen):   ple):
... 1948. 3v.
.1-2-1   behandlar delar av sta-   considering certain statistics
tistiken över kön, ålder och ci-   according to sex, age, marital
vilstånd, äktenskapens varakti-   status, duration of marriage,
ghet, födelseort och yrke./trai-   place of birth, and occupation.
tant certaines parties de la   [LC, UN, PRC, RPI
statistique suivant le sexe,
l'âge et l'état civil, la durée
des mariages, le lieu de naissance et les professions. x,
44, 38p.
.1-2-2   behandlar delar av sta-   considering certain statistics
tistiken över yrke och över sko-   of occupation and of educational
loch yrkesutbildring samt sta-   and work training, as well as statistiken över simkunnighet./trai-   tistics on persons who know how
tant certaines parties de la sta-   to swim.
tistique des professions et rela-   [LC, UN, PRC, RPI
tive à l'instruction scolaire et
et professionnelle, ainsi que la
statistique sur les personnes
sachant nager. x, 37, 33p.
.1-2-3   behandlar delar av sta-   considering certain statistics
tistiken över yrke./traitant cer-   of occupation.

taines parties de la statistique
des professions. xii, 73, 32p.

 III. Partiella undersök-
ningar (tolvtedelssamplingen):
... 1949. 3v.

1945.1-3-1   behandlar delar av statistiken över inkomst./traitant
certaines parties de la statistique des revenus. xii, 53, 41p.

.1-3-2   behandlar delar av statistiken över förmögenhet./trai-
tant certaines parties de la
statistique des fortunes. xi,
56, 21p.

.1-3-3   behandlar delar av statistiken över beskattningsför-
hållanden./traitant certains
parties de la statistique des
impositions. x, 35, 29, [3]p.

.1-4   IV. Totala räkningen:
behandlar statistiken över lapp-
befolkningen./Recensement total:
traitant la statistique sur la
population lapone. 1949. xi,
37, 28, [3]p.

.1-5   V. Totala räkningen:
folkmängden kommunvis efter ålder och kön samt efter yrke m.m./
Recensement total: population
par âge et par sexe, par branches d'activité économique, etc.,
dans les divisions communales.
1949. vi, 5, 413p.

.1-6   VI. Totala räkningen:
folkmängden efter ålder, kön och
civilstånd. Dödlighets- och
livslängdstabeller./Recensement
total: la population par âge,
par sexe et par état civil.
Tables de mortalité et de sur-
vie. 1950. viii, 29, 55, [3]p.

 VII. Partiella undersök-
ningar (tolvtedelssamplingen):
behandlar delar av familjestis-
tiken./Enquêtes partielles
(échantillon de 8 pourcent):
traitant certaines parties de la
statistique des familles. 2v.

.1-7-1   1950. xvi, 123, 86,
[3]p.

.1-7-2   1954. xii, 77, 38p.

[LC, UN, PRC, RPI

Sample survey (eight percent sample): ...

considering certain statistics
about income.
[LC, UN, PRC, RPI

considering certain statistics
about wealth.
[LC, UN, PRC, RPI

considering certain statistics
about taxation.
[LC, UN. PRC, RPI

Complete census: concerning certain statistics on the Lapp population.
[LC, UN, PRC, RPI

Complete census: population by
age and sex, by branch of economic activity, etc., in communal
divisions.
[LC, UN, PRC, RPI

Complete census: population by
age, sex and marital status.
Life tables.
[LC, UN, PRC, RPI

Sample survey (eight percent sample): considering certain statistics of families.

[LC, UN, PRC, RPI
[LC, UN, PRC, RPI

VIII. Partiella undersök-
ningar (bottensamplingen): behandlar av statistiken.../Enquê-
tes partielles (échantillon de
2 pour cent): traitant certaines
parties de la statistique des...

.1-8-1   inkomst./revenus. 1951.
x, 101, 69, [3]p.

.1-8-2   förmögenhet./fortunes.
1951. x, 67, 51, [3]p.

.1-9   IX. Totala räkningen:
folkmängden efter yrke, utländska undersåtar m.m./Recensement
total: population par branches
d'activité économique, sujets
étrangers, etc. 1952. ix, 30,
110, [3]p.

X. Partiella undersöknin-
gar (tolvtedelssamplingen): .../
Enquêtes partielles (échantillon
de 8 pourcent): ... 1952. 2v.

.1-10-1   behandler statistiken
över inrikes omflyttning, yrkes-
växling, m.m./traitant les statistiques des mouvements migra-
toires à l'intérieur du pays,
des changements de profession,
etc. x, 79, 53, [3]p.

.1-10-2   specialundersökningar
rörande yrkesverksamheten./rap-
ports supplémentaires sur l'activité professionnelle. xi, 103,
[3]p.

.1-11   XI. Redogörelse för råta-
bellernas innehåll m.m./Compte-
rendus des tableaux bruts, leur
contenu, etc. 1954. xi, 8, 363p.

Sweden. Statistiska Centralbyrån.
Folkräkningen den 31 december
1950. Stockholm, 1952-1956.
Vol. I-VIII.

1950.1-1   I. Areal och fölkmangd
inom särskilda förvaltningsom-
råden m.m. Tätorter. 1952.
xi, 57, 313, [3]p.

.1-2   II. Urvalsundersökningar:
statistiken över ålder, kön,
civilstånd, yrke och familjer.
1953. xi, 86, [3]p.

.1-3   III. Totala räkningen:
folkmängden efter ålder och kön

Sample survey (two percent sample): considering certain statistics of...

income.
[LC, UN, PRC, RPI
wealth.
[LC, UN, PRC, RPI
Complete census: population by
branches of economic activity,
foreign subjects, etc.
[LC, UN, PRC, RPI

Sample survey (eight percent sample): ...

concerning statistics of internal
migration, of change of occupation,
etc.
[LC, UN, PRC, RPI

supplementary reports on occupational activities.
[LC, UN, PRC, RPI

Account of the crude tables, their
content, etc.
[LC, UN, PRC, RPI

Population census of December 31,
1950.

area and population in different
administrative divisions, etc.
Population clusters.
[LC, UN, PRC, RPI
Sample survey: statistics of age,
sex, marital status, occupation
and families.
[LC, UN, PRC, RPI
Total enumeration: population by
age and sex in communes, parishes

i kommuner, församlingar och tätorter. 1954. vi, 6, 317, [5]p.

.1-4   IV. Totala räkningen:
fölkmangden efter yrke i kommuner, församlingar, och tätorter.
1954. vii, 6, 489, [6]p.

.1-5   V. Totala räkningen:
fölkmangden efter ålder, kön och
civilstånd. 1955. xii, 138,
[6]p.

.1-6   VI. Totala räkningen:
fölkmangden efter yrke; hushåll;
utrikes födda och utlänningar.
1955. xiv, 244p.

.1-7   VII. Urvalsundersökningar:
statistiken över inkomst. 1956.
xvi, 78, 93p.

.1-8   VIII. Urvalsundersökningar: statistiken över förmögenhet. 1956. xiv, 66, 77p.

Sweden. Statistiska Centralbyrån.
   Folkräkningen den 1 november
1960. Stockholm, 1961-1965.
Vol. I-XI.

1960.1-1   I. Folkmängd inom kommuner och församlingar efter kön,
ålder, civilstånd m.m. 1961.
vii, 4, 214p.

.1-2   II. Folkmängd inom tätorter efter kön, ålder och civilstånd. 1961. vi, 6, 137p.

.1-3   III. Folkmängd i hela riket och länen efter kön, ålder
och civilstånd m.m. 1961. vii,
3, 145p.

.1-4   IV. Folkmängd inom särskilda områden, utlänningar m.m.
1962. x, 5, 147p.

.1-5   V. Indelningar, tätorts-
avgränsning, befolkningsutveckling m.m. 1962. xv, 118p.

.1-6   VI. Förvärvsarbetande befolkning efter näringsgren och
yrkesställning m.m. inom kommuner, församlingar och tätorter.
1963. viii, 416p. map.

.1-7   VII. Förvärvsarbetande
befolkning efter yrke samt hushåll efter hushållsstorlek m.m.

and population clusters.
[LC, UN, PRC, RPI
Total enumeration: population by
occupation in communes, parishes
and population clusters.
[LC, UN, PRC, RPI
Total enumeration: population by
age, sex, and marital status.
[LC, UN. PRC, RPI

Total enumeration: population by
occupation; households; persons
born abroad and aliens.
[LC, UN, PRC, RPI
Sample surveys: statistics of
income.
[LC, UN, PRC, RPI
Sample surveys: statistics of
property.
[LC, UN, PRC, RPI

Population census of November 1,
1960.

Population in communities and
parishes by sex, age and marital
status, etc.
[LC, UN, BC, PRC, RPI, RIR
Population in localities by sex,
age and marital status.
[LC, UN, BC, PRC, RPI, RIR
Population in the whole country
and in the counties by sex, age
and marital status, etc.
[LC, UN, BC, PRC, RPI, RIR
Population in different divisions,
aliens, etc.
[LC, UN, BC, PRC, RPI, RIR
Divisions, demarcations of local-
ities, development of the popula-
tion, etc.
[LC, UN, BC, PRC, RPI, RIR
Economically active population by
industry and status, etc., in com-
munes, parishes and localities.
[LC, UN, BC, PRC, RPI, RIR

Economically active population
by occupation and households by
size, etc., within communes and

inom kommuner och större tätorter. 1963. viii, 224p.
.1-8   VIII. Förvärvsarbetande
dagbefolkning efter näringsgren
samt utpendling och inpendling
i kommuner och landsförsamlin-
gar. 1963. viii, 242p.
.1-9   IX. Näringsgren, yrke,
pendling, hushåll och utbildning
i hela riket, länsvis m.m. 1964.
xii, 244p.
.1-10   X. Huvudsysselsättning,
åker- och skogsareal, person-
bilsinnehav samt nationalitet.
1964. x, 138p. map.
.1-11   XI. Urvalsbearbetning:
familjer, inkomst, inrikes omflyttning och näringsgrensvax-
ling. 1965. xii, 23, 107p.

Sweden. Statistiska Centralby-
     rån och Bostadsstyrelsen.
.2   Folk- och bostadsräkningen
den 1 november 1960. Redogörelse för folk- och bostadsräkningens uppläggning och utförande. Stockholm, 1965.
ix, 150p.

Sweden. Statistiska Centralbyrån
     Folk- och bostadsräkningen den
1 november 1965. Stockholm,
1966-1969. Vol. I-IX.
1965.1-1   I. Folkmängd inom kommuner och församlingar samt kommunblock efter kön, ålder, civilstånd m.m. 1966. [9], 236p.
.1-2   II. Folkmängd inom tätorter efter kön, ålder och civilstånd. 1967. 16, 142p.
.1-3   III. Folkmängd i hela riket och länen efter kön, ålder
och civilstånd m.m. 1967. 23,
105p.
.1-4   IV. Förvärvsarbetande
befolkning efter näringsgren och
yrkesstallning m.m. inom kommunblock, kommuner, församling och
tätorter. 1967. 536p.
.1-5   V. Lägenhater och hushåll
inom kommunblock, kommuner och
tätorter. 1968. 435p.

larger localities.
[LC, UN, BC, PRC, RPI, RIR
Economically active day-popula-
tion by industry and outgoing
and incoming commuting in communes and rural parishes.
[LC, UN, BC, PRC, RPI, RIR
Industry, occupation, commuting,
households, and education in the
whole country, by county, etc.
[LC, UN, BC, PRC, RPI, RIR
main occupation, arable and for-
est acreage, private car owners
and nationality.
[LC, UN, BC, PRC, RPI, RIR
Sample surveys: families, income,
internal migration and change of
industry.
[LC, UN, BC, PRC, RPI, RIR

Census of population and housing
in 1960. Report on the planning
and processing of the census of
population and housing.
[LC, BC, PRC, RPI

Population and housing census of
November 1, 1965.

Population in communes, parishes
and cooperating communes by sex,
age and marital status, etc.
[LC, UN, PRC, RPI
Population in localities by sex,
age and marital status.
[LC, UN, PRC, RPI
Population in the whole country
and in the counties by sex, age
and marital status, etc.
[LC, UN, PRC, RPI
Economically active population
by industry and status, etc., in
cooperating communes, communes,
parishes and localities.
[LC, UN, PRC, RPI
Dwellings and households in cooperating communes, communes and
localities.
[LC, UN, PRC, RPI

.1-6   VI. Förvärsarbetande dagbefolkning efter näringsgren samt
utpendling och inpendling i kommuner och kommunblock. 1968.
242p.

Economically active day-time population by industry and outgoing
and incoming commuters in communes
and cooperating communes.
[LC, UN, PRC, RPI

.1-7   VII. Förvärvsarbetande
befolkning efter näringsgren
yrkesställning och arbetsplat-
sens belägenhet m.m. i hela
riket, länen och kommunblock-
sanpassade A-regioner. 1968.
176p.

Economically active population
by industry, status and place of
work, etc., in the whole country,
counties and regions of cooperative communes.
[LC, UN, PRC, RPI

.1-8   VIII. Lägenheter och hushåll i hela riket, län och kom-
munblocksanpassade A-regioner.
1969. 221p.

Dwellings and households in the
whole country, counties and regions of cooperative communes.
[LC, UN, PRC, RPI

.1-9   IX. Urvalsbearbetning:
inkomst, yrke m.m. Redogörelse
för folk- och bostadsräkningens
uppläggning och utförande. 1969.
217p.

Sample surveys: income, occupations, etc. Report on the planning and processing of the population and housing census.
[LC, UN, PRC, RPI

Sweden. Statistiska Centralbyrån.
Folk- och bostadsräkningen,
1970. Stockholm, 1972-1975.
Vol. 1-14.

Population and housing census,
1970.

1970.1-1   Befolkning i kommuner och
församlingar m.m. 1972. 258p.

Population in communes and parishes, etc.
[PRC

.1-2   Befolkning i tätorter.
1972. 148p.

Population in localities.
[PRC

.1-3   Befolkning i hela riket
och länen utlänningar och utrikes födda personer m.m. 1972.
223p.

Population in the whole country
and in the counties, aliens and
foreign-born presons, etc.
[PRC

.1-4   Den demografiska statistiken. Definitioner, metoder,
befolkningsutveckling m.m. 1974.
111p.

Demographic statistics. Definitions, methods, population development, etc.
[PRC

.1-5   Förvärvsarbetande befolkning efter näringsgren m.m. i
kommunblock, kommuner och tätorter. 1973. 385p.

Economically active population
by industry, age, etc., in cooperating communes, communes and
localities.
[PRC

.1-6   Lägenheter och hushåll i
kommunblock och tätorter m.m.
1973. 296p.

Dwellings and households in cooperating communes and localities,
etc.
[PRC

.1-7   Förvärvsarbetande befolkning efter yrke m.m. i kimmun-
block, kommuner och tätorter.
1973. 421p.

Economically active population
by occupation, etc., in cooperating communes, communes and localities.
[PRC

.1-8   Förvärvsarbetande dagbefolkning efter näringsgren,
yrke m.m. samt utpendling och
inpendling i kommunblock, kommuner och tätorter. 1974.
796p.

Economically active day-time population by industry and occupation
and commuting in cooperating communes, communes and localities.
[PRC

.1-9   Lägenheter, hushåll och
familjer i hela riket, länen m.
m. 1974. 236p.

Dwellings, households, and families in the whole country, counties, etc.
[PRC

.1-10   Näringsgren, yrke och utbildning i hela riket, länen m.
m. 1974. 213p.

Industry, occupation and education
in the whole country, by county,
etc.
[PRC

.1-11   Inkomst. 1975. 221p.

Income.
[PRC

.1-12   Redogörelse för folk- och
bostadsräkningens uppläggning
och utförande. 1974. 143p.

Report on the planning and processing of the population and housing
census 1970.
[PRC

.1-13   Sysselsättning och utbildning. Definitioner, jämförbar-
het och utveckling m.m. 1975.
120p. appendices.

Economic activity and education.
Definitions, comparability, devel-
opment, etc.
[PRC

.1-14   Bostäder och hushåll 1960-
1970. 1975. 153p.

Dwellings and households 1960-1970.
[PRC

Sweden. Statistiska Centralbyrån.
Folk- och bostadsräkningen,
1975. Stockholm, 1976-   .
Vol. 1-11 in 21v.
    1. Råtabellplaner. No.
1-3.

Population and housing census,
1975.

Tabulation programme.

1975.1-1-1   ...1975. 1977. 108p.

... for 1975.
[PRC, LC

.1-1-2   ...1975 (forts) och
1970. 1977. 222p.

... for 1975 (Cont'd) and 1970.
[PRC, LC

.1-1-3   ...1965 och 1960.
197 .   p.

... for 1965 and 1960.
[

    2. Utveckling mellan 1970
och 1975. Nos. 1-4 in 3v.

Development between 1970 and 1975.

.1-2-1   Lägenheter. 1977. 76p.

Dwellings.
[PRC, LC

.1-2-2&3   Hushåll och sysselsatt-
ning. 1978. 84p.

Households and type of activity.
[PRC

.1-2-4   Tätorternas areal och
folkmängd. 1977. 77p.

Area and population of localities.
[PRC, LC

    3. Folkmängd... Nos. 1-3.

Population...

.1-3-1   ... i kommuner och församlingar. 1977. 148p.

... in communes and parishes.
[PRC

1975.1-3-2   ... i tätorter. 1976. 104p.

.1-3-3   ... i hela riket och länen m.m. samt utländska medborgare och utrikes födda i hela riket. 1977. 126p.

.1-4   4. Lägenheter i hela riket, länen, kommuner och tätorter. 1977. 407p.
5. Hushåll och familjer. No. 1-2.

.1-5-1   ... i kommuner och tätorter. 1978. 283p.

.1-5-2   ... i hela riket och länen m.m. 1978. 270p.

6. Förvärvsarbetande nattbefolkning... Nos. 1-2.

.1-6-1   ... i kommuner och tätorter. 1978. 339p.

.1-6-2   ... i hela riket och länen m.m. 1979. 194p.

7. Förvärvsarbetande dagbefolkning samt pendling... Nos. 1-2.

.1-7-1   ... i kommuner och tätorter. 1979. 351p.

.1-7-2   Pendling mellan enskilda tätorter. 1979. 349p.

.1-8   8. Inkomst. Bilinnhav. 1978. 256p.
9. Resultat från evalveringsstudier. Nos. 1-2.

.1-9-1   ... avseende bostadsdata för smhus. 1977. 109p. specimen forms.

.1-9-2   ... avseende sysselsättningsdata. 1978. 100p.

.1-10   10. Grafisk redovisning. 1979. 103p.

.1-11   11. Folk- och bostadsräkningens uppläggning och genomförande.

... in localities.
[PRC, LC
... in the whole country and in the counties, etc., aliens and foreign-born persons in the whole country.
[PRC, LC
Dwellings in the whole country, counties, communes and localities.
[PRC, LC
Households and families.

... in communes and localities.
[PRC, OPR, PSC
... in the whole country, counties, etc.
[PRC, OPR, PSC
Economically active resident population...
... in communes and localities.
[PRC, OPR, PSC
... in the whole country and the counties, etc.
[PRC, PSC
Economically active day-time population and commuting...

... in communes and localities.
[PRC, PSC, OPR
Commuting between localities.
[OPR, PSC
Income. Car ownership.
[PRC, PSC, OPR
Results from the evaluation study.

... concerning housing data for one and two dwelling houses.
[LC, OPR, PRC
... concerning economic activity.
[PRC
Graphic presentation.
[PRC

[

SWITZERLAND

Swiss Confederation   Capital: Bern.
Statistical Agency: Federal Bureau of Statistics
                     [Eidgenössisches Statistisches Amt]
                     Hallwylstrasse 15
                     Ch-3003 Berne,
Publications Distributor: same

         Switzerland. Eidgenössisches
             Statistisches Amt.
           Eidgenössische Volkszählung,   Federal census of population, Dec-
         1 dezember 1950./Recensement   ember 1, 1950.
         fédéral de la population, 1er   [In German, French, Italian]
         décembre 1950./Censimento fede-
         rale della popolazione.   Bern,
         1951-1957. Vol. 1-27. (Statis-
         tische quellenwerke der Schweiz).
1950.1-1   Wohnbevölkerung der Ge-   Resident population in the com-
         meinden; ungeprüfte Ergebniss./   munes; uncertified results.
         Population résidente des commu-   [PRC, BC, LC, RPI
         nes; résultats non contrôlés.
         1951. 9, 69p. (Heft 230)
1950.1-2 through 1950.1-23. 2. Aargau. 1954. 152p. (255)/3. Appenzell-
         Inner and Outer Rhodes. 1955. 200p. (270)/4. Basel, city and dis-
         trict. 1955. 224p. (268)/5. Bern. 1954. 354p. (251)/6. Fribourg.
         1955. 150p. (269)/7. Geneva. 1955. 197p. (278)/8. Glarus. 1954.
         106p. (263)/9. Graubünden. 1954. 150p. (257)/10. Lucerne. 1955.
         193p. (279)/11. Neuchâtel. 1955. 185p. (266)/12. Saint Gall. 1953.
         207p. (245)/13. Schaffhausen. 1954. 114p. (265)/14. Schwyz. 1953.
         116p. (241)/15. Solothurn. 1954. 138p. (254)/16. Thurgau. 1954.
         142p. (260)/17. Ticino. 1954. 154p. (262)/18. Unterwalden. 1952.
         190p. (237)/19. Uri. 1952. 102p. (239)/20. Valais. 1954. 134p.
         (261)/21. Vaud. 1954. 257p. (253)/22. Zurich. 1953. 296p. (247)/
         23. Zug. 1954. 108p. (264) [BC, PRC, LC, RPI
     .1-24   Schweiz. Tabellenteil I/   Switzerland. Tables, part I.
         Suisse. Tableaux 1ère partie.   [BC, LC, PRC, RPI
         1956. 206p. (288).
     .1-25   Schweiz. Tabellenteil II/   Switzerland. Tables, part II.
         Suisse. Tableaux 2éme partie.   [BC, LC, PRC, RPI
         1957. 433p. (289).
     .1-26   Schweizerbürger nach Hei-   Swiss population classified ac-
         matkantonen und -gemeinden./Popu-   cording to native communes.
         lation suisse répartie par can-   [BC, LC, PRC, RPI
         tons et communes d'origine. 1955.
         81p. (280).
     .1-27   Berufstätige nach Arbeits-   Gainfully employed population
         und Wohnort./Personnes exerçant   according to workplace and dom-
         une profession d'après le lieu   icile.
         de travail et le domicile. 1956.   [BC, LC, PRC, RPI
         91p. (281).

Switzerland. Eidgenössisches
Statistisches Amt.
Eidgenössische Volkszählung,
1 dezember 1960./Recensement
fédéral de la population 1er
décembre 1960. Bern, 1961-1969.
Vol. 1-33. (Statistische quellenwerke der Schweiz). (Heft)

Federal population census, December 1, 1960.

1960.1-1 Wohnbevölkerung der Gemeinden 1850-1960./Population
résidente des communes, 1850-
1960. 1961. 87p. (326).

Resident population of the communes, 1850-1960.
[BC, PRC, RPI, RIR

1960.1-2 through 1960.1-26. [Cantons]. 2. Aargau. 1964. 157p. (367)/3.
Appenzell-Outer Rhodes. 1963. 107p. (343)/4. Appenzell-Inner Rhodes.
1963. 103p. (337)/5. Basel-District. 1963. 133p. (355)/6. Basel-
City. 1963. 175p. (354)/7. Bern. 1964. 351p. (364)/8. Fribourg.
1964. 171p. (371)/9. Geneva. 1963. 191p. (360)/10. Glarus. 1963.
109p. (349)/11. Graubünden. 1964. 147p. (374)/12. Lucerne. 1964.
191p. (370)/13. Neuchâtel. 1964. 135p. (359)/14. Saint Gall. 1964.
194p. (369)/15. Schaffhausen. 1963. 115p. (356)/16. Schwyz. 1963.
111p. (351)/17. Solothurn. 1963. 143p. (362)/18. Thurgau. 1964.
151p. (372)/19. Ticino. 1963. 155p. (352)/20. Unterwalden (Nidwalden). 1963. 105p. (348)/21. Unterwalden (Obwalden). 1963. 105p.
(347)/22. Uri. 1963. 107p. (345)/23. Valais. 1964. 153p. (373)/
24. Vaud. 1964. 254p. (365)/25. Zug. 1963. 107p. (350)/26. Zurich. 1963. 293p. (350). [BC, PRC, RPI, RIR

.1-27 Schweiz. Teil I. Geschlecht, Heimat, Geburtsort,
Konfession, Muttersprache, Zivilstand, Alter, Schulbesuch./
Suisse. 1ère partie. Sexe,
origine, lieu de naissance, religion, langue maternelle, état
civil, âge, formation scolaire.
1964. 187p. (366).

Switzerland. Part I. Sex, origin, birthplace, religion, mother
tongue, marital status, age, and
education.
[BC, LC, PRC, RPI, RIR

.1-28 Schweiz. Teil II. Erwerb
und Beruf./Suisse. 2ème partie.
Branches économiques et professions. 1965. 377p. (385).

Switzerland. Part II. Economic
branches and occupations.
[BC, LC, PRC, RPI, RIR

.1-29 Schweiz. Teil III. Wohnungen./Suisse. 3ème partie.
Logements. 1964. 319p. (379).

Switzerland. Part III. Housing.
[BC, LC, PRC, RPI, RIR

.1-30 Schweiz. Teil IV. Wohn-
und Arbeitsort der Berufstätigen
(Pendelwanderung)./Domicile et
lieu de travail des personnes
exerçant une profession. (Migrations alternantes). 1965.
97p. (383).

Switzerland. Part IV. Residence
and place of work of the gainfully employed population (commuting).
[BC, LC, PRC, RPI, RIR

.1-31 Schweiz. Teil V. Heimat-
gemeinden der Schweizerburger./

Switzerland. Part V. Counties
of birth of Swiss nationals.

Communes d'origine des ressor-
tissants Suisses. 1965. 86p.
(387).

.1-32   Schweiz. Teil VI. Haushaltungen./Ménages. 1966. 129p.
(396).

.1-33   Gesammelte Textbeiträge./
Recueil de commentaires. 1969.
409p. (446).

Switzerland. Eidgenössisches
      Statistisches Amt.
   Eidgenössische Volkszählung
1970./Recensement fédéral 1970.
Bern, 1971-1976. Vol. 1-12 in
38v. (Statistische quellenwerke
der Schweiz) (Heft).

1970.1-1   Wohnbevölkerung der Gemeinden, 1850-1970./Population
résidente des communes, 1850-
1970. 1971. 85p. map. (467).

.1-2   Gemeinden. Demographische
Merkmale, Wirtschaftssektoren,
Haushaltungen./Communes. Caractéristiques démographiques, secteurs économiques, ménages.
1972. 407p. (476).

.1-2a   Gemeinden. Erwerb./Com-
munes. Activité économique.
1974. 145p. (535).

1970.1-3-1 through 1970.1-3-25. [Cantons]. 1. Zurich. 1974. 411p. (517)/
2. Bern. 1974. 417p. (498)/3. Lucerne. 1974. 261p. (503)/4. Uri.
1974. 129p. (513)/5. Schwyz. 1974. 153p. (509)/6. Obwalden. 1974.
129p. (506)/7. Nidwalden. 1974. 129p. (505)/8. Glarus. 1974.
137p. (501)/9. Zug. 1974. 147p. (516)/10. Fribourg. 1974. 181p.
(499)/11. Solothurn. 1974. 177p. (510)/12. Basel-City. 1974. 263p.
(497)/13. Basel-District. 1974. 175p. (496)/14. Schaffhausen. 1974.
153p. (508)/15. Appenzell Outer Rhodes. 1974. 141p. (494)/16. Appenzell Inner Rhodes. 1974. 121p. (495)/17. Saint Gall. 1974. 267p.
(507)/18. Graubünden. 1974. 177p. (502)/19. Aargau. 1974. 189p.
(493)/20. Thurgau. 1974. 177p. (511)/21. Ticino. 1974. 185p.
(512)/22. Vaud. 1974. 315p. (515)/23. Valais. 1974. 173p. (514)/
24. Neuchâtel. 1974. 169p. (504)/25. Geneva. 1974. 277p. (500).
[PRC, LC

.1-4   Schweiz 1. Geschlecht,
Heimat, Konfession, Muttterspra-
che, Zivilstand, Alter./Suisse
1. Sexe, origine, religion.
langue maternelle, état civil,
âge. 1972. 164p. (479).

[BC, LC, PRC, RPI, RIR

Switzerland. Part VI. House-
holds.
[BC, LC, PRC, RPI, RIR
Collection of commentaries.
[BC, PRC, RPI, RIR

Federal population census, 1970.

Resident population of the communes, 1850-1970.
[PRC, LC

Communes. Demographic characteristics, economic sectors, households.
[PRC, LC

Communes. Economic activity.
[PRC, LC

Switzerland 1. Sex, origin, religion, mother tongue, marital
status, age.
[PRC

1970.1-5   Schweiz 2. Erwerb und
       Beruf. 1974. 333p. (533)

   .1-6   Schweiz 3. Pendler, Ar-
       beitsweg, Verkehrsmittel./Suisse
       3. Navettes de travailleurs,
       trajets effectués et moyens de
       transport utilisés pour se ren-
       dre au travail. 1974. 176p.
       (549).

   .1-7   Schweiz 4. Heimat, Geburt-
       sort, Schulbesuch usw./Origine,
       lieu de naissance, formation
       scolaire, etc. 1974. 100p.
       (547).

   .1-7a   Kantone. Heimat, Geburt-
       sort, Schulbesuch usw./Cantons.
       Origine, lieu de naissance, for-
       mation scolaire, etc. 1974.
       291p. (545).

   .1-8   Schweiz 5. Haushaltungen./
       Suisse 5. Ménages. 1975. 123p.
       (561).

   .1-9   Gemeinden. Gebäude und
       Wohnungen./Communes. Immeubles
       et logements. 1973. 343p.
       (518).

   .1-10   Kantone. Gebäude und
       Wohnungen./Cantons. Immeubles
       et logements. 1974. 164p.
       (530).

   .1-11   Suisse 6. Immeubles et
       logements. 1974. 221p. (537).

   .1-12   Allgemeines, Textbeträge,
       Erhebungspapier./Généralités,
       textes, formules de relevé.
       1976. 262p. 2 maps. 50 unnum-
       bered pages. (579).

Switzerland 2. Economic branches
and occupations.
[PRC, LC
Switzerland 3. Commuters, routes
and means of transport to work.
[PRC, LC

Switzerland 4. Origin, birthplace, education, etc.
[PRC, LC

Cantons. Origin, birthplace,
education, etc.
[PRC, LC

Switzerland 5. Households.
[PRC, LC

Communes. Buildings and dwellings.
[PRC, LC

Cantons. Buildings and dwellings.
[PRC, LC

Switzerland 6. Buildings and
dwellings.
[PRC, LC
Generalities, texts, census forms.
[PRC, LC

SYRIA

Syrian Arab Republic.   Capital: Damascus
Statistical Agency: Central Bureau of Statistics
                      Office of the Prime Minister
                      Damascus,
Publications Distributor: same

      Syria.   Ministry of Planning.   Directorate of Statistics.
         Census of population 1960.   Damascus, Jomhoria Press, 1965.   15v.
1960.1-1 through 1960.1-14.   1. Dar'a Mohafaza.   xxv, 225p./1. [i.e. 2] Sweida
      Mohafaza.   xxv, 222p./3. Damascus City.   xxv, 157p./4. Aleppo City.
      xxi, 157p./5. Damascus Mohafaza.   xxiii, 232p./6. Aleppo Mohafaza.
      xxiii, 272p./7. Homs Mohafaza.   xxv, 246p./8. Hama Mohafaza.   xxv,
      246p./9. Latakia Mohafaza.   xxv, 312p./10. Idleb Mohafaza.   xxvi,
      281p./11. Hasakeh Mohafaza.   xxv, 300p./12. Deir-ez-Zor.   xxv, 234p./
      13. Al-Rakka Mohafaza.   xxv, 236p./14. Bedowins.   xvi, 45p.   [PRC,
      BC, RPI
   .1-15   Syrian Arab Republic.   xxii, 287, ii p.   [PRC, BC, RPI

      Syria.   Central Bureau of Statistics.
         Population census, 1970.   Syrian Arab Republic.   Damascus, 197?
      Vol. 1-2.
1970.1-1   Syrian Arab Republic.   310p.   [PRC, LC
   .1-2   Syrian Arab Republic.   Pp. 311-646.   [PRC, LC

      Syria.   Central Bureau of Statistics.
         Population census, 1970.   [Governorates and cities].   Damascus,
      197?.   Vol. 1-14 in   v.
1970.2-1 through 1970.2-14.   1. Damascus City.   162p./2. Damascus Governorate.
      195p./3. Aleppo Governorate.   305p./3a. Annex.   Population's aggre-
      gates in Aleppo Governorate.   91p./4. Hama Governorate.   333p./5. Homs
      Governorate.   326p./6. Rakka Governorate.   331p./7.
            /8. Lattakia Governorate.   341p./9. Edleb Governorate.   333p./
      10. Deir-ez-Zor Governorate.   300p./11. Al-Hasakeh Governorate.   400p./
      12. Al-Sweida Governorate.   301p./13. Dar'a Governorate.   293p./14.
                              [PRC

      Syria.   Central Bureau of Statistics.
   .3   Summary bulletin: 1970 population census data of Syrian Arab Re-
      public.   Damascus, 1973.   19p.   [OPR

TAIWAN AND FUKIEN OFF-SHORE ISLANDS

Republic of China.   Capital: Taipei, Taiwan Island.
Statistical Agency: Department of Population
                     Ministry of the Interior
                     107, Sec. 4, Roosevelt Road
                     Taipei,
                              and
                     Directorate General of Budget, Accounting and Statistics.
                     Executive Yuan
                     1, Chung Hsiao East Rd., Sec. 1
                     Taipei
Publications Distributor: both

Taiwan sheng hu k'ou p'u ch'a ch'u pien yin.	Taiwan. Bureau of the Census.
Chung hua min kuo hu k'ou p'u ch'a pao kao shu. [Taipei], 1959. Vol. I-III in 8v.	Report on the household population census of the Republic of China [1956].
1956.1-1 I. T'ai min ti ch'ü. Hu k'ou p'u ch'a chi shu chi tieng chi t'i yao. 2, 216p.	Taiwan and Fukien area. Descriptive report on the census and a statistical summary. [BC, PRC, RPI
II. Taiwan sheng. 8v.	Taiwan Province.
.1-2-1 Hu k'ou tsung piao chi jen k'ou chi pien. 816p.	General household population tables and population registration characteristics. [BC, PRC, RPI
.1-2-2 Jen k'ou chih nien ling chi hun yin chuang k'uang. 360p.	Age and marital status of the population. [BC, PRC, RPI
Jen k'ou chih chiao yü ch'eng tu. 2v.	Educational levels of the population.
.1-2-3-1 (Shang). 888p.	First part. [BC, PRC, RPI
.1-2-3-2 (Hsia). pp. 889-1680.	Last part. [BC, PRC, RPI
.1-2-4 Jen k'ou chih hang yet. 838p.	Industries of the population. [BC, PRC, RPI
.1-2-5 Jen k'ou chih chih yeh. 1140p.	Occupations of the population. [BC, PRC, RPI
Jen k'ou chih hang yeh yü chih yeh. 2v.	Industry and occupation of the population.
.1-2-6-1 (Shang). 728p.	First part. [BC, PRC, RPI
.1-2-6-2 (Hsia). pp. 729-1390.	Last part. [BC, PRC, RPI
III. Fukien sheng.	Fukien Province.
.1-3 Chin ma ti ch'u. Hu k'ou tsung piao chi fen lei t'ung chi. 566p.	Quemoy and Matsu. General tables on household population and detailed characteristics. [BC, PRC, RPI

[Taiwan.　Bureau of the Census]
　.2　　Hu k'ou p'u ch'a jen yuan
　shou ts'e.　242p.

　　　　Handbook for census personnel.
　　　　[BC, RPI

Taiwan sheng hu k'ou p'u ch'a
　　ch'u pien yin.
　　T'ai min ti ch'u hu k'ou chi
chu chai p'u ch'a pao kao shu.
[Taipei], 1969.　Vol. 1-3 in 21v.
1966.1-1　　1.　T'ai min ti ch'u.　Hu
k'ou chi chu chai p'u ch'a tsun
shuo ming chi t'ung chi t'i yao.
378p.
　　　　2.　Taiwan sheng.　11 parts
in 18v.

　　　　Taiwan Provincial Census Office.

　　　　1966 Taiwan and Fukien Off-shore
　　　　Islands.　Census of population
　　　　and Housing.
　　　　General explanatory document of
　　　　census and residence, and a sum-
　　　　mary of statistics.
　　　　[PRC, CPC
　　　　Taiwan Province.

　.1-2-1　　Hu k'ou tsun piao chi
　jen k'ou chih chi pein, nien
　ling, ch'ien i.　724p.
　.1-2-2　　Jen k'ou chih hun yin
　chuang k'uang.　Fu nu sheng yu
　li.　176p.
　　　　Jen k'ou chi chiao yu
ch'eng tu.　2v.
　.1-2-3-1　　(Shang).　766p.

　.1-2-3-2　　(Hsia).　pp. 767-
　1536.
　.1-2-4　　Jen k'ou chih ching
　chi hua tung lei pieh.　360p.

　　　　Jen k'ou chi hang yeh.
　3v.
　.1-2-5-1　　(Shang).　820p.

　.1-2-5-2　　(Chung).　pp. 821-
　1684.
　.1-2-5-3　　(Hsia).　pp. 1685-
　2494.
　　　　Jen k'ou chih chih yeh.
　3v.
　.1-2-6-1　　(Shang).　992p.

　.1-2-6-2　　(Chung).　pp. 993-
　1932.
　.1-2-6-3　　(Hsia).　pp. 1933-
　2892.
　.1-2-7　　Jen k'ou chih hang yeh
　yü chih yeh.　1048p.

　.1-2-8　　Shih yeh jen k'ou.
　475p.

　　　　Census tables of origin, age,
　　　　and mobility of the population.
　　　　[PRC, CPC
　　　　Marital status and fertility of
　　　　women.
　　　　[PRC, CPC
　　　　Educational level of the popula-
　　　　tion.
　　　　First part.
　　　　[PRC, CPC
　　　　Last part.
　　　　[PRC, CPC
　　　　Categories of economic status of
　　　　the population.
　　　　[PRC, CPC
　　　　Industries of the population.

　　　　First part.
　　　　[PRC, CPC
　　　　Second part.
　　　　[PRC, CPC
　　　　Last part.
　　　　[PRC, CPC
　　　　Occupations of the population.

　　　　First part.
　　　　[PRC, CPC
　　　　Second part.
　　　　[PRC, CPC
　　　　Last part.
　　　　[PRC, CPC
　　　　Industry and occupation of the
　　　　population.
　　　　[PRC, CPC
　　　　The unemployed.
　　　　[PRC, CPC

.1-2-9	Chu chu tan wei. 312p.	Housing.
		[PRC, CPC
	Yu jen chu chu tang	Inhabited housing units.
	wei. 3v.	
.1-2-10-1	(Shang). 1064p.	First part.
		[PRC, CPC
.1-2-10-2	(Chung). pp. 1065-	Second part.
	2136.	[PRC, CPC
.1-2-10-3	(Hsia). pp. 2137-	Last part.
	3168.	[PRC, CPC
.1-2-11	Yu jen chu chu tang	Usual residents of inhabited hous-
	wei chih p'u tung chu hu.	ing units.
		[PRC, CPC
	3. Fukien sheng. Chin	Fukien Province. Quemoy and Matsu
	ma ti ch'u. 2v.	area.
.1-3-1	Hu k'ou chuang k'uang.	Population condition.
	1148p.	[PRC, CPC
.1-3-2	Chu chai chuang k'uang.	Housing condition.
	200p.	[PRC, CPC

Taiwan Provincial Government. Census Office.
.2   An extract report on the 1966 population and housing censuses of
Taiwan Province and Fukien Off-shore Islands of the Republic of China.
[Taipei], 1969. iii, 183p. specimen forms. [PRC

Taiwan Provincial Government. Census Office.
.3   The manual of the population census and household registration data.
Taipei, 1972.   173p. [CPC

Taiwan. Executive Yuan. Census Office.
    The 1970 sample census of population and housing. Taiwan-Fukien
area, Republic of China. General report. [Taipei], 1972. Vol. I-
IV in 6v.
1970.1-1   I. General description and abstracts of statistics. 5, 302p.
7 fold. pages. [PRC
.1-2   II. Population by sex, age, nativity, marital status, and educational attainment. 5, 301p. [PRC
    III. Population by economic characteristics. Parts 1-3.
.1-3-1   5, 647p. [PRC
.1-3-2   5, 757p. [PRC
.1-3-3   5, 539p. [PRC
.1-4   IV. Housing conditions. 5, 196p. [PRC

Taiwan. Executive Yuan. Census Office.
.2   An extract report on the 1970 sample census of population and housing. Taiwan-Fukien area, Republic of China.   Taipei, 1972. ix, 448p.
[PRC

Taiwan. Executive Yuan. Census Office.
    The 1975 sample census of population and housing. Taiwan-Fukien
area, Republic of China. General report. [Taipei], 1976. Vol. I-
IV in 6v.

1975.1-1   I.   General description.   Abstracts of statistics and regulations.
        xxx, 294p.   [PRC
    .1-2   II.   Population by sex, age domicile, marital status, and educa-
        tional attainment.   685p.   [PRC, OPR
             III.   Population by economic characteristics.   Parts 1-3.
    .1-3-1   [vii], 645p.   [PRC, OPR
    .1-3-2   [vii], 865p.   [PRC, OPR
    .1-3-3   [ix], 839p.   [OPR
    .1-4   IV.   Housing conditions.   [ix], 471p.   [PRC, OPR

     Taiwan.   Executive Yuan.   Population Census Office.
    .2   An extract report on the 1975 sample census of population and hous-
        ing.   Taiwan-Fukien area, Republic of China.   [Taipei], 1976.   [250]p.
        [PRC, E-W, OPR

TANGANYIKA AND ZANZIBAR

United Republic of Tanzania.   Capital: Dar es Salaam
Statistical Agency: Bureau of Statistics
                      P.O. Box 796
                      Dar es Salaam,
Publications Distributor: Government Bookshop
                            P.O. Box 1801
                            Dar es Salaam,

East Africa High Commission. Statistical Department.
1948.1   African population of Tanganyika Territory; geographical and tribal studies.   Nairobi, 1950. 89p. [TXU, UN, RPI

Tanganyika. Superintendent of Census.
.2   Report on the census of the non-native population taken on the
night of 25th February 1948.   Dar es Salaam, Government Printer,
1953. [2], 73p. 31 charts. [UN, NWU, LC, PRC, RPI

Great Britain. Colonial Office.
.3   Census of February 1948: population by sex and ethnic group for
country and population of city of Zanzibar. In: Report on Zanzibar
for the years 1949-1950. London, 1952. p.5. [UN, RPI

Zanzibar Protectorate.
.4   Notes on the census of the Zanzibar Protectorate, 1948.   Zanzibar,
Government Printer, 1948. [2], 14p. [LC, RPI

East Africa High Commission. Statistical Department.
1952.1   Tanganyika. Report on the census of the non-African population
taken on the night of 13th February 1952.   Dar es Salaam, 1954.
iv, 51p. [UN, NWU, RPI

East Africa High Commission. Statistical Department.
.2   Tanganyika population census, 1952. Nairobi, 1952. In: Quarterly
economic and statistical bulletin, no. 17. Sept. 1952. Pp. 14-18 &
ff. [UN

East Africa High Commission. Statistical Department.
.3   The main characteristics of the non-African population at Tanganyika as reported in the census taken on the 13th February, 1952. In:
Quarterly economic and statistical bulletin, no. 22. Dec. 1953. Pp.
vi-viii. [UN

East Africa High Commission. Statistical Office.
1957.1   Report on the census of the non-African population on the night of
20th-21st February, 1957. Dar es Salaam, Government Printer, 1958.
[3], 63p. [BC, TXU, NWU, LC, RPI

East Africa High Commission. Statistical Office.
.2   Tanganyika population census, 1957. Analysis of total population;

certain analyses by race and sex, geographical area, age, religion and nationality.   [Nairobi], 1958.   [10]p.   [BC, TXU, NWU, LC, RPI

East Africa High Commission. Statistical Department.
.3   Tanganyika African population census 1957: analysis by sex and age for province, district, and territorial census areas.   [Nairobi], 1958. [20]p. [TXU, NWU, LC, RPI

East Africa High Commission. Statistical Department.
.4   Tanganyika population census 1957. Tribal analysis.   Nairobi, 1958. 249p. [NWU, PRC, LC, RPI

Tanganyika. Central Statistical Bureau.
.5   African census report, 1957.   Dar es Salaam, Government Printer, 1963. [6], 109p. maps. specimen forms. [PRC, NWU, LC, RPI

Zanzibar Protectorate.
1958.1   Report on the census of the population of Zanzibar Protectorate taken on the night of the 19th and 20th March, 1958.   Zanzibar, Government Printer, 1960. [2], 111p. [PRC, LC, RPI

Tanzania. Central Statistical Bureau.
       1967 population census.   Dar es Salaam, 1969-1973. Vol. I-VI.
1967.1-1   I. Statistics for enumeration areas. 1969. [2], xxvi, [1], 342p. [BC, PRC, NWU, LC, RPI
.1-2   II. Statistics for urban areas. 1970. [1], xx, [1], 304p. specimen forms. [BC, PRC, NWU, LC, RPI
.1-3   III. Demographic statistics. 1971. xxii, 490p. [BC, PRC, NWU, LC
.1-4   IV. Economic statistics. 1971. xxxvi, 476p. [PRC, NWU, BC, LC
.1-5   V. Census methodology. 1971. x, 270, [2]p. [BC, LC, PRC, NWU, RPI
.1-6   [VI]. The population of Tanzania: an analysis of the 1967 population census. Edited by Bertil Egero and Roushdi A. Henin.   Dar es Salaam, 1973. xv, 292p. [LC

Tanzania. Bureau of Statistics and Bureau of Resource Assessment and Land Use Planning.
       1973 national demographic survey of Tanzania.   Dar es Salaam, 1976. Vol. I-VI.
1973.1-1   I. Regional and national data. xvii, 428p. [OPR, LC
.1-2   II. Data for socioeconomic groups. xxv, 258p. [OPR, LC
.1-3   III. Summary data for survey clusters. By R.A. Henin and D.C. Ewbank. xxvii, 155p. [OPR, LC
.1-4   IV. The methods report. By R.A. Henin and others. x, 360p. [OPR, LC
.1-5   V. Training manual. By R.A. Henin and I.D. Thomas. 72p. [OPR, LC
.1-6   VI. The demography of Tanzania. xviii, 423p. [PRC

The next census was proposed for 1978 but no publications have been seen as yet.

THAILAND

Kingdom of Thailand.   Capital: Bangkok.
Statistical Agency: National Statistical Office
                     Larnluang Road.
                     Bangkok,
Publications Distributor: same

Thailand. Central Statistical Office.
          [Census of population and agriculture of Thailand]. Bangkok, n.d.
     Vol. I-VII in 8v.   [This census is totally in the Thai language.]
1947.1-1   I. Population by locality. [397]p. [BC, PRC, RPI
   .1-2   II. Population by principal characteristics. [470]p. [BC, PRC,
     RPI
   .1-3   III. Population by marital status. [830]p. [BC, PRC, RPI
   .1-4   IV. Education. [320]p. [BC, PRC, RPI
   .1-5   V. Population by nationality-race. [316]p. [BC, PRC, RPI
            VI. Population by age and nationality. Parts 1-2.
   .1-6-1   1. [1570]p. [BC, PRC, RPI
   .1-6-2   2. [10], [1336]p. [BC, PRC, RPI
   .1-7   VII. Population by occupation. [828]p. [BC, PRC, RPI

Thailand. Central Statistical Office.
   .2   Census of population 1947: final figures. In: Statistical year-
    book Thailand, 1952. Pp. 3-63. [In Thai and English]. [BC, PRC, RPI

Thailand. Central Statistical Office.
1954.1   Final report of the demographic and economic survey 1954. General
    information and tables. [Bangkok, n.d.] 532p. 25 tables. [PRC, RPI

Thailand. Central Statistical Office.
     Population census. Changwad series. Bangkok, 1961-1962. 71v.
1960.1-1 through 1960.1-71. 1. Angthong. 1962. c, 33p./2. Buri-Ram. 1961.
    c, 33p./3. Cha-Choengsao. 1961. c, 33p./4. Chai-Nat. 1961. c, c,
    33p./5. Chanthaburi. 1962. c, 33p./6. Chayaphum. 1961. c, 33p./7.
    Chiengmai. 1961. c, 35p./8. Chieng-Rai. 1962. c, 35p./9. Chonburi.
    1962. c, 33p./10. Chumphorn. 1962. c, 35p./11. Kalasin. 1961. c,
    33p./12. Kamphaengphet. c, 33p./13. Kanchanaburi. 1962. c, 33p./14.
    Khonkaen. 1961. c, 35p./15. Krabi. 1961. c, 33p./16. Lampang. 1961.
    c, 33p./17. Lamphun. 1962. c, 33p./18. Loei. 1961. c, 33p./19. Lop-
    buri. 1962. c, 33p./20. Mae-Hongson. 1962. c, 30p./21. Mahasarakham.
    1961. c, 33p./22. Nakhornnayok. 1961. c, 33p./23. Nakhornpathom.
    1962. c, 33p./24. Nakhornphanom. 1962. c, 33p./
         25. Nakhornratchsima. 1961. c, 35p./26. Nakhornsawan. 1961. c,
    33p./27. Nakhornsrithamrat. 1961. c, 35p./28. Nan. 1961. c, 33p./
    29. Nara-Thiwat. 1961. c, 33p./30. Nongkhai. 1961. c, 33p./31. Non-
    thaburi. 1962. c, 33p./32. Pathumthani. 1961. c, 33p./33. Pattani.
    1961. c, 33p./34. Phang-Nga. 1961. c, 33p./35. Phatalung. 1961.
    c, 33p./36. Phetburi. 1962. c, 33p./37. Phetchbun. 1962. c, 33p./
    38. Phichit. 1962. c, 33p./39. Phitsnulok. 1961. c, 33p./40. Phrae.
    1962. c, 33p./41. Phranakhorn. 1962. [2], c, 55p./42. Phranakhorn-

sri-Ayuthya. 1961. c, 35p./43. Phuket. 1961. c, 33p./44. Prachin-
buri. 1962. c, 33p./45. Prachuap-Khirkhan. 1961. c, 33p./46. Ranong.
1962. c, 33p./47. Ratburi. 1961. c, 33p./48. Rayong. 1962. c, 33p./
49. Roy Et. 1961. [2], c, 33p./
     50. Sakannakhorn. 1961. c, 36p./51. Samutprakan. 1961. c, 33p./
52. Samutsakhorn. 1962. c, 33p./53. Samutsongkhram. 1962. c, 33p./
54. Saraburi. 1962. c, 33p./55. Satun. 1961. c, 33p./56. Singhburi.
1962. c, 33p./57. Sonkhla. 1961. c, 33p./58. Srisaket. 1961. c,
33p./59. Sukho-Thai. 1962. c, 33p./60. Suphanburi. 1962. c, 33p./
61. Suratthani. 1961. c, 33p./62. Surin. 1962. c, 33p./63. Tak.
1962. c, 33p./64. Thonburi. 1961. c, 53p./65. Trang. 1962. c, 35p./
66. Trat. 1962. c, 29p./67. Ubonratch-Thani. 1961. c, 43p./68.
Udornthani. 1961. c, 33p./69. Uthai-Thani. 1962. c, 33p./70. Uttaradit. 1961. c, 33p./71. Yala. 1961. c, 33p. [TXU, RPI

Thailand. Central Statistical Office.
     Thailand population census 1960. Bangkok, n.d. 2v.
.2-1   Northeast region. [10], 48p. [BC, PRC, RPI
.2-2   Whole kingdom. v, 59, vi-x p. [BC, PRC, RPI

Thailand. Central Statistical Office.
     Special reports. Bangkok, 1962-1963. Nos. 1-10.
.3-1   Number of employed 11 years of age... 1962. 2p. [BC, PRC, RPI
.3-2   Percent literate 10 years of age... 1962. 3p. [BC, PRC, RPI
.3-3   Percent literate 10 years of age... 1962. 2p. [BC, PRC, RPI
.3-4   Economically active population... 1962. 8p. [BC, PRC, RPI
.3-5   Fertility. 1962. 6p. [BC, PRC, RPI
.3-6   Education and economic activity... 1963. 6p. [BC, PRC, RPI
.3-7   Education and occupation. 1963. 7p. [BC, PRC, RPI
.3-8   Education and industry. 1963. 7p. [BC, PRC, RPI
.3-9   Size of place. 1963. 1p. [BC, PRC, RPI
.3-10   Foreign born. 1963. 1p. [BC, PRC, RPI

Thailand. Central Statistical Office.
.4   1960 population census - Muban series. Population of Changwad Nam
by amphur, tambol, and muban. [n.p., n.d.] 4 mimeographed pages.
[BC, RPI

Thailand. National Statistical Office.
     1970 population and housing census. Chanwat... Bangkok, 1972-
1973. 71v.
1970.1-1 through 1970.1-71. 1. Ang Thong. 1973. xviii, 66p./2. Buri Ram.
1973. xviii, 68p./3. Chachoengsao. 1972. xviii, 66p./4. Chai Nat.
1973. xviii, 66p./5. Chanthaburi. 1973. xvi, 66p./6. Chaiyaphum.
1972. xvi, 68p./7. Chiang Mai. 1972. xviii, 128p./8. Chiang Rai.
1973. xviii, 116p./9. Chon Buri. 1972. xvi, 68p./10. Chumphon.
1973. xviii, 66p./11. Kalasin. 1973. xviii, 66p./12. Kamphaeng.
Phet. 1973. xviii, 64p./13. Kanchanaburi. 1973. xvi, 68p./14. Khon
Kaen. 1972. xvi, 124p./15. Krabi. 1973. xviii, 66p./16. Lampang.
1973. xviii, 68p./17. Lamphun. 1973. xviii, 66p./18. Loei. 1972.
xvi, 66p./19. Lop Buri. 1973. xviii, 66p./20. Mae Hong Son. 1973.
xviii, 66p./21. Maha Sarakham. 1973. xvi, 68p./22. Nakhon Nayok.

1973. xviii, 64p./23. Nakhon Pathom. 1972. xvi, 66p./24. Nakhon
Phanom. 1972. xviii, 68p./
    25. Nakhon Ratchasima. 1973. xviii, 120p./26. Nakhon Sawan. 1973.
xviii, 70p./27. Nakhon Si Thammarat. 1973. xvi, 70p./28. Nana. 1973.
xviii, 66p./29. Narathiwat. 1973. xviii, 68p./30. Nong Khai. 1973.
xviii, 66p./31. Nonthaburi. 1972. xviii, 66p./32. Pathum Thani. 1972.
xvi, 66p./33. Pattani. 1972. xviii, 66p./34. Phangnga. 1973. xviii,
66p./35. Phatthalung. 1973. xvi, 64p./36. Phetchaburi. 1973. xviii,
66p./37. Phetchabuni. 1973. xviii, 66p./38. Phichit. 1973. xviii,
66p./39. Phitsanulok. 1973. xviii, 66p./40. Phrae. 1973. xvi, 66p./
41. Phra Nakhon. 1973. xviii, 146p./42. Phra Nakhon Si Ayutthaya.
1972. xviii, 72p./43. Phuket. 1973. xvi, 64p./44. Prachin Buri.
1973. xvi, 64p./45. Prachuap Khiri Khan. 1973. xviii, 66p./46. Ranong. 1972. xvi, 64p./47. Ratchaburi. 1973. xvi, 66p./48. Rayong.
1973. xvi, 64p./49. Roi Et. 1973. xvi, 70p./
    50. Sakon Nakhon. 1973. xvi, 68p./51. Samut Prakan. 1972. xviii,
64p./52. Samut Sakhon. 1972. xviii, 64p./53. Samut Songkhram. 1973.
xviii, 64p./54. Saraburi. 1973. xviii, 68p./55. Satun. 1973. xviii,
64p./56. Sing Buri. 1973. xviii, 66p./57. Songkhla. 1973. xviii,
116p./58. Si Sa Ket. 1973. xvi, 68p./59. Sukhothai. 1973. xvi,
68p./60. Suphan Buri. 1973. xvi, 66p./61. Surat Thani. 1973. xvii,
70p./62. Surin. 1973. xvi, 68p./63. Tak. 1973. xviii, 66p./64.
Thon Buri. 1972. xviii, 142p./65. Trang. 1973. xviii, 66p./66.
Trat. 1972. xvi, 64p./67. Ubon Ratchathani. 1973. xvi, 124p./68.
Udon Thani. 1973. xviii, 114p./69. Uthai Thani. 1973. xvi, 66p./
70. Uttaradit. 1973. xvi, 66p./71. Yala. 1972. xviii, 66p. [PRC,
BC

Thailand. National Statistical Office.
    1970 population and housing census. Bangkok, 1973. 5v.
1970.2-1   Central region. 1973. xvi, 136p. [PRC
  .2-2   Southern region. 1973. xviii, 124p. [PRC
  .2-3   Northern region. 1973. xviii, 124p. [PRC
  .2-4   Northeastern region. 1973. xvi, 126p. [PRC
  .2-5   Whole kingdom. 1973. xviii, 158p. [PRC, BC

Thailand. National Statistical Office.
  .3   Selected tables from 1 percent sample, 1970 population and housing
    census. Bangkok, 1973. xx, 14p. [PRC, BC

Thailand. National Statistical Office.
    1970 population and housing census. Subject reports. Bangkok,
    1976- . Nos. 1- .
  .4-1   Economic characteristics. By Fred Arnold and Supani Boonpratu-
    ang. 1976. 77p. illus. [PRC, UN, E-W, OPR
  .4-2   Migration. By Fred Arnold and Supani Boonpratuang. 1976. 73p.
    illus. [UN, E-W, OPR
  .4-3   Fertility. By Aphichat Chamrathrithirang and Supani Boonpra-
    tuang. 1977. 75p. [E-W, OPR

TIMOR

[Since 1976 a province of Indonesia].   Capital: Dili.
Statistical Agency: Central Bureau of Statistics
                      [Biro Pusat Statistik]
                      P.O. Box 3
                      Djakarta,
Publications Distributor: same

        Portugal.   Instituto Nacional
           de Estatística.
1950.1   Censo da população do ultra-   Census of the population in the
       mar de 1950:   9, Provincia de   overseas territories in 1950:
       Timor./Recensement de la popu-   9, Province of Timor.
       lation dans les territoires d'   [Harvard, UN, LC, PRC, RPI
       outre-mer en 1950:   9, Province
       de Timor.   In: Boletin mensal
       do INE, Ano 24, no. 1, Janeiro
       1952.   Pp. 7-9.

        Timor.   Repartição Provincial
           dos Serviços de Estatís-
           tica.
1960.1   População por sexos, con-   Population by sex, councils and
       celhos e circunscrição, segun-   areas, according to the census
       do o censo de 1960.   n.p., n.   of 1960.
       d. 1 typewritten page.   [PRC

        Portugal.   Instituto Nacional de Estatística.
1970   [1970 recenseamento da população...
           [See Portugal 1970.3]

TOGO

Republic of Togo.   Capital: Lomé
Statistical Agency: Statistical Office
                     [Direction de la Statistique]
                     B.P. No. 118
                     Lomé,
Publications Distributor: same

	France. INSEE [and] Service Colonial des Statistiques.	
1946	Résultats du recensement de 1946...	
	[See French Overseas Territories, Nos. 1946.1-1, 2 and 3.]	

         France. INSEE [and] Service des Statistiques.
            Les français d'origine métropolitaine...
            [See French Overseas Territories, No. 1946.2.]

         France. INSEE.
1951   Le recensement de la population non originaire...
            [See French Overseas Territories, No. 1951.1.]

	France. INSEE.	
.2	Premiers résultats du recensement de 1951 dans les territoires d'outre-mer (population non originaire): 2ème partie, Togo-Cameroun. Paris, n.d. [12], 87, [2]p. (BMSOM, supplément série "statistiques," No. 15).	First results of the census of 1951 in the overseas territories (non-indigenous population): Part 2, Togo-Cameroon. [UN, RPI

	Togo. Service de la Statistique Générale.	
	Recensement général de la population du Togo, 1958/60. Lomé, 1959-1963. Fasc. 1-6 in 7v.	General census of the population of Togo, 1958/60.
1960.1-1	Le recensement de la population urbaine du Togo, 1958-59. (Premiers résultats). 1959. 107p.	Census of the urban population of Togo, 1958-59. First results. [PRC, RPI
.1-2	Recensement général de la population (1958-1960). (Liste des villages). 1961. 45, 81p.	General census of the population (1958-1960). List of villages. [NWU, LC, RPI
	Présentation d'ensemble. 1962. 2v.	Total results.
.1-3-1	I. Étude régionale. 69p.	Regional study. [LC, RPI
.1-3-2	II. Répartition des ethnies. 165p.	Distribution of ethnics. [LC, RPI
.1-4	Méthodologie. 1962. 98p.	Methodology. [LC, RPI

1960.1-5	Résultats définitifs.	Final results.
	1962. 135p.	[NWU, LC, OPR, RPI
.1-6	Résultats défintifs hors	Final results outside of urban
	communes urbaines. 1963. 51p.	communes.
		[NWU, PRC, OPR, LC, RPI

Togo. Service de la Statisti-
    que Générale.
    Enquête démographique, 1961.   Demographic survey, 1961.
    1963-1965. Fasc. 1-2.

1961.1-1	Méthodologie. 1963. [ii],	Methodology.
	144p.	[NWU, RPI
.1-2	Résultats définitifs.	Final results.
	1965. [ii], 137p.	[NWU, PRC, LC, RPI

Togo. Service de la Statistique.
1970.0-1	Recensement général de la	General census of the population.
	population. Résultats provi-	Provisional summary results of
	soires sommaires du recensement.	the census.
	Lomé, 1973. 1 table.	[PRC

Togo. Direction de la Statis-
    tique.
.1	Recensement général de la	General census of the population
	population (mars-avril 1970).	(March-April 1970).
	Lomé, 1974. 80p.	[UN, RPI

Togo. Direction de la Statis-
    tique.
    Recensement général de la
    population (mars-avril 1970).
    Lomé, 1974-1979. Vol. I-IV.
.2-1	I. Méthodologie et pre-	Methodology and first results.
	miers résultats. 1974. 146p.	[NWU, PRC, LC, UN, RPI
.2-2	II. Résultats détaillés	Detailed results by circonscrip-
	par circonscription. 1975. [6],	tions.
	ii, 662p.	[NWU, PRC, LC, UN, RPI
.2-3		
.2-4		

It is presumed that the next census will be taken in 1980.

TOKELAU ISLANDS

Tokelau Islands Dependency (New Zealand)   Capital: Administered from Apia,
Statistical Agency: Department of Statistics   Western Samoa.
                     Private Bag
                     Wellington C.1., NEW ZEALAND
Publications Distributor: Government Printing Office
                           Private Bag
                           Wellington, NEW ZEALAND

     Note: Numbers are those of the New Zealand set where applicable.

     New Zealand. Census and Statistics Department.
1945.2-2   Population census, 1945. Volume II, Island Territories: Cook
     Islands and Niue, Tokelau Islands, Western Samoa.   Auckland, Leigh-
     tons Ltd., 1947. [4], 14p. [PRC, RPI

     New Zealand. Department of Island Territories.
1951.1   Population census, 25 September 1951. Wellington, Government
     Printer, 1954. 28p. maps. [PRC, UN, BC, RPI

     New Zealand. House of Representatives.
1956.1   Journal of the House of Representatives of New Zealand, 1957.
     Appendix A-3. Wellington, Government Printer, 1957. P. 107. [NYPL,
     RPI

     New Zealand. House of Representatives.
1961.1   Journal of the House of Representatives of New Zealand, 1962.
     Appendix A-3. Wellington, Government Printer, 1962. P.   [

     New Zealand. Department of Statistics.
1966.4-1   New Zealand census of population and dwellings, 1966. Volume 1.
     Increase and location of population. Wellington, Government Printer,
     1967. P. 10. [PRC

     New Zealand. Department of Statistics.
1971.2-1   New Zealand census of population and dwellings, 1971. Volume 1.
     Increase and location of population. Wellington, Government Printer,
     1972. P. 15. [PRC

TONGA

Kingdom of Tonga.   Capital: Nuku' Alofa
Statistical Agency: Statistics Department
                     P.O. Box 149
                     Nuku' Alofa,
Publications Distributor: same

        Tonga. Census Office.
1956.1   Report on the results of the 1956 census. By M.U. Tupouniua.
          Nuku' Alofa, Government Printer, 1958. iv, 101, [2]p. [PRC, BC, LC,
          RPI

        Tonga. Census Office.
1966.1   Report on the results of the 1966 census. By Sione N. Fiefia.
          [Nuku' Alofa], 1968. 116p. [PRC, OPR, RPI

        Tonga. Census Office.
1975.1   Population and housing. Nuku' Alofa, 1975. 16p. [E-W, OPR

TRANSKEI

[Independence from South Africa, 1976]   Capital: Umtata

No country but South Africa has recognized this black homeland as a separate nation.

The 1970 South Africa census has figures for economic regions and districts (Bantu Homelands) that correspond more or less to this area. See economic area No. 73, Transkei, also South Africa 1970.2-19-1 (Xhosa).

TRIESTE

[Trieste is now divided between Italy and Yugoslavia.]

Trieste. British–United States Zone.
1949.1   Report on the administration of the British/United States zone of
the Free Territory of Trieste, 1 April to 30 June 1949. Report No. 7.
15, xiv p. [UN, RPI

Italy. Istituto Central de
          Statistica.
1951.1   IX censimento generale della   Ninth general census of popula-
popolazione e rikazione delle   tion and housing. Third general
abitazioni. III censimento gene-   census of industry and commerce,
rale dell'industria e del com-   4–5 November 1951. First general
mercio, 4 e 5 novembre 1951.   results of the census; de jure
Primi risultati generali dei   and de facto population; housing
censimenti; popolazione residen-   ...preliminary data. Part 28.
te e presente; abitazioni e...   Territory of Trieste.
dati provisori. Fascicolo 28.   [TXU, RPI
Territorio de Trieste.   Roma,
Tipografia Failli, 1956. 19p.

Yugoslavia. Inštut za Narod-
          nostna Upravanja.
.2   Tržaško ozemlje ter goriška   Territory of Trieste and regions
in videmska pokrajina. Po ljud   of Gorizia and Udine. According
skem štetju 4. novembra 1951.   to the population census of 4
(S sloven skimi in italijan-   November 1951 (with Slovenian
skimi krajevnimi imeni). [By]   and Italian place names. Compiled
Dr. Lavo Čermelj. Ljubljana,   by Dr. Lavo Čermelj.
1958. 84p. 4 maps.   [LC, RPI

Note: The Trieste area west of the new Yugoslav territory was made a
free territory after WW II. In 1954 the city and 90 square miles were
transferred to Italy and the rest went to Yugoslavia.

TRINIDAD AND TOBAGO

Republic of Trinidad and Tobago   Capital: Port of Spain
Statistical Agency: Central Statistical Office
                      2 Edward Street, Textel Building
                      Port of Spain,
Publications Distributor: same

Jamaica.   Central Bureau of Statistics.
1946   West Indian census, 1946.   Kingston, Government Printer, 1948-
           1950.
               [See Commonwealth Caribbean, Nos. 1946.1-A and G.]

           Trinidad and Tobago.   Register-General Department.
     .2   Census of the Colony of Trinidad and Tobago, 1946.   [Port of Spain],
           1948.   iii, 616p.   [LC

           Trinidad and Tobago.   Central Statistical Office.
1960   East Caribbean population census of 1960.   Port of Spain, 1963-
           1970.
               [See Commonwealth Caribbean, Nos. 1960.1-1-A, B and S.
                                         1960.1-2-T-A and B
                                         1960.1-3-T-1 through 9.]

           West Indies.   University.   Census Research Programme.
1970   1970 population census of the Commonwealth Caribbean.   Kingston,
           Herald Limited, 1973-   .
               [See Commonwealth Caribbean, Nos. 1970.1-1
                                                  1970.1-2-?
                                                  1970.1-3
                                                  1970.1-4-2 and 16
                                                  1970.1-5
                                                  1970.1-6-1
                                                  1970.1-7
                                                  1970.1-8-a, b, and c.
                                                  1970.1-9-1
                                                  1970.1-10-1 and 4.]

           Trinidad and Tobago.   Central Statistical Office.   Population Census
               Division.
               1970 population census.   Bulletin.   Port of Spain, 1971-1975.   6v.
     .2-1   [Population and housing by sex and administrative area].   1971.
           6p.   [BC, PRC
     .2-1a   [Non-institutional population].   1974.   19p.   [PRC
     .2-2   Housing.   1974.   p.   [IASI
     .2-3   Fertility.   1974.   [IASI
     .2-4   Education.   1975.   17p.   [PRC
     .2-5   Religion.   1975.   23p.   [PRC

TUNISIA

Tunisian Republic.   Capital: Tunis
Statistical Agency: National Institute of Statistics
                       [Institut National de la Statistique]
                       27 rue du Liban/B.P. No. 65
                       Tunis,
Publications Distributor: same

> Tunisia. Service Tunisien des
>   Statistiques.

1946.1   Dénombrement de la population   Enumeration of the European and
civile européenne et tunisienne   Tunisian civilian population as
en Tunisie au 1er novembre 1946.   of November 1, 1946.
Tunis, 1947. In: Bulletin du   [UN, PRC, RPI
service tunisien des statisti-
ques, 2ème trimestre 1947. Pp.
41-73.

> Tunisia. Service des Statis-
>   tiques.

1956.1   Recensement général de la   General census of the population
population de la Tunisie du 1   of Tunisia as of February 1, 1956:
febrier 1956: répartition géo-   geographic distribution of the
graphique de la population.   population.
Tunis, Impr. Officielle, 1957.   [BC, PRC
191p.

[Other data from the 1956 census can be found in various editions of
the Annuaire Statistique de la Tunisie, e.g. 1960.]

> Tunisia. Service des Statisti-
>   ques Démographiques.

Recensement général de la   General census of population and
population et des logements, 3   housing, May 3, 1966.
mai 1966.   [Tunis, 1968] Fasc.
1-3.
1966.1-1   Population par âge, sexe   Population by age, sex and marital
et état matrimonial. unpaged.   status.
                                              [UN, LC, PRC, RPI
  .1-2   Population par division   Population by administrative divi-
administrative. [3], 94p.   sions.
                                              [UN, PRC, RPI
  .1-3   Migration. [2], 106p.   Migration.
                                              [UN, PRC, RPI

> Tunisia. Institut National de
>   la Statistique.

Recensement général de la   General census of population and
population et des logements du   housing, May 3, 1966.
3 mai 1966.   Tunis, 1973. Vol.
I-IV.

.2-1   I. Population par division administrative, caractéristiques démographiques, fécondité,
population étrangère. 271p.
.2-2   II. Migrations. 157p.

.2-3   III. Caractéristiques
educationnelles, caractéristiques économiques. 271p.
.2-4   IV. Ménages, logements.
106p.

Population by administrative divi-
sion, demographic characteristics,
fertility, foreign population.
[PRC, NWU
Migration.
[PRC, NWU
Educational characteristics, eco-
nomic characteristics.
[PRC, NWU
Households, dwellings.
[PRC, NWU

Tunisia. Institut National de
la Statistique.
1975.1   Recensement général de la
population et des logements, 8
mai 1975. Population par division administrative. Tunis,
1975. 242, [18]p.

General census of population and
housing, May 8, 1975. Population
by administrative division.
[PRC, OPR, LC, BC

Tunisia. Institut National de
la Statistique.
Recensement général de la
population et des logements, 8
mai 1975. Tableaux et analyses
des résultats du sondage au 1/
10éme. Tunis, 1975-   . Vol.
I-IV.

General census of population and
housing, May 8, 1975. Tables and
analyses of the results of the one-
in-ten sample.

.2-1   I. Logements. 1975.
221p.
.2-2   II. Ménages et chefs de
ménage. n.d. 237p.
.2-3

.2-4   IV. Caractéristiques d'
education. 1975. 201p.

Housing.
[PRC, LC
Households and heads of households.
[PRC, UN

Educational characteristics.
[PRC, UN

TURKEY

Republic of Turkey.   Capital: Ankara.
Statistical Agency: State Institute of Statistics
                     [Devlet Istatistik Enstitüsü (DIE)]
                     Bakanliklar
                     Ankara,
Publications Distributor: same.

Turkey. Istatistik Genel Müdür-
       lüğü.
     21 ekim 1945 genel nüfus sa-   General census of the population.
yimi./Recensement général de la   October 21, 1945.
population au 21 octobre 1945.
Ankara, 1948-1950. Cilt 1-65.
(Publication no. 286).
1945.1-1   Il, ilçe, bucak ve muh-   Population by provinces, districts,
tarliklar itibarile nüfus./Popu-   communes and villages.
lation par provinces, districts,   [PRC, UN, BC, RPI
communes et villages. 1948.
1v, 619p.
1945.1-2 through 1945.1-64. 2. Afyonkarahisar. 1949. 24p./3. Ağri. 1949.
22p./4. Amasya. 1949. 31p./5. Ankara. 1949. 56p./6. Antalya. 1949.
27p./7. Aydin. 1949. 37p./8. Balikeshir. 1949. 52p./9. Bilecik.
1949. 24p./10. Bingöl. 1949. 20p./11. Bitlis. 1949. 22p./12. Bolu.
1949. 24p./13. Burdur. 1949. 18p./14. Bursa. 1949. 60p./15. Çanak-
kale. 1949. 29p./16. Çankiri. 1949. 24p./17. Çoruh. 1949. 22p./
18. Çorum. 1949. 30p./19. Denizli. 1949. 22p./20. Diyarbakir. 1949.
32p./21. Edirne. 1949. 24p./22. Elâzig. 1949. 25p./23. Erzincan.
1949. 25p./24. Erzurum. 1949. 30p./
     25. Eskişehir. 1949. 33p./26. Gaziantep. 1949. 42p./27. Giresun.
1949. 22p./28. Gümüşane. 1949. 22p./29. Hakâri. 1949. 20p./30.
Hatay. 1949. 35p./31. Içel. 1949. 39p./32. Istanbul. 1949. 55p./
33. Izmir. 1949. 100p./34. Isparta. 1949. 22p./35. Kars. 1949.
26p./36. Kastamonu. 1949. 30p./37. Kayseri. 1949. 36p./38. Kirkla-
reli. 1949. 30p./39. Kirşehir. 1949. 25p./40. Kocaeli. 1949.
25p./41. Konya. 1949. 52p./42. Kütahya. 1949. 30p./43. Malatya.
1949. 38p./44. Manisa. 1949. 50p./45. Maras. 1949. 29p./46. Mar-
din. 1949. 26p./47. Muğla. 1949. 24p./48. Muş. 1949. 22p./48. [i.
e. 49] Niğde. 1950. 36p./
     50. Ordu. 1950. 24p./51. Rize. 1950. 22p./52. Samsun. 1950.
40p./53. Seyhan. 1950. 48p./54. Siirt. 1950. 26p./55. Sinop. 1950.
22p./56. Sivas. 1950. 32p./57. Tekirdağ. 1950. 32p./58. Tokat.
1950. 32p./59. Trabzon. 1950. 24p./60. Tuncili. 1950. 24p./61.
Urfa. 1950. 42p./62. Van. 1950. 24p./63. Yozgat. 1950. 25p./64.
Zonguldak. 1950. 42p. [BC, PRC, RPI
   .1-65   Türkiye nüfusu./Population   Population of Turkey.
de la Turquie. 1950. vi, 342p.   [BC, PRC, RPI

Turkey. Istatistik Genel Müdür-
       lüğü.
1948.1   1948 köy sayimi hülâsa sonu-   1948 village census summary re-
çlari. Ankara, 1952. [4], 43p.   sults.

specimen forms. (Publication no. 320).

[BC, PRC, RPI

Turkey. Istatistik Umum Müdürlüğü.
Genel nüfus sayimi, 22 ekim
1950./Recensement général de la
population au 22 octobre 1950.
Ankara, 1950-1951. Cilt 1-65.
(Publication no. 316).

General census of the population,
October 22, 1950.

1950.1-1   Muvakkat raklamar./Chif-
fres provisoires. 1950. 32p.
1950.1-2 through 1950.1-64.
.1-65   Türkiye nüfusu./Population
de la Turquie.   p.

Provisional figures.
[UN
[Same order and 1945.1-2, etc., above.] [
Population of Turkey.
[

Turkey. Istatistik Umum Müdürlüğü.
.2   Nüfusun vilâyet ve kazalar
itibarile. Köylerin de nüfus
gruplarina göre dağilisi 1950.
Ankara, n.d. 38p. (Publication no. 358).

Population by provinces and districts. Also population of villages by size groups 1950.
[PRC, RPI

Turkey. Istatistik Umum Müdürlüğü.
.3   Umumî nüfus sayimi 22 ekim
1950. Vilâyat, kaza, nahiye ve
köyler itibariyle nüfus./Recen-
sement général de la population
du 22 octobre 1950. Population
par provinces, districts, communes, et villages. Ankara,
n.d. 395p. (Publication no.
359).

General population census of October 22, 1950. Population by province, district, communes, and
villages.
[PRC, BC, Harvard, RPI

Turkey. Istatistik Genel
Müdürlüğü.
.4   22 ekim 1950, genel nüfus sayimi. Türkiye nüfusu. Istanbul, 1961. xiii, xiii, 400p.
specimen forms. (Publication
no. 410).

General population census, October 22, 1950. Population of Turkey.
[PRC, BC, OPR, RPI

Turkey. Istatistik Umum
Müdürlüğü.
1955.0-1   1955 genel nüfus sayimi.
Telgrafla alinan neticelar.
[Ankara?], 1955. [2], 16p.

1955 general population census.
First results by telegraph.
[PRC, BC, RPI

Turkey. Istatistik Umum
    Müdürlüğü.
.1   1955 genel nüfus sayimi. °/o   1955 general population census.
10 örnekleme usulü ile elde edi-   Estimated national totals based
len Türkiye neticeleri.   Ankara,   on a 10 per cent sample.
1956. 51p.   [BC, UN, PRC, RPI

.1e [Turkish-English version of the above.] Ankara, 1957. 65p. (Publication no. 372). [PRC, LC, UN, RPI

Turkey. Istatistik Umum
    Müdürlüğü.
.2   Nüfus gruplari itibarile se-   Population of cities and villages
hirler ve köyler 1955.   Ankara,   by size groups 1955.
1959. 46p. (Publication no.   [PRC, BC, LC, RPI
389).

Turkey. Istatistik Genel
    Müdürlüğü.
    23 ekim 1955, genel nüfus sa-   General population census, Octo-
yimi. Ankara, 1960-1961.   ber 23, 1955.
Parts 1-67. (Publication no.
399).
1955.3-1 through 1955.3-66. [One volume for each province.] [
.3-67. Türkiye nüfusu.   Istanbul,   Population of Turkey.
1961. xii, 387, ix p. (Publi-   [BC, PSC, PRC, RPI
cation no. 399).

Turkey. IGM.
.4   23 ekim 1955, genel nüfus   Census of population, October 23,
sayimi. Vilâyet, kaza, nihiye   1955. Population by province,
ve köyler itibariyle nüfus.   district, subdistricts and vil-
Ankara, 1961. lxxii, 572, [1]p.   lages.
(Publication no. 412).   [PRC, BC, OPR, RPI

Turkey. IGM.
1960.0-1   1960 genel nüfus sayimi.   1960 general population census.
Telgrafla alinan ilk neticeler.   First results by telegraph.
[Ankara], n.d. [4], 20p. (Pub-   [PRC, UN, RPI
lication no. 408).

Turkey. Devlet Istatistik
    Enstitüsü.
.1   1960 genel nüfus sayimi. °/o   1960 general population census.
1 örnekleme usulü ile elde edi-   Estimated national totals based
len Türkiye neticeleri.   Ankara,   on 1 per cent sample.
1962. viii, 38p. (Publication   [PRC, BC, UN, OPR, RPI
no. 433).

Turkey. DIE.
.2   23 ekim 1960, genel nüfus   General population census, Octo-
sayimi. Il, ilçe, bucak ve köy-   ber 23, 1960. Population by pro-

ler itibariyle nüfus. Ankara, 1963. lvi, 601p. (Publication no. 444).

vinces, districts, subdistricts and villages.
[BC, UN, PRC, OPR, RPI

Turkey. DIE.
.3   23 ekim 1960, genel nüfus sayimi. Türkiye nüfusu. Ankara, 1964. [12], lii, 514p. specimen forms. (Publication no. 452).

General population census, October 23, 1960. Population of Turkey.
[PRC, BC, PSC, LC, UN, OPR, RPI

Turkey. DIE.
.4   23 ekim 1960, genel nüfus sayimi.

(Publication no. 468).

General population census, October 23, 1960.

[

Turkey. DIE.
1965.0-1   1965 genel nüfus sayimi. Telgrafla alinan geçici neticeler./Recensement général de la population, 1965. Résultats provisoires reçus par télégramme. Ankara, 1965. 19p.

1965 general population census. Provisional results obtained by telegraph.
[PRC

Turkey. DIE.
.1   24 ekim 1965, genel nüfus sayimi. °/o 1 örnekleme sonuçlari. Türkiye toplami, Ankara, Istanbul ve Izmir sehirleri. Ankara, 1966. xvi, 97p. specimen forms. (Publication no. 508).

General population census, October 24, 1965. 1 per cent sample results. Totals for Turkey and the cities of Ankara, Istanbul and Izmir.
[PRC, BC, OPR

Turkey. DIE.
.2   Genel nüfus sayimi. Idari bölünüs. [Il, ilçe, bucak ve koy (muhtarlik) nüfuslari], 24. 10.1965. Ankara, 1968. xlvii, 673p. (Publication no. 537).

General population census. Administrative divisions [province, district, subdistrict and village (muhtarlik) populations].
[PRC, BC, PSC

Turkey. DIE.
.3   Genel nüfus sayimi. Nüfusun sosyal ve ekonomik, nitelikleri, 24.10.1965. Ankara, 1969. xi, [5], 708p. (Publication no. 568).

General population census. Social and economic characteristics of the population.
[PRC, BC, PSC

Turkey. DIE.
1970.0-1 25 ekim 1970, genel nüfus sayimi. Telgrafla alinan geçici sonuçlar. Ankara, [1970]. 19p. (Publication no. 616).

General population census, October 25, 1970. Provisional results obtained by telegraph.
[PRC, OPR

Turkey. DIE.
.1   25 ekim 1970, genel nüfus
sayimi. °/o 1 örnekleme sonuçlari.   Ankara, n.d.   28p.

General population census, October 25, 1970.   Results of 1 per
cent sampling.
[PRC, BC

Turkey. DIE.
.2   Genel nüfus sayimi, 25 ekim
1970. örnekleme sonuçlari.
Ankara, 1972. xii, 399p. (Publication no. 659).

General population census, October 25, 1970.   Sampling results.
[PRC, OPR, BC, LC

Turkey. DIE.
.3   Genel nüfus sayimi, idari
bölünus: il, ilçe, bucak ve
koy (muhtarlik) nüfuslari, 25.
10.1970.   Ankara, 1973. xlviii,
616p. (Publication no. 672).

General population census, administrative divisions: province,
district, subdistrict and village
(muhtarlik) populations.
[BC

Turkey. DIE.
       Genel nüfus sayimi, 25 ekim
1970.   Ankara, 1976?.   Cilt 1-
66. (Publication no. 690).

General population census, October 25, 1970.

1970.4-1 through 1970.4-66. [Only the following have been seen.] 1. Adana
ili. xiv, 107p./2. Adiyaman ili. xiv, 107p./6. Ankara ili.   xiv,
107p./16. Bursa ili. xiv, 107p./26. Eskişehir ili. xiv, 107p./34.
Istanbul ili. xiv, 107p./35. Izmir ili. xiv, 107p. [PSC

Turkey. DIE.
.5   Genel nüfus sayimi. Nüfusun
sosyal ve ekonomik nitelikleri,
25.10.1970.   Ankara, 1977.
222p. (Publication no. 756).

General population census. Social and economic characteristics
of the population.
[OPR

Turkey. DIE.
1975.0-1   26 ekim 1975, genel nüfus
sayimi. Telgrafla alinan geçici sonuçlar.   Ankara, 1975.
20p. (Publication no. 739).

General population census, October 26, 1975. Provisional results
obtained by telegraph.
[PSC

Turkey. DIE.
.1   26 ekim 1975, genel nüfus
sayimi. °/o 1 örnekleme sonuçlari (ikinci baski).   Ankara,
1976. xv, 49p. (Publication
no. 771).

General population census, October 26, 1975. 1 per cent sampling
results (2nd printing).
[PRC, UN, PSC, OPR

Turkey. DIE.
.2   Genel nüfus sayimi, idari
bölünüs. Il, ilçe, bucak ve
koy (muhtarlik) nüfusleri, 26.

General population census. Administrative divisions: province,
district, subdistrict and village

10.1975.   Ankara, 1977.   xliv,   population.
var. pag.   (Publication no. 813).   [PRC, UN, PSC

TURKS AND CAICOS ISLANDS.

Colony of the Turks and Caicos Islands.   Capital: Grand Turk.
Statistical Agency: Department of Statistics
                      9 Swallowfield Road
                      Kingston 5, JAMAICA
Publications Distributor: same

The 1943 census was included in order to complete the West Indian
census taken in 1946.

Jamaica.   Central Bureau of Statistics.
1943   Eighth census of Jamaica and its dependencies, 1943...
            [See Commonwealth Caribbean, No. 1943.1.]

Jamaica.   Department of Statistics.   Jamaica Tabulation Centre.
1960   West Indies population census.   Census of the Turks and Caicos...
            [See Commonwealth Caribbean, Nos. 1960.2-TC-1 and 2.]

West Indies.   University.   Census Research Programme.
1970   1970 population census of the Commonwealth Carubbean...
            [See Commonwealth Caribbean, Nos. 1970.1-1
                                          1970.1-2-?
                                          1970.1-3
                                          1970.1-4-15 and 16
                                          1970.1-6-3
                                          1970.1-7
                                          1970.1-8-a, b, and c
                                          1970.1-9-4
                                          1970.1-10-3 and 4.]

UGANDA

Republic of Uganda.   Capital: Kampala
Statistical Agency: The Statistics Division
                     Ministry of Finance, Planning and Economic Development
                     P.O. Box 13
                     Entebbe,
Publications Distributor: same

        East Africa High Commission. Statistical Department.
1948.1   African population of Uganda protectorate: geographical and tribal
        studies. East African population census, 1948. Nairobi, 1950. 59p.
        [LC, UN, TXU, NWU, PRC, RPI

        East Africa High Commission. Statistical Department.
  .2   Report on the census of the non-native population of Uganda protec-
        torate, taken on the night of the 25th February, 1948. Nairobi, W.
        Boyd, 1953. [5], 136p. [LC, UN, TXU, NWU, PRC, RPI

        East Africa High Commission. Statistical Department.
1959.1   Uganda census, 1959: non-African population. Nairobi/Entebbe,
        1960. [2], iv, 110p. specimen forms. [UN, TXU, NWU, PRC, RPI

        East Africa High Commission. Statistical Department.
        Uganda, General African census, 1959. Nairobi, 1960. Vol. 1-2
        in 6v.
  .2-1   I. Population by sex and age group for protectorate, provinces,
        districts, counties, divisions and parishes. 2, 189p. [UN, TXU, LC
        NWU, PRC, RPI
              II. Tribal analysis for... Parts 1-5.
  .2-2-1   ...protectorate, provinces, districts and counties. 2, 129p.
        [UN, TXU, LC, NWU, PRC, RPI
  .2-2-2   ...Buganda province, districts, counties and divisions. [2],
        pp. 130-277. [UN, TXU, LC, NWU, PRC, RPI
  .2-2-3   ...Eastern province, districts, counties and divisions. [2],
        pp. 278-450. [UN, TXU, LC, NWU, PRC, RPI
  .2-2-4   ...Northern provinces, districts, counties and divisions.
        [2], pp. 451-566. [UN, TXU, LC, NWU, PRC, RPI
  .2-2-5   ...Western province, districts, counties and divisions. [2],
        pp. 567-680. [UN, TXU, LC, NWU, PRC, RPI

        Uganda. Ministry of Economic Affairs. Statistical Branch.
  .3   Uganda census, 1959. African population. Nairobi, 1961. v, [2],
        103p. specimen forms. fold. map. [UN, BC, TXU, NWU, PRC, RPI

        Uganda. Ministry of Planning and Economic Development. Statistics
              Division.
        Report on the 1969 population census. Entebbe, 1971-1974. Vol.
        I-III.
1969.1-1   I. The population of administrative areas. 1971. iv, [2],
        469p. [PRC, OPR, NWU, LC
  .1-2   II. The administrative report. 1974. ii, 95p. [LC, OPR, PRC,
        NWU

1969.1-3   III.   Additional tables.   1973.   ii, ii, 257p.   [PRC, OPR, JB-F,
        NWU, LC

        Uganda.   [Ministry of Planning and Economic Development.   Statistics
              Division.]
     .2   Atlas of population census 1969 in Uganda.   By B.W. Langlands.
        [Entebbe], 1974.   200p.   [NWU, OPR

        The next census is to take place in 1979.

U.S.S.R.

Union of Soviet Socialist Republics   Capital: Moscow
Statistical Agency: Central Statistical Board
                     [TSentral'noe Statisticheskoe Upravlenie (TSU)]
                     Ulitsa Kirova 39
                     Moscow 103450,
Publications Distributor: Victor Kamkin, Inc.
                           12224 Parklawn Drive
                           Rockville, Maryland 20852

USSR. TSentral'noe Statisti-
     cheskoe Upravlenie.

1959.0-1   Vsesoiuznaia perepis' na-   All-union census of population
    seleniia 1959 goda. Moscow,   of 1959.
    Gospolitizdat, 1958. 51p.   [UN, RPI

USSR. TSU.

.1   Uroven' obrazovaniia, natsio-   Level of education, national com-
    nal'nyĭ sostav, vozrastnaia struk-   position, age and distribution of
    tura i razmeshchenie naseleniia   the population of the USSR by re-
    SSSP po respublikam, kraiam i ob-   public, region and province based
    lastiam po dannya vsesoiuznoĭ   on data from the all-union popu-
    perepisi naseleniia 1959 goda.   lation census of 1959.
    Moscow, Gosstatizdat, 1960. 38p.   [BC, UN, PRC, RPI

USSR. TSU.

    Itogi vsesoiuznoĭ perepisi   Results of the all-union popula-
naseleniia 1959 goda. Moscow,   tion census of 1959.
1962-1963. 16v.

.2-1   SSSP. 1962. 284p.   USSR [Whole country].
                       [UN, BC, PRC, RPI

1959.2-2 through 1959.2-16. [Republics]. 2. Russian Soviet Federated Social-
    ist Republic. 1963. 456p./3. Armenia. 1963. 116p./4. Azerbaijan.
    1963. 158p./5. Belorussia. 1963. 146p./6. Georgia. 1963. 162p./
    7. Kazakhstan. 1962. 202p./8. Kirgizia. 1963. 150p./9. Moldavia.
    1962. 104p./10. Tadzhikstan. 1963. 140p./11. Turkmenistan. 1963.
    150p./12. Ukraine. 1963. 210p./13. Uzbekistan. 1962. 168p./14.
    Estonia. 1962. 108p./15. Latvia. 1962. 106p./16. Lithuania. 1963.
    179p. [BC, LC, PRC, RPI

USSR. TSU.

1970.0-1   Vsesoiuznaia perepis' nase-   All-union census of population.
    leniia, 1970. Usenarodnoe delo.   General census business.
    Moscow, 1969. 63p. specimen   [PRC, LC
    forms.

USSR. Central Statistical Board.

.0-2   1970 population census in the USSR. Moscow, 1970. 19p. [PRC

USSR. TSU.
1970.1   Chislennost', razmeshchenie,
vozrastnaia struktura, uroven'
obrazovaniia, natsional'nyĭ sostav, iazyki i istochniki sredstav
sushchestvovaniia naseleniia SSSP.
Po dannym vsesoiuznoĭ perepisi
naseleniia 1970 goda.   Moscow,
Statistika, 1971.   34p.

Number, location, age composition,
education, nationality (ethnic)
group, languages and sources of
income of the population of the
USSR.   According to the data from
the all-union population census
of 1970.
[PRC, LC

USSR. TSU.
.2   O vozrastnoĕ strukture, urov-
ne obrazovaniia, natsional'nom
sostove, iazykakh i istochnikakh
sredstv sushchestvovaniia naseleniia na 15 ianvaria 1970 goda.
Moscow, 1971. 19p.

Age structure, educational level,
national (ethnic) composition,
languages and means of livelihood
of the USSR population according
to the data from the all-union
population census of January 15,
1970.
[BC, PRC

USSR. TSU.
     Itogi vsesoiuznoĭ perepisi
naseleniia 1970 goda.   Moscow,
Statistika, 1972-1974.   Vo. 1-7.
.3-1   Chislennost' naseleniia
SSSR, soiuznykh i avtonomnykh
respublik, kraev i oblasteĭ.
1972. 176p.
.3-2   Pol, vozrast i sostoianie
v brake naseleniia SSSR, soiuznykh i avtonomnykh respublik,
kraev i oblasteĭ. 1972. 272p.

.3-3   Uroven' obrazovaniia naseleniia SSSR, soiuznykh i avtonomnykh respublic, kraev i oblasteĭ. 1972. 576p.

.3-4   Natsional'nyĭ sostav naseleniia SSSR, soiuznykh i avtonomnykh respublik, kraev, oblasteĭ
i natsional'nykh okrugov. 1973.
648p.

.3-5   Raspredlenie naseleniia
SSSR po obschestvennim gryppam,
istochnikam cpedstv syschestovo-
vaniia i otrasliam narodnogo
khoziastva. 1973. 295p.
.3-6   Raspredlenie naseleniia
SSSR i soiuznykh respublik po
zaniatiiam. 1973. 807p.

Results of the all-union population census of 1970.

Population of the USSR, union and
autonomous republics, regions and
oblasts.
[PRC, LC
Sex, age and marital status of
the population of the USSR, by
union and autonomous republics,
regions and oblasts.
[PRC, LC
Educational level of the population of the USSR by union and
autonomous republic, region and
oblasts.
[PRC, LC
Nationality (ethnic) groups of
the population of the USSR, by
union and autonomous republic,
regions, oblasts and national
regions.
[PRC, LC
Distribution of the population
of the USSR by social group,
source of income, and industry
of employment.
[PRC, LC
Distribution of the USSR population, union and republics, by
occupation.
[PRC, LC

1970.3-7   Migratsiia naseleniia,   Migration of the population, size
   chislo i sostav semeĭ v SSSR.   and composition of families of
   Soiuznykh i avtonomnykh respub-   the USSR, union and autonomous
   likakh, kraiekh i oblastiakh.   republics, territories and ob-
   1974. 454p.   lasts.
                                             [PRC, LC

Note: There are also a number of articles published in VESTNIK STA-
TISTIKI [Statistical Bulletin] 1971 and following.

     Pravda.
1979.0-   The 1979 census: a preliminary report. In: Current digest of
   the Soviet Press (Columbus, Ohio), 31(16):1-6. May 16, 1979. [

UNITED ARAB EMIRATES

Capital: Abu Dhabi

Statistical Agency: Statistical Section
                      Department of Planning
                      Abu Dhabi,
Publications Distributor: Ministry of Foreign Affairs
                          P.O. Box 1
                          Abu Dhabi,

          Dubai. Government. Central Accounts Section.
1965.1   [Letter containing estimates of population for the Trucial States.]
          1965. 1p. [PRC

          Trucial States. Middle East Development Division.
1968.0-1   First population census of the Trucial States, March/April 1968.
          Methods report. [Abu Dhabi], 1968. [51]p. [PRC

          Trucial States. Middle East Development Division.
   .1   Trucial States census figures, 1968. [Abu Dhabi], 1970. 4, 11p.
          [PRC, LC

          United Arab Emirates. Central Department of Statistics.
             Population census 1975 of United Arab Emirates. [Abu Dhabi], 1977.
          Parts I-
1975.1-1

UNITED STATES

United States of America.   Capital: Washington, D.C.
Statistical Agency: U.S. Bureau of the Census
                    Washington, D.C. 20233
Publications Distributor: U.S. Government Printing Office
                    Washington, D.C. 20402

      U.S. Bureau of the Census.
         Census of population: 1950. A report of the seventeenth decennial
      census of the United States. Washington, D.C., GPO, 1952-1957. Vol.
      I-IV in 175v.
1950.1-1   I. Number of inhabitants. 1952. 1428p. maps. [PRC, RPI
            II. Characteristics of the population: number of inhabitants,
      general and detailed characteristics of the population. 1952-1953.
      Nos. 1-54 in 51v.
.1-2-1   United States summary. 1953. xi, 486p. [PRC, RPI
1950.1-2-2 through 1950.1-2-51/54. 2. Alabama. 1952. xxxi, 258p./3. Arizona
      1952. xxxi, 144p./4. Arkansas. 1952. xxxi, 208p./5. California.
      1952. xxxi, 483p./6. Colorado. 1952. xxxi, 182p./7. Connecticut.
      1952. xxxi, 242p./8. Delaware. 1952. xxxi, 132p./9. District of Col-
      umbia. 1952. xxviii, 106p./
         10. Florida. 1952. xxxi, 307p./11. Georgia. 1952. xxxi, 350p./
      12. Idaho. 1952. xxxi, 140p./13. Illinois. 1952. xxxi, 347p./14.
      Indiana. 1952. xxxi, 290p./15. Iowa. 1952. xxxi, 238p./16. Kansas.
      1952. xxxi, 222p./17. Kentucky. 1952. xxxi, 263p./18. Louisiana.
      1952. xxxi, 248p./19. Maine. 1952. xxxi, 132p./
         20. Maryland. 1952. xxxi, 178p./21. Massachusetts. 1952. 308p./
      22. Michigan. 1952. xxxi, 348p./23. Minnesota. 1952. xxxi, 259p./
      24. Mississippi. 1952. xxxi, 206p./25. Missouri. 1952. xxxi, 304p./
      26. Montana. 1952. xxxi, 144p./27. Nebraska. 1952. xxxi, 204p./28.
      Nevada. 1952. xxxi, 104p./29. New Hampshire. 1952. xxxi, 108p./
         30. New Jersey. 1952. xxxi, 272p./31 New Mexico. 1952. xxxi,
      138p./32. New York. 1952. xxxi, 460p./33. North Carolina. 1952.
      xxxi, 284p./34. North Dakota. 1952. xxxi, 140p./35. Ohio. 1952.
      xxxi, 520p./36. Oklahoma. 1952. xxxi, 256p./37. Oregon. 1952. xxxi,
      174p./38. Pennsylvania. 1952. xxxi, 544p./39. Rhode Island. 1952.
      xxxi, 134p./
         40. South Carolina. 1952. xxxi, 199p./41. South Dakota. 1952.
      xxxi, 156p./42. Tennessee. 1952. xxxi, 328p./43. Texas. 1952. xxxi,
      607p./44. Utah. 1952. xxxi, 154p./45. Vermont. 1952. xxxi, 104p./
      46. Virginia. 1952. xxxi, 310p./47. Washington. 1952. xxxi, 239p./
      48. West Virginia. 1952. xxxi, 230p./49. Wisconsin. 1952. xxxi,
      230p./
         50. Wyoming. 1952. xxix, 116p./51-54. Territories and possessions
      (Alaska, Hawaii, Puerto Rico, American Samoa, Canal Zone, Guam, and
      Virgin Islands). 1953. Var. pag. [PRC, RPI
            III. Census tract statistics. 1952-1953. 64v.
1950.1-3-1 through 1950.1-3-64. 1. Akron./2. Atlanta./3. Austin./4. Balti-
      more./5. Birmingham./6. Boston./7. Bridgeport./8. Buffalo./9. Chatta-
      nooga./10. Chicago./11. Cincinnati./12. Cleveland./13. Columbus./14.
      Dallas./15. Dayton./16. Denver./17. Detroit./18. Duluth./19. Durham./

20. Flint./21. Fort Worth./22. Greensboro./23. Hartford./24. Houston./25. Indianapolis./26. Kalamazoo./27. Kansas City./28. Los Angeles./29. Louisville./30. Memphis./31. Miami./32. Milwaukee./33. Minneapolis-St. Paul./34. Nashville./35. New Haven./36. New Orleans./37. New York./38. Norfolk./39. Oklahoma City./

40. Omaha./41. Paterson./42. Philadelphia./43. Pittsburgh./44. Providence./45. Richmond./46. Sacramento./47. St. Louis./48. San Diego./49. San Francisco-Oakland./50. San Jose./51. Seattle./52. Spokane./53. Springfield./54. Syracuse./55. Tacoma./56. Toledo./57. Trenton./58. Utica./59. Washington, D.C./

60. Westchester County./61. Wichita./62. Honolulu./63. Portland./64. Rochester. [TXU, RPI

IV. Special reports. 1953-1957. 20v.

1950.1-4-1A	Employment and personal characteristics. 1953. 145p. [PRC, RPI	
.1-4-1B	Occupational characteristics. 1956. 262p. [PRC, RPI	
.1-4-1C	Occupation by industry. 1954. 75p. [PRC, RPI	
.1-4-1D	Industrial characteristics. 1955. 82p. [PRC, RPI	
.1-4-2A	General characteristics of families. 1955. 225p. [PRC, RPI	
.1-4-2B	Detailed characteristics of families. [Never published]	
.1-4-2C	Institutional population. 1953. 209p. [PRC, RPI	
.1-4-2D	Marital status. 1953. 64p. [PRC, RPI	
.1-4-2E	Duration of current marital status. 1955. 51p. [PRC, RPI	
.1-4-3A	Nativity and parentage. 1954. 296p. [BC, RPI	
.1-4-3B	Nonwhite population by race. 1953. 88p. [BC, RPI	
.1-4-3C	Persons of Spanish surname. 1953. 70p. [PRC, RPI	
.1-4-3D	Puerto Ricans in continental United States. 1953. 18p. [PRC, RPI	
.1-4-4A	State of birth. 1953. 108p. [PRC, RPI	
.1-4-4B	Population mobility: States and state economic areas. 1956. 311p. [PRC, RPI	
.1-4-4C	Population mobility: Farm-nonfarm movers. 1957. 244p. [PRC, RPI	
.1-4-4D	Population mobility: Characteristics of migrants. 1957. 335p. [PRC, RPI	
.1-4-5A	Characteristics by size of place. 1953. 64p. [PRC, RPI	
.1-4-5B	Education. 1953. 129p. [PRC, RPI	
.1-4-5C	Fertility. 1955. 184p. [PRC, RPI	

Note: The following two entries contain information not printed in any other reports.

U.S. Bureau of the Census.
Census of population: 1950. Advance report. Washington, D.C., GPO, 1951-1956. 2 parts in 8.
PC-10: Population (specified cities and adjacent tracted areas), by census tracts. 1951. 6v.
.2-10-(Number). 3. Atlantic City./4. Augusta./19. Des Moines./33. Macon./43. Northeastern New Jersey./57. Savannah. [BC, RPI
PC-14: Summary reports of population characteristics (various areas). 2v.

1950.2-14-21   Fertility by social and economic status, for Puerto Rico:
　　　1950. 1954. 28p. [PRC
　.2-14-22   Fertility by duration of marriage: 1950. 1956. 16p. [BC

　　　　U.S. Bureau of the Census.
　　　　　Census of population: 1950. Washington, D.C., GPO, 1950-1951.
　　　4v.
　.3-1   Alphabetical index of occupations and industries: 1950. 1950.
　　　374p. [BC, RPI
　.3-2   Alphabetical index of occupations and industries: 1950. (Re-
　　　vised edition). 1950. xxiv, 374p. [BC, RPI
　.3-3   Classified index of occupations and industries. 1951. xviii,
　　　228p. [BC, RPI
　.3-4   Puerto Rico censo de población: 1950. Indice alfabético de
　　　ocupaciones e industrias. 1951. xxxii, 81p. [BC, RPI

　　　　U.S. Bureau of the Census.
　.4   United States censuses of population and housing: 1950. Key to
　　　published and tabulated data for small areas. Washington, D.C., GPO,
　　　1951. v, 50p. appendices. [PRC, RPI

　　　　U.S. Bureau of the Census.
　.5   Principal data collections forms used in the 1950 censuses. Wash-
　　　ington, D.C., GPO, 1952. 41p. [PRC, RPI

　　　　U.S. Bureau of the Census.
　.6   County outline maps of the United States; county boundaries as of
　　　April 1, 1950. Washington, D.C., GPO, 1952. 2 maps. [BC, RPI

　　　　U.S. Bureau of the Census.
　.7   Portfolio of United States census maps: 1950. Washington, D.C.,
　　　GPO, 1953. 28p. [BC, RPI

　　　　U.S. Bureau of the Census.
　.8   United States population distribution, urban and rural: 1950.
　　　[Map]. Washington, D.C., GPO, 1953. 1 map. [BC, RPI

　　　　U.S. Bureau of the Census.
　　　　　Procedural studies of the 1950 censuses. Washington, D.C., GPO,
　　　1953-1955. Nos. 1-2.
　.9-1   Infant enumeration study, 1950. Completeness of enumeration of
　　　infants related to: residence, race, birth month, age and education
　　　of mother, occupation of father. 1953. vi, 64p. [PRC, RPI
　.9-2   The 1950 censuses - how they were taken. Population, housing,
　　　agriculture, irrigation, drainage. 1955. vii, [1], 222p. [PRC, RPI

　　　　U.S. Bureau of the Census.
　　　　　Census of population: 1960. The eighteenth decennial census of
　　　the United States. Washington, D.C., GPO, 1961-1968. Vol. I-IV in
　　　92v.
　　　　　　I. Characteristics of the population. Number of inhabitants,

general population characteristics, general social and economic characteristics, and detailed characteristics. 1963-1964. [Part A, Number of inhabitants, was also issued as a single volume. 1961. 1470p.]
57 parts in 54v.

1960.1-1-1   U.S. Summary. 1964. cxxvii, S-64, 821p. [PRC, RPI

1960.1-1-2 through 1960.1-1-54/57. [All are 1963 imprint date except Puerto
    Rico (1964)]. 2. Alabama. xlviii, 492p./3. Alaska. xlviii, 231p./
    4. Arizona. xlviii, 320p./5. Arkansas. xlvii, 392p./6. California.
    xlviii, 990p./7. Colorado. xlvii, 376p./8. Connecticut. xlviii,
    420p./9. Delaware. xlvii, 271p./10. District of Columbia. xlvii,
    191p./11. Florida. xlviii, 678p./12. Georgia. xlvii, 616p./13. Hawaii.
    xlviii, 272p./14. Idaho. xlvii, 255p./15. Illinois. xlviii, 776p./16.
    Indiana. xlvii, 552p./17. Iowa. xlvii, 503p./18. Kansas. xlvii,
    464p./19. Kentucky. xlviii, 487p./
        20. Louisiana. xlvii, 496p./21. Maine. xlviii, 247p./22. Maryland.
    xlviii, 379p./23. Massachusetts. xlviii, 519p./24. Michigan. xlvii,
    675p./25. Minnesota. xlvii, 539p./26. Mississippi. xlvii, 384p./27.
    Missouri. xlvii, 588p./28. Montana. xlviii, 275p./29. Nebraska.
    xlvii, 440p./30. Nevada. xlvii, 219p./31 New Hampshire. xlvii, 208p./
    32. New Jersey. xlviii, 687p./33. New Mexico. xlvii, 300p./34. New
    York. xlviii, 904p./35. North Carolina. xlvii, 527p./36. North Dakota.
    xlvii, 312p./37. Ohio. xlvii, 970p./38. Oklahoma. xlvii, 508p./39.
    Oregon. xlvii, 332p./
        40. Pennsylvania. xlviii, 1030p./41. Rhode Island. xlvii, 251p./
    42. South Carolina. xlvii, 387p./43. South Dakota. xlvii, 339p./44.
    Tennessee. xlvii, 600p./45. Texas. xlviii, 1112p./46. Utah. xlviii,
    291p./47. Vermont. xlviii, 208p./48. Virginia. xlvii, 564p./49. Wash-
    ington. xlvii, 428p./50. West Virginia. xlviii, 400p./51. Wisconsin.
    xlvii, 483p./52. Wyoming. xlvii, 219p./53. Puerto Rico. 1964. lxxv,
    400p./54-57. Outlying areas (Virgin Islands, Guam, American Samoa,
    and Canal Zone). [218]p. [PRC, RPI
        II. Subject reports. 1963-1968. 33v.

.1-2-1A   Nativity and parentage. 1965. 167p. [PRC, RPI
.1-2-1B   Persons of Spanish surname. 1963. xvii, 202p. [PRC, RPI
.1-2-1C   Nonwhite population by race. 1963. 274p. [PRC, RPI
.1-2-1D   Puerto Ricans in the United States. 1963. xiv, 104p. [PRC,
    RPI
.1-2-1E   Mother tongue of the foreign born. 1966. xiii, 25p. [PRC,
    RPI
.1-2-2A   State of birth. 1963. xiii, 176p. [PRC, RPI
.1-2-2B   Mobility for states and state economic areas. 1963. 490p.
    [PRC, RPI
.1-2-2C   Mobility for metropolitan areas. 1963. xvii, 348p. [PRC,
    RPI
.1-2-2D   Lifetime and recent migration. 1963. 506p. [PRC, RPI
.1-2-2E   Migration between state economic areas. 1967. xvi, 372, [1]p.
    [PRC, RPI
.1-2-3A   Women by number of children ever born. 1964. 343p. [PRC,
    RPI
.1-2-3B   Childspacing. 1968. xvi, 185p. [PRC, RPI
.1-2-3C   Current fertility by social and economic characteristics of
    women and their families. 1968. xx, 140p. [PRC, RPI

.1-2-4A   Families. 1963. xxiv, 453p. [PRC, RPI
.1-2-4B   Persons by family characteristics. 1964. xxii, 205p. [PRC
    RPI
.1-2-4C   Sources and structure of family income. 1964. 255p. [PRC,
    RPI
.1-2-4D   Age at first marriage. 1966. vii, 172p. [PRC, RPI
.1-2-4E   Marital status. [1965]. 180p. [PRC, RPI
.1-2-5A   School enrollment. 1964. xvii, 132p. [PRC, RPI
.1-2-5B   Educational attainment. 1963. xvi, 188p. [PRC, RPI
.1-2-5C   Socioeconomic status. 1967. xix, 268p. [PRC, RPI
.1-2-6A   Employment status and work experience. 1963. xviii, 226p.
    [PRC, RPI
.1-2-6B   Journey to work. 1963. xv, 564p. [PRC, RPI
.1-2-6C   Labor reserve. 1966. xix, 199p. [PRC, RPI
.1-2-7A   Occupational characteristics. 1963. xxxi, 530p. [PRC, RPI
.1-2-7B   Occupation by earnings and education. 1963. xiv, 304p.
    [PRC, RPI
.1-2-7C   Occupation by industry. 1963. xvii, 146p. [PRC, RPI
.1-2-7D   Characteristics of teachers. 1964. xvi, 58p. [PRC, RPI
.1-2-7E   Characteristics of professional workers. 1964. xvi, 145p.
    [PRC, RPI
.1-2-7F   Industrial characteristics. 1967. xx, 195p. [PRC, RPI
.1-2-8A   Inmates of institutions. 1963. xix, 303p. [PRC, RPI
.1-2-8B   Income of the elderly population. 1963. xii, 207p. [PRC,
    RPI
.1-2-8C   Veterans. 1964. xv, 99p. [PRC, RPI
    III. Selected area reports. 1963-1964. 5v.
.1-3-1A   State economic areas. 1963. xvii, 464p. [PRC, RPI
.1-3-1B   Size of place. 1964. xix, 78p. [PRC, RPI
.1-3-1C   Americans overseas. 1964. 151p. [PRC, RPI
.1-3-1D   Standard metropolitan statistical areas. 1963. xv, 747p.
    [PRC, RPI
.1-3-1E   Type of place. 1964. xxii, 459p. [PRC, RPI
    IV. Summary and analytical report. [Not published].

    U.S. Bureau of the Census.
      U.S. censuses of population and housing: 1960. Final reports.
    Washington, D.C., GPO, 1961-1962. Vol. 1-3 in 250v.
        1. Census tracts. 1961-1962. 180 parts in 181v.
1960.2-1-1 through 1960.2-1-180. 1. Abilene./2. Akron./3. Albany-Schenectady-
    Troy./4. Albuquerque./5. Allentown-Bethlehem-Easton./6. Altoona./7. Ann
    Arbor./8. Atlanta./9. Atlantic City./10. Augusta./11. Austin./12. Bing-
    hamton./17. Birmingham./18. Boston./19. Bridgeport./20. Brockton./21.
    Buffalo./22. Canton./23. Charleston./24. Charlotte./25. Chattanooga./
    26. Chicago./27. Cincinnati./28. Cleveland./29. Colorado Springs./30.
    Columbia./31. Columbus. GA./32. Columbus. OH./33. Corpus Christi./34.
    Dallas./35. Davenport-Rock Island-Moline./36. Dayton./37. Decatur./38.
    Denver./39. Des Moines./
        40. Detroit./41. Duluth-Superior./42. Durham./43. El Paso./44. Erie./
    45. Evansville./46. Fall River./47. Flint./48. Fort Smith./49. Fort
    Wayne./50. Fort Worth./51. Fresno./52. Gadsden./53. Galveston-Texas
    City./54. Gary-Hammond-East Chicago./55. Grand Rapids./56. Green Bay./

57. Greensboro-High Point./58. Greenville./59. Hamilton-Middletown./
60. Harrisburg./61 Hartford./62. Honolulu./63. Houston./64. Indianapolis./65. Jackson./66. Jacksonville./67. Jersey City./68. Johnstown./
69. Kalamazoo./70. Kansas City./71. Knoxville./72. Lancaster./73. Lansing./74. Laredo./75. Las Vegas./76. Lawrence-Haverhill./77. Lexington./
78. Lima./79. Lincoln./
    80. Little Rock-North Little Rock./81. Lorain-Elyria./82. Los Ange-
les-Long Beach./83. Louisville./84. Lowell./85. Lubbock./86. Macon./
87. Madison./88. Manchester./89. Memphis./90. Miami./91. Middlesex
County./92. Milwaukee./93. Minneapolis-St. Paul./94. Mobile./95. Monroe./96. Montgomery./97. Muncie./98. Muskegon-Muskegon Heights./99.
Nashville./100. New Bedford./101. New Britain./102. New Haven./103.
New Orleans./104-1. New York City./104-2. Outside New York City./105.
Newark./106. Newport News-Hampton./107. Norfolk-Portsmouth./108. Norwalk./109. Odessa./110. Ogden./111. Oklahoma City./112. Omaha./113.
Orlando./114. Paterson-Clifton-Passaic./115. Peoria./116. Philadelphia./
117. Phoenix./118. Pittsburgh./119. Pittsfield./
    120. Portland, ME./121. Portland. OR./122. Providence-Pawtucket./
123. Pueblo./124. Raleigh./125. Reading./126. Richmond./127. Roches-
ter, VA./128. Rockford, IL./129. Sacramento./130. Saginaw./131. St.
Louis./132. Salt Lake City./133. San Angelo./134. San Antonio./135.
San Bernadino-Riverside-Ontario./136. San Diego./137. San Francisco-
Oakland/. 138. San Jose./139 Santa Barbara./140. Savannah./141. Scranton./142. Seattle./143. Shreveport./144. Sioux City./145. Somerset
County./146. South Bend./147. Spokane./148. Springfield, MO./149.
Springfield, OH./150. Springfield-Chicopee-Holyoke, MS./151. Stamford./
152. Steubenville-Weirton./153. Stockton./154. Syracuse./155. Tacoma./
156. Tampa-St. Petersburg./157. Texarkana./158. Toledo./159. Topeka./
    160. Trenton./161. Tuscon./162. Tulsa./163. Tyler./164. Utica-Rome./
165. Waco./166. Washington, D.C./167. Waterbury./168. Waterloo./169.
Wheeling./170. Wichita./171. Wichita Falls./172. Wilkes-Barre-Hazel-
ton./173. Wilmington./174. Winston-Salem./175. Worcester./176. York./
177. Youngstown-Warren./178. Mayaguez./179. Ponce./180. San Juan.
[BC, RPI
    2. Geographic identification code scheme. 1961. 51v.
1960.2-2-1 through 1960.2-2-51. U.S. Summary and 50 state reports (District
of Columbia and Delaware under same cover). [BC, RPI
    3. Census county division boundary descriptions. 1962. 18v.
1960.2-3-1 through 1960.2-3-18. 1. Alabama. 41p./2. Arizona. 11p./3.
California. 53p./4. Colorado. 26p./5. Florida. 34p./6. Georgia.
64p./7. Hawaii. 8p./8. Idaho. 24p./9. Kentucky. 53p./10. Montana.
26p./11. New Mexico. 16p./12. Oregon. 31p./13. South Carolina. 34p./
14. Tennessee. 49p./15. Texas. 93p./16. Utah. 16p./17. Washington.
40p./18. Wyoming. 11p. [BC, RPI

U.S. Bureau of the Census.
    Census of population: 1960. Washington, D.C., GPO, 1960. 2v.
 .3-1   Alphabetical index of occupations and industries. (Rev'd ed.)
    673p. [PRC, RPI
 .3-2   Classified index of occupations and industries. 403p. [PRC, RPI

U.S. Bureau of the Census.
1960.4   U.S. census of population: 1960. Availability of published and
unpublished data. Washington, D.C., GPO, 1961. 35p. [Rev'd 1964.
36p.] [PRC, RPI

U.S. Bureau of the Census.
.5   United States censuses of population and housing, 1960: principal
data-collection forms and procedures. Washington, D.C., GPO, 1961.
iv, 62p. [BC, RPI

U.S. Bureau of the Census.
.6   Minor civil divison (or census county division) maps: 1960.
Washington, D.C., GPO, 1962. 47 maps. [BC, RPI

U.S. Bureau of the Census.
.7   United States censuses of population and housing, 1960: procedural
history. Washington, D.C. GPO, 1966. vi, [2], 387p. [PRC, RPI

U.S. Bureau of the Census.
Evaluation and research program of the censuses of population and
housing: 1960. Washington, D.C., GPO, 1963-1973. Nos. 1-11.
.8-1   Background, procedures, and forms. 1963. 112p. [BC
.8-2   Record check studies of population coverage. 1964. 14p. [BC
.8-3   Accuracy of data on housing characteristics. 1964. 28p. [BC
.8-4   Accuracy of data on population characteristics as measured by
reinterviews. 1964. 27p. [BC
.8-5   Accuracy of data on population characteristics as measured by
CPS-Census match. 1965. 63p. [BC
.8-6   The employer record check. 1965. 18p. [BC
.8-7   Effects of interviewers and crew leaders. 1968. 91p. [BC
.8-8   Record check study of accuracy of income reporting. 1970. 22p.
[BC
.8-9   Effect of coders. 1972. 29p. [BC
.8-10   Accuracy of data on population characteristics for sub-groups
of the population. 1973.   p. [BC
.8-11   Effects of different reinterview techniques on estimates of simple response variance. 1972. 106p. [BC

U.S. Bureau of the Census.
1960 census monograph series. Washington, D.C., GPO, 1966-1971.
5v.
.9-1   Income distribution in the United States. By Herman P. Miller.
1966. 314p. [BC. LC
.9-2   Education of the American population. By John F. Folger and
Charles B. Nam. 1967. 299p. [BC, LC
.9-3   People of rural America. By Dale E. Hathaway, J. Allen Beegle,
and W. Keith Bryant. 1969. 292p. [BC, LC
.9-4   Changing characteristics of the Negro population. By Daniel O.
Price. 1970. 263p. [BC, LC
.9-5   People of the United States in the 20th Century. By Irene B and
Conrad Taeuber. 1971. 1083p. [PRC, BC, LC

U.S.   Bureau of the Census.
    Census of population: 1970.   Washington, D.C., GPO, 1972-1975.
    Vol. I-II in 101v.
1970.1-1-A   Number of inhabitants. 1972. 2v. [PRC, BC
            I.   Characteristics of the population. 1973-1974.
    .1-1-1   U.S. summary. 1974. 2v. [PRC
1970.1-1-2 through 1970.1-1-54/58. [All have 1973 imprint date except where
    noted.] 2. Alabama./3. Alaska./4. Arizona./5. Arkansas./6-1 & 2. Cali-
    fornia. 1974./7. Colorado./8. Connecticut./9. Delaware./10. District
    of Columbia./11-1 & 2. Florida./12. Georgia./13. Hawaii./14. Idaho./
    15-1 & 2. Illinois./16. Indiana. 1974./17. Iowa./18. Kansas./19. Ken-
    tucky./20. Louisiana./21. Maine./22. Maryland./23. Massachusetts./24.
    24. Michigan./
        25. Minnesota./26. Mississippi./27. Missouri./28. Montana./29. Neb-
    raska./30. Nevada./31. New Hampshire./32-1 & 2. New Jersey./33. New
    Mexico./34-1 & 2. New York./35. North Carolina./36. North Dakota./37-1
    & 2. Ohio. 1973-74./38. Oklahoma./39. Oregon./40-1 & 2. Pennsylvania./
    41. Rhode Island./42. South Carolina./43. South Dakota./44. Tennessee./
    45-1 & 2. Texas. 1974./46. Utah./47. Vermont./48. Virginia./49. Wash-
    ington./50. West Virginia./51. Wisconsin./52. Wyoming./53. Puerto Rico.
    1974./54-58. Guam, Virgin Islands, American Samoa, Canal Zone, Trust
    Territory of the Pacific Islands. [BC, LC, PRC
            II.   Subject reports. 40v.
    .1-2-1A   National origin and language. 1973. xi, 505, A-21p. [PRC,
    BC,
    .1-2-1B   Negro population. 1973. x, 207, A-24p. [PRC, BC
    .1-2-1C   Persons of Spanish origin. 1973. x, 199, A-24p. [PRC, BC
    .1-2-1D   Persons of Spanish surname. 1973. vii, 122, A-24p. [PRC,
    BC
    .1-2-1E   Puerto Ricans in the United States. 1973. xi, 123, A-24p.
    [PRC, BC
    .1-2-1F   American Indians. 1973. xvi, 192, A-24p. [PRC, BC
    .1-2-1G   Japanese, Chinese, and Filipinos in the United States. 1973.
    xi, 181, A-24p. [PRC, BC
    .1-2-2A   State of birth. 1973. viii, 277, A-14p. [PRC, BC
    .1-2-2B   Mobility for states and the nation. 1973. xi, 422, A-24p.
    [PRC, BC
    .1-2-2C   Mobility for metropolitan areas. 1973. xv, 424, A-20p.
    [PRC, BC
    .1-2-2D   Lifetime and recent migration. 1973. viii, 521, A-21p. [PRC
    BC
    .1-2-2E   Migration between state economic areas. 1972. x, 361, A-24p.
    [PRC, BC
    .1-2-3A   Women by number of children ever born. 1973. xvii, 379, A-
    25p. [PRC, BC
    .1-2-3B   Childspacing and current fertility. 1975. xxix, 463, A-22p.
    [PRC, BC
    .1-2-4A   Family composition. 1973. x, 298, A-24p. [PRC, BC
    .1-2-4B   Persons by family characteristics. 1973. xi, 168, A-21p.
    [PRC, BC
    .1-2-4C   Marital status. 1972. x, 299, A-21p. [PRC, BC

.1-2-4D   Age at first marriage. 1973. ix, 277, A-20p. ⌐PRC, BC

.1-2-4E   Persons in institutions and other group quarters. 1973. xiv, 518, A-21p. ⌐PRC, BC

.1-2-5A   School enrollment. 1973. ix, 344, A-21p. ⌐PRC, BC

.1-2-5B   Educational attainment. 1973. x, 252, A-21p. ⌐PRC, BC

.1-2-5C   Vocational training. 1973. xxi, 336, A-21p. ⌐PRC, BC

.1-2-6A   Employment status and work experience. 1973. xi, 421, A-21p. ⌐PRC, BC

.1-2-6B   Persons not employed. 1973. xx, 242, A-21p. ⌐PRC, BC

.1-2-6C   Persons with work disability. 1973. v, 174, A-21p. ⌐PRC, BC

.1-2-6D   Journey to work. 1973. xvii, 1132, A-21p. ⌐PRC, BC

.1-2-6E   Veterans. 1973. ix, 199, A-24p. ⌐PRC, BC

.1-2-7A   Occupational characteristics. 1973. xix, 805, A-21p. ⌐PRC, BC

.1-2-7B   Industrial characteristics. 1973. xiv, 376, A-21p. ⌐PRC, BC

.1-2-7C   Occupation by industry. 1972. xvi, 504, A-12p. ⌐PRC, BC

.1-2-7D   Government workers. 1973. xvi, 271, A-21p. ⌐PRC, BC

.1-2-7E   Occupation and residence in 1965. 1973. xiv, 116, A-21p. ⌐PRC, BC

.1-2-7F   Occupations of persons with high earnings. 1973. xiii, 119, A-21p. ⌐PRC, BC

.1-2-8A   Sources and structure of family income. 1973. xii, 475, A-21p. ⌐PRC, BC

.1-2-8B   Occupation by earnings and education. 1973. x, 407, A-21p. ⌐PRC, BC

.1-2-8C   Income of the farm-related population. 1973. xi, 820, A-24p. ⌐PRC, BC

.1-2-9A   Low-income population. 1973. xi, 465, A-24p. ⌐PRC, BC

.1-2-9B   Low-income areas in large cities. 1973. xxxiv, 853, A-24p. ⌐PRC, BC

.1-2-10A   Americans living abroad. 1973. vii, 153, A-19p. ⌐PRC, BC

.1-2-10B   State economic areas. 1972. x, 425, A-47p. ⌐PRC, BC

U.S. Bureau of the Census.

Census of population and housing: 1970. Washington, D.C., GPO, 1971-1972. Vol. 1-3 in 369v.

1. Census tracts. 1972. 241v.

1970.3-1-1 through 1970.3-1-241. 1. Abilene./2. Akron./3. Albany, GA./4. Albany-Schenectady-Troy./5. Albuquerque./6. Allentown-Bethlehem-Easton./ 7. Altoona./8. Amarillo./9. Anaheim-Santa Ana-Garden Grove./10. Anderson./11. Ann Arbor./12. Appleton-Oshkosh./13. Asheville./14. Atlanta./ 15. Atlantic City./16. Augusta./17. Austin./18. Bakersfield./19. Baltimore./20. Baton Rouge./21. Bay City./22. Beaumont-Port Arthur-Orange./ 23. Billings./24. Biloxi-Gulfport./

25. Binghamton./26. Birmingham./27. Bloomington-Normal./28. Boise City./29. Boston./20. Bridgeport./31. Bristol./32. Brockton./33. Brownsville-Harlingen-San Benito./34. Bryan-College Station./35. Buffalo./ 36. Canton./37. Cedar Rapids./38. Champaign-Urbana./39. Charleston, SC./ 40. Charleston, W.VA./41. Charlotte./42. Chattanooga./43. Chicago./44. Cincinnati./45. Cleveland./46. Colorado Springs./47. Columbia, MO./48. Columbia, SC./49. Columbus, GA./

50. Columbus, OH./51. Corpus Christi./52. Dallas./53. Davenport-

Rock Island–Moline./54. Dayton./55. Decatur./56. Denver./57. Des Moines./
58. Detroit./59. Dubuque./60. Duluth–Superior./61. Durham./62. El Paso./
63. Erie./64. Eugene./65. Evansville./66. Fall River./67. Fargo–Moor-
head./68. Fayetteville./69. Fitchburg–Leominster./70. Flint./71. Fort
Lauderdale–Hollywood, FL./72. Fort Smith./73. Fort Wayne./74. Fort
Worth./
  75. Fresno./76. Gadsden./77. Gainesville./78. Galveston–Texas City./
79. Gary–Hammond–East Chicago./80. Grand Rapids./81 Great Falls./82.
Green Bay./83. Greensboro–Winston-Salem–High Point./84. Greenville./85.
Hamilton–Middletown./86. Harrisburg./87. Hartford./88. Honolulu./89.
Houston./90. Huntington–Ashland./91. Huntsville, AL./92. Indianapolis./
93. Jackson, MI./94. Jackson, Miss./95. Jacksonville./96. Jersey City./
97. Johnstown./98. Kalamazoo./99. Kansas City./
  100. Kenosha./101. Knoxville./102. Lafayette, LA./103. Lafayette-
West Lafayette, Ind./104. Lake Charles./105. Lancaster./106. Lansing./
107. Laredo./108. Las Vegas./109. Lawrence–Haverhill./110. Lawton./111.
Lewiston–Auburn./112. Lexington./113. Lima./114. Lincoln./115. Little
Rock–North Little Rock./116. Lorain–Elyria./117. Los Angeles–Long Beach./
118. Louisville./119. Lowell./120. Lubbock./121. Lynchburg./122. Macon./
123. Madison./124. Manchester./
  125. Mansfield./126. McAllen–Pharr–Edinburg./127. Memphis./128. Meri-
den./129. Miami./.30. Midland./131. Milwaukee./132. Minneapolis–St.
Paul./133. Mobile./134. Modesto./135. Monroe./136. Montgomery./137.
Muncie./138. Muskegon–Muskegon Heights./139. Nashville–Davidson./140.
New Bedford./141. New Britain./142. New Haven./143. New London–Groton-
Norwich./144. New Orleans./145. New York./146. Newark./147. Newport
News–Hampton./148. Norfolk–Portsmouth./149. Norwalk./
  150. Odessa./151. Ogden./152. Oklahoma City./153. Omaha./154. Orlan-
do./155. Oxnard–Ventura./156. Paterson–Clifton–Passaic./157. Pensacola./
158. Peoria./159. Philadelphia./160. Phoenix./161. Pine Bluff./162.
Pittsburgh./163. Pittsfield./164. Portland, ME./165. Portland, OR./166.
Providence–Pawtucket–Warwick./167. Provo–Orem./168. Pueblo./169. Racine./
170. Raleigh./171. Reading./172. Reno./173. Richmond./174. Roanoke./
  175. Rochester, Minn./176. Rochester, NY./177. Rockford./178. Sacramento./179. Saginaw./180. St. Joseph./181. St. Louis./182. Salem./183.
Salinas–Monterey./184. Salt Lake City./185. San Angelo./186. San Antonio./187. San Bernardino–Riverside–Ontario./188. San Diego./189. San
Francisco–Oakland./190. San Jose./191. Santa Barbara./192. Santa Rosa./
193. Savannah./194. Scranton./195. Seattle–Everett./196. Sherman–Deni-
son./197. Shreveport./198. Sioux City./199. Sioux Falls./
  200. South Bend./201. Spokane./202. Springfield, Ill./203. Springfield, MO./204. Springfield, OH./205. Springfield–Chicopee–Holyoke./
206. Stamford./207. Steubenville–Weirton./208. Stockton./209. Syracuse./210. Tacoma./211. Tallahassee./212. Tampa–St. Petersburg./213.
Terre Haute./214. Texarkana./215. Tolego./216. Topeka./217. Trenton./
218. Tucson./219. Tulsa./220. Tuscaloosa./221. Tyler./222. Utica–Rome./
223. Vallejo–Napa./224. Vineland–Millville–Bridgeton./
  225. Waco./226. Washingotn, D.C./227. Waterbury./228. Waterloo./
229. West Palm Beach./230. Wheeling./231. Wichita./232. Wichita Falls./
233. Wilkes–Barre–Hazleton./234. Wilmington, Del./235. Wilmington, NC./
236. Worcester./237. York./238. Youngstown–Warren./239. Mayagüez./240.
Ponce./241. San Juan. [BC, LC

2. General demographic trends for metropolitan areas, 1960-
1970. 52v.
.3-2-1   U.S. summary. 1971. 120p. [PRC
1970.3-2-2 through 1970.3-2-52. [States]. [Same listing as for 1970.1-1-2
through 1970.1-1-52.] [PRC
3. Employment profiles of selected low-income areas. 1971-
1972. 76v.
.3-3-1   U.S. Summary-urban areas. 1971. xii, 216, A-31p. [PRC
1970.3-3-2 through 1970.3-3-76. 2. New York, NY--All survey areas./3. New
York, NY--Puerto Rican population of survey areas./4. Manhattan Borough, New York City--Summary./5. Manhattan Borough, New York City--
Summary./8. Brooklyn Borough, NYC--Area I./9. Brooklyn Borough, NYC--
Area II./10. Brooklyn Borough, NYC--Area III./11. Bronx Borough, NYC./
12. Queens Borough, NYC./13. Los Angeles, CA.--Summary./14. Los Angeles, CA--Area I./15. Los Angeles, CA.--Area II./
16. Chicago, IL--Summary./17. Chicago, IL--Area I./18. Chicago, IL--
Area II./19. Philadelphia, PA--Summary./20. Philadelphia, PA--Area I./
21. Philadelphia, PA--Area II./22. Detroit, MI./23. San Francisco./
24. Washington, D.C./25. Boston./26. Pittsburgh./27. St. Louis./28.
Baltimore./29. Cleveland./30. Houston./
31 Newark./32. Dallas./33. Minneapolis./34. St. Paul./35. Milwaukee./36. Atlanta./37. Cincinnati./38. Buffalo./39. San Diego./40.
Miami./41. Kansas City./42. Denver./43. Indianapolis./44. New Orleans./
45. Oakland./
46. Tampa./27. Portland, OR./48. Phoenix./49. Columbus./50. San
Antonio./51. Dayton./42. Rochester, NY./53. Louisville./54. Memphis./
55. Fort Worth./56. Birmingham./57. Toledo./58. Akron./59. Norfolk./
60. Oklahoma City./
61. Jersey City./62. Providence./63. Omaha./64. Youngstown./65.
Tulsa./66. Charlotte./67. Wichita./68. Bridgeport./69. Selected rural
counties in Alabama./70. Selected rural counties in Appalachia./71.
Selected rural counties in Arkansas./72. Selected rural counties in
California./73. Selected rural counties in Missouri./74. Selected rural counties in North Carolina./75. Selected rural counties in New
Mexico./76. Zuni Reservation, New Mexico. [BC, LC, PRC

U.S. Bureau of the Census.
Census of population: 1970. Washington, D.C., GPO, 1971. 2v.
.4-1   Alphabetical index of industries and occupations. xiv, I-165,
0-201p. [BC, PRC
.4-2   Classified index of industries and occupations. xiv, I-114,
0-137p. [BC, PRC

U.S. Bureau of the Census.
Census of population and housing: 1970. Evaluation and research
program. Washington, D.C., GPO, 1973-1975. Nos. 1-11.
.5-1   The quality of residential geographic coding. 1973. 15p. [BC,
PRC
.5-2   Test of birth registration completeness, 1964 to 1968. 1973.
8p. [BC, PRC
.5-3   Results and analysis of the experimental mail extension test.
1973. 25p. [BC, PRC

1970.5–4   Estimates of coverage of population by sex, race, and age: de-
       mographic analysis. 1974. 31p. [BC, PRC
    .5–5   The coverage of housing in the 1970 census. 1973. 48p. [BC, PRC
    .5–6   Effect of special procedures to improve coverage in the 1970
       census. 1974. 24p. [BC
    .5–7   The Medicare record check: an evaluation of the coverage of per-
       sons 65 years of age and over in the 1970 census. 1973. 28p. [BC,
       PRC
    .5–8   Coding performance in the 1970 census. 1974. 36p. [BC, PRC
    .5–9   Accuracy of data for selected population characteristics as mea-
       sured by reinterviews. 1974. 71p. [BC, PRC
    .5–10

    .5–11   Accuracy of data for selected population characteristics as mea-
       sured by the 1970 CPS-Census match. 1975. 122p. [BC, PRC

       U.S. Bureau of the Census.
          Census of population and housing: 1970.   Washington, D.C., GPO,
       1971–1976. Nos. 1-3 in 6v.
    .6–1   Procedural history. 1976. var. pag. [BC, PRC
    .6–2   Data-Collection forms and procedures. 1971. 115p. [BC, PRC
          Geographic identification code scheme. 1972. 4 parts.
    .6–3–1   Northeast region. var. pag. [BC, PRC
    .6–3–2   North Central region. var. pag. [BC, PRC
    .6–3–3   South region. var. pag. [BC, PRC
    .6–3–4   West region. var. pag. [BC, PRC

UPPER VOLTA

Republic of Upper Volta.   Capital: Ougadougou
Statistical Agency: National Institute of Statistics and Demography.
                     [Institut National de la Statistique et de la Démogra-
                        phie]
                     Ministère du Plan, du Développement Rural, de l'Environ-
                        nement et du Tourisme.
                     Ouagadougou,
Publications Distributor: same

        French West Africa. Service de
           la Statistique Générale.
1951.1   Population de l'A.O.F. en   Population of French West Africa
           1950-1951 par canton et groupe   in 1950-51 by canton and ethnic
           éthnique, chiffres provisoires.   group, provisional figures.
           Dakar, 1953. [135]p.   [UN, PRC, RPI

        French West Africa. Service de
           la Statistique Générale.
           Recensement de la population non autochtone...
           [See French Overseas Territories, No. 1951.2.]

        Note: The demographic inquiry of 1960-61 covered the entire country
        except for the urban centers of Ougadougou and Bobo Dioulasso.

        Upper Volta. Service de Statis-
           tique et de la Mécanographie.
1961.1   Enquête démographique par   Demographic survey by sampling
           sondage, 1960-61. Résultats dé-   1960-61. Final results.
           finitifs. Paris, INSEE, 1970.   [OPR
           466p.

        France. SEDES.
           Étude socio-economique de   Socio-economic study of Bobo
           Bobo Dioulasso. Paris, 1961.   Dioulasso.
           2 fasc.
    .2-1   Rapport principal.   Main report.
                                              [
    .2-2   Annexes.   Appendices.
                                              [

        Upper Volta. Service de la
           Statistique Générale.
1962.1   Recensement démographique: Demographic census: Ouagadougou,
           Ouagadougou, 1961-1962. Résul-   1961-1962. Final results.
           tats définitifs. Paris, INSEE,   [NWU, PRC, RPI
           1964. 93p.

        Provisional total population figures from the 1975 census has been
        released but citation to that publication has not been seen as yet.

URUGUAY

Oriental Republic of Uruguay.   Capital: Montevideo
Statistical Agency: General Bureau of Statistics and Censuses
                    [Dirección General de Estadística y Censos (DGEC)]
                    Cuareim 2052
                    Montevideo,
Publications Distributor: same

Uruguay. Dirección General de
    Estadística y Censos.
    IV censo general de pobla-
ción y II de vivienda, 16 de
octubre de 1963. Distribución
territorial de la población y
vivienda. Montevideo, 1963–
1965. 11v.

Fourth general census of population and second of housing, October 16, 1963. Territorial distribution of the population and
housing.

1963.1-1 through 1963.1-18. [Departamentos] 1. Artigas. 1964. iv, [1],
    22p./2. Canelones. 1965. iv, 33p./3. Cerro Largo.   /
    4. Colonia. 1964. 49p./5. Durazno. 1963.   p./6. Flores. 1964.
    iv, [1], 16p./7. Florida. 1963. iv, 28p./8. Lavalleja. 1963.   /
    9. Maldonado. 1964. iv, [1], 27p./10. Paysandú. 1963.   /11.
    Río Negro. 1963.   /12. Rivera. 1964. iv, 30p./13. Rocha.
    1964. iv, 30p./14. Salto. 1965. iv, 28p. /15. San José. 1964. iv,
    25p./16. Soriano. 1964. iv, [1], 31p./17. Tacuarembo. 1964. iv,
    27p./18. Treinta y Tres. 1964. iv, 24p. [BC, UN, LC, PRC, RPI

Uruguay. DGEC.
    Censo general IV de pobla-
ción, II de vivienda. Anticipación de resultados censales.
Analisis por muestreo. Montevideo, 1965. Vol. 1-2.
.2-1   1. 23p.
.2-2   2. 52p.

Fourth general census of population, second of housing. Advance
census results. Analysis by sample.

[UN, PRC, RPI
[UN, PRC, RPI

Uruguay. DGEC.
.3   Un ensayo de evaluación del
    IV censo general de población
    (Encuesta de cobertura). [Mon-
    tevideo, n.d.] [6], 23, 14, 1,
    14p.

Essay on the evaluation of the
fourth general census of population. (Coverage inquiry).
[UN, PRC, RPI

Uruguay. DGEC.
.4   IV censo de población, II de
    vivienda. Datos definitivos,
    cifras principales. Montevi-
    deo, 1969. 55p.

Fourth census of population, second of housing. Final data,
main figures.
[LC, PRC

Uruguay. DGEC.
.5   IV censo de población y II
    de vivienda, año 1963. Muestra

Fourth census of population and
second of housing, 1963.

de anticipación de resultados
censales. [Montevideo, 1964?]
xii, 109p.

Advance sample of census results.
[LC

Uruguay. DGEC.
    IV censo de población y II
de vivienda, año 1963. [Monte-
video, 1963-1973]. Vol. I-V.

Fourth census of population and
second of housing, 1963.

1963.6-1   I. Demografía. 1963.
  184p.

Demography.
[PRC, BC, LC

.6-2   II. Educación. 1973.
  83p.

Education.
[PRC, BC, LC

.6-3   III. Población económicamente activa. 1973. xxiv, 83p.

Economically active population.
[PRC, BC, LC

.6-4   IV. Migración interna.
  1973. 121p.

Internal migration.
[PRC, BC, LC

.6-5   V. Vivienda. 1963. 28p.

Housing.
[PRC, BC, LC

Uruguay. DGEC.
1975.0-1   V censo general de población; III de vivienda, año 1973
[sic]. Métodos y procedimientos.
Montevideo, 1975.   p.

Fifth general census of population; third of housing, 1973 [sic].
Methods and procedures.
[

Uruguay. DGEC.
.0-2   Plan preliminar de tabulaciones del V censo general de
población y III de vivienda, año
1975. Montevideo, 1975. [125]p.

Preliminary tabulation plan of
the fifth general census of population and third of housing, 1975.
[OPR

Uruguay. DGEC.
.0-3   V censo general de población, III de viviendas, año 1975.
Datos preliminares. 2da. ed.
[Montevideo], [1976]. [132]p.
maps.

Fifth general census of popula-
tion, third of housing, 1975.
Preliminary data.
[LC, NYPL

Uruguay. DGEC.
.0-4   V censo general de población, III de viviendas, año 1975.
Encuesta de cobertura. Montevideo, [1978]. 16, [4]p.

Fifth general census of population, third of housing, 1975.
Survey of coverage.
[

Uruguay. DGEC.
.1   V censo general de población
y III de viviendas. Muestra de
anticipación de resultados censales. [Cifras y comentarios].
3d. ed. Montevideo, 1977. iv,
224, 55p.

Fifth general census of population and third of housing. Advance sample of census results.
[Figures and commentaries].
[UN, IASI, LC, NYPL, BC

VATICAN CITY

State of the Vatican City.   Capital: Vatican City
Statistical Agency: Secretary of State
                     Government of the Holy See
                     Vatican City (Rome), ITALY
Publications Distributor: same

The population of the State of the Vatican City is published in "Ati-
vità della Santa Sede" which is edited annually by the Secretary of
State of the Vatican City.

VENEZUELA

Republic of Venezuela.   Capital: Caracas
Statistical Agency: General Bureau of Statistics and National Censuses
                     [Dirección General de Estadística y Censos Nacionales
                      (DGE y CN)]
                     Ministerio de Fomento
                     Centro Simón Bolívar
                     Caracas,
Publications Distributor: same

    Venezuela. DGE y CN.
      Octavo censo general de pob-   Eighth general census of popula-
lación.   Caracas. 1954-1957.   tion.
Parts 1-9 in 11v.
1950.1-1   Resúmenes principales.   Principal summaries.
   [1954]. 8p.   [TXU, PRC, RPI
 .1-2   Relación de localidades   Report of localities (capitals
  (capitales y no capitales) de   and non-capitals) of 1,000 and
  1.000 y más habitantes. [1954].   more inhabitants.
  10p.   [TXU, PRC, RPI
 .1-3   Resultados generales por   General results for states and
  entidades, distritos y munici-   territories, districts, and muni-
  pios. 1954. viii, 66, [3]p.   cipal districts.
    [TXU, LC, PRC, RPI
 .1-3a   Resultados generales por   General results for states and
  entidades, distritos y munici-   territories, districts and muni-
  pios. 1955. xv, 88p.   cipal districts.
    [TXU, LC, UN, PRC, RPI
 .1-4   Edad y estado civil, por   Age and marital status for states
  entidades y distritos y resumen   and territories and districts and
  nacional. 1954. 138p.   national summary.
    [TXU, LC, PRC, RPI
 .1-5   Población urbana y rural   Urban and rural population and
  y lugar de nacimiento. 1955.   birthplace.
  148p.   [UN, LC, PRC, RPI
 .1-6   Resúmenes principales de   Principal summaries of census
  grupos censales y viviendas   groups and domestic housing.
  familiares. 1955. 8p.   [TXU, PRC, RPI
 .1-7   Alfabetismo, asistencia   Literacy, school enrollment and
  escolar y nivel educacional   educational attainment.
  1955. [6], 121, [3]p.   [UN, PRC, RPI
 .1-8   Principales resultados   Principal national results--mini-
  nacionales--clasificaciones mí-   mal classifications in accordance
  nimas de acuerdo con el progra-   with the Census of the Americas
  ma del Censo de las Américas de   Program of 1950.
  1950. 1955. 56p.   [TXU, LC, PRC, RPI
 .1-8a   Principales resultados   Principal national results...(2d.
  nacionales...(reedición ampli-   printing amplified).
  ada). 1957. 94p.   [TXU, LC, PRC, RPI

.1-9   Nomenclador nacional de   National list of population cen-
centros poblados y divisiones   ters and political-territorial
político-territoriales. 1958.   divisions.
xxiv, 866p.   [TXU, LC, PRC, RPI

Venezuela. DGE y CN.
   Octavo censo general de pob-   Eighth general census of popula-
lación, 26 de noviembre de 1950.   tion, November 26, 1950.
Caracas, 1955-1960. Vol. I-XII
in 25v.
1950.2-1-1 through 1950.2-11-2.   [State volumes] 1-1. Distrito Federal. 1955.
xl, [19], 229p./1-2. Anzoátegui. 1955. xlii, [17], 422p./2-1. Apure.
1955. xliii, [16], 259p./2-2. Aragua. 1955. xxxvi, [17], 291p./3-1.
Barinas. 1956. xliv, [16], 276p./3-2. Bolívar. 1956. xxxviii, [16],
297p./4-1. Carabobo. 1956. xlvi, [16], 289p./4-2. Cojedes. 1956.
xxvi, [16], 233p./5-1. Falcón. 1957. li, [16], 412p./5-2. Guárico.
1957. xli, [16], 298p./6-1. Lara. 1957. xlix, [16], 333p./6-2. Mérida. 1957. xlii, [16], 352p./7-1. Miranda. 1958. liii, [16],
374p./7-2. Monogas. n.d. xliv, [16], 260p./8-1. Nueva Esparta. 1958.
xlvii, [16], 231p./8-2. Portuguesa. 1958. xlii, [16], 259p./9-1.
Sucre. 1959. xxxviii, [16], 380p./9-2. Táchira. 1959. xl, [16],
402p./10-1. Trujillo. 1960. xliv, [16], 381p./10-2. Yaracuy. 1960.
xli, [16], 292p./11-1. Zulia. 1959. lvi, [16], 369p./11-2. Territorios y dependencias federales. 1959. xxx, [1], 327p. [TXU, LC, PRC,
RPI
         Resumen general de la   General summary of the Republic:
   República:
.2-12-A   Población. 1957. xlix,   Population.
   [17], 669p.   [TXU, LC, JB-F, PRC, RPI
.2-12-B   Familias y viviendas.   Families and housing.
   1957. xliii, [9], 360p.   [TXU, LC, JB-F, PRC, RPI

Venezuela. DGE y CN.
.3   Empadronamiento especial de   Special enumeration of the Indian
la población indígena. n.d.   population.
117p.   [BC, PRC, RPI

Venezuela. DGE y CN.
   Croquis de municipios y loca-   Rough sketch of the municipal dis-
lidades. Programa censal de 1960.   tricts and towns. Census program
n.p., n.d. Vol. I-XXIII.   of 1960.
1961.1-1 through 1961.1-23.   1. Distrito Federal. 2p. 31 maps./2. Anzoátegui. 2p. 58 maps./3. Apure. 2p. 27 maps./4. Aragua. 2p. 35 maps./
5. Barinas. 2p. 37 maps./6. Bolívar. 2p. 23 maps./7. Carabobo. 2p.
48 maps./8. Cojedes. 2p. 23 maps./9. Falcón. 2p. 74 maps./10. Guárico. 2p. 42 maps./11. Lara. 2p. 44 maps./12. Mérida. 2p. 57 maps./
13. Miranda. 2p. 47 maps./14. Monagas. 2p. 24 maps./15. Nueva Esparta.
2p. 12 maps./16. Portuguesa. 2p. 27 maps./17. Sucre. 2p. 49 maps./
18. Táchira. 2p. 45 maps./19. Trujillo. 2p. 48 maps./20. Yaracuy.
2p. 30 maps./21. Zulia. 2p. 47 maps./22. Territorio Federal Amazonas.
2p. 6 maps./23. Territorio Federal Delta Amacuro. 2p. 5 maps. [TXU,
PRC, RPI

Venezuela. DGE y CN.
IX censo nacional de población.   Caracas, Taller Gráfico,
1962.

Ninth national census of population.

.3-1   Resultados comparativos
de población por distritos, municipios y sus capitales según
los censos de 1941, 1950, y
1961. 1962. 79p.

Comparative population results by
districts, municipal districts
and their capitals according to
the censuses of 1941, 1950 and
1960.
[TXU, LC, PRC, RPI

.3-2   Población urbana, inter-
media y rural, censos de 1961,
1950, 1941 y 1936. 1962. 87p.

Urban, intermediate and rural population, censuses of 1961, 1950,
1941 and 1936.
[TXU, LC, PRC, RPI

Venezuela. DGE y CN.
Noveno censo general de población (26 de febrero de 1961).
Caracas, Taller Gráfico, 1964-
1969. Parts 1-24 in 26v.

Ninth general census of population (February 26, 1961).

1961.4-1 through 1961.4-23-2. 1. Distrito Federal. 1964. lxii, 728p./2.
Area Metropolitana de Caracas. 1964. lxi, 344p./3. Anzoátegui. 1966.
lxxii, 776p./4. Apure. 1969. lxxiv, [8], 648p./5. Aragua. 1967.
lxxv, 678p./6. Barinas. 1968. lxxvii, [7], 674p./7. Bolívar. 1964.
lx, 734p./8. Carabobo. 1966. lxx, 692p./9. Cojedes. 1965. lxv,
618p./10. Falcón. 1966. lxxvi, 840p./11. Guárico. 1967. lxxxiv,
690p./12. Lara. 1964. lxvi, 796p./13. Mérida. 1967. lxxiii, 750p./
14. Miranda. 1965. lxiv, 804p./15. Monagas. 1967. lxxv, 644p./16.
Nueva Esparta. 1969. lxxv, [7], 640p./17. Portuguesa. 1969. lxxviii,
[2], 676p./18. Sucre. 1965. lxii, 724p./19. Táchira. 1965. lxvi,
700p./20. Trujillo. 1967. lxxvii, 758p./21. Yaracuy. 1964. lxviii,
726p./22. Zulia. 1964. lxviii, 810p./23-1. Territorios federales
Amazonas y delta Amacuro y dependencias federales. 1970. lxi, 659p./
23-2. Territorios federales... 1970. Pp. 663-1345. [TXU, LC, PRC,
RPI

Resumen general de la
República: 1966-1967. Parts
A & B.

General summary of the Republic.

.4-24-A   A. [Población]. 1966.
xiv, 23 graphs, 241p.

Population.
[TXU, BC, LC, JB-F, PRC, RPI

.4-24-B   B. [Vivienda y pobla-
ción]. 1967. xiv, 737p.

Housing and population.
[TXU, LC, JB-F, PRC, RPI

Venezuela. DGE y CN.
Noveno censo general de población (26 de febrero de 1961).
Nomenclador de centros poblados
y divisiones político-territoriales.   Caracas, Taller Gráfico,
1966. Vol. I-VI in 5v.

Ninth general census of population (February 26, 1961). List
of populated centers and politico-
territorial divisions.

.5-1   Región I. xxii, 150p.

(Distrito Federal, Aragua, Carabobo,
Miranda).
[TXU, LC, PRC, RPI

.5-2   Región II.   xxiv, 229p.   (Falcón, Lara, Yaracuy, Zulia).
                                        [TXU, LC, PRC, RPI
.5-3   Región III. xxiv, 186p.   (Mérida, Táchira, Trujillo).
                                        [TXU, LC, PRC, RPI
.5-4   Región IV.   xxiv, 186p.   (Anzoátegui, Monagas, Nueva Es-
                                        parta, Sucre).
                                        [TXU, LC, PRC, RPI
.5-5&6 Región V.   xxvi, 204p.   (Apure, Barinas, Cojedes, Guári-
        Región VI. xvi, 97p.   co, Portuguesa). (Bolívar, Terr.
                                        Amazonas, Terr. Delta Amacuro).
                                        [TXU, UN, LC, PRC, RPI

        Venezuela. DGE y CN.
.6   Noveno censo general de pog-   Ninth general census of popula-
      lación (26 de febrero de 1961).   tion (February 26, 1961). Poli-
      Division político-territorial.   tico-territorial division.
      Caracas, Taller Gráfico, 1966.   [LC, RPI
      132p.
.6a   (Revised edition). 1968.
      132p.   [PRC, RPI

        Venezuela. DGE y CN.
      X censo general de población   Tenth general census of popula-
      (2 de noviembre 1971). Resulta-   tion (November 2, 1971). Com-
      dos comparativos.   Caracas,   parative results.
      1972-1973. 4 parts in 58v.
.1-1   Venezuela. 1972. 25p.   Whole country.
                                         [PRC
        Areas metropolitanas. 1972.   Metropolitan areas:
1971.1-2-1 through 1971.1-2-25. 1. Caracas./2. Departamento Vargas/3. Los
      Teques./4. Maracay./5. Valencia./6. Puerto Cabello./7. Barquisimeto./
      8. Coro./9. Punto Fijo./10. Acarigua-Araure./11. Maracaibo./12. Cabi-
      mas./13. Lagunillas./14. Mérida./15. San Cristobal./16. Valera./17.
      Barinas./18. Maturin./19. Cumaná./20. Carupano./21. Ciudad Bolívar./
      22. Distrito municipal Caroni (San Felix)./23. Barcelona./24. Puerto
      La Cruz./25. El Tigre.   [LC
        Entidades federales. 1972.   Federal entities (States & Terr.)
1971.1-3-1 through 1971.1-3-24. 1. Anzoátegui./2. Apure./3. Aragua./4. Bari-
      nas./5. Bolívar./6. Carabobo./7. Cojedes./8. Distrito Federal./9. Fal-
      cón./10. Guárico./11. Lara./12. Mérida./13. Miranda./14. Monagas./15.
      Nueva Esparta./16. Portuguesa./17. Sucre./18. Táchira./19. Trujillo./
      20. Yaracuy./21. Zulia./22. Terr. Fed. Amazonas./23. Terr. Fed. Delta
      Amacuro./24. Dependencias federales. [PRC, RPI
        Regiones. 1973.
1971.1-4-1 through 1971.1-4-8. 1. Capital./2. Central./3. Centro-Occidental./
      4. Zuliana./5. de los Andes./6. Sur./7. Nor-Oriental./8. de Guayana.
      [JB-F

        Venezuela. DGE y CN.
.2   X censo de población y vivi-   Tenth census of population and
      endas. Venezuela. Resumen   housing. Venezuela. General
      general. 1974. xxxvi, 102p.   summary.
                                        [PRC, LC

Venezuela. DGE y CN.
    X censo de población y vivi-   Tenth census of population and
endas. Caracas, 1974–1977.   housing.
Parts 1–8 in 16v.
      Resumen nacional. 1974–   National summary.
1975. Parts 1–6.

1971.3-1   Características gene-   General characteristics.
rales. 1974. lxi, 321p.   [PRC
.3-2   Características gene-   General characteristics.
rales. 1974. 426p.   [PRC
.3-3   Características por   Characteristics by size of popu-
tamaño de centros poblados   lated centers.
1975. xix, 107p.   [PRC
.3-4   Residencia y lugar de   Residence and birthplace.
nacimiento. 1975. xxiii, 176p.   [PRC
.3-5   Características educa-   Educational characteristics.
tivas. 1975. xxiii, 221p.   [PRC
.3-6   Fuerza de trabajo.   Labor force.
1975. xxi, 253p.   [PRC, LC
      Resumen por entidades   Summary for federal entities
federales. 1975–1976. Part 7   (States and Territories).
in 4v.
.3-7-A   [Características gene-   General characteristics.
rales]. 1975. 736p.   [PRC
.3-7-B   [Fuerza de trabajo].   Labor force.
1975. xvii, [6], 1223p.   [PRC
.3-7-C   [Fuerza de trabajo].   Labor force.
1976. xvii, 1177p.   [PRC, LC
.3-7-D   [Viviendas familiares].   Domestic housing.
1975. 799p.   [PRC, LC
      Areas metropolitanas.   Metropolitan areas.
1976–1977. Part 8 in 6v.
.3-8-A   Carácterísticas gene-   General characteristics (Caracas
rales. 1976. [10], 653p.   to Lagunillas).
       [PRC, LC
.3-8-B   Carácterísticas gene-   General characteristics (Mérida
rales. 1976. [10], 561p.   to El Tigre).
       [PRC, IASI, LC
.3-8-C   Fuerza de trabajo.   Labor force (Caracas to Punto
1976. xvii, 810p.   Fijo).
       [PRC, IASI, LC
.3-8-D   Fuerza de trabajo.   Labor force (Acariga-Araure to
1976. xvii, 720p.   Barinas).
       [PRC, IASI, LC
.3-8-E   Fuerza de trabajo.   Labor force (Maturin to El Tigre).
1976. xvii, 720p.   [PRC
.3-8-F   Vivienda. 1977. [xii],   Housing.
554p.   [PRC

Venezuela. DGE y CN.
    Nomenclador de centros pob-   List of populated centers. 1971

lados.   Censos 71.   Región...   census.   ...region.
Caracas, 1974-1975.   8v.
1971.4-1   Capital. 1974. 137p.   (Metropolitan Caracas, Distrito
                                                   Federal, Miranda, Dependencia
                                                   Federal).
                                                   [PRC, LC, NYPL
.4-2   Central. 1974. 245p.   (Aragua, Carabobo, Cojedes and
                                                   Guárico).
                                                   [PRC, LC, NYPL
.4-3   Centro occidental. 1974.   (Falcón, Lara, Portuguesa and
   365p.   Yaracuy).
                                                   [PRC, NYPL
.4-4   Zuliana. 1974. 95p.   (Zulia).
                                                   [PRC, LC, NYPL
.4-5   de los Andes. 1974.   (Barinas, Mérida, Táchira, Tru-
   422p.   jillo & Distrito Páez of Apure).
                                                   [LC, NYPL
.4-6   Sur. 1975. 88p.   (Apure, Distrito Cedeño of Bolí-
                                                   var, Terr, Amazonas).
                                                   [Yale, NYPL, RPI
.4-7   Nor-oriental. 1974. 312p.   (Anzoátegui, Monagas, Nueva Es-
                                                   parta and Sucre).
                                                   [Yale, NYPL, RPI
.4-8   de Guayana. 1975. 63p.   (Bolívar, Terr. Delta Amacuro).
                                                   [Yale, NYPL, RPI

   Venezuela.   DGE y CN.
.5   X censo general de población   Tenth general population census
   (2 de noviembre 1971). Venezuela.   (November 2, 1971). Venezuela.
   Nivel educativo, fuerza de traba-   Level of education, labor force
   jo y vivienda.   Caracas, 1973.   and housing.
   [6], 47p.   [OPR, PRC

VIETNAM

Socialist Republic of Vietnam.   Capital: Hanoi
Statistical Agency: National Institute of Statistics. (as of late 1960's)
                    [Institut National de la Statistique]
                    Hanoi,
Publications Distributor: same?

France. INSEE.
1946.2-1   Résultats statistiques du   Statistical results of the general
recensement général de la popu-   census of population taken March
lation effectué le 10 mars 1946.   10, 1946. Vol. I, De jure popula-
Vol. I, Population légale.   tion. Appendix: area, population
Paris, 1948. Appendix, pp. 145-   and density of the population of
147.   the French Union countries around
                                             1946.
                                             [PRC, RPI

France. INSEE.
1946   Les français d'origine métropolitaine...
         [See French Overseas Territories, No. 1946.2.]

Vietnam (South). Institut Na-
         tional de la Statistique.
1958.1   Enquêtes démographiques au   Demographic surveys in Vietnam in
Vietnam en 1958.   Saigon, 1960.   1958.
122p. app.   [PRC, RPI

Vietnam (South). Institut Na-
         tional de la Statistique.
.2   Interprétation des résultats   Interpretation of the results of
de l'enquête démographique à   the demographic survey in Saigon
Saigon en juillet 1958.   Sai-   in July 1958.
gon, 1958.   p.   [

Vietnam (South). Institut Na-
         tional de la Statistique.
1959.1   Recensement pilote de la   Trial census of the province of
Province de Phuoc-Tuy effectué   Phuoc-Tuy taken November 6, 1959.
le 6 novembre 1959.   [Saigon,   [PRC, RPI
1959]. [v], x, 68p.

Vietnam (North). Central Census Steering Committee.
1960.1   [Official government report on 1960 census in North Vietnam]. In:
Nhah dan, no. 2419. (2 Nov. 1960). Hanoi, 1960. 3p. [In: Translations on North Vietnam, March 1961. U.S. Joint Publications Research
Service, no. 6570. Washington, D.C., 1961. 7p.] [Berkeley, PRC, RPI

Vietnam (North). Central Census Steering Committee.
.2   [Government resolutions and directives and census figures on Hanoi,
North Vietman]. In: Translations on North Vietnam, JPRS 6823. New
York, 1961. [

Vietnam (South). Institut National de la Statistique.

1962.1   Enquête démographique à Saigon en 1962.   Saigon, 1963. 231p.

Demographic survey in Saigon in 1962.
[

Vietnam (South). Institut National de la Statistique.

1964.1   Dân sô Viêt-Nam theo do'n-vi hanh chanh, 1964.   Saigon, Viên quoc-gia thông-kê, 1965.
                p.

Population of Vietnam according to administrative units, 1964.
[

Demeny, Paul G.

1967.1   A population survey in Viet-Nam: Final report.   Cambridge, Mass., Simulmatics Corp., 1967. 51p. (U.S. Dept. of Defence, Advanced Research Projects Agency. SIM/CAM/10/67). [Harvard

VIRGIN ISLANDS (U.S.)

Virgin Islands of the United States   Capital: Charlotte
Statistical Agency: U.S. Bureau of the Census   Amalie
                     Washington, D.C. 20233
                          and
                     Office of Territorial Affairs
                     Department of the Interior
                     Washington, D.C., 20240
Publications Distributor: U.S. Government Printing Office
                     Washington, D.C. 20402

      U.S. Bureau of the Census.
1950.1-2-51/54   Census of population: 1950. A report of the seventeenth
      decennial census of the United States. Volume II. Characteristics of
      the population. Part 51-54. Territories and possessions (Alaska,
      Hawaii, Puerto Rico, American Samoa, Canal Zone, Guam and Virgin Is-
      lands). 1953. var. gap. [PRC, LC, BC, RPI

      U.S. Bureau of the Census.
1960.1-1-54/57   Census of population: 1960. The eighteenth decennial cen-
      sus of the United States. Volume I. Characteristics of the population.
      Part 54-57. Outlying areas (Virgin Islands, Guam, American Samoa, and
      Canal Zone). 1963. [218]p. [PRC, BC, LC, RPI

      U.S. Bureau of the Census.
1970.1-1-54/58   Census of population: 1970. Volume I. Characteristics of
      the population. Part 54-58. Guam, Virgin Islands, American Samoa,
      Canal Zone, Trust Territory of the Pacific Islands. 1973. var. pag.
      [PRC, LC, BC, RPI

WAKE ISLAND

United States Unincorporated Territory.   Capital: Administered from Wash-
                                                              ington, D.C.

The U.S. censuses for 1950, 1960 and 1970 carry only total numbers of
inhabitants in Table 1 of the U.S. Summary volume for those years.

WALLIS AND FUTUNA

Territory of Wallis and Futuna (France)   Capital: Mata Utu.
Statistical Agency: INSEE
                    18, Blvd Adolphe-Pinard
                    75675 Paris, Cedex 14, FRANCE
Publications Distributor: Observatoire Économique de Paris.
                          195, rue de Bercy, Tour Gamma A
                          75582 Paris, Cedex 12, FRANCE

France. INSEE.
1969.1   Recensement de la population   Census of the population of Wallis
          de Wallis et Futuna, Mars 1969;   and Futuna, March 1969: main re-
          principaux résultats.   Paria,   sults.
          1970? 55p.   [BC, E-W, LC

France. INSEE.
1976.1   Résultats statistiques du   Statistical results of the general
          recensement général de la popu- census of the population of the
          lation des îles Wallis et Futuna, Wallis and Futuna islands, March
          26 mars 1976.   Paris, 1976?   26, 1976.
          16p.   [BC

France. INSEE.
  .2   Résultats du recensement de   Results of the census of popula-
          la population des Wallis et Fu-   tion of the Wallis and Futuna Is-
          tuna, 26 mars 1976.   Paris, 1978. lands, March 26, 1976.
          161p. specimen forms.   [OPR, E-W

WESTERN SAHARA

[Divided between Morocco and Mauritania.]   Capital: El Aaiún.
Statistical Agency: National Statistical Institute
                     [Instituto Nacional de Estadística (INE)]
                     Avenida Generalísimo, 91
                     Madrid 16, SPAIN
Publications Distributor: Administración de Publicaciones
                           (of the above).

Spain. Instituto Nacional de
       Estadística.
1950.1-1 Censo de la población de Es-   Census of the population of Spain
paña y territorios de su sobe-   and the territories under its
ranía y protectorado, según el   sovereignty and protectorship,
empadronamiento realizado el 31   according to the enumeration of
de diciembre de 1950: Tomo I,   December 31, 1950. Part I, Gen-
Cifras generales de habitantes.   eral data on inhabitants.
Madrid, 1952. 1v, 415p.   [UN, BC, PRC, RPI, RIR

Spain. INE.
1960.2-1   Censo de la población y   Census of the population and hous-
de las viviendas de Estaña, se-   ing of Spain, according to the
gún la inscripción realizada el   enumeration taken December 31,
31 de diciembre de 1960. Tomo   1960. Part I. General data of
I. Cifras generales de habitan-   inhabitants.
tes.   Madrid, 1962. xl,404p.   [PRC, BC, UN, RPI, RIR

Spain. INE.
1970.1   Censo de la población de Es-   Census of the population of Spain,
paña, año 1970. Poblaciones de   1970. De jure and de facto popu-
derecho y de hecho de los muni-   lation of the municipalities.
cipios.   Madrid, 1971. 126p.   [PRC, LC

Spain. INE.
.3-3   Censo de la población de   Census of the population of Spain,
España, según la inscripción   according to the enumeration taken
realizada el 31 de diciembre de   December 31, 1970. Part III.
1970. Tomo III. Característi-   Population characteristics. Na-
cas de la población. Total na-   tional total. (Annex).
cional.   Madrid, 1974. xxii,   [PRC
185p. (Anexo).

WESTERN SAMOA

The Independent State of Western Samoa.   Capital: Apia
Statistical Agency: Department of Statistics
                     P.O. Box 1151
                     Apia,
Publications Distributor: same

New Zealand. Census and Statistical Department.
1945.2-2   Population census, 1945. Volume II, Island Territories: Cook
    Islands and Nieu, Tokelau Island, Western Samoa. Auckland, Leightons
    Ltd., 1947. [4], 14p. [PRC, BC, RPI

New Zealand. Department of Island Territories.
1951.1   Population census, 25 September 1951. Wellington, Government
    Printer, 1954. 28p. maps. [UN, LC, BC, PRC, RPI

Western Samoa. Census Commissioner's Office.
1956.1   Report on the population census, 1956. By Kathleen M. Jupp. Wel-
    lington, Government Printer, 1958. 127, [1], 13p. maps. [UN, LC,
    TXU, PRC, RPI

New Zealand. Department of Island Territories.
1961.1   Population census 1961. Apia, Census Commissioner's Office, 1962.
    133p. 2 maps. [UN, TXU, BC, PRC, RPI

    Western Samoa. Bureau of Statistics.
1966.1   Population census, 1966. Apia, 1968. vi, 249p. [PRC, LC

    Western Samoa. Bureau of Statistics.
  .2   Apia urban area population census, 1966. Apia, 1968.   p. [LC

    Western Samoa. Department of Statistics.
1971.1   Census of population and housing, 1971. Apia, n.d. vi, 612p.
    [PRC, E-W, UN

    Western Samoa. Department of Statistics.
1976.1   Census of population and housing, 1976. Apia, 1978. 389p. [E-W

YEMEN (ADEN)

People's Democratic Republic of Yemen.   Capital: Aden.
Statistical Agency: Central Statistical Office
                      Central Planning Commission
                      P.O. Box 4147
                      Crater, Aden,
Publications Distributor: same

     Aden State.   Superintendent of Census.
1946.0-1   Census of Aden, 1946.   First report [Civil population by sex].
     [Aden], 1946.   1p.   [LC, BC, PRC, RPI

     Aden State.   Superintendent of Census.
   .1   Census of Aden, 1946.   Interim report.   Civil population of Aden
     by races.   [Aden], 1947.   1p.   [LC, BC, PRC, RPI

     Aden State.   Superintendent of Census.
   .2   Census of Aden: report and tables.   [Aden, 1947].   130p.   [PRC,
     Berkeley, RPI

     Aden State.   District Commissioner.
1955.1   Census report, 1955.   Aden, Government Printer, 1955.   31p.   [PRC,
     UN, LC, BC, RPI

     Note: There was a one-in-fifteen sample in 1973 and a pilot study of
     the nomads in 1974 but no citation of publications has been seen.

YEMEN (SANA'A)

Yemen Arab Republic.   Capital: Sana'a
Statistical Agency: Statistics Department
                     Central Planning Organisation
                     P.O. Box 175
                     Sana'a,
Publications Distributor: same

There was a census of Sana'a in 1972 but no citation of publications has been seen.

Yemen (Sana'a). Central Planning Organisation. Statistics Department.
1975.0-1   The housing and population census, Feb. 1975. Preliminary re-
    sults. 2d ed. Sana'a, 1976. [32]p. [Mostly Arabic]. [PRC, BC

Yemen (Sana'a). Central Planning Organisation; and Switzerland. Ser-
    vice de la Cooperation Technique.
.0-2   Databank of Yemen's population and housing census 1975: country-
    wide demographic figures by districts and district centres and detailed
    demographic records of over 10,000 settlements in 36 selected districts.
    By H. Steffen and U. Geiser. Zurich, University of Zurich, Dept. of
    Geography, 1977. 261p. (Airphoto Interpretation Project, preliminary
    report, no. 5). [

Yemen (Sana'a). Central Planning Organisation. Statistics Department.
.1   [Census analysis]. Sana'a, 1976? [64]p. [Arabic with English
    table headings] [PRC

Yemen (Sana'a). Central Planning Organisation. Statistics Department.
.2   Population. Chapter 2 of Statistical Year Book, 1976-1977. [Sana'a],
    n.d. Pp. 37-64. [PRC

Note: The above is "complimentary to the results of the sample and
should be used in connection with it."

Yemen (Sana'a). Central Planning Organization [and] Switzerland. Ser-
    vice de la Cooperation Technique.
.3   Yemen Arab Republic: final report on the airphoto interpretation
    project. The major findings of the population and housing census of
    February 1975. Volume 1. Zurich, Univ. of Zurich, Dept. of Geography,
    1978. [232]p. [

YUGOSLAVIA

Socialist Federal Republic of Yugoslavia.   Capital: Belgrade.
Statistical Agency: Federal Statistical Office
                     [Savezni Zavod za Statistika (SZS)]
                     P.O. Box 203
                     11000 Beograd,
Publications Distributor: same.

Yugoslavia. Savezni Zavod za
      Statistiku i Evidenciju.
      Konačni resultati popisa sta-   Final results of the census of
novništva od 15 marta 1948 godi-   population of March 15, 1948.
ne./Résultats définitifs du re-
censement de la population du 15
mars 1948.   Belgrade, 1951-1956.
Vol. I-X.
1948.1-1   I. Stanovništvo po polu   Population by sex and households.
      i domaćinstva./Population par   [UN, LC, TXU, RPI
      sexe et ménages. 1951. 430p.

  .1-2   II. Stanovništvo po sta-   Population by age and sex.
      rosti i polu./Population par âge   [UN, LC, TXU, RPI
      et sexe. 1951. xxxv, 91p.

  .1-3   III. Stanovništvo po   Population according to occupa-
      zanimanju./Population d'après   tion.
      les professions. 1954. cxi,   [UN, LC, TXU, RPI
      496p.

  .1-4   IV. Stanovništvo po škol-   Population by formal education.
      skoj spremi./Population par in-   [UN, LC, TXU, RPI
      struction scolaire. 1952. lii,
      125, [2]p.

  .1-5   V. Stanovništvo po pis-   Population according to literacy.
      mentosti./Population d'après   [UN, LC, TXU, RPI
      l'aptitude à lire et à écrire.
      1955. lxiv, 384p.

  .1-6   VI. Stanovništvo po rod-   Population according to birth-
      nom kraju./Population d'après   place.
      le lieu de naissance. 1955.   [UN, LC, TXU, RPI
      xlviii, 95p.

  .1-7   VII. Stanovništvo prema   Population according to marital
      braćnom stanju./Population d'   status.
      après l'état matrimonial. 1954.   [UN, LC, TXU, RPI
      lxxii, 475p.

  .1-8   VIII. Žensko stanovništvo   Female population by number of
      prema broju žiborotene dece./   children born alive.
      Population féminine d'après le   [UN, LC, TXU, RPI
      nombre des enfants nés vivants.
      lxx, 176p.

  .1-9   IX. Stanovništvo po narod-   Population by ethnic nationality.
      nosti./Population d'après la   [UN, LC, TXU, RPI
      nationalité ethnique. 1954.
      xliv, 494p.

.1-10　　X.　Domaćinstva./Ménages.
1956.　lix, 186, [2]p.

Households.
[UN, LC, TXU, RPI

Yugoslavia.　SZS.
　Popis stanovištva 1953.　Belgrade, 1958-1962.　Vol. 1-16.

Population census 1953.

1953.1-1　　Vitalna i etnička obeležja.
Konačni rezultati za FNRJ i Narodne Republike.　1959.　civ,
287p.

Vital and ethnic characteristics.
Final results for the Federal Re-
public and the National Republics.
[UN, LC, TXU, RPI

.1-2　　Ekonomska obeležja stanovništva.　Konačni rezultati za
FNRJ i Narodne Republike.　1960.
xvii, 555p.

Economic characteristics of the
population.　Final results for the
Federal Republic and the National
Republics.
[UN, LC, TXU, RPI

.1-3　　Pismenosti i školska sprema.　Konačni rezultati za FNRJ
i Narodne Republike.　1960.
lxxxvii, 359p.

Literacy and educational attainment.　Final results for the Federal Republic and the National
Republics.
[UN, LC, TXU, RPI

.1-4　　Fertilna obeležja.　Konačni rezultati za FNRJ i Narodne
Republike.　1960.　xviii, 321p.

Fertility characteristics.　Final
results for the Fed. Rep. and the
National Republics.
[UN, LC, TXU, RPI

.1-5　　Delatnost i poljoprivredno
stanovništvo podaci za srezove
prema upravnoj podeli u 1953 godini.　1960.　xxx, 403p.

Industrial and agricultural population data by districts according
to the administrative areas of 1953.
[UN, LC, TXU, RPI

.1-6　　Zanimanje.　Podaci za srezove prema upravnoj podeli u
1953 godini.　1960.　xxix, 377p.

Occupations.　Data by districts
according to the administrative
areas of 1953.
[UN, LC, TXU, RPI

.1-7　　Bračno stanje.　Podaci za
srezove prema upravnoj podeli u
1953 godini.　1959.　xxx, 377p.

Marital status.　Data by districts
according to the administrative
areas of 1953.
[UN, LC, TXU, RPI

.1-8　　Narodnost i maternji jezik.
Podaci za srezove prema upravnoj
podeli u 1953 godini.　1959.
xxvii, 395p.

Nationality and mother tongue.
Data by districts according to
the administrative areas of 1953.
[UN, LC, TXU, RPI

.1-9　　Pismenost i školska sprema.
Podaci za srezove prema upravnoj
podeli u 1953 godini.　1960.
xxvii, 416p.

Literacy and schooling.　Data by
districts according to the administrative areas of 1953.
[UN, LC, TXU, RPI

.1-10　　Fertilitet.　Podaci za
srezove prema upravnoj podeli u
1953 godini.　1960.　xxviii,
377p.

Fertility.　Data by districts according to the administrative
areas of 1953.
[UN, LC, TXU, RPI

.1-11　　Starost, pismenost i narodnost.　Podaci za opštine prema upravnoj podeli u 1953 godini.
1960.　xxvi, 531p.

Age, literacy and nationality.
Data by districts according to
the administrative areas of 1953.
[UN, LC, TXU, RPI

.1-12 Ekonomska obeležja stanovništva. Podaci za opštine prema
upravnoj podeli u 1953 godini.
1960. xxvi, 557p.

Economic characteristics of the
population. Data by districts
according to the administrative
areas of 1953.
[UN, LC, TXU, RPI

.1-13 Stanovištvo i domaćinstva.
Podaci za naselji i delove naselja prema upravnoj podeli u
1953 godini. 1959. xxviii, 484p.

Population and households. Data
for localities and the occupants
of localities by the administrative divisions of 1953.
[UN, LC, TXU, RPI

.1-14 Osnovni podaci o stanovništvo. Podaci za naselja prema
upravnoj podeli u 1953 godini.
1958. xxix, 635p.

Basic population data. Data for
localities by the administrative
divisions of 1953.
[UN, LC, TXU, RPI

.1-15 Osnovni podaci o stanovništvo. Podaci za naselja prema
upravnoj podeli 30-VI-1958 godini.
1960. xviii, 568p.

Basic data about the population.
Data on localities by the administrative divisions of June 30,
1958.
[UN, LC, TXU, RPI

.1-16 Domaćinstva i porodice.
Rezultati potpune obrade i po
uzorku. 1962. xliii, 399p.

Households and families. Complete
results compared with those con-
verted from sample.
[UN, LC, TXU, RPI

Yugoslavia. SZS.
Popis stanovništva 1961.
Belgrade, 1965-1973. Vol. 1-16.

Census of population 1961.

1961.1-1 Vitalna, etnička i migraciona obeležja. Rezultati za
Republike i demografske rejone.
1970. 16, xc, 144, [8]p. map.

Vital, ethnic, and migration
characteristics. Results for the
Republic and the demographic regions.
[UN, LC, PRC, RPI

.1-2 Pismenost i školovanost.
Rezultati za socijalističke republike i demografske rejone.
1971. xc, 345, [21]p. map.

Literacy and educational attainment. Results for the socialist
republic and the demographic regions.
[UN, LC, PRC, RPI

.1-3 Ekonomske karakteristike.
I deo. (Ukupni i aktivno stanovništvo). Rezultati za socijalističke republike i demografske rejone. 1970. xcii,
329, [15]p. map.

Economic characteristics. Part I.
(Total and economically active
population). Results for the
socialist republic and for the
demographic regions.
[UN, LC, PRC, RPI

.1-4 Ekonomska obeležja stanovništva. II deo. (Radnici -
Službenici). Rezultati za socijalističke republike i demografske rejone. 1969. xcvii,
[3], 429p. map.

Economic characteristics of the
population. Part II. (Manual
and non-manual workers). Results
for the socialist republic and
the demographic regions.
[UN, LC, PRC, RPI

.1-5 Karakteristike domaćin-
stava i porodica. 1973. cxxvii,
472p.

Household and family characteristics.
[UN, LC, PRC, RPI

.1-6   Vitalna, etnička i migraciona obeležja. Rezultati za
opštine. 1967. lxxi, 334, [6]p.
map.

Vital, ethnic and migration characteristics. Results by districts.
[UN, LC, PRC, RPI

.1-7   Pismenost, školska sprema
i kvalifikacija. Rezultati za
opštine. 1968. lxii, [5], w73p.
maps.

Literacy, educational attainment
and qualification. Results by
districts.
[UN, LC, PRC, RPI

.1-8   Ekonomska obeležja stanovništva. Rezultati za opštine.
1966. lxxi, 297p.

Economic characteristics of the
population. Results by districts.
[UN, LC, PRC, RPI

.1-9   Domaćinstva i stanovništvo
prema karakteristikama domaćinstva. Rezultati za opštine.
1966. lxxiii, 287p.

Households and population accord-
ing to household characteristics.
Results by district.
[UN, LC, PRC, RPI

.1-10   Stanovništvo i comaćinstva.
u 1948, 1953, i 1961. Rezultati
za naselja. 1965. xliii, 531p.
maps.

Population and households in 1948,
1953, and 1961. Results by localities.
[UN, LC, PRC, RPI

.1-11   Pol i starost. Rezultati
za naselja. 1965. xlvii, 369p.
maps.

Sex and age. Results by localities.
[UN, LC, PRC, RPI

.1-12   Migraciona obeležja. Rezultati za naselja. 1966.
lxviii, 376p.

Migration characteristics. Results
by localities.
[UN, LC, PRC, RPI

.1-13   Školska sprema i pismenost.
Rezultati za naselja. 1965.
lxvii, 369p. maps.

Educational attainment and literacy. Results for localities.
[UN, LC, PRC, RPI

.1-14   Aktivnost i delatnost.
Rezultati za naselja. 1965.
lix, 369p. maps.

Activity and industry. Results
for localities.
[UN, LC, PRC, RPI

.1-15   Poljoprivredno stanovništvo. Rezultati za naselja.
1966. lxviii, 368p.

Agricultural population. Results
for localities.
[UN, LC, PRC, RPI

.1-16   Veličina i izvori prihoda
domaćinstva. Rezultati za naselja. 1965. lvi, 369p. maps.

Size and source of income of households. Results for localities.
[UN, LC, PRC, RPI

Yugoslavia. SZS.
.2   Popis stanovništva 1961: Re-
gistri nazava opština i naselja,
sa objašnjenjima promena. Belgrade, 1965. 531p.

Population census 1961: registry
of district and commune names,
with commentary on changes.
[LC

Yugoslavia. SZS.
Popis stanovništva i stanova
1971. Stanovništva. Belgrade,
1974-1975. Vol. I-XII in 13v.

Census of population and housing
1971. Population.

1971.1-1   I. Vitalna, etnička i migraciona obeležja. Rezultati po
republikama i pokrajinama. 1974.
lix, 108p. specimen forms.

Vital, ethnic and migration characteristics. Results for the republics and provinces.
[PRC, LC

1971.1-2   II. Pismenost i školova-   Literacy and educational charact-
      nost. 1974. 1x, 341p.   eristics.
                                                 [PRC, LC

  .1-3   III. Ekonomske karakteris-   Economic characteristics. Part I.
      tike. I deo (Ukupno i aktivno   (Total and economically active
      stanovništvo). 1974. lix, 190p.   population).
                                                 [PRC, LC

  .1-4   IV. Ekonomske karakteris-   Economic characteristics. Part II.
      tike. II deo (Zaposleno osoblje).   (Employed persons).
      1974. lix, 326p.   [PRC, LC

  .1-5   V. Domaćinstva i porodice.   Households and families.
      1974. lxiii, 628p. sample forms.   [PRC, LC

  .1-6   VI. Etnička, prosvetna i   Ethnic, educational and economic
      ekonomske obeležja stanovništva   characteristics of the population
      i domaćinstva prema broju člano-   and households according to num-
      va. 1974. xxix, 248p.   bers of members.
                                                 [PRC, LC

  .1-7   VII. Stanovništvo i doma-   Population and households in 1948,
      ćinstva u 1948, 1953, 1961 i 1971   1953, 1961 and 1971 and housing
      i stanovi u 1971. Rezultati po   in 1971. Results for communes
      naseljima i opštinama. 1975.   and districts.
      xvii, 503p.   [PRC, LC
                VIII. Pol i starost.   Age and sex.
  .1-8-1   I deo. 1973. xviii,   Part I.
      352p.   [PRC, LC
  .1-8-2   II deo. 1973. Pp. 355-   Part II.
      647.   [PRC, LC
  .1-9   IX. Migraciona obeležja.   Migration characteristics.
      1973. xviii, 381p. w/Eng. trans-   [PRC, LC
      lation.
  .1-10   X. Delatnost. 1974.   Industry.
      xviii, 383p.   [PRC, LC
  .1-11   XI. Poljoprivredno sta-   Agricultural population.
      novništvo. 1973. xviii, 381p.   [PRC, LC
      w/Eng. translation.
  .1-12   XII. Veličina poseda i   Size of estate and sources of
      izvori prihoda comaćinstva. 1974.   household income.
      xviii, 382p.   [PRC, LC

      Yugoslavia. SZS.
  .2   Popis stanovništva i stanova   Census of population and housing
      1971. Registri naziva opština   1971. Register of district and
      i naselja sa objašnjenjima pro-   commune names with commentary on
      mena od 1963 do 1971. Belgrade,   changes from 1963 to 1971.
      1974. 120p.   [PRC

      Yugoslavia. SZS.
  .3   Popis stanovništva i stanova   Census of population and housing
      1971. Program obrade i publiko-   1971. Processing and publications
      vanja--šeme tabeliranja, tabele   program--Scheme of tabulation,
      i klasificacije--. Belgrade,   tables and classification--.
      1975. 332p.   [PRC, LC

ZAIRE

Republic of Zaïre.   Capital: Kinshasa
Statistical Agency: Institute of Scientific Research
                     [Institut de Recherche Scientifique]
                     B.P. No. 20
                     Kinshasa/Gombe,
Publications Distributor: Bureau d'Information
                           Ministère de l'Intérieur
                           B.P. No. 1142
                           Kinshasa/Gombe,

         Belgian Congo. Gouvernement
             Général. Section Statis-
             tique.
1952.1   Résultats du recensement gé-   Results of the general census of
          néral de la population non-indi-   the non-indigenous populatio of
          gène du Congo Belge et du Ruanda-   the Belgian Congo and of Ruanda-
          Urundi du 3 janvier 1952. [Léo-   Urundi of January 3, 1952.
          poldville], 1952. 87p. (Bulle-   [UN, PRC, RPI
          tin mensuel des statistiques du
          Congo Belge et du Ruanda-Urundi,
          3ème année, no. 21).

         Belgian Congo. Direction de la
             Statistique et des Études
             Économiques.
           Enquête démographique, 1955-   Demographic survey, 1955-1957.
         1957. Léopoldville, 1957-196?.
         13 parts in 12v.
1957.1-1   Cité indigène de Léopold-   Central city of Leopoldville.
          ville. 1957. 6, 35p.   [LC, JB-F, RPI
     .1-2   Territoire suburbain de   Suburban territory of Leopoldville.
          Léopoldville. 1957. 1, 11p.   [LC, JB-F, RPI
     .1-3&4 Districts du Bas-Congo et   Districts of Lower Congo and the
          des Cataractes. 1957. vii, [2],   Falls.
          73p.   [LC, JB-F, RPI
     .1-5   District de la Tshuapa.   Tshuapa district.
          1958.   p.   [JB-F
     .1-6   Province du Kasaï. 1958.   Kasai province.
               p.   [JB-F
     .1-7   District du Maniema.   Maniema district.
          1959.   p.   [
     .1-8   Province de l'Equateur   Equator province (except Tshuapa
          (sauf District de la Tshuapa).   district).
          1959. 16, [2], 172p.   [TXU
     .1-9   Province du Kasaï (4 dis-   Kasai province (4 districts).
          tricts). 1959. [3], 236p.   [TXU
     .1-10   Province du Katanga. 1960.   Katanga province.
          iii, 207p.   [TXU

.1-11   Districts du Kwilu, du   Kwilu, Kwango and Lake Leopold II
Kwango, et du Lac Léopold II.   districts.
1961.   p.   [
.1-12   Districts du Nord- et du   North and South Kivu districts.
Sud-Kivu. 1961.   p.   [
.1-13   Province Orientale. 196?.   Eastern province
         p.   [

Belgian Congo. Direction de la
        Statistique et des Études
        Économiques.
.2   Enquête démographique, 1955-   Demographic survey, 1955-57.
57. Tableau général de la démo-   General table of Congolese demographie congolaise. Analyse   graphy. General analysis of the
générale des résultats statis-   statistical results.
tiques. Léopoldville, 1961.   [UN, NWU, PRC, JB-F
214p. maps.

Belgian Congo. Direction de la
        Statistique.
        Résultats du recensement de   Results of the census of the non-
la population non-indigène au   indigenous population of January
3-1-1958.   Leopoldville,1959-   3, 1958.
1960. Fasc a-f. (Bulletin
mensuel des statistiques générales du Congo Belge et du Ruanda-Urundi, série speciale, no.1)
        A. Race blanche. Popula-   A. White race. Population...
tion...
1958.1-1   a. ...par nationalité   ...by nationality and occupation-
et groupe professionnel. 1959.   al group.
[2], 136p.   [BC, NWU, PRC, RPI
.1-2   b. ...par état civil.   ...by marital status. Missionar-
Missionnaires. 1959. 9, pp.   ies.
137-255.   [BC, NWU, PRC, RPI
.1-3   c. ...par âge. ...   ...by age. ...by duration of
durée du séjour... 1959. 12,   residence.
pp. 259-351.   [BC, NWU, PRC, RPI
.1-4   d. ...active...   Economically active... Business
Agents d'entreprise... 1959.   agents...
14, pp. 349-488.   [BC, PRC, NWU, RPI
.1-5   e. Chefs de ménage...   Household heads...
1960. 14, pp. 490-646.   [BC, NWU, PRC, RPI
        B. Population totale des   Total population of other races.
autres races.
.1-6   f. 1960. 14, pp. 650-
700.   [BC, NWU, PRC, RPI

Congo (Democratic Republic).
        INS [and] France. Assis-
        tance Technique.
1967.1   Étude socio-démographique de   Socio-demographic study of Kin-
Kinshasa 1967. Rapport général.   shasa 1967. General report.

Paris, Société Française d'Étu-   [NWU
des et de Développement, 1969.
iii, 192p.

Congo (Democratic Republic).
    Cabinet du Ministère d'État.
1970.1   Résultats officiels du recen-   Official results of the general
sement général de la population   census of the population of the
de la République Démocratique du   Democratic Republic of the Congo,
Congo, 1970.   Kinshasa, 1970.   1970.
24p.   [PRC, BC, NWU, LC
.1a   Annex. 14 tables.   Appendix.
                         [PRC, BC, NWU

Zaïre. Institut National de la
    Statistique.
.2   Recueil des rapports et to-   Collection of reports and totals:
taux: calculés à partir des   calculated from the official re-
résultats officiels du recense-   sults of the 1970 population cen-
ment de la population de la R.   sus of the Democratic Republic of
D.C. en 1970.   Kinshasa, 1971.   the Congo.
i, iv, 94p.   [NWU, LC

Zaïre. INS.
.3   Population des villes, recen-   Population of towns, census 1970.
sement 1970.   Kinshasa, n.d.   [BC
        p.

The proposed date for the next census is 1980.

ZAMBIA

Republic of Zambia.   Capital: Lusaka
Statistical Agency: Central Statistical Office
                      P.O. Box 1908
                      Lusaka,
Publications Distributor: same

        Rhodesia (Northern). Central African Statistical Office.
1946.1   Census, 1946. The European, Coloured and Asiatic populations and
        Africans in employment as disclosed by the census taken on the 15th
        October, 1946.   Lusaka, Government Printer, 1947. 7p. [LC, PRC, RPI

        Rhodesia (Northern). Central African Statistical Office.
   .2   Report on the census of population of Northern Rhodesia held on
        15th October, 1946.   Lusaka, 1949. 125p. schedules. [UN, NWU, RPI

        Rhodesia (Northern). Central African Statistical Office.
1950.1   Report on the 1950 demographic sample survey of the African popula-
        tion of Northern Rhodesia.   Salisbury, 1952. 43p. [LC, UN, NWU, RPI

        Rhodesia (Northern). Central African Statistical Office.
1951.1   Census, 1951. The European, Coloured and Asiatic population and
        Africans in employment as disclosed by the census taken on the 8th May,
        1951.   Lusaka, Government Printer, 1951. 8p. [UN, LC, NWU, RPI

        Rhodesia (Northern). Central African Statistical Office.
   .2   Report on the census of population, 1951. Northern Rhodesia.   Lu-
        saka, Government Press, 1954. 70p. schedules. [LC, UN, NWU, PRC, RPI

        Rhodesia and Nyasaland. Central Statistical Office.
1956.1   Census of population, 1956. Salisbury, 1960. 167p. [TXU, RPI

        Rhodesia (Northern). Central Statistical Office.
1960.1   Report on Northern Rhodesia African demographic surveys, May to Aug-
        ust 1960.   Salisbury, 1961. 74p. [NWU, LC

        Zambia. Central Statistical Office.
1961.1   Final report of the September 1961 censuses of non-Africans and
        employees.   Lusaka, 1965. 70p. [NWU

        Zambia. Central Statistical Office.
1963.1   Second [i.e. Final] report of the May/June, 1963, census of Africans
        in Northern Rhodesia.   Lusaka, 1964. ii, 74p. [BC, NWU, LC

        Zambia. Central Statistical Office.
          Census of Africans, May/June 1963. Village populations.   Lusaka,
        1965-1968. 43v.
1963.2-1 through 1963.2-43. [Districts]. 1. Abercorn. 1965. [64]p./2. Balo-
        vale. 1967. [80]p./3. Bancroft. 1965. [19]p./4. Broken Hill. 1966.
        [115]p./5. Chadiza. 1968. [26]p./6. Chingola. 1965. [22]p./7. Chin-
        sali. 1965. [71]p./8. Choma. 1966. [57]p./9. Feika. 1965. [11]p./

10. Fort Jameson. 1967. [104]p./11. Fort Rosebery. 1965. [68]p./
12. Gwembe. 1965. [63]p./13. Isoka. 1965. [45]p./14. Kabompo.
1967. [64]p./15. Kalabo. 1967. [101]p./16. Kalomo. 1965. [65]p./
17. Kalulushi. 1965. [20]p./18. Kasama. 1965. [103]p./19. Kasempa.
1968. [61]p./20. Katete. 1968. [42]p./21. Kawambwa. 1965. [94]p./
22. Kitwe. 1965. [33]p./23. Livingstone. 1965. [20]p./24. Luanshya.
1965. [31]p./25. Lundazi. 1965. [93]p./26. Lusaka. 1965. [89]p./
27. Luwingu. 1967. [73]p./28. Mankoya. 1968. [98]p./29. Mazabuka.
1965. [106]p./30. Mongu. 1967. [109]p./31 Mpika. 1966. [54]p./
32. Mporokoso. 1968. [47]p./33. Mufulira. 1965. [32]p./34. Mumbwa.
1965. [57]p./35. Mwinilunga. 1968. [89]p./36. Namwala. 1966.
[29]p./37. Ndola. 1965. [126]p./38. Petauke. 1968. [85]p./39. Samfya. 1965. [86]p./40. Sananga. 1968. [98]p./41 Serenje. 1965.
[89]p./42. Sesheke. 1967. [39]p./43. Solwezi. 1965. [46]p. [PRC,
UN, LC

Zambia. Central Statistical Office.
1969.1   Census of population and housing, 1969. First report. Lusaka,
1970. 90p. [NWU, BC, LC

Zambia. Central Statistical Office.
Census of population and housing 1969. Final report. Lusaka,
1973- . Vol. I-IV in 45v.
.2-1   I. Total Zambia. 1973. [3], 54p. [PRC, NWU, BC, LC
        II. (By province). 1973. 8v.
1969.2-2-A through 1969.2-2-H. A. Central. [6], 160p./B. Copperbelt. [7],
178p./C. Eastern. [6], 106p./D. Luapula. [5], 106p./E. Northern.
[7], 178p./F. North-Western. [8], 124p./G. Southern. [11], 215p./H.
Western. [8], 142p. [PRC, NWU, LC
.2-3   III. Demographic analysis. 1974. iv, 43p. [NWU, PRC
        IV. (By Polling district populations). 1974-1976. 35v.
1969.2-4-A1 through 1969.2-4-I [Central] A1. Kabwe rural district. 1974.
107p./A2. Lusaka rural district. 1974. 77p./A3. Mkushi district.
1974. 145p./A4. Mumbwa district. 1974. 55p./A5. Serenje district.
1974. 93p./ [Copperbelt] B1. Ndola rural district. 1974. 125p./
[Eastern] C1. Chipata district. 1974. 203p./C2. Lundazi district.
1974. 120p./C3. Petauke district. 1974. 102p./[Luapula] D1. Kawambwa district. 1974. 86p./D2. Mansa district. 1974. 50p./D3. Samfya
district. 1974. 55p./ [Northern] E1. Chinsali district. 1974. 43p./
E2. Isoka district. 1974. 55p./E3. Kasama district. 1974. 66p./E4.
Luwingu district. 1974. 72p./E5.Mbala district. 1974. 57p./E6.
Mpika district. 1974. 59p./E7. Mporokoso district. 1974. 45p./
[North-Western] F1. Kabompo district. 1974. 73p./F2. Kasempa district.
1974. 59p./F3. Mwinilunga district. 1975. 78p./F4. Solwezi district.
1974. 101p./F5. Zambezi district. 1975. 99p./ [Southern] G1. Choma
District. 1975. 47p./G2. Gwembe district. 1975. 39p./G3. Kalomo
and Livingstone rural districts. 1975. 58p./G4. Mazabuku district.
1975. 85p./G5. Namwala district. 1975. 30p./ [Western] H1. Kalabo
district. 1975. 104p./H2. Kaoma district. 1975. 103p./H3. Mongu
district. 1976. 136p./H4. Senanga district. 1976. 87p./H5. Sesheke
district. 1975. 54p./I. Urban districts. 1975. 41p. [PRC, NWU, LC

Zambia.   Central Statistical Office.
1974.0-1   Sample census of population, 1974. Preliminary report.   Lusaka,
     1975. 10p. [PRC, BC

The next census is due to be taken in 1980.

BIBLIOGRAPHY

Allen, C.G. A manual of European languages for librarians. New York, Bowker, cl975. xiii, 803p.

Cason, Maidel. Censuses in the Melville J. Herskovits Library of African Studies. Evanston, Ill, Northwestern University, 1978. 33p.

CICRED Monographs (World Population Year). The population of... (fifty-six countries to date). Paris, 1974-

East-West Center. Introduction to censuses of Asia and the Pacific, 1970-74. Edited by Lee-Jay Cho, with the assistance of David B. Johnson and Milann Gannaway. Honolulu, 1976. xi, 198p.

France. INSEE. Situation des recensements et des enquêtes démographiques dans les états Africains et Malgache au ler janvier 1970. Paris, 1970. 63p.

Goyer, Doreen S. National population censuses, 1945-1976: some holding libraries. Clarion, PA, APLIC, 1979. [ii], 44p. (APLIC Special Publication, No. 1)

Hall, G.K. and Co. The developing areas; a classed bibliography of the Joint Bank-Fund library. Boston, 1976. Vols. 1-3.

McAfee, Judith L. Censuses in the Melville J. Herskovits Library of African Studies. Evanston, Ill., Northwestern Univ., 1975. 19p.

OAS. Inter-American Statistical Institute. Estadística: journal of the IASI. Washington, D.C. Monthly.

_____. _____. List of statistical publications received. Washington, D.C. Bimonthly.

Office of Population Research and Population Association of America. Population Index. Princeton, N.J. Quarterly.

Population Research Center. International population census bibliography. Austin, Univ. of Texas, Bureau of Business Research, 1965-1968. Nos. 1-6 and supplement.

United Nations. Dag Hammarskjold Library. Current bibliographical information. New York, N.Y. Semimonthly.

_____. Department of Economic and Social Affairs. Demographic yearbook, 1948- . New York, 1949- . Annual.

_____. Multilingual demographic dictionary. Prepared by the Demographic Dictionary Committee of the IUSSP. (English, French, Spanish, Brazilian, CZech, Russian). New York, 1958- . Irregular.

United Nations. Department of Economic and Social Affairs. Population and
     vital statistics report. Data available as of... New York. At
     first quarterly, now semiannual.

United Nations. Department of Economic and Social Affairs. Principles and
     recommendations for the 1970 population censuses. New York, 1967.
     vii, 163p. (Statistical papers, Series M, no. 44).

United States. Bureau of the Census. Library notes. Washington, D.C.
     Monthly.

United States. Department of State. Countries of the world and their lead-
     ers. 4th ed. Detroit, Gale, 1978. [8], 1154p.

University Microfilms Internationa. The Library of Congress shelflist.
     (H schedules). Ann Arbor, Mich. Microfiche.

The World almanac and book of facts. New York. Annual.

Accessions lists from the East-West Center, Office of Population Research,
     Population Studies Center, Population Council.

APPENDIX A

Continental Division Corresponding to Original IPCB

Vol. 1 - Latin America and the Caribbean.

Antigua	Guyana
Argentina	Haiti
Bahamas	Honduras
Barbados	Jamaica
Belize	Martinique
Bermuda	Mexico
Bolivia	Montserrat
Brazil	Netherlands Antilles
British Virgin Islands	Nicaragua
Cayman Islands	Panama
Chile	Panama Canal Zone
Colombia	Paraguay
Commonwealth Caribbean	Peru
Costa Rica	Puerto Rico
Cuba	St. Kitts-Nevis-Anguilla
Dominica	St. Lucia
Dominican Republic	St. Vincent
Ecuador	Suriname
El Salvador	Trinidad and Tobago
Falkland Islands	Turks and Caicos Islands
Grenada	Uruguay
Guadeloupe	Venezuela
Guatemala	Virgin Islands (U.S.)

Vol. 2 - Africa.

Algeria	Guinea
Angola	Guinea-Bissau
Benin	Ivory Coast
Bophuthatswana	Kenya
British Indian Ocean Terr.	Liberia
Burundi	Libya
Cameroon	Madagascar
Cape Verde	Malawi
Central Africa	Mali
Ceuta and Melilla	Mauritania
Chad	Mauritius
Comoros	Morocco
Congo	Mozambique
Djibouti	Namibia
Egypt	Niger
Equatorial Guinea	Nigeria
Ethiopia	Reunion
French Overseas Territories	Rhodesia
Gabon	Rwanda
Gambia, The	St. Helena and Ascension Islands
Ghana	São Tomé and Principe

Vol. 2 - Africa (Cont'd)
    Senegal   Togo
    Seychelles   Transkei
    Sierra Leone   Tunisia
    Somalia   Uganda
    South Africa   Upper Volta
    Sudan   Western Sahara
    Swaziland   Zaïre
    Tanganyika and Zanzibar   Zambia

Vol. 3 - Oceania.
    American Samoa   New Hebrides
    Australia   New Zealand
    Canton and Enderbury Islands   Niue
    Christmas Island   Norfolk Islands
    Cocos (Keeling) Islands   Pacific Islands, Trust Territory
    Cook Islands   Papua New Guinea
    Fiji   Pitcairn
    French Polynesia   Solomon Islands
    Gilbert Islands   Tokelau Islands
    Guam   Tonga
    Johnston Island   Wake Island
    Midway Islands   Wallis and Futuna
    Nauru   Western Samoa
    New Caledonia

Vol. 4 - North America.
    Canada   St. Pierre and Miquelon
    Greenland   United States

Vol. 5 - Asia.
    Afghanistan   Kuwait
    Bahrain   Laos
    Bangladesh   Lebanon
    Bhutan   Macao
    Bonin Islands   Malaysia
    Brunei   Maldives
    Burma   Mongolia
    Cambodia   Nepal
    China (Mainland)   Oman
    Cyprus   Pakistan
    Hong Kong   Philippines
    India   Qatar
    Indonesia   Ryukyu Islands
    Iran   Saudi Arabia
    Iraq   Singapore
    Israel   Sri Lanka
    Japan   Syria
    Jordan   Taiwan and Fukien
    Korea, North   Thailand
    Korea, South   Timor